RENNY DARLING'S

These Are a Few of Your Favorite Things!

A Treasury of Recipes to Enjoy with Love

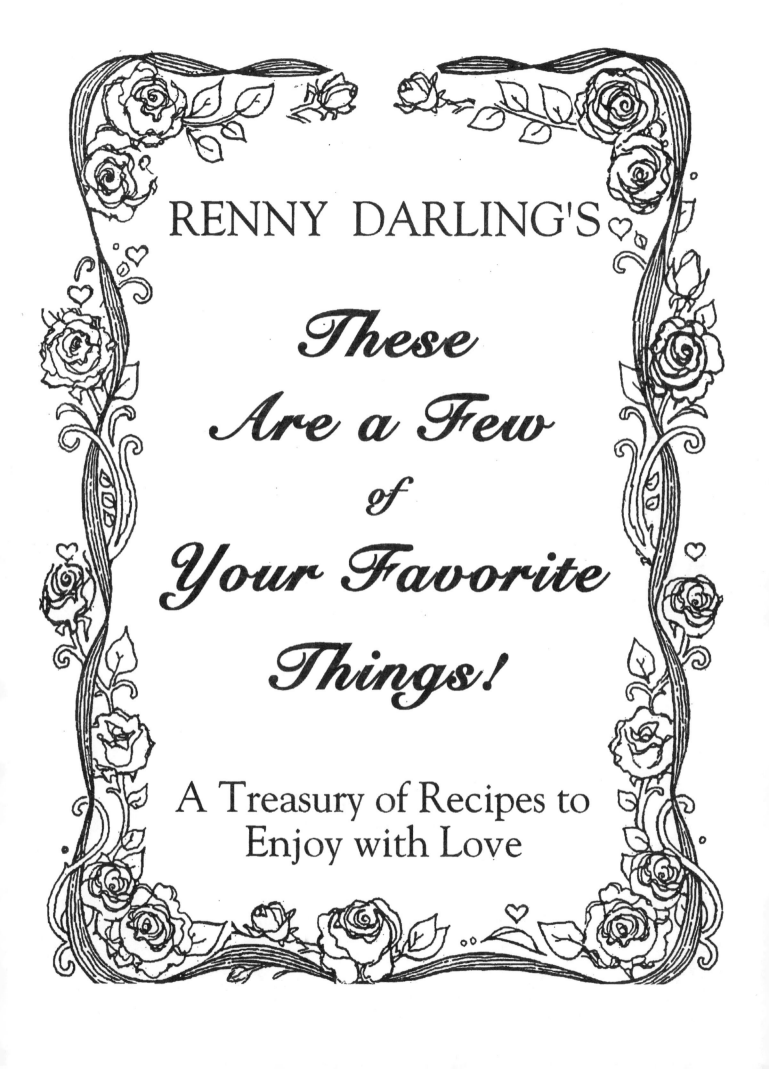

Simply Delicious Cookbooks
by Renny Darling

The Joy of Eating
The Love of Eating
The Joy of Entertaining
The Joy of Eating French Food
Great Beginnings & Happy Endings
With Love from Darling's Kitchen
Easiest & Best Coffee Cakes & Quick Breads
Entertaining Fast & Fancy
The Moderation Diet
The New Joy of Eating
Happy Holidays & Great Celebrations
Vegetarian Fast & Fancy
These Are A Few Of Your Favorite Things

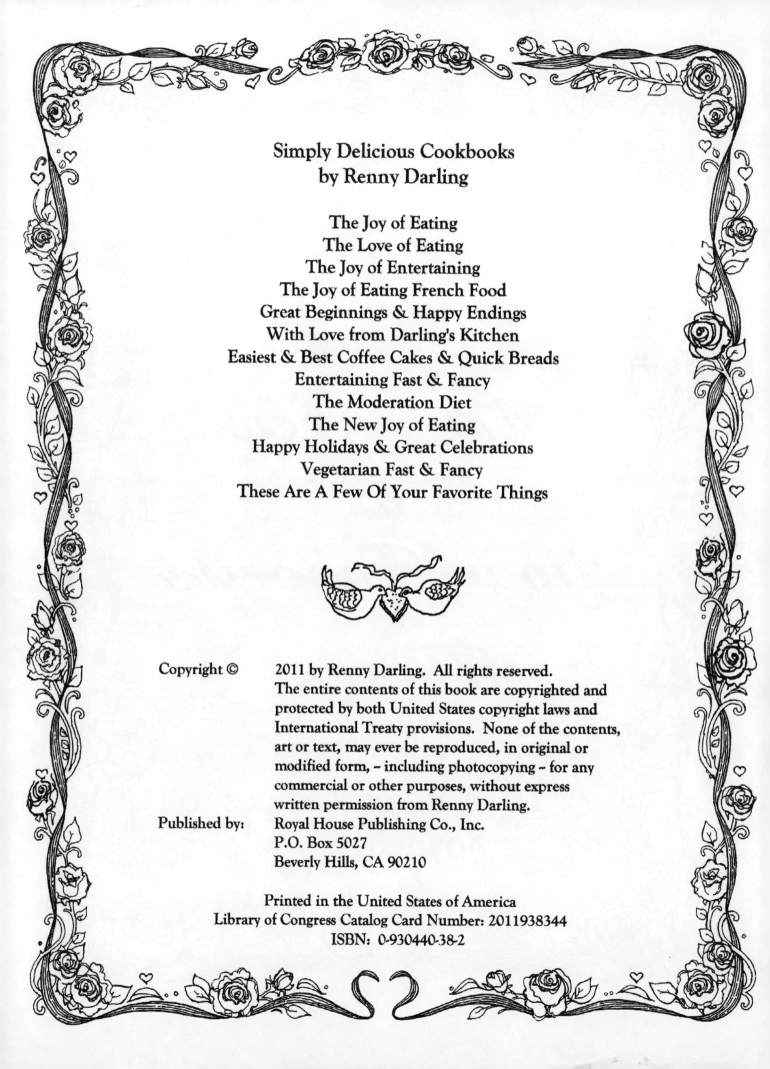

Published by: Royal House Publishing Co., Inc.
P.O. Box 5027
Beverly Hills, CA 90210

Printed in the United States of America
Library of Congress Catalog Card Number: 2011938344
ISBN: 0-930440-38-2

The Contents

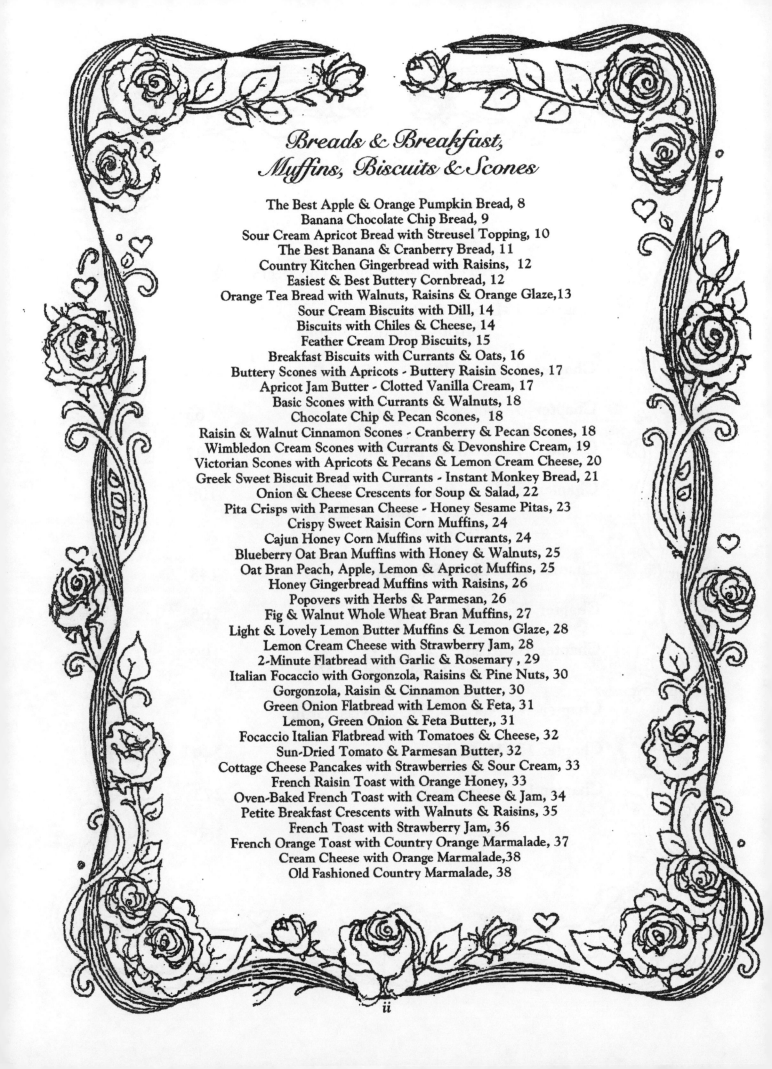

Breads & Breakfast, Muffins, Biscuits & Scones

Hors d'Oeuvres & Small Entrees

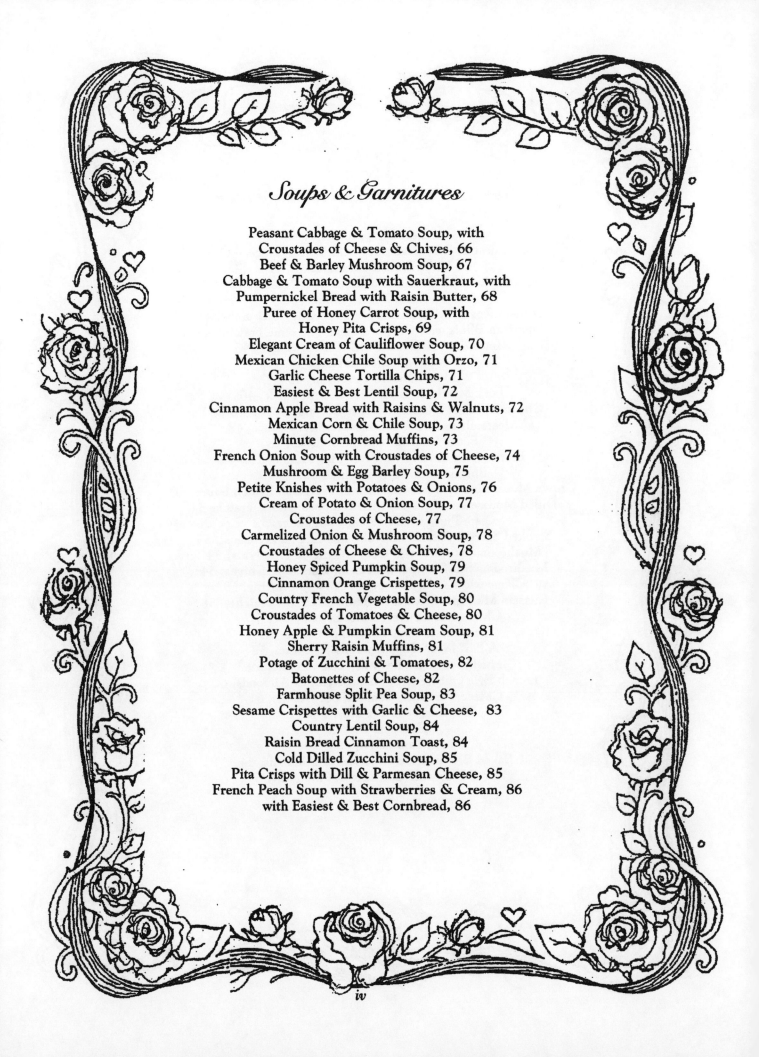

Soups & Garnitures

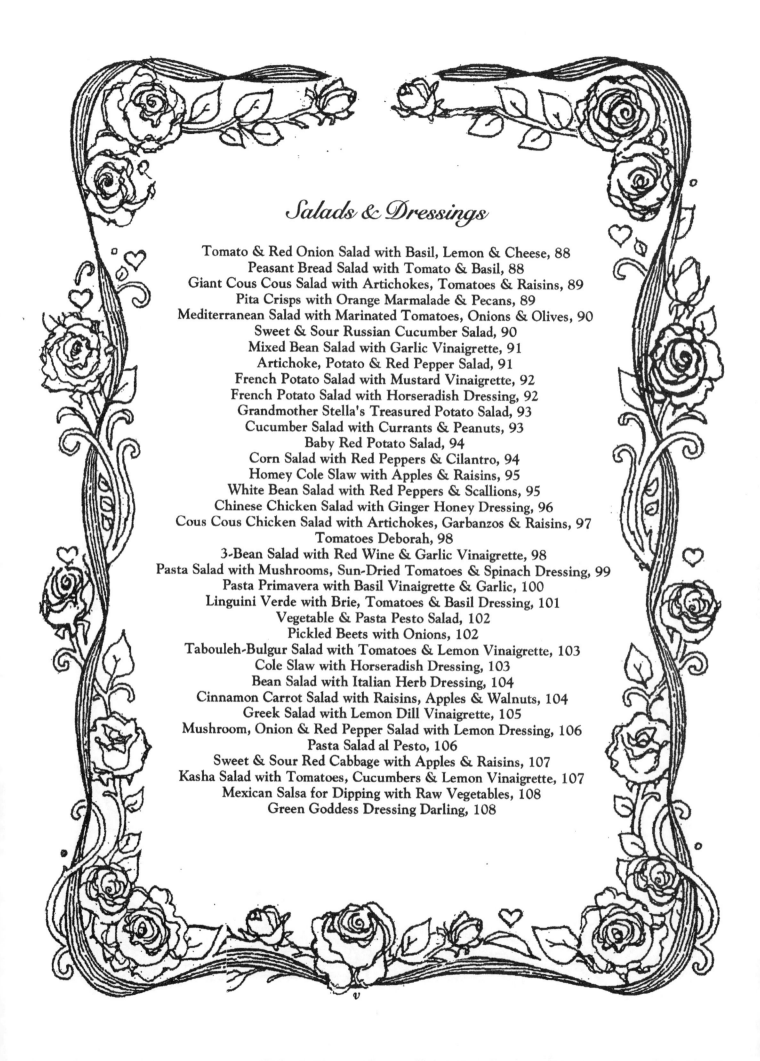

Salads & Dressings

Tomato & Red Onion Salad with Basil, Lemon & Cheese, 88
Peasant Bread Salad with Tomato & Basil, 88
Giant Cous Cous Salad with Artichokes, Tomatoes & Raisins, 89
Pita Crisps with Orange Marmalade & Pecans, 89
Mediterranean Salad with Marinated Tomatoes, Onions & Olives, 90
Sweet & Sour Russian Cucumber Salad, 90
Mixed Bean Salad with Garlic Vinaigrette, 91
Artichoke, Potato & Red Pepper Salad, 91
French Potato Salad with Mustard Vinaigrette, 92
French Potato Salad with Horseradish Dressing, 92
Grandmother Stella's Treasured Potato Salad, 93
Cucumber Salad with Currants & Peanuts, 93
Baby Red Potato Salad, 94
Corn Salad with Red Peppers & Cilantro, 94
Homey Cole Slaw with Apples & Raisins, 95
White Bean Salad with Red Peppers & Scallions, 95
Chinese Chicken Salad with Ginger Honey Dressing, 96
Cous Cous Chicken Salad with Artichokes, Garbanzos & Raisins, 97
Tomatoes Deborah, 98
3-Bean Salad with Red Wine & Garlic Vinaigrette, 98
Pasta Salad with Mushrooms, Sun-Dried Tomatoes & Spinach Dressing, 99
Pasta Primavera with Basil Vinaigrette & Garlic, 100
Linguini Verde with Brie, Tomatoes & Basil Dressing, 101
Vegetable & Pasta Pesto Salad, 102
Pickled Beets with Onions, 102
Tabouleh-Bulgur Salad with Tomatoes & Lemon Vinaigrette, 103
Cole Slaw with Horseradish Dressing, 103
Bean Salad with Italian Herb Dressing, 104
Cinnamon Carrot Salad with Raisins, Apples & Walnuts, 104
Greek Salad with Lemon Dill Vinaigrette, 105
Mushroom, Onion & Red Pepper Salad with Lemon Dressing, 106
Pasta Salad al Pesto, 106
Sweet & Sour Red Cabbage with Apples & Raisins, 107
Kasha Salad with Tomatoes, Cucumbers & Lemon Vinaigrette, 107
Mexican Salsa for Dipping with Raw Vegetables, 108
Green Goddess Dressing Darling, 108

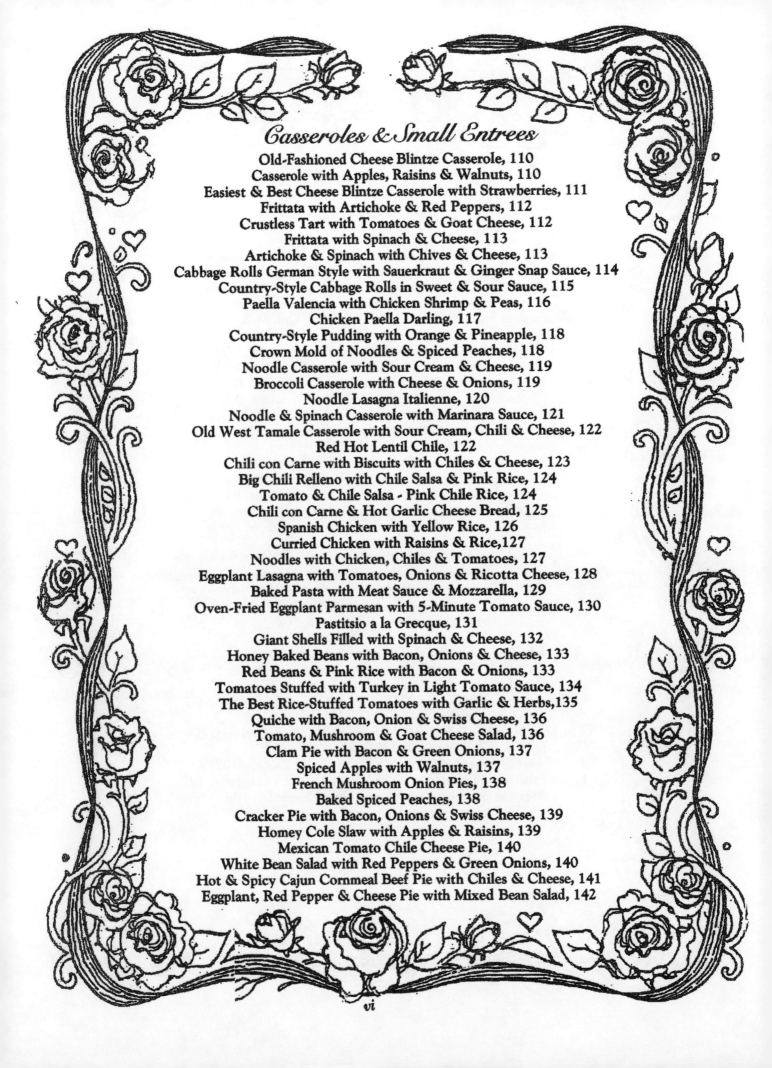

Casseroles & Small Entrees

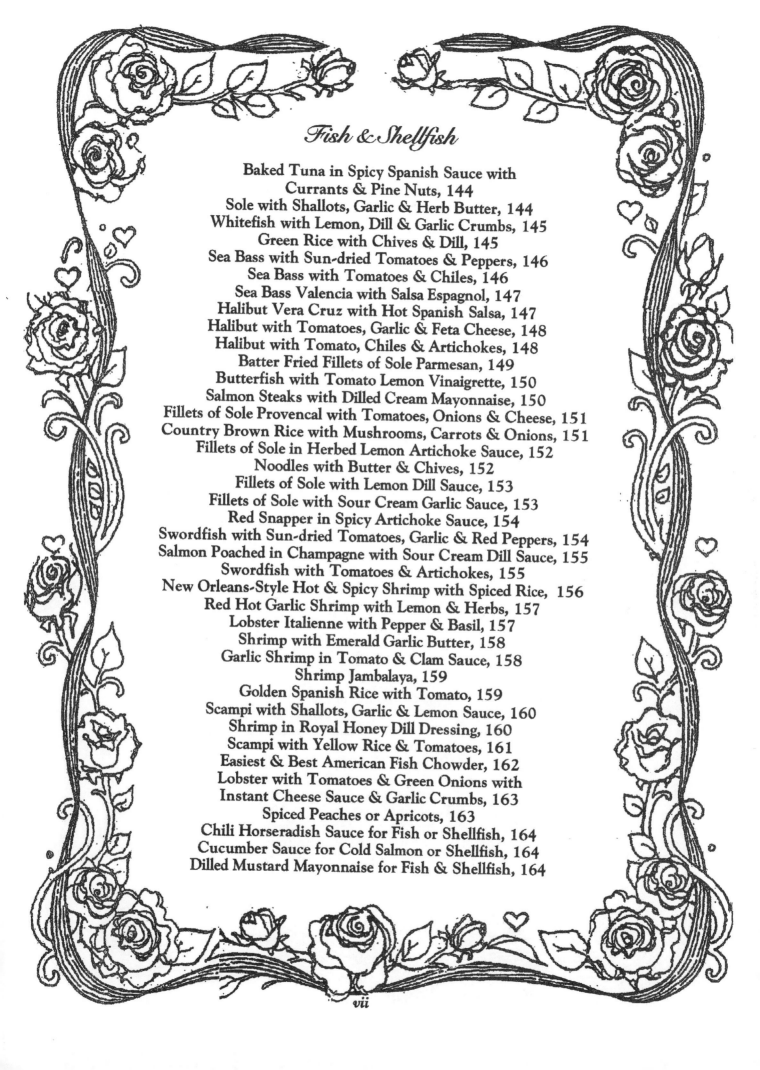

Fish & Shellfish

Poultry & Dressing

Meats
Beef, Lamb, Pork & Veal

Barbecued Brisket & Honey Barbecue Sauce, 200
Brisket with Peaches & Sweet Potatoes, 200
Minute Chile Meat Loaf, 201
To Make Dried Bread Crumbs, 201
Farmhouse Sweet & Sour Pot Roast with Apples & Raisins, 202
Garlic Mashed Potatoes, 202
Family Night Meat Loaf, 203
Meatballs is Chili Currant Sauce, 203
Old-Fashioned Hungarian Goulash, 204
Buttered Noodles with Poppyseeds, 204
Easiest & Best Hungarian Spaetzel, 205
Sweet & Sour Red Cabbage, 205
Butterflied Roast Leg of Lamb with
Lemon, Garlic & Yogurt, 206
Crown Roast of Lamb, with
Bulgur, Lamb, Lemon, & Chive Dressing, 207
Greek-Styled Lamb Shanks in a Tomato Garlic Wine Sauce, 208
Rack of Lamb with Garlic & Herbs, 209
Rack of Lamb with Orange Lemon Glaze, 209
Cassoulet of Lamb Shanks with Beans, 210
Dilled Lamb with Yogurt, Lemon & Garlic Sauce, 211
Brown Rice with Mushrooms & Onions, 211
Teriyaki Pork Roast with Apple Jelly Glaze, 212
Country Spareribs with Honey Barbecue Sauce, 212
Plum-Glazed Barbecued Spare Ribs, 213
Apricot Glazed Canadian Bacon, 213
Roast Tendeloin of Port with Apple Jelly, 214
Roast Tenderloin of Pork with Orange Glaze, 214
Pork Dumplings & Apricot Peanut Sauce, 215
Sweet & Sour Barbecued Loin of Pork with Baked Apples & Raisins, 216
Honey Glazed Ham with Glazed Cinnamon Apple Rings, 217
Baked Ham with Apple & Pecan Cornbread Pudding, 218
Easiest & Best Osso Bucco alla Milanese, 219
Pink Risotto alla Milanese, 219
Herb Stuffed Breast of Veal with Currant Wine Sauce, 220
Veal Meatloaf with Brandied Apple Rings, 221
Rice Pilaf with Herbs, 221
Pate of Veal & Red Peppers with Herbed Tomato Sauce, 222

Rice, Noodles, Grains & Pastas

Lemon Rice with Peas & Parmesan, 224
Rice with Tomato, Parsley & Chives, 224
Pink Rice with Chili Beans, 225
Vegetable Fried Rice, 226
Lemon Rice with Chives & Cheese, 226
Oven-Baked Rice & Vermicelli with Onions & Mushrooms, 227
Brown Rice & Lentil Casserole with Carrots & Onions, 227
Timbales of Rice & Carrots, 228
Green Rice with Lemon & Herbs, 228
Casserole of Wild Rice with Apples & Chives, 229
Golden Mexican Rice with Tomatoes & Chiles, 229
Casserole of Brown Rice with Cabbage & Onions, 230
Brown Rice with Mushrooms & Onions, 230
Curried Rice with Mushrooms & Peas, 231
Yellow Rice India with Onions & Almonds, 231
Noodle Pudding with Apples & Raisins, 232
The Best Noodle Pudding with Sour Cream & Raisins, 233
Noodle Pudding with Sweet Red Peppers & Cheese, 234
Toasted Barley with Mushrooms & Onions, 234
Toasted Vermicelli in Chicken Broth, 235
Fideos with Onions & Mushroom, 235
Ramekins of Noodles with Red Peppers & Cheese, 236
Easiest & Best Barbecued Baked Beans, 237
Red Beans, Pink Rice & Green Onions, 237
Kasha with Mushrooms & Onions, 238
Cous Cous with Mushrooms & Red Peppers, 238
Bulgur with Dried Cherries & Pecans, 239
Bulgur Pilaf with Red Peppers & Cheese, 239
Bulgur with Ground Lamb, 240
Bulgur Pilaf with Garbanzos, 240
Kasha with Dried Cherries & Pecans, 241
Bulgur with Lemon, Currants & Pine Nuts, 241
Bulgur with Apricots, Raisins & Pine Nuts, 242
Bulgur with Lemon & Chives, 242
Garbanzos with Tomatoes & Onion Curry, 243
Red Lentils with Tomatoes & Fried Onions, 243
Toasted Orzo with Mushrooms & Onions, 244
Orzo with Tomatoes, Onions & Peas, 244
Spaghetti alla Bolognese, 245
Fettuccini alla Romano with Onions, Pepper & Cheese, 246
Fresh Linguini with Basil & Sun-Dried Tomato Sauce. 247
Angel Hair Pasta with Fresh Tomatoes, Garlic & Basil. 247
Baked Ziti with Ricotta & Mozzarella in Instant Tomato Sauce, 248

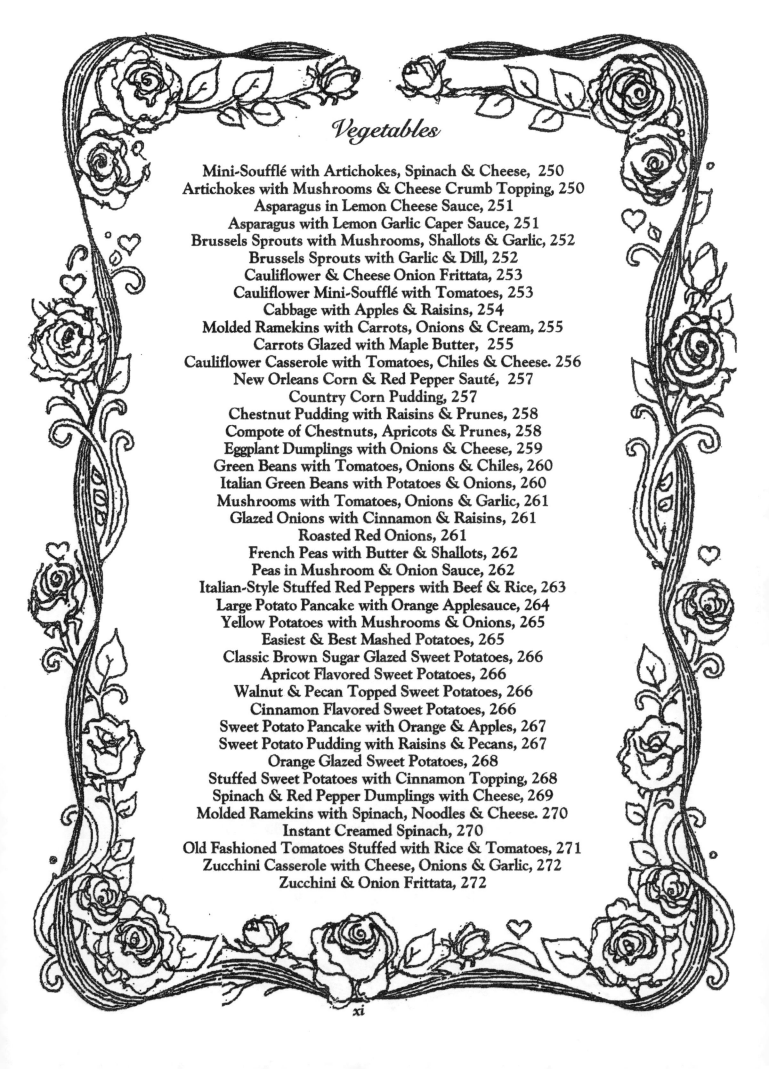

Vegetables

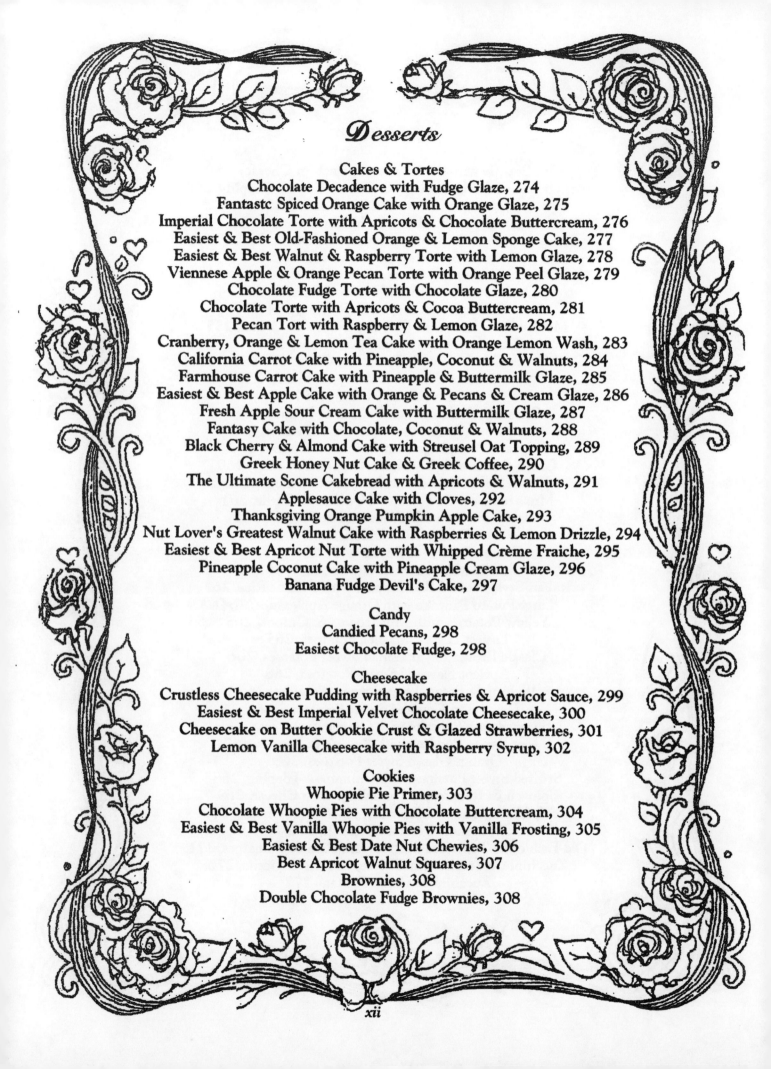

Desserts

Cakes & Tortes

Candy

Cheesecake

Cookies

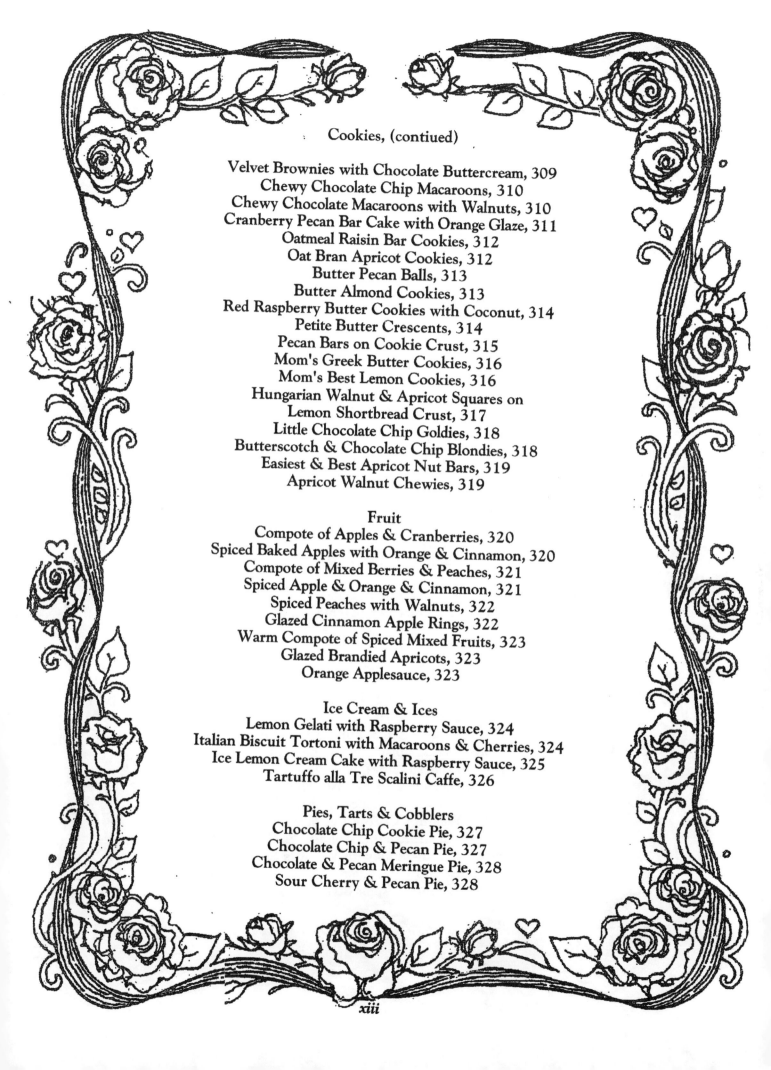

Cookies, (contiued)

Fruit

Ice Cream & Ices

Pies, Tarts & Cobblers

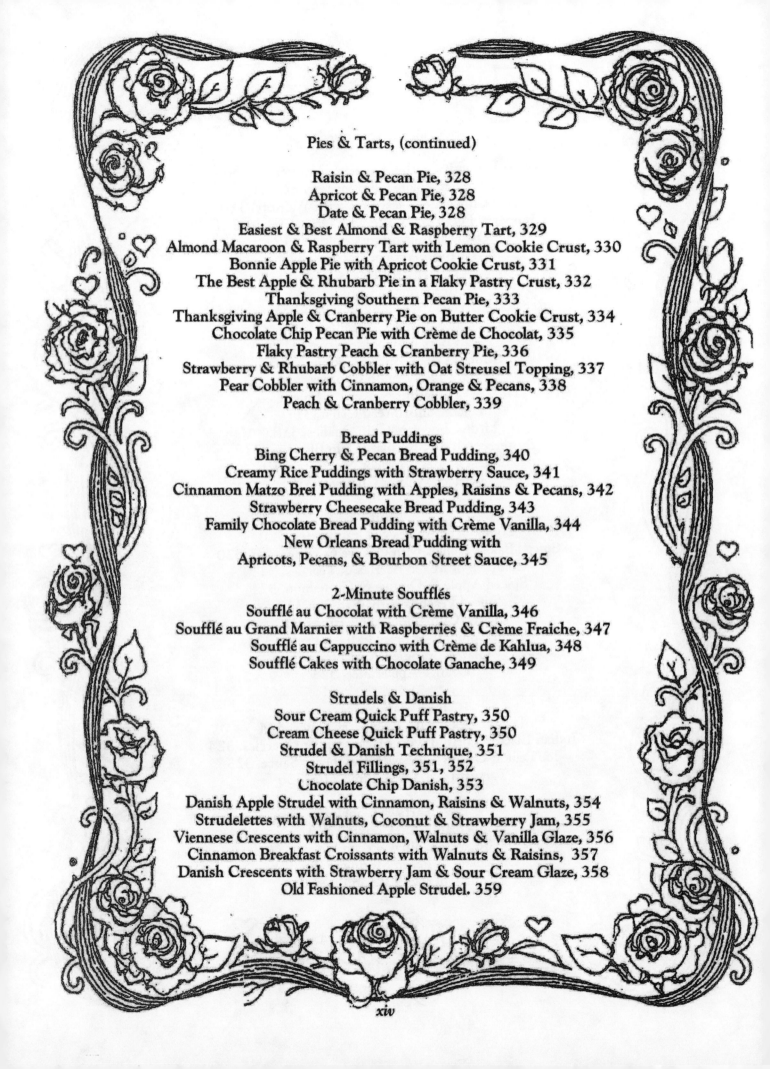

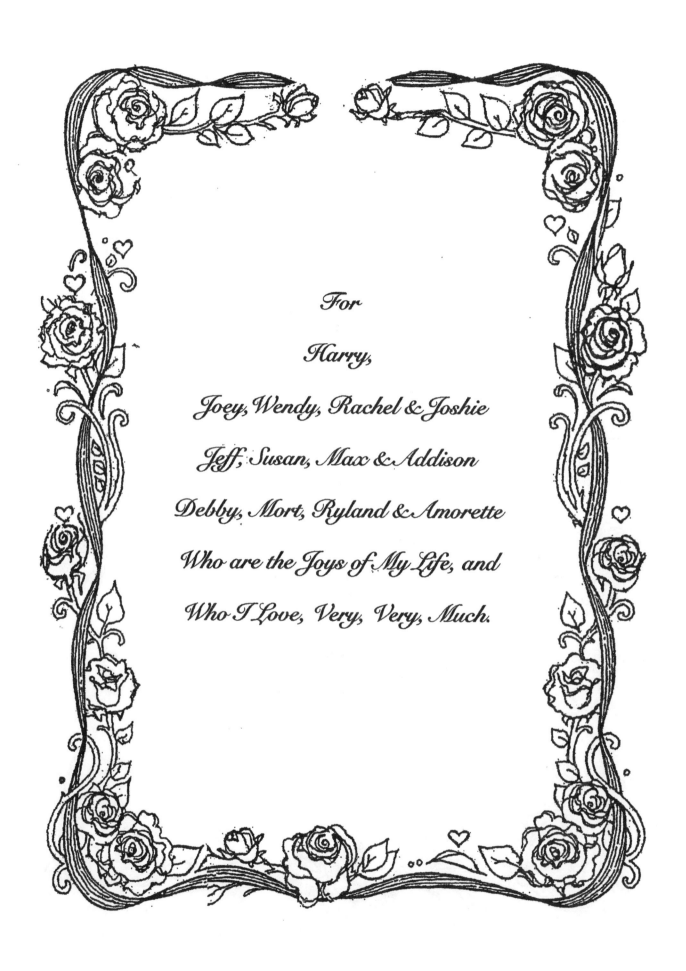

For

Harry,

Joey, Wendy, Rachel & Joshie

Jeff, Susan, Max & Addison

Debby, Mort, Ryland & Amorette

Who are the Joys of My Life, and

Who I Love, Very, Very, Much.

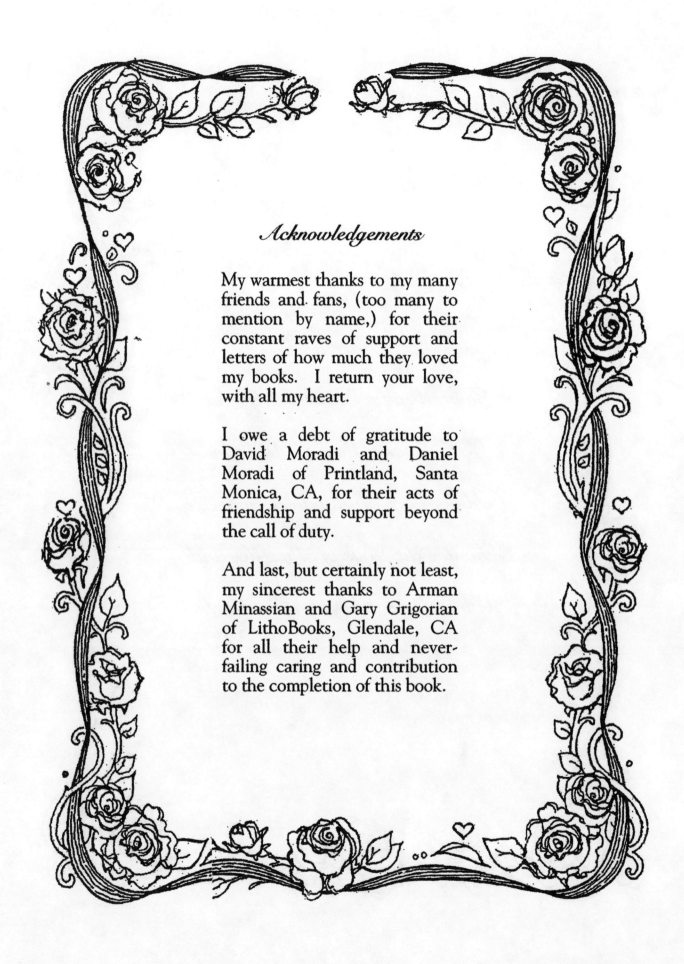

Acknowledgements

My warmest thanks to my many friends and fans, (too many to mention by name,) for their constant raves of support and letters of how much they loved my books. I return your love, with all my heart.

I owe a debt of gratitude to David Moradi and Daniel Moradi of Printland, Santa Monica, CA, for their acts of friendship and support beyond the call of duty.

And last, but certainly not least, my sincerest thanks to Arman Minassian and Gary Grigorian of LithoBooks, Glendale, CA for all their help and never-failing caring and contribution to the completion of this book.

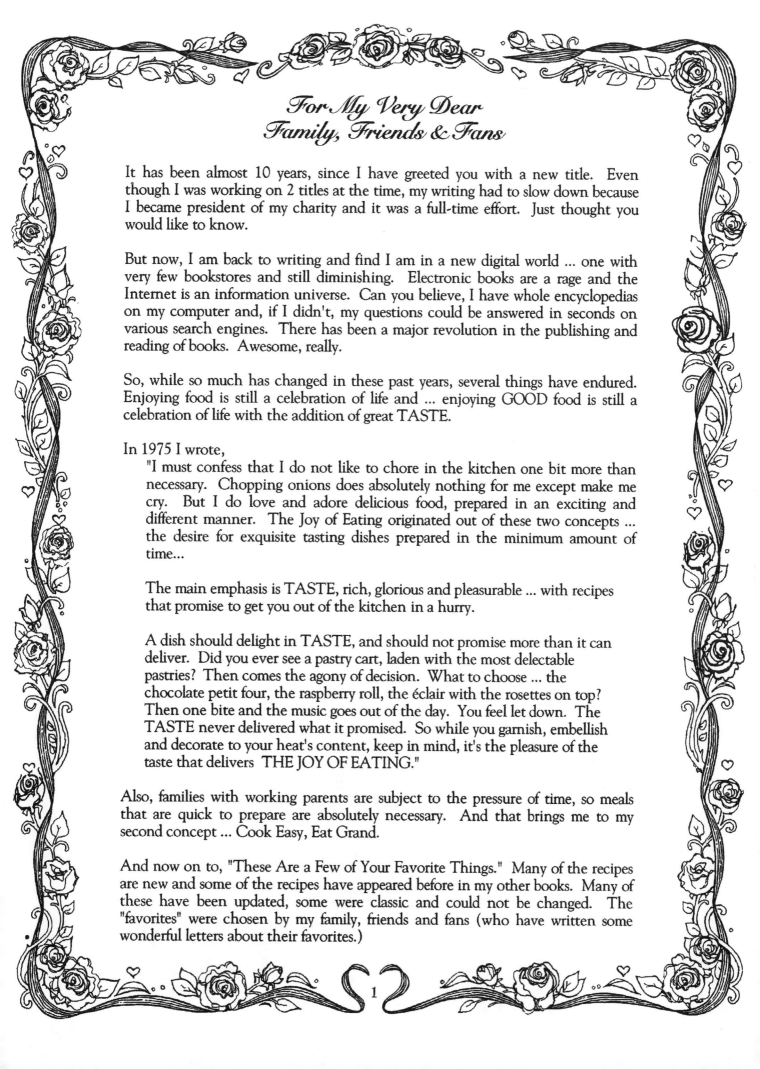

For My Very Dear Family, Friends & Fans

It has been almost 10 years, since I have greeted you with a new title. Even though I was working on 2 titles at the time, my writing had to slow down because I became president of my charity and it was a full-time effort. Just thought you would like to know.

But now, I am back to writing and find I am in a new digital world ... one with very few bookstores and still diminishing. Electronic books are a rage and the Internet is an information universe. Can you believe, I have whole encyclopedias on my computer and, if I didn't, my questions could be answered in seconds on various search engines. There has been a major revolution in the publishing and reading of books. Awesome, really.

So, while so much has changed in these past years, several things have endured. Enjoying food is still a celebration of life and ... enjoying GOOD food is still a celebration of life with the addition of great TASTE.

In 1975 I wrote,
"I must confess that I do not like to chore in the kitchen one bit more than necessary. Chopping onions does absolutely nothing for me except make me cry. But I do love and adore delicious food, prepared in an exciting and different manner. The Joy of Eating originated out of these two concepts ... the desire for exquisite tasting dishes prepared in the minimum amount of time...

The main emphasis is TASTE, rich, glorious and pleasurable ... with recipes that promise to get you out of the kitchen in a hurry.

A dish should delight in TASTE, and should not promise more than it can deliver. Did you ever see a pastry cart, laden with the most delectable pastries? Then comes the agony of decision. What to choose ... the chocolate petit four, the raspberry roll, the éclair with the rosettes on top? Then one bite and the music goes out of the day. You feel let down. The TASTE never delivered what it promised. So while you garnish, embellish and decorate to your heat's content, keep in mind, it's the pleasure of the taste that delivers THE JOY OF EATING."

Also, families with working parents are subject to the pressure of time, so meals that are quick to prepare are absolutely necessary. And that brings me to my second concept ... Cook Easy, Eat Grand.

And now on to, "These Are a Few of Your Favorite Things." Many of the recipes are new and some of the recipes have appeared before in my other books. Many of these have been updated, some were classic and could not be changed. The "favorites" were chosen by my family, friends and fans (who have written some wonderful letters about their favorites.)

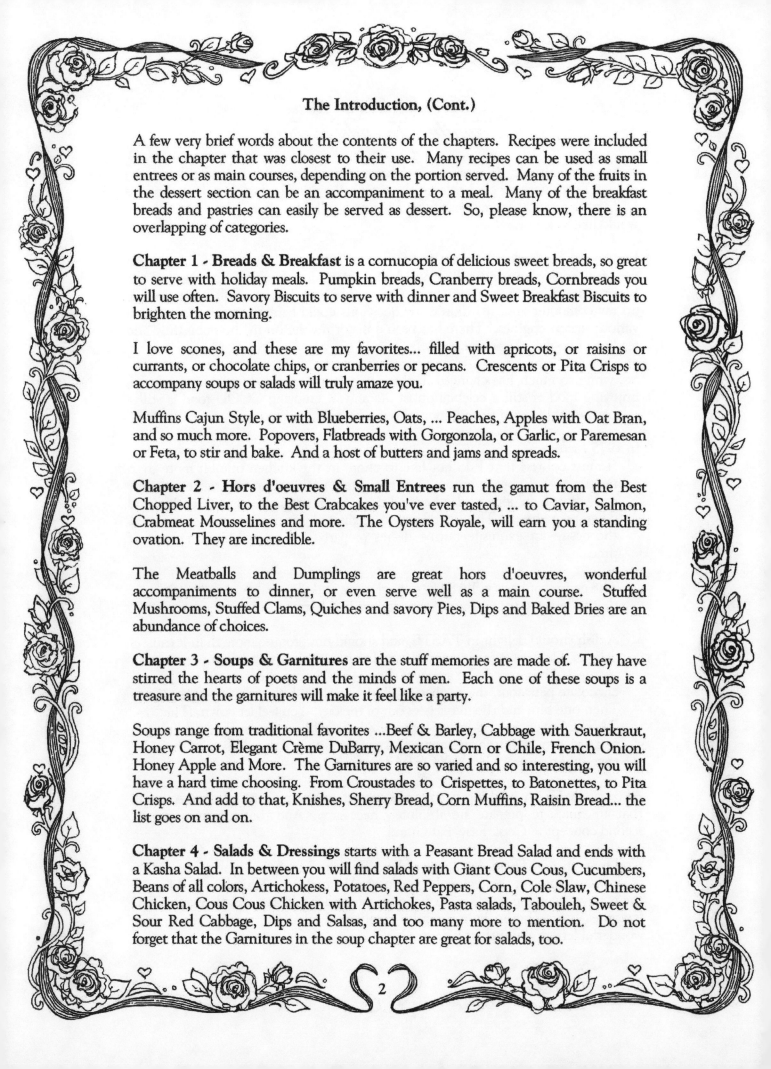

The Introduction, (Cont.)

A few very brief words about the contents of the chapters. Recipes were included in the chapter that was closest to their use. Many recipes can be used as small entrees or as main courses, depending on the portion served. Many of the fruits in the dessert section can be an accompaniment to a meal. Many of the breakfast breads and pastries can easily be served as dessert. So, please know, there is an overlapping of categories.

Chapter 1 - Breads & Breakfast is a cornucopia of delicious sweet breads, so great to serve with holiday meals. Pumpkin breads, Cranberry breads, Cornbreads you will use often. Savory Biscuits to serve with dinner and Sweet Breakfast Biscuits to brighten the morning.

I love scones, and these are my favorites... filled with apricots, or raisins or currants, or chocolate chips, or cranberries or pecans. Crescents or Pita Crisps to accompany soups or salads will truly amaze you.

Muffins Cajun Style, or with Blueberries, Oats, ... Peaches, Apples with Oat Bran, and so much more. Popovers, Flatbreads with Gorgonzola, or Garlic, or Paremesan or Feta, to stir and bake. And a host of butters and jams and spreads.

Chapter 2 - Hors d'oeuvres & Small Entrees run the gamut from the Best Chopped Liver, to the Best Crabcakes you've ever tasted, ... to Caviar, Salmon, Crabmeat Mousselines and more. The Oysters Royale, will earn you a standing ovation. They are incredible.

The Meatballs and Dumplings are great hors d'oeuvres, wonderful accompaniments to dinner, or even serve well as a main course. Stuffed Mushrooms, Stuffed Clams, Quiches and savory Pies, Dips and Baked Bries are an abundance of choices.

Chapter 3 - Soups & Garnitures are the stuff memories are made of. They have stirred the hearts of poets and the minds of men. Each one of these soups is a treasure and the garnitures will make it feel like a party.

Soups range from traditional favorites ...Beef & Barley, Cabbage with Sauerkraut, Honey Carrot, Elegant Crème DuBarry, Mexican Corn or Chile, French Onion. Honey Apple and More. The Garnitures are so varied and so interesting, you will have a hard time choosing. From Croustades to Crispettes, to Batonettes, to Pita Crisps. And add to that, Knishes, Sherry Bread, Corn Muffins, Raisin Bread... the list goes on and on.

Chapter 4 - Salads & Dressings starts with a Peasant Bread Salad and ends with a Kasha Salad. In between you will find salads with Giant Cous Cous, Cucumbers, Beans of all colors, Artichokess, Potatoes, Red Peppers, Corn, Cole Slaw, Chinese Chicken, Cous Cous Chicken with Artichokes, Pasta salads, Tabouleh, Sweet & Sour Red Cabbage, Dips and Salsas, and too many more to mention. Do not forget that the Garnitures in the soup chapter are great for salads, too.

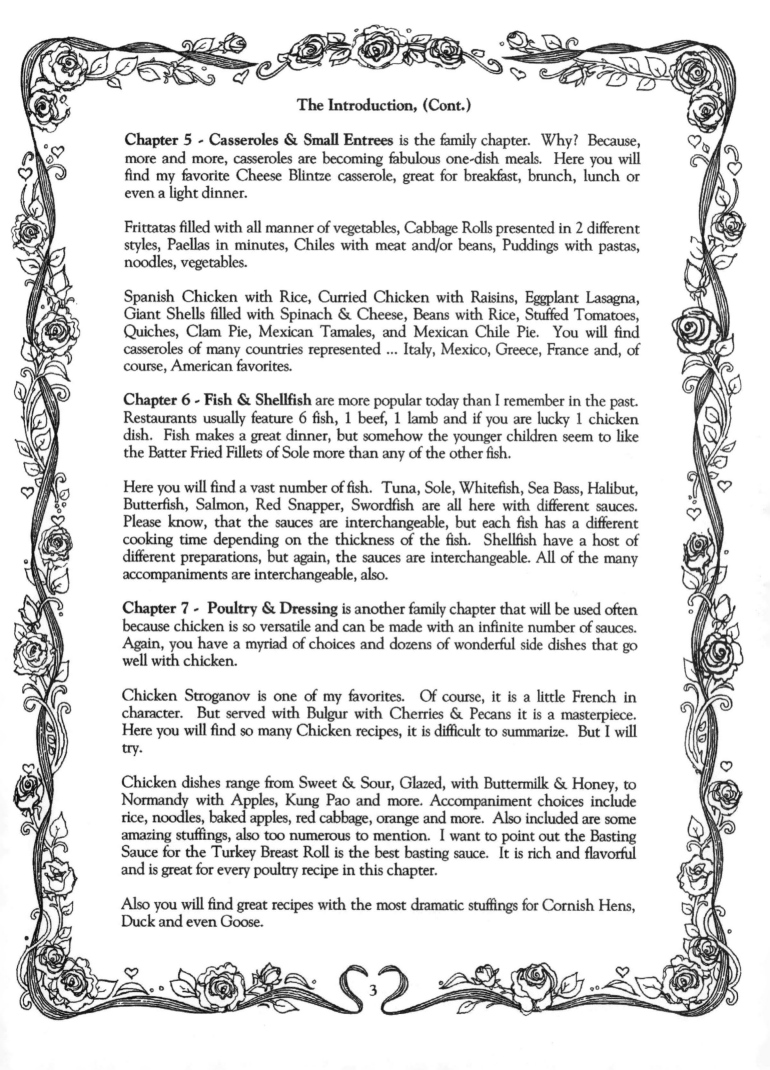

Chapter 5 - Casseroles & Small Entrees is the family chapter. Why? Because, more and more, casseroles are becoming fabulous one-dish meals. Here you will find my favorite Cheese Blintze casserole, great for breakfast, brunch, lunch or even a light dinner.

Frittatas filled with all manner of vegetables, Cabbage Rolls presented in 2 different styles, Paellas in minutes, Chiles with meat and/or beans, Puddings with pastas, noodles, vegetables.

Spanish Chicken with Rice, Curried Chicken with Raisins, Eggplant Lasagna, Giant Shells filled with Spinach & Cheese, Beans with Rice, Stuffed Tomatoes, Quiches, Clam Pie, Mexican Tamales, and Mexican Chile Pie. You will find casseroles of many countries represented ... Italy, Mexico, Greece, France and, of course, American favorites.

Chapter 6 - Fish & Shellfish are more popular today than I remember in the past. Restaurants usually feature 6 fish, 1 beef, 1 lamb and if you are lucky 1 chicken dish. Fish makes a great dinner, but somehow the younger children seem to like the Batter Fried Fillets of Sole more than any of the other fish.

Here you will find a vast number of fish. Tuna, Sole, Whitefish, Sea Bass, Halibut, Butterfish, Salmon, Red Snapper, Swordfish are all here with different sauces. Please know, that the sauces are interchangeable, but each fish has a different cooking time depending on the thickness of the fish. Shellfish have a host of different preparations, but again, the sauces are interchangeable. All of the many accompaniments are interchangeable, also.

Chapter 7 - Poultry & Dressing is another family chapter that will be used often because chicken is so versatile and can be made with an infinite number of sauces. Again, you have a myriad of choices and dozens of wonderful side dishes that go well with chicken.

Chicken Stroganov is one of my favorites. Of course, it is a little French in character. But served with Bulgur with Cherries & Pecans it is a masterpiece. Here you will find so many Chicken recipes, it is difficult to summarize. But I will try.

Chicken dishes range from Sweet & Sour, Glazed, with Buttermilk & Honey, to Normandy with Apples, Kung Pao and more. Accompaniment choices include rice, noodles, baked apples, red cabbage, orange and more. Also included are some amazing stuffings, also too numerous to mention. I want to point out the Basting Sauce for the Turkey Breast Roll is the best basting sauce. It is rich and flavorful and is great for every poultry recipe in this chapter.

Also you will find great recipes with the most dramatic stuffings for Cornish Hens, Duck and even Goose.

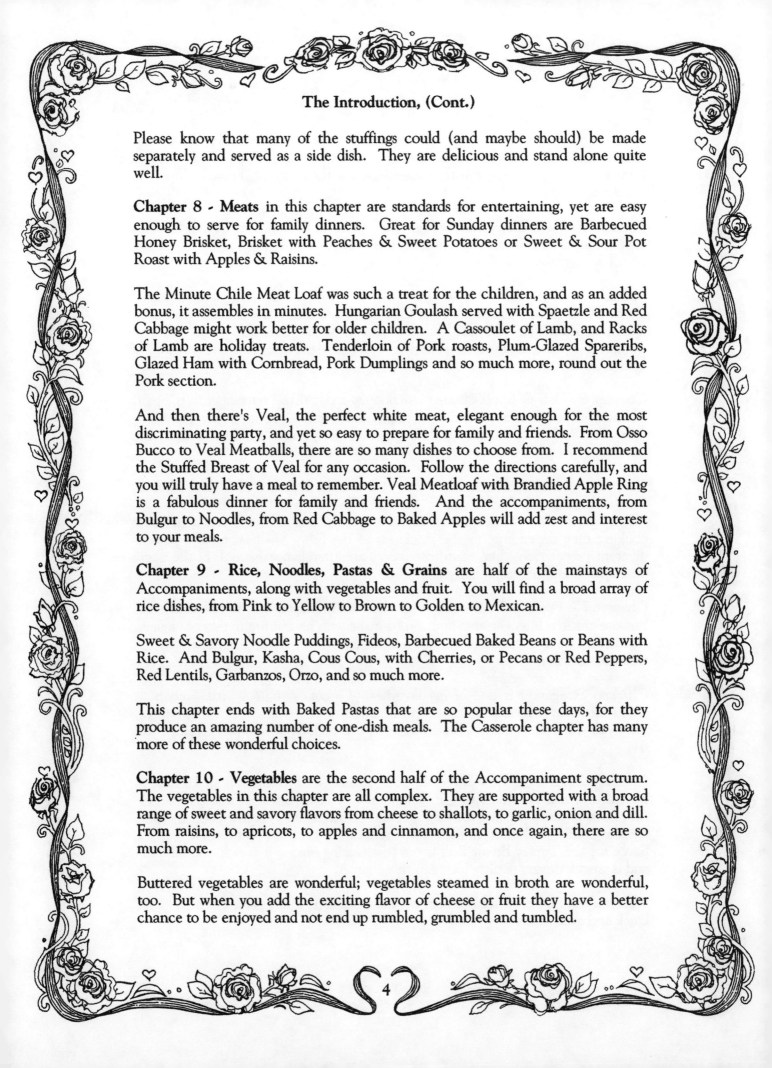

Please know that many of the stuffings could (and maybe should) be made separately and served as a side dish. They are delicious and stand alone quite well.

Chapter 8 - Meats in this chapter are standards for entertaining, yet are easy enough to serve for family dinners. Great for Sunday dinners are Barbecued Honey Brisket, Brisket with Peaches & Sweet Potatoes or Sweet & Sour Pot Roast with Apples & Raisins.

The Minute Chile Meat Loaf was such a treat for the children, and as an added bonus, it assembles in minutes. Hungarian Goulash served with Spaetzle and Red Cabbage might work better for older children. A Cassoulet of Lamb, and Racks of Lamb are holiday treats. Tenderloin of Pork roasts, Plum-Glazed Spareribs, Glazed Ham with Cornbread, Pork Dumplings and so much more, round out the Pork section.

And then there's Veal, the perfect white meat, elegant enough for the most discriminating party, and yet so easy to prepare for family and friends. From Osso Bucco to Veal Meatballs, there are so many dishes to choose from. I recommend the Stuffed Breast of Veal for any occasion. Follow the directions carefully, and you will truly have a meal to remember. Veal Meatloaf with Brandied Apple Ring is a fabulous dinner for family and friends. And the accompaniments, from Bulgur to Noodles, from Red Cabbage to Baked Apples will add zest and interest to your meals.

Chapter 9 - Rice, Noodles, Pastas & Grains are half of the mainstays of Accompaniments, along with vegetables and fruit. You will find a broad array of rice dishes, from Pink to Yellow to Brown to Golden to Mexican.

Sweet & Savory Noodle Puddings, Fideos, Barbecued Baked Beans or Beans with Rice. And Bulgur, Kasha, Cous Cous, with Cherries, or Pecans or Red Peppers, Red Lentils, Garbanzos, Orzo, and so much more.

This chapter ends with Baked Pastas that are so popular these days, for they produce an amazing number of one-dish meals. The Casserole chapter has many more of these wonderful choices.

Chapter 10 - Vegetables are the second half of the Accompaniment spectrum. The vegetables in this chapter are all complex. They are supported with a broad range of sweet and savory flavors from cheese to shallots, to garlic, onion and dill. From raisins, to apricots, to apples and cinnamon, and once again, there are so much more.

Buttered vegetables are wonderful; vegetables steamed in broth are wonderful, too. But when you add the exciting flavor of cheese or fruit they have a better chance to be enjoyed and not end up rumbled, grumbled and tumbled.

Chapter 11 - Desserts are the Grand Dames of dinner. It is the course that almost everybody looks forward to even when they feel they cannot eat another bite. Then something magical happens ... they can. Also, more time is spent lingering over dessert than any other course in the meal. That's when everyone is talking and laughing and all at the same time.

If I had to point out certain favorites, it would take too long ... they all are. But I will mention my Torte recipes, that are assembled in minutes, are processed for 1 minute and then baked. These tortes produce the finest-tasting cakes, with no fats, little flour, and one index-finger press on the food processor. I also would be remiss if I did not remind you about my 2-minute Soufflés that do not need separating eggs, making a white sauce and beating whites at the last minute. Again, one index finger does all the work, and it can be prepared in advance and baked just before serving. Also, please try the Candied Pecans. The compliments I have received for these gorgeous pecans would fill a book. The only problem is that everyone cannot stop eating them.

And now, Dear Family, Dear Friends, Dear Fans, I cannot close without a few remarks about how you have added to my life with your loving compliments, loving support and loving letters. After the earthquake in 1994, we had piles of boxes to be discarded with damage from that shake. However, my tons of boxes of letters from you were on one side of the yard and the other side had the items that were destroyed. And, sad to say, when the boxes were picked up, my treasured mail was taken also. I cried, but it was too late. They could not be retrieved. I have some mail that was saved, and about 500 letters that were excerpted to include in a book, but that is all that is left.

I would like to end with a few words written by Marc Chagall. It is not a direct quote but they are the words I wish to express. "In my art I have hidden my love." It is my hope that I have touched upon your lives in some happy and magical way and given you some joyful memories. I can go on and on, but I must close now ... but my good wishes go on forever.

Enjoy with Love,

Renny Darling

Renny Darling
Beverly Hills, California
October, 2011

A Few Words Before You Begin...

The Basics:

-At the start, always read a recipe very carefully and then assemble all the ingredients. I also measure the ingredients before I start, so there is no last minute fidgeting.

-Always preheat the oven.

-Cooking times are approximate due to variations in oven temperatures. Look for the alternative description to guide you...such as "when a cake tester, inserted in center, comes out clean" or "when top is lightly browned".

-The number of servings is also approximate, depending on courses served, the accompaniments and, of course, appetites.

Helpful Tips:

-The low-fat sour cream, cottage cheese, cream cheese and yogurt, are excellent substitutes for their richer cousins. These have been very reliable in all the recipes I tried. With the current emphasis on fats and oils, every recipe I have made, substituting these low-fat substitutes has worked exceedingly well.

-I have a dislike for recipes that are cross-referred. Some recipes even have three cross-references... which means, the dough is on one page, the sauce on the other, storing instructions in the introduction and wrapping instructions in the index. Turning pages, back and forth is not to my liking. Why am I telling you this??? Because, I repeat certain short recipes over and over. I try to have all the instruction on one page as best as I can. The recipe for Toast Points is often repeated. So is the recipe for Cinnamon Sugar. There are others, but I don't want you to think that this is an error, but my personal choice.

-Do not dilute canned BROTHS, even if they are labeled "double strength."

-Always use sweet or unsalted BUTTER. When a recipe calls for "softened butter", it is butter that is still slightly chilled, yet soft and pliable. "Butter at room temperature" refers to butter that is softer, but not to the point where it is oily.

-When a recipe calls for ORANGE ZEST or LEMON ZEST, it calls for grating only the orange or yellow part of the peel. When GRATED ORANGE or GRATED LEMON is called for, this refers to grating the whole fruit. Grate on the 3rd largest side of a 4-sided grater with short brisk strokes. This adds a great deal of flavor to the recipe. However, you need to use a thin-skinned fruit. If the peel is too thick, then you will have to grate the zest and the fruit separately.

-LEMON JUICE is always freshly squeezed.

-FLOUR used, unless otherwise stated, is all-purpose, unbleached flour. Not necessary to sift. But do spoon it lightly into a meassuring cup.

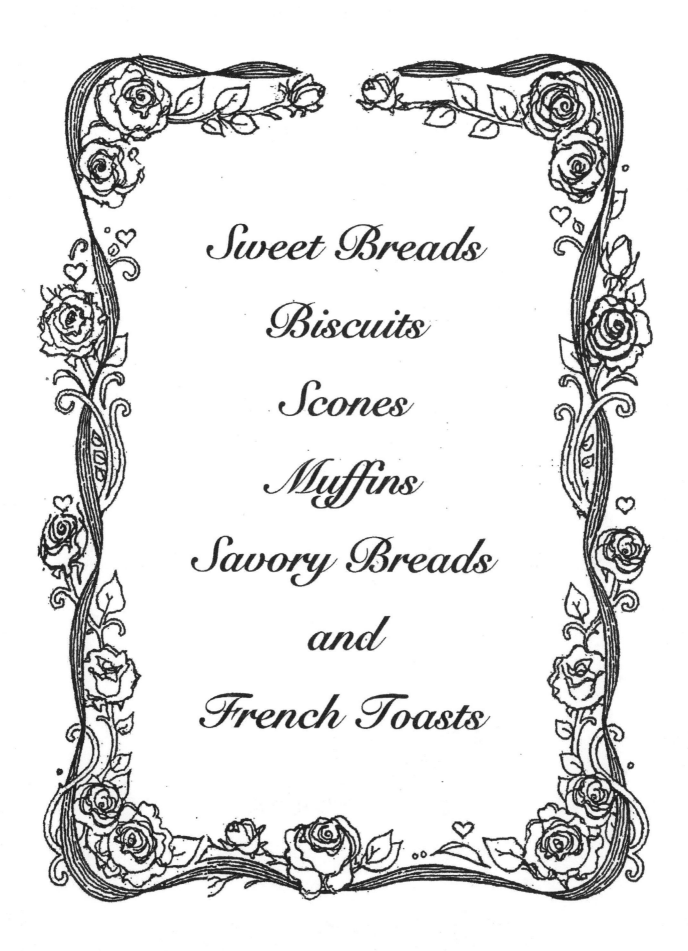

Sweet Breads

Biscuits

Scones

Muffins

Savory Breads

and

French Toasts

The Best Apple & Orange Pumpkin Bread

This bread is truly a little treasure. The flavors of apple and orange and spices make this pumpkin bread deeply fragrant and totally irresistible. It is one of our favorite Thanksgiving breads. These freeze beautifully, wrapped in double thicknesses of plastic wrap and then foil. Remove wrappers to defrost.

2	cups sugar
2	eggs
1	cup canned pumpkin puree
1/2	cup oil
1/2	orange, grated (about 3 tablespoons fruit, juice and peel). Remove any large pieces of membrane.
1	apple, peeled, cored and grated

2 1/2	cups flour
1 1/2	teaspoons baking soda
2	teaspoons pumpkin pie spice
1	teaspoon cinnamon
1/2	cup yellow raisins
1/2	cup chopped walnuts

Beat together first 4 ingredients until blended. Stir in the orange and apple until blended. Stir in the remaining ingredients until blended. Do not overmix.

Divide batter between 4 greased and lightly floured mini-loaf pans (6x3x2-inches), place pans on a cookie sheet and bake at 325° for 45 to 50 minutes, or until a cake tester, inserted in center, comes out clean.

Allow to cool in pans for 15 minutes and then, remove from pans and continue cooling on a rack. Yields 4 mini-loaves.

Banana Chocolate Chip Bread

I like preparing these breads in smaller loaves for several reasons. First, because, they are easier to store. Second, if you eat half a loaf, then the other half feels like a leftover. Third, if you wish to share a loaf with a neighbor, it is so much nicer than sharing a few slices. But, a large loaf has its place also. It is nice on a buffet, and travels well to a potluck.

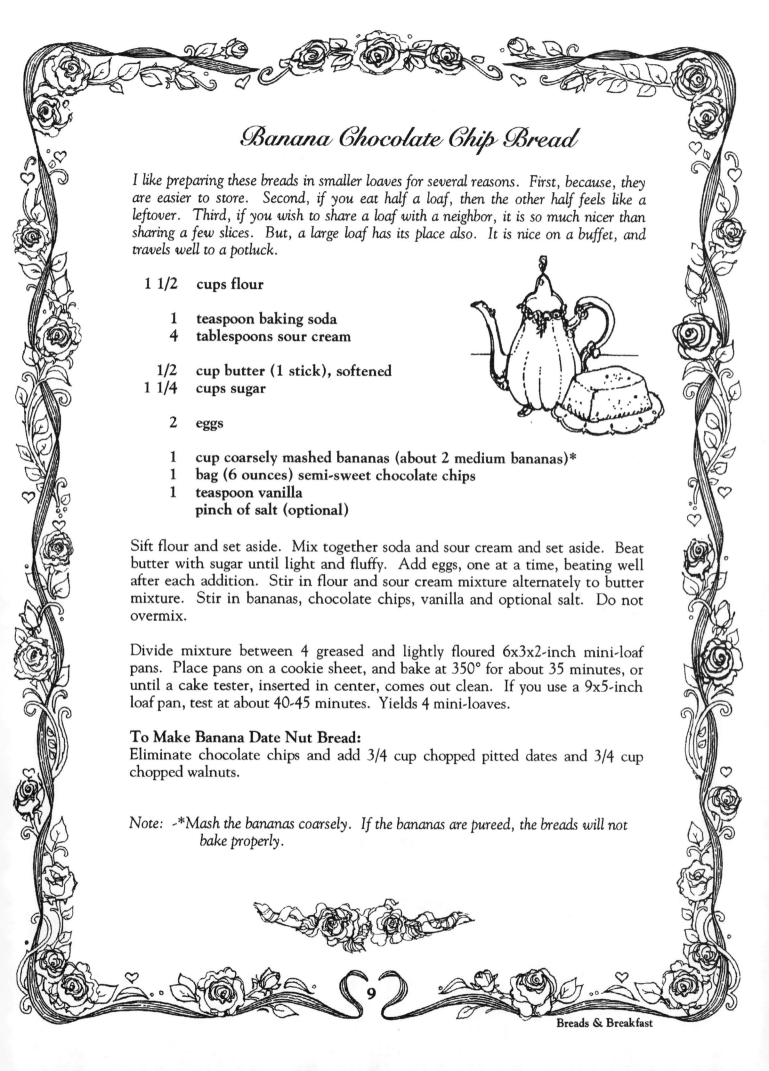

1 1/2	cups flour
1	teaspoon baking soda
4	tablespoons sour cream
1/2	cup butter (1 stick), softened
1 1/4	cups sugar
2	eggs
1	cup coarsely mashed bananas (about 2 medium bananas)*
1	bag (6 ounces) semi-sweet chocolate chips
1	teaspoon vanilla
	pinch of salt (optional)

Sift flour and set aside. Mix together soda and sour cream and set aside. Beat butter with sugar until light and fluffy. Add eggs, one at a time, beating well after each addition. Stir in flour and sour cream mixture alternately to butter mixture. Stir in bananas, chocolate chips, vanilla and optional salt. Do not overmix.

Divide mixture between 4 greased and lightly floured 6x3x2-inch mini-loaf pans. Place pans on a cookie sheet, and bake at 350° for about 35 minutes, or until a cake tester, inserted in center, comes out clean. If you use a 9x5-inch loaf pan, test at about 40-45 minutes. Yields 4 mini-loaves.

To Make Banana Date Nut Bread:
Eliminate chocolate chips and add 3/4 cup chopped pitted dates and 3/4 cup chopped walnuts.

*Note: -*Mash the bananas coarsely. If the bananas are pureed, the breads will not bake properly.*

Sour Cream Apricot Bread with Streusel Topping

This is a nice bread to consider as a gift from your kitchen. The Streusel Topping is a dressy cover-up and optional. The bread stands alone quite well.

1/2	cup butter, softened
1	cup sugar
3	eggs
3/4	cup sour cream
2	teaspoons vanilla
2	cups flour
1 1/2	teaspoons baking powder
1/2	teaspoon baking soda
1	cup chopped dried apricots
1/2	cup chopped walnuts

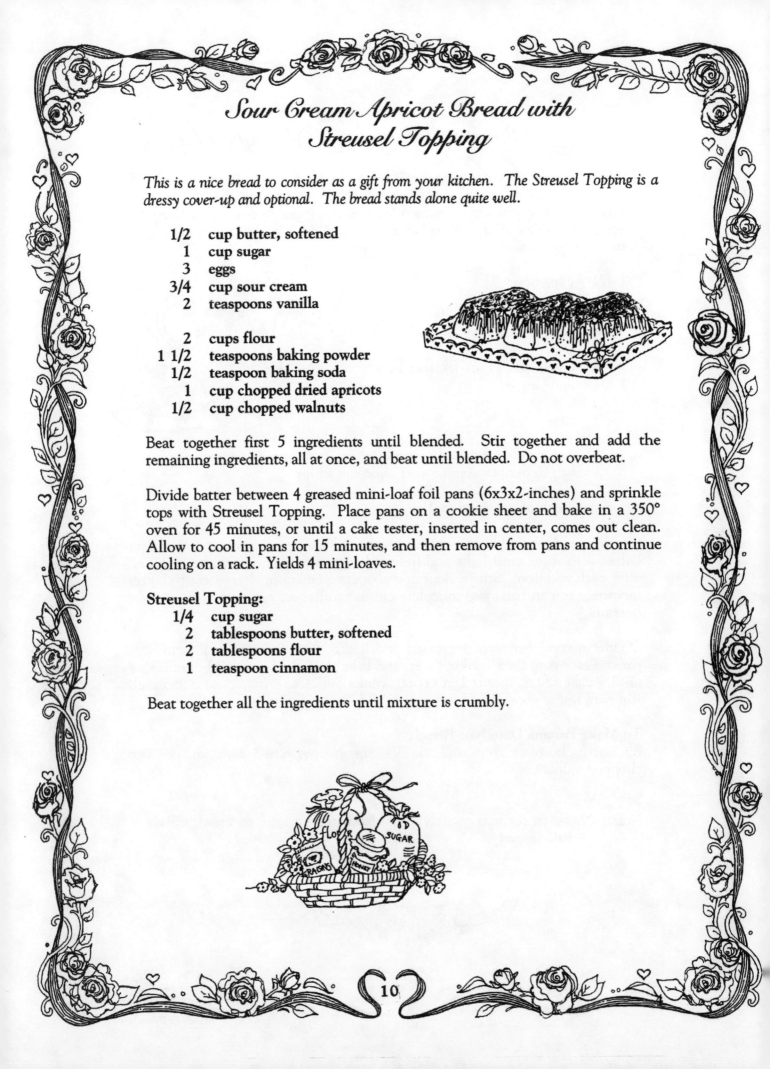

Beat together first 5 ingredients until blended. Stir together and add the remaining ingredients, all at once, and beat until blended. Do not overbeat.

Divide batter between 4 greased mini-loaf foil pans (6x3x2-inches) and sprinkle tops with Streusel Topping. Place pans on a cookie sheet and bake in a 350° oven for 45 minutes, or until a cake tester, inserted in center, comes out clean. Allow to cool in pans for 15 minutes, and then remove from pans and continue cooling on a rack. Yields 4 mini-loaves.

Streusel Topping:

1/4	cup sugar
2	tablespoons butter, softened
2	tablespoons flour
1	teaspoon cinnamon

Beat together all the ingredients until mixture is crumbly.

The Best Banana & Cranberry Bread

This is one of my favorite breads. It is a poetry of flavors and textures. It has a great "crumb" and can be cut into the thinnest slices. To insure success, do not puree the bananas. Mash them coarsely with a fork and then stir them in. If the bananas are pureed, it will take forever to bake the breads and results will be less than satisfactory.

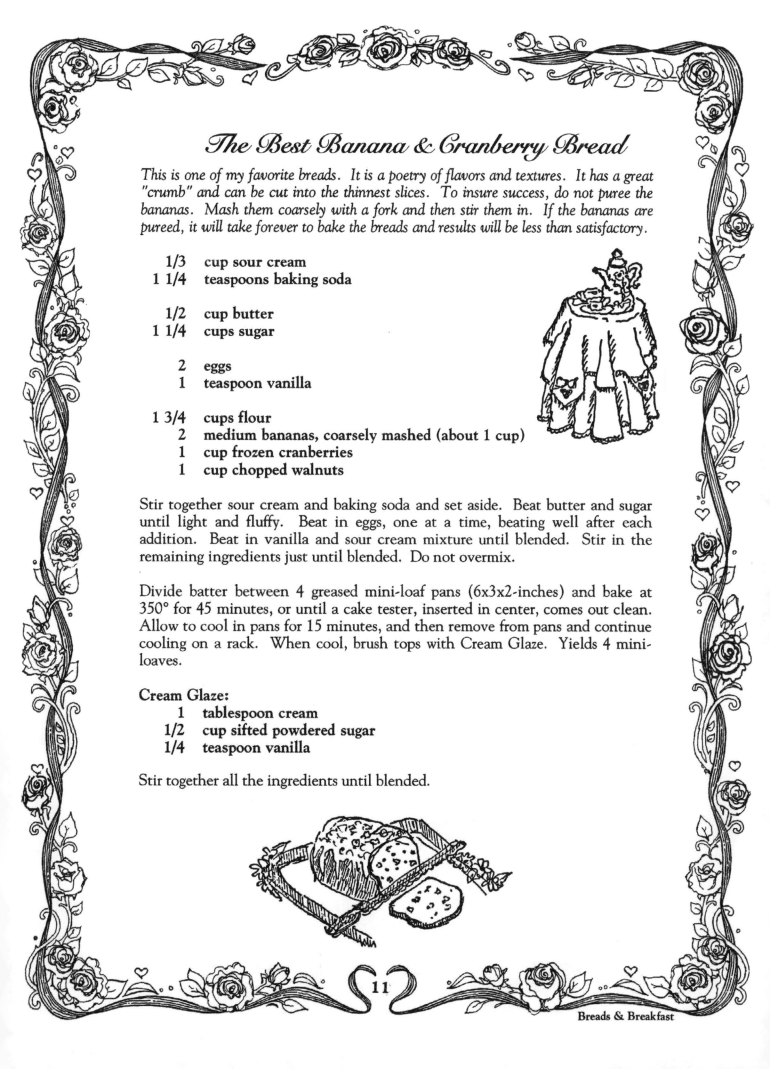

1/3	cup sour cream
1 1/4	teaspoons baking soda
1/2	cup butter
1 1/4	cups sugar
2	eggs
1	teaspoon vanilla
1 3/4	cups flour
2	medium bananas, coarsely mashed (about 1 cup)
1	cup frozen cranberries
1	cup chopped walnuts

Stir together sour cream and baking soda and set aside. Beat butter and sugar until light and fluffy. Beat in eggs, one at a time, beating well after each addition. Beat in vanilla and sour cream mixture until blended. Stir in the remaining ingredients just until blended. Do not overmix.

Divide batter between 4 greased mini-loaf pans (6x3x2-inches) and bake at 350° for 45 minutes, or until a cake tester, inserted in center, comes out clean. Allow to cool in pans for 15 minutes, and then remove from pans and continue cooling on a rack. When cool, brush tops with Cream Glaze. Yields 4 mini-loaves.

Cream Glaze:
1	tablespoon cream
1/2	cup sifted powdered sugar
1/4	teaspoon vanilla

Stir together all the ingredients until blended.

11

Country Kitchen Gingerbread with Raisins

2	cups sifted flour
2	teaspoons baking powder
1/2	teaspoon baking soda
1	teaspoon cinnamon
1	teaspoon ginger
1/4	teaspoon ground cloves
1/2	teaspoon salt
1/2	cup shortening
3/4	cup brown sugar
1	egg
3/4	cup boiling water
3/4	cup molasses
1/2	cup yellow raisins

Combine first 7 ingredients and set aside. Beat together the shortening and sugar until blended. Beat in the egg and continue beating until mixture is light and fluffy. Combine the hot water and molasses.

Now, add the dry ingredients and the molasses and water to the shortening mixture, alternating a little at a time, stirring only until blended and smooth. Stir in the raisins.

Spoon batter into a greased 8x8-inch pan and bake at 350° for 45 minutes. Cut into squares and serve with cream cheese, sliced strawberries and toasted pecans. Yields 16 2-inch squares.

Easiest & Best Buttery Cornbread

1/2	cup butter, melted
1/2	cup milk
1	egg, beaten
1	cup Bisquick
1/2	teaspoon baking soda
4	tablespoons cornmeal
6	tablespoons sugar

In a bowl, stir together the butter, milk and egg. Add the remaining ingredients, all at once, and stir until partially blended. Batter will be a little lumpy. Pour batter into a greased 8x8-inch pan. Bake at 350° for about 25 minutes or until top is light brown. Yields 16 2-inch squares

Orange Tea Bread with
Walnuts & Raisins & Orange Glaze

This dense bread, filled with orange, walnuts and raisins is just lovely for breakfast, brunch or tea time. The Orange Glaze is very festive and adds a delicious touch.

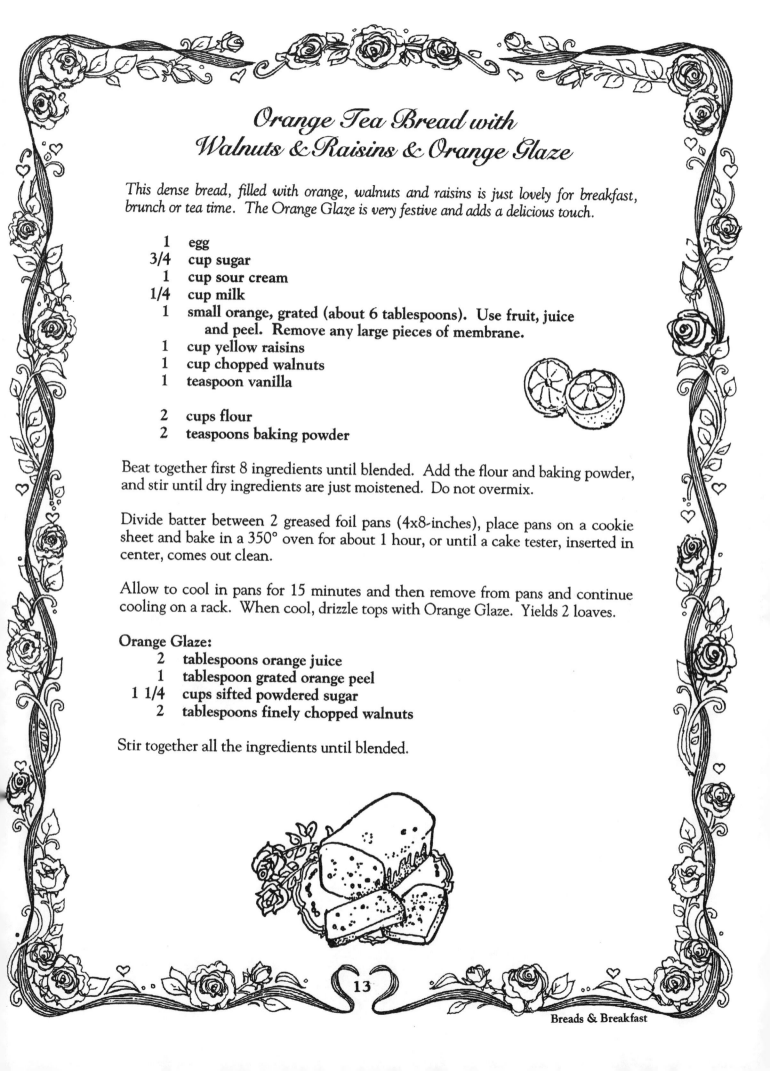

1	egg
3/4	cup sugar
1	cup sour cream
1/4	cup milk
1	small orange, grated (about 6 tablespoons). Use fruit, juice and peel. Remove any large pieces of membrane.
1	cup yellow raisins
1	cup chopped walnuts
1	teaspoon vanilla
2	cups flour
2	teaspoons baking powder

Beat together first 8 ingredients until blended. Add the flour and baking powder, and stir until dry ingredients are just moistened. Do not overmix.

Divide batter between 2 greased foil pans (4x8-inches), place pans on a cookie sheet and bake in a 350° oven for about 1 hour, or until a cake tester, inserted in center, comes out clean.

Allow to cool in pans for 15 minutes and then remove from pans and continue cooling on a rack. When cool, drizzle tops with Orange Glaze. Yields 2 loaves.

Orange Glaze:

2	tablespoons orange juice
1	tablespoon grated orange peel
1 1/4	cups sifted powdered sugar
2	tablespoons finely chopped walnuts

Stir together all the ingredients until blended.

13

Sour Cream Biscuits with Dill

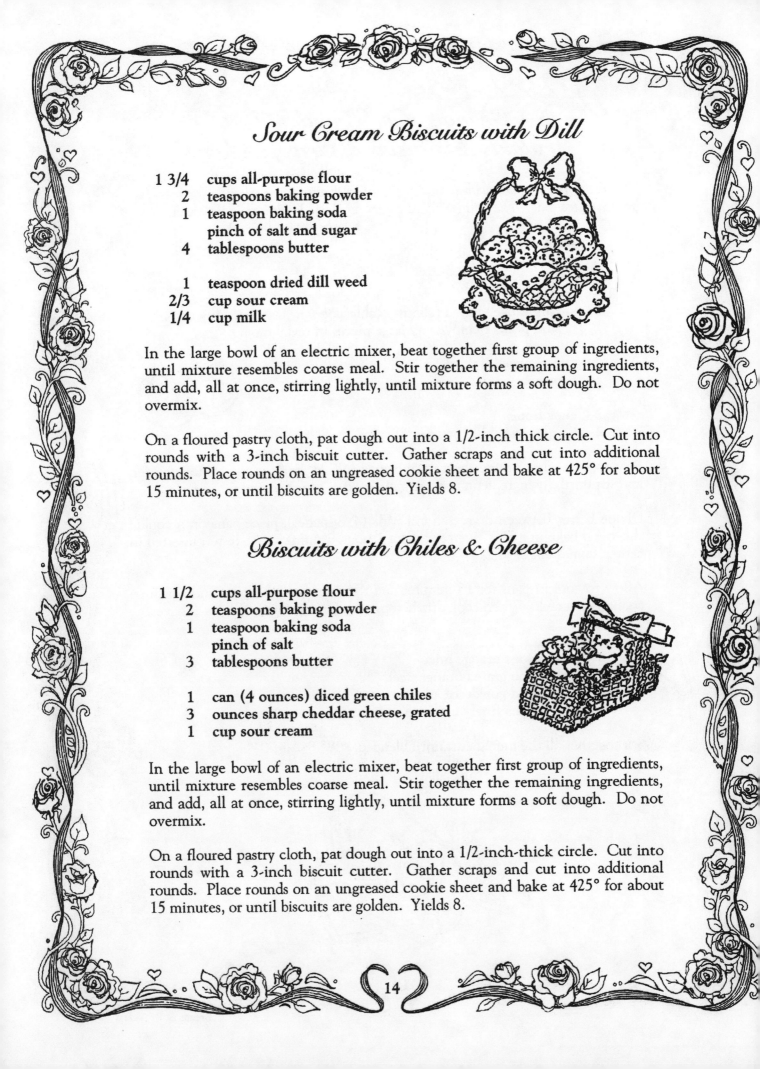

1 3/4	cups all-purpose flour
2	teaspoons baking powder
1	teaspoon baking soda
	pinch of salt and sugar
4	tablespoons butter
1	teaspoon dried dill weed
2/3	cup sour cream
1/4	cup milk

In the large bowl of an electric mixer, beat together first group of ingredients, until mixture resembles coarse meal. Stir together the remaining ingredients, and add, all at once, stirring lightly, until mixture forms a soft dough. Do not overmix.

On a floured pastry cloth, pat dough out into a 1/2-inch thick circle. Cut into rounds with a 3-inch biscuit cutter. Gather scraps and cut into additional rounds. Place rounds on an ungreased cookie sheet and bake at 425° for about 15 minutes, or until biscuits are golden. Yields 8.

Biscuits with Chiles & Cheese

1 1/2	cups all-purpose flour
2	teaspoons baking powder
1	teaspoon baking soda
	pinch of salt
3	tablespoons butter
1	can (4 ounces) diced green chiles
3	ounces sharp cheddar cheese, grated
1	cup sour cream

In the large bowl of an electric mixer, beat together first group of ingredients, until mixture resembles coarse meal. Stir together the remaining ingredients, and add, all at once, stirring lightly, until mixture forms a soft dough. Do not overmix.

On a floured pastry cloth, pat dough out into a 1/2-inch-thick circle. Cut into rounds with a 3-inch biscuit cutter. Gather scraps and cut into additional rounds. Place rounds on an ungreased cookie sheet and bake at 425° for about 15 minutes, or until biscuits are golden. Yields 8.

Feather Cream Drop Biscuits

This is my favorite biscuit, light as a feather and very easy to prepare. Biscuits are dropped from a tablespoon which eliminates kneading, rolling and cutting. Follow the directions carefully, and your biscuits will be perfect every time.

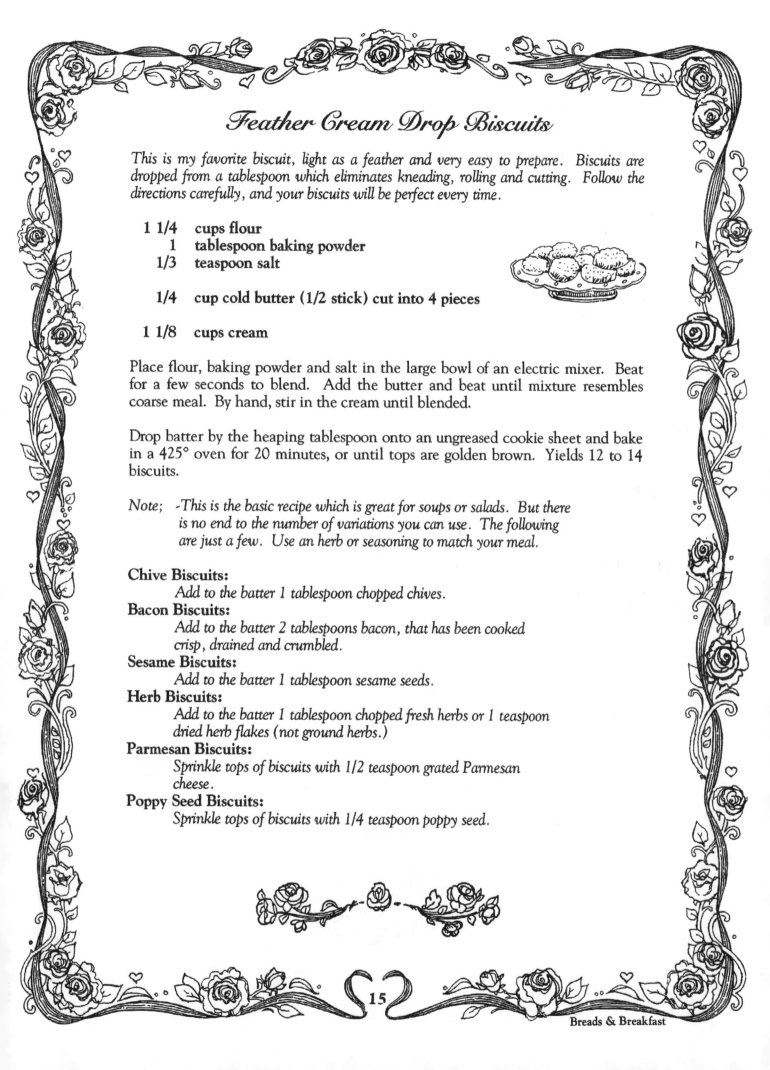

1 1/4	cups flour
1	tablespoon baking powder
1/3	teaspoon salt
1/4	cup cold butter (1/2 stick) cut into 4 pieces
1 1/8	cups cream

Place flour, baking powder and salt in the large bowl of an electric mixer. Beat for a few seconds to blend. Add the butter and beat until mixture resembles coarse meal. By hand, stir in the cream until blended.

Drop batter by the heaping tablespoon onto an ungreased cookie sheet and bake in a 425° oven for 20 minutes, or until tops are golden brown. Yields 12 to 14 biscuits.

Note; -This is the basic recipe which is great for soups or salads. But there is no end to the number of variations you can use. The following are just a few. Use an herb or seasoning to match your meal.

Chive Biscuits:
> *Add to the batter 1 tablespoon chopped chives.*

Bacon Biscuits:
> *Add to the batter 2 tablespoons bacon, that has been cooked crisp, drained and crumbled.*

Sesame Biscuits:
> *Add to the batter 1 tablespoon sesame seeds.*

Herb Biscuits:
> *Add to the batter 1 tablespoon chopped fresh herbs or 1 teaspoon dried herb flakes (not ground herbs.)*

Parmesan Biscuits:
> *Sprinkle tops of biscuits with 1/2 teaspoon grated Parmesan cheese.*

Poppy Seed Biscuits:
> *Sprinkle tops of biscuits with 1/4 teaspoon poppy seed.*

Breakfast Biscuits with Currants & Oats

These are nice to serve at breakfast, with sweet butter and jam. Preparing them in a food processor is totally foolproof…although they can be prepared in a mixer, using a paddle beater. Do not overbeat. This is not a fluffy biscuit, so don't think anything went wrong.

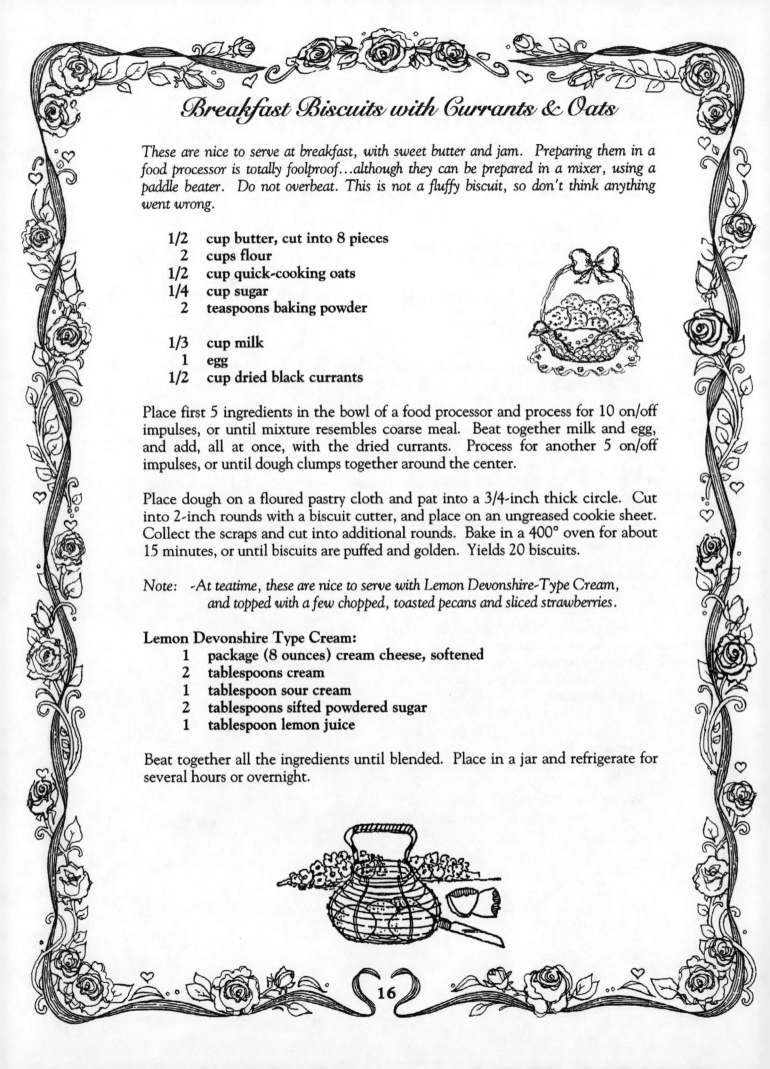

1/2	cup butter, cut into 8 pieces
2	cups flour
1/2	cup quick-cooking oats
1/4	cup sugar
2	teaspoons baking powder
1/3	cup milk
1	egg
1/2	cup dried black currants

Place first 5 ingredients in the bowl of a food processor and process for 10 on/off impulses, or until mixture resembles coarse meal. Beat together milk and egg, and add, all at once, with the dried currants. Process for another 5 on/off impulses, or until dough clumps together around the center.

Place dough on a floured pastry cloth and pat into a 3/4-inch thick circle. Cut into 2-inch rounds with a biscuit cutter, and place on an ungreased cookie sheet. Collect the scraps and cut into additional rounds. Bake in a 400° oven for about 15 minutes, or until biscuits are puffed and golden. Yields 20 biscuits.

Note: -At teatime, these are nice to serve with Lemon Devonshire-Type Cream, and topped with a few chopped, toasted pecans and sliced strawberries.

Lemon Devonshire Type Cream:

1	package (8 ounces) cream cheese, softened
2	tablespoons cream
1	tablespoon sour cream
2	tablespoons sifted powdered sugar
1	tablespoon lemon juice

Beat together all the ingredients until blended. Place in a jar and refrigerate for several hours or overnight.

Buttery Scones with Apricots

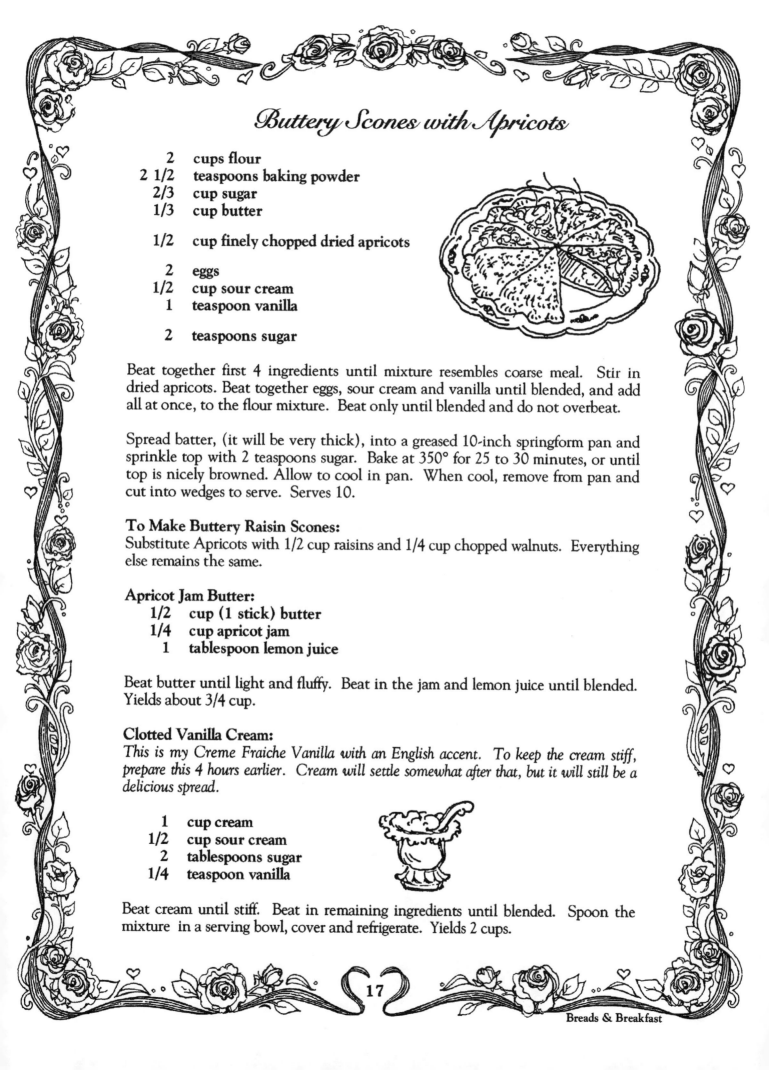

2	cups flour
2 1/2	teaspoons baking powder
2/3	cup sugar
1/3	cup butter
1/2	cup finely chopped dried apricots
2	eggs
1/2	cup sour cream
1	teaspoon vanilla
2	teaspoons sugar

Beat together first 4 ingredients until mixture resembles coarse meal. Stir in dried apricots. Beat together eggs, sour cream and vanilla until blended, and add all at once, to the flour mixture. Beat only until blended and do not overbeat.

Spread batter, (it will be very thick), into a greased 10-inch springform pan and sprinkle top with 2 teaspoons sugar. Bake at 350° for 25 to 30 minutes, or until top is nicely browned. Allow to cool in pan. When cool, remove from pan and cut into wedges to serve. Serves 10.

To Make Buttery Raisin Scones:
Substitute Apricots with 1/2 cup raisins and 1/4 cup chopped walnuts. Everything else remains the same.

Apricot Jam Butter:

1/2	cup (1 stick) butter
1/4	cup apricot jam
1	tablespoon lemon juice

Beat butter until light and fluffy. Beat in the jam and lemon juice until blended. Yields about 3/4 cup.

Clotted Vanilla Cream:
This is my Creme Fraiche Vanilla with an English accent. To keep the cream stiff, prepare this 4 hours earlier. Cream will settle somewhat after that, but it will still be a delicious spread.

1	cup cream
1/2	cup sour cream
2	tablespoons sugar
1/4	teaspoon vanilla

Beat cream until stiff. Beat in remaining ingredients until blended. Spoon the mixture in a serving bowl, cover and refrigerate. Yields 2 cups.

Basic Scones with Currants & Walnuts

This recipe serves well as a basic scone. It can be added to in so many different ways. You can change the dry fruit to dry apricots, dates, raisins, cranberries or cherries...all very delicious.

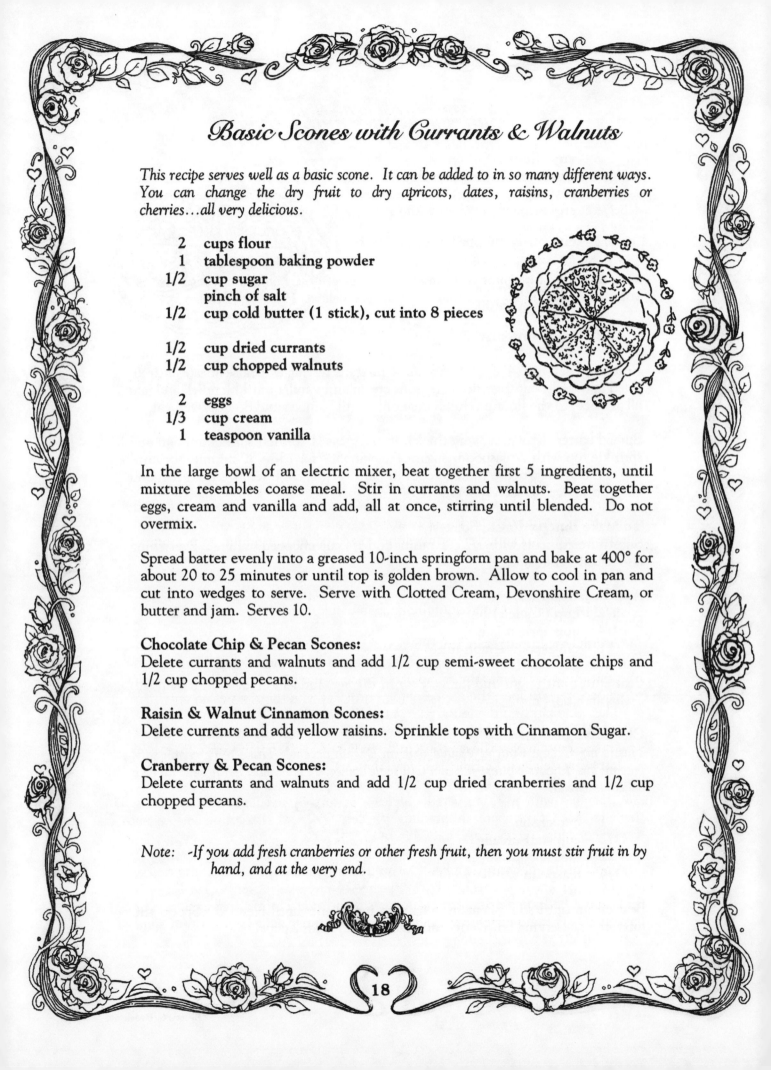

2	cups flour
1	tablespoon baking powder
1/2	cup sugar
	pinch of salt
1/2	cup cold butter (1 stick), cut into 8 pieces
1/2	cup dried currants
1/2	cup chopped walnuts
2	eggs
1/3	cup cream
1	teaspoon vanilla

In the large bowl of an electric mixer, beat together first 5 ingredients, until mixture resembles coarse meal. Stir in currants and walnuts. Beat together eggs, cream and vanilla and add, all at once, stirring until blended. Do not overmix.

Spread batter evenly into a greased 10-inch springform pan and bake at 400° for about 20 to 25 minutes or until top is golden brown. Allow to cool in pan and cut into wedges to serve. Serve with Clotted Cream, Devonshire Cream, or butter and jam. Serves 10.

Chocolate Chip & Pecan Scones:
Delete currants and walnuts and add 1/2 cup semi-sweet chocolate chips and 1/2 cup chopped pecans.

Raisin & Walnut Cinnamon Scones:
Delete currents and add yellow raisins. Sprinkle tops with Cinnamon Sugar.

Cranberry & Pecan Scones:
Delete currants and walnuts and add 1/2 cup dried cranberries and 1/2 cup chopped pecans.

Note: -If you add fresh cranberries or other fresh fruit, then you must stir fruit in by hand, and at the very end.

Wimbledon Cream Scones with Currants

This is a variation of my Victorian Cream Scones. Serve it with Devonshire Cream and Strawberries for an English breakfast treat. This recipe is a little more moist and tender than the traditional scone. Chopped dried apricots can be substituted for the currants. As a variation, add 2 tablespoons of chopped pecans.

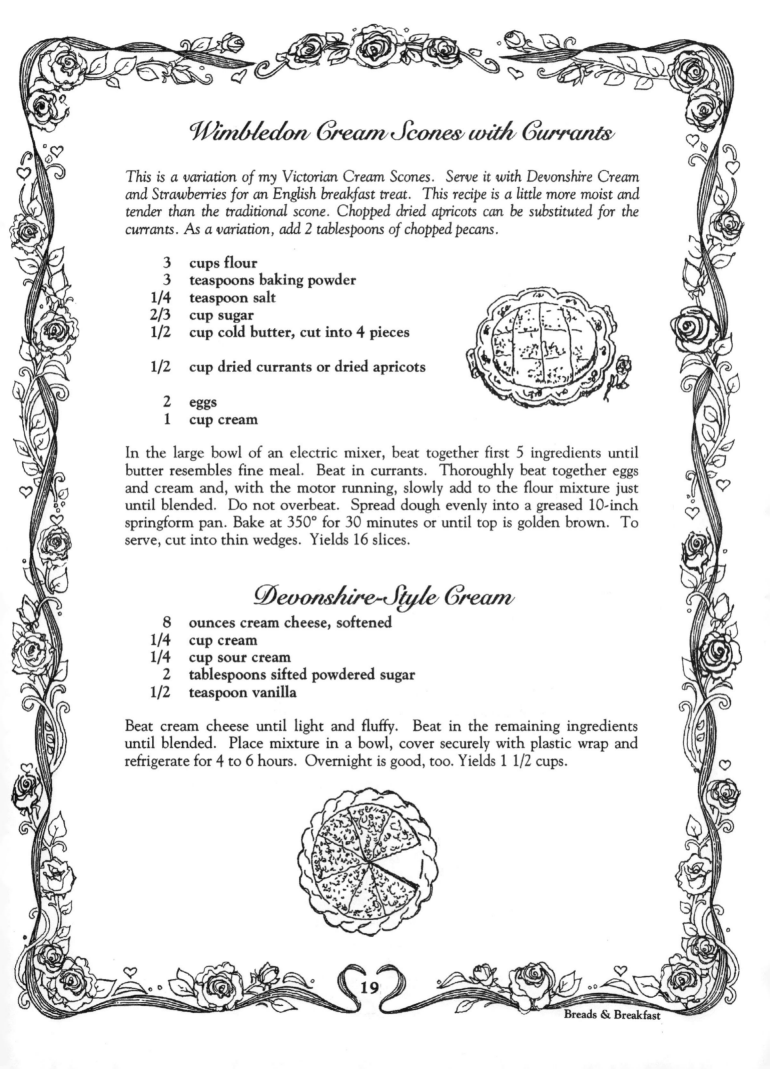

3	cups flour
3	teaspoons baking powder
1/4	teaspoon salt
2/3	cup sugar
1/2	cup cold butter, cut into 4 pieces
1/2	cup dried currants or dried apricots
2	eggs
1	cup cream

In the large bowl of an electric mixer, beat together first 5 ingredients until butter resembles fine meal. Beat in currants. Thoroughly beat together eggs and cream and, with the motor running, slowly add to the flour mixture just until blended. Do not overbeat. Spread dough evenly into a greased 10-inch springform pan. Bake at 350° for 30 minutes or until top is golden brown. To serve, cut into thin wedges. Yields 16 slices.

Devonshire-Style Cream

8	ounces cream cheese, softened
1/4	cup cream
1/4	cup sour cream
2	tablespoons sifted powdered sugar
1/2	teaspoon vanilla

Beat cream cheese until light and fluffy. Beat in the remaining ingredients until blended. Place mixture in a bowl, cover securely with plastic wrap and refrigerate for 4 to 6 hours. Overnight is good, too. Yields 1 1/2 cups.

Victorian Scones with Apricots & Pecans

- 2 cups flour
- 1 tablespoon baking powder
- 1/2 cup sugar
- pinch of salt
- 1/2 cup cold butter (1 stick), cut into 8 pieces

- 1/2 cup chopped dried apricots
- 1/2 cup chopped pecans

- 2 eggs
- 1/3 cup cream
- 1 teaspoon vanilla

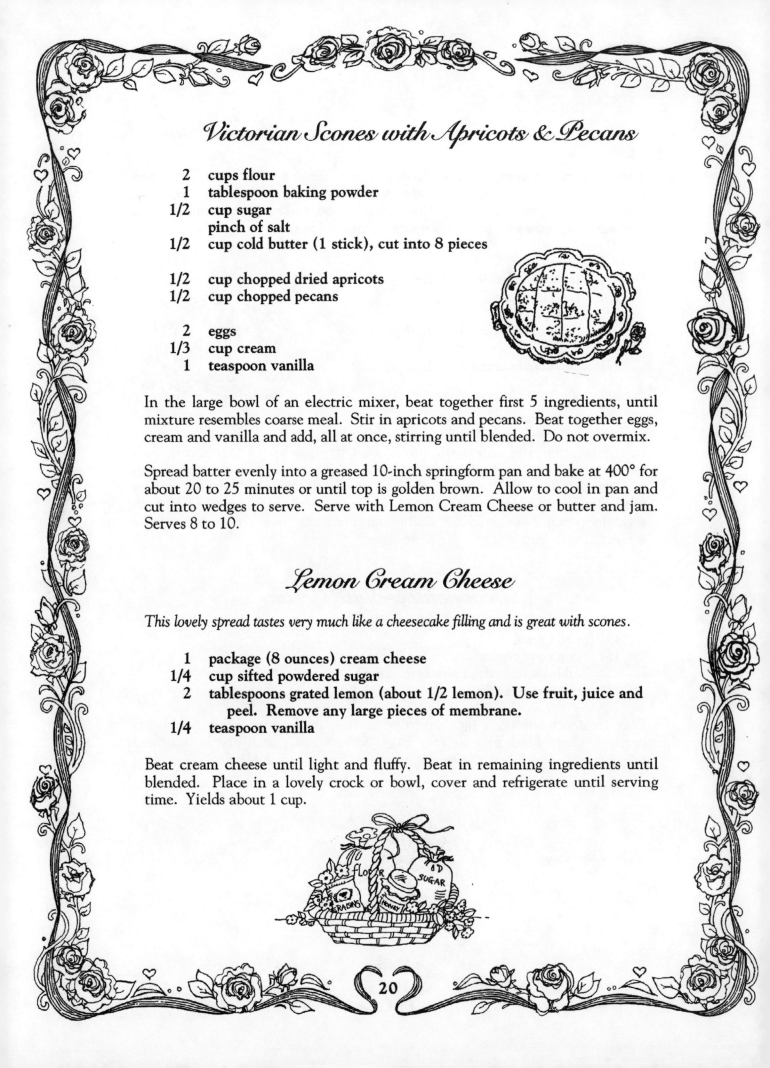

In the large bowl of an electric mixer, beat together first 5 ingredients, until mixture resembles coarse meal. Stir in apricots and pecans. Beat together eggs, cream and vanilla and add, all at once, stirring until blended. Do not overmix.

Spread batter evenly into a greased 10-inch springform pan and bake at 400° for about 20 to 25 minutes or until top is golden brown. Allow to cool in pan and cut into wedges to serve. Serve with Lemon Cream Cheese or butter and jam. Serves 8 to 10.

Lemon Cream Cheese

This lovely spread tastes very much like a cheesecake filling and is great with scones.

- 1 package (8 ounces) cream cheese
- 1/4 cup sifted powdered sugar
- 2 tablespoons grated lemon (about 1/2 lemon). Use fruit, juice and peel. Remove any large pieces of membrane.
- 1/4 teaspoon vanilla

Beat cream cheese until light and fluffy. Beat in remaining ingredients until blended. Place in a lovely crock or bowl, cover and refrigerate until serving time. Yields about 1 cup.

Greek Sweet Biscuit Bread with Currants

This is an interesting and versatile bread. It is moist, tender and delicious and serves well with sweet or savory spreads. Far more interesting than a cracker, it is equally good served with cream cheese, sliced strawberries and a sprinkling of pecans...or with cheese, pâté and wine.

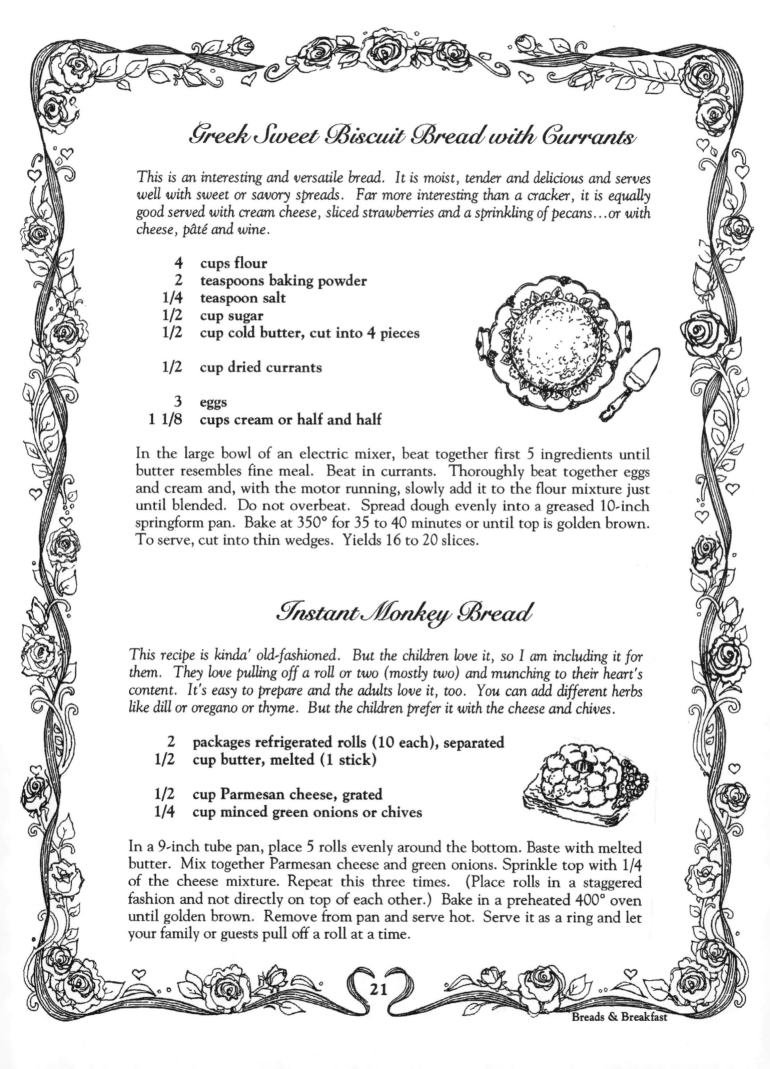

4	cups flour
2	teaspoons baking powder
1/4	teaspoon salt
1/2	cup sugar
1/2	cup cold butter, cut into 4 pieces
1/2	cup dried currants
3	eggs
1 1/8	cups cream or half and half

In the large bowl of an electric mixer, beat together first 5 ingredients until butter resembles fine meal. Beat in currants. Thoroughly beat together eggs and cream and, with the motor running, slowly add it to the flour mixture just until blended. Do not overbeat. Spread dough evenly into a greased 10-inch springform pan. Bake at 350° for 35 to 40 minutes or until top is golden brown. To serve, cut into thin wedges. Yields 16 to 20 slices.

Instant Monkey Bread

This recipe is kinda' old-fashioned. But the children love it, so I am including it for them. They love pulling off a roll or two (mostly two) and munching to their heart's content. It's easy to prepare and the adults love it, too. You can add different herbs like dill or oregano or thyme. But the children prefer it with the cheese and chives.

2	packages refrigerated rolls (10 each), separated
1/2	cup butter, melted (1 stick)
1/2	cup Parmesan cheese, grated
1/4	cup minced green onions or chives

In a 9-inch tube pan, place 5 rolls evenly around the bottom. Baste with melted butter. Mix together Parmesan cheese and green onions. Sprinkle top with 1/4 of the cheese mixture. Repeat this three times. (Place rolls in a staggered fashion and not directly on top of each other.) Bake in a preheated 400° oven until golden brown. Remove from pan and serve hot. Serve it as a ring and let your family or guests pull off a roll at a time.

Onion & Cheese Crescents for Soup and Salad

This is a delightful bread to accompany soup or salad. Serve these warm and no need to serve with butter.

1	cup cottage cheese
3	ounces butter (3/4 stick), softened
1	cup flour
2	tablespoons grated Parmesan cheese
1	tablespoon dried onion flakes

Topping:

2	tablespoons melted butter
3	tablespoons grated Parmesan cheese

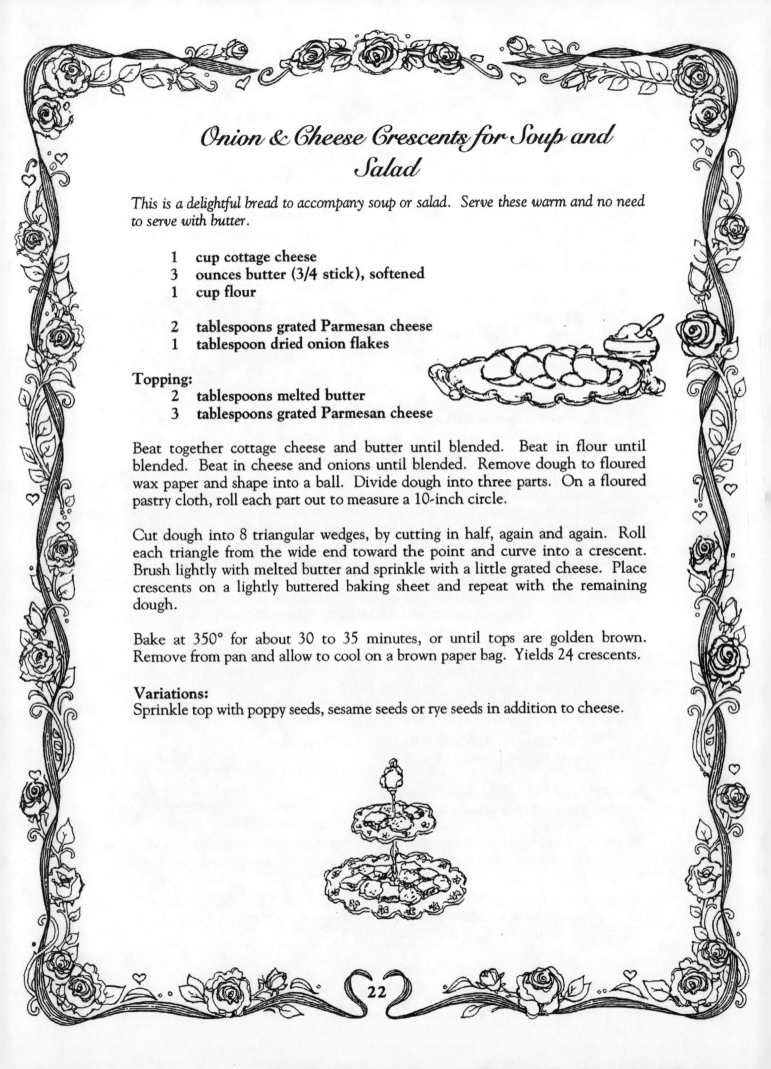

Beat together cottage cheese and butter until blended. Beat in flour until blended. Beat in cheese and onions until blended. Remove dough to floured wax paper and shape into a ball. Divide dough into three parts. On a floured pastry cloth, roll each part out to measure a 10-inch circle.

Cut dough into 8 triangular wedges, by cutting in half, again and again. Roll each triangle from the wide end toward the point and curve into a crescent. Brush lightly with melted butter and sprinkle with a little grated cheese. Place crescents on a lightly buttered baking sheet and repeat with the remaining dough.

Bake at 350° for about 30 to 35 minutes, or until tops are golden brown. Remove from pan and allow to cool on a brown paper bag. Yields 24 crescents.

Variations:
Sprinkle top with poppy seeds, sesame seeds or rye seeds in addition to cheese.

Pita Crisps with Parmesan Cheese

    6   6-inch pita breads
    12   teaspoons butter
    12   teaspoons grated Parmesan cheese or more to taste

Cut off 1/8-inch around the edge of pitas and separate them into halves. Place pitas, rough side up, in one layer in a baking pan. Spread 1 teaspoon butter on each rough side of pita bread. Sprinkle with 1 teaspoon grated Parmesan.

Bake at 350° for 3 to 4 minutes or until cheese starts to bubble. Careful, for there are only a few seconds between crisp and burnt. Serve with soup or salads. Can be prepared earlier in the day and stored in a plastic bag. Serve at room temperature. Yields 12 servings.

Note: -Make extras, these get gobbled up very, very quickly. Everybody loves them.

Honey Sesame Pitas

Crisp and sweet, these are a lovely accompaniment to a Cous Cous Salad. They can be prepared earlier in the day and stored in plastic bags at room temperature.

    8   pitas

    1/3 cup butter
    1/3 cup honey
    8   teaspoons sesame seeds

Cut off 1/8-inch around the edge of pitas and separate them into halves. In batches, place pitas in one layer in a baking pan, rough side up. Heat together butter and honey until nicely blended and brush tops of pitas with the mixture.

Sprinkle each top with 1/2 teaspoon of sesame seeds. Bake in a 350° oven for about 5 minutes until edges are beginning to take on color. Watch carefully, for there are only a few seconds between brown and burnt. Remove from oven and cool. They will be chewy and crisp. Repeat with remaining pitas. Serves 8.

Note: -Warming the butter and honey makes it easy to spread. You could spread 1 teaspoon of butter and honey on each half. Just a suggestion.

Crispy Sweet Raisin Corn Muffins

If you enjoy muffins that are crisp and crunchy, you will love this little treasure. These are on the sweet side and are delicious served warm for breakfast with a little cream cheese and jam. These, also, are a nice accompaniment to a Mexican soup or salad.

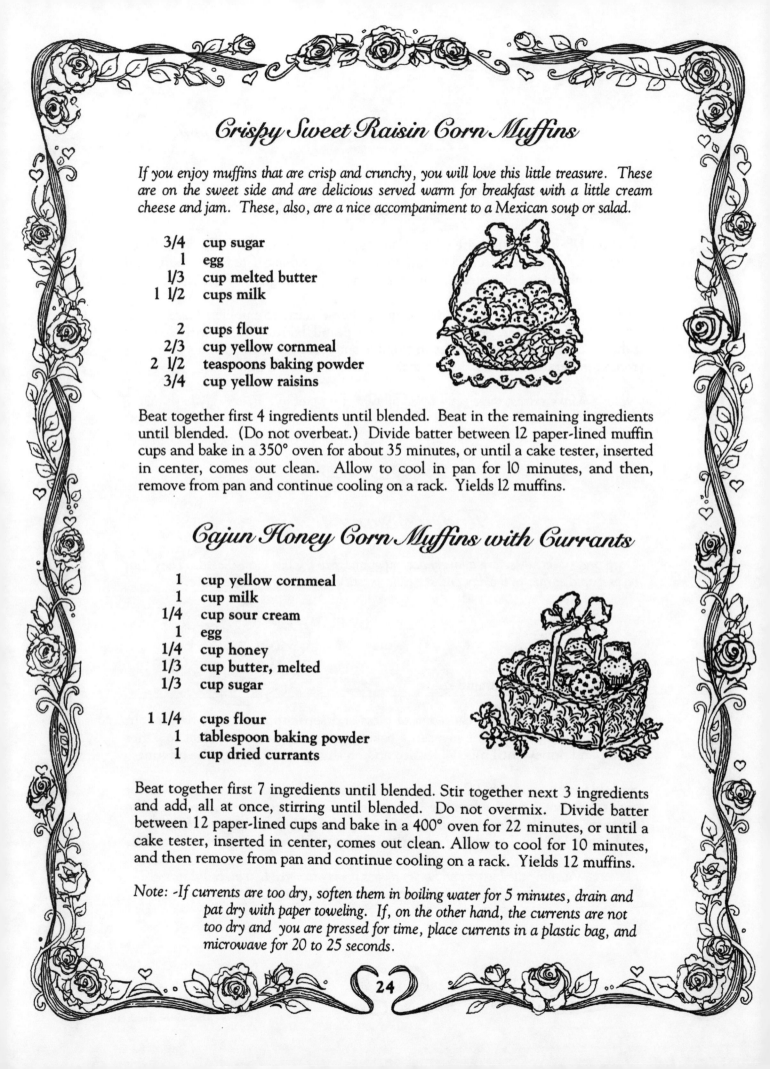

3/4	cup sugar
1	egg
1/3	cup melted butter
1 1/2	cups milk
2	cups flour
2/3	cup yellow cornmeal
2 1/2	teaspoons baking powder
3/4	cup yellow raisins

Beat together first 4 ingredients until blended. Beat in the remaining ingredients until blended. (Do not overbeat.) Divide batter between 12 paper-lined muffin cups and bake in a 350° oven for about 35 minutes, or until a cake tester, inserted in center, comes out clean. Allow to cool in pan for 10 minutes, and then, remove from pan and continue cooling on a rack. Yields 12 muffins.

Cajun Honey Corn Muffins with Currants

1	cup yellow cornmeal
1	cup milk
1/4	cup sour cream
1	egg
1/4	cup honey
1/3	cup butter, melted
1/3	cup sugar
1 1/4	cups flour
1	tablespoon baking powder
1	cup dried currants

Beat together first 7 ingredients until blended. Stir together next 3 ingredients and add, all at once, stirring until blended. Do not overmix. Divide batter between 12 paper-lined cups and bake in a 400° oven for 22 minutes, or until a cake tester, inserted in center, comes out clean. Allow to cool for 10 minutes, and then remove from pan and continue cooling on a rack. Yields 12 muffins.

Note: -If currents are too dry, soften them in boiling water for 5 minutes, drain and pat dry with paper toweling. If, on the other hand, the currents are not too dry and you are pressed for time, place currants in a plastic bag, and microwave for 20 to 25 seconds.

Blueberry Oat Bran Muffins with Honey & Walnuts

These plump muffins are filled with all manner of good things, including oat bran, honey and blueberries. These are on the dense side because of the high content of oat bran. An excellent choice for breakfast.

2	eggs
3/4	cup milk
1/4	cup honey
1/2	cup sugar
1/4	cup oil
1/2	cup flour
2 1/4	cups oat bran cereal
1	tablespoon baking powder
1	cup blueberries
1/2	cup chopped walnuts

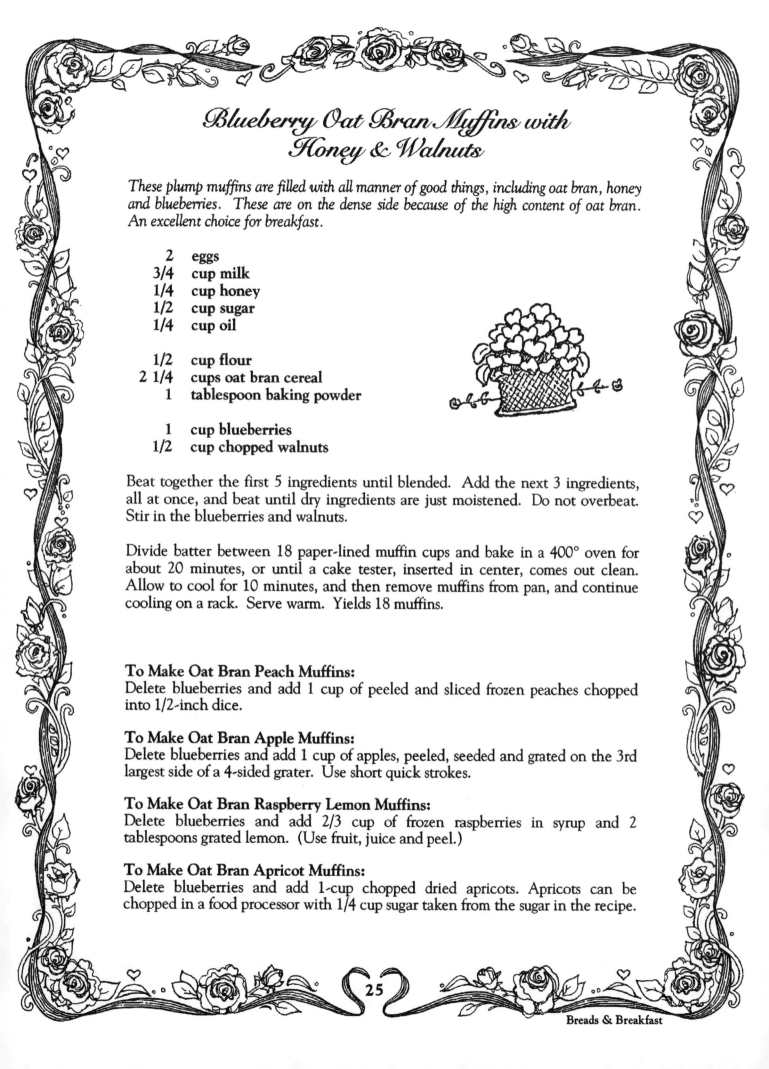

Beat together the first 5 ingredients until blended. Add the next 3 ingredients, all at once, and beat until dry ingredients are just moistened. Do not overbeat. Stir in the blueberries and walnuts.

Divide batter between 18 paper-lined muffin cups and bake in a 400° oven for about 20 minutes, or until a cake tester, inserted in center, comes out clean. Allow to cool for 10 minutes, and then remove muffins from pan, and continue cooling on a rack. Serve warm. Yields 18 muffins.

To Make Oat Bran Peach Muffins:
Delete blueberries and add 1 cup of peeled and sliced frozen peaches chopped into 1/2-inch dice.

To Make Oat Bran Apple Muffins:
Delete blueberries and add 1 cup of apples, peeled, seeded and grated on the 3rd largest side of a 4-sided grater. Use short quick strokes.

To Make Oat Bran Raspberry Lemon Muffins:
Delete blueberries and add 2/3 cup of frozen raspberries in syrup and 2 tablespoons grated lemon. (Use fruit, juice and peel.)

To Make Oat Bran Apricot Muffins:
Delete blueberries and add 1-cup chopped dried apricots. Apricots can be chopped in a food processor with 1/4 cup sugar taken from the sugar in the recipe.

Honey Gingerbread Muffins with Raisins

These muffins are dark and chewy and quite spicy. They are a good choice to serve with a hot and spicy soup or stew.

1/2	cup butter
1/2	cup sugar
1	egg
3/4	cup honey
1	cup sour milk (made with 1 cup milk and 1 teaspoon vinegar)

2 1/2	cups flour
1 1/2	teaspoons baking soda
1	teaspoon cinnamon
1	teaspoon ground ginger
1/4	teaspoon nutmeg
1	cup raisins
1/2	cup chopped walnuts

Beat together first 5 ingredients until blended. Stir together the remaining ingredients and add, all at once, beating until blended. Do not overbeat. Divide batter between 18 paper-lined muffin cups and bake in a 350° oven for about 25 minutes, or until a cake tester, inserted in center, comes out clean. Allow to cool for 10 minutes, and then remove from pans and continue cooling on rack. Yields 18 muffins.

Popovers with Herbs & Parmesan

3	eggs
1	cup flour
1/4	teaspoon salt
1	cup milk
1	tablespoon dried parsley flakes
1	tablespoon dried chopped chives

grated Parmesan cheese

Beat together all the ingredients except the grated cheese. Let batter rest for at least 1 hour. Heavily butter 18 muffin molds. (Use the basic size muffin pans.) Divide mixture evenly into the 18 muffin molds and sprinkle lightly with grated Parmesan.

Bake in a preheated 400° oven for 25 to 30 minutes or until popovers are puffed and golden brown. Serve immediately. Serves 8.

Fig & Walnut Whole Wheat Bran Muffins

This is a very tasty muffin that is filled with all manner of good things ... whole wheat, bran, figs. The recipe is a good basic one and can also be prepared with dates or apricots or raisins, instead of figs.

1 1/2	cups 100% all bran cereal (not bran flakes)
1 1/2	cups milk

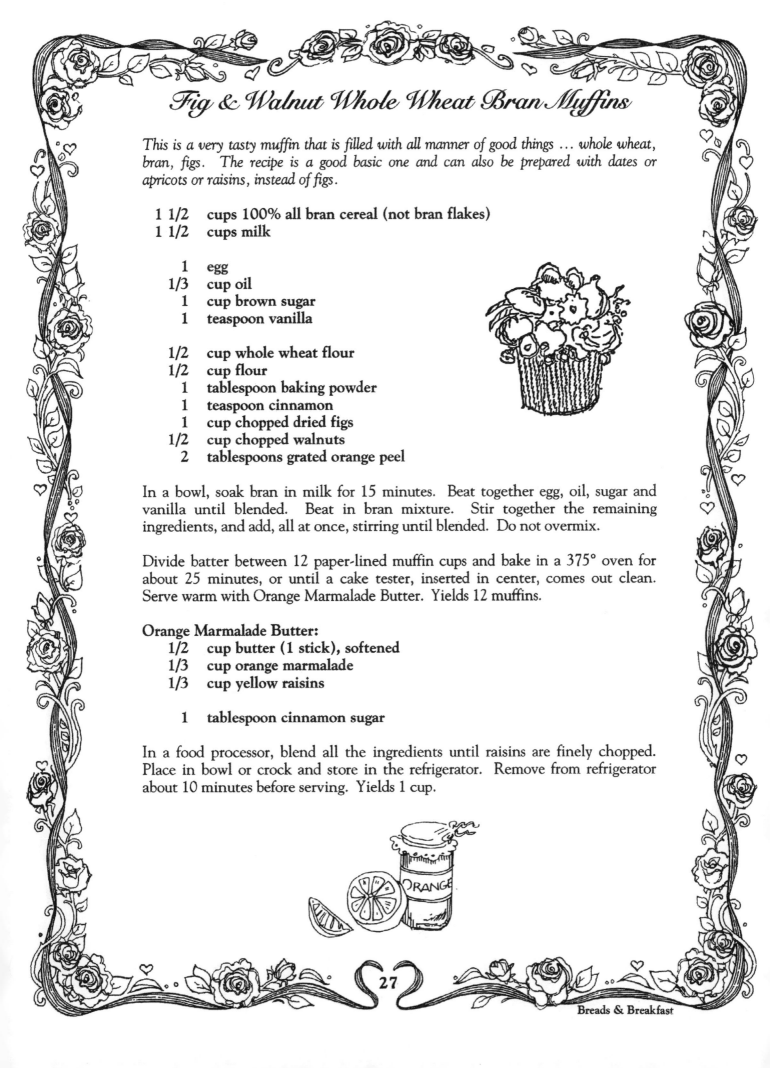

1	egg
1/3	cup oil
1	cup brown sugar
1	teaspoon vanilla

1/2	cup whole wheat flour
1/2	cup flour
1	tablespoon baking powder
1	teaspoon cinnamon
1	cup chopped dried figs
1/2	cup chopped walnuts
2	tablespoons grated orange peel

In a bowl, soak bran in milk for 15 minutes. Beat together egg, oil, sugar and vanilla until blended. Beat in bran mixture. Stir together the remaining ingredients, and add, all at once, stirring until blended. Do not overmix.

Divide batter between 12 paper-lined muffin cups and bake in a 375° oven for about 25 minutes, or until a cake tester, inserted in center, comes out clean. Serve warm with Orange Marmalade Butter. Yields 12 muffins.

Orange Marmalade Butter:

1/2	cup butter (1 stick), softened
1/3	cup orange marmalade
1/3	cup yellow raisins
1	tablespoon cinnamon sugar

In a food processor, blend all the ingredients until raisins are finely chopped. Place in bowl or crock and store in the refrigerator. Remove from refrigerator about 10 minutes before serving. Yields 1 cup.

Light & Lovely Lemon Butter Muffins

These muffins are lovely to serve at a ladies brunch or luncheon. They are delicate and very light.

    1/2   cup butter, softened
    2   eggs
    2/3   cup sugar
    4   tablespoons grated lemon. Use fruit, juice and peel. Remove any
           large pieces of membrane.

    2   cups flour
    3   teaspoons baking powder

    12   sprinkles sugar for topping

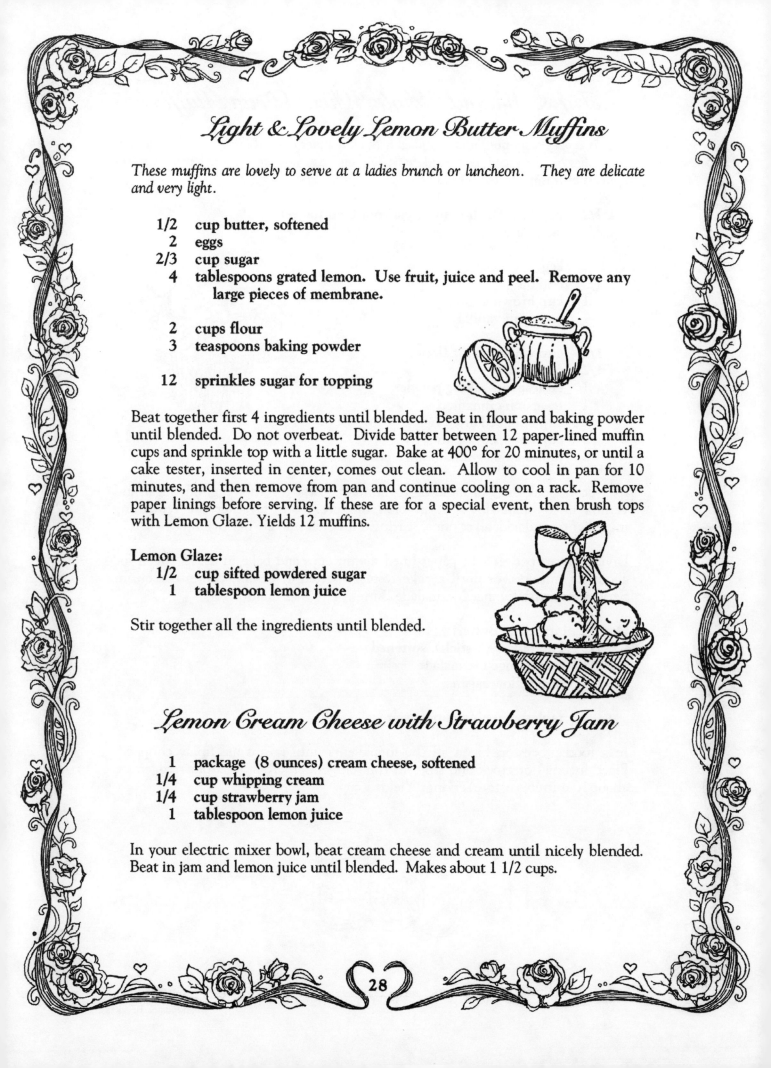

Beat together first 4 ingredients until blended. Beat in flour and baking powder until blended. Do not overbeat. Divide batter between 12 paper-lined muffin cups and sprinkle top with a little sugar. Bake at 400° for 20 minutes, or until a cake tester, inserted in center, comes out clean. Allow to cool in pan for 10 minutes, and then remove from pan and continue cooling on a rack. Remove paper linings before serving. If these are for a special event, then brush tops with Lemon Glaze. Yields 12 muffins.

Lemon Glaze:
    1/2   cup sifted powdered sugar
    1   tablespoon lemon juice

Stir together all the ingredients until blended.

Lemon Cream Cheese with Strawberry Jam

    1   package (8 ounces) cream cheese, softened
    1/4   cup whipping cream
    1/4   cup strawberry jam
    1   tablespoon lemon juice

In your electric mixer bowl, beat cream cheese and cream until nicely blended. Beat in jam and lemon juice until blended. Makes about 1 1/2 cups.

2-Minute Flatbread with Garlic & Rosemary

This is a variation of the popular beer bread, but heightened with the addition of garlic and rosemary. The cheese rounds out the taste beautifully. This is a great bread to serve with a meal in an Italian mood. If preparing bread earlier in the day, leave it in the pan and wrap pan securely with plastic wrap. The first 3 ingredients are basic and flavorings can be mixed and matched. Match the spices to your dinner, or add sesame seeds, poppy seeds, caraway seeds, etc. for a bread with a totally different character.

Basic Bread:

3	cups self-rising flour
3	tablespoons sugar
1	can (12 ounces) beer, cold or at room temperature. (I have found no difference in results using either.)
3	tablespoons crumbled rosemary
6	cloves minced garlic
4	teaspoons oil
2	tablespoons grated Parmesan cheese

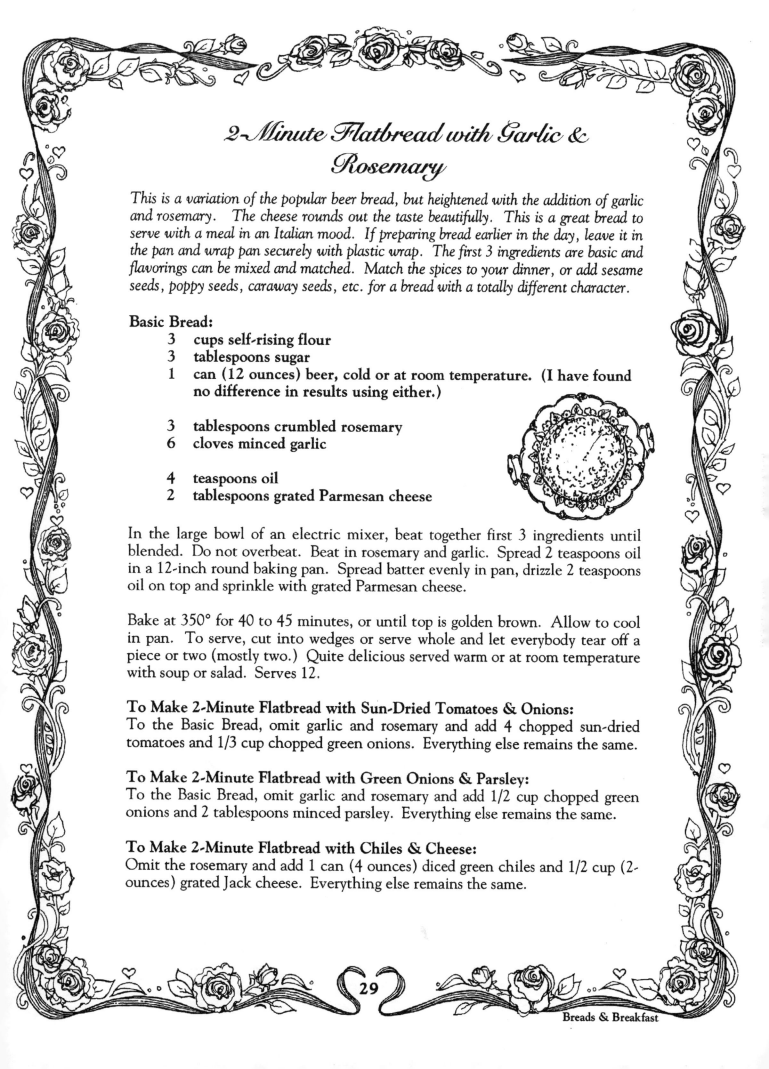

In the large bowl of an electric mixer, beat together first 3 ingredients until blended. Do not overbeat. Beat in rosemary and garlic. Spread 2 teaspoons oil in a 12-inch round baking pan. Spread batter evenly in pan, drizzle 2 teaspoons oil on top and sprinkle with grated Parmesan cheese.

Bake at 350° for 40 to 45 minutes, or until top is golden brown. Allow to cool in pan. To serve, cut into wedges or serve whole and let everybody tear off a piece or two (mostly two.) Quite delicious served warm or at room temperature with soup or salad. Serves 12.

To Make 2-Minute Flatbread with Sun-Dried Tomatoes & Onions:
To the Basic Bread, omit garlic and rosemary and add 4 chopped sun-dried tomatoes and 1/3 cup chopped green onions. Everything else remains the same.

To Make 2-Minute Flatbread with Green Onions & Parsley:
To the Basic Bread, omit garlic and rosemary and add 1/2 cup chopped green onions and 2 tablespoons minced parsley. Everything else remains the same.

To Make 2-Minute Flatbread with Chiles & Cheese:
Omit the rosemary and add 1 can (4 ounces) diced green chiles and 1/2 cup (2-ounces) grated Jack cheese. Everything else remains the same.

Italian Focaccia with Gorgonzola, Raisins & Pine Nuts

This bread will add excitement to the most sedate party. Truly a masterpiece of taste, it will transform the most ordinary salad into an exciting course. No butter is necessary, just slice and enjoy.

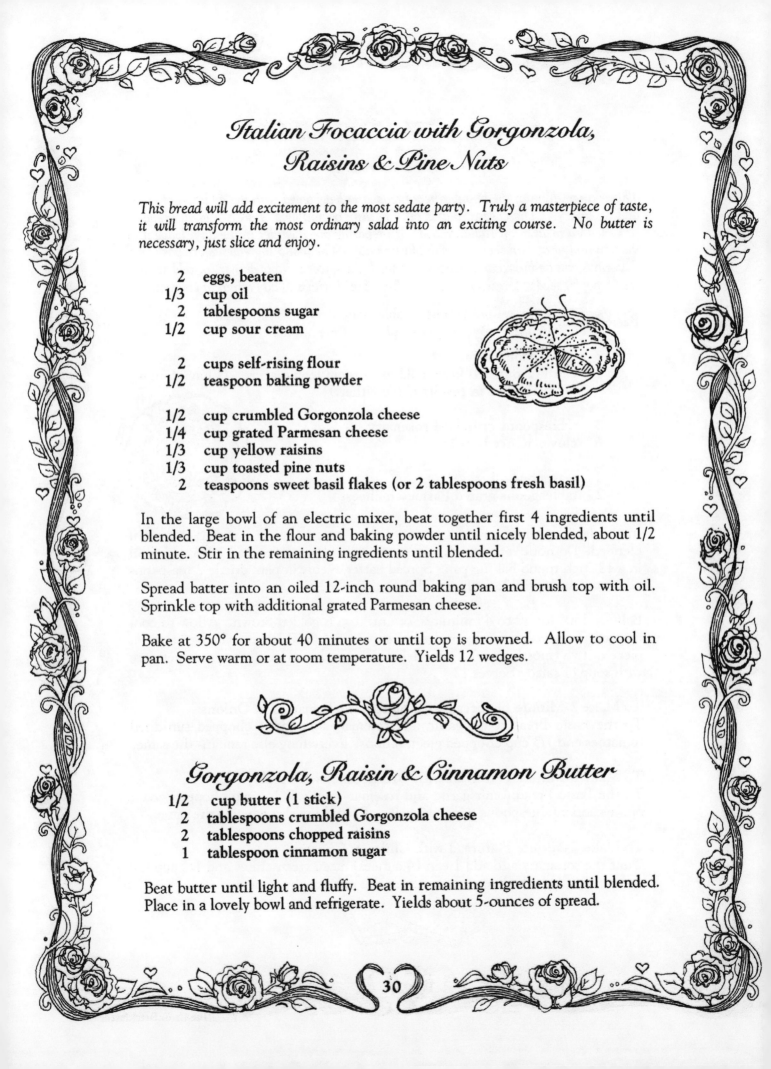

2	eggs, beaten
1/3	cup oil
2	tablespoons sugar
1/2	cup sour cream
2	cups self-rising flour
1/2	teaspoon baking powder
1/2	cup crumbled Gorgonzola cheese
1/4	cup grated Parmesan cheese
1/3	cup yellow raisins
1/3	cup toasted pine nuts
2	teaspoons sweet basil flakes (or 2 tablespoons fresh basil)

In the large bowl of an electric mixer, beat together first 4 ingredients until blended. Beat in the flour and baking powder until nicely blended, about 1/2 minute. Stir in the remaining ingredients until blended.

Spread batter into an oiled 12-inch round baking pan and brush top with oil. Sprinkle top with additional grated Parmesan cheese.

Bake at 350° for about 40 minutes or until top is browned. Allow to cool in pan. Serve warm or at room temperature. Yields 12 wedges.

Gorgonzola, Raisin & Cinnamon Butter

1/2	cup butter (1 stick)
2	tablespoons crumbled Gorgonzola cheese
2	tablespoons chopped raisins
1	tablespoon cinnamon sugar

Beat butter until light and fluffy. Beat in remaining ingredients until blended. Place in a lovely bowl and refrigerate. Yields about 5-ounces of spread.

Green Onion Flatbread with Lemon & Feta

A marvelous bread to serve with dinner in a Greek mood, very different and very interesting. It is an excellent accompaniment to soup or salad, and will create a great deal of excitement at the table.

1/4	cup oil
1	egg
1 1/2	cups buttermilk
3	tablespoons sugar
1/2	cup chopped green onions
1	tablespoon grated lemon. Use fruit, juice and peel.
3	cups flour
4	teaspoons baking powder
1/4	pound (4 ounces) feta cheese, crumbled
2	tablespoons oil
2	tablespoons sesame seeds
2	tablespoons grated Parmesan cheese

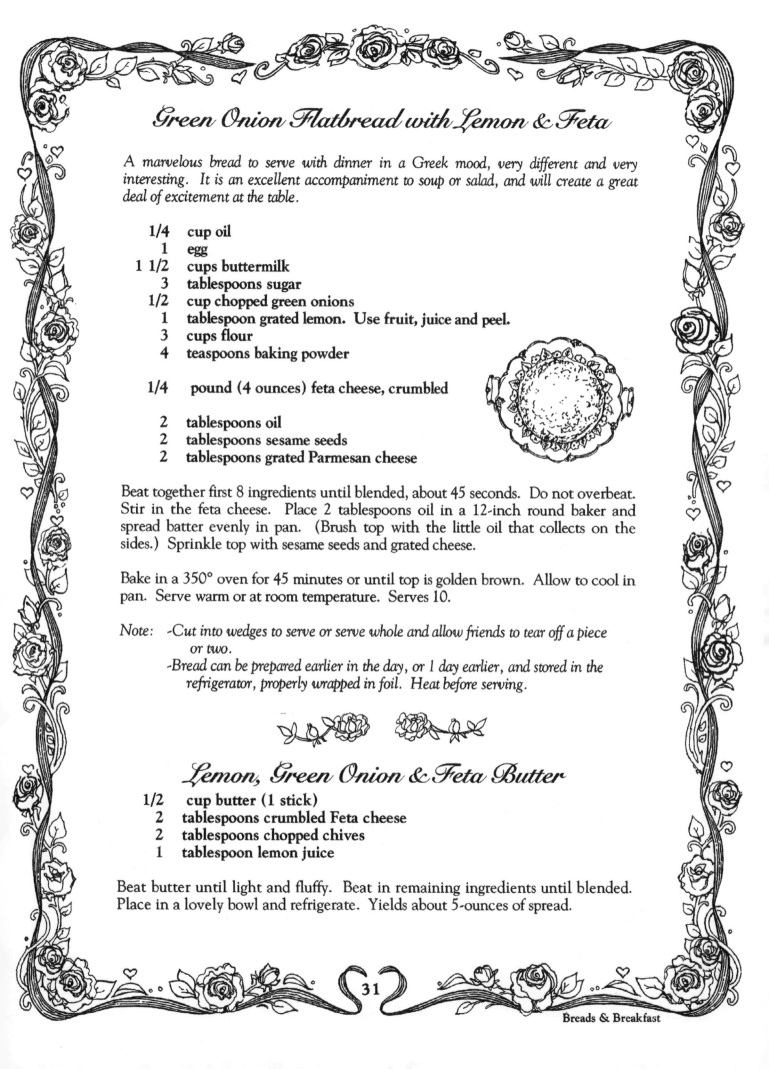

Beat together first 8 ingredients until blended, about 45 seconds. Do not overbeat. Stir in the feta cheese. Place 2 tablespoons oil in a 12-inch round baker and spread batter evenly in pan. (Brush top with the little oil that collects on the sides.) Sprinkle top with sesame seeds and grated cheese.

Bake in a 350° oven for 45 minutes or until top is golden brown. Allow to cool in pan. Serve warm or at room temperature. Serves 10.

Note: -Cut into wedges to serve or serve whole and allow friends to tear off a piece or two.
-Bread can be prepared earlier in the day, or 1 day earlier, and stored in the refrigerator, properly wrapped in foil. Heat before serving.

Lemon, Green Onion & Feta Butter

1/2	cup butter (1 stick)
2	tablespoons crumbled Feta cheese
2	tablespoons chopped chives
1	tablespoon lemon juice

Beat butter until light and fluffy. Beat in remaining ingredients until blended. Place in a lovely bowl and refrigerate. Yields about 5-ounces of spread.

Focaccio Italian Flatbread with Tomatoes & Cheese

When you serve this bread with Cioppino, the excitement will truly amaze you. This is truly a delicious bread and a wonderful blend of flavors. I do hope you love it as much as our friends did.

2	medium tomatoes, chopped and seeded, fresh or canned
1/4	cup chopped green onions
2	cloves garlic, minced
3/4	cup grated Swiss cheese
1/4	cup grated Parmesan cheese
1/3	cup oil
2	tablespoons sugar
1/2	cup buttermilk
2	cups flour
3 1/2	teaspoons baking powder
1	teaspoon Italian Herb Seasoning
1	teaspoon sweet basil flakes

Beat together first group of ingredients until blended. Beat in the remaining ingredients until blended, about 1 minute.

Spread batter into a heavily oiled 12-inch round baking pan and brush top with a little oil that collects on the sides. Bake in a 350° oven for about 40 minutes or until top is browned. Serve warm, or at room temperature, and cut into wedges to serve. Serves 6.

Note: -Bread can be prepared earlier in the day, or 1 day earlier, securely wrapped in foil and stored in the refrigerator Heat bread in a 350° oven for 10 minutes before serving.

Sun-Dried Tomatoes & Parmesan Butter

1/2	cup butter (1 stick)
2	tablespoons sun-dried tomatoes
2	tablespoons grated Parmesan cheese
1	tablespoon finely chopped green onions
	pinch of sweet basil flakes

Beat butter until light and fluffy. Beat in remaining ingredients until blended. Place in a lovely bowl and refrigerate. Yields about 5-ounces of spread.

Cottage Cheese Pancakes with Strawberries & Sour Cream

1   cup non-fat cottage cheese
3   eggs
     pinch of salt
2   tablespoons sugar
2   tablespoons melted butter
1/3 cup flour
1   teaspoon baking powder
1/2 teaspoon vanilla

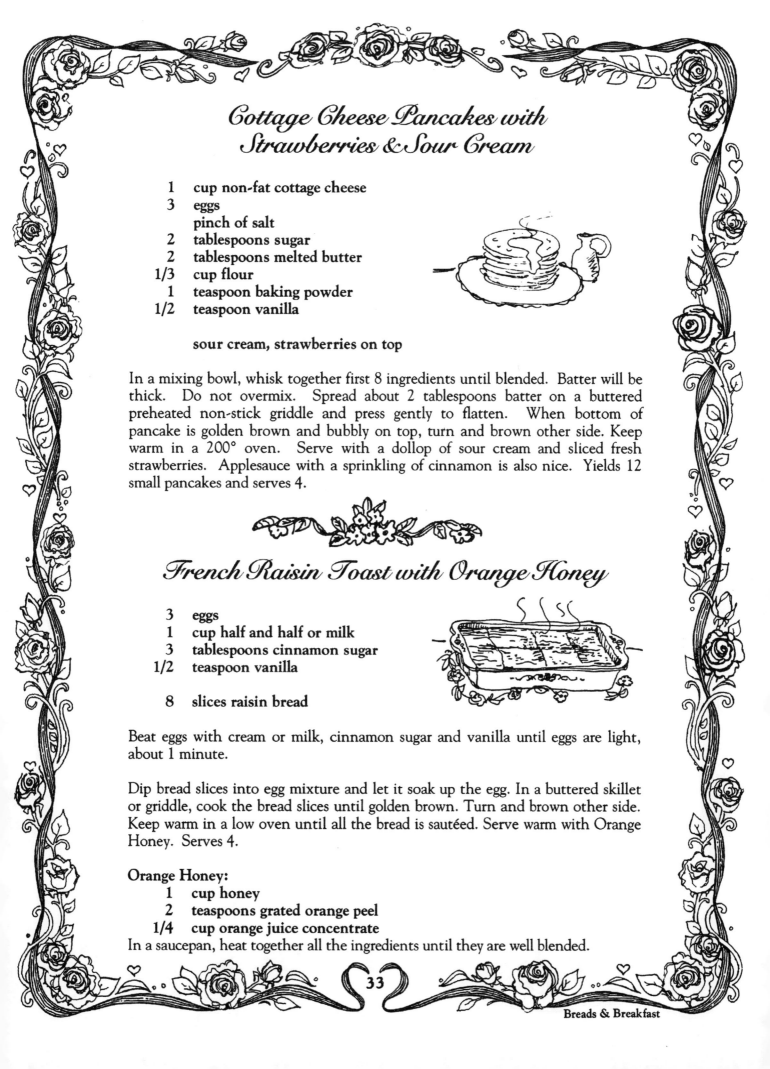

sour cream, strawberries on top

In a mixing bowl, whisk together first 8 ingredients until blended. Batter will be thick. Do not overmix. Spread about 2 tablespoons batter on a buttered preheated non-stick griddle and press gently to flatten. When bottom of pancake is golden brown and bubbly on top, turn and brown other side. Keep warm in a 200° oven. Serve with a dollop of sour cream and sliced fresh strawberries. Applesauce with a sprinkling of cinnamon is also nice. Yields 12 small pancakes and serves 4.

French Raisin Toast with Orange Honey

3   eggs
1   cup half and half or milk
3   tablespoons cinnamon sugar
1/2 teaspoon vanilla

8   slices raisin bread

Beat eggs with cream or milk, cinnamon sugar and vanilla until eggs are light, about 1 minute.

Dip bread slices into egg mixture and let it soak up the egg. In a buttered skillet or griddle, cook the bread slices until golden brown. Turn and brown other side. Keep warm in a low oven until all the bread is sautéed. Serve warm with Orange Honey. Serves 4.

Orange Honey:
1   cup honey
2   teaspoons grated orange peel
1/4 cup orange juice concentrate
In a saucepan, heat together all the ingredients until they are well blended.

33

Oven-Baked French Toast with Cream Cheese & Jam

You will love serving this delicious casserole for a breakfast or brunch. Casserole can be prepared in advance and baked before serving. Everyone loves it. It is very attractive surrounded with small bowls of strawberries, sour cream and maple syrup and everyone can choose the topping.

12	slices thinly sliced egg bread or white bread, crusts removed
6	tablespoons cream cheese
6	tablespoons strawberry jam
3	eggs
2	cups milk
1	cup low-fat sour cream
1/2	cup sugar
1	teaspoon vanilla
2	teaspoons cinnamon sugar

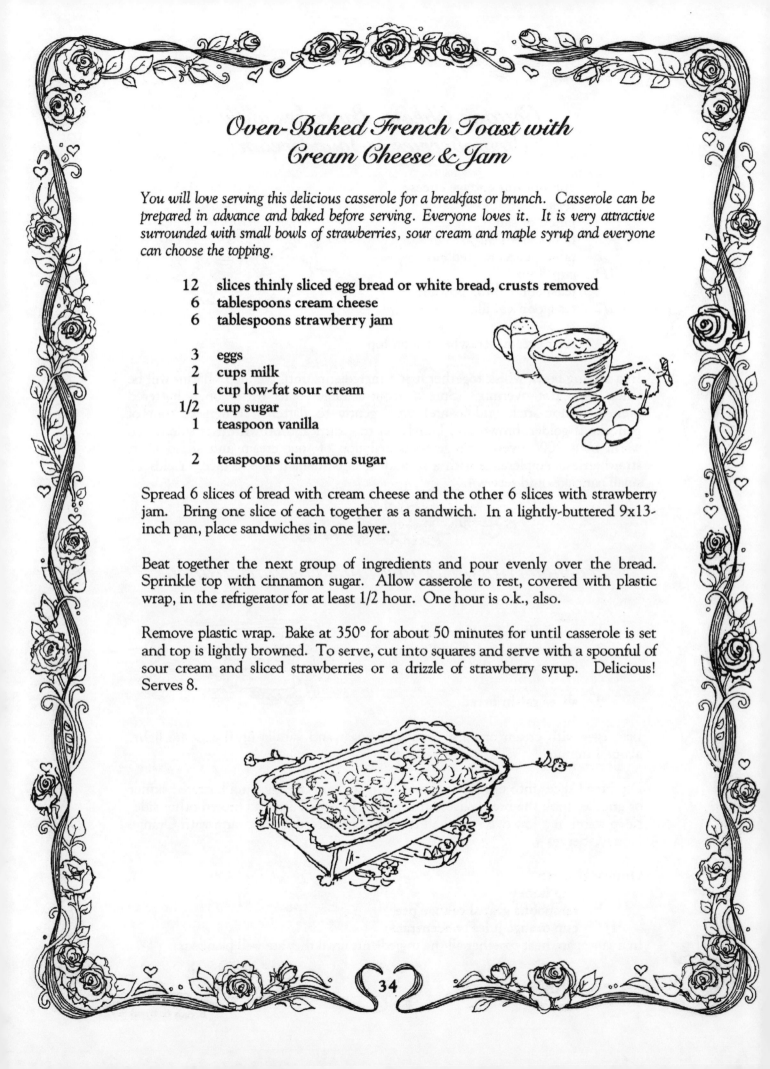

Spread 6 slices of bread with cream cheese and the other 6 slices with strawberry jam. Bring one slice of each together as a sandwich. In a lightly-buttered 9x13-inch pan, place sandwiches in one layer.

Beat together the next group of ingredients and pour evenly over the bread. Sprinkle top with cinnamon sugar. Allow casserole to rest, covered with plastic wrap, in the refrigerator for at least 1/2 hour. One hour is o.k., also.

Remove plastic wrap. Bake at 350° for about 50 minutes for until casserole is set and top is lightly browned. To serve, cut into squares and serve with a spoonful of sour cream and sliced strawberries or a drizzle of strawberry syrup. Delicious! Serves 8.

Petite Breakfast Crescents with Walnuts & Raisins

These delicate little crescents are assembled in minutes and look and taste as if they were made with yeast. The dough is easily handled and very easy to work with.

> 1   cup cottage cheese
> 3   ounces butter (3/4 stick), softened
> 1   cup flour

Filling Ingredients:
> 1/2   cup finely chopped walnuts
> 1/2   cup finely chopped raisins
> 1/2   cup sugar
> 1   teaspoon cinnamon
>
> cinnamon sugar

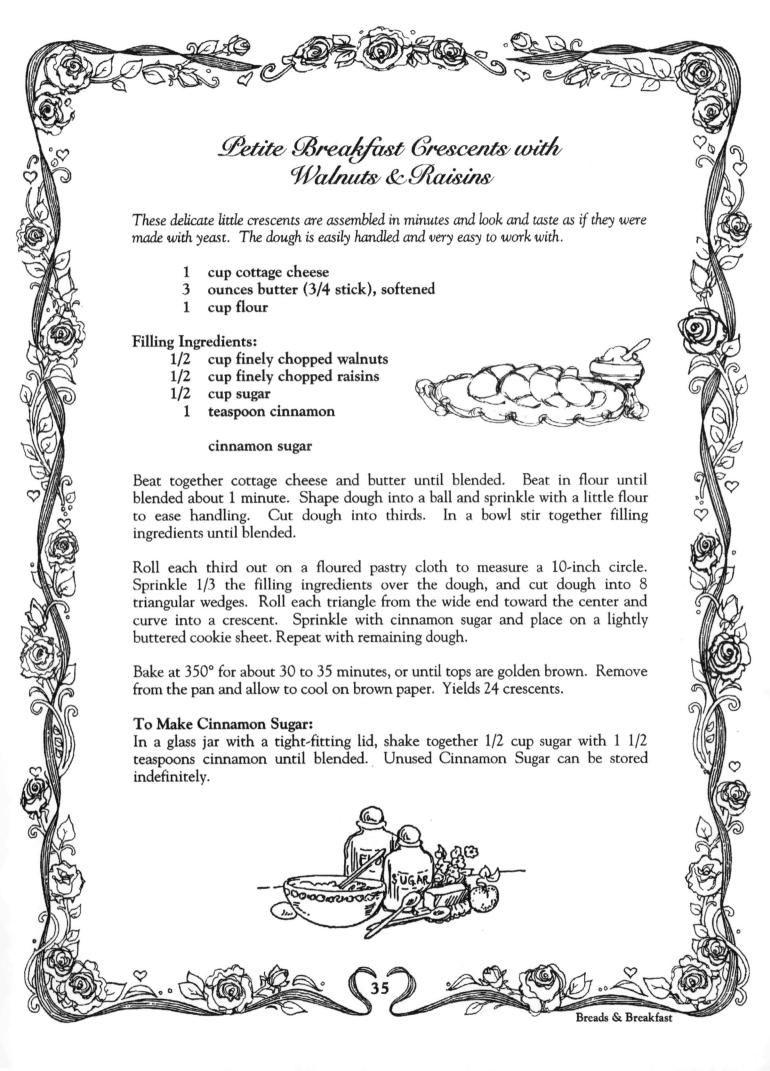

Beat together cottage cheese and butter until blended. Beat in flour until blended about 1 minute. Shape dough into a ball and sprinkle with a little flour to ease handling. Cut dough into thirds. In a bowl stir together filling ingredients until blended.

Roll each third out on a floured pastry cloth to measure a 10-inch circle. Sprinkle 1/3 the filling ingredients over the dough, and cut dough into 8 triangular wedges. Roll each triangle from the wide end toward the center and curve into a crescent. Sprinkle with cinnamon sugar and place on a lightly buttered cookie sheet. Repeat with remaining dough.

Bake at 350° for about 30 to 35 minutes, or until tops are golden brown. Remove from the pan and allow to cool on brown paper. Yields 24 crescents.

To Make Cinnamon Sugar:
In a glass jar with a tight-fitting lid, shake together 1/2 cup sugar with 1 1/2 teaspoons cinnamon until blended. Unused Cinnamon Sugar can be stored indefinitely.

French Toast with Strawberry Jam

You will love serving this delicious casserole for a breakfast or brunch. Casserole can be prepared in advance and baked before serving. Everyone loves it. It is very attractive surrounded with small bowls of strawberries, sour cream and maple syrup and everyone can choose the topping.

12	slices thinly sliced egg bread or white bread, crusts removed
6	tablespoons strawberry jam (or your favorite)
6	tablespoons sour cream.
4	eggs
2	cup milk
1	cup low-fat sour cream
1/2	cup sugar
1	teaspoon vanilla
3	teaspoons cinnamon sugar

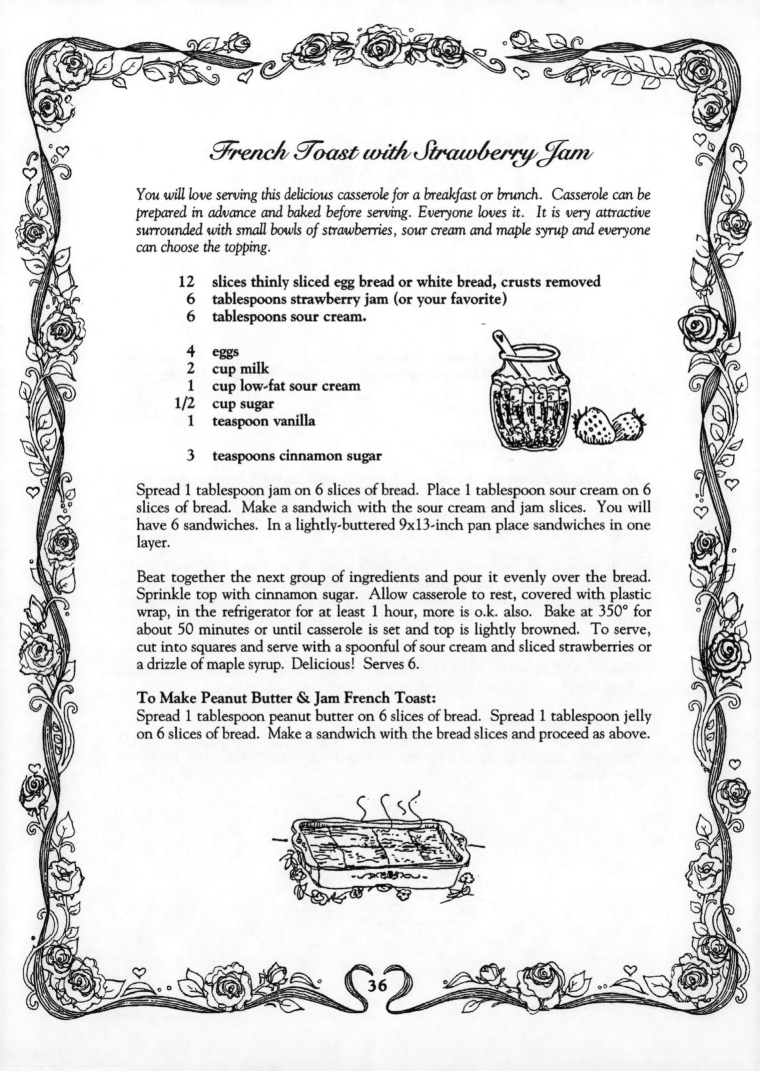

Spread 1 tablespoon jam on 6 slices of bread. Place 1 tablespoon sour cream on 6 slices of bread. Make a sandwich with the sour cream and jam slices. You will have 6 sandwiches. In a lightly-buttered 9x13-inch pan place sandwiches in one layer.

Beat together the next group of ingredients and pour it evenly over the bread. Sprinkle top with cinnamon sugar. Allow casserole to rest, covered with plastic wrap, in the refrigerator for at least 1 hour, more is o.k. also. Bake at 350° for about 50 minutes or until casserole is set and top is lightly browned. To serve, cut into squares and serve with a spoonful of sour cream and sliced strawberries or a drizzle of maple syrup. Delicious! Serves 6.

To Make Peanut Butter & Jam French Toast:
Spread 1 tablespoon peanut butter on 6 slices of bread. Spread 1 tablespoon jelly on 6 slices of bread. Make a sandwich with the bread slices and proceed as above.

French Orange Toast
with Country Orange Marmalade

8   1-inch slices French bread

3   eggs
1   cup cream or half and half
2   tablespoons grated orange zest (orange part of the peel)
1/4   cup cinnamon sugar

butter
Country Orange Marmalade

In a 9x13-inch pan, place bread slices in one layer. Beat together eggs, orange juice, cream and cinnamon sugar until blended. Pour egg mixture evenly over the bread. Allow bread to soak up egg, turning now and again until evenly moistened.

In a large skillet, heat 1 tablespoon butter until sizzling hot. Sauté bread slices until golden brown on both sides. Use more butter as needed. Serve with Country Orange Marmalade or your favorite syrup. Serves 4.

Note: -The French toast can be baked in the oven for a slightly different effect. After the eggs are nicely soaked up, place pan in a 350° oven and bake until bread is golden and puffed. Do not overbake.

Country Orange Marmalade

This little gem produces the finest tasting marmalade. The lemon adds a beautiful flavor to the orange, the walnuts add texture and the cherries add color. I hope you try it soon. This is also a lovely gift from your kitchen.

1   cup orange marmalade
2   tablespoons lemon juice
4   tablespoons chopped walnuts
3   tablespoons yellow raisins
2   tablespoons chopped Maraschino cherries

Combine all the ingredients and stir until blended. Store in the refrigerator until ready to use.

Cream Cheese with Orange Marmalade

Basic Recipe:

- 1 package (8 ounces) cream cheese, softened
- 1/4 cup whipping cream
- 1/4 cup orange marmalade

In your electric mixer bowl, beat cream cheese and cream until nicely blended. Beat in marmalade until blended. Makes about 1 1/2 cups.

Note: You can substitute orange marmalade with any fruit jam that is your favorite. Strawberry, apricot, plum jams are wonderful. If the fruit is in large chunks, then cut them up a bit, so they can be spread easily.

Old Fashioned Country Marmalade

You know, a gift from your kitchen is like a kiss and a hug. It's a warm and loving way of saying, "Happy Holiday." or "Thank you for having us." or simply "Hello, from our house to yours." Old Fashioned Country Marmalade is a wonderful little marmalade that will delight your family and friends. It can be assembled literally in minutes which is so good around holiday time.

Use some pretty, transparent glass containers. Yellow and amber are especially lovely and easily found at the import stores. Look for some smashing labels and present them to the beautiful people you know.

- 3 pounds orange marmalade
- 1 jar (8 ounces) Maraschino Cherries, drained and coarsely chopped
- 3 tablespoons fresh lemon juice
- 1 cup walnuts, coarsely chopped
- 1 cup golden raisins
- 1/2 cup currants

Simply mix all the ingredients together and spoon the mixture into pretty jars. Yields about 8 cups.

Hors d'Oeuvres

and

Small Entrees

The Best Chopped Liver

The difference between paté and chopped liver is "panache." This is the homey kind, filled with the tastiest fried onions. While it appears to be made with an inordinate number of onions, do no despair. The end result is delicious. Leave the thin layer of fried onions on the bottom as a surprise.

- 6   large onions, chopped
- 6   tablespoons butter

- 1 1/2   pounds chicken livers, connective membranes removed, and cut into 1-inch pieces
- 2   tablespoons butter

- 4   hard-boiled eggs

In a large skillet, over high heat, fry onions in butter until onions are a deep golden brown. Reserve 1/4 of the onions and place 3/4 of the onions in a food processor.

Sauté chicken livers in butter until meat loses its pinkness. Do not over cook, but do not undercook, either. Place chicken livers and eggs in the food processor with the onions. Pulse mixture until everything is very finely chopped, but not pureed.

Line a 4-cup mold with plastic wrap and press chopped liver evenly into it. Place reserved onions on the top. Cover mold with plastic wrap and refrigerate for several hours. Overnight is good, too.

To unmold, remove plastic cover, invert mold onto a serving platter, and remove plastic lining. Voilá, the most intricate mold is uncovered, intact and without fuss. The thin layer of onions will be on the bottom. (This is the easiest and best way to unmold patés and sticky fillings.) Serve with thin slices of cocktail rye bread. Champagne Crackers are very good, too. Yields about 4 cups. Serves 20.

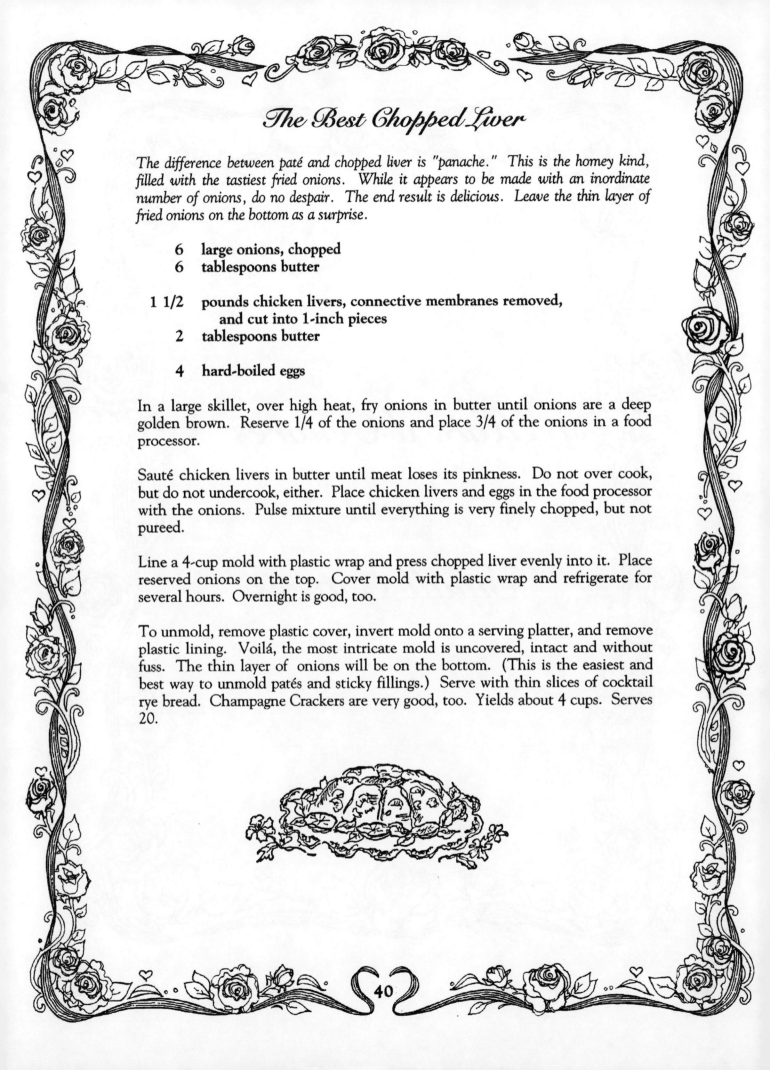

Easiest & Best Crab Cakes with Tartar Sauce

You will love these delicious little crab cakes that serve well for an hors d'oeuvre, first course, or even a main course. This is truly a simple little recipe that everyone loved at our New Year's Eve party. Hope you enjoy them as much as they did. The Tartar Sauce is not traditional, as it is much lighter, and a very pleasant change.

1	pound crabmeat, picked over for bones, and torn into coarse shreds
1/2	cup finely chopped green onions or chives
2	cups fresh bread crumbs
1	teaspoon dried dill weed
3/4	cup mayonnaise
2	eggs, beaten
3	tablespoons lemon juice
	salt to taste

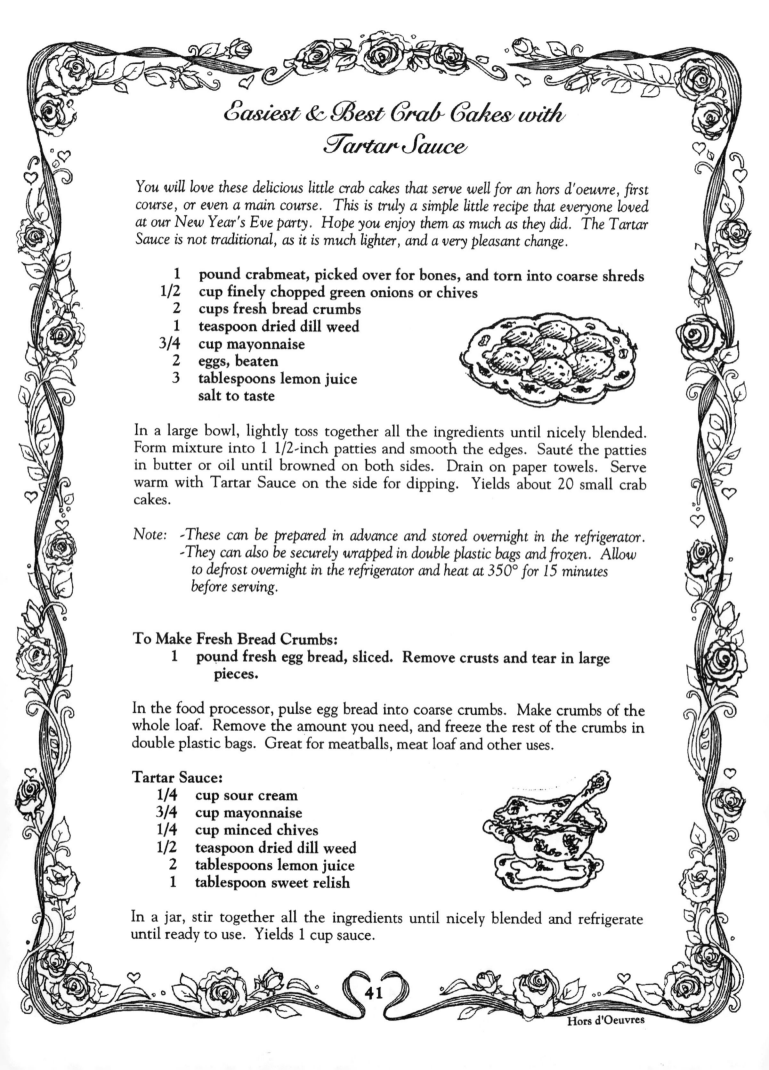

In a large bowl, lightly toss together all the ingredients until nicely blended. Form mixture into 1 1/2-inch patties and smooth the edges. Sauté the patties in butter or oil until browned on both sides. Drain on paper towels. Serve warm with Tartar Sauce on the side for dipping. Yields about 20 small crab cakes.

Note: -These can be prepared in advance and stored overnight in the refrigerator.
-They can also be securely wrapped in double plastic bags and frozen. Allow to defrost overnight in the refrigerator and heat at 350° for 15 minutes before serving.

To Make Fresh Bread Crumbs:

    1   pound fresh egg bread, sliced. Remove crusts and tear in large pieces.

In the food processor, pulse egg bread into coarse crumbs. Make crumbs of the whole loaf. Remove the amount you need, and freeze the rest of the crumbs in double plastic bags. Great for meatballs, meat loaf and other uses.

Tartar Sauce:

1/4	cup sour cream
3/4	cup mayonnaise
1/4	cup minced chives
1/2	teaspoon dried dill weed
2	tablespoons lemon juice
1	tablespoon sweet relish

In a jar, stir together all the ingredients until nicely blended and refrigerate until ready to use. Yields 1 cup sauce.

Hors d'Oeuvres

Caviar with Crème Fraiche & Toast Points

My favorite way to relish caviar is simply to spread it on Toast Points. Toast points are delicate and do not interfere with the taste of the caviar. Chopped chives and Crème Fraiche are optional but a nice addition.

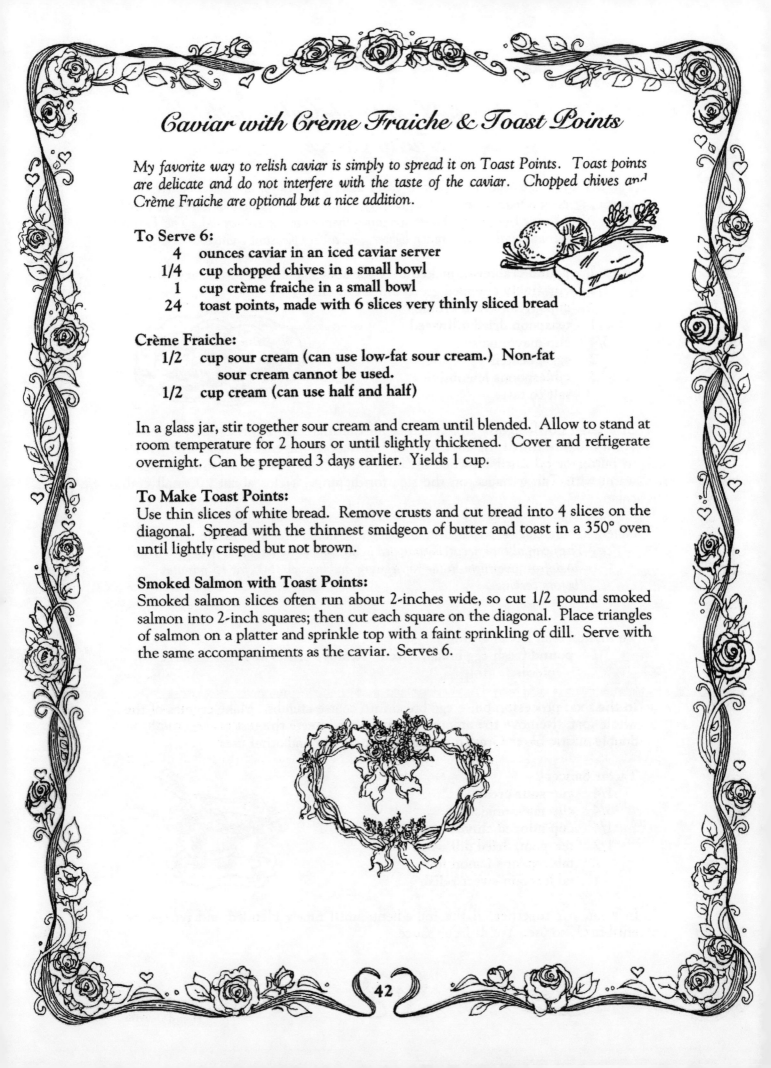

To Serve 6:

4	ounces caviar in an iced caviar server
1/4	cup chopped chives in a small bowl
1	cup crème fraiche in a small bowl
24	toast points, made with 6 slices very thinly sliced bread

Crème Fraiche:

1/2	cup sour cream (can use low-fat sour cream.) Non-fat sour cream cannot be used.
1/2	cup cream (can use half and half)

In a glass jar, stir together sour cream and cream until blended. Allow to stand at room temperature for 2 hours or until slightly thickened. Cover and refrigerate overnight. Can be prepared 3 days earlier. Yields 1 cup.

To Make Toast Points:
Use thin slices of white bread. Remove crusts and cut bread into 4 slices on the diagonal. Spread with the thinnest smidgeon of butter and toast in a 350° oven until lightly crisped but not brown.

Smoked Salmon with Toast Points:
Smoked salmon slices often run about 2-inches wide, so cut 1/2 pound smoked salmon into 2-inch squares; then cut each square on the diagonal. Place triangles of salmon on a platter and sprinkle top with a faint sprinkling of dill. Serve with the same accompaniments as the caviar. Serves 6.

Oysters Royale with Garlic, Herbs & Cheese Crumbs

If you are serving this as a casserole, it is best served as a small entree with hors d'oeuvres and drinks. Simply have a large serving spoon and a few small plates close by. To serve as a first course at dinner, I suggest you make individual servings. This can be prepared in individual ramekins. Simply layer crumb mixture, oysters, crumb mixture and a generous sprinkling of grated Parmesan cheese on top. Heat for about 20 minutes at 350° until heated through. Casserole, or individual ramekins, can be prepared earlier in the day, stored in the refrigerator and heated before serving.

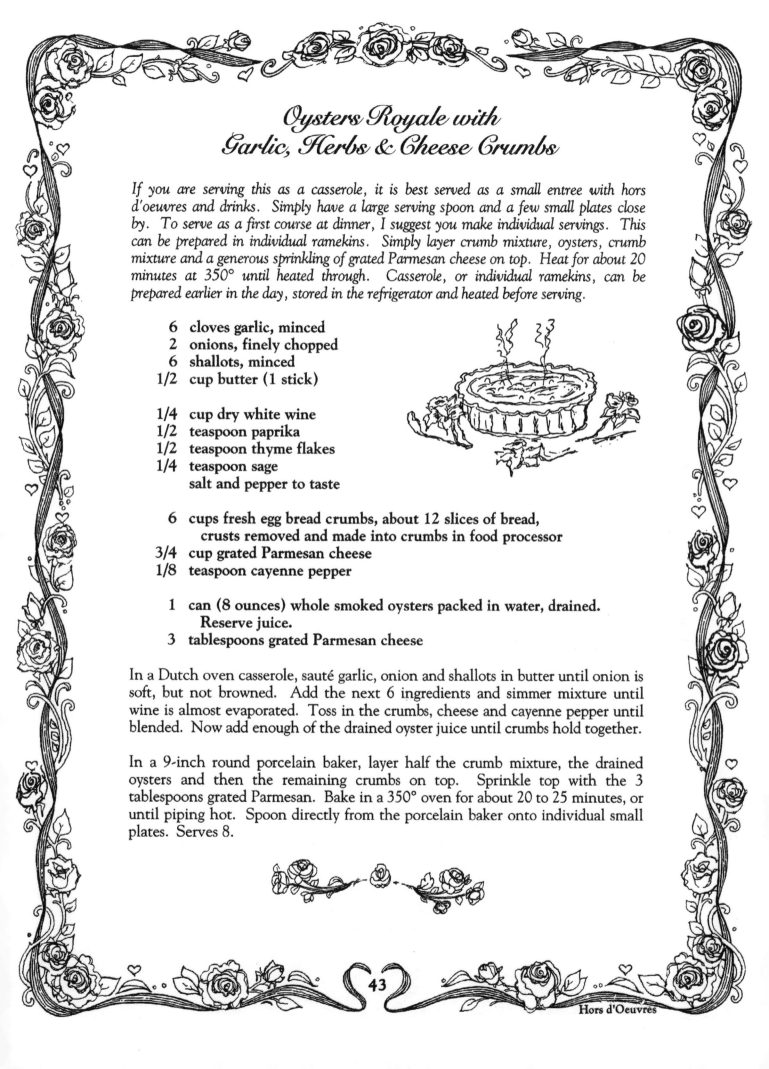

6	cloves garlic, minced
2	onions, finely chopped
6	shallots, minced
1/2	cup butter (1 stick)
1/4	cup dry white wine
1/2	teaspoon paprika
1/2	teaspoon thyme flakes
1/4	teaspoon sage
	salt and pepper to taste
6	cups fresh egg bread crumbs, about 12 slices of bread, crusts removed and made into crumbs in food processor
3/4	cup grated Parmesan cheese
1/8	teaspoon cayenne pepper
1	can (8 ounces) whole smoked oysters packed in water, drained. Reserve juice.
3	tablespoons grated Parmesan cheese

In a Dutch oven casserole, sauté garlic, onion and shallots in butter until onion is soft, but not browned. Add the next 6 ingredients and simmer mixture until wine is almost evaporated. Toss in the crumbs, cheese and cayenne pepper until blended. Now add enough of the drained oyster juice until crumbs hold together.

In a 9-inch round porcelain baker, layer half the crumb mixture, the drained oysters and then the remaining crumbs on top. Sprinkle top with the 3 tablespoons grated Parmesan. Bake in a 350° oven for about 20 to 25 minutes, or until piping hot. Spoon directly from the porcelain baker onto individual small plates. Serves 8.

American Blinis with Golden Caviar & Crème Fraiche

I call these "American" because they are made with white flour instead of the usual buckwheat. These are interesting little rounds of dough, deeply flavorful and aromatic. Serve them with a dollop of Crème Fraiche and a dot of caviar or smoked salmon on top. A faint sprinkle of chopped chives or dill is very nice, also. Serve these warm. They can be prepared in advance and heated before serving.

1	package (1/4 ounce) dry yeast
1/2	teaspoon sugar
1/3	cup warm water (105°)
2 1/4	cups flour
1 3/4	cups warm milk (105°)
1	egg, beaten
1	teaspoon sugar
1/4	teaspoon salt
4	tablespoons butter, melted and cooled
1/4	cup water

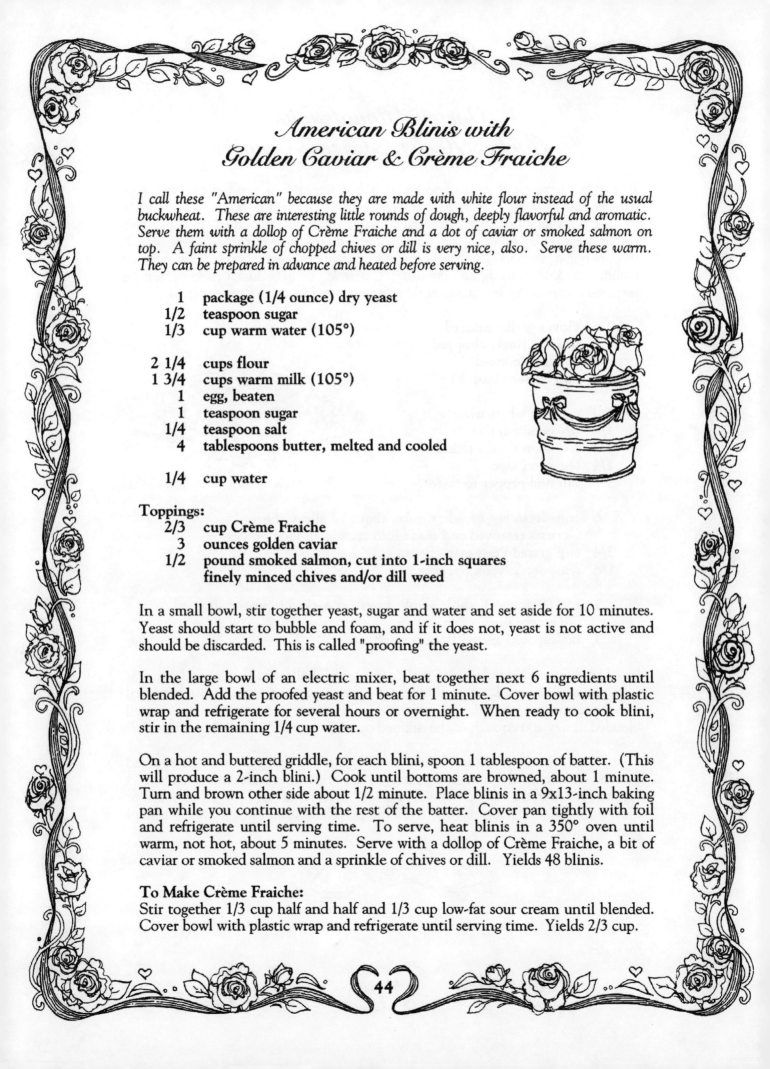

Toppings:

2/3	cup Crème Fraiche
3	ounces golden caviar
1/2	pound smoked salmon, cut into 1-inch squares
	finely minced chives and/or dill weed

In a small bowl, stir together yeast, sugar and water and set aside for 10 minutes. Yeast should start to bubble and foam, and if it does not, yeast is not active and should be discarded. This is called "proofing" the yeast.

In the large bowl of an electric mixer, beat together next 6 ingredients until blended. Add the proofed yeast and beat for 1 minute. Cover bowl with plastic wrap and refrigerate for several hours or overnight. When ready to cook blini, stir in the remaining 1/4 cup water.

On a hot and buttered griddle, for each blini, spoon 1 tablespoon of batter. (This will produce a 2-inch blini.) Cook until bottoms are browned, about 1 minute. Turn and brown other side about 1/2 minute. Place blinis in a 9x13-inch baking pan while you continue with the rest of the batter. Cover pan tightly with foil and refrigerate until serving time. To serve, heat blinis in a 350° oven until warm, not hot, about 5 minutes. Serve with a dollop of Crème Fraiche, a bit of caviar or smoked salmon and a sprinkle of chives or dill. Yields 48 blinis.

To Make Crème Fraiche:

Stir together 1/3 cup half and half and 1/3 cup low-fat sour cream until blended. Cover bowl with plastic wrap and refrigerate until serving time. Yields 2/3 cup.

Mousseline of Salmon with Chives & Dill

I do believe that this recipe is the one that almost everyone who has tasted it has asked for the recipe. It has literally traveled around the world. It is amazingly delicious and amazingly versatile. I will tell you just a few of the different ways you can use this very simple recipe. It is an oldie but goodie and I am certain it will become one of your favorites, too. Lining the mold with plastic wrap takes all the worry out of unmolding. Remember to have Toast Points close by for spreading.

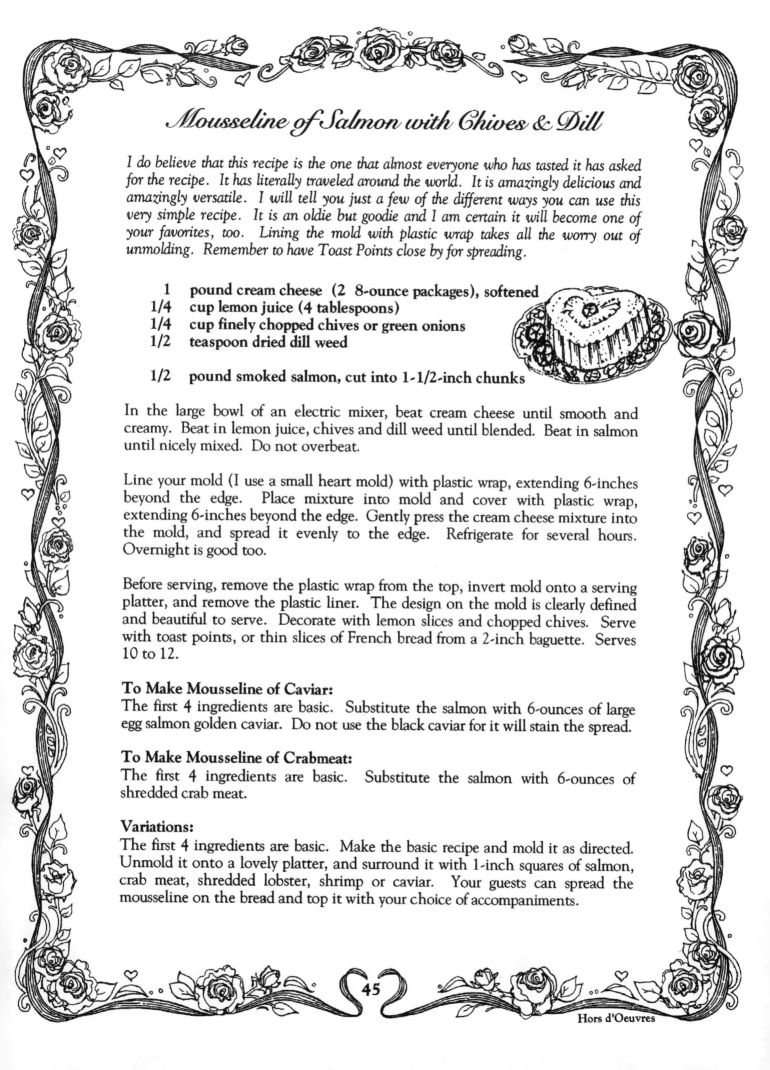

1	pound cream cheese (2 8-ounce packages), softened
1/4	cup lemon juice (4 tablespoons)
1/4	cup finely chopped chives or green onions
1/2	teaspoon dried dill weed
1/2	pound smoked salmon, cut into 1-1/2-inch chunks

In the large bowl of an electric mixer, beat cream cheese until smooth and creamy. Beat in lemon juice, chives and dill weed until blended. Beat in salmon until nicely mixed. Do not overbeat.

Line your mold (I use a small heart mold) with plastic wrap, extending 6-inches beyond the edge. Place mixture into mold and cover with plastic wrap, extending 6-inches beyond the edge. Gently press the cream cheese mixture into the mold, and spread it evenly to the edge. Refrigerate for several hours. Overnight is good too.

Before serving, remove the plastic wrap from the top, invert mold onto a serving platter, and remove the plastic liner. The design on the mold is clearly defined and beautiful to serve. Decorate with lemon slices and chopped chives. Serve with toast points, or thin slices of French bread from a 2-inch baguette. Serves 10 to 12.

To Make Mousseline of Caviar:
The first 4 ingredients are basic. Substitute the salmon with 6-ounces of large egg salmon golden caviar. Do not use the black caviar for it will stain the spread.

To Make Mousseline of Crabmeat:
The first 4 ingredients are basic. Substitute the salmon with 6-ounces of shredded crab meat.

Variations:
The first 4 ingredients are basic. Make the basic recipe and mold it as directed. Unmold it onto a lovely platter, and surround it with 1-inch squares of salmon, crab meat, shredded lobster, shrimp or caviar. Your guests can spread the mousseline on the bread and top it with your choice of accompaniments.

Hors d'Oeuvres

Pork Meatballs with Coconut and Hot Apricot Dipping Sauce

This is a nice hors d'oeuvre that everybody loves.   Somehow, pork and coconut and hot apricot sauce go so well together.

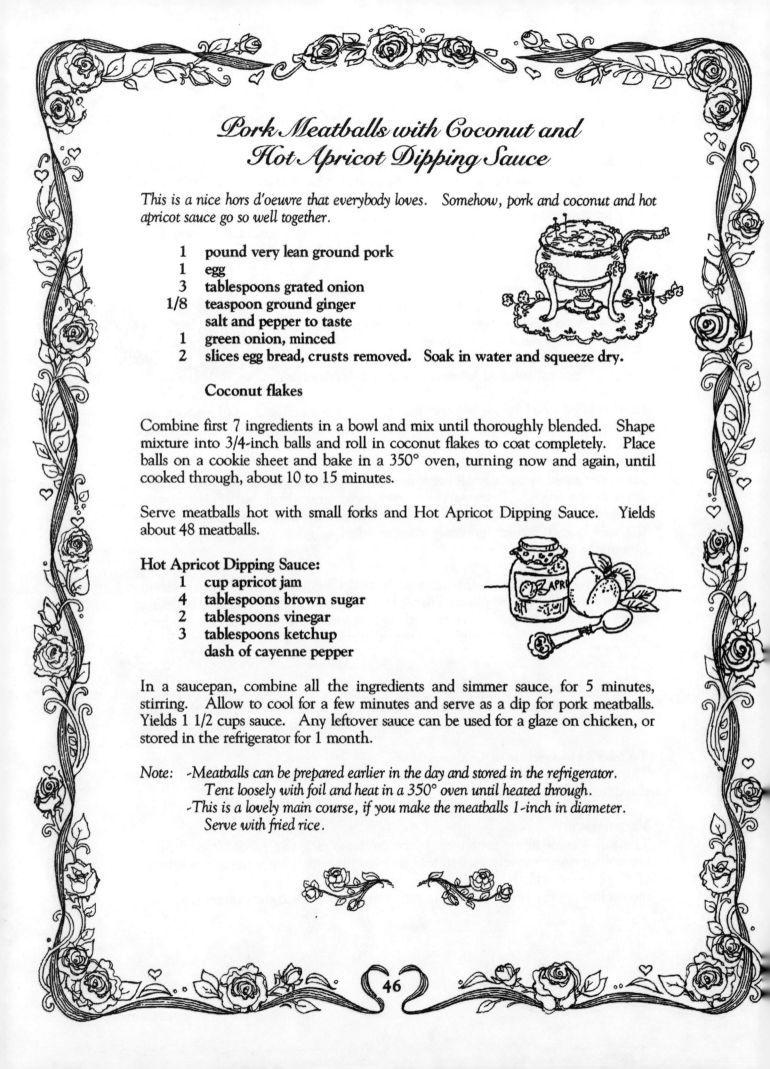

1	pound very lean ground pork
1	egg
3	tablespoons grated onion
1/8	teaspoon ground ginger
	salt and pepper to taste
1	green onion, minced
2	slices egg bread, crusts removed. Soak in water and squeeze dry.

Coconut flakes

Combine first 7 ingredients in a bowl and mix until thoroughly blended.   Shape mixture into 3/4-inch balls and roll in coconut flakes to coat completely.   Place balls on a cookie sheet and bake in a 350° oven, turning now and again, until cooked through, about 10 to 15 minutes.

Serve meatballs hot with small forks and Hot Apricot Dipping Sauce.   Yields about 48 meatballs.

Hot Apricot Dipping Sauce:

1	cup apricot jam
4	tablespoons brown sugar
2	tablespoons vinegar
3	tablespoons ketchup
	dash of cayenne pepper

In a saucepan, combine all the ingredients and simmer sauce, for 5 minutes, stirring.   Allow to cool for a few minutes and serve as a dip for pork meatballs. Yields 1 1/2 cups sauce.   Any leftover sauce can be used for a glaze on chicken, or stored in the refrigerator for 1 month.

Note: -Meatballs can be prepared earlier in the day and stored in the refrigerator.
Tent loosely with foil and heat in a 350° oven until heated through.
-This is a lovely main course, if you make the meatballs 1-inch in diameter.
Serve with fried rice.

Chicken Ginger Dumplings with Coconut in Apricot Peanut Sauce

This is a lovely small entree for a backyard picnic or barbecue with a tropical island theme. If you make the dumplings small, they will serve as a wonderful hors d'oeuvre.

1	pound boned chicken breasts (about 2 medium breasts), cubed
2	eggs
1	shallot
1	clove garlic
2	tablespoons chopped chives
1/2	cup fresh bread crumbs, soaked in 1/4 cup cream
1/4	teaspoon ground ginger
	salt and pepper to taste
1/2	cup coconut flakes

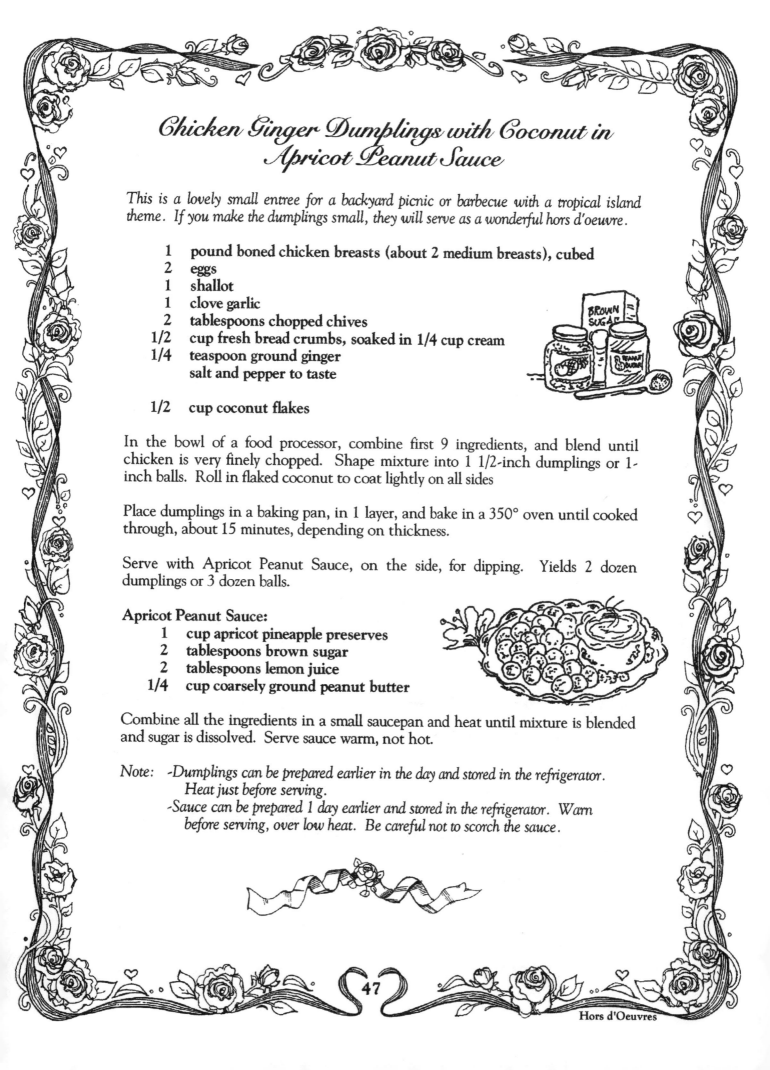

In the bowl of a food processor, combine first 9 ingredients, and blend until chicken is very finely chopped. Shape mixture into 1 1/2-inch dumplings or 1-inch balls. Roll in flaked coconut to coat lightly on all sides

Place dumplings in a baking pan, in 1 layer, and bake in a 350° oven until cooked through, about 15 minutes, depending on thickness.

Serve with Apricot Peanut Sauce, on the side, for dipping. Yields 2 dozen dumplings or 3 dozen balls.

Apricot Peanut Sauce:

1	cup apricot pineapple preserves
2	tablespoons brown sugar
2	tablespoons lemon juice
1/4	cup coarsely ground peanut butter

Combine all the ingredients in a small saucepan and heat until mixture is blended and sugar is dissolved. Serve sauce warm, not hot.

Note: -*Dumplings can be prepared earlier in the day and stored in the refrigerator. Heat just before serving.*
-*Sauce can be prepared 1 day earlier and stored in the refrigerator. Warm before serving, over low heat. Be careful not to scorch the sauce.*

Hors d'Oeuvres

Meatballs in Sweet & Sour Cranberry Sauce

1 1/2	pounds ground beef
1	package dehydrated onion soup
2	eggs
1/2	cup herb seasoned stuffing mix, soaked in 3 tablespoons water
2	tablespoons dried parsley flakes
	salt and pepper to taste

Combine all the ingredients and shape into 1/2-inch balls. Brown the meatballs in a large skillet, shaking the pan frequently so that the meatballs will brown on all sides. If the meat is very lean, add a little butter. Place meatballs and hot Sweet and Sour Cranberry Sauce in a chafing dish. Makes about 50 to 60 meatballs.

Sweet & Sour Cranberry Sauce:

1	cup cranberry sauce, whole berry
1/2	cup ketchup
2	tablespoons grated onion
1	teaspoon vinegar
2	tablespoons brown sugar

Combine all the ingredients and simmer over low heat for 15 to 20 minutes. Add meatballs and heat through.

Petite Cheddar Cheese Soufflés

This is a lovely luncheon dish, light and very delicious. And this soufflé is guaranteed not to make you nervous. There is no white sauce, no separating eggs, no beating the whites at the last minute. Just place all the ingredients in a processor, let it run for about 1 minute and Voila! a beautiful soufflé, light as air.

5	eggs
1	package (8 ounces) cream cheese
1/2	cup cream
1/4	pound Cheddar cheese, cut into cubes
1/2	cup grated Parmesan cheese
1/2	teaspoon curry powder
	salt and pepper to taste

Place eggs in blender container or processor bowl and blend for a few seconds. Now with the motor running, add the remaining ingredients in the order listed and blend for 10 seconds after the last addition.

Divide mixture evenly between 6 buttered ramekins and bake in a 375° oven for about 20 minutes or just until the center is set. Do not overbake. Serve at once. Serves 6.

Note: - Entire dish can be assembled earlier in the day and refrigerated.

Crème Mousseline of Crabmeat with Horseradish Lemon Sauce

There are few hors d'oeuvres that you can make that are more delicious and elegant than this one. Serve it with small triangle toasted points. Do not use flavored crackers for this one, as it will interfere with the delicate balance of flavors.

1	package gelatin
1/3	cup water
1/2	pound crabmeat, picked over for particles of shells
3/4	cup sour cream
3/4	cup cream
2	tablespoons chopped chives
1/4	teaspoon dill weed
3	tablespoons lemon juice

In a metal measuring cup, soften gelatin in water. Place cup in a pan with simmering water, and stir until gelatin is dissolved. Set aside.

In the bowl of a food processor, place the remaining ingredients, and blend until crabmeat is very finely chopped, but not pureed. Beat in the gelatin until blended.

Line a flower mold (about 2-cup capacity and without a hole in the center) with plastic wrap. Press mousseline firmly into the mold, cover with another sheet of plastic wrap and refrigerate until firm.

To serve, remove plastic cover and invert mold on serving dish. Carefully peel off plastic lining. Decorate with scored lemon slices sprinkled with dill and parsley bouquets. Place Horseradish Lemon Sauce on the side, surrounded with toast points. Now, if the party is a very special one, spoon top in a decorative fashion with golden caviar. Just beautiful. Serves as an hors d'oeuvre

Horseradish Lemon Sauce:

1/4	cup sour cream
1/4	cup cream
1	tablespoon lemon juice
1	tablespoon prepared horseradish
1	tablespoon chopped chives
1/8	teaspoon dried dill weed

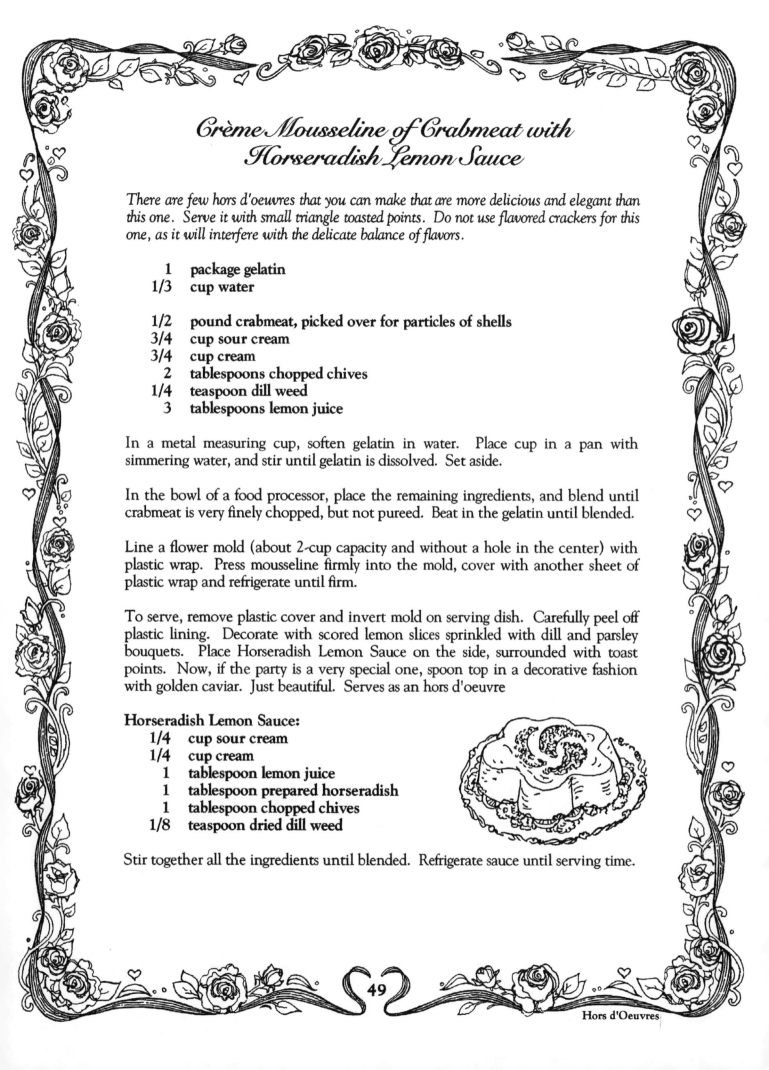

Stir together all the ingredients until blended. Refrigerate sauce until serving time.

Batter-Fried Shrimp with Hot Plum Sauce

2   pounds shrimp, shelled and deveined and dusted with flour

Batter:
1/2   cup flour
1/2   cup corn starch
3/4   cup cold water
1   egg
1/8   teaspoon salt

oil for frying

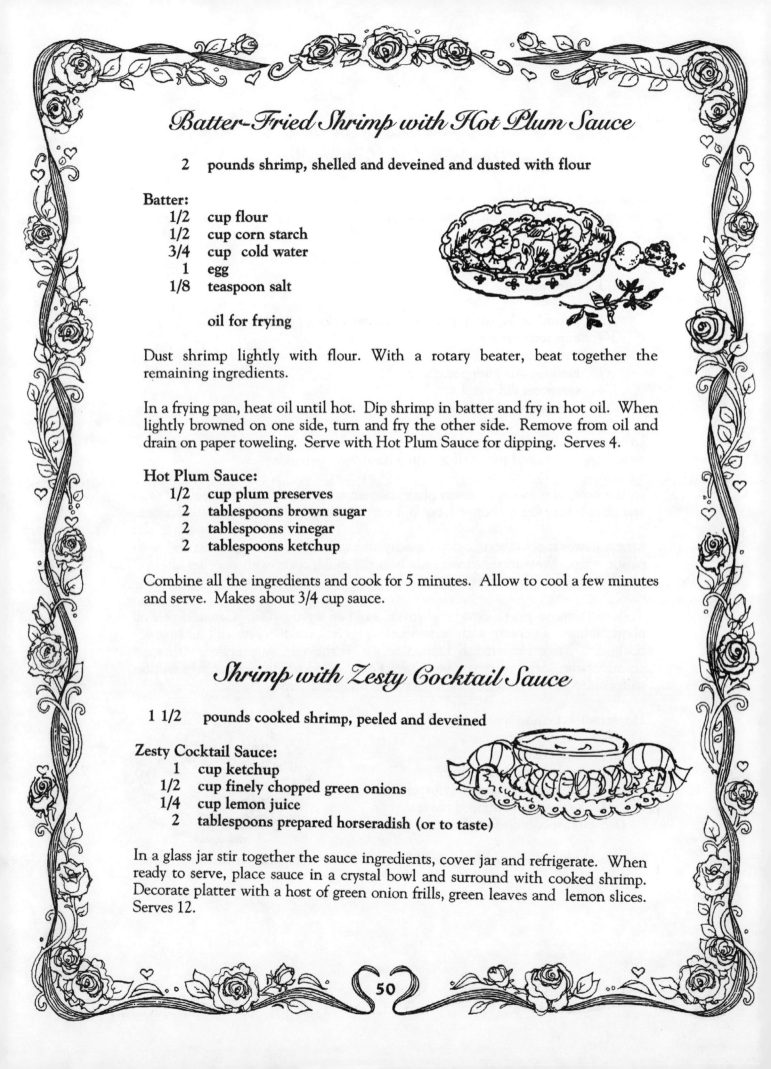

Dust shrimp lightly with flour. With a rotary beater, beat together the remaining ingredients.

In a frying pan, heat oil until hot. Dip shrimp in batter and fry in hot oil. When lightly browned on one side, turn and fry the other side. Remove from oil and drain on paper toweling. Serve with Hot Plum Sauce for dipping. Serves 4.

Hot Plum Sauce:
1/2   cup plum preserves
2   tablespoons brown sugar
2   tablespoons vinegar
2   tablespoons ketchup

Combine all the ingredients and cook for 5 minutes. Allow to cool a few minutes and serve. Makes about 3/4 cup sauce.

Shrimp with Zesty Cocktail Sauce

1 1/2   pounds cooked shrimp, peeled and deveined

Zesty Cocktail Sauce:
1   cup ketchup
1/2   cup finely chopped green onions
1/4   cup lemon juice
2   tablespoons prepared horseradish (or to taste)

In a glass jar stir together the sauce ingredients, cover jar and refrigerate. When ready to serve, place sauce in a crystal bowl and surround with cooked shrimp. Decorate platter with a host of green onion frills, green leaves and lemon slices. Serves 12.

Dilled Mousseline of Caviar with Whipped Crème Fraiche

This s a very romantic hors d'oeuvre, that is so nice to serve with champagne, for a late evening get-together. Serve it with triangle toasted points, very thinly spread with sweet butter.

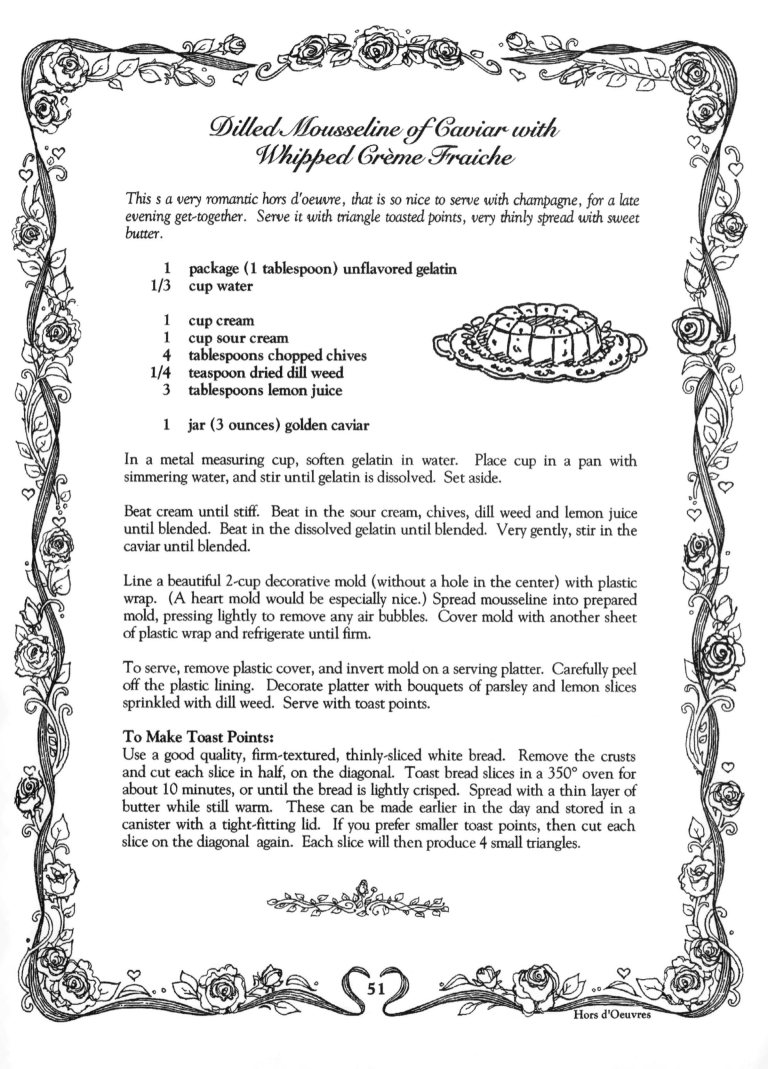

1	package (1 tablespoon) unflavored gelatin
1/3	cup water
1	cup cream
1	cup sour cream
4	tablespoons chopped chives
1/4	teaspoon dried dill weed
3	tablespoons lemon juice
1	jar (3 ounces) golden caviar

In a metal measuring cup, soften gelatin in water. Place cup in a pan with simmering water, and stir until gelatin is dissolved. Set aside.

Beat cream until stiff. Beat in the sour cream, chives, dill weed and lemon juice until blended. Beat in the dissolved gelatin until blended. Very gently, stir in the caviar until blended.

Line a beautiful 2-cup decorative mold (without a hole in the center) with plastic wrap. (A heart mold would be especially nice.) Spread mousseline into prepared mold, pressing lightly to remove any air bubbles. Cover mold with another sheet of plastic wrap and refrigerate until firm.

To serve, remove plastic cover, and invert mold on a serving platter. Carefully peel off the plastic lining. Decorate platter with bouquets of parsley and lemon slices sprinkled with dill weed. Serve with toast points.

To Make Toast Points:
Use a good quality, firm-textured, thinly-sliced white bread. Remove the crusts and cut each slice in half, on the diagonal. Toast bread slices in a 350° oven for about 10 minutes, or until the bread is lightly crisped. Spread with a thin layer of butter while still warm. These can be made earlier in the day and stored in a canister with a tight-fitting lid. If you prefer smaller toast points, then cut each slice on the diagonal again. Each slice will then produce 4 small triangles.

Clam Puffs with Red Cocktail Sauce

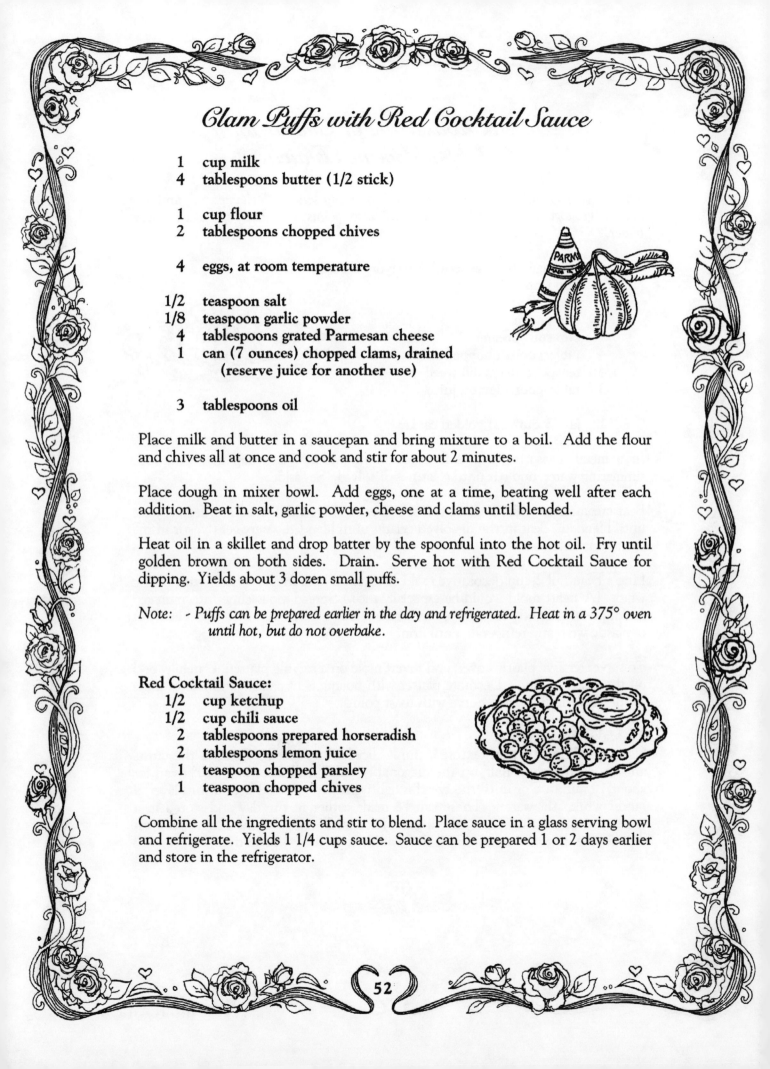

1   cup milk
4   tablespoons butter (1/2 stick)

1   cup flour
2   tablespoons chopped chives

4   eggs, at room temperature

1/2   teaspoon salt
1/8   teaspoon garlic powder
4   tablespoons grated Parmesan cheese
1   can (7 ounces) chopped clams, drained
    (reserve juice for another use)

3   tablespoons oil

Place milk and butter in a saucepan and bring mixture to a boil. Add the flour and chives all at once and cook and stir for about 2 minutes.

Place dough in mixer bowl. Add eggs, one at a time, beating well after each addition. Beat in salt, garlic powder, cheese and clams until blended.

Heat oil in a skillet and drop batter by the spoonful into the hot oil. Fry until golden brown on both sides. Drain. Serve hot with Red Cocktail Sauce for dipping. Yields about 3 dozen small puffs.

Note: - Puffs can be prepared earlier in the day and refrigerated. Heat in a 375° oven until hot, but do not overbake.

Red Cocktail Sauce:
1/2   cup ketchup
1/2   cup chili sauce
2   tablespoons prepared horseradish
2   tablespoons lemon juice
1   teaspoon chopped parsley
1   teaspoon chopped chives

Combine all the ingredients and stir to blend. Place sauce in a glass serving bowl and refrigerate. Yields 1 1/4 cups sauce. Sauce can be prepared 1 or 2 days earlier and store in the refrigerator.

Smoked Salmon Paté Cheesecake in Cheese & Dill Cracker Crust

This is delicately flavored with salmon and dill with just a hint of garlic and lemon. While it is simple to prepare, it does serve in a grand manner. Decorated with rosettes of cream cheese and a sprinkle of dill and surrounded with cherry tomatoes and chive-sprinkled lemon slices, it is beautiful and delicious. This can be prepared a day earlier and stored in the refrigerator.

1	package (4 ounces) creamy cheese with garlic and herbs. (Sold as Boursin or Rondole or Alouette.)
4	ounces cream cheese, softened
1/4	cup chopped chives
1/2	teaspoon dried dill weed (or 2 teaspoons fresh dill weed)
3	eggs
3/4	cup cream
2	tablespoons lemon juice
2	ounces smoked salmon, cut into 1-inch pieces

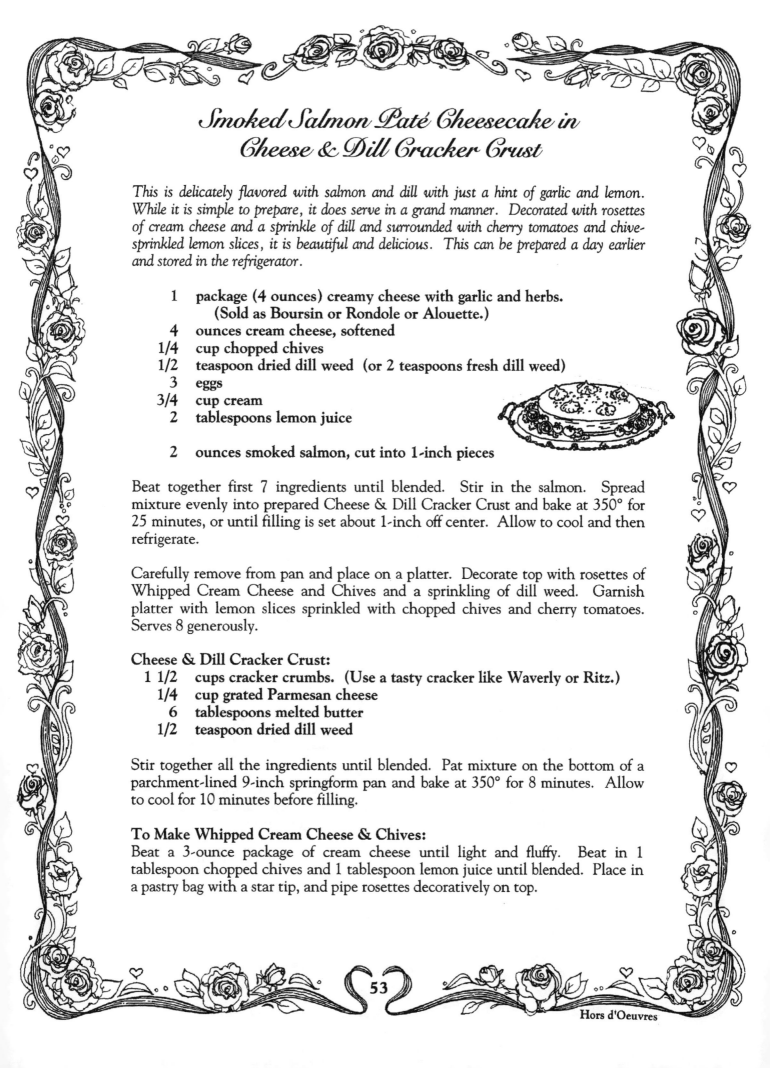

Beat together first 7 ingredients until blended. Stir in the salmon. Spread mixture evenly into prepared Cheese & Dill Cracker Crust and bake at 350° for 25 minutes, or until filling is set about 1-inch off center. Allow to cool and then refrigerate.

Carefully remove from pan and place on a platter. Decorate top with rosettes of Whipped Cream Cheese and Chives and a sprinkling of dill weed. Garnish platter with lemon slices sprinkled with chopped chives and cherry tomatoes. Serves 8 generously.

Cheese & Dill Cracker Crust:

1 1/2	cups cracker crumbs. (Use a tasty cracker like Waverly or Ritz.)
1/4	cup grated Parmesan cheese
6	tablespoons melted butter
1/2	teaspoon dried dill weed

Stir together all the ingredients until blended. Pat mixture on the bottom of a parchment-lined 9-inch springform pan and bake at 350° for 8 minutes. Allow to cool for 10 minutes before filling.

To Make Whipped Cream Cheese & Chives:
Beat a 3-ounce package of cream cheese until light and fluffy. Beat in 1 tablespoon chopped chives and 1 tablespoon lemon juice until blended. Place in a pastry bag with a star tip, and pipe rosettes decoratively on top.

Mushrooms Stuffed with Goat Cheese & Pine Nuts

Goat Cheese & Pine Nut Filling:

1/4	pound log chevre goat cheese, softened	
1/4	pound low-fat cream cheese, softened	
3/4	cup garlic croutons, crushed into crumbs	
1/4	cup minced chives	
1/4	cup finely chopped pine nuts	

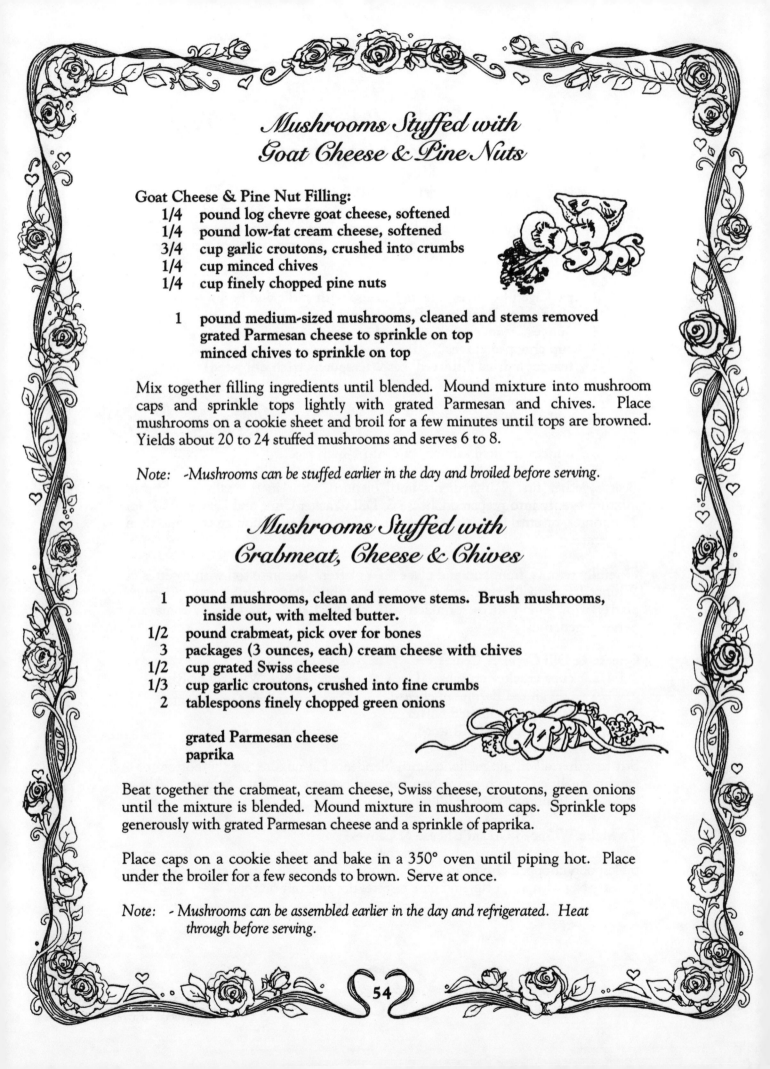

1	pound medium-sized mushrooms, cleaned and stems removed
	grated Parmesan cheese to sprinkle on top
	minced chives to sprinkle on top

Mix together filling ingredients until blended. Mound mixture into mushroom caps and sprinkle tops lightly with grated Parmesan and chives. Place mushrooms on a cookie sheet and broil for a few minutes until tops are browned. Yields about 20 to 24 stuffed mushrooms and serves 6 to 8.

Note: -Mushrooms can be stuffed earlier in the day and broiled before serving.

Mushrooms Stuffed with Crabmeat, Cheese & Chives

1	pound mushrooms, clean and remove stems. Brush mushrooms, inside out, with melted butter.
1/2	pound crabmeat, pick over for bones
3	packages (3 ounces, each) cream cheese with chives
1/2	cup grated Swiss cheese
1/3	cup garlic croutons, crushed into fine crumbs
2	tablespoons finely chopped green onions

grated Parmesan cheese
paprika

Beat together the crabmeat, cream cheese, Swiss cheese, croutons, green onions until the mixture is blended. Mound mixture in mushroom caps. Sprinkle tops generously with grated Parmesan cheese and a sprinkle of paprika.

Place caps on a cookie sheet and bake in a 350° oven until piping hot. Place under the broiler for a few seconds to brown. Serve at once.

Note: - Mushrooms can be assembled earlier in the day and refrigerated. Heat through before serving.

Clams with Garlic, Parmesan & Herb Stuffing

This is a spectacular introduction to dinner in an Italian mood. Highly flavored with garlic and herbs and sparkled with a little Parmesan. Everybody savors every last crumb.

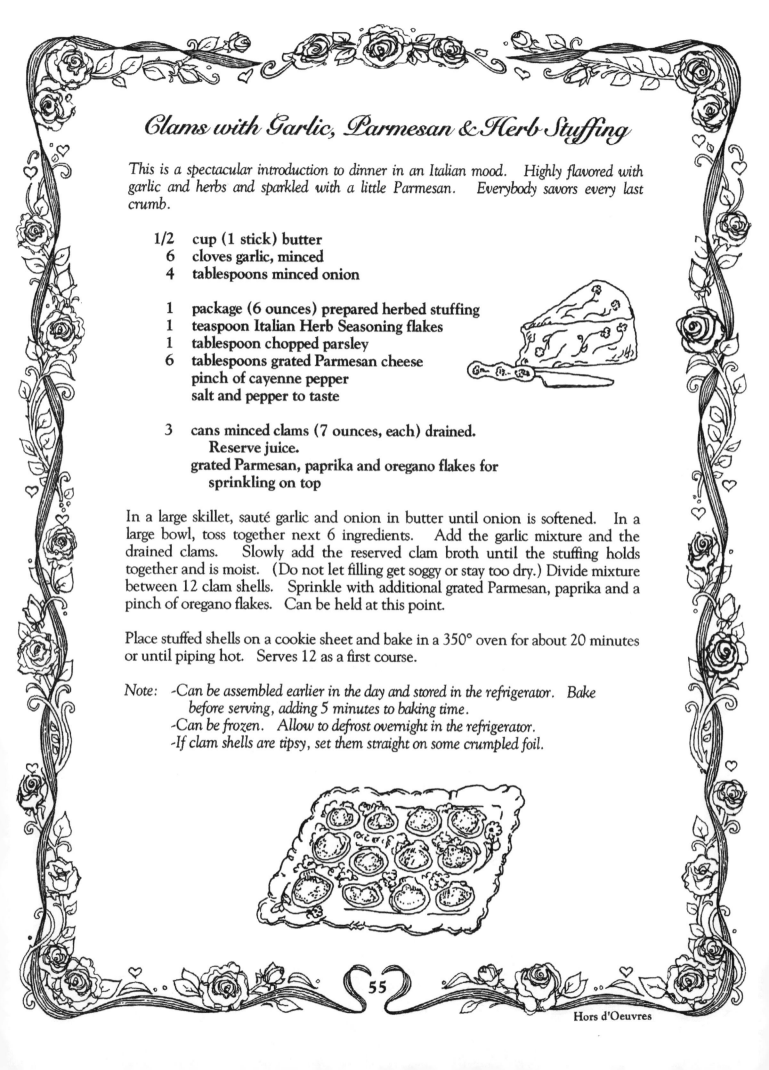

1/2   cup (1 stick) butter
6   cloves garlic, minced
4   tablespoons minced onion

1   package (6 ounces) prepared herbed stuffing
1   teaspoon Italian Herb Seasoning flakes
1   tablespoon chopped parsley
6   tablespoons grated Parmesan cheese
     pinch of cayenne pepper
     salt and pepper to taste

3   cans minced clams (7 ounces, each) drained.
     Reserve juice.
     grated Parmesan, paprika and oregano flakes for
     sprinkling on top

In a large skillet, sauté garlic and onion in butter until onion is softened. In a large bowl, toss together next 6 ingredients. Add the garlic mixture and the drained clams. Slowly add the reserved clam broth until the stuffing holds together and is moist. (Do not let filling get soggy or stay too dry.) Divide mixture between 12 clam shells. Sprinkle with additional grated Parmesan, paprika and a pinch of oregano flakes. Can be held at this point.

Place stuffed shells on a cookie sheet and bake in a 350° oven for about 20 minutes or until piping hot. Serves 12 as a first course.

Note: -*Can be assembled earlier in the day and stored in the refrigerator. Bake before serving, adding 5 minutes to baking time.*
       -*Can be frozen. Allow to defrost overnight in the refrigerator.*
       -*If clam shells are tipsy, set them straight on some crumpled foil.*

Hors d'Oeuvres

Russian Mini-Muffins with Salmon & Crème Fraiche with Lemon & Dill

While this recipe yields more muffins than you will need, unused muffins can be frozen. Mini-muffins are served warm, not hot or cold. Room temperature is O.K. Crème Fraiche can be made with the light cream and light sour cream. However, non-fat sour cream cannot be substituted.

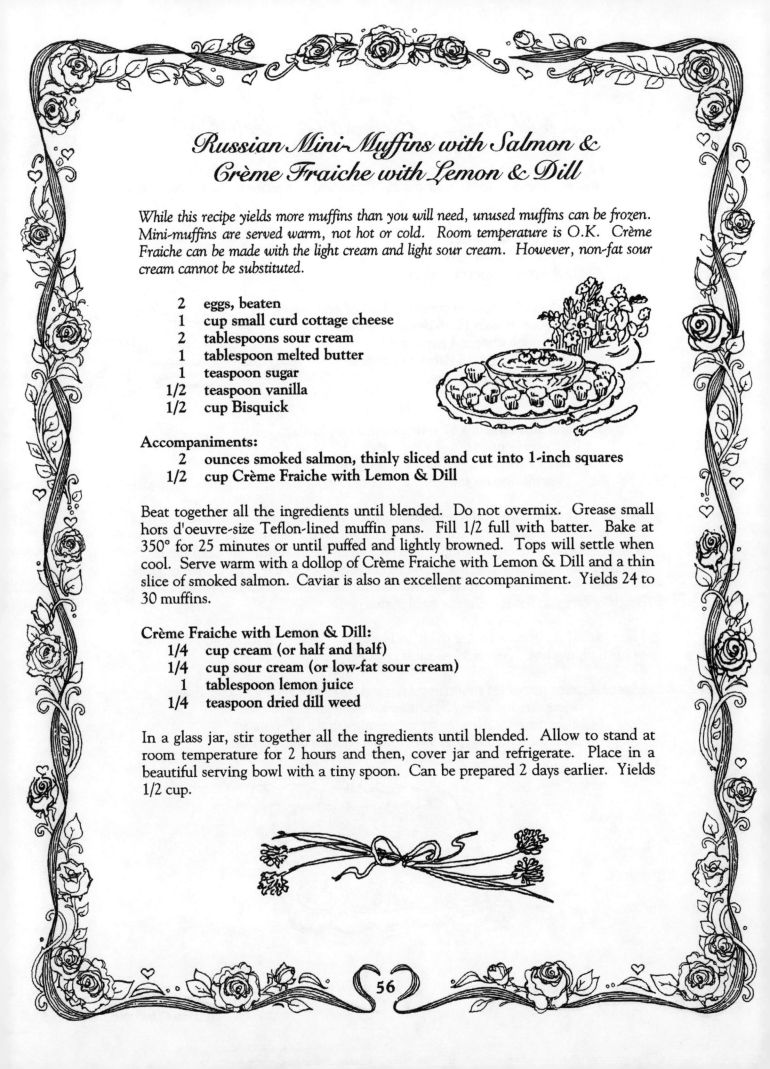

2	eggs, beaten
1	cup small curd cottage cheese
2	tablespoons sour cream
1	tablespoon melted butter
1	teaspoon sugar
1/2	teaspoon vanilla
1/2	cup Bisquick

Accompaniments:

2	ounces smoked salmon, thinly sliced and cut into 1-inch squares
1/2	cup Crème Fraiche with Lemon & Dill

Beat together all the ingredients until blended. Do not overmix. Grease small hors d'oeuvre-size Teflon-lined muffin pans. Fill 1/2 full with batter. Bake at 350° for 25 minutes or until puffed and lightly browned. Tops will settle when cool. Serve warm with a dollop of Crème Fraiche with Lemon & Dill and a thin slice of smoked salmon. Caviar is also an excellent accompaniment. Yields 24 to 30 muffins.

Crème Fraiche with Lemon & Dill:

1/4	cup cream (or half and half)
1/4	cup sour cream (or low-fat sour cream)
1	tablespoon lemon juice
1/4	teaspoon dried dill weed

In a glass jar, stir together all the ingredients until blended. Allow to stand at room temperature for 2 hours and then, cover jar and refrigerate. Place in a beautiful serving bowl with a tiny spoon. Can be prepared 2 days earlier. Yields 1/2 cup.

Chicken & Gruyere Puffed Pastry Pie

Exciting, delicious and very easy is this lovely dish of flaky pastry filled with a delicate blend of chicken, sour cream and Gruyere cheese.

1   package frozen patty shells (6 shells), thawed
1   egg, beaten
2   tablespoons grated Parmesan cheese

On a floured surface, stack 3 patty shells and roll out to measure about 8 or 9-inches round. Place on a lightly greased cookie sheet. Brush edges with beaten egg. Place Chicken Gruyere Filling on pastry, leaving a one-inch border of dough without filling.

Stack and roll remaining shells in the same manner. Place pastry over the first shell. Press edges down with the tines of a fork to seal, Scallop edges for a lovely touch if you have the time. Brush top with beaten egg and pierce with a fork. Sprinkle top with grated Parmesan cheese.

Bake in a 400° oven for 25 to 30 minutes or until pastry is puffed and top is golden brown. Serve in wedges with fresh fruit or buttered vegetables and serve 6.

Chicken Gruyere Filling:
2   cups cooked chicken, cut into small dice
1   cup sour cream
1   cup grated Gruyere or Swiss cheese
1/4   cup chopped chives (or 2 tablespoons dried chives)
1   tablespoon lemon juice
      salt and pepper to taste
1/4   teaspoon thyme

Combine all the ingredients and toss until blended.

Note: - *Entire dish can be assembled a day earlier and refrigerated, unbaked.*
          Add 5 minutes to baking time.
        - *You can substitute leftover turkey for the chicken.*

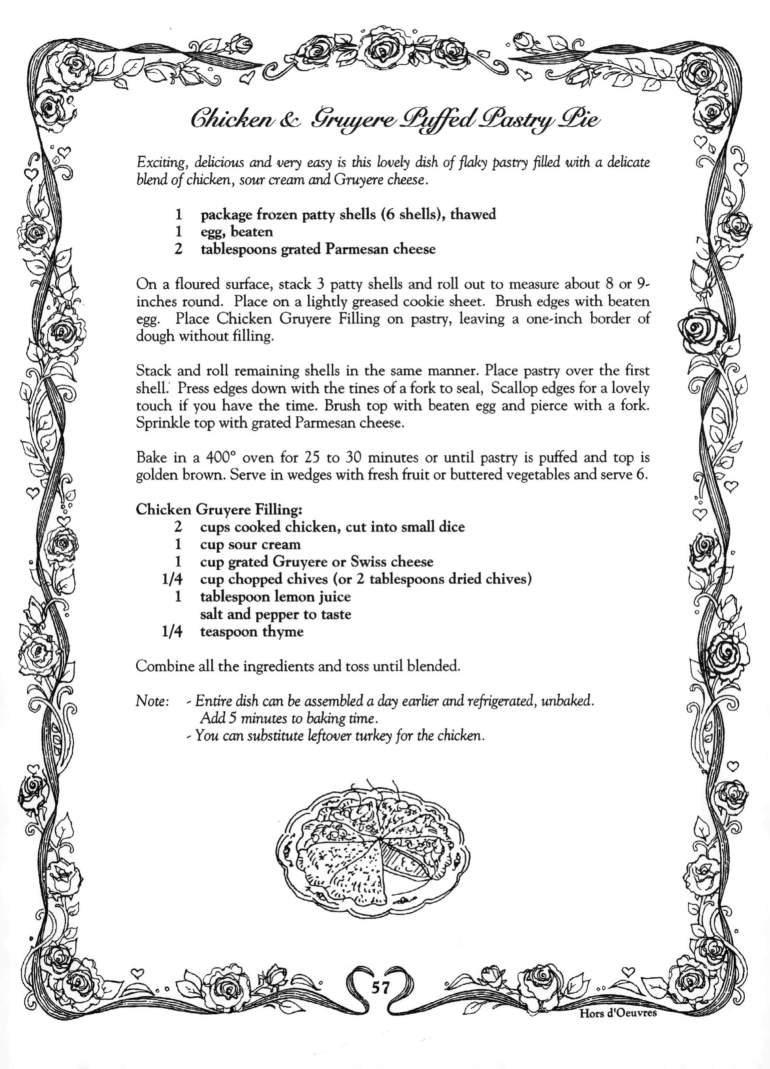

Hors d'Oeuvres

Bruschetta with Tomato & Garlic
(Tomato & Garlic Salad with Parmesan Bread)

This is a very popular salad featured in most Italian restaurants. Spooned on Parmesan Toast it is recklessly delicious. It is easy to prepare, can be made earlier in the day and stored in the refrigerator. Parmesan bread can be assembled earlier in the day, covered securely with plastic wrap and broiled before serving.

Tomato & Garlic Salad:

4	medium tomatoes, seeded and diced
3	cloves garlic, minced
3	tablespoons olive oil
2	tablespoons lemon juice
2	tablespoons chopped fresh basil (or 1 teaspoon sweet basil flakes)
	salt and pepper to taste

In a bowl, toss together all the ingredients until nicely mixed. Cover bowl and refrigerate until serving time. To serve, place tomatoes in a bowl and surround with Parmesan Bread. Allow guests to spoon the salad on the bread to taste. Serves 6.

Bruschetta (Parmesan Bread):

12	thin slices (1/4-inch thick) crusty Italian bread
6	teaspoons butter
12	teaspoons grated Parmesan cheese

Spread each slice of bread with 1/2 teaspoon butter and 1 teaspoon of grated cheese. Place slices on a cookie sheet and broil for 1 minute, or until cheese melts and just begins to color. Watch carefully for there are only seconds between brown and burnt.

A Few More Toppings for Bruschetta

Tomato & Garlic Spread:
Finely chop together 1/2 pound Italian plum tomatoes, 2 cloves garlic, 1 tablespoon chopped basil leaves, salt and pepper to taste. Place mixture in a bowl and stir in 2 tablespoons olive oil, 2 tablespoons lemon juice and salt and pepper to taste. Yields about 1 1/4 cups.

Mushroom & Garlic Spread:
In a skillet, sauté together 2 cloves minced garlic and 1/2 pound finely chopped mushrooms in 1 tablespoon olive oil, until mushrooms are tender and liquid rendered is evaporated. Place mixture in a bowl and add 2 tablespoons minced parsley leaves, 2 tablespoons lemon juice, 2 tablespoons olive oil and salt and pepper to taste. Yields about 1 1/4 cups.

Mushrooms Duxelles with Toast Points

You will enjoy serving this incredible mushroom delicacy with simple toast points as a light introduction to dinner. This can be served warm (not hot) or cool (not cold). It is light and delicate and very flavorful.

1	onion, minced
1	tablespoon butter
1	pound mushrooms, thinly sliced
3	tablespoons lemon juice
	salt and pepper to taste
1/4	cup sour cream
1/4	cup chopped chives

In a large skillet, sauté onion in butter until onion is soft. Add the mushrooms, lemon juice and seasonings and sauté mushrooms until mushrooms are tender and liquid rendered is evaporated. Place mushroom mixture in a bowl and stir in sour cream and chives. Serve with Toast Points. Yields 6 small servings.

To Make Toast Points:

4	slices thin-sliced white bread, crusts removed
4	teaspoons butter

Spread each slice of bread with a thin coating of butter. Cut bread slices on the diagonal. Cut each diagonal into 2 triangles. You will have 16 toast points. Place on a cookie sheet and bake at 350° for just a few minutes, or until toast points are dry, but not browned. Time will vary depending on the freshness of the bread, so keep an eye on the bread as it bakes. Place on a serving platter covered with plastic wrap until ready to serve.

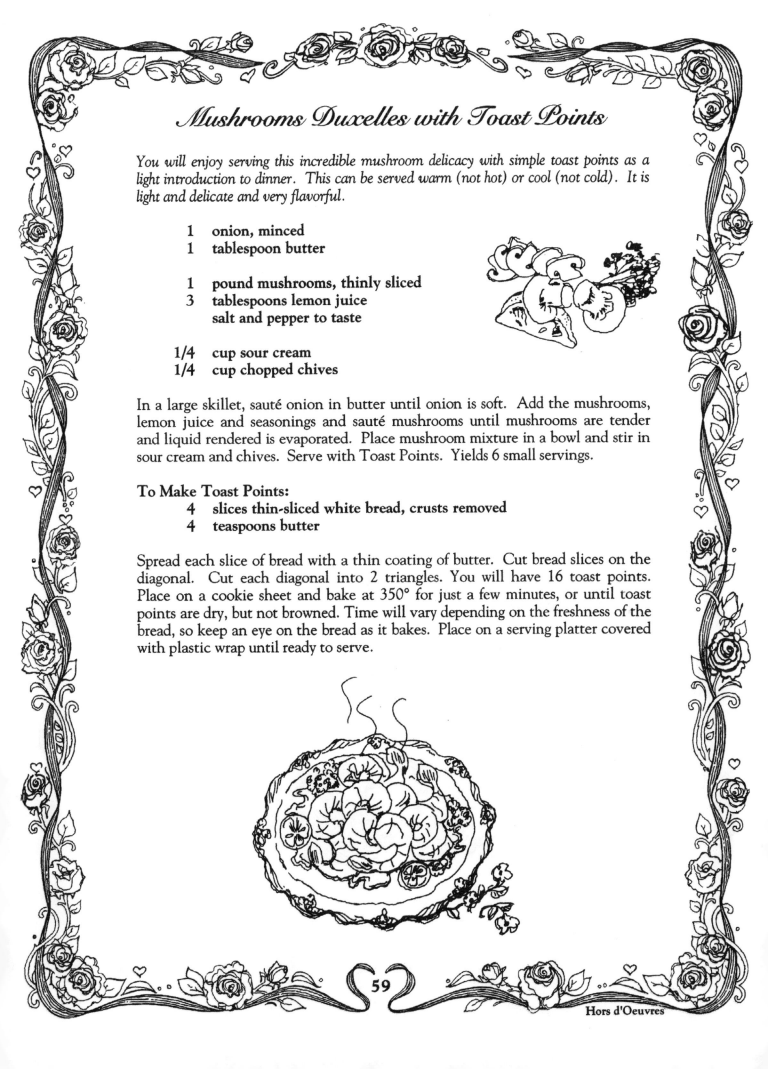

French Brie Quiche with Strawberries & Toasted Almonds

Brie, served with fresh fruit and almonds, is a lovely combination of flavors and colors. Here, they are combined in a quiche that has flair and panache. It can be prepared in advance and stored in the refrigerator. Heat through before serving.

1   deep dish frozen pie shell, baked in a 400° oven for about 8 minutes, or until just beginning to take on color. Leave shell in pan.

6   ounces French Brie. Remove the outer moldy rind and cut the remaining Brie into small dice.
1   package (3 ounces) cream cheese, cut into 1/2-inch dice
1/3 cup sliced toasted* almonds

4   eggs
1   cup half and half

1   cup strawberries sliced in halves and sprinkled with 1 teaspoon sugar

Place prepared pie shell on a cookie sheet. Place Brie evenly in shell. Place cream cheese evenly in shell. Sprinkle almonds over all.

Beat together eggs and half-and-half and pour evenly in shell. Bake at 350° for 45 minutes. Remove from the oven and place strawberries decoratively along the rim and in the center. Serves 6.

*To Toast Almonds:
Place sliced almonds in a pie plate and toast at 350° for 5 or 6 minutes. Watch carefully as almonds are thinly sliced. They should be just beginning to take on color.

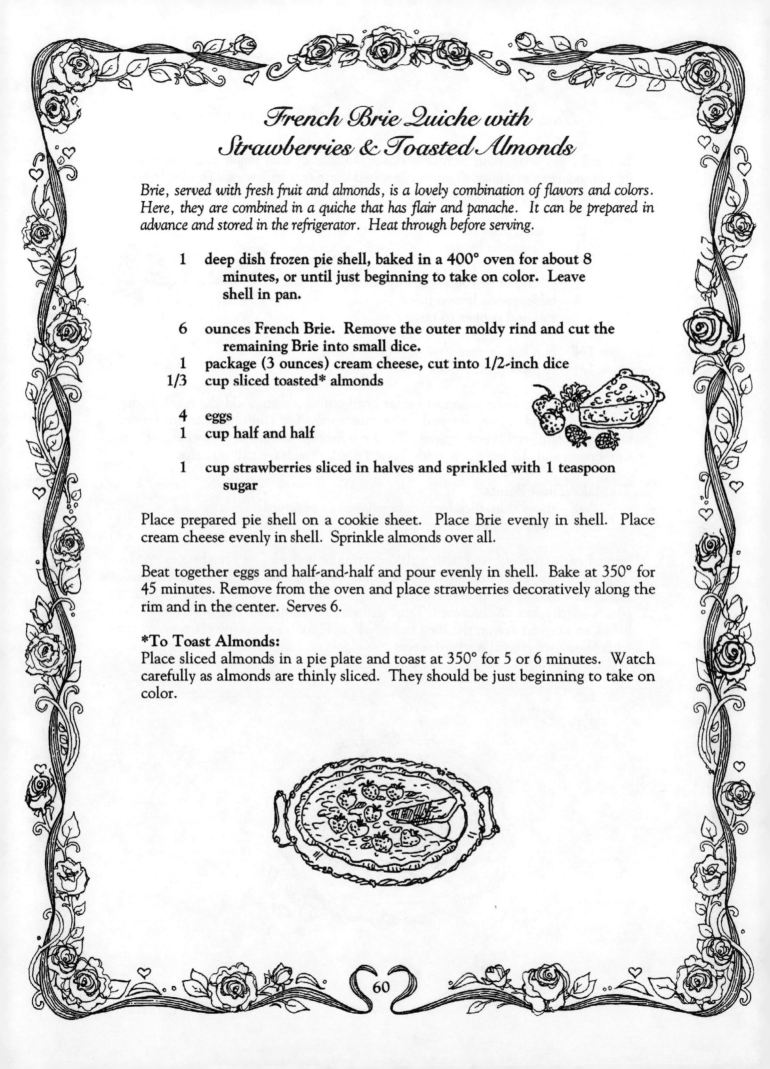

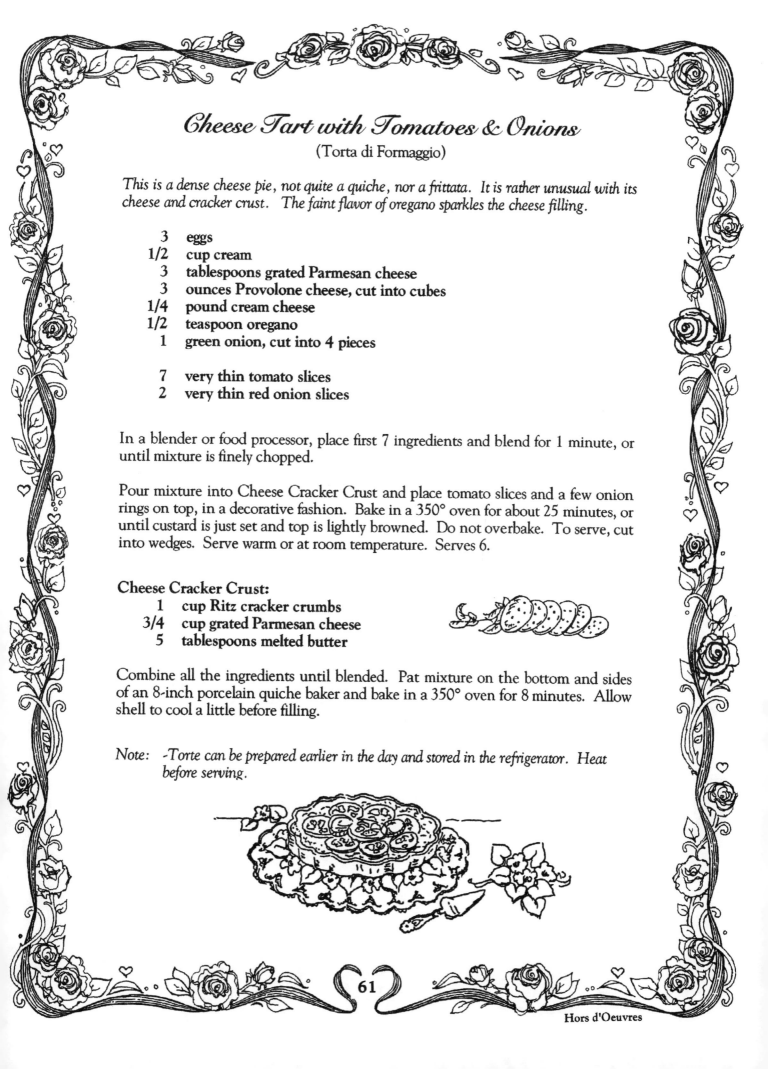

Cheese Tart with Tomatoes & Onions
(Torta di Formaggio)

This is a dense cheese pie, not quite a quiche, nor a frittata. It is rather unusual with its cheese and cracker crust. The faint flavor of oregano sparkles the cheese filling.

3	eggs
1/2	cup cream
3	tablespoons grated Parmesan cheese
3	ounces Provolone cheese, cut into cubes
1/4	pound cream cheese
1/2	teaspoon oregano
1	green onion, cut into 4 pieces
7	very thin tomato slices
2	very thin red onion slices

In a blender or food processor, place first 7 ingredients and blend for 1 minute, or until mixture is finely chopped.

Pour mixture into Cheese Cracker Crust and place tomato slices and a few onion rings on top, in a decorative fashion. Bake in a 350° oven for about 25 minutes, or until custard is just set and top is lightly browned. Do not overbake. To serve, cut into wedges. Serve warm or at room temperature. Serves 6.

Cheese Cracker Crust:

1	cup Ritz cracker crumbs
3/4	cup grated Parmesan cheese
5	tablespoons melted butter

Combine all the ingredients until blended. Pat mixture on the bottom and sides of an 8-inch porcelain quiche baker and bake in a 350° oven for 8 minutes. Allow shell to cool a little before filling.

Note: -Torte can be prepared earlier in the day and stored in the refrigerator. Heat before serving.

Hors d'Oeuvres

Piroshki Logs a la Muscovite

Using the prepared puff pastry cuts preparation time to a minimum. And preparing these in 8-inch logs that you will later cut into slices is another timesaver.

Mushroom & Herb Filling:

2	tablespoons butter
4	shallots, minced
2	cloves garlic, minced
1	large onion, minced
1/2	pound mushrooms, minced
2	teaspoons lemon juice
1/4	teaspoon ground poultry seasoning
1/8	teaspoon thyme flakes
	salt and pepper to taste
2	tablespoons flour
1	cup sour cream

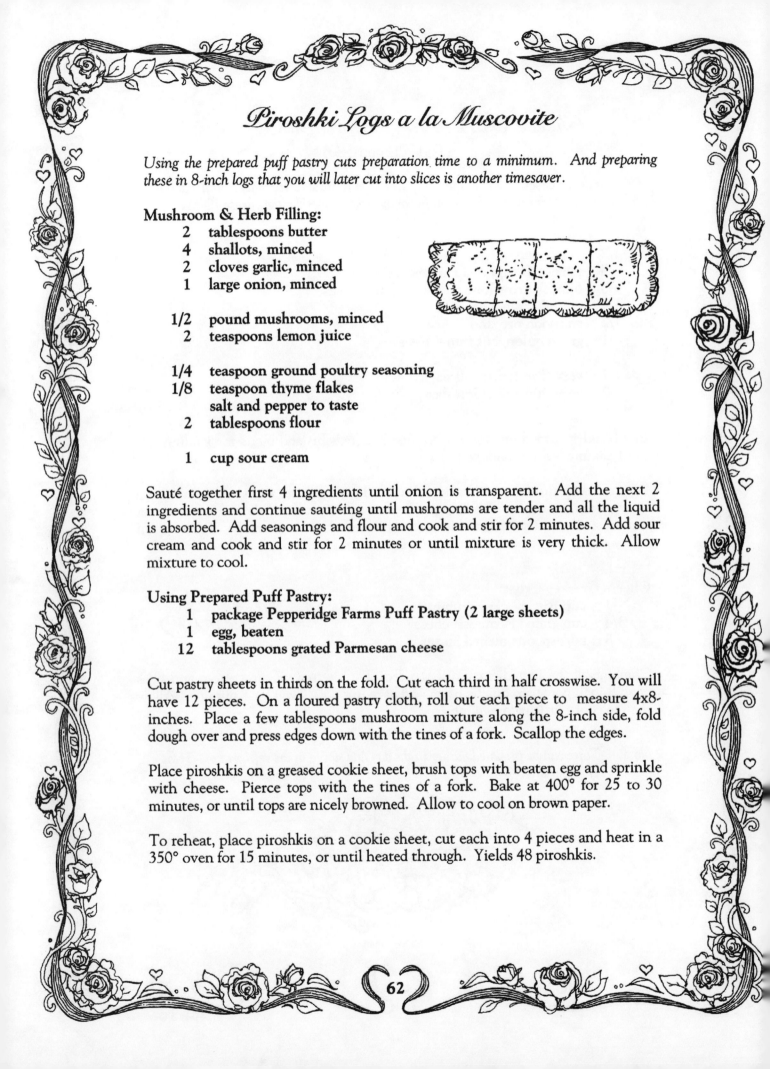

Sauté together first 4 ingredients until onion is transparent. Add the next 2 ingredients and continue sautéing until mushrooms are tender and all the liquid is absorbed. Add seasonings and flour and cook and stir for 2 minutes. Add sour cream and cook and stir for 2 minutes or until mixture is very thick. Allow mixture to cool.

Using Prepared Puff Pastry:

1	package Pepperidge Farms Puff Pastry (2 large sheets)
1	egg, beaten
12	tablespoons grated Parmesan cheese

Cut pastry sheets in thirds on the fold. Cut each third in half crosswise. You will have 12 pieces. On a floured pastry cloth, roll out each piece to measure 4x8-inches. Place a few tablespoons mushroom mixture along the 8-inch side, fold dough over and press edges down with the tines of a fork. Scallop the edges.

Place piroshkis on a greased cookie sheet, brush tops with beaten egg and sprinkle with cheese. Pierce tops with the tines of a fork. Bake at 400° for 25 to 30 minutes, or until tops are nicely browned. Allow to cool on brown paper.

To reheat, place piroshkis on a cookie sheet, cut each into 4 pieces and heat in a 350° oven for 15 minutes, or until heated through. Yields 48 piroshkis.

Hummus

This Middle Eastern chick pea dip is delicious served with small wedges of fresh pita bread. The "tahini" can be purchased in most supermarkets and health food stores. This can be prepared in minutes using the food processor. Also, it can be prepared 2 days in advance and stored, covered, in the refrigerator.

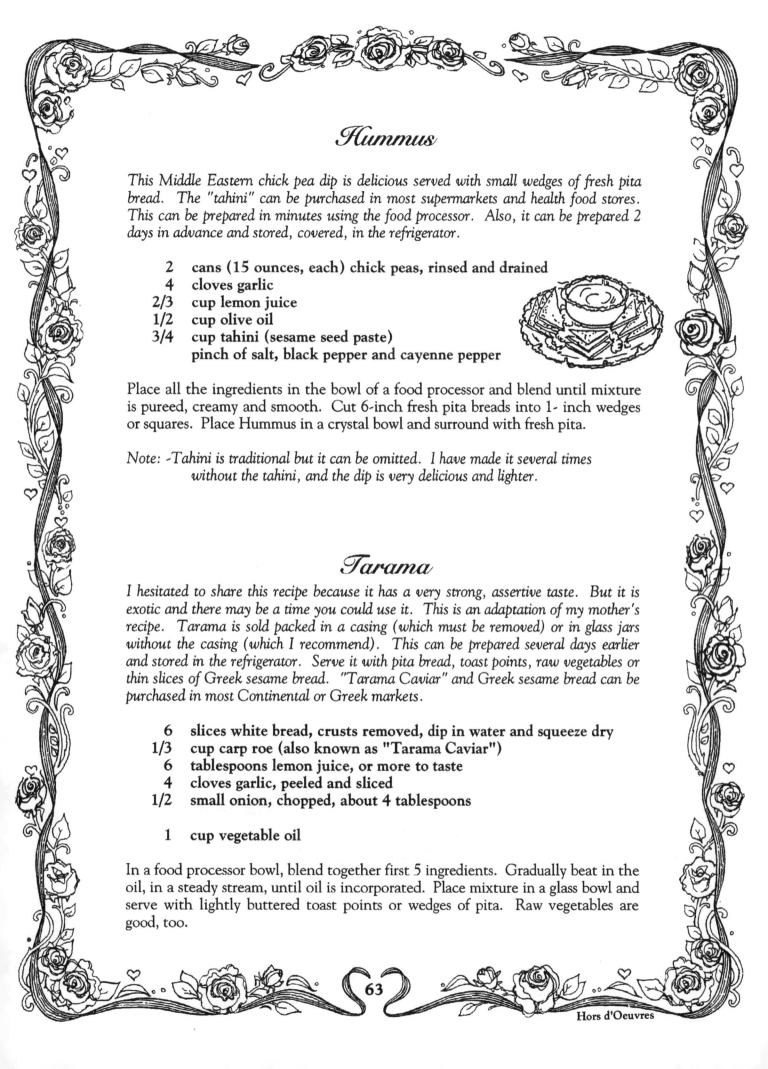

2   cans (15 ounces, each) chick peas, rinsed and drained
4   cloves garlic
2/3 cup lemon juice
1/2 cup olive oil
3/4 cup tahini (sesame seed paste)
     pinch of salt, black pepper and cayenne pepper

Place all the ingredients in the bowl of a food processor and blend until mixture is pureed, creamy and smooth. Cut 6-inch fresh pita breads into 1- inch wedges or squares. Place Hummus in a crystal bowl and surround with fresh pita.

Note: -Tahini is traditional but it can be omitted. I have made it several times without the tahini, and the dip is very delicious and lighter.

Tarama

I hesitated to share this recipe because it has a very strong, assertive taste. But it is exotic and there may be a time you could use it. This is an adaptation of my mother's recipe. Tarama is sold packed in a casing (which must be removed) or in glass jars without the casing (which I recommend). This can be prepared several days earlier and stored in the refrigerator. Serve it with pita bread, toast points, raw vegetables or thin slices of Greek sesame bread. "Tarama Caviar" and Greek sesame bread can be purchased in most Continental or Greek markets.

6   slices white bread, crusts removed, dip in water and squeeze dry
1/3 cup carp roe (also known as "Tarama Caviar")
6   tablespoons lemon juice, or more to taste
4   cloves garlic, peeled and sliced
1/2 small onion, chopped, about 4 tablespoons

1   cup vegetable oil

In a food processor bowl, blend together first 5 ingredients. Gradually beat in the oil, in a steady stream, until oil is incorporated. Place mixture in a glass bowl and serve with lightly buttered toast points or wedges of pita. Raw vegetables are good, too.

Hors d'Oeuvres

Baked Brie with Strawberries & Almonds

1   wheel of Brie (8-inch circle) weighing about 2 pounds. Remove
      the outer rind of mold from the top. Place Brie in an 8-inch
      round quiche dish or porcelain baker.
1/2 cup chopped almonds

1   cup sliced fresh strawberries

Mark the top of the Brie into 4 wedges. Fill alternate wedges with almonds and
leave alternate wedges unfilled. Pace Brie in a 350° oven and bake for about 20
minutes, or until Brie is soft. Fill unfilled wedges with sliced strawberries. Serve
at once with small toast points or pale soda crackers.

Baked Brie with Currants & Pine Nuts

1   wheel of Brie (8-inch circle) weighing about 2 pounds. Remove
      the outer rind of mold from the top. Place Brie in an 8-inch
      round quiche dish or porcelain baker.
3/4 cup currants
3/4 cup pine nuts

Mark the top of the Brie into 4 wedges. Fill alternate wedges with currants and
pine nuts. Place Brie in a 350° oven and bake for 20 minutes, or until Brie is soft.
Serve at once with small toast points or pale soda crackers.

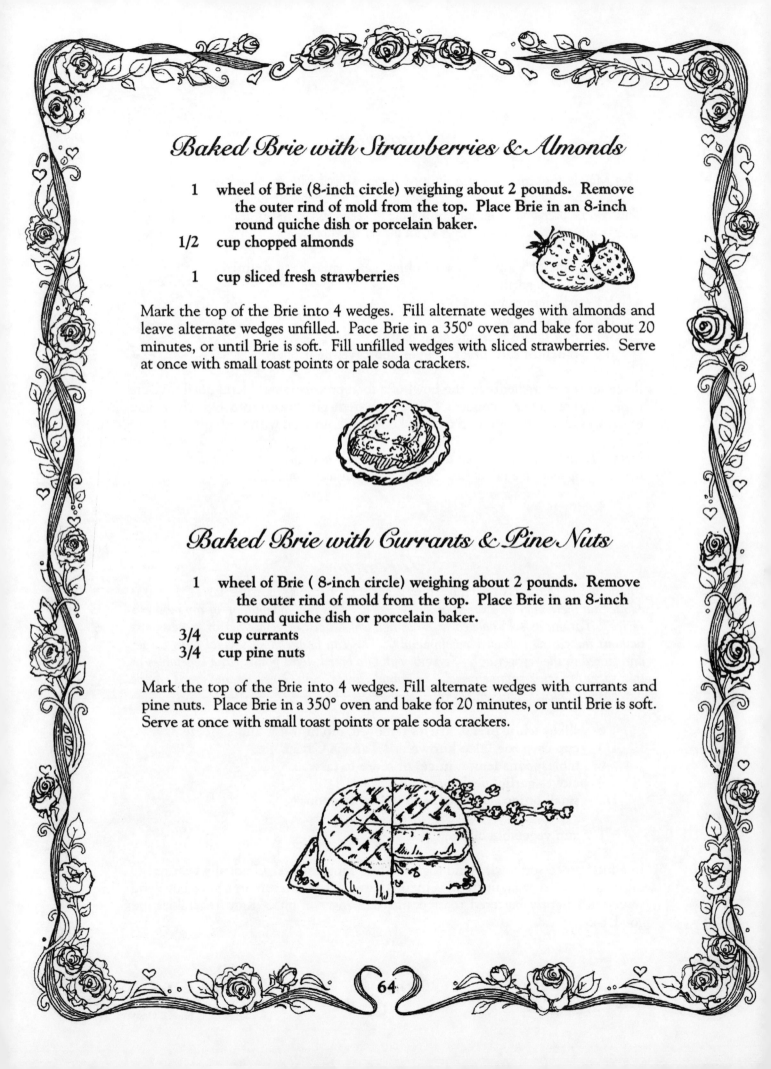

Soups

and

Garnitures

Peasant Cabbage & Tomato Soup

This is nice homey soup to serve on a Sunday night when the family joins together for dinner. The Croustades are especially delicious, and a few extras would be in order.

2	onions, chopped
2	shallots, minced
6	cloves garlic, minced
2	tablespoons butter

1	small cabbage (about 1 pound) coarsely chopped
1	can (1 pound) stewed tomatoes, chopped. Do not drain.
3	cans (10 1/2 ounces, each) chicken broth
1	tablespoon lemon juice
1	teaspoon sugar
1	teaspoon sweet basil flakes
1/2	teaspoon oregano flakes
	salt and pepper to taste
1 or 2	shakes of cayenne pepper

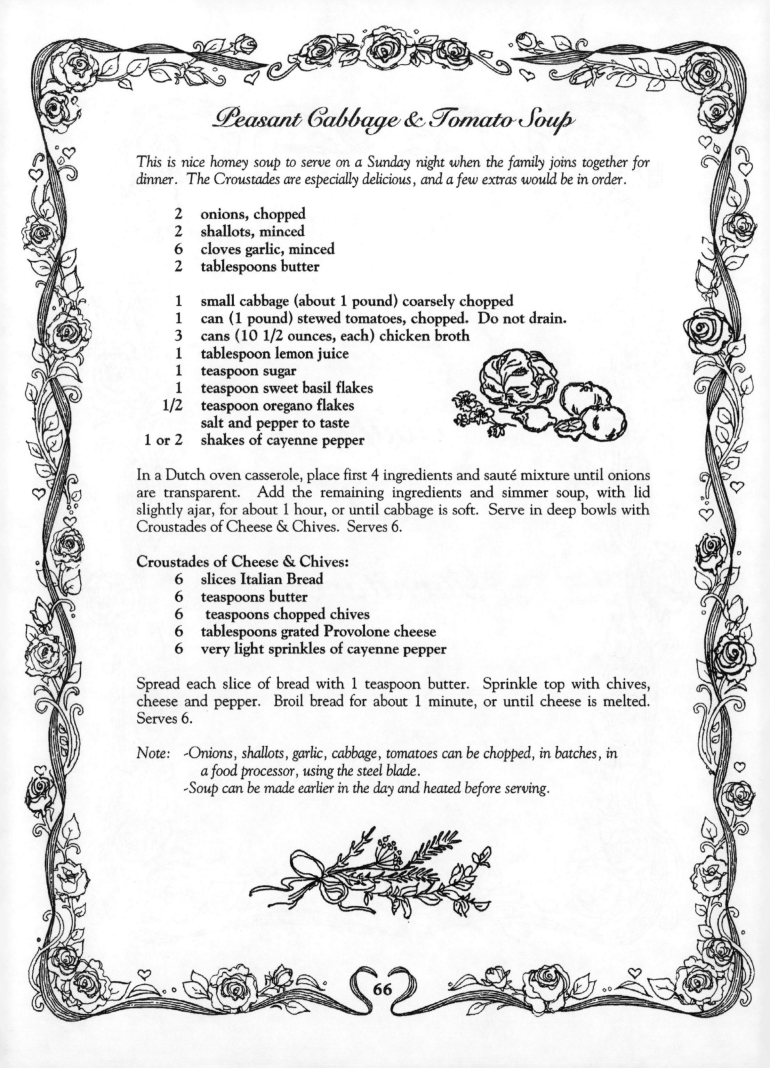

In a Dutch oven casserole, place first 4 ingredients and sauté mixture until onions are transparent. Add the remaining ingredients and simmer soup, with lid slightly ajar, for about 1 hour, or until cabbage is soft. Serve in deep bowls with Croustades of Cheese & Chives. Serves 6.

Croustades of Cheese & Chives:

6	slices Italian Bread
6	teaspoons butter
6	teaspoons chopped chives
6	tablespoons grated Provolone cheese
6	very light sprinkles of cayenne pepper

Spread each slice of bread with 1 teaspoon butter. Sprinkle top with chives, cheese and pepper. Broil bread for about 1 minute, or until cheese is melted. Serves 6.

Note: -Onions, shallots, garlic, cabbage, tomatoes can be chopped, in batches, in a food processor, using the steel blade.
-Soup can be made earlier in the day and heated before serving.

Beef & Barley Mushroom Soup

This is a nice, thick homey soup that is a good choice for an informal Sunday night dinner with family and friends. It can be prepared a day earlier, stored in the refrigerator, and heated before serving.

2	cans (10 1/2 ounces, each) beef broth
1	cup chicken broth
1	large onion, finely chopped
4	cloves minced garlic
2	carrots, grated
1/2	cup pearl barley
1/2	pound boneless chuck, cut into 1/2-inch cubes
1/2	pound mushrooms
4	cloves minced garlic
2	teaspoons oil
1	tablespoon chopped parsley
	salt and pepper to taste

In a covered Dutch oven casserole, place first group of ingredients and simmer mixture until barley and beef are tender, about 1 hour. Meanwhile, sauté mushrooms in oil until they are tender and add to soup. Stir in the parsley and seasonings and heat through. Serves 8.

Note: -*If you have the extra time, I would recommend this. Pearl barley is a little starchy when cooked and it takes an hour to soften. I usually make 1 pound of barley at a time, separate it in 4 small plastic bags and freeze it. Each little bag will be about 1/2 cup uncooked barley. To make the barley, place it in a large pot, cover it generously with water, and simmer it until it is tender. This way, you can use the cooked barley in soup at a moment's notice.*

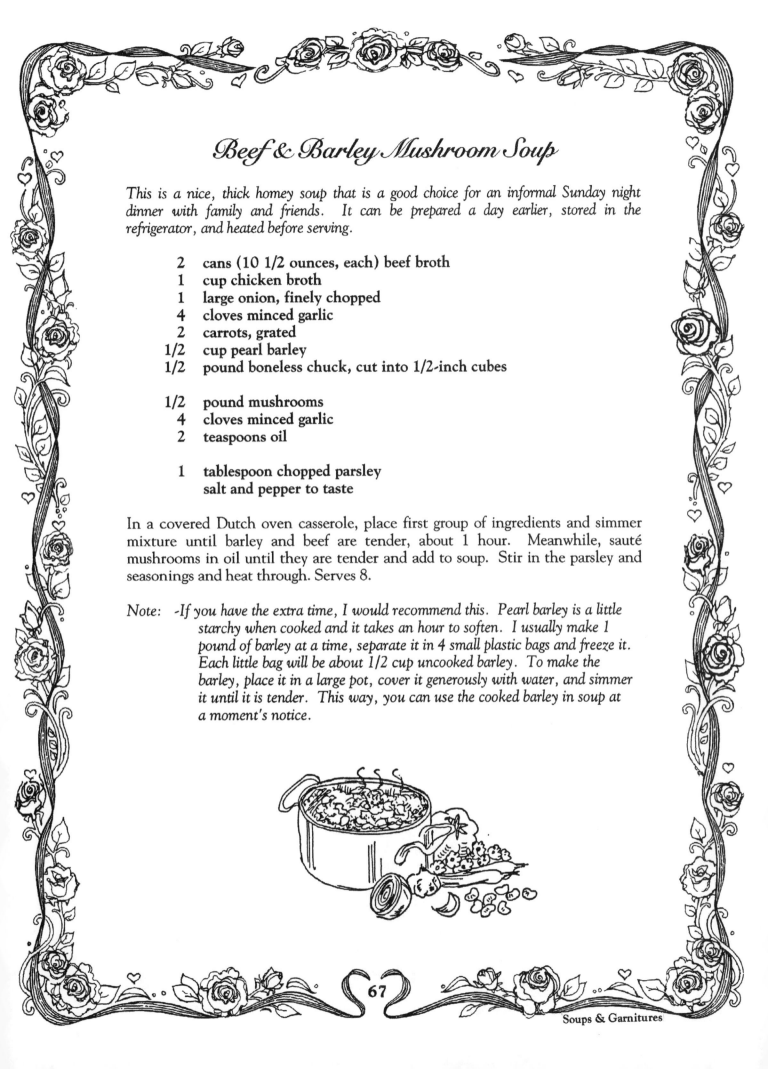

Cabbage & Tomato Soup with Sauerkraut

2   pounds chuck flanken-style ribs, meaty and lean (sometimes called short ribs)
1   small head of cabbage (about 1 1/2 pounds), grated or coarsely chopped
1   cup sauerkraut
1   can (1 pound) stewed tomatoes, finely chopped
3   cans (10 1/2 ounces, each) chicken broth
1   can (10 1/2 ounces) beef broth
1   teaspoon Bovril, meat extract base
3   onions, chopped
2   cloves garlic, put through a press
1   carrot, finely grated

2   tablespoons lemon juice
2   tablespoons sugar

salt and pepper to taste

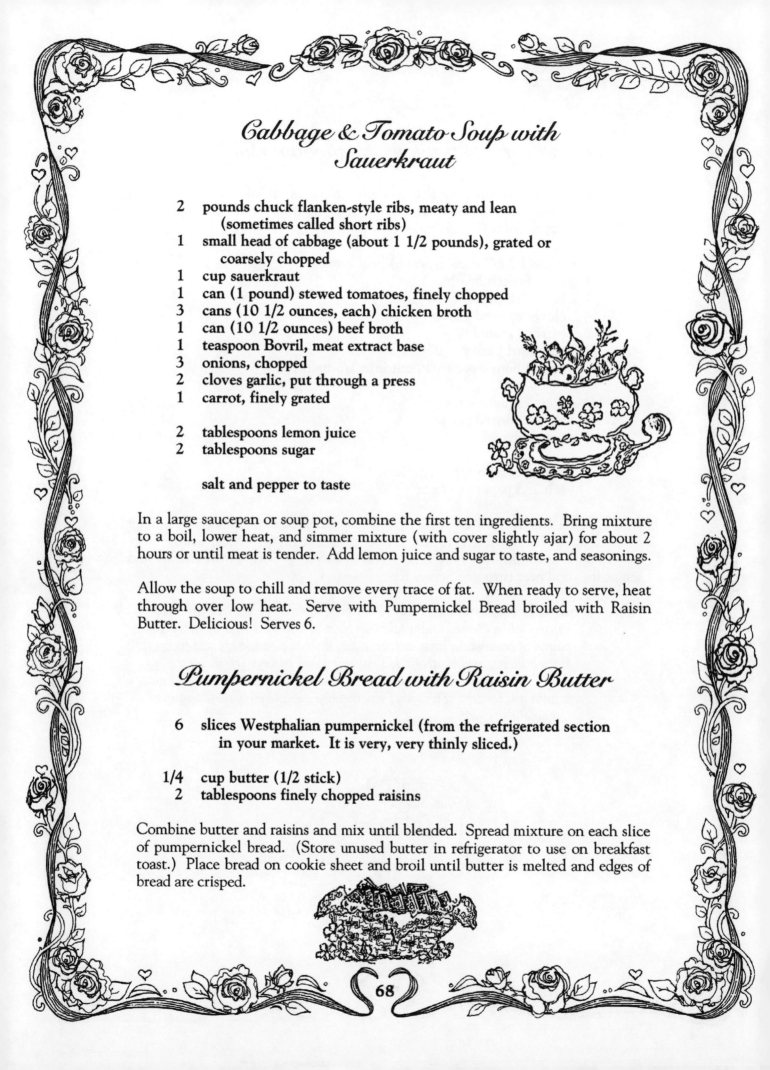

In a large saucepan or soup pot, combine the first ten ingredients. Bring mixture to a boil, lower heat, and simmer mixture (with cover slightly ajar) for about 2 hours or until meat is tender. Add lemon juice and sugar to taste, and seasonings.

Allow the soup to chill and remove every trace of fat. When ready to serve, heat through over low heat. Serve with Pumpernickel Bread broiled with Raisin Butter. Delicious! Serves 6.

Pumpernickel Bread with Raisin Butter

6   slices Westphalian pumpernickel (from the refrigerated section in your market. It is very, very thinly sliced.)

1/4   cup butter (1/2 stick)
2   tablespoons finely chopped raisins

Combine butter and raisins and mix until blended. Spread mixture on each slice of pumpernickel bread. (Store unused butter in refrigerator to use on breakfast toast.) Place bread on cookie sheet and broil until butter is melted and edges of bread are crisped.

Puree of Honey Carrot Soup with Apples & Cinnamon

This is one of the nicest soups to start a holiday feast. It is festive and interesting with a promise of good things to come.

1	pound fresh baby carrots
2	apples, peeled, cored and sliced
2	onions, chopped
6	shallots, chopped
2	cloves garlic, chopped
6	cups chicken broth
1	tablespoon honey
	salt to taste
1	cup half and half
12	teaspoons low-fat sour cream
12	sprinkles cinnamon sugar

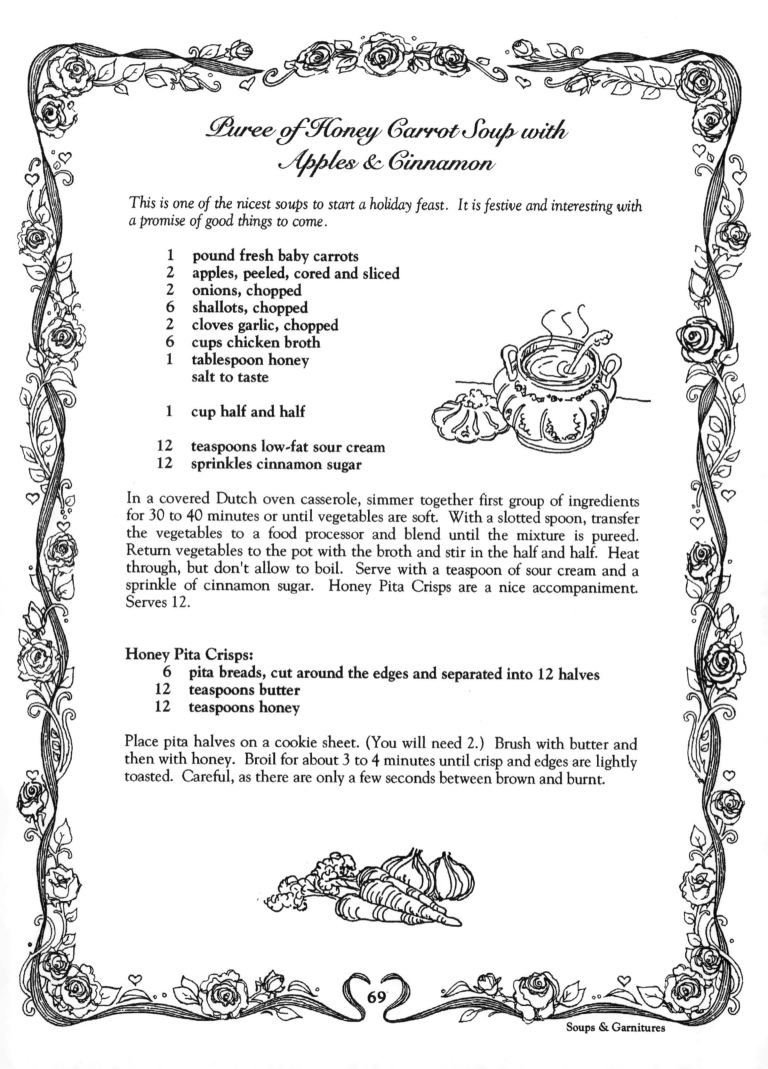

In a covered Dutch oven casserole, simmer together first group of ingredients for 30 to 40 minutes or until vegetables are soft. With a slotted spoon, transfer the vegetables to a food processor and blend until the mixture is pureed. Return vegetables to the pot with the broth and stir in the half and half. Heat through, but don't allow to boil. Serve with a teaspoon of sour cream and a sprinkle of cinnamon sugar. Honey Pita Crisps are a nice accompaniment. Serves 12.

Honey Pita Crisps:

6	pita breads, cut around the edges and separated into 12 halves
12	teaspoons butter
12	teaspoons honey

Place pita halves on a cookie sheet. (You will need 2.) Brush with butter and then with honey. Broil for about 3 to 4 minutes until crisp and edges are lightly toasted. Careful, as there are only a few seconds between brown and burnt.

An Elegant Cream of Cauliflower Soup
(Crème Du Barry)

As many times as I have prepared this soup, someone always remarks that it is the best soup they have ever tasted. It is one of my very favorites, as well. When you consider its utter simplicity in preparation and the incredible results, I hope you enjoy this often.

1	cup cream
1	cup sour cream
2	packages (10 ounces, each) frozen cauliflower florets, defrosted
2	onions, chopped
2	shallots, minced (about 2 heaping tablespoons)
2	cloves garlic, minced
2	tablespoons lemon juice
1/4	cup butter (1/2 stick)
3	cans (10 1/2 ounces, each) chicken broth
	salt and white pepper to taste
1	tablespoon minced parsley
2	tablespoons minced chives
1/4	teaspoon dill weed

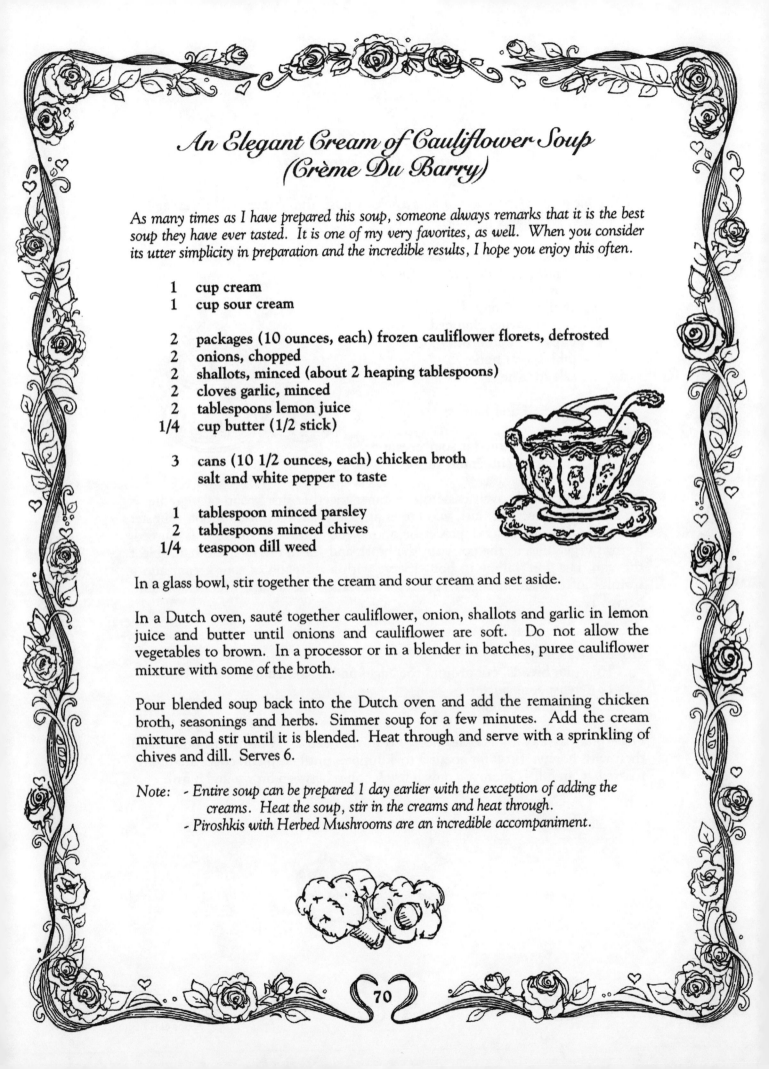

In a glass bowl, stir together the cream and sour cream and set aside.

In a Dutch oven, sauté together cauliflower, onion, shallots and garlic in lemon juice and butter until onions and cauliflower are soft. Do not allow the vegetables to brown. In a processor or in a blender in batches, puree cauliflower mixture with some of the broth.

Pour blended soup back into the Dutch oven and add the remaining chicken broth, seasonings and herbs. Simmer soup for a few minutes. Add the cream mixture and stir until it is blended. Heat through and serve with a sprinkling of chives and dill. Serves 6.

Note: - Entire soup can be prepared 1 day earlier with the exception of adding the creams. Heat the soup, stir in the creams and heat through.
- Piroshkis with Herbed Mushrooms are an incredible accompaniment.

Mexican Chicken Chile Soup with Orzo

This is delicious soup, very new and very different. It is a medley of Mexican tastes and flavors. It is also very hearty, and will serve well as a complete meal. My Easiest & Best Cornbread is another lovely accompaniment.

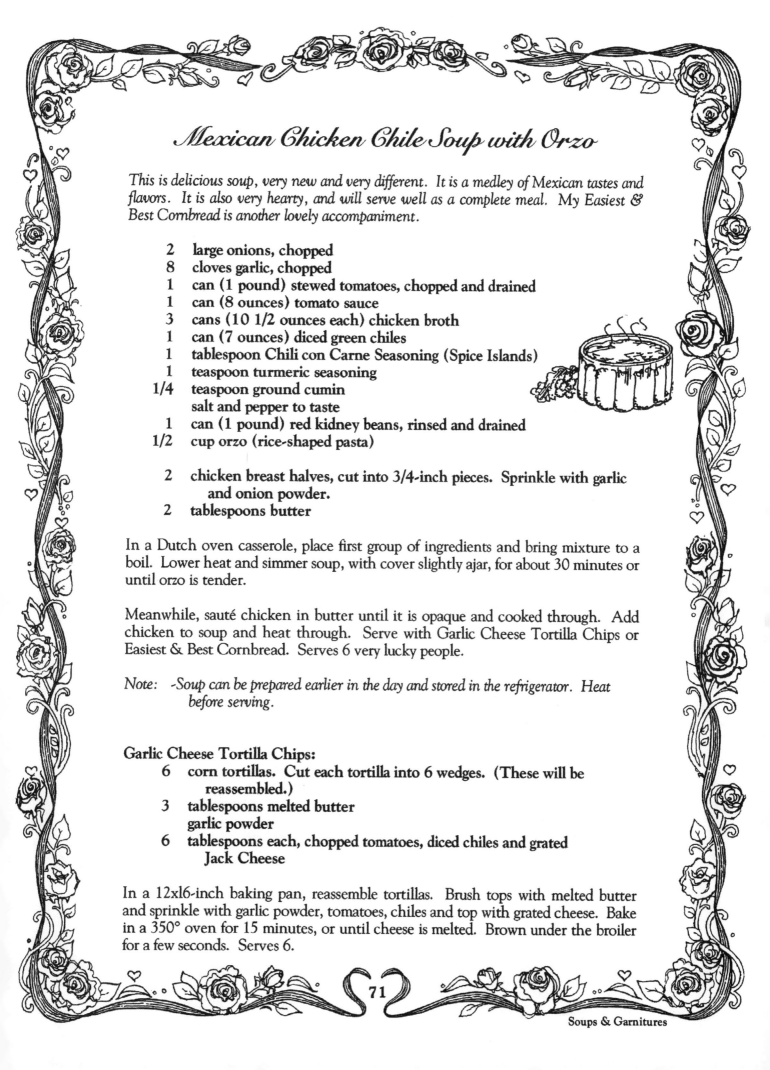

2	large onions, chopped
8	cloves garlic, chopped
1	can (1 pound) stewed tomatoes, chopped and drained
1	can (8 ounces) tomato sauce
3	cans (10 1/2 ounces each) chicken broth
1	can (7 ounces) diced green chiles
1	tablespoon Chili con Carne Seasoning (Spice Islands)
1	teaspoon turmeric seasoning
1/4	teaspoon ground cumin
	salt and pepper to taste
1	can (1 pound) red kidney beans, rinsed and drained
1/2	cup orzo (rice-shaped pasta)
2	chicken breast halves, cut into 3/4-inch pieces. Sprinkle with garlic and onion powder.
2	tablespoons butter

In a Dutch oven casserole, place first group of ingredients and bring mixture to a boil. Lower heat and simmer soup, with cover slightly ajar, for about 30 minutes or until orzo is tender.

Meanwhile, sauté chicken in butter until it is opaque and cooked through. Add chicken to soup and heat through. Serve with Garlic Cheese Tortilla Chips or Easiest & Best Cornbread. Serves 6 very lucky people.

Note: -Soup can be prepared earlier in the day and stored in the refrigerator. Heat before serving.

Garlic Cheese Tortilla Chips:

6	corn tortillas. Cut each tortilla into 6 wedges. (These will be reassembled.)
3	tablespoons melted butter
	garlic powder
6	tablespoons each, chopped tomatoes, diced chiles and grated Jack Cheese

In a 12x16-inch baking pan, reassemble tortillas. Brush tops with melted butter and sprinkle with garlic powder, tomatoes, chiles and top with grated cheese. Bake in a 350° oven for 15 minutes, or until cheese is melted. Brown under the broiler for a few seconds. Serves 6.

Easiest & Best Lentil Soup

1   pound lentils, rinsed in a strainer
2   cans (10 1/2 ounces, each) beef broth
4   cups water
2   cups chopped onions
3   carrots, thinly sliced
      salt and pepper to taste
1   package onion soup

Place all the ingredients in a Dutch oven, cover and simmer soup for 1 1/2 hours or until lentils are tender. This produces an exceedingly thick and hearty soup and it couldn't be easier. Serve it with thin slices of Apple Bread and sweet butter. Serves 6 to 8.

Cinnamon Apple Bread with Raisins & Walnuts

2   eggs
1   cup sugar
1/2   cup oil
1   teaspoon vanilla

1 1/2   cups flour
1   teaspoon baking powder
1/2   teaspoon baking soda
1/8   teaspoon salt
2   teaspoons cinnamon

1   cup grated apples
1/2   cup raisins
1/2   cup walnuts

Beat together eggs, sugar, oil and vanilla until thoroughly blended, about 1 minute. Stir in flour, baking powder, soda, salt and cinnamon until blended. Stir in apples, raisins and walnuts. Pour mixture into a 9 x 5 x3-inch loaf pan that has been greased and floured. Bake in a 350° oven for about 50 minutes to 1 hour or until a cake tester, inserted in center, comes out clean.

Cool pan for 10 minutes, then remove pan and cool on rack. Yields 1 loaf.

Mexican Corn & Chile Soup

Please note that in the following recipe, "corn" appears twice. In the first group of ingredients, it is coarsely chopped. In the second group of ingredients, it is left whole.

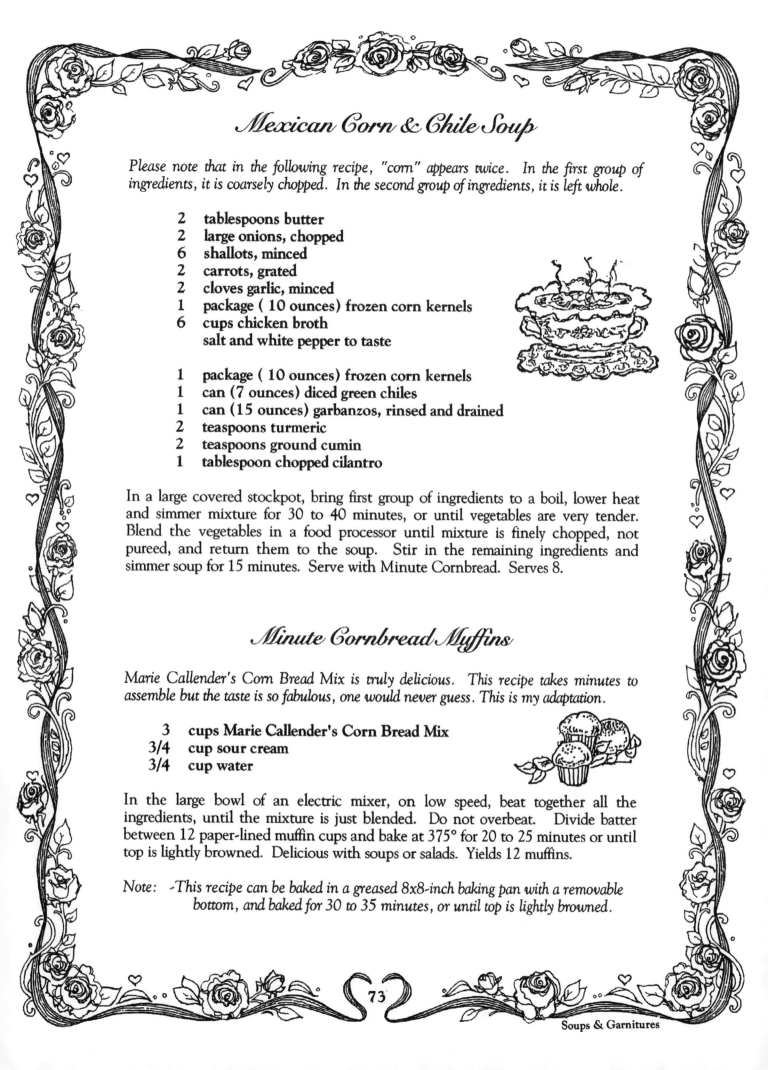

2	tablespoons butter
2	large onions, chopped
6	shallots, minced
2	carrots, grated
2	cloves garlic, minced
1	package (10 ounces) frozen corn kernels
6	cups chicken broth
	salt and white pepper to taste

1	package (10 ounces) frozen corn kernels
1	can (7 ounces) diced green chiles
1	can (15 ounces) garbanzos, rinsed and drained
2	teaspoons turmeric
2	teaspoons ground cumin
1	tablespoon chopped cilantro

In a large covered stockpot, bring first group of ingredients to a boil, lower heat and simmer mixture for 30 to 40 minutes, or until vegetables are very tender. Blend the vegetables in a food processor until mixture is finely chopped, not pureed, and return them to the soup. Stir in the remaining ingredients and simmer soup for 15 minutes. Serve with Minute Cornbread. Serves 8.

Minute Cornbread Muffins

Marie Callender's Corn Bread Mix is truly delicious. This recipe takes minutes to assemble but the taste is so fabulous, one would never guess. This is my adaptation.

3	cups Marie Callender's Corn Bread Mix
3/4	cup sour cream
3/4	cup water

In the large bowl of an electric mixer, on low speed, beat together all the ingredients, until the mixture is just blended. Do not overbeat. Divide batter between 12 paper-lined muffin cups and bake at 375° for 20 to 25 minutes or until top is lightly browned. Delicious with soups or salads. Yields 12 muffins.

Note: -This recipe can be baked in a greased 8x8-inch baking pan with a removable bottom, and baked for 30 to 35 minutes, or until top is lightly browned.

French Onion Soup with Croustades of Cheese

The essence of a good onion soup is made when the onions are cooked very slowly in butter...the longer, the better. What you are actually doing, is sweating or melting the onions and releasing their intense flavor. As far as ingredients go, there is very little that varies one soup recipe from another. The distinguishing factor is usually in technique. The onions, when sautéed very, very slowly, will turn into a rich brown color and become limp. Important: There should be no evidence of the edges becoming crisp or fried.

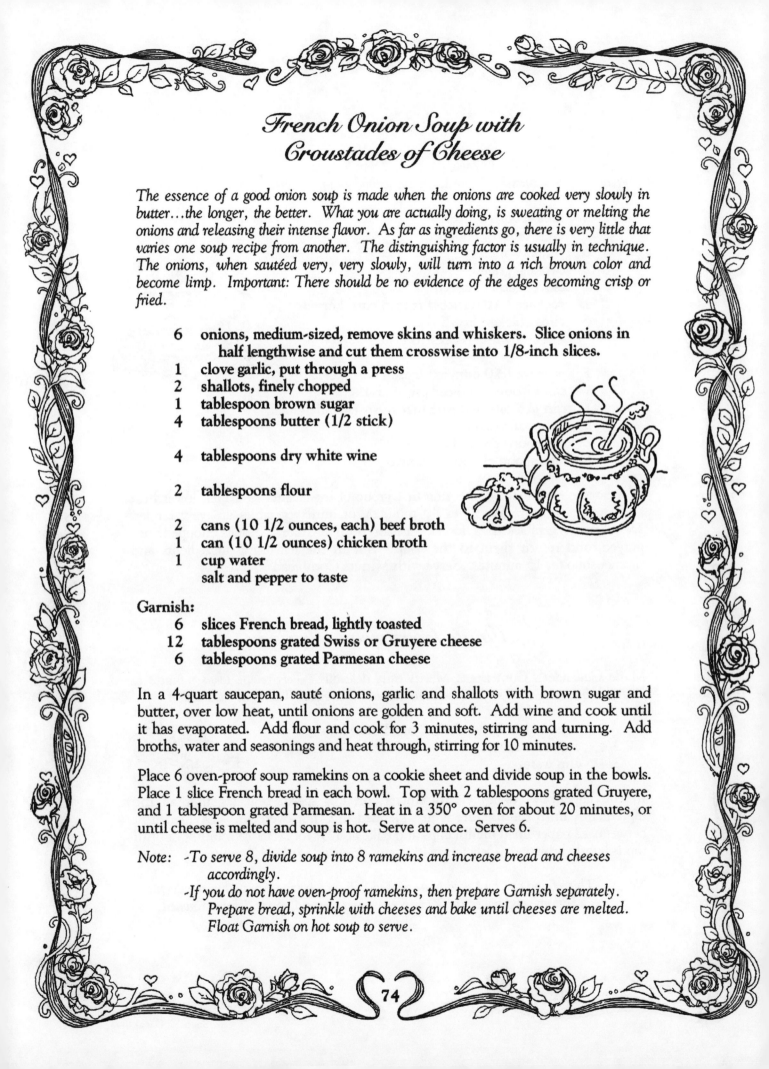

6	onions, medium-sized, remove skins and whiskers. Slice onions in half lengthwise and cut them crosswise into 1/8-inch slices.
1	clove garlic, put through a press
2	shallots, finely chopped
1	tablespoon brown sugar
4	tablespoons butter (1/2 stick)
4	tablespoons dry white wine
2	tablespoons flour
2	cans (10 1/2 ounces, each) beef broth
1	can (10 1/2 ounces) chicken broth
1	cup water
	salt and pepper to taste

Garnish:

6	slices French bread, lightly toasted
12	tablespoons grated Swiss or Gruyere cheese
6	tablespoons grated Parmesan cheese

In a 4-quart saucepan, sauté onions, garlic and shallots with brown sugar and butter, over low heat, until onions are golden and soft. Add wine and cook until it has evaporated. Add flour and cook for 3 minutes, stirring and turning. Add broths, water and seasonings and heat through, stirring for 10 minutes.

Place 6 oven-proof soup ramekins on a cookie sheet and divide soup in the bowls. Place 1 slice French bread in each bowl. Top with 2 tablespoons grated Gruyere, and 1 tablespoon grated Parmesan. Heat in a 350° oven for about 20 minutes, or until cheese is melted and soup is hot. Serve at once. Serves 6.

Note: -To serve 8, divide soup into 8 ramekins and increase bread and cheeses accordingly.
-If you do not have oven-proof ramekins, then prepare Garnish separately. Prepare bread, sprinkle with cheeses and bake until cheeses are melted. Float Garnish on hot soup to serve.

Mushroom & Egg Barley Soup with Petite Knishes with Potatoes & Onions

You would have to go far and wide to find a more "comforting" soup. This is a great soup and a joy to serve. The Petite Knishes is one of my favorites and I hope you enjoy them as much as my family and friends do. Please boil the egg barley separately so as to remove the starch.

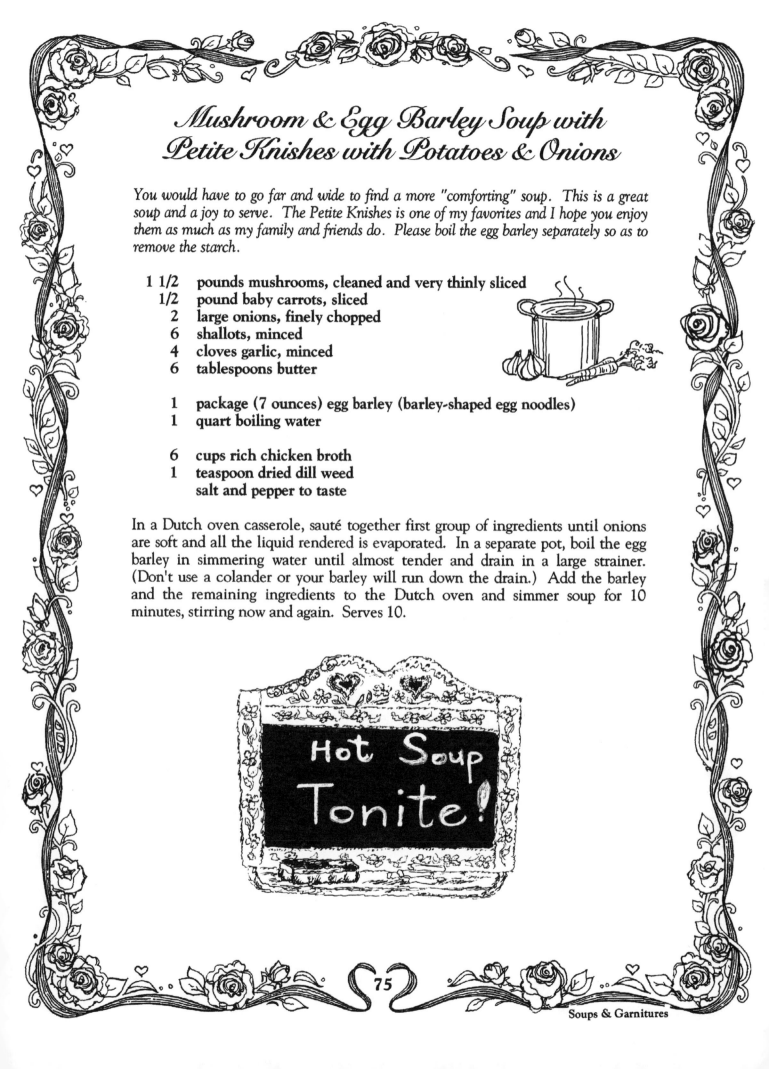

1 1/2	pounds mushrooms, cleaned and very thinly sliced
1/2	pound baby carrots, sliced
2	large onions, finely chopped
6	shallots, minced
4	cloves garlic, minced
6	tablespoons butter
1	package (7 ounces) egg barley (barley-shaped egg noodles)
1	quart boiling water
6	cups rich chicken broth
1	teaspoon dried dill weed
	salt and pepper to taste

In a Dutch oven casserole, sauté together first group of ingredients until onions are soft and all the liquid rendered is evaporated. In a separate pot, boil the egg barley in simmering water until almost tender and drain in a large strainer. (Don't use a colander or your barley will run down the drain.) Add the barley and the remaining ingredients to the Dutch oven and simmer soup for 10 minutes, stirring now and again. Serves 10.

75

Petite Knishes with Potatoes & Onions

Let me say, right at the start, that the Potato & Onion Filling gives these the name of "knishes." Fill them with mushrooms and they become Piroshkis. These little knishes have to be one of the best-tasting hors d'oeuvres. They are also a great accompaniment to a hearty soup, like Mushroom Barley. I recently prepared these for a Super Bowl game and everybody loved them. Traditionally made with a heavy-duty dough, making these with puff pastry truly elevates them to gastronomical heights. I have further simplified preparation using the potato flakes. This is o.k. as the flavor of the onions takes over.

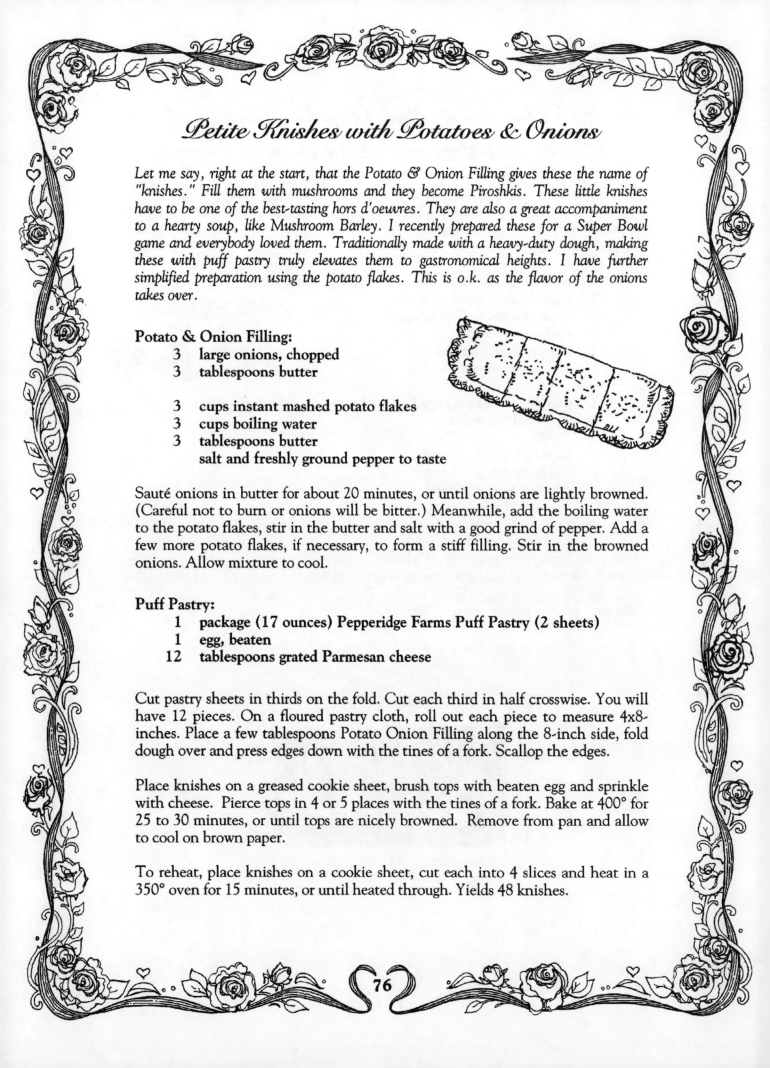

Potato & Onion Filling:

3	large onions, chopped
3	tablespoons butter
3	cups instant mashed potato flakes
3	cups boiling water
3	tablespoons butter
	salt and freshly ground pepper to taste

Sauté onions in butter for about 20 minutes, or until onions are lightly browned. (Careful not to burn or onions will be bitter.) Meanwhile, add the boiling water to the potato flakes, stir in the butter and salt with a good grind of pepper. Add a few more potato flakes, if necessary, to form a stiff filling. Stir in the browned onions. Allow mixture to cool.

Puff Pastry:

1	package (17 ounces) Pepperidge Farms Puff Pastry (2 sheets)
1	egg, beaten
12	tablespoons grated Parmesan cheese

Cut pastry sheets in thirds on the fold. Cut each third in half crosswise. You will have 12 pieces. On a floured pastry cloth, roll out each piece to measure 4x8-inches. Place a few tablespoons Potato Onion Filling along the 8-inch side, fold dough over and press edges down with the tines of a fork. Scallop the edges.

Place knishes on a greased cookie sheet, brush tops with beaten egg and sprinkle with cheese. Pierce tops in 4 or 5 places with the tines of a fork. Bake at 400° for 25 to 30 minutes, or until tops are nicely browned. Remove from pan and allow to cool on brown paper.

To reheat, place knishes on a cookie sheet, cut each into 4 slices and heat in a 350° oven for 15 minutes, or until heated through. Yields 48 knishes.

Cream of Potato & Onion Soup

This is a fascinating soup because it is made with instant mash potato flakes. It can be prepared quickly and does not at all appear as a "jiffy" dish. If you have the time to prepare 1 cup of mashed potatoes from scratch, that is very good, too.

1   large onion, minced
2   cloves garlic, put through a press
2   shallots, minced
2   tablespoons butter

3   cans (10 1/2 ounces, each) chicken broth
3   tablespoons chopped chives
2   tablespoons chopped parsley
    salt and pepper to taste

1   cup instant mash potato flakes (use straight from the box)

1/2   cup cream

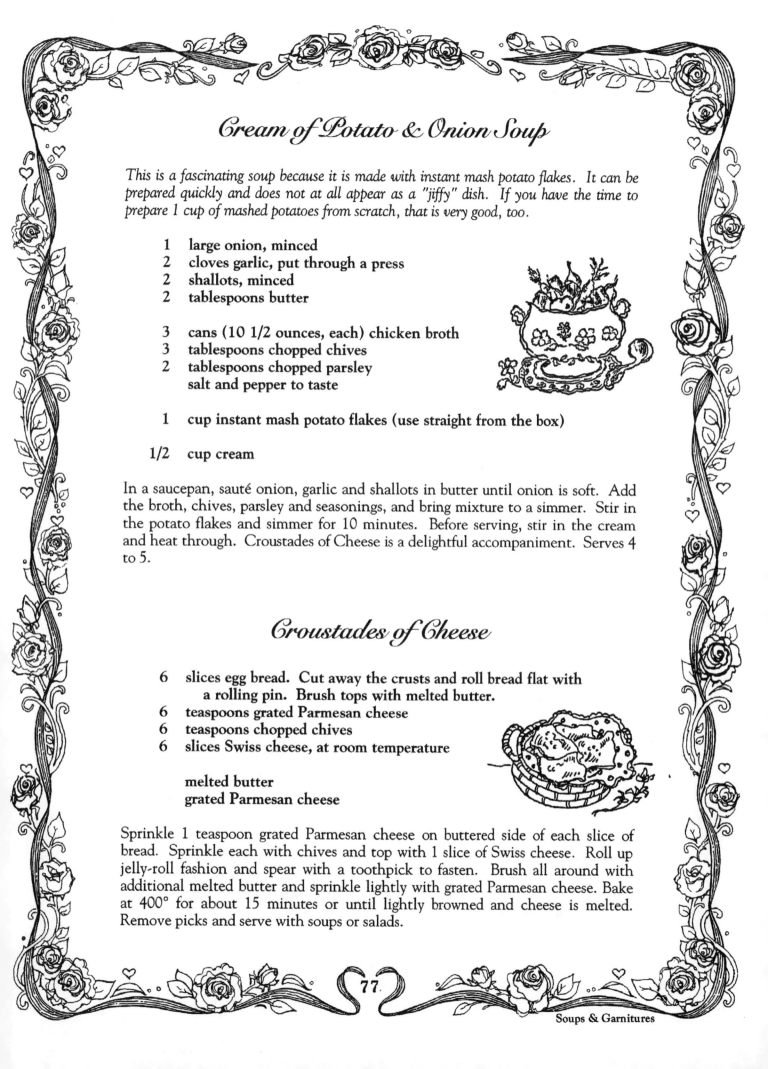

In a saucepan, sauté onion, garlic and shallots in butter until onion is soft. Add the broth, chives, parsley and seasonings, and bring mixture to a simmer. Stir in the potato flakes and simmer for 10 minutes. Before serving, stir in the cream and heat through. Croustades of Cheese is a delightful accompaniment. Serves 4 to 5.

Croustades of Cheese

6   slices egg bread. Cut away the crusts and roll bread flat with
      a rolling pin. Brush tops with melted butter.
6   teaspoons grated Parmesan cheese
6   teaspoons chopped chives
6   slices Swiss cheese, at room temperature

    melted butter
    grated Parmesan cheese

Sprinkle 1 teaspoon grated Parmesan cheese on buttered side of each slice of bread. Sprinkle each with chives and top with 1 slice of Swiss cheese. Roll up jelly-roll fashion and spear with a toothpick to fasten. Brush all around with additional melted butter and sprinkle lightly with grated Parmesan cheese. Bake at 400° for about 15 minutes or until lightly browned and cheese is melted. Remove picks and serve with soups or salads.

Caramelized Onion & Mushroom Soup & Croustades of Cheese & Chives

4	medium onions, chopped
4	cloves garlic, minced
4	shallots, chopped
1	teaspoon honey
3	tablespoons butter
1	pound mushrooms, cleaned and very thinly sliced
2	tablespoons butter
1/4	cup dry white wine
	salt and pepper to taste
2	tablespoons flour
5	cups chicken broth
1/2	cup cream

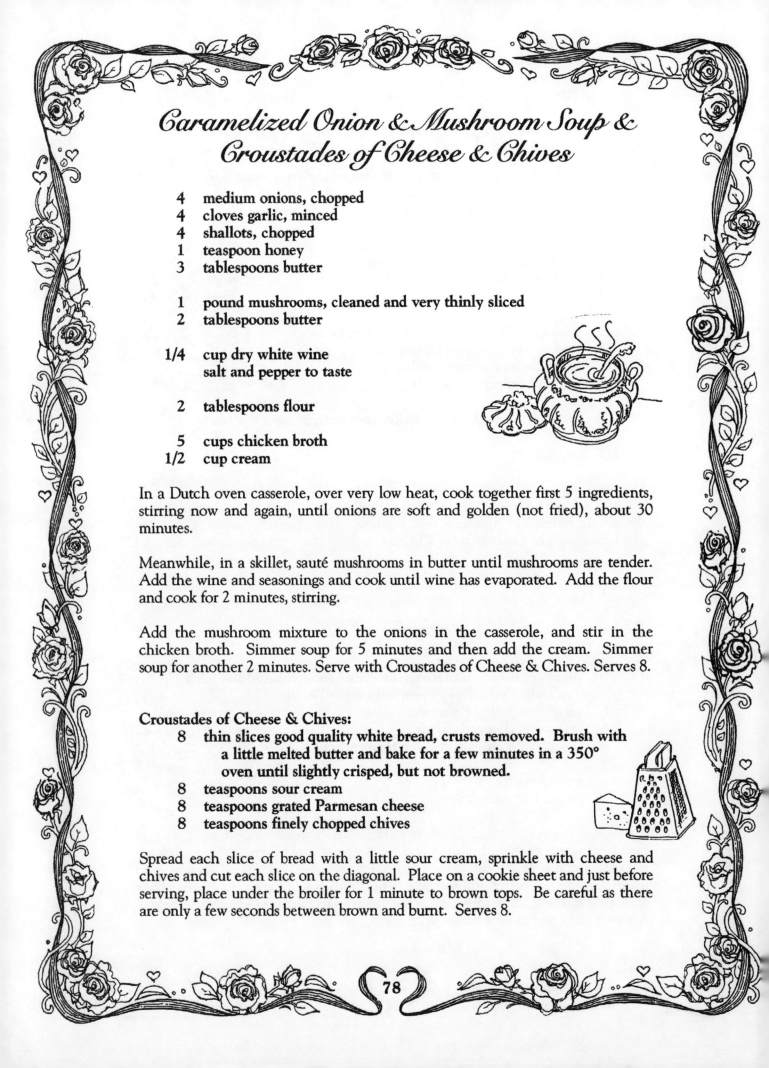

In a Dutch oven casserole, over very low heat, cook together first 5 ingredients, stirring now and again, until onions are soft and golden (not fried), about 30 minutes.

Meanwhile, in a skillet, sauté mushrooms in butter until mushrooms are tender. Add the wine and seasonings and cook until wine has evaporated. Add the flour and cook for 2 minutes, stirring.

Add the mushroom mixture to the onions in the casserole, and stir in the chicken broth. Simmer soup for 5 minutes and then add the cream. Simmer soup for another 2 minutes. Serve with Croustades of Cheese & Chives. Serves 8.

Croustades of Cheese & Chives:

8	thin slices good quality white bread, crusts removed. Brush with a little melted butter and bake for a few minutes in a 350° oven until slightly crisped, but not browned.
8	teaspoons sour cream
8	teaspoons grated Parmesan cheese
8	teaspoons finely chopped chives

Spread each slice of bread with a little sour cream, sprinkle with cheese and chives and cut each slice on the diagonal. Place on a cookie sheet and just before serving, place under the broiler for 1 minute to brown tops. Be careful as there are only a few seconds between brown and burnt. Serves 8.

Honey Spiced Pumpkin Soup with Cinnamon Orange Crispettes

1 large onion, finely chopped
2 shallots, finely chopped
2 tablespoons butter

3 cans (10 1/2 ounces, each) chicken broth
1 can (1 pound) pumpkin puree
1/4 cup honey
1 cup half and half
1 apple, peeled, cored and grated
3/4 teaspoon pumpkin pie spice
    salt to taste

1/4 cup cream (Can use half-and-half.)
1/4 cup sour cream (Can use low-fat sour cream.)

Sauté onion and shallots in butter until onions are soft, but not browned. Add the next 7 ingredients and simmer soup for 10 minutes. Stir together the cream and sour cream until blended and add it to the soup. Heat soup through. Serve with a dollop of sour cream on top and a faint sprinkling of cinnamon. Crispettes flavored with Cinnamon & Orange are a lovely accompaniment. Serves 6.

Cinnamon Orange Crispettes

3 pita breads, split in halves
6 teaspoons butter
6 teaspoons orange marmalade

cinnamon

Spread 1 teaspoon of butter and 1 teaspoon of marmalade on each half of pita bread. Sprinkle top lightly with a dash of cinnamon.

Place bread on a cookie sheet and bake in a 350° oven until lightly browned and crisped. Serves 6.

Note: -Soup can be prepared earlier in the day and heated at time of serving.
       -Bread can be prepared earlier in the day and stored in a covered plastic
        container, at room temperature.

Country French Vegetable Soup with Croustades of Tomato & Cheese

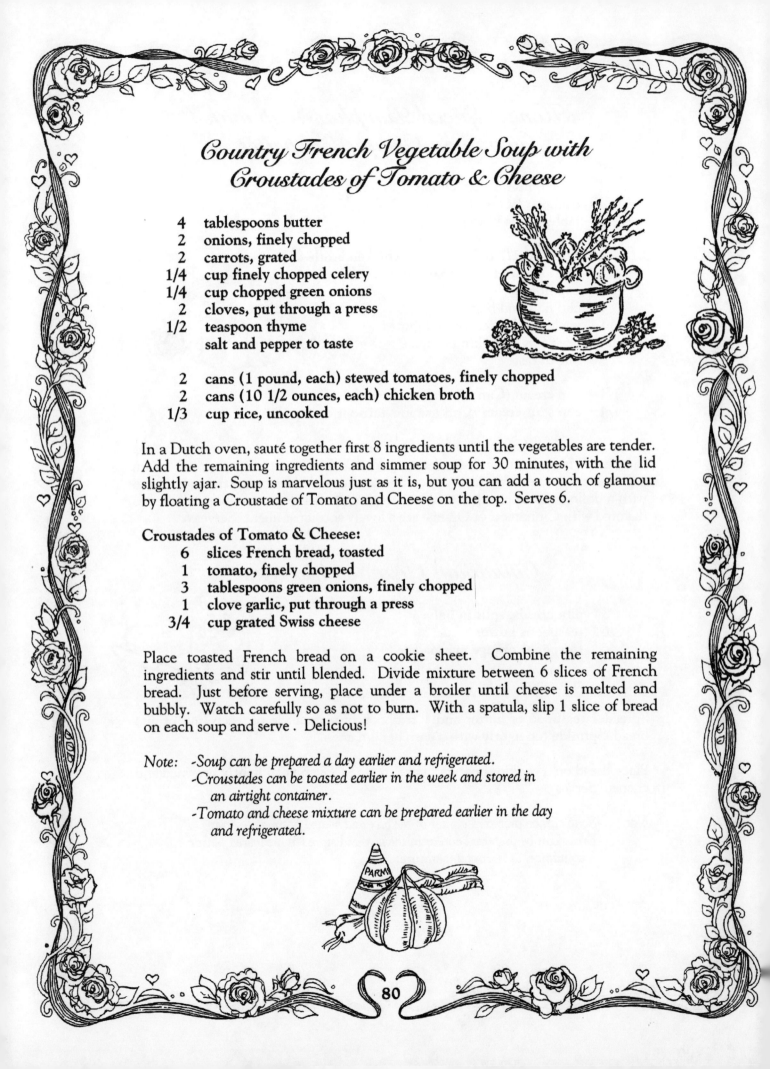

4	tablespoons butter
2	onions, finely chopped
2	carrots, grated
1/4	cup finely chopped celery
1/4	cup chopped green onions
2	cloves, put through a press
1/2	teaspoon thyme
	salt and pepper to taste

2	cans (1 pound, each) stewed tomatoes, finely chopped
2	cans (10 1/2 ounces, each) chicken broth
1/3	cup rice, uncooked

In a Dutch oven, sauté together first 8 ingredients until the vegetables are tender. Add the remaining ingredients and simmer soup for 30 minutes, with the lid slightly ajar. Soup is marvelous just as it is, but you can add a touch of glamour by floating a Croustade of Tomato and Cheese on the top. Serves 6.

Croustades of Tomato & Cheese:

6	slices French bread, toasted
1	tomato, finely chopped
3	tablespoons green onions, finely chopped
1	clove garlic, put through a press
3/4	cup grated Swiss cheese

Place toasted French bread on a cookie sheet. Combine the remaining ingredients and stir until blended. Divide mixture between 6 slices of French bread. Just before serving, place under a broiler until cheese is melted and bubbly. Watch carefully so as not to burn. With a spatula, slip 1 slice of bread on each soup and serve . Delicious!

Note: -*Soup can be prepared a day earlier and refrigerated.*
-Croustades can be toasted earlier in the week and stored in
    an airtight container.
-Tomato and cheese mixture can be prepared earlier in the day
    and refrigerated.

Honey Apple & Pumpkin Cream Soup

This delicious soup is a good choice for Thanksgiving dinner or on any frosty night, when the weather is raging outside. It is deeply flavored with spices and should be served with a sweetened quick bread or muffins.

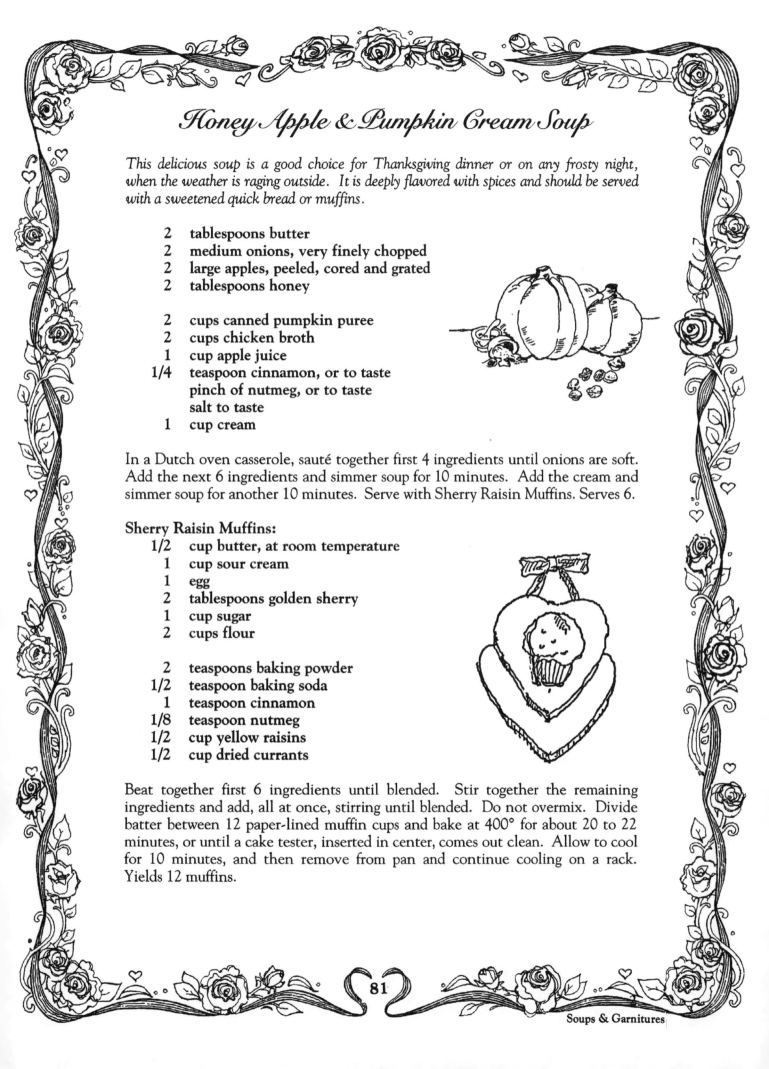

2	tablespoons butter
2	medium onions, very finely chopped
2	large apples, peeled, cored and grated
2	tablespoons honey
2	cups canned pumpkin puree
2	cups chicken broth
1	cup apple juice
1/4	teaspoon cinnamon, or to taste
	pinch of nutmeg, or to taste
	salt to taste
1	cup cream

In a Dutch oven casserole, sauté together first 4 ingredients until onions are soft. Add the next 6 ingredients and simmer soup for 10 minutes. Add the cream and simmer soup for another 10 minutes. Serve with Sherry Raisin Muffins. Serves 6.

Sherry Raisin Muffins:

1/2	cup butter, at room temperature
1	cup sour cream
1	egg
2	tablespoons golden sherry
1	cup sugar
2	cups flour
2	teaspoons baking powder
1/2	teaspoon baking soda
1	teaspoon cinnamon
1/8	teaspoon nutmeg
1/2	cup yellow raisins
1/2	cup dried currants

Beat together first 6 ingredients until blended. Stir together the remaining ingredients and add, all at once, stirring until blended. Do not overmix. Divide batter between 12 paper-lined muffin cups and bake at 400° for about 20 to 22 minutes, or until a cake tester, inserted in center, comes out clean. Allow to cool for 10 minutes, and then remove from pan and continue cooling on a rack. Yields 12 muffins.

Potage of Zucchini & Tomatoes
with Batonettes of Cheese

What a sublime soup, marvelously flavored with onions and garlic and herbs. The Batonettes are incredibly good, and exceptionally easy to prepare, starting, as they do, with frozen puff pastry. This soup can be served either warm or chilled.

6   medium zucchini, scrubbed, but do not peel. Cut into thin slices.
2   large onions, chopped
4   cloves garlic, minced
2   shallots, chopped
2   tablespoons butter

1   can (1 pound) stewed tomatoes, finely chopped. Do not drain.
2   cans (10 1/2 ounces, each) chicken broth
2   teaspoons lemon juice
1/2   teaspoon sugar
1   tablespoon chopped parsley
1/2   teaspoon dried dill weed or more to taste
    salt to taste

1/2   cup half and half

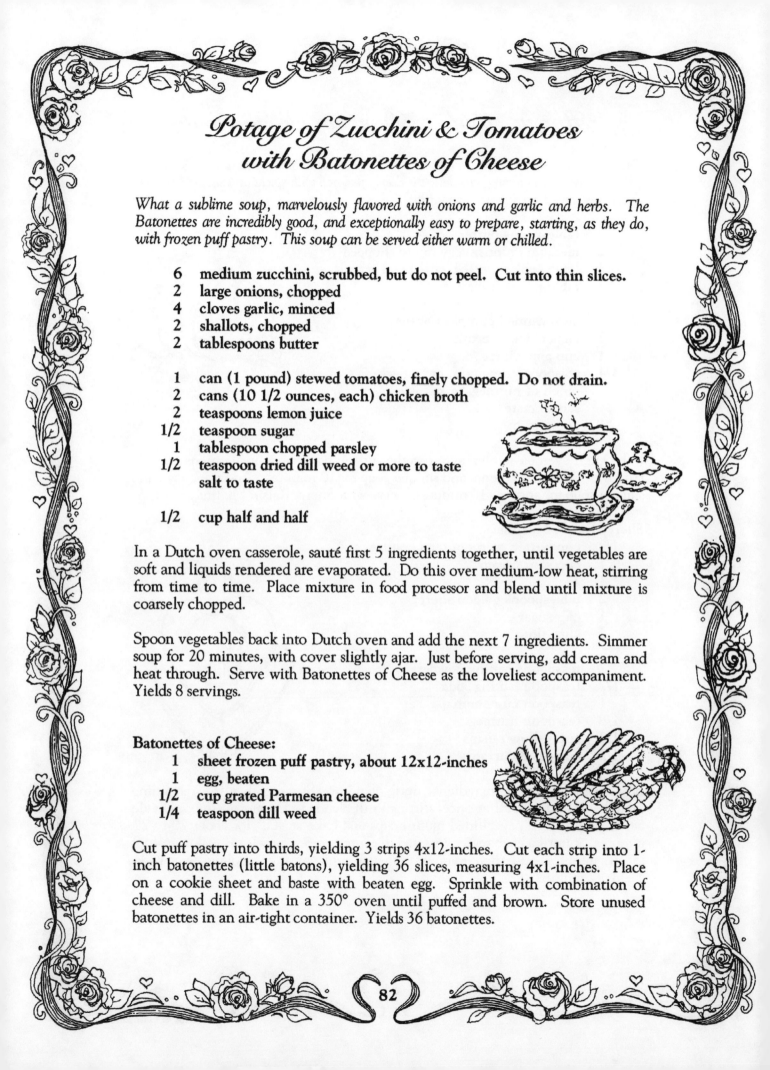

In a Dutch oven casserole, sauté first 5 ingredients together, until vegetables are soft and liquids rendered are evaporated. Do this over medium-low heat, stirring from time to time. Place mixture in food processor and blend until mixture is coarsely chopped.

Spoon vegetables back into Dutch oven and add the next 7 ingredients. Simmer soup for 20 minutes, with cover slightly ajar. Just before serving, add cream and heat through. Serve with Batonettes of Cheese as the loveliest accompaniment. Yields 8 servings.

Batonettes of Cheese:
1   sheet frozen puff pastry, about 12x12-inches
1   egg, beaten
1/2   cup grated Parmesan cheese
1/4   teaspoon dill weed

Cut puff pastry into thirds, yielding 3 strips 4x12-inches. Cut each strip into 1-inch batonettes (little batons), yielding 36 slices, measuring 4x1-inches. Place on a cookie sheet and baste with beaten egg. Sprinkle with combination of cheese and dill. Bake in a 350° oven until puffed and brown. Store unused batonettes in an air-tight container. Yields 36 batonettes.

Farmhouse Split Pea Soup

This is another one of my favorite soups. As you probably have guessed by now, I like soups that are thick and hearty and just bursting with flavor and goodness. Consommés are lovely, and do have their place, but when the weather is storming, there is nothing like a bowl of thick soup, filled with all manner of good things.

1	pound dried split peas, rinsed and picked over for foreign particles
1	pound cooked ham, cut into 1/2-inch cubes
2	onions, chopped
3	carrots, grated
1	can (1 pound) stewed tomatoes, chopped. Do not drain.
3	cans (10 1/2 ounces, each) beef broth
1 1/2	cups water
2	tablespoons butter
	salt and pepper to taste

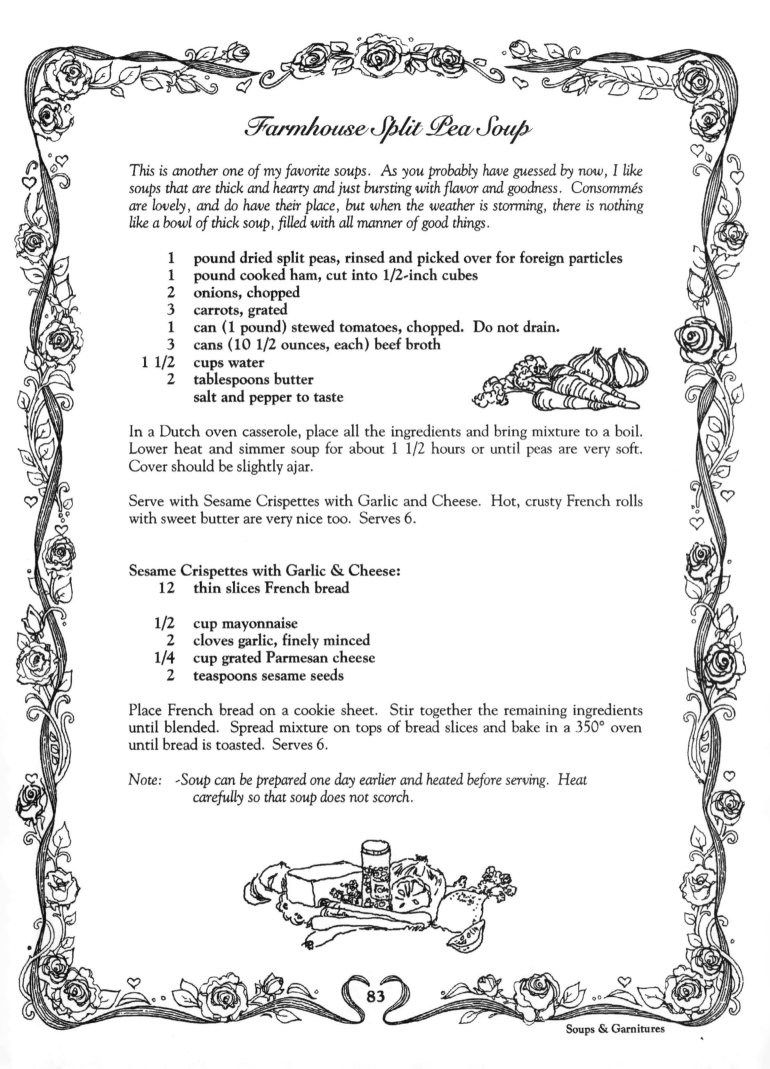

In a Dutch oven casserole, place all the ingredients and bring mixture to a boil. Lower heat and simmer soup for about 1 1/2 hours or until peas are very soft. Cover should be slightly ajar.

Serve with Sesame Crispettes with Garlic and Cheese. Hot, crusty French rolls with sweet butter are very nice too. Serves 6.

Sesame Crispettes with Garlic & Cheese:

12	thin slices French bread
1/2	cup mayonnaise
2	cloves garlic, finely minced
1/4	cup grated Parmesan cheese
2	teaspoons sesame seeds

Place French bread on a cookie sheet. Stir together the remaining ingredients until blended. Spread mixture on tops of bread slices and bake in a 350° oven until bread is toasted. Serves 6.

Note: -Soup can be prepared one day earlier and heated before serving. Heat carefully so that soup does not scorch.

Country Lentil Soup with Raisin Bread Cinnamon Toast

What a nice soup to enjoy on nights when family and friends get together. It is thick and satisfying and the Raisin Bread is the perfect accompaniment.

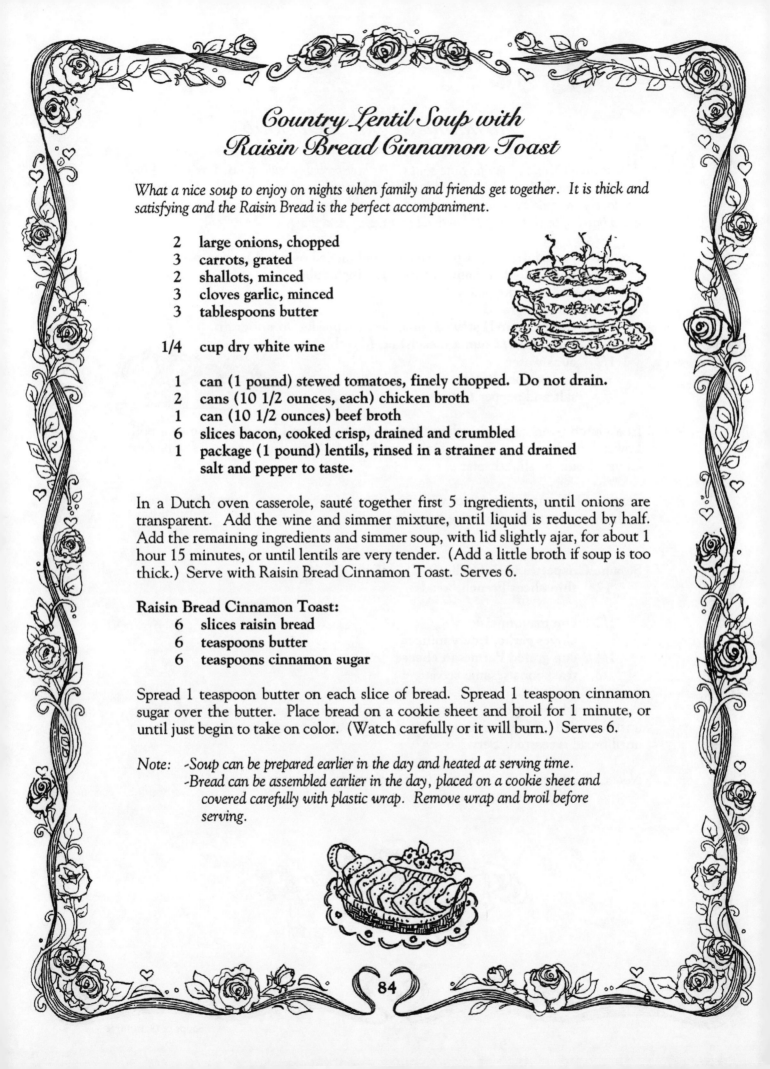

2	large onions, chopped
3	carrots, grated
2	shallots, minced
3	cloves garlic, minced
3	tablespoons butter

1/4   cup dry white wine

1	can (1 pound) stewed tomatoes, finely chopped. Do not drain.
2	cans (10 1/2 ounces, each) chicken broth
1	can (10 1/2 ounces) beef broth
6	slices bacon, cooked crisp, drained and crumbled
1	package (1 pound) lentils, rinsed in a strainer and drained
	salt and pepper to taste.

In a Dutch oven casserole, sauté together first 5 ingredients, until onions are transparent. Add the wine and simmer mixture, until liquid is reduced by half. Add the remaining ingredients and simmer soup, with lid slightly ajar, for about 1 hour 15 minutes, or until lentils are very tender. (Add a little broth if soup is too thick.) Serve with Raisin Bread Cinnamon Toast. Serves 6.

Raisin Bread Cinnamon Toast:
- 6   slices raisin bread
- 6   teaspoons butter
- 6   teaspoons cinnamon sugar

Spread 1 teaspoon butter on each slice of bread. Spread 1 teaspoon cinnamon sugar over the butter. Place bread on a cookie sheet and broil for 1 minute, or until just begin to take on color. (Watch carefully or it will burn.) Serves 6.

Note: -Soup can be prepared earlier in the day and heated at serving time.
-Bread can be assembled earlier in the day, placed on a cookie sheet and covered carefully with plastic wrap. Remove wrap and broil before serving.

Cold Dilled Zucchini Soup with Crème Fraiche

There is probably no soup you can make that is more elegant and delicious than this one. It is gloriously thick and flavorful and can be served for the most special of all occasions. However, its simplicity makes it a good choice for anytime.

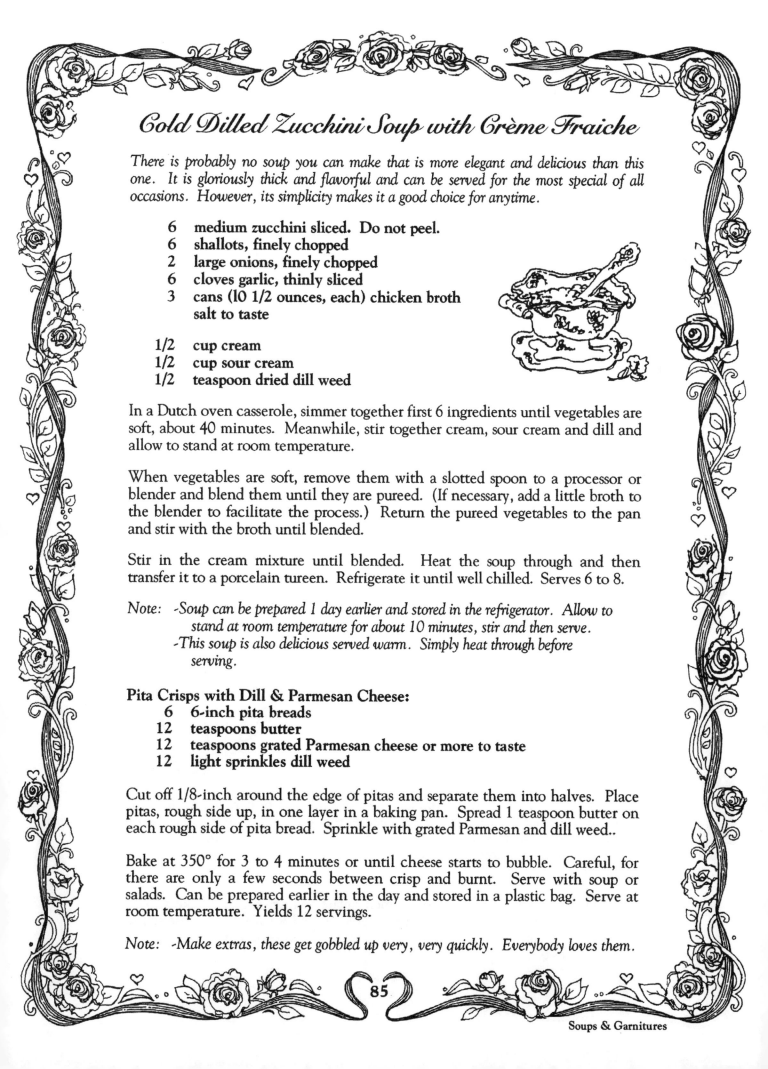

- 6 medium zucchini sliced. Do not peel.
- 6 shallots, finely chopped
- 2 large onions, finely chopped
- 6 cloves garlic, thinly sliced
- 3 cans (10 1/2 ounces, each) chicken broth
  salt to taste

- 1/2 cup cream
- 1/2 cup sour cream
- 1/2 teaspoon dried dill weed

In a Dutch oven casserole, simmer together first 6 ingredients until vegetables are soft, about 40 minutes. Meanwhile, stir together cream, sour cream and dill and allow to stand at room temperature.

When vegetables are soft, remove them with a slotted spoon to a processor or blender and blend them until they are pureed. (If necessary, add a little broth to the blender to facilitate the process.) Return the pureed vegetables to the pan and stir with the broth until blended.

Stir in the cream mixture until blended. Heat the soup through and then transfer it to a porcelain tureen. Refrigerate it until well chilled. Serves 6 to 8.

Note: -Soup can be prepared 1 day earlier and stored in the refrigerator. Allow to stand at room temperature for about 10 minutes, stir and then serve.
-This soup is also delicious served warm. Simply heat through before serving.

Pita Crisps with Dill & Parmesan Cheese:
- 6 6-inch pita breads
- 12 teaspoons butter
- 12 teaspoons grated Parmesan cheese or more to taste
- 12 light sprinkles dill weed

Cut off 1/8-inch around the edge of pitas and separate them into halves. Place pitas, rough side up, in one layer in a baking pan. Spread 1 teaspoon butter on each rough side of pita bread. Sprinkle with grated Parmesan and dill weed..

Bake at 350° for 3 to 4 minutes or until cheese starts to bubble. Careful, for there are only a few seconds between crisp and burnt. Serve with soup or salads. Can be prepared earlier in the day and stored in a plastic bag. Serve at room temperature. Yields 12 servings.

Note: -Make extras, these get gobbled up very, very quickly. Everybody loves them.

Fresh Peach Soup with Strawberries & Cream

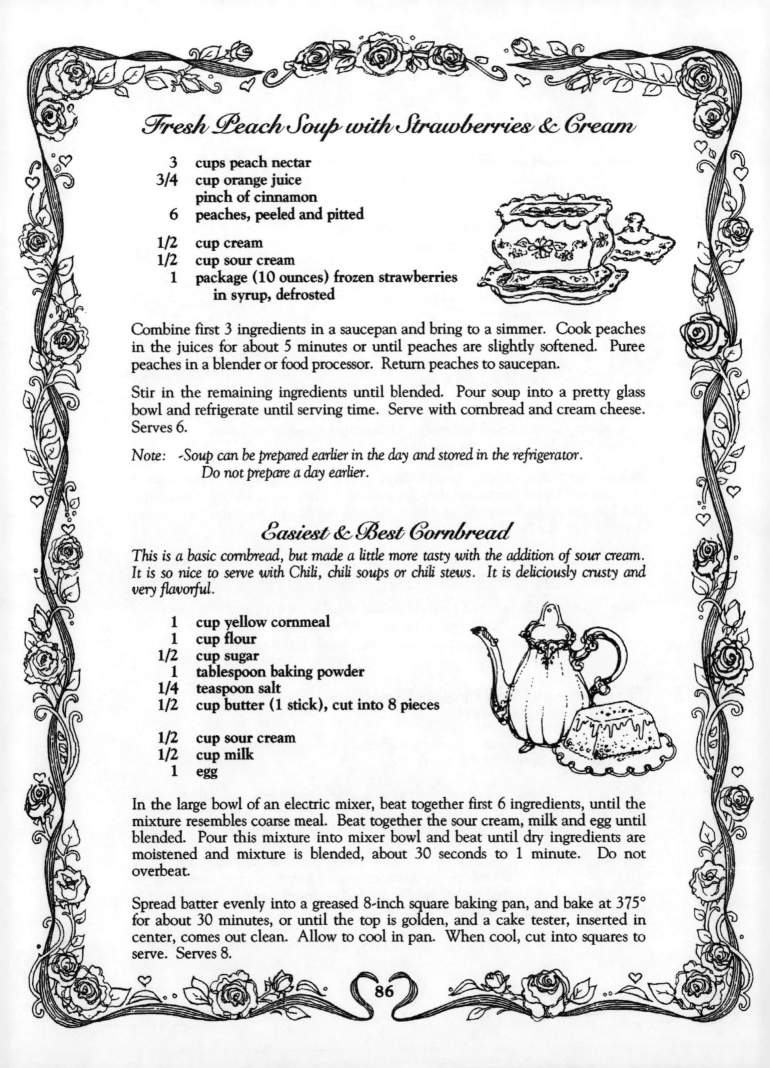

 3   cups peach nectar
 3/4 cup orange juice
      pinch of cinnamon
 6   peaches, peeled and pitted

 1/2 cup cream
 1/2 cup sour cream
 1   package (10 ounces) frozen strawberries
        in syrup, defrosted

Combine first 3 ingredients in a saucepan and bring to a simmer. Cook peaches in the juices for about 5 minutes or until peaches are slightly softened. Puree peaches in a blender or food processor. Return peaches to saucepan.

Stir in the remaining ingredients until blended. Pour soup into a pretty glass bowl and refrigerate until serving time. Serve with cornbread and cream cheese. Serves 6.

Note: -Soup can be prepared earlier in the day and stored in the refrigerator.
        Do not prepare a day earlier.

Easiest & Best Cornbread

This is a basic cornbread, but made a little more tasty with the addition of sour cream. It is so nice to serve with Chili, chili soups or chili stews. It is deliciously crusty and very flavorful.

 1   cup yellow cornmeal
 1   cup flour
 1/2 cup sugar
 1   tablespoon baking powder
 1/4 teaspoon salt
 1/2 cup butter (1 stick), cut into 8 pieces

 1/2 cup sour cream
 1/2 cup milk
 1   egg

In the large bowl of an electric mixer, beat together first 6 ingredients, until the mixture resembles coarse meal. Beat together the sour cream, milk and egg until blended. Pour this mixture into mixer bowl and beat until dry ingredients are moistened and mixture is blended, about 30 seconds to 1 minute. Do not overbeat.

Spread batter evenly into a greased 8-inch square baking pan, and bake at 375° for about 30 minutes, or until the top is golden, and a cake tester, inserted in center, comes out clean. Allow to cool in pan. When cool, cut into squares to serve. Serves 8.

Salads

and

Dressings

Tomato & Red Onion Salad with Basil, Lemon and Cheese

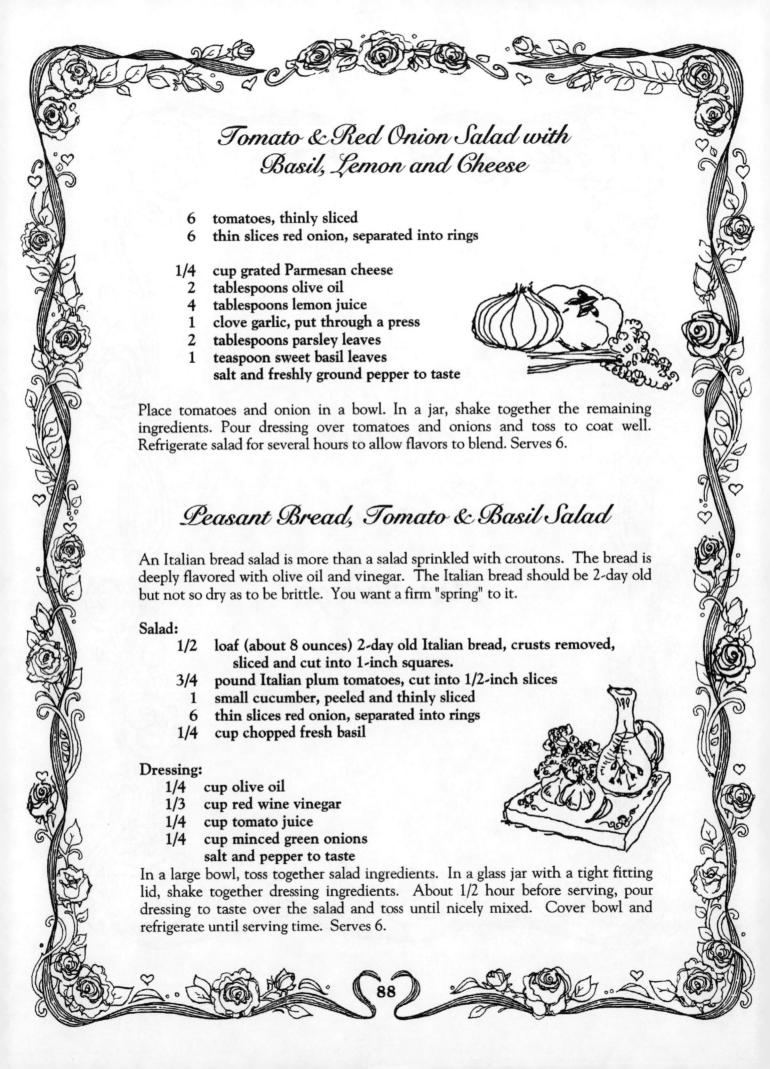

6   tomatoes, thinly sliced
6   thin slices red onion, separated into rings

1/4 cup grated Parmesan cheese
2   tablespoons olive oil
4   tablespoons lemon juice
1   clove garlic, put through a press
2   tablespoons parsley leaves
1   teaspoon sweet basil leaves
     salt and freshly ground pepper to taste

Place tomatoes and onion in a bowl. In a jar, shake together the remaining ingredients. Pour dressing over tomatoes and onions and toss to coat well. Refrigerate salad for several hours to allow flavors to blend. Serves 6.

Peasant Bread, Tomato & Basil Salad

An Italian bread salad is more than a salad sprinkled with croutons. The bread is deeply flavored with olive oil and vinegar. The Italian bread should be 2-day old but not so dry as to be brittle. You want a firm "spring" to it.

Salad:
1/2 loaf (about 8 ounces) 2-day old Italian bread, crusts removed,
        sliced and cut into 1-inch squares.
3/4 pound Italian plum tomatoes, cut into 1/2-inch slices
1   small cucumber, peeled and thinly sliced
6   thin slices red onion, separated into rings
1/4 cup chopped fresh basil

Dressing:
1/4 cup olive oil
1/3 cup red wine vinegar
1/4 cup tomato juice
1/4 cup minced green onions
     salt and pepper to taste

In a large bowl, toss together salad ingredients. In a glass jar with a tight fitting lid, shake together dressing ingredients. About 1/2 hour before serving, pour dressing to taste over the salad and toss until nicely mixed. Cover bowl and refrigerate until serving time. Serves 6.

Giant Cous Cous Salad with Artichokes, Tomatoes & Raisins

Using the large-sized cous cous makes for a very dramatic presentation. It is not often used, so it attracts everyone's attention. As with the smaller-size, this Cous Cous can be served hot or cold, and is great in salads or as an accompaniment to dinner. It can be enriched with onions and mushrooms, raisins and pine nuts, dried cherries and pecans, and so much more. It is often called Israeli Cous Cous.

1	cup large-sized cous cous
1	tablespoon oil
1 1/2	cups chicken broth

1	jar (6-ounces) marinated artichoke hearts, sliced. Use the marinade in the salad.
3/4	cup cherry tomatoes, halved. Scoop out the seeds.
1/4	cup finely chopped green onions
2	tablespoons minced parsley leaves
1/2	cup yellow raisins
2	tablespoons lemon juice
1/8	teaspoon coarse-grind garlic powder

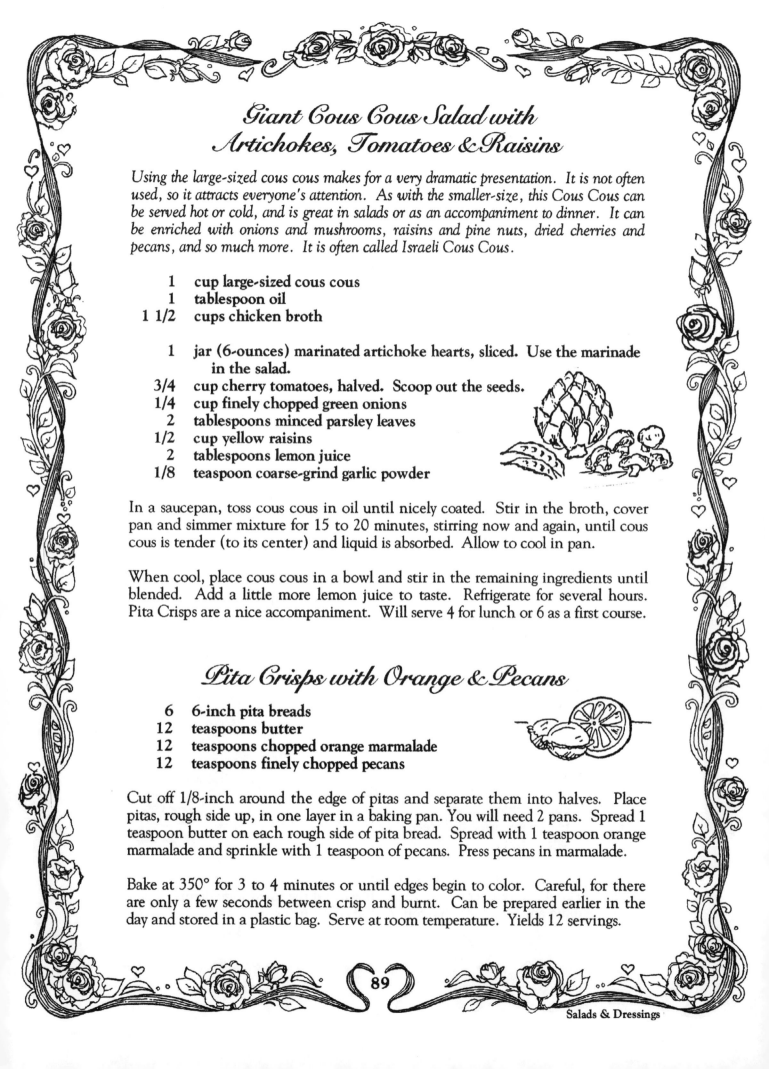

In a saucepan, toss cous cous in oil until nicely coated. Stir in the broth, cover pan and simmer mixture for 15 to 20 minutes, stirring now and again, until cous cous is tender (to its center) and liquid is absorbed. Allow to cool in pan.

When cool, place cous cous in a bowl and stir in the remaining ingredients until blended. Add a little more lemon juice to taste. Refrigerate for several hours. Pita Crisps are a nice accompaniment. Will serve 4 for lunch or 6 as a first course.

Pita Crisps with Orange & Pecans

6	6-inch pita breads
12	teaspoons butter
12	teaspoons chopped orange marmalade
12	teaspoons finely chopped pecans

Cut off 1/8-inch around the edge of pitas and separate them into halves. Place pitas, rough side up, in one layer in a baking pan. You will need 2 pans. Spread 1 teaspoon butter on each rough side of pita bread. Spread with 1 teaspoon orange marmalade and sprinkle with 1 teaspoon of pecans. Press pecans in marmalade.

Bake at 350° for 3 to 4 minutes or until edges begin to color. Careful, for there are only a few seconds between crisp and burnt. Can be prepared earlier in the day and stored in a plastic bag. Serve at room temperature. Yields 12 servings.

Mediterranean Salad with Marinated Tomatoes, Onions & Olives

1 pound tomatoes, cut into 1/4-inch slices
1/2 medium red onion, very thinly sliced and separated into rings
1 can (2 ounces) sliced black olives
2 tablespoons chopped parsley leaves
4 ounces crumbled feta cheese

Dressing:
1/4 cup olive oil
1/4 cup white wine vinegar
1/4 cup grated Parmesan cheese
1 clove garlic, minced
salt and pepper to taste

1/2 cup garlic croutons. (Use the croutons that resemble pennies.)

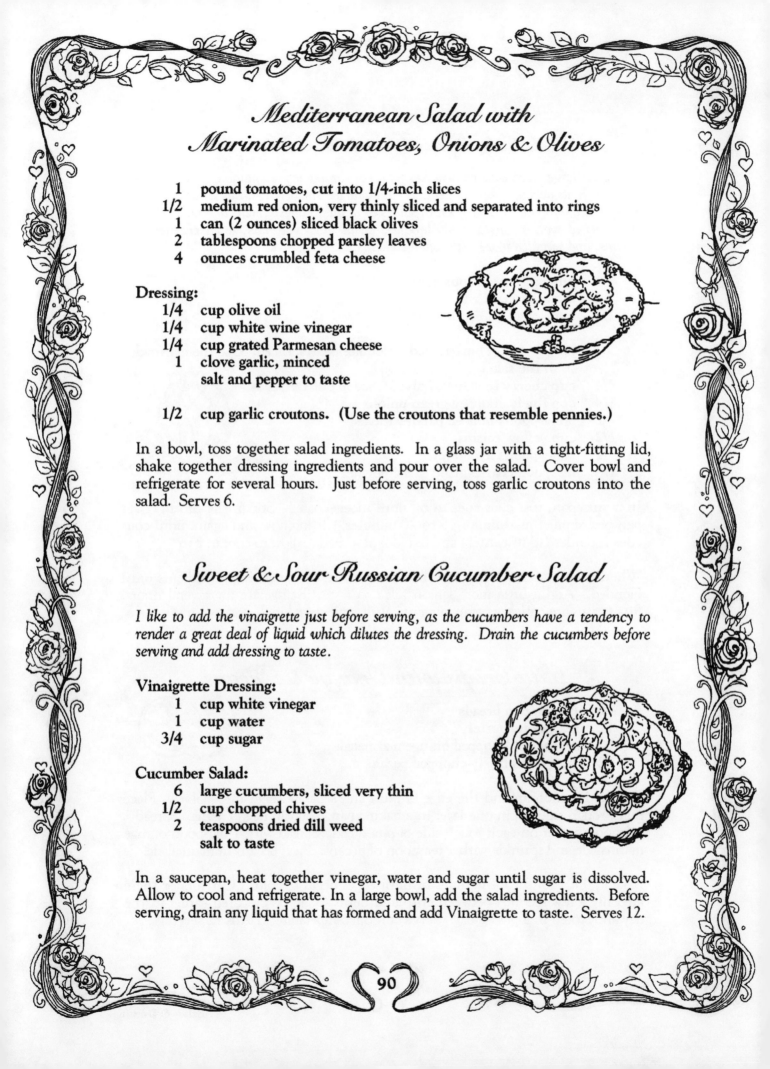

In a bowl, toss together salad ingredients. In a glass jar with a tight-fitting lid, shake together dressing ingredients and pour over the salad. Cover bowl and refrigerate for several hours. Just before serving, toss garlic croutons into the salad. Serves 6.

Sweet & Sour Russian Cucumber Salad

I like to add the vinaigrette just before serving, as the cucumbers have a tendency to render a great deal of liquid which dilutes the dressing. Drain the cucumbers before serving and add dressing to taste.

Vinaigrette Dressing:
1 cup white vinegar
1 cup water
3/4 cup sugar

Cucumber Salad:
6 large cucumbers, sliced very thin
1/2 cup chopped chives
2 teaspoons dried dill weed
salt to taste

In a saucepan, heat together vinegar, water and sugar until sugar is dissolved. Allow to cool and refrigerate. In a large bowl, add the salad ingredients. Before serving, drain any liquid that has formed and add Vinaigrette to taste. Serves 12.

Mixed Bean Salad with Garlic Vinaigrette

Using the canned beans saves you hours of preparation time, and the results are very good, indeed. This is a good choice for a dinner in a Spanish or Italian mood. It is better prepared 1 day earlier and stored in the refrigerator.

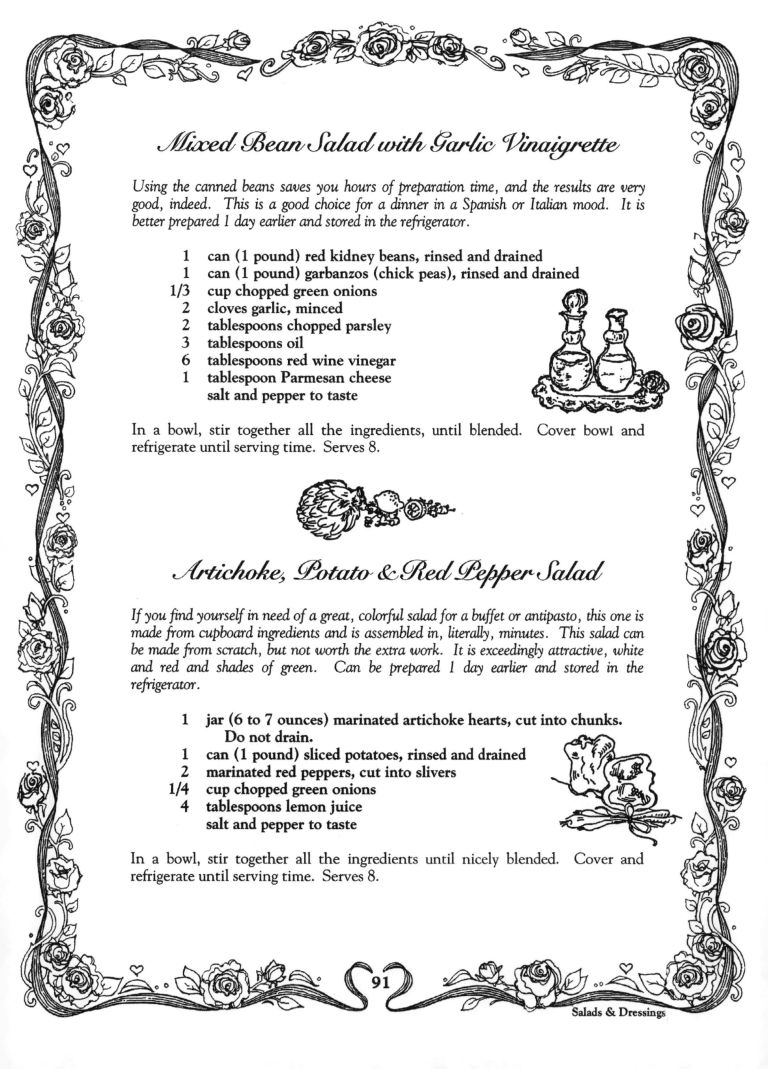

1	can (1 pound) red kidney beans, rinsed and drained
1	can (1 pound) garbanzos (chick peas), rinsed and drained
1/3	cup chopped green onions
2	cloves garlic, minced
2	tablespoons chopped parsley
3	tablespoons oil
6	tablespoons red wine vinegar
1	tablespoon Parmesan cheese
	salt and pepper to taste

In a bowl, stir together all the ingredients, until blended. Cover bowl and refrigerate until serving time. Serves 8.

Artichoke, Potato & Red Pepper Salad

If you find yourself in need of a great, colorful salad for a buffet or antipasto, this one is made from cupboard ingredients and is assembled in, literally, minutes. This salad can be made from scratch, but not worth the extra work. It is exceedingly attractive, white and red and shades of green. Can be prepared 1 day earlier and stored in the refrigerator.

1	jar (6 to 7 ounces) marinated artichoke hearts, cut into chunks. Do not drain.
1	can (1 pound) sliced potatoes, rinsed and drained
2	marinated red peppers, cut into slivers
1/4	cup chopped green onions
4	tablespoons lemon juice
	salt and pepper to taste

In a bowl, stir together all the ingredients until nicely blended. Cover and refrigerate until serving time. Serves 8.

French Potato Salad with Mustard Vinaigrette

When you are looking for a change from the traditional potato salad, this is a good one to consider. It is a nice accompaniment to meat loaf. While traditionally served cold, this is very delicious served warm (not hot.)

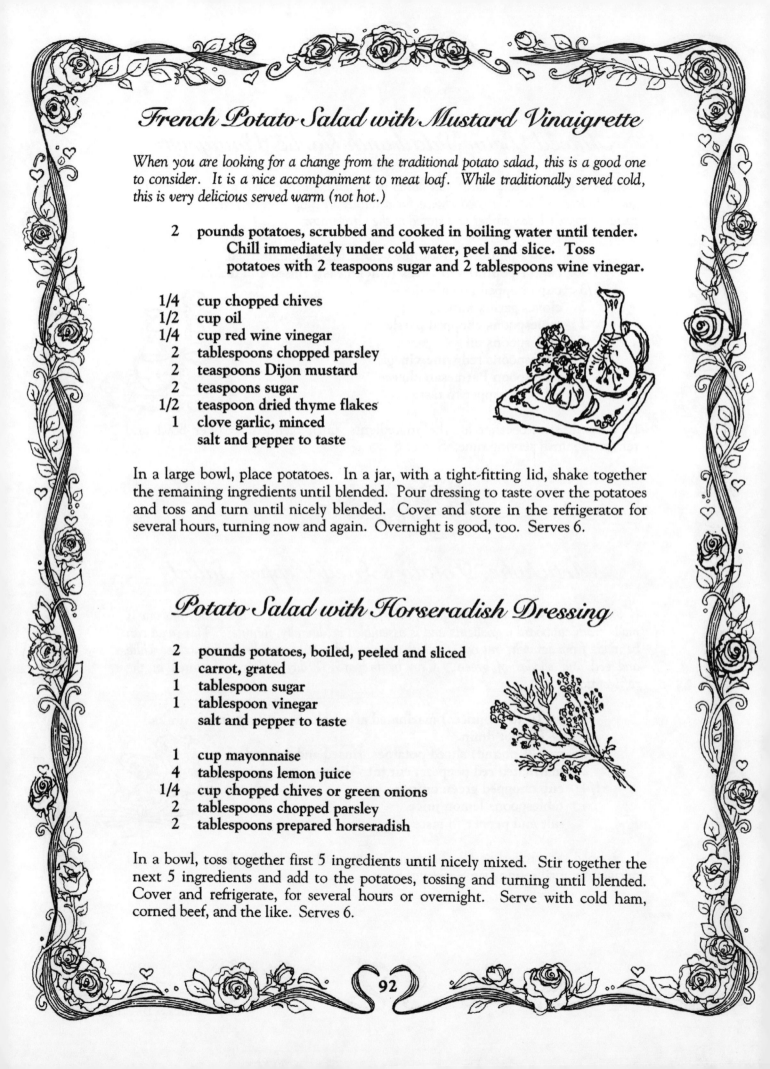

2   pounds potatoes, scrubbed and cooked in boiling water until tender. Chill immediately under cold water, peel and slice. Toss potatoes with 2 teaspoons sugar and 2 tablespoons wine vinegar.

1/4   cup chopped chives
1/2   cup oil
1/4   cup red wine vinegar
2   tablespoons chopped parsley
2   teaspoons Dijon mustard
2   teaspoons sugar
1/2   teaspoon dried thyme flakes
1   clove garlic, minced
    salt and pepper to taste

In a large bowl, place potatoes. In a jar, with a tight-fitting lid, shake together the remaining ingredients until blended. Pour dressing to taste over the potatoes and toss and turn until nicely blended. Cover and store in the refrigerator for several hours, turning now and again. Overnight is good, too. Serves 6.

Potato Salad with Horseradish Dressing

2   pounds potatoes, boiled, peeled and sliced
1   carrot, grated
1   tablespoon sugar
1   tablespoon vinegar
    salt and pepper to taste

1   cup mayonnaise
4   tablespoons lemon juice
1/4   cup chopped chives or green onions
2   tablespoons chopped parsley
2   tablespoons prepared horseradish

In a bowl, toss together first 5 ingredients until nicely mixed. Stir together the next 5 ingredients and add to the potatoes, tossing and turning until blended. Cover and refrigerate, for several hours or overnight. Serve with cold ham, corned beef, and the like. Serves 6.

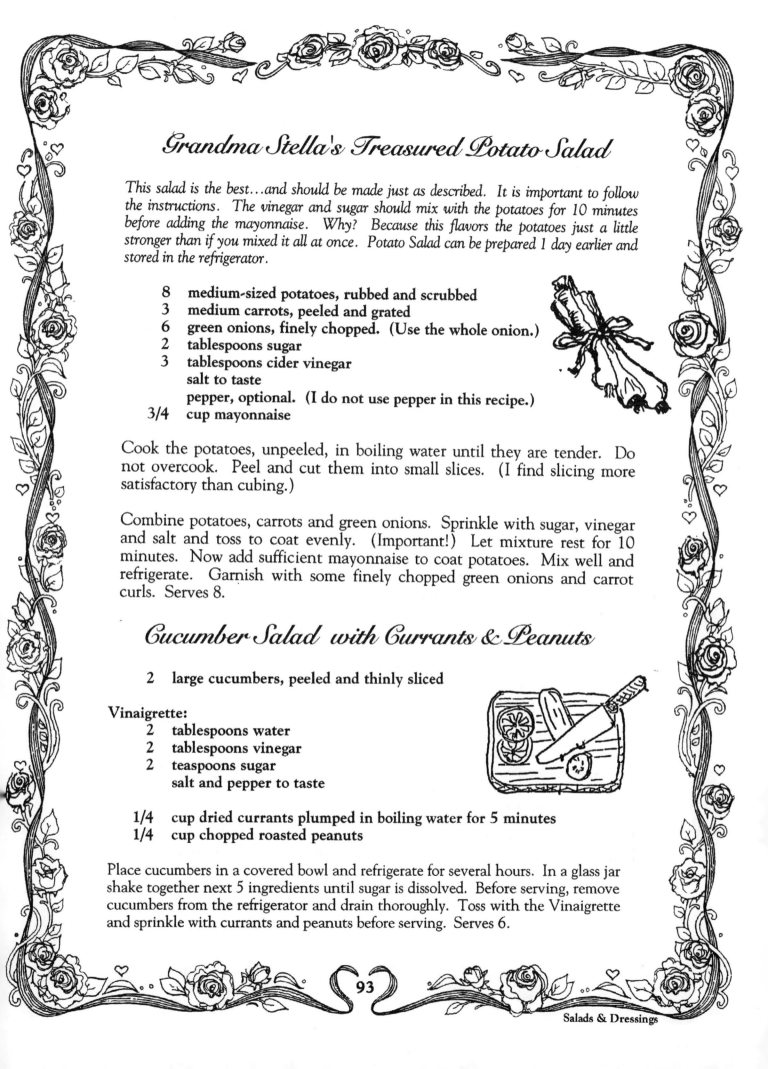

Grandma Stella's Treasured Potato Salad

This salad is the best…and should be made just as described. It is important to follow the instructions. The vinegar and sugar should mix with the potatoes for 10 minutes before adding the mayonnaise. Why? Because this flavors the potatoes just a little stronger than if you mixed it all at once. Potato Salad can be prepared 1 day earlier and stored in the refrigerator.

8   medium-sized potatoes, rubbed and scrubbed
3   medium carrots, peeled and grated
6   green onions, finely chopped. (Use the whole onion.)
2   tablespoons sugar
3   tablespoons cider vinegar
     salt to taste
     pepper, optional. (I do not use pepper in this recipe.)
3/4 cup mayonnaise

Cook the potatoes, unpeeled, in boiling water until they are tender. Do not overcook. Peel and cut them into small slices. (I find slicing more satisfactory than cubing.)

Combine potatoes, carrots and green onions. Sprinkle with sugar, vinegar and salt and toss to coat evenly. (Important!) Let mixture rest for 10 minutes. Now add sufficient mayonnaise to coat potatoes. Mix well and refrigerate. Garnish with some finely chopped green onions and carrot curls. Serves 8.

Cucumber Salad with Currants & Peanuts

2   large cucumbers, peeled and thinly sliced

Vinaigrette:
2   tablespoons water
2   tablespoons vinegar
2   teaspoons sugar
     salt and pepper to taste

1/4 cup dried currants plumped in boiling water for 5 minutes
1/4 cup chopped roasted peanuts

Place cucumbers in a covered bowl and refrigerate for several hours. In a glass jar shake together next 5 ingredients until sugar is dissolved. Before serving, remove cucumbers from the refrigerator and drain thoroughly. Toss with the Vinaigrette and sprinkle with currants and peanuts before serving. Serves 6.

Salads & Dressings

Baby Red Potato Salad

You will love this salad on a buffet for its attractive and exciting colors. This is an adaptation of my Mom's potato salad so you will be enjoying the same delicious taste.

2 1/2 pounds baby red potatoes, scrubbed and cooked, unpeeled, in boiling water until fork tender. Do not overcook. Drain potatoes and refrigerate until chilled.

3   carrots, peeled and grated
6   green onions, finely chopped. Use the white and green parts.
2   tablespoons sugar
3   tablespoons cider vinegar
       salt and pepper to taste

3/4   cup mayonnaise

Cut potatoes into 1/4-inch wedges and place in a large bowl. Add the next 6 ingredients and toss potatoes to coat evenly. Allow mixture to rest for 10 minutes. Now add sufficient mayonnaise to coat potatoes and mix well. Cover bowl and refrigerate. To serve, decorate platter with green onion frills and carrot curls. Serves 8.

Corn Salad with Red Peppers & Cilantro

Corn salads are becoming more and more popular lately. This colorful salad is lovely to serve on a buffet.

3   packages (10 ounces, each) frozen corn
1   marinated red pepper, cut into small dice
1/4   cup chopped chives
2   tablespoons finely chopped cilantro
1   tablespoon chopped parsley leaves
3   tablespoons seasoned rice vinegar
1   tablespoon lemon juice
       pepper to taste

Cook the corn for 2 minutes in a saucepan. In a large bowl, place the corn with the remaining ingredients and toss to blend. Refrigerate until serving time. Serves 8 to 10.

Homey Cole Slaw with Apples & Raisins

Apples and raisins add a delicious sweetness to this Cole Slaw. This recipe is a nice change from the more-often-used crushed pineapple.

1/2	cup low-fat mayonnaise
1/2	cup low-fat sour cream
1	teaspoon sugar
2	apples, peeled, cored, grated and tossed with 1/4 cup lemon juice
1	small head of cabbage, about 1 pound, shredded
2	carrots, peeled and grated
1/3	cup yellow raisins
1/2	teaspoon celery seed
	salt to taste

Stir together first 3 ingredients until blended. Toss apples in lemon juice until nicely coated. In a large bowl, toss together all the ingredients until well mixed. Serves 6 to 8.

White Bean Salad with Red Peppers & Scallions

Here is a nice salad with the colors of the Italian flag and just right for an antipasto. Using the canned beans saves hours of preparation and is recommended.

1	can (15 ounces) Cannellini or Great Northern beans, rinsed and drained
2	marinated red peppers, cut into slivers
1/3	cup minced green onion
4	tablespoons minced red onions
1	clove garlic, minced
1/3	cup red wine vinegar
2	tablespoons oil
1	teaspoon Italian Herb Seasoning
	salt and pepper to taste

In a large bowl, toss together all the ingredients until nicely blended. Cover bowl and refrigerate until serving time. Serves 6.

Chinese Chicken Salad

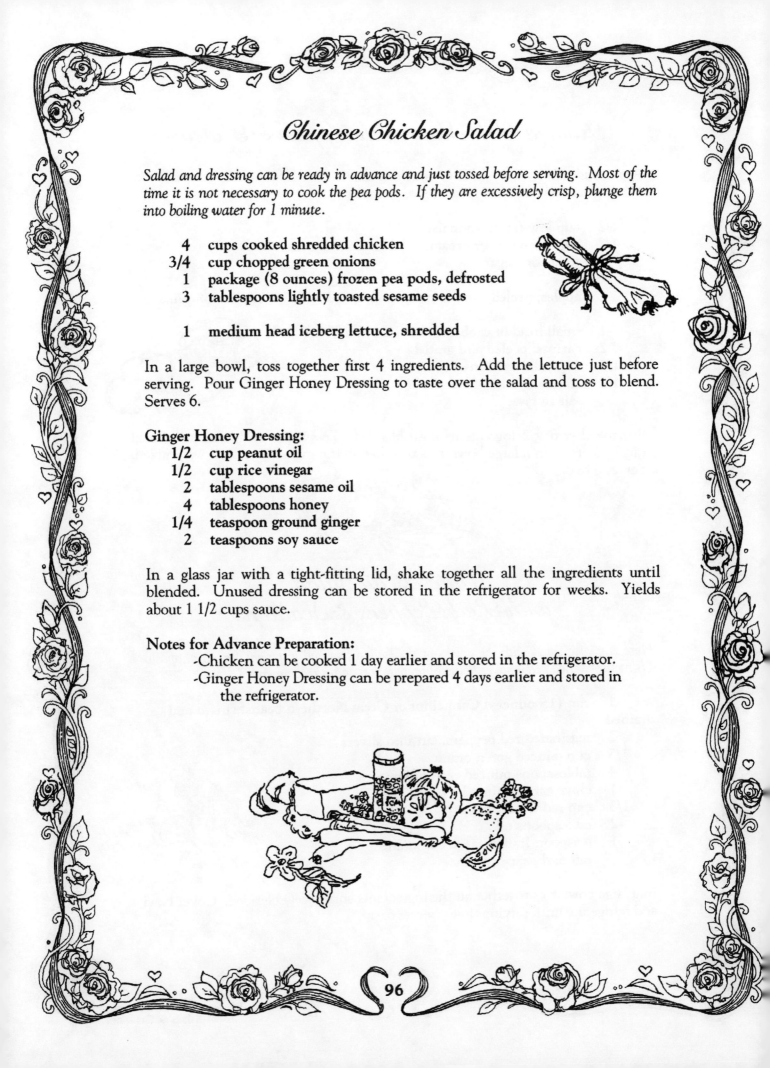

Salad and dressing can be ready in advance and just tossed before serving. Most of the time it is not necessary to cook the pea pods. If they are excessively crisp, plunge them into boiling water for 1 minute.

4	cups cooked shredded chicken
3/4	cup chopped green onions
1	package (8 ounces) frozen pea pods, defrosted
3	tablespoons lightly toasted sesame seeds
1	medium head iceberg lettuce, shredded

In a large bowl, toss together first 4 ingredients. Add the lettuce just before serving. Pour Ginger Honey Dressing to taste over the salad and toss to blend. Serves 6.

Ginger Honey Dressing:

1/2	cup peanut oil
1/2	cup rice vinegar
2	tablespoons sesame oil
4	tablespoons honey
1/4	teaspoon ground ginger
2	teaspoons soy sauce

In a glass jar with a tight-fitting lid, shake together all the ingredients until blended. Unused dressing can be stored in the refrigerator for weeks. Yields about 1 1/2 cups sauce.

Notes for Advance Preparation:
- Chicken can be cooked 1 day earlier and stored in the refrigerator.
- Ginger Honey Dressing can be prepared 4 days earlier and stored in the refrigerator.

Cous Cous Chicken Salad with Artichokes, Red Peppers, Garbanzos & Raisins

This salad is gorgeous and so easy to prepare. It is a great dish to serve a large group, as it can be prepared a day before serving and stored in the refrigerator. As an added touch, before serving, sprinkle top with whole cashews and a few additional raisins. Do not add the cashew nuts earlier as they can become too soggy for my taste. Chopped dried apricots can be substituted for the raisins.

3	cups water
2	cups pre-cooked cous cous
2	jars (7 ounces) marinated artichoke hearts, chopped. Do not drain.
4	marinated red peppers, cut into 1/4-inch strips
1	can (1 pound) garbanzos, rinsed and drained
1/2	cup dark raisins, (plumped in orange juice and drained)
1/2	cup chopped green onions
1/4	cup lemon juice, or more to taste
2	cups cooked and chopped boneless chicken breasts

Sprinkle on Top:
1	cup cashew nuts
	additional raisins or chopped dried apricots

In a saucepan, bring water to a boil. Sprinkle in the cous cous, cover pan and cook for 1 minute. Remove pan from the heat. After another minute, fluff the cous cous several times, to separate the grains. Allow to cool. In a large bowl, toss the cous cous with the remaining ingredients, cover bowl and refrigerate. Serve with spiced apples, peaches or apricots. Serves 8.

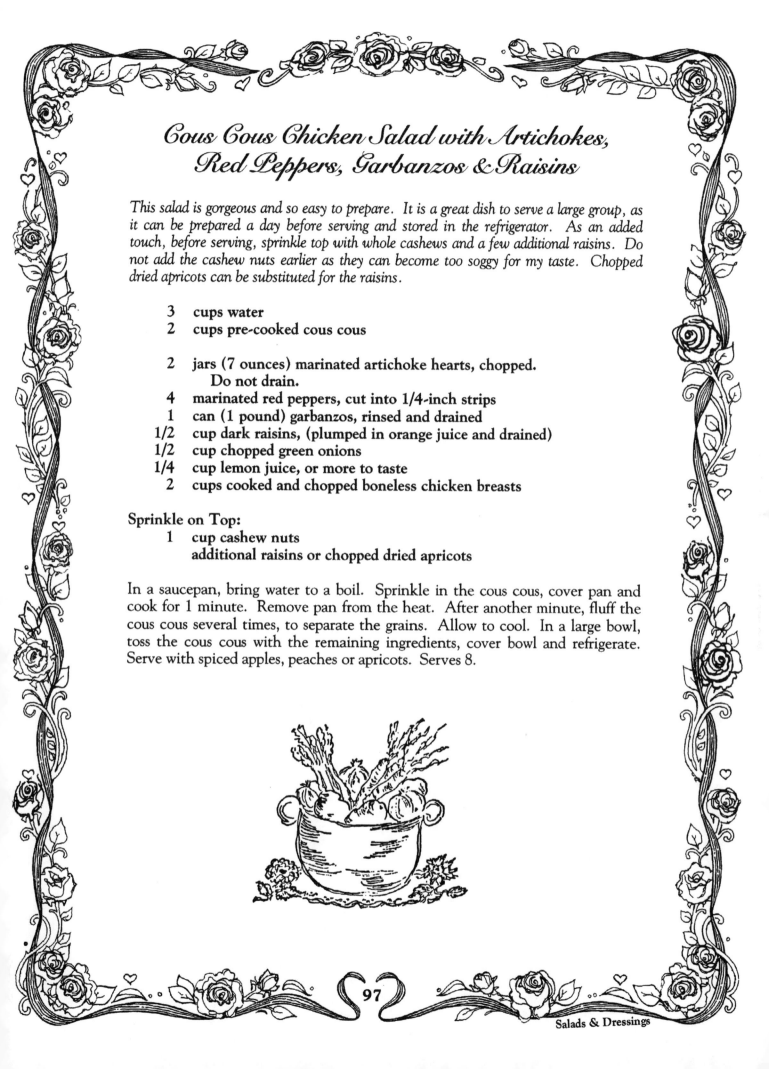

Tomatoes Deborah

Years and years ago, this was a favorite salad with our friends. And yet, to this day, when I serve it, everyone still loves it.

3   large tomatoes, cut into 1/2-inch slices

2   tablespoons dried toasted onion flakes*
1   tablespoon chopped parsley leaves
6   tablespoons salad oil
3   tablespoons white wine vinegar
    salt to taste
1   clove garlic, minced
4   tablespoons grated Parmesan cheese

Place the tomatoes in a lovely glass serving dish with a rim. Combine the remaining ingredients and mix well. Pour dressing over the tomatoes and marinate for at least 4 to 6 hours. Serves 4.

*To Toast Dried Onion Flakes:
Toasted Dried Onion Flakes are difficult to find nowadays. But they are easy to make. In a small pan or pie pan, lay dried onion flakes in one layer. Bake in a 350° oven until they are a light brown. This takes a few minutes, but will depend on the pan and the number you are toasting at one time. Leftover toasted flakes can be stored in a small glass jar. You will be amazed at the wonderful addition of flavor that toasted onion flakes brings to salads. Keep them on hand. They are wonderful.

3-Bean Salad with Red Wine & Garlic Vinaigrette

1   can (1 pound) red kidney beans, rinsed and drained
1   can (1 pound) cut green beans, rinsed and drained
1   can (1 pound) cici peas (garbanzos), rinsed and drained
3/4 cup chopped green onions
2   cloves garlic, minced
2   tablespoons minced parsley
1   jar (2 ounces) pimiento strips
1/4 cup red wine vinegar
1/2 cup oil
1/2 teaspoon sugar
    salt and pepper to taste

In a large bowl, toss together all the ingredients until thoroughly mixed. Cover and refrigerate for several hours before serving. Serves 8.

Pasta Salad with Mushrooms, Sun-Dried Tomatoes & Spinach Dressing

This is a rather assertive dressing, as the pasta soaks up so much taste. You might even need a little more lemon juice. The addition of 2 cups diced, cooked, white chicken meat will transform this salad into a main course for a luncheon.

Spinach Dressing:

1/2	cup mayonnaise
1/2	cup low-fat sour cream
2	medium green onions, cut up. Use white and green parts.
4	tablespoons lemon juice
	salt and freshly ground pepper to taste
1	package (10 ounces) frozen chopped spinach, defrosted and drained. (Place spinach in a strainer and press out liquid.)

Salad:

1	pound penne pasta, cooked al dente (tender but firm), and drained
1/2	pound mushrooms, cleaned and sliced
4	sun-dried tomatoes, packed in oil, drained and chopped

To Make the Spinach Dressing:
In a food processor, blend together first 6 ingredients until onions are very finely chopped. Place mixture in a large bowl and stir in the spinach.

To Assemble the Salad:
In a large bowl, toss together pasta, mushrooms and tomatoes until nicely mixed. Toss with dressing to taste. Serve in a large bowl and decorate with lemon slices and green onion frills. Serves 8.

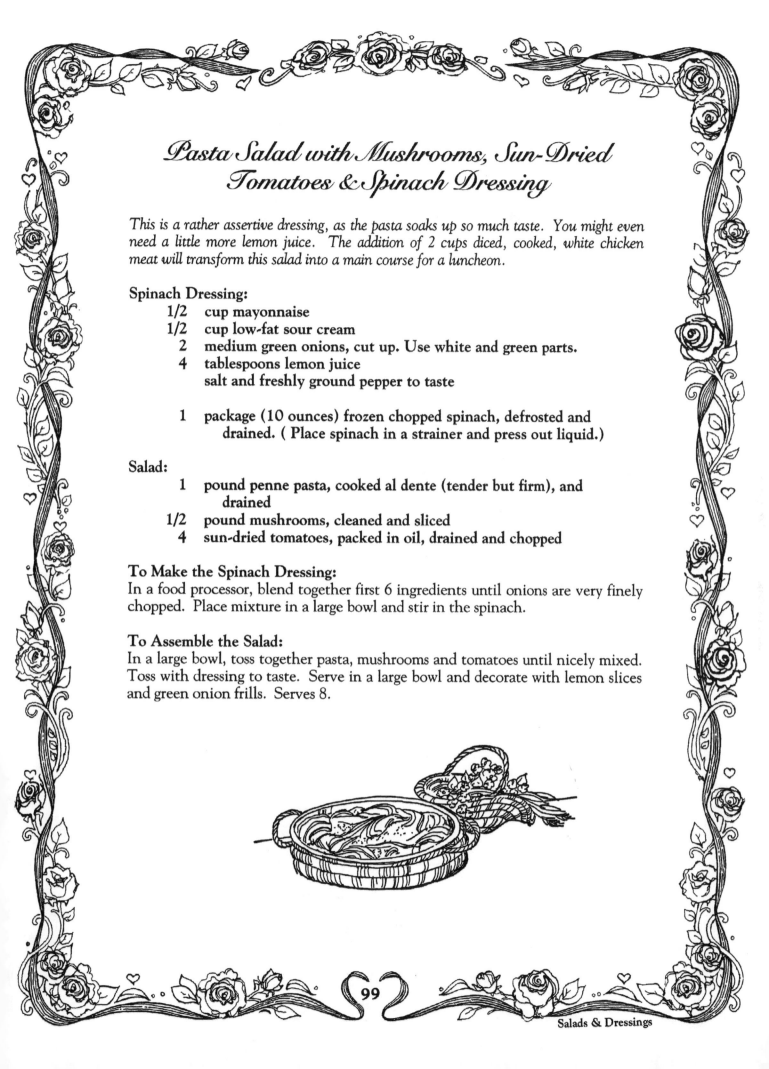

Pasta Primavera with Basil Vinaigrette with Garlic

3/4   pound spiral pasta, cooked tender but firm (al dente)

1   bag (1 pound) Del Sol vegetables, defrosted. (Del Sol is a combination of broccoli, cauliflower and carrots. Many food companies make this combination.) Cook the vegetables according to the directions on the package until tender.

In a large bowl, toss together pasta and vegetables until nicely mixed. Now, pour Basil Vinaigrette with Garlic over all and toss until pasta and vegetables are evenly coated. Refrigerate for several hours. Overnight is good, too.

To serve, decorate top with an additional sprinkling of grated cheese and minced green onion. Serves 6 as a small entree.

Basil Vinaigrette with Garlic:

1/4   cup grated Parmesan cheese

1/2   cup oil (use part olive oil)

1/4   cup red wine vinegar

2   tablespoons lemon juice

1   tablespoon Dijon mustard

1   shallot, minced

2   cloves garlic, minced

2   green onions, minced

1   teaspoon sweet basil flakes

    salt and pepper to taste

Place all the ingredients in a jar with a tight fitting lid and shake until blended. Refrigerate for several hours. Yields about 1 cup dressing.

Note: -Pasta is bland and absorbs dressing like a sponge. Dressing may need a bit more vinegar. Taste after tossing.

       -Dressing can be prepared 1 day earlier and stored in the refrigerator. But, please know that the shallots intensify in flavor if allowed to sit in the dressing for too long.

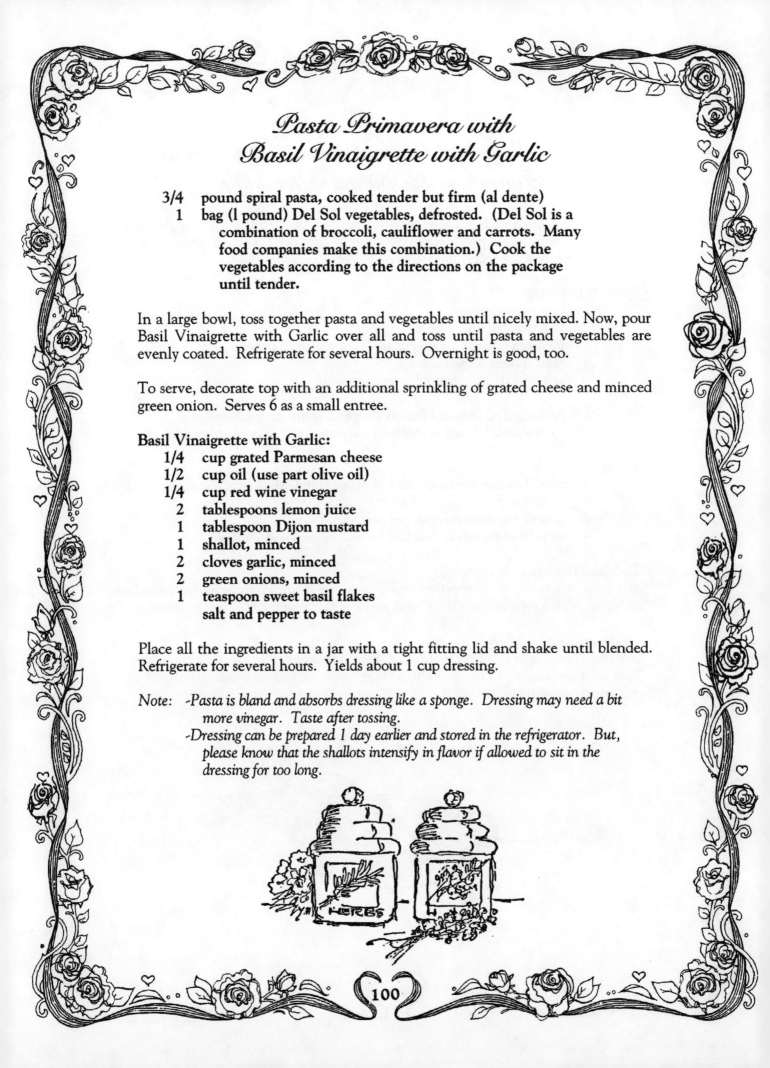

Linguini Verde with Brie, Tomatoes & Basil Dressing

Pasta salads are so popular nowadays. Pasta shops are springing up all over and the combinations are exciting and creative. It is a far cry from the macaroni salads I had as a child. This is an exceptionally attractive salad, bright red and green.

1	pound semi-ripe Brie. Remove rind and cut into small pieces while Brie is chilled.
4	tomatoes, peeled, seeded and chopped
3	cloves garlic, minced
1/4	cup chopped green onions
1/2	cup oil (can use part olive oil)
1/4	cup red wine vinegar
2	teaspoons dried sweet basil flakes
1/2	cup grated Parmesan cheese
	salt and freshly ground pepper to taste
1	pound linguini verde, broken into 2-inch pieces, cooked firm but tender and drained

In a large bowl, place first 9 ingredients and toss to blend. Cook linguini, until tender, in a spaghetti cooker and then, plunge basket in cold water until linguini is chilled. Drain thoroughly.

Toss linguini in bowl with Brie mixture until nicely mixed. Refrigerate until serving time. Serves 6.

Note: -Can be prepared 4 to 6 hours before serving and stored in the refrigerator.
*   -Linguini should be broken into small pieces so that tomato and Brie can better combine.*
*   -Ziti or rotini or similar small pasta can be substituted. Leave pasta whole.*

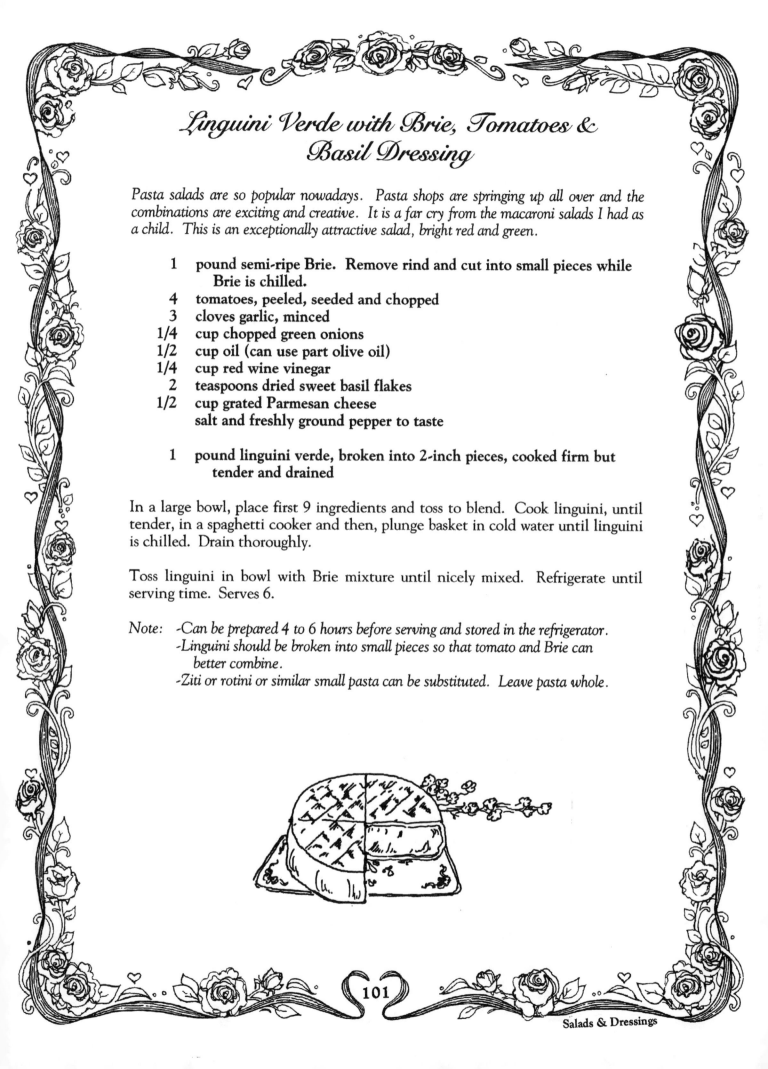

101

Vegetable & Pasta Pesto Salad

This is an interesting pasta salad as it is filled with vegetables. The number of vegetables can be doubled for a very low-calorie dinner. If you are pressed for time, using the frozen vegetables is recommended in this recipe, as they are cut to perfect size, do not contain stalks or stems, and include only the florets of the vegetables.

1   package (8 ounces) corkscrew pasta or any small-sized pasta, cooked until tender and drained
2   jars (6 ounces, each) marinated artichoke hearts, undrained
4   tablespoons lemon juice
1/2 cup chopped chives
2   teaspoons sweet basil flakes
1   package (1 pound) frozen Del Sol vegetables, parboiled and drained. (This is a combination of carrot sticks, broccoli florets and cauliflower florets in perfectly cut sizes.)

In a large bowl, toss together all the ingredients and taste if more lemon juice is needed. Refrigerate until serving time. Taste again, as pasta has a way of soaking up all the flavor. Serves 8.

Pickled Beets with Onions

1   can (1 pound) sliced beets, drained. Reserve 1/2 cup beet juice.
1   onion, thinly sliced in rings

4   tablespoons wine vinegar
1   teaspoon sugar
1   tablespoon olive oil
1   clove garlic, cut in half
    salt and pepper to taste

In a glass jar with a tight-fitting lid, combine all the ingredients with reserved 1/2 cup beet juice. Refrigerate for at least 2 days. Serve chilled. Serves 6.

Tabouleh-Bulgur Salad with Tomatoes & Lemon Vinaigrette

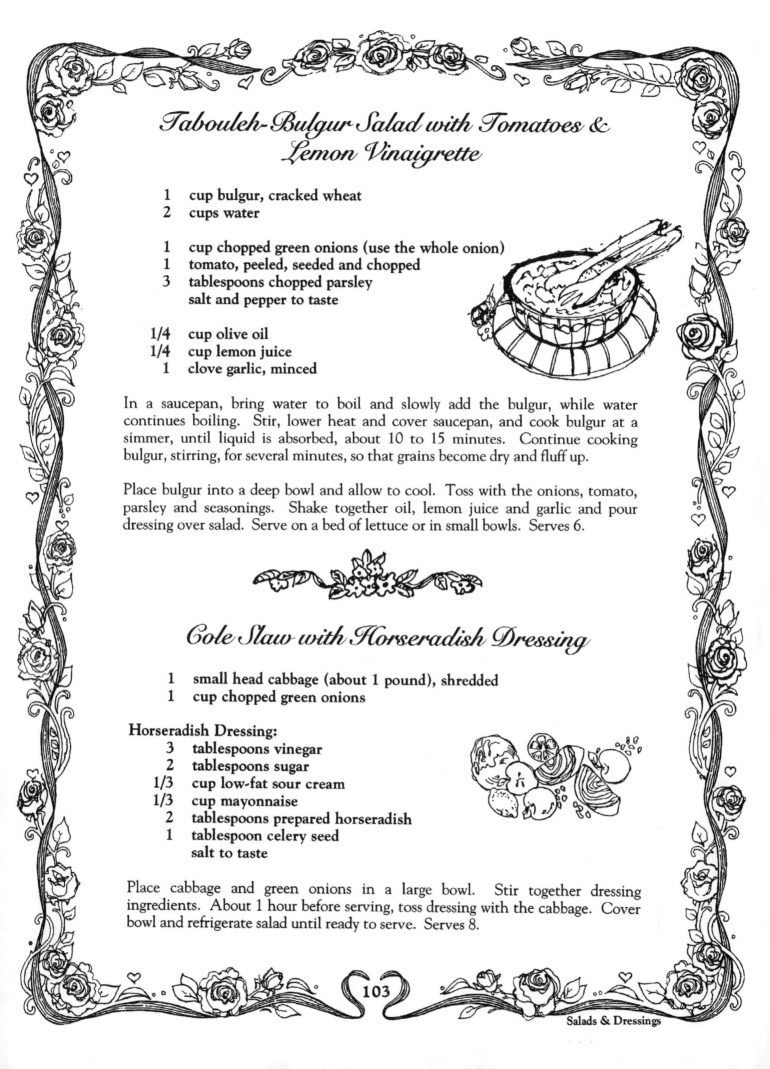

1	cup bulgur, cracked wheat
2	cups water

1	cup chopped green onions (use the whole onion)
1	tomato, peeled, seeded and chopped
3	tablespoons chopped parsley
	salt and pepper to taste

1/4	cup olive oil
1/4	cup lemon juice
1	clove garlic, minced

In a saucepan, bring water to boil and slowly add the bulgur, while water continues boiling. Stir, lower heat and cover saucepan, and cook bulgur at a simmer, until liquid is absorbed, about 10 to 15 minutes. Continue cooking bulgur, stirring, for several minutes, so that grains become dry and fluff up.

Place bulgur into a deep bowl and allow to cool. Toss with the onions, tomato, parsley and seasonings. Shake together oil, lemon juice and garlic and pour dressing over salad. Serve on a bed of lettuce or in small bowls. Serves 6.

Cole Slaw with Horseradish Dressing

1	small head cabbage (about 1 pound), shredded
1	cup chopped green onions

Horseradish Dressing:

3	tablespoons vinegar
2	tablespoons sugar
1/3	cup low-fat sour cream
1/3	cup mayonnaise
2	tablespoons prepared horseradish
1	tablespoon celery seed
	salt to taste

Place cabbage and green onions in a large bowl. Stir together dressing ingredients. About 1 hour before serving, toss dressing with the cabbage. Cover bowl and refrigerate salad until ready to serve. Serves 8.

Salads & Dressings

Bean Salad with Italian Herb Dressing

This simple little dressing can be used over an antipasto or mixed green salad.

Bean Salad:
- 1   can (15 ounces) garbanzo beans, rinsed and drained
- 1   can (15 ounces) red kidney beans, rinsed and drained
- 1/3   cup chopped green onions
- 1/4   cup chopped red onions

Italian Herb Dressing:
- 1/4   cup oil
- 1/4   cup red wine vinegar
- 1   shallot, minced
- 1   teaspoon oregano flakes
- 1   teaspoon sweet basil flakes
- 1/4   teaspoon thyme flakes
- 2   cloves garlic, put through a press
  - salt and freshly ground pepper to taste

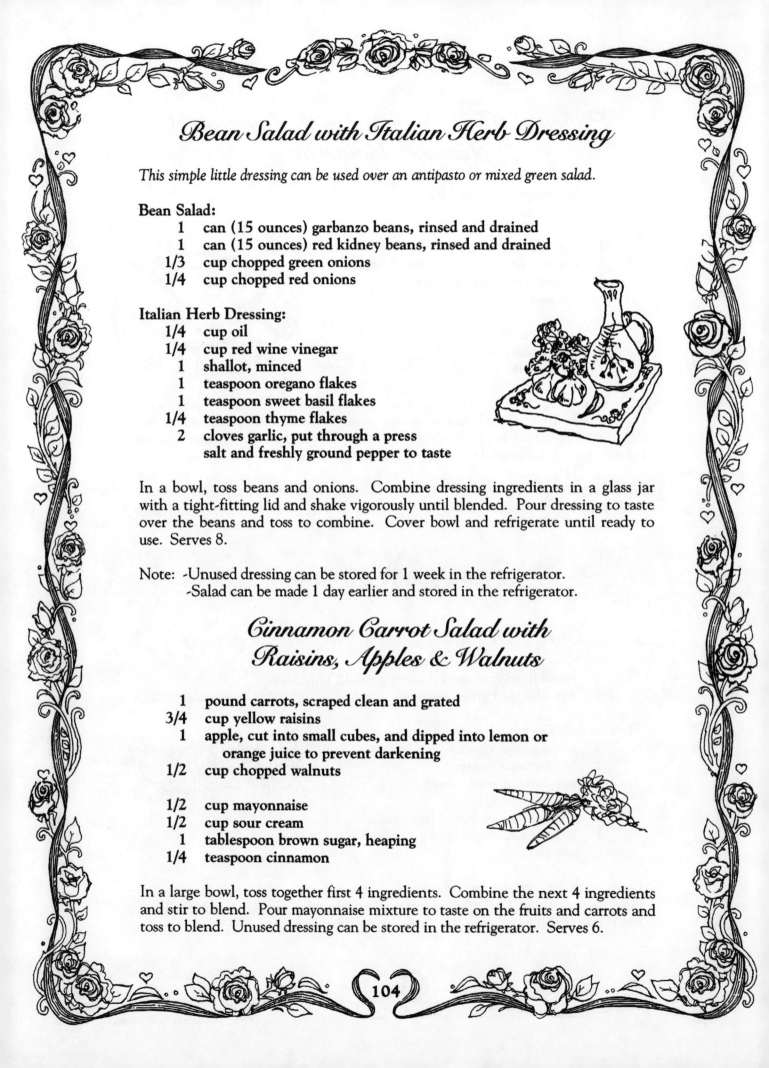

In a bowl, toss beans and onions. Combine dressing ingredients in a glass jar with a tight-fitting lid and shake vigorously until blended. Pour dressing to taste over the beans and toss to combine. Cover bowl and refrigerate until ready to use. Serves 8.

Note: -Unused dressing can be stored for 1 week in the refrigerator.
        -Salad can be made 1 day earlier and stored in the refrigerator.

Cinnamon Carrot Salad with Raisins, Apples & Walnuts

- 1   pound carrots, scraped clean and grated
- 3/4   cup yellow raisins
- 1   apple, cut into small cubes, and dipped into lemon or orange juice to prevent darkening
- 1/2   cup chopped walnuts

- 1/2   cup mayonnaise
- 1/2   cup sour cream
- 1   tablespoon brown sugar, heaping
- 1/4   teaspoon cinnamon

In a large bowl, toss together first 4 ingredients. Combine the next 4 ingredients and stir to blend. Pour mayonnaise mixture to taste on the fruits and carrots and toss to blend. Unused dressing can be stored in the refrigerator. Serves 6.

Greek Salad with Lemon Dill Vinaigrette

A Greek salad can be made in any number of ways, but they seem to always include lettuce, tomatoes and cucumbers. The addition of olives and feta cheese makes it a little more festive. And while the anchovies are optional, in this salad, they add depth.

- 1   medium head lettuce cut up, about 4 cups
- 4   medium tomatoes, thinly sliced
- 1   large cucumber peeled and cut into thin slices. (If you have a few seconds, run a fork down the sides of the peeled cucumber, and then, when it is sliced, it will look faintly scalloped.)
- 1/4   cup pitted olive slices
- 4   ounces feta cheese, crumbled
- 3   green onions, finely chopped
- 2   tablespoons chopped parsley
-     salt and freshly ground pepper to taste
- 2   anchovies, mashed (optional)

Toss together all the ingredients in a large bowl and refrigerate. Just before serving pour Lemon Dill Vinaigrette over the salad and toss until evenly coated. Serves 6.

Lemon Dill Vinaigrette:
- 1/4   cup lemon juice
- 1   tablespoon wine vinegar
- 1   tablespoon water
- 3/4   cup oil
- 1/2   teaspoon dried dill weed
- 1   clove garlic, minced or put through a press
- 2   tablespoons grated Parmesan cheese
- 1   tablespoon minced parsley
-     salt and pepper to taste

Place all the ingredients in a jar with a tight-fitting lid and shake vigorously. Refrigerate dressing until serving time. Yields about 1 cup dressing.

Note: -Salad can be cut up earlier in the day. Dressing can be prepared 1 day earlier and stored in the refrigerator.

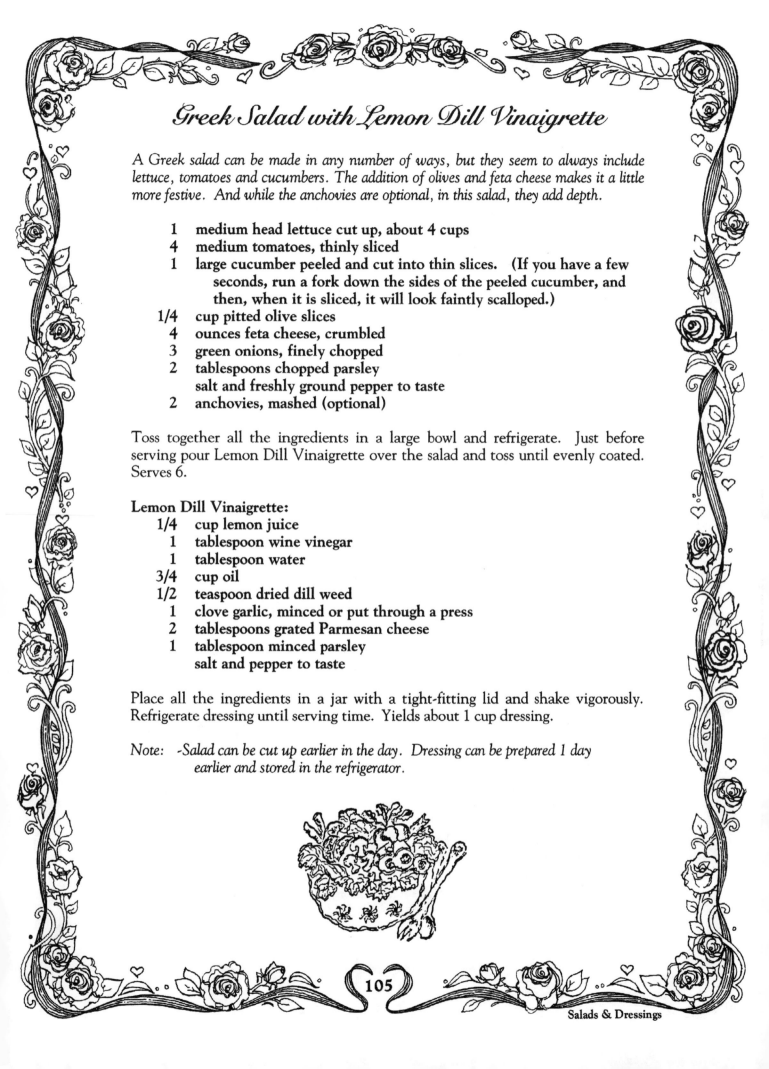

Mushroom, Onion & Red Pepper Salad with Lemon Dressing

1   jar (1 pound) roasted sweet red peppers, drained and cut into strips
1   pound button mushrooms, stemmed and caps left whole. Reserve stems for another use.
1/2 pound frozen baby pearl onions, blanched in boiling water for 3 minutes and drained

1/2 cup lemon juice, freshly squeezed
1   cup oil (can use 1/2 olive oil)
1   teaspoon sugar
1/3 cup chopped green onions
1/4 teaspoon garlic powder
1/2 teaspoon, each, sweet basil flakes and oregano flakes
     salt and pepper to taste

12   pitted black olives, optional
6   anchovies, optional

In a bowl, toss together peppers, mushrooms and onions. In a glass jar, shake together next 8 ingredients until blended. Pour dressing to taste, over the vegetables. Serve with black olives and anchovies on top. Serves 6.

Pasta Salad al Pesto

1   pound medium-sized pasta, such as penne, ziti or rotini. Cook in a spaghetti cooker until firm but tender and drain. Plunge into cold water until chilled.

1/2 cup sour cream
1/2 cup cream
1/2 cup grated Parmesan cheese
2   teaspoons dried sweet basil flakes
2   cloves garlic, minced
4   tablespoons pine nuts

Place cooked pasta in a large bowl. Combine the remaining ingredients in a food processor and blend until pine nuts are pureed. Pour dressing to taste over cooked pasta and toss to blend. Refrigerate until serving time. Can be prepared earlier in the day and stored in the refrigerator. Unused dresing can be stored in a glass jar in the refrigerator. Serves 6.

Sweet & Sour Red Cabbage with Apples & Raisins

1   red cabbage, (about 1 pound), remove the hard central core and grate. This can be done with the grating attachment in a food processor.
2   large apples, peeled, cored and grated in a food processor
1   large onion, chopped
1   cup chicken broth
     salt and pepper to taste

3   tablespoons lemon juice
1   tablespoon sugar
1/2   cup yellow raisins

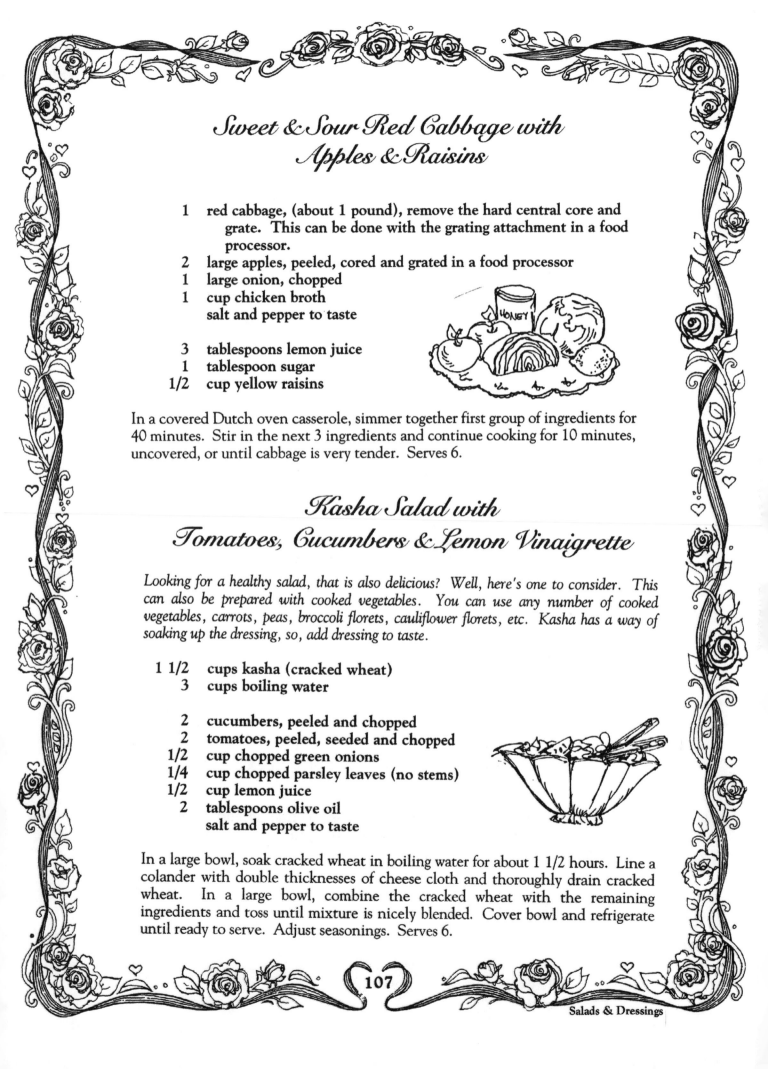

In a covered Dutch oven casserole, simmer together first group of ingredients for 40 minutes. Stir in the next 3 ingredients and continue cooking for 10 minutes, uncovered, or until cabbage is very tender. Serves 6.

Kasha Salad with Tomatoes, Cucumbers & Lemon Vinaigrette

Looking for a healthy salad, that is also delicious? Well, here's one to consider. This can also be prepared with cooked vegetables. You can use any number of cooked vegetables, carrots, peas, broccoli florets, cauliflower florets, etc. Kasha has a way of soaking up the dressing, so, add dressing to taste.

1 1/2   cups kasha (cracked wheat)
3   cups boiling water

2   cucumbers, peeled and chopped
2   tomatoes, peeled, seeded and chopped
1/2   cup chopped green onions
1/4   cup chopped parsley leaves (no stems)
1/2   cup lemon juice
2   tablespoons olive oil
     salt and pepper to taste

In a large bowl, soak cracked wheat in boiling water for about 1 1/2 hours. Line a colander with double thicknesses of cheese cloth and thoroughly drain cracked wheat. In a large bowl, combine the cracked wheat with the remaining ingredients and toss until mixture is nicely blended. Cover bowl and refrigerate until ready to serve. Adjust seasonings. Serves 6.

Mexican Salsa for Dipping with Raw Vegetables

1   can (1 pound) stewed tomatoes, finely chopped. Do not drain.
1/3   cup chopped green onions
2   tablespoons minced red onions
1   can (4 ounces) diced green chiles
1   clove garlic, minced
2   tablespoons chopped parsley
2   tablespoons red wine vinegar
2   tablespoons lemon juice
1   tablespoon oil
1/4   teaspoon ground cumin
      pinch of sugar
      salt and pepper to taste

In a quart-jar with a tight-fitting lid, shake together all the ingredients until mixture is nicely blended. Refrigerate salsa for several hours. Overnight is good, too. Serve with raw vegetables, cut on the diagonal, to make more room for the sauce. You probably should have a few corn chips close by, and they are ideal, but higher in calories. Yields 2 1/2 cups sauce.

Green Goddess Dressing Darling

This salad dressing is also exceptionally good as a dip for a cold vegetable platter.

1   cup mayonnaise
1/4   cup half and half
1/4   teaspoon garlic powder
1/4   cup parsley leaves
3   green onions, medium-sized, use the whole onion
      pinch of salt

Combine all the ingredients in food processor container and blend at high speed until mixture is smooth. Pour dressing into a glass jar, cover and refrigerate. Makes 1 1/2 cups.

Note: -Dressing will keep for a week in the refrigerator.

Casseroles

and

Small Entrees

Old-Fashioned Cheese Blintze Casserole

4	tablespoons butter, melted
12	cheese blintzes, purchased from a deli
4	eggs
1	pint sour cream
3	tablespoons lemon juice
3/4	cup sugar
1	teaspoon vanilla
1/2	cup yellow raisins, plumped in orange juice
2	tablespoons cinnamon sugar

In a 9x13-inch baking pan, spread melted butter and place cheese blintzes. Beat together next 6 ingredients until blended and pour over the blintzes. Sprinkle top with cinnamon sugar. (Press down into the custard any raisins that have floated to the top.) Bake at 350° for 45 minutes or until custard is set and top is golden. Serve with a dollop of sour cream and strawberry jam. Fresh strawberries in syrup is also lovely. Serves 6 to 12 depending on what else is being served.

Casserole with Apples, Raisins and Walnuts

6	eggs, well beaten
3	tablespoons flour
3	tablespoons sugar
1/2	cup cream
1	teaspoon vanilla
2	apples, peeled, cored and grated
1/2	cup golden raisins, plumped in boiling water and drained
1/2	cup chopped walnuts
1	teaspoon orange zest
3	tablespoons butter
3	tablespoons cinnamon sugar

Beat eggs with flour, sugar, cream and vanilla until light. Add apples, raisins, walnuts and orange zest and mix well.

Melt butter in a 12-inch baking pan or oval baker. Add egg mixture to pan and sprinkle top with cinnamon sugar. Bake in a 350° oven for about 50 minutes or until eggs are set and top is golden brown. Serve with a dollop of sour cream and a tablespoonful of defrosted strawberry slices in syrup. Serves 4 to 6.

Note: -I have not found it satisfactory to assemble this dish earlier in the day, so prepare it before baking.

Easiest & Best Cheese Blintze Casserole with Strawberries & Sour Cream

This is an oldie but goodie. Nothing could be easier to prepare than this delicious casserole. It has all the character and flavor of cheese blintzes with none of the work. This is a good choice for a breakfast or brunch, as it can be prepared in advance and heated before serving. The original of this recipe appeared in my newsletter in 1968. To this day, it is still enjoyed by everyone. This version is a little lighter.

Batter:

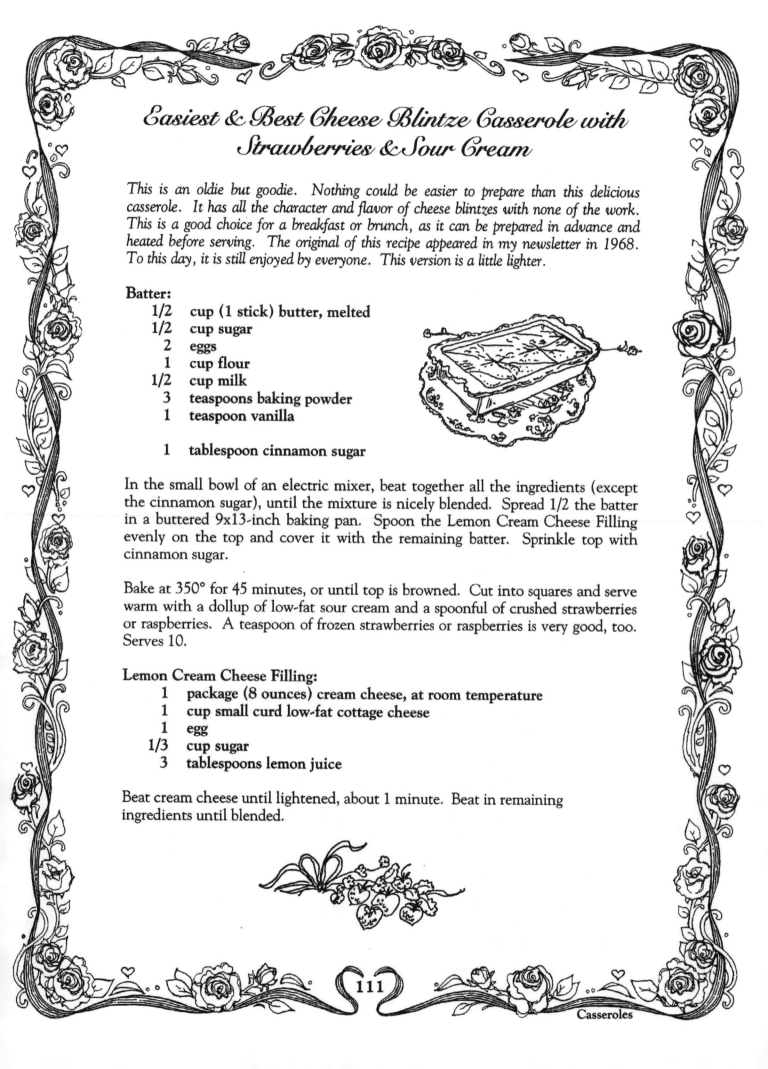

1/2	cup (1 stick) butter, melted
1/2	cup sugar
2	eggs
1	cup flour
1/2	cup milk
3	teaspoons baking powder
1	teaspoon vanilla
1	tablespoon cinnamon sugar

In the small bowl of an electric mixer, beat together all the ingredients (except the cinnamon sugar), until the mixture is nicely blended. Spread 1/2 the batter in a buttered 9x13-inch baking pan. Spoon the Lemon Cream Cheese Filling evenly on the top and cover it with the remaining batter. Sprinkle top with cinnamon sugar.

Bake at 350° for 45 minutes, or until top is browned. Cut into squares and serve warm with a dollup of low-fat sour cream and a spoonful of crushed strawberries or raspberries. A teaspoon of frozen strawberries or raspberries is very good, too. Serves 10.

Lemon Cream Cheese Filling:

1	package (8 ounces) cream cheese, at room temperature
1	cup small curd low-fat cottage cheese
1	egg
1/3	cup sugar
3	tablespoons lemon juice

Beat cream cheese until lightened, about 1 minute. Beat in remaining ingredients until blended.

Frittata with Artichokes and Red Peppers

4   eggs
1   cup low-fat milk
1/2 teaspoon oregano flakes
    white pepper to taste

1   jar (8 ounces) marinated artichoke hearts, drained and cut
      into fourths
4   marinated red peppers, drained and cut into strips
1/2 cup chopped green onions
1   clove garlic, minced

2   tablespoons grated Parmesan cheese

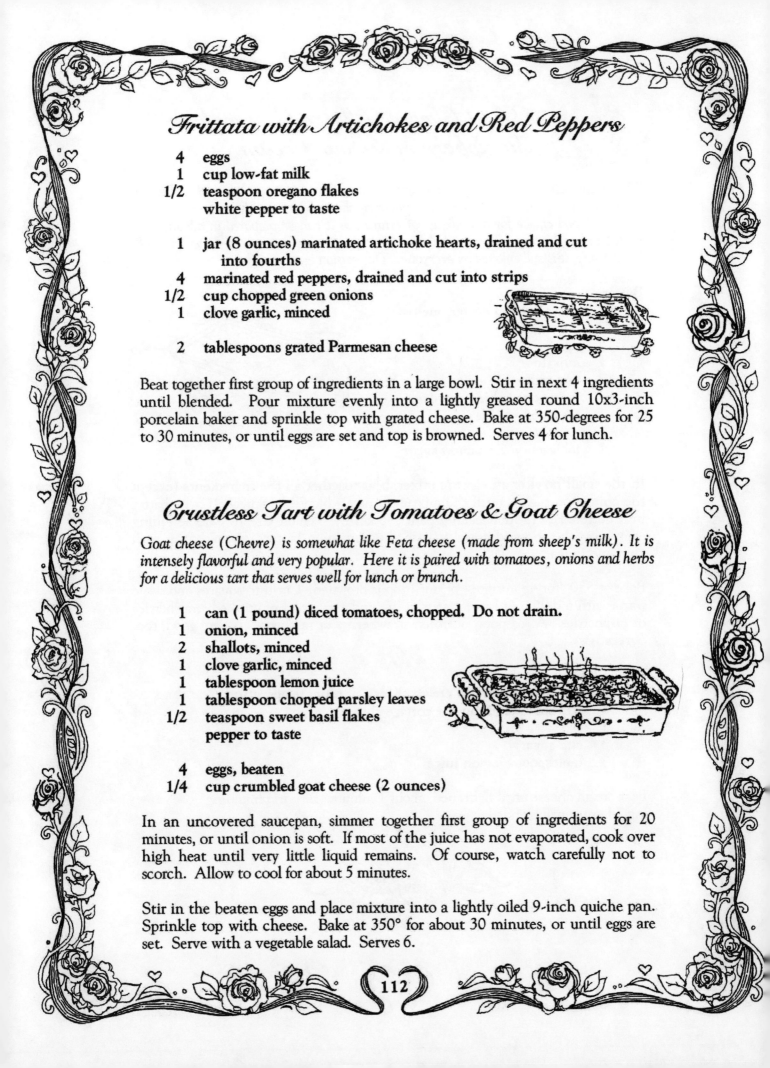

Beat together first group of ingredients in a large bowl. Stir in next 4 ingredients until blended. Pour mixture evenly into a lightly greased round 10x3-inch porcelain baker and sprinkle top with grated cheese. Bake at 350-degrees for 25 to 30 minutes, or until eggs are set and top is browned. Serves 4 for lunch.

Crustless Tart with Tomatoes & Goat Cheese

Goat cheese (Chevre) is somewhat like Feta cheese (made from sheep's milk). It is intensely flavorful and very popular. Here it is paired with tomatoes, onions and herbs for a delicious tart that serves well for lunch or brunch.

1   can (1 pound) diced tomatoes, chopped. Do not drain.
1   onion, minced
2   shallots, minced
1   clove garlic, minced
1   tablespoon lemon juice
1   tablespoon chopped parsley leaves
1/2 teaspoon sweet basil flakes
    pepper to taste

4   eggs, beaten
1/4 cup crumbled goat cheese (2 ounces)

In an uncovered saucepan, simmer together first group of ingredients for 20 minutes, or until onion is soft. If most of the juice has not evaporated, cook over high heat until very little liquid remains. Of course, watch carefully not to scorch. Allow to cool for about 5 minutes.

Stir in the beaten eggs and place mixture into a lightly oiled 9-inch quiche pan. Sprinkle top with cheese. Bake at 350° for about 30 minutes, or until eggs are set. Serve with a vegetable salad. Serves 6.

112

Frittata with Spinach & Cheese

This is my latest version of my Spinach Frittata, in a Greek mood. It is filled with vegetables and cheese. Also high in protein and very low in fats, this is a good dish to consider for lunch or brunch or an accompaniment to dinner. As an added bonus, it is almost a perfect food, containing eggs, vegetable, cheese and carbs. This version is also great served as an hors d'oeuvre.

3   eggs, beaten
1   pound bag frozen chopped spinach, slightly defrosted
1   pint small-curd cottage cheese (regular, low-fat or non-fat)
1   cup grated Parmesan cheese
1   cup Ritz cracker coarse crumbs (about 22 crackers)

2   tablespoons grated Parmesan cheese for topping

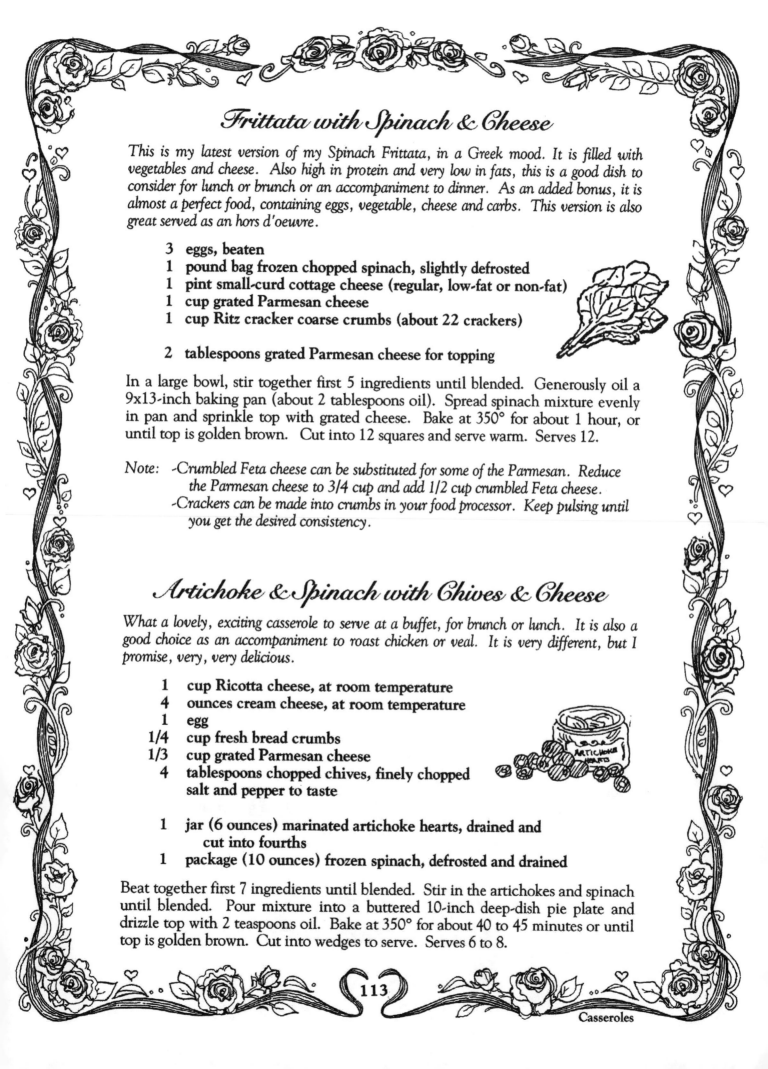

In a large bowl, stir together first 5 ingredients until blended. Generously oil a 9x13-inch baking pan (about 2 tablespoons oil). Spread spinach mixture evenly in pan and sprinkle top with grated cheese. Bake at 350° for about 1 hour, or until top is golden brown. Cut into 12 squares and serve warm. Serves 12.

Note: -Crumbled Feta cheese can be substituted for some of the Parmesan. Reduce the Parmesan cheese to 3/4 cup and add 1/2 cup crumbled Feta cheese.
-Crackers can be made into crumbs in your food processor. Keep pulsing until you get the desired consistency.

Artichoke & Spinach with Chives & Cheese

What a lovely, exciting casserole to serve at a buffet, for brunch or lunch. It is also a good choice as an accompaniment to roast chicken or veal. It is very different, but I promise, very, very delicious.

1   cup Ricotta cheese, at room temperature
4   ounces cream cheese, at room temperature
1   egg
1/4   cup fresh bread crumbs
1/3   cup grated Parmesan cheese
4   tablespoons chopped chives, finely chopped
     salt and pepper to taste

1   jar (6 ounces) marinated artichoke hearts, drained and cut into fourths
1   package (10 ounces) frozen spinach, defrosted and drained

Beat together first 7 ingredients until blended. Stir in the artichokes and spinach until blended. Pour mixture into a buttered 10-inch deep-dish pie plate and drizzle top with 2 teaspoons oil. Bake at 350° for about 40 to 45 minutes or until top is golden brown. Cut into wedges to serve. Serves 6 to 8.

Casseroles

Cabbage Rolls German Style with Sauerkraut & Ginger Snap Sauce

1   large head cabbage

1   onion, chopped, sautéed in 1 tablespoon butter
1   pound lean ground beef
1/2 cup raw rice
1   egg
1/4 cup cold water
     pinch of garlic powder
     salt and pepper to taste

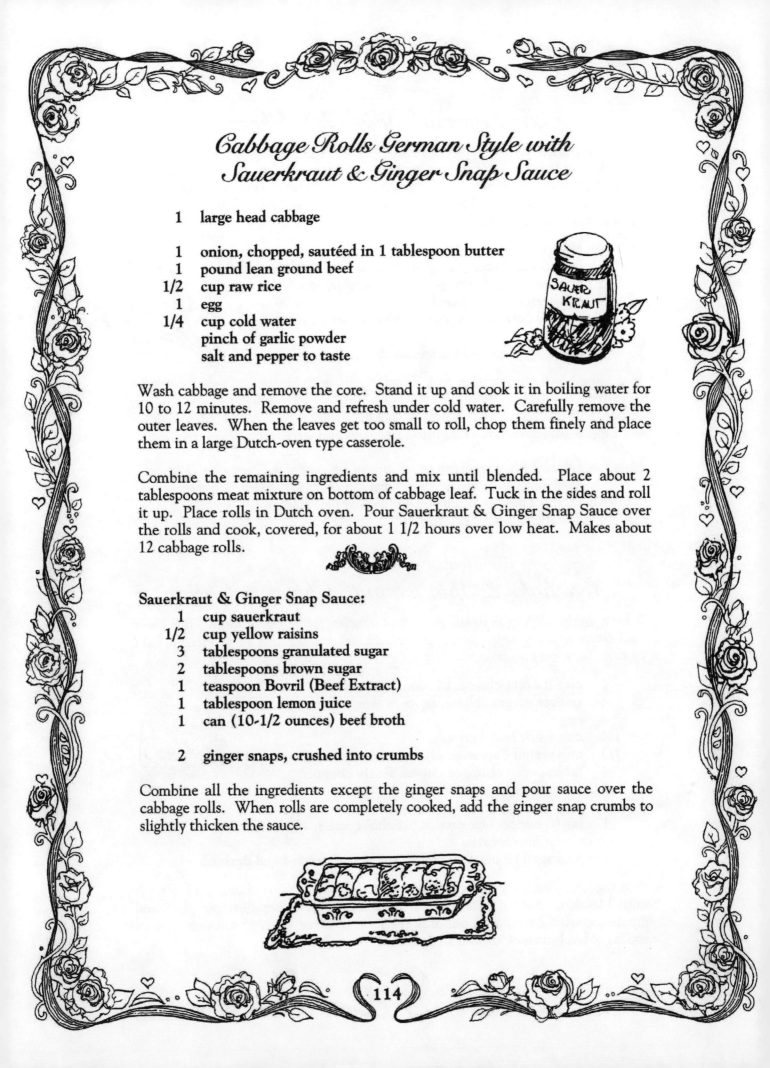

Wash cabbage and remove the core. Stand it up and cook it in boiling water for 10 to 12 minutes. Remove and refresh under cold water. Carefully remove the outer leaves. When the leaves get too small to roll, chop them finely and place them in a large Dutch-oven type casserole.

Combine the remaining ingredients and mix until blended. Place about 2 tablespoons meat mixture on bottom of cabbage leaf. Tuck in the sides and roll it up. Place rolls in Dutch oven. Pour Sauerkraut & Ginger Snap Sauce over the rolls and cook, covered, for about 1 1/2 hours over low heat. Makes about 12 cabbage rolls.

Sauerkraut & Ginger Snap Sauce:
1   cup sauerkraut
1/2 cup yellow raisins
3   tablespoons granulated sugar
2   tablespoons brown sugar
1   teaspoon Bovril (Beef Extract)
1   tablespoon lemon juice
1   can (10-1/2 ounces) beef broth

2   ginger snaps, crushed into crumbs

Combine all the ingredients except the ginger snaps and pour sauce over the cabbage rolls. When rolls are completely cooked, add the ginger snap crumbs to slightly thicken the sauce.

Country-Style Cabbage Rolls in Sweet & Sour Sauce

1   large head of cabbage (about 1 1/2 pounds). Rinse cabbage and remove the core. Cook it, core side down, in boiling water for about 12 to 15 minutes. Remove and refresh under cold water. Carefully remove the outer leaves. When the leaves get too small to roll, finely chop them and place them in a large Dutch-oven casserole.

Meat, Onion & Rice Filling:

1	pound lean ground beef
1	egg
1/2	onion, grated, about 6 tablespoons
1 1/2	cups cooked rice*
1/8	teaspoon garlic powder
	salt and pepper to taste

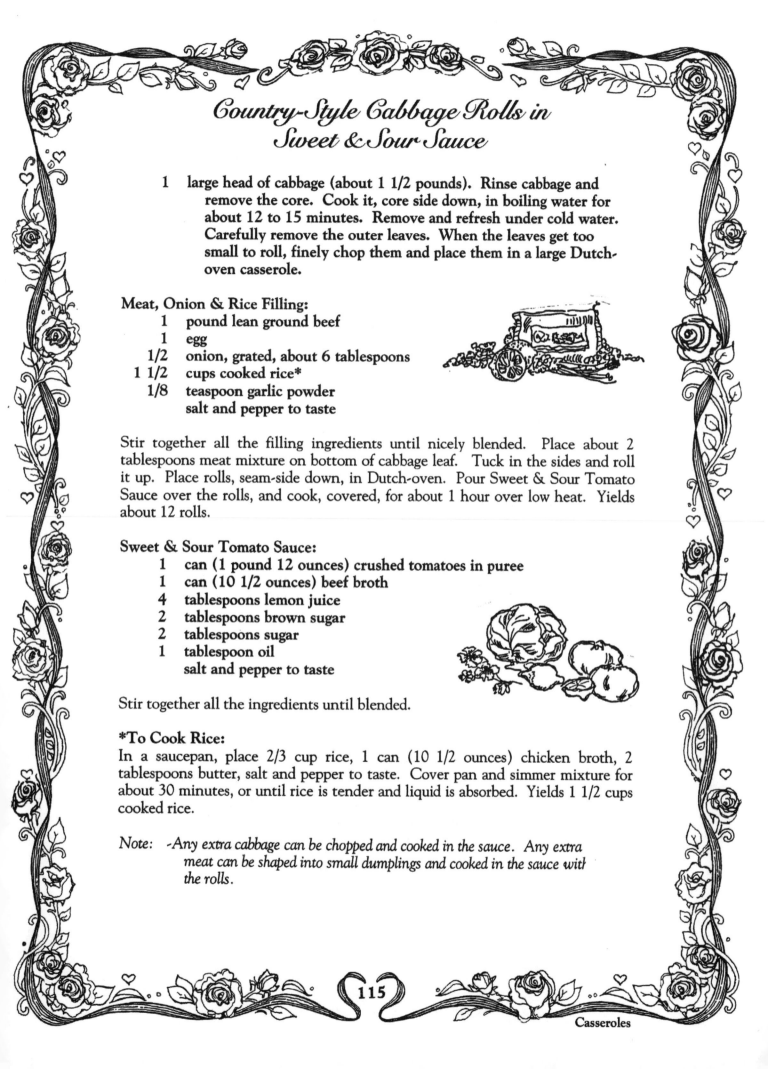

Stir together all the filling ingredients until nicely blended. Place about 2 tablespoons meat mixture on bottom of cabbage leaf. Tuck in the sides and roll it up. Place rolls, seam-side down, in Dutch-oven. Pour Sweet & Sour Tomato Sauce over the rolls, and cook, covered, for about 1 hour over low heat. Yields about 12 rolls.

Sweet & Sour Tomato Sauce:

1	can (1 pound 12 ounces) crushed tomatoes in puree
1	can (10 1/2 ounces) beef broth
4	tablespoons lemon juice
2	tablespoons brown sugar
2	tablespoons sugar
1	tablespoon oil
	salt and pepper to taste

Stir together all the ingredients until blended.

*To Cook Rice:

In a saucepan, place 2/3 cup rice, 1 can (10 1/2 ounces) chicken broth, 2 tablespoons butter, salt and pepper to taste. Cover pan and simmer mixture for about 30 minutes, or until rice is tender and liquid is absorbed. Yields 1 1/2 cups cooked rice.

Note: *-Any extra cabbage can be chopped and cooked in the sauce. Any extra meat can be shaped into small dumplings and cooked in the sauce with the rolls.*

Paella Valencia with Chicken, Shrimp & Peas

1   fryer chicken (about 2 1/2 pounds) cut into 8 serving pieces. Sprinkle with salt, pepper and garlic powder.

1   large onion, chopped
1   red pepper, chopped
3   cloves garlic, minced
4   tablespoons butter

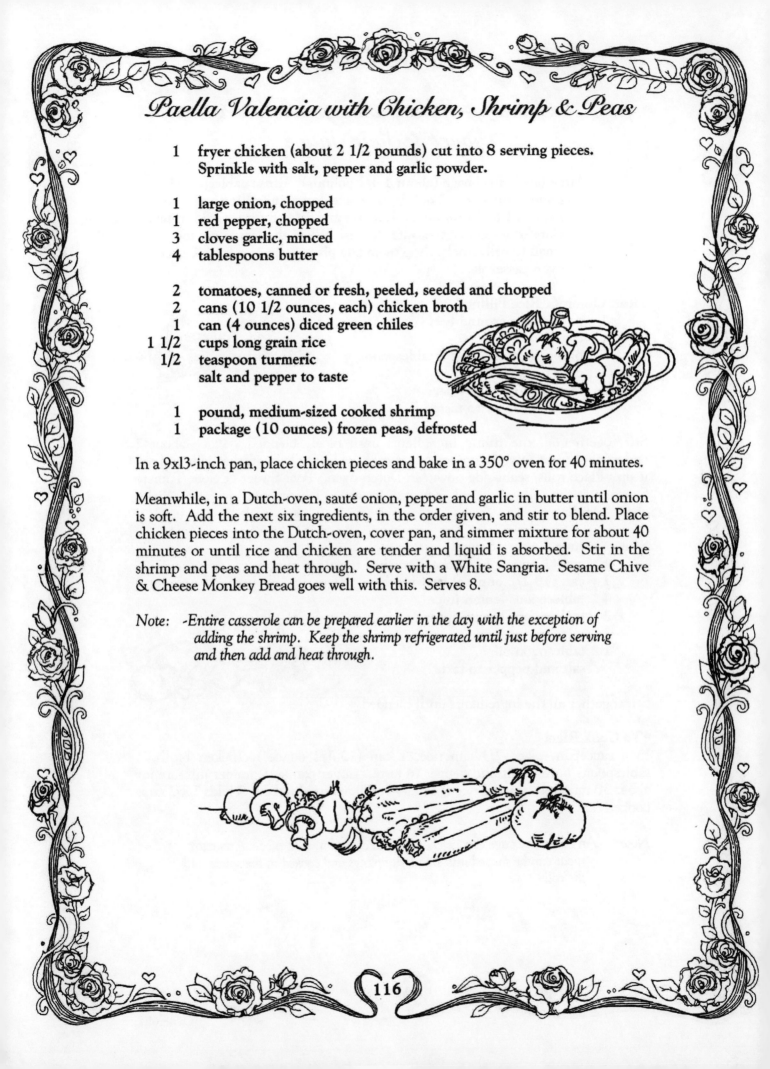

2   tomatoes, canned or fresh, peeled, seeded and chopped
2   cans (10 1/2 ounces, each) chicken broth
1   can (4 ounces) diced green chiles
1 1/2   cups long grain rice
1/2   teaspoon turmeric
     salt and pepper to taste

1   pound, medium-sized cooked shrimp
1   package (10 ounces) frozen peas, defrosted

In a 9x13-inch pan, place chicken pieces and bake in a 350° oven for 40 minutes.

Meanwhile, in a Dutch-oven, sauté onion, pepper and garlic in butter until onion is soft. Add the next six ingredients, in the order given, and stir to blend. Place chicken pieces into the Dutch-oven, cover pan, and simmer mixture for about 40 minutes or until rice and chicken are tender and liquid is absorbed. Stir in the shrimp and peas and heat through. Serve with a White Sangria. Sesame Chive & Cheese Monkey Bread goes well with this. Serves 8.

Note: -Entire casserole can be prepared earlier in the day with the exception of adding the shrimp. Keep the shrimp refrigerated until just before serving and then add and heat through.

Chicken Paella Darling

This is a very delicious, jiffy paella, that makes leftover chicken or turkey festive enough for a dinner party. Please do not cook the chicken with the rice, as it will toughen up. Cook the rice separately and then mix in the chicken with the chile mixture

3	cups cooked chicken or turkey, cut into large dice
2	large onions, chopped
3	tablespoons oil
1	can (4 ounces) Ortega diced green chiles
2	tomatoes, chopped coarsely

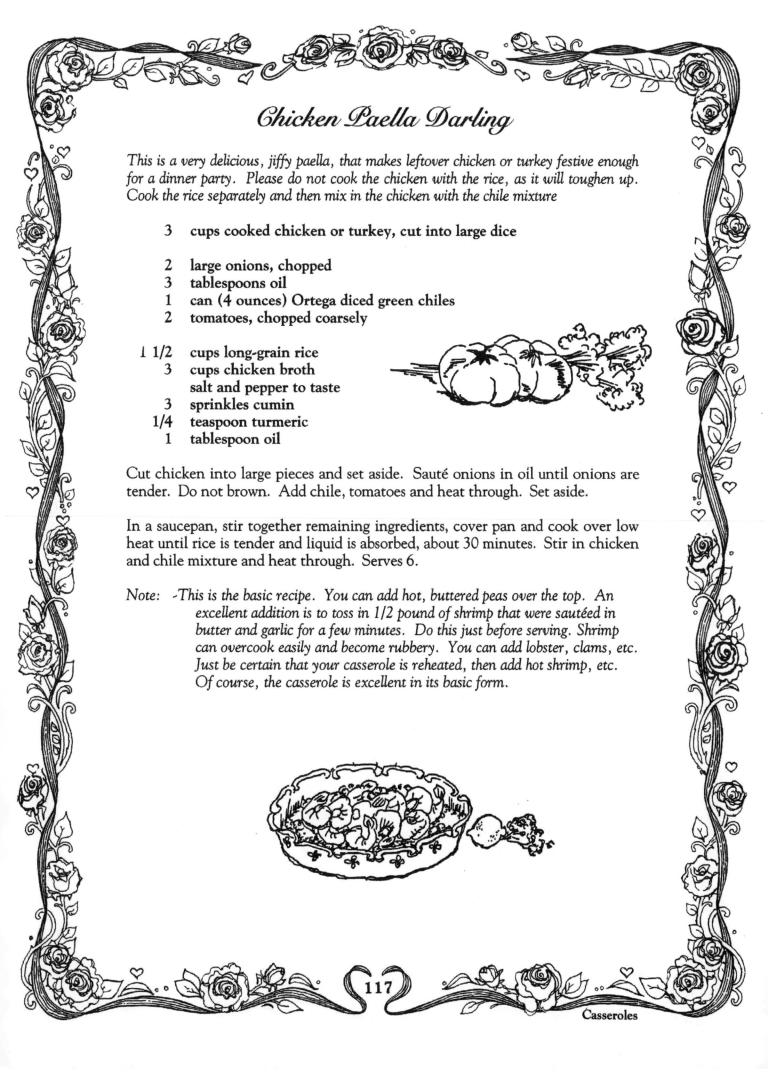

1 1/2	cups long-grain rice
3	cups chicken broth
	salt and pepper to taste
3	sprinkles cumin
1/4	teaspoon turmeric
1	tablespoon oil

Cut chicken into large pieces and set aside. Sauté onions in oil until onions are tender. Do not brown. Add chile, tomatoes and heat through. Set aside.

In a saucepan, stir together remaining ingredients, cover pan and cook over low heat until rice is tender and liquid is absorbed, about 30 minutes. Stir in chicken and chile mixture and heat through. Serves 6.

Note: -This is the basic recipe. You can add hot, buttered peas over the top. An excellent addition is to toss in 1/2 pound of shrimp that were sautéed in butter and garlic for a few minutes. Do this just before serving. Shrimp can overcook easily and become rubbery. You can add lobster, clams, etc. Just be certain that your casserole is reheated, then add hot shrimp, etc. Of course, the casserole is excellent in its basic form.

Country-Style Pudding with Orange & Pineapple

What a delectable pudding to serve with roast chicken on Sunday night when the whole family gets together. Invite a few friends for this recipe serves 12.

1	package (8 ounces) medium noodles, cooked according to the directions on the package.
1/2	cup (1 stick) melted butter
4	eggs
1	cup sugar
2	cups sour cream
1	teaspoon vanilla
1/4	teaspoon salt
1	can (8 ounces) crushed pineapple. Do not drain.
1/2	orange, grated. Use fruit, juice and peel.
1	cup yellow raisins
2	tablespoons cinnamon sugar

In a 9x13-inch pan, toss together cooked noodles with melted butter until blended.

Beat together next 5 ingredients until blended. Stir in pineapple, orange and yellow raisins. Pour mixture evenly over the noodles and ease noodles so that the filling flows to the bottom. Sprinkle top with cinnamon sugar. Bake in a 350° oven for 1 hour or until top is golden brown. Cut into squares and serve warm. Serves 10 to 12.

Crown Mold of Noodles & Spiced Peaches

1	package (8 ounces) medium noodles, cooked and drained
1/2	cup (1 stick) butter, melted
4	tablespoons cinnamon sugar
1	can (1 pound) spiced peaches, drained, pitted and chopped. Reserve juice for another use.
1/2	cup yellow raisins
3	eggs
1 1/2	cups sour cream
3/4	cup sugar
1	teaspoon vanilla
1/4	teaspoon salt

In a bowl, toss together first 5 ingredients and pour mixture into a 2-quart round, smooth, greased mold. Beat together remaining ingredients, and pour into the mold. Place mold on a cookie sheet and bake in a 350° oven for about 1 hour or until top is golden and custard is set. Unfold onto a lovely platter and serve warm. Serves 10.

Noodle Casserole with Sour Cream and Cheese

1/2   pound wide egg noodles, cooked and drained
1/4   cup butter, (1/2 stick), melted

4   eggs
1   pint sour cream
1   cup cottage cheese

1/2   cup chopped green onions
2   tablespoons finely chopped parsley
1/8   teaspoon garlic powder
1/2   cup Parmesan cheese, grated
     salt and pepper to taste

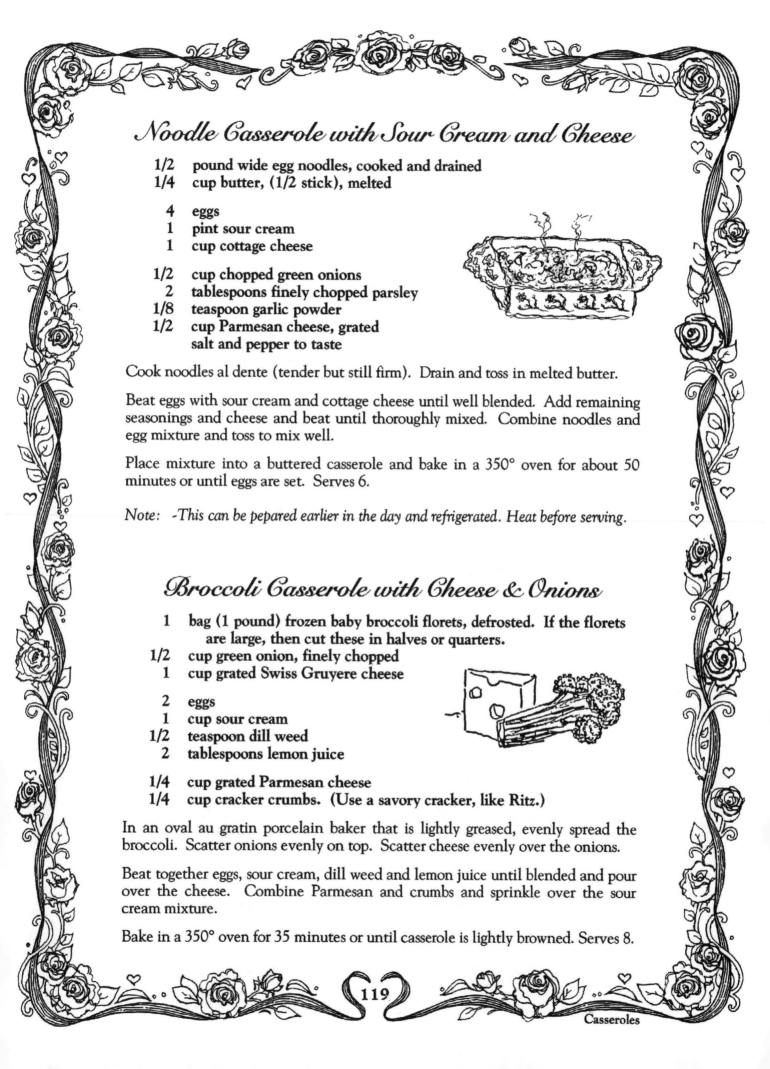

Cook noodles al dente (tender but still firm). Drain and toss in melted butter.

Beat eggs with sour cream and cottage cheese until well blended. Add remaining seasonings and cheese and beat until thoroughly mixed. Combine noodles and egg mixture and toss to mix well.

Place mixture into a buttered casserole and bake in a 350° oven for about 50 minutes or until eggs are set. Serves 6.

Note: -This can be pepared earlier in the day and refrigerated. Heat before serving.

Broccoli Casserole with Cheese & Onions

1   bag (1 pound) frozen baby broccoli florets, defrosted. If the florets are large, then cut these in halves or quarters.
1/2   cup green onion, finely chopped
1   cup grated Swiss Gruyere cheese

2   eggs
1   cup sour cream
1/2   teaspoon dill weed
2   tablespoons lemon juice

1/4   cup grated Parmesan cheese
1/4   cup cracker crumbs. (Use a savory cracker, like Ritz.)

In an oval au gratin porcelain baker that is lightly greased, evenly spread the broccoli. Scatter onions evenly on top. Scatter cheese evenly over the onions.

Beat together eggs, sour cream, dill weed and lemon juice until blended and pour over the cheese. Combine Parmesan and crumbs and sprinkle over the sour cream mixture.

Bake in a 350° oven for 35 minutes or until casserole is lightly browned. Serves 8.

Noodle Lasagna Italienne

3/4   pound wide egg noodles, cooked and drained

Sauce:
- 1   onion, finely chopped
- 1   tablespoon oil
- 1   pound ground beef
- 1   can (1 pound 12 ounces) diced tomatoes
- 1   can (6 ounces) tomato paste
- 1   teaspoon sugar
- 1   teaspoon Italian Herb Seasoning
  salt and pepper to taste

Cheese Filling:
- 1   pound Ricotta cheese
- 3   eggs
- 1/2   cup grated Parmesan cheese

Sauté onion in oil until onion is soft. Add ground beef and continue sautéing, crumbling the beef, until beef is cooked through. Add tomatoes, tomato paste, sugar and seasonings and simmer gently for 20 minutes. Set sauce aside.

Beat together the Ricotta cheese, eggs and grated cheese.

Spread a thin layer of sauce in a 9x13-inch baking pan. Place half the noodles over the sauce. Follow with half the cheese mixture and half the sauce. Repeat, layering the remaining noodles, cheese mixture and sauce. Sprinkle top generously with additional grated Parmesan cheese.

Bake casserole in a 350° oven for about 35 minutes or until piping hot. Serve with some Hot Garlic Cheese Bread. Serves 6.

Note: -Entire casserole can be assembled earlier in the day and refrigerated. When reheating, allow to come to room temperature and heat as described above.

Hot Garlic Cheese Bread:
- 12   slices thinly sliced Italian bread (about 1/4-inch thick)
- 1   egg, beaten
- 6   tablespoons grated Parmesan cheese
- 1/4   teaspoon coarse-grind garlic powder

Place bread in 1 layer on a cookie sheet. Beat together egg, cheese and garlic powder until blended. Brush mixture on top of bread slices. Bake in a 350° oven for 10 minutes or until topping is starting to bubble. Broil for a few seconds to brown tops. Serve at once. Yields 12 slices.

Noodle & Spinach Casserole with Marinara Sauce

1	pound wide egg noodles, cooked until tender but firm. Drain and toss noodles in 1/2 cup (1 stick) butter.
1	package (8 ounces) cream cheese
2	cups Ricotta cheese
1	package (8 ounces) Mozzeralla cheese, grated
2	green onions, finely chopped
1	package (10 ounces) frozen spinach, defrosted and drained
2	eggs
1/2	teaspoon Italian Herb Seasoning
	salt and pepper to taste
1/2	cup grated Parmesan cheese

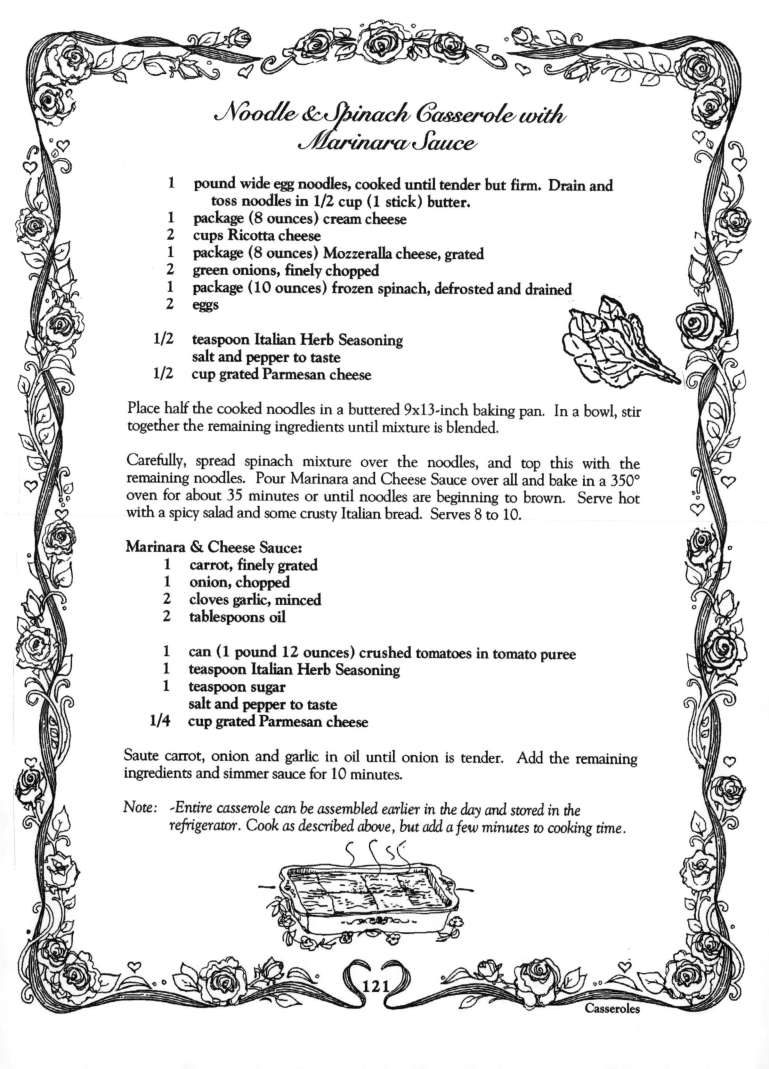

Place half the cooked noodles in a buttered 9x13-inch baking pan. In a bowl, stir together the remaining ingredients until mixture is blended.

Carefully, spread spinach mixture over the noodles, and top this with the remaining noodles. Pour Marinara and Cheese Sauce over all and bake in a 350° oven for about 35 minutes or until noodles are beginning to brown. Serve hot with a spicy salad and some crusty Italian bread. Serves 8 to 10.

Marinara & Cheese Sauce:

1	carrot, finely grated
1	onion, chopped
2	cloves garlic, minced
2	tablespoons oil
1	can (1 pound 12 ounces) crushed tomatoes in tomato puree
1	teaspoon Italian Herb Seasoning
1	teaspoon sugar
	salt and pepper to taste
1/4	cup grated Parmesan cheese

Saute carrot, onion and garlic in oil until onion is tender. Add the remaining ingredients and simmer sauce for 10 minutes.

Note: -Entire casserole can be assembled earlier in the day and stored in the refrigerator. Cook as described above, but add a few minutes to cooking time.

121

Old West Tamale Casserole with Sour Cream, Chili & Cheese

There is probably no dish that you can make that is easier than this one or more fun to eat. Everybody loves it. Serve it with hot corn tortillas, spread with a little sweet butter.

- 8 prepared tamales (about 3 ounces, each) from the refrigerated section in your market. Cut tamales into 1-inch slices.
- 1 chili brick (1 pound) from the refrigerated section in your market
- 1 can (1 pound) stewed tomatoes, chopped. Do not drain.

- 1 cup sour cream
- 2 cups medium sharp Cheddar cheese, grated (4 ounces)
- 1/2 cup chopped green onions

In a 12-inch porcelain baker, place tamale slices evenly. Heat together the chili brick and stewed tomatoes until mixture is blended. (If chile is very thick, dilute with 1/2 cup beef broth.)

Spread chile mixture over the tamale slices. Spread sour cream on top and sprinkle with grated cheese and green onions. Heat in a 350° oven for about 30 to 40 minutes or until casserole is heated through and cheese is melted. Serve with pink rice. Serves 8.

Red Hot Lentil Chili

Lentils are becoming more and more popular in recipes other than soup. Here, I spice them with chili, cumin and cayenne pepper. An interesting dish and simple to prepare.

- 1 package (1 pound) lentils, rinsed and picked over for particles
- 2 large onions, chopped
- 6 cloves garlic, minced
- 3 carrots, grated
- 1 can (28 ounces) crushed tomatoes in puree
- 8 cups chicken broth
- 4 tablespoons chili powder
- 2 teaspoons ground cumin
- 2 teaspoons sugar
- 1 teaspoon oregano flakes
- 1/8 teaspoon cayenne pepper
  salt and pepper to taste

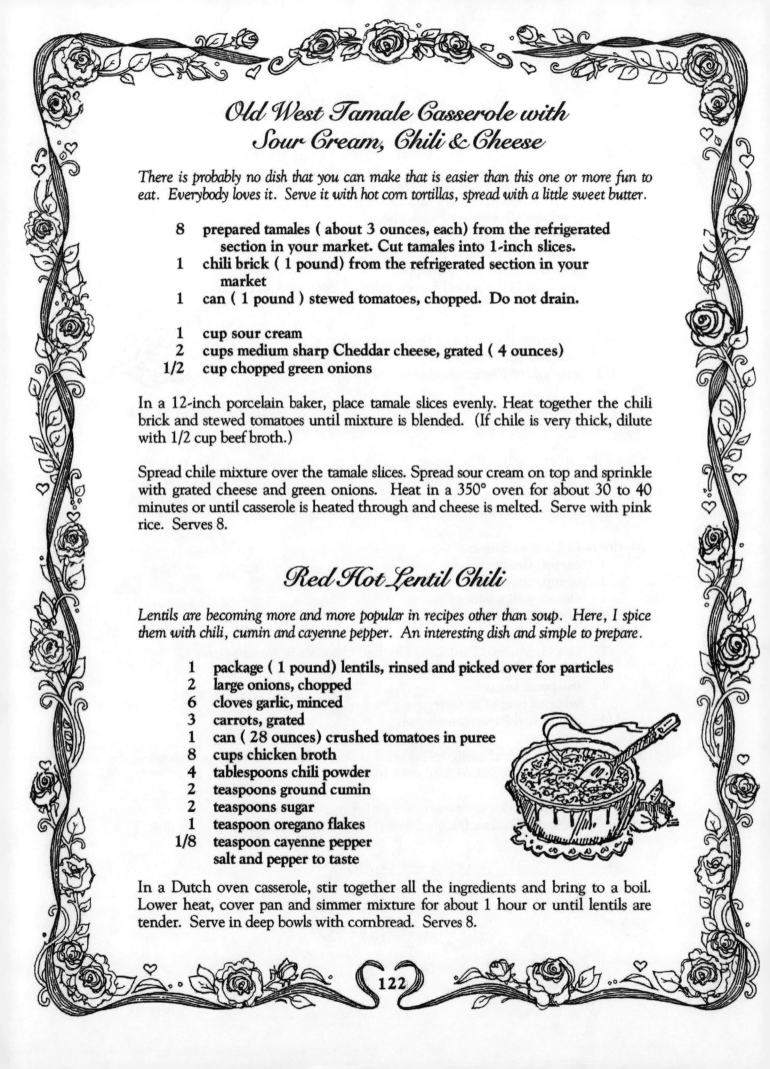

In a Dutch oven casserole, stir together all the ingredients and bring to a boil. Lower heat, cover pan and simmer mixture for about 1 hour or until lentils are tender. Serve in deep bowls with cornbread. Serves 8.

Chili con Carne

This is another Chili con Carne, but made with beans. The flavor is wonderful. If your family does not like beans, then omit them.

3	onions, chopped
6	cloves garlic, minced
2	tablespoons oil
3	pounds boneless chuck steak, coarsely ground ("chili grind")
2	cans (10 1/2 ounces, each) beef broth
3	tablespoons Masa Harina (finely ground corn meal)
4	tablespoons chili powder (or more to taste)
1	tablespoon cumin powder
1	tablespoon paprika
1	tablespoon dried oregano flakes
1	can (16 ounces) tomato sauce
2	teaspoons sugar
1/4	teaspoon red pepper flakes, (or more to taste)
1	can (1 pound) red kidney beans, rinsed and drained (optional)
1	can (7 ounces) diced green chiles

In a Dutch oven casserole, sauté onions and garlic in oil until onions are softened. Add the beef and cook until the meat loses its pinkness. Stir beef broth with Masa Harina and add to casserole. Stir in the remaining ingredients and simmer mixture, partially uncovered, for 45 minutes, or until meat is tender and mixture is thickened. Serve with Biscuits with Chile & Cheese. Serves 8.

Biscuits with Chiles & Cheese:

1 1/2	cups all-purpose flour
2	teaspoons baking powder
1	teaspoon baking soda
	pinch of salt
3	tablespoons butter
1	can (4 ounces) diced green chiles
3	ounces sharp cheddar cheese, grated
1	cup sour cream

In the large bowl of an electric mixer, beat together first group of ingredients, until mixture resembles coarse meal. Stir together the remaining ingredients, and add, all at once, stirring lightly, until mixture forms a soft dough. Do not overmix.

On a floured pastry cloth, pat dough out into a 1/2-inch-thick circle. Cut into rounds with a 3-inch biscuit cutter. Gather scraps and cut into additional rounds. Place rounds on an ungreased cookie sheet and bake at 425° for about 15 minutes, or until biscuits are golden. Yields 8.

Big Chile Relleno with Chile Salsa & Pink Rice

There is no way you would judge this delicious Mexican dish as a diet casserole, but at approximately 350 calories, including the rice, it most assuredly is. This will appeal to those with a keen and spicy palate. You may add an extra dash or two of Tabasco Sauce to the salsa, if you like it very hot.

- 4 ounces low-fat Mozzarella cheese, grated
- 6 ounces cooked chicken, coarsely chopped (white meat only)
- 2 tablespoons grated Parmesan cheese
- 2 tablespoons chopped green onions
- 2 tablespoons chopped cilantro

- 1 can (7 ounces) whole green chiles. Carefully remove seeds.
- 4 teaspoons low-fat sour cream

In a bowl, stir together first 5 ingredients until nicely mixed. Divide mixture and stuff the chiles. Place chiles in one layer in an 8x12-inch baking pan and spread Tomato & Chile Salsa over the top.

Bake in a 350° oven for about 15 minutes, or until cheese is melted. Serve with a teaspoon of sour cream on top. Pink Chile Rice is an excellent accompaniment. Serves 4.

Tomato & Chile Salsa:
Stir together until blended:
1/2 cup canned chopped stewed tomatoes, 1 can (4 ounces) diced green chiles, 4 tablespoons finely chopped green onions, 4 tablespoons finely chopped cilantro, 2 tablespoons vinegar, 1/8 teaspoon garlic powder, dash of Tabasco Sauce.

Pink Chile Rice:
In a saucepan, stir together 3/4 cup rice, 1 1/2 cups chicken broth, 1/4 cup chopped stewed tomatoes, 1/2 teaspoon chili powder, 1/2 teaspoon ground cumin. Cover pan and simmer mixture for 30 minutes, or until rice is tender and liquid is absorbed. Serves 4.

Note: -If the whole chiles are small, then sprinkle any left-over stuffing over the tops of the chiles in the pan.
-1 can (1 pound) stewed tomatoes, drained and chopped will be sufficient for the rice and salsa. Use juice for another use.
-Entire dish can be assembled earlier in the day and heated before serving.

Another Family Favorite,
Chile Con Carne & Hot Garlic Cheese Bread

This is my son's favorite chili. It is very traditional and does not include beans. When we were young, my mother always served it with beans and pink rice on the side. This might offend purists, but as children we loved it . . . and I still do.

3	onions, chopped
2	teaspoons minced garlic (about 6 cloves)
2	tablespoons oil
2	pounds coarsely ground lean beef (chili grind)
1	pound coarsely ground lean pork (chili grind)
2	cans (10-1/2 ounces, each) beef broth
3	tablespoons Masa Harina (finely ground corn meal)
1	can (1 pound 12 ounces) crushed tomatoes in tomato puree
1	can (7 ounces) diced green chiles
4 to 6	tablespoons chili powder
2	teaspoons sugar
1	teaspoon oregano
1	teaspoon cumin
	salt to taste

In a Dutch oven casserole, sauté onions and garlic in oil, until onions are transparent. Add the beef and pork, and cook until the meat loses its pinkness. Stir beef broth with Masa Harina and add to casserole. Stir in the remaining ingredients and simmer mixture, partially uncovered, for about 45 minutes. Mixture should be very thick. Serve with thick slices of Hot Garlic Cheese Bread. Yields about 2 quarts chili ... and will serve from 4 to 6.

Hot Garlic Cheese Bread:

12	slices thinly sliced French bread (about 1/4-inch thick)
1	egg, beaten
6	tablespoons grated Parmesan cheese
1/4	teaspoon garlic powder

Place bread in 1 layer on cookie sheet. Beat together egg, cheese, and garlic powder until blended. Brush mixture on top of bread slices. Bake for 5 minutes at 350°. Broil for a few seconds to brown tops. Serve at once.

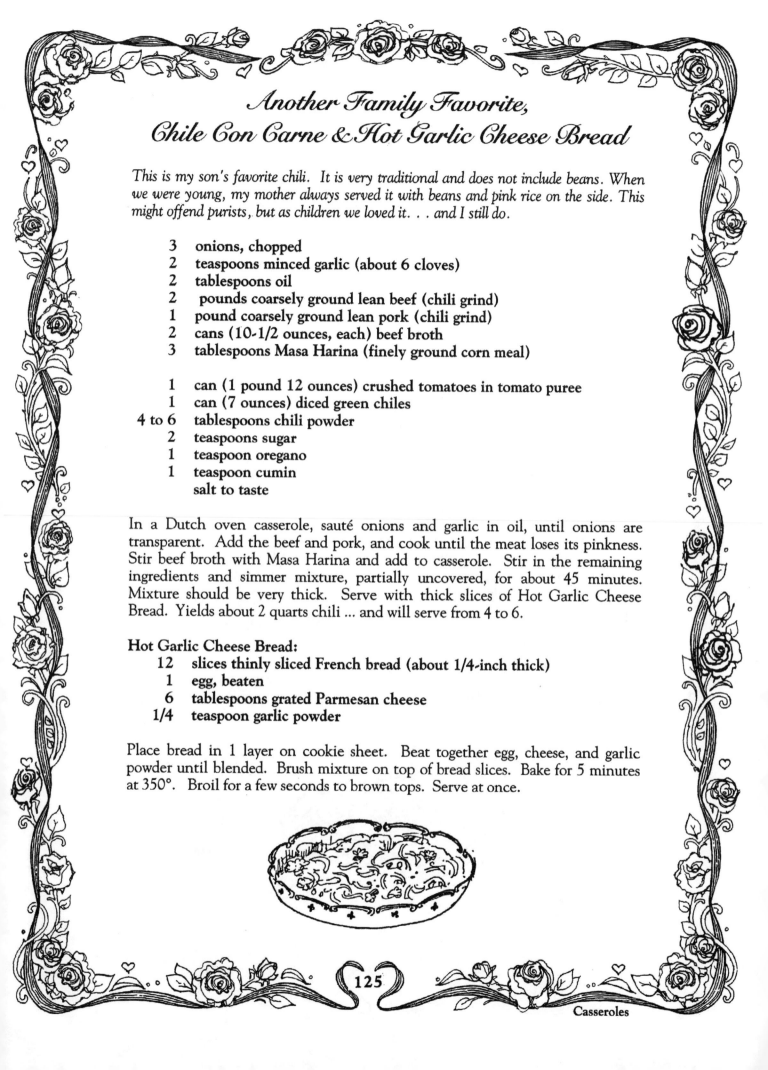

Spanish Chicken with Yellow Rice

This is a very delicious casserole and the only work is slicing the few sauce ingredients. It is great to prepare with leftover chicken or turkey. This is a fun meal and has the meat, vegetable and starch all in one. I think you will enjoy it a lot. This can be prepared earlier in the day, and heated before serving.

For the Sauce:

2	onions, chopped
2	cloves garlic, mashed
3	tablespoons butter
1/2	pound sliced mushrooms
2	tomatoes, coarsely chopped
1	package (10 ounces) frozen petite green peas
3	cups cooked chicken cubes

For the Rice:

1 1/2	cups rice
3	cups chicken broth
2	tablespoons oil
1/2	teaspoon turmeric
	salt and pepper to taste

In a saucepan, simmer together Sauce ingredients until onions and mushrooms are soft. Add the peas and cook for about 5 minutes, or until peas are tender. Stir in the cooked chicken.

Meanwhile, in another saucepan, stir together Rice ingredients, cover pan and simmer mixture for 30 minutes, or until rice is tender.

When ready to serve, stir together rice and sauce and heat through. Serve with some warm tortillas, and enjoy.

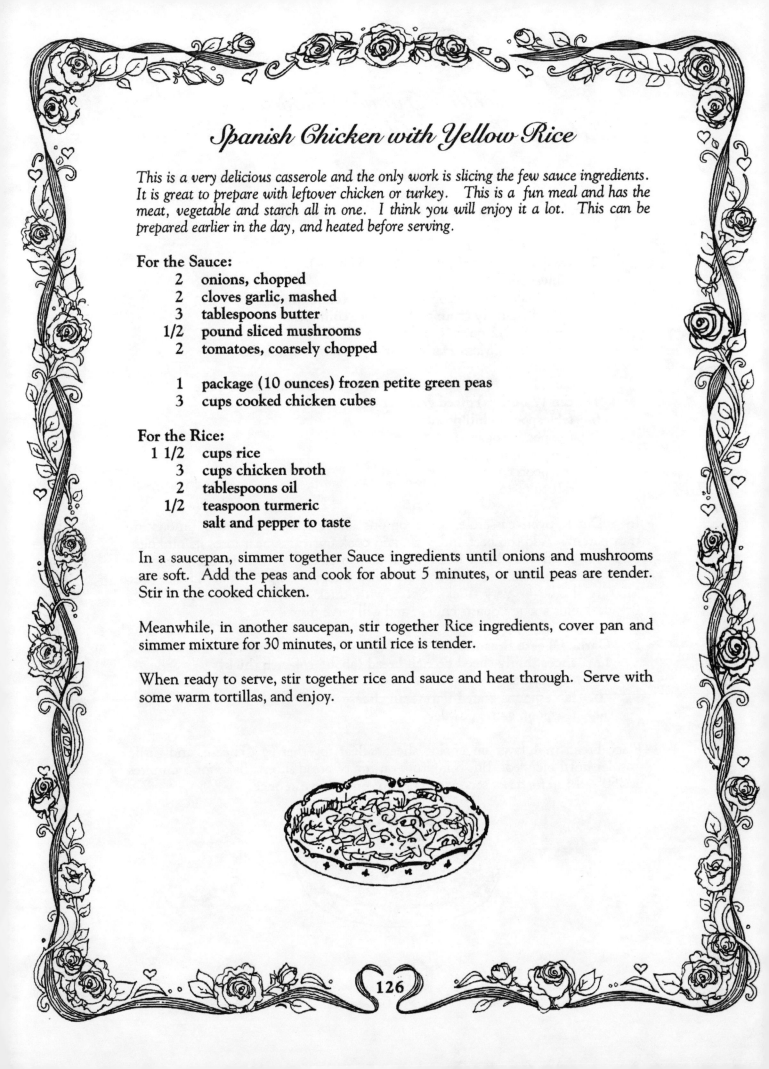

Curried Chicken with Raisins & Rice

This is a very delicious and quick curry dish that can make leftover chicken or turkey grand enough for a dinner party and yet is easy enough to serve on an evening when you are running late.

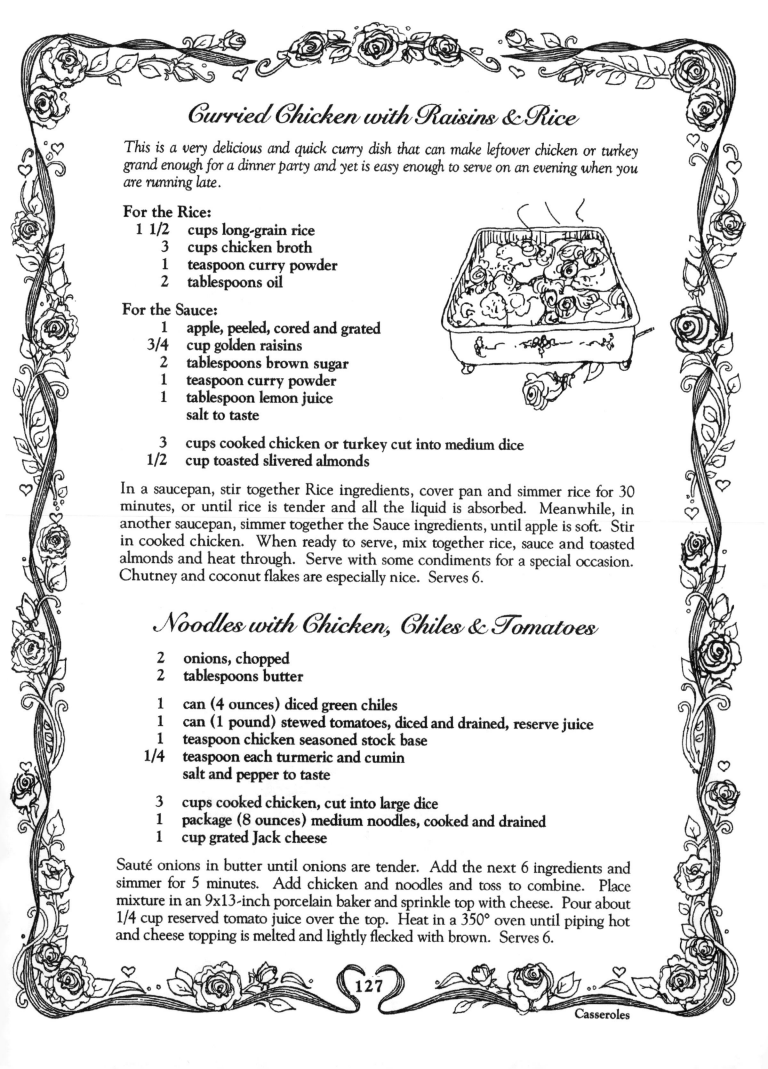

For the Rice:

1 1/2	cups long-grain rice
3	cups chicken broth
1	teaspoon curry powder
2	tablespoons oil

For the Sauce:

1	apple, peeled, cored and grated
3/4	cup golden raisins
2	tablespoons brown sugar
1	teaspoon curry powder
1	tablespoon lemon juice
	salt to taste
3	cups cooked chicken or turkey cut into medium dice
1/2	cup toasted slivered almonds

In a saucepan, stir together Rice ingredients, cover pan and simmer rice for 30 minutes, or until rice is tender and all the liquid is absorbed. Meanwhile, in another saucepan, simmer together the Sauce ingredients, until apple is soft. Stir in cooked chicken. When ready to serve, mix together rice, sauce and toasted almonds and heat through. Serve with some condiments for a special occasion. Chutney and coconut flakes are especially nice. Serves 6.

Noodles with Chicken, Chiles & Tomatoes

2	onions, chopped
2	tablespoons butter
1	can (4 ounces) diced green chiles
1	can (1 pound) stewed tomatoes, diced and drained, reserve juice
1	teaspoon chicken seasoned stock base
1/4	teaspoon each turmeric and cumin
	salt and pepper to taste
3	cups cooked chicken, cut into large dice
1	package (8 ounces) medium noodles, cooked and drained
1	cup grated Jack cheese

Sauté onions in butter until onions are tender. Add the next 6 ingredients and simmer for 5 minutes. Add chicken and noodles and toss to combine. Place mixture in an 9x13-inch porcelain baker and sprinkle top with cheese. Pour about 1/4 cup reserved tomato juice over the top. Heat in a 350° oven until piping hot and cheese topping is melted and lightly flecked with brown. Serves 6.

Eggplant Lasagna with Tomatoes, Onion & Ricotta Cheese

6   Japanese eggplants, sliced. (Or 1 medium eggplant, cut into quarters and thinly sliced.) About 1 pound. Do not peel.
1   can (1 pound) stewed tomatoes. Do not drain.
1   can (8 ounces) tomato sauce
1   onion, chopped
3   cloves garlic, minced
1/2   teaspoon sweet basil flakes
1/2   teaspoon Italian Herb Seasoning
1   teaspoon sugar (optional)
     salt and pepper to taste

1   pint Ricotta cheese
2   eggs
1/3   cup grated Parmesan cheese
1   teaspoon sweet basil flakes

In a Dutch oven casserole, place first 9 ingredients and simmer mixture for about 30 minutes, or until eggplant is soft.

Meanwhile, beat together Ricotta, eggs, Parmesan and sweet basil until blended.

In a 9x13-inch baking pan, spread 1/2 the eggplant mixture. Top with Ricotta cheese mixture and then, remaining eggplant mixture. Sprinkle top with 1 tablespoon grated Parmesan (optional).

Bake in a 350° oven for about 20 minutes or until cheese layer is set. Cut into squares and serve 8.

Note: -Casserole can be baked earlier in the day and heated at serving time.

Baked Pasta with Meat Sauce & Mozzarella

3/4 pound noodles, cooked and drained (use the wide egg noodles or the extra-wide lasagna noodles)
1   cup grated Mozzarella cheese
1   pound Ricotta cheese
1/2 cup grated Parmesan cheese

1/2 cup additional Mozzarella cheese, grated

Mix together the noodles, Mozzarella, Ricotta and Parmesan cheese. In a 9x13-inch lasagna pan, lay alternate layers of Meat Sauce and noodle mixture, starting and ending with the meat sauce. Sprinkle top with additional Mozzarella.

Bake casserole in a 350° oven for 30 minutes or until heated through. Yields 6 servings.

Meat Sauce:
1   onion, finely chopped
1   tablespoon butter
1   pound lean ground beef

1   can (1 pound 12 ounces) crushed tomatoes in puree
1   tablespoon sugar
1   teaspoon Italian Herb Seasoning
1   bay leaf
1   tablespoon chopped parsley
     salt and pepper to taste

Sauté onion in butter until onions are soft. Add ground beef and sauté until meat loses its pinkness. Add the remaining ingredients and simmer mixture for 10 minutes. Remove bay leaf. Use on spaghetti and lasagna.

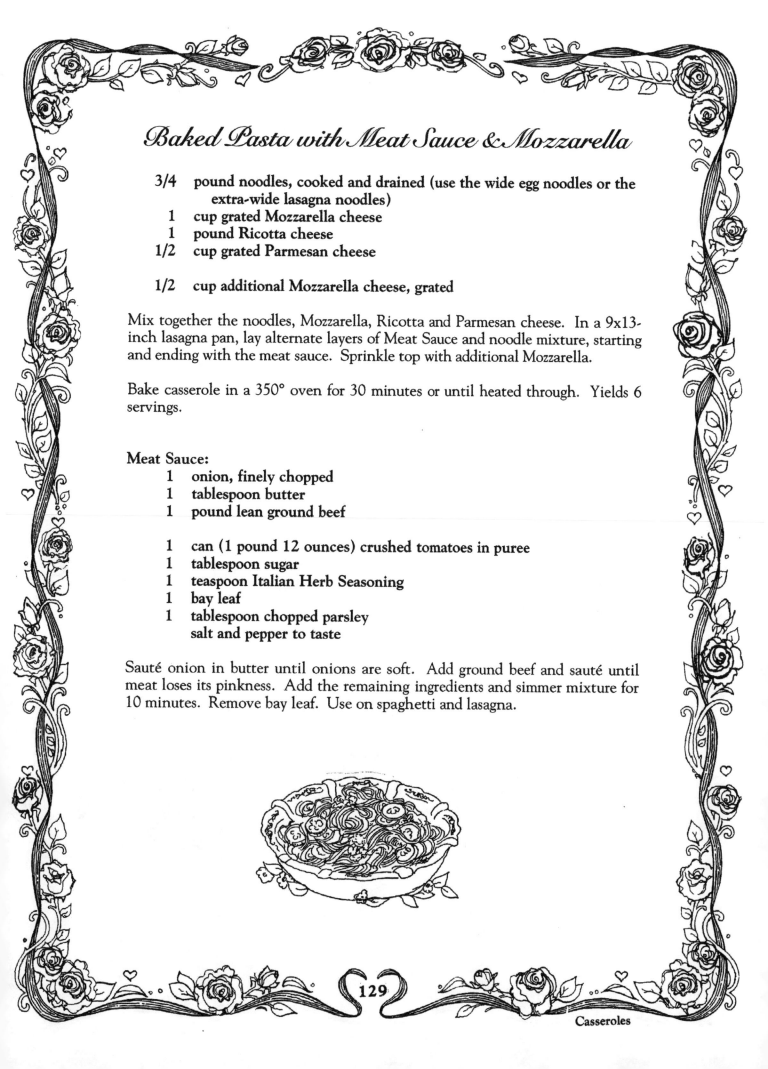

Oven-Fried Eggplant Parmesan with 5-Minute Tomato Sauce

This is a delicious side dish or a great first course. It can be prepared earlier in the day and heated before serving. The sauce is one of the best...very simple, rich and flavorful. Sauce is wonderful over pasta, too.

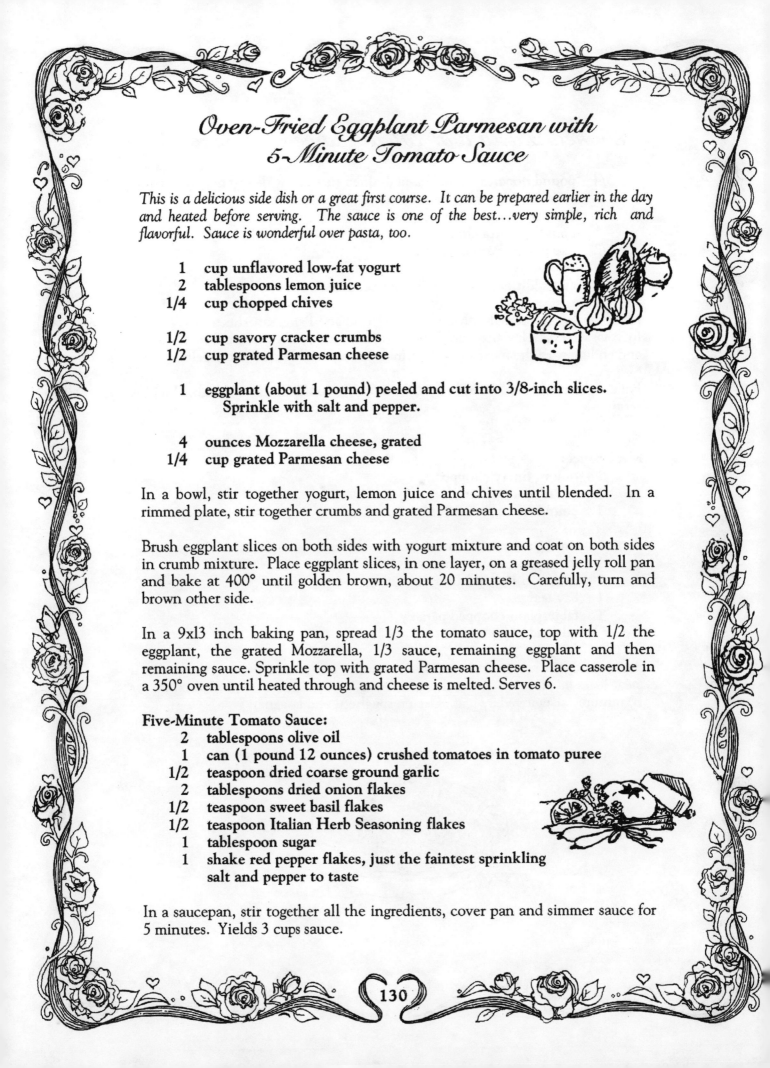

1	cup unflavored low-fat yogurt
2	tablespoons lemon juice
1/4	cup chopped chives
1/2	cup savory cracker crumbs
1/2	cup grated Parmesan cheese
1	eggplant (about 1 pound) peeled and cut into 3/8-inch slices. Sprinkle with salt and pepper.
4	ounces Mozzarella cheese, grated
1/4	cup grated Parmesan cheese

In a bowl, stir together yogurt, lemon juice and chives until blended. In a rimmed plate, stir together crumbs and grated Parmesan cheese.

Brush eggplant slices on both sides with yogurt mixture and coat on both sides in crumb mixture. Place eggplant slices, in one layer, on a greased jelly roll pan and bake at 400° until golden brown, about 20 minutes. Carefully, turn and brown other side.

In a 9x13 inch baking pan, spread 1/3 the tomato sauce, top with 1/2 the eggplant, the grated Mozzarella, 1/3 sauce, remaining eggplant and then remaining sauce. Sprinkle top with grated Parmesan cheese. Place casserole in a 350° oven until heated through and cheese is melted. Serves 6.

Five-Minute Tomato Sauce:

2	tablespoons olive oil
1	can (1 pound 12 ounces) crushed tomatoes in tomato puree
1/2	teaspoon dried coarse ground garlic
2	tablespoons dried onion flakes
1/2	teaspoon sweet basil flakes
1/2	teaspoon Italian Herb Seasoning flakes
1	tablespoon sugar
1	shake red pepper flakes, just the faintest sprinkling
	salt and pepper to taste

In a saucepan, stir together all the ingredients, cover pan and simmer sauce for 5 minutes. Yields 3 cups sauce.

Pastitsio a la Grecque

Pastitsio is a Greek version of pasta and meat in casserole. It is basically easy to prepare and very easy to serve. Traditionally topped with a cream sauce, I prefer to omit it. Beef or lamb can be used in the filling.

Meat Filling:

2	large onions, chopped
6	cloves garlic, minced
2	tablespoons olive oil
2	pounds lean ground lamb or beef
1	can (1 pound 12 ounces) chopped tomatoes in puree
1	can (3 ounces) tomato sauce
3	tablespoons chopped parsley leaves
1/4	teaspoon, each, cinnamon and nutmeg
	salt and pepper to taste

In a Dutch oven casserole, sauté onions and garlic in olive oil until onions are transparent. Add the ground meat and cook and stir, crumbling the meat until it is no longer pink. Stir in tomatoes, parsley and seasonings, cover pan and simmer mixture for 15 minutes or until sauce has thickened slightly.

Cheese Crumb Mixture:

1/2   cup grated Parmesan cheese mixed with 1/2 cup stale bread crumbs

Pasta:

1   pound pasta (ziti, penne or other small pasta), cooked in boiling water until tender, but firm and thoroughly drained. Toss with 2 tablespoons olive oil.

To Assemble:

In a 9x13-inch baking pan, layer half the meat filling, half the pasta, half the cheese/crumb mixture. Continue layering with the remaining meat, pasta and cheese/crumb mixture. Pat top down to settle the casserole. Bake in a 350° oven for 30 minutes, or until heated through and top is crusty brown. Serves 8 to 10.

Giant Shells Filled with Spinach & Cheese

This is a grand family dish, exceedingly attractive and simple to prepare. It can be prepared ahead and heated at serving time.

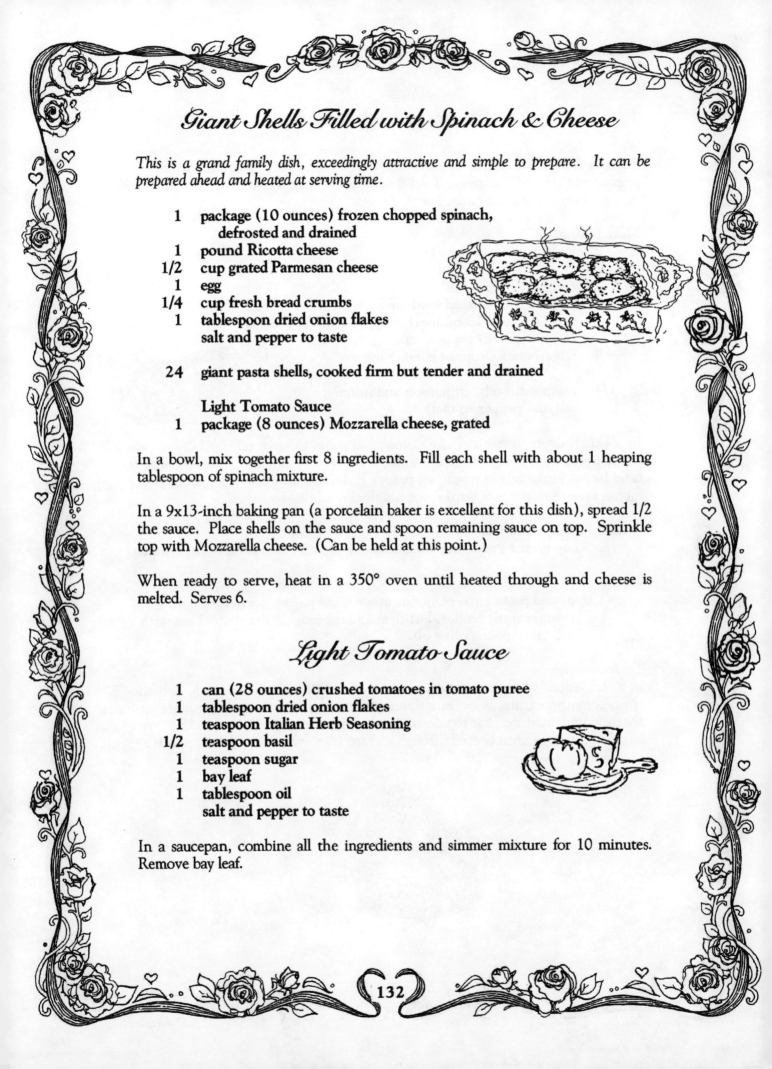

1   package (10 ounces) frozen chopped spinach,
       defrosted and drained
1   pound Ricotta cheese
1/2   cup grated Parmesan cheese
1   egg
1/4   cup fresh bread crumbs
1   tablespoon dried onion flakes
      salt and pepper to taste

24   giant pasta shells, cooked firm but tender and drained

      Light Tomato Sauce
1   package (8 ounces) Mozzarella cheese, grated

In a bowl, mix together first 8 ingredients. Fill each shell with about 1 heaping tablespoon of spinach mixture.

In a 9x13-inch baking pan (a porcelain baker is excellent for this dish), spread 1/2 the sauce. Place shells on the sauce and spoon remaining sauce on top. Sprinkle top with Mozzarella cheese. (Can be held at this point.)

When ready to serve, heat in a 350° oven until heated through and cheese is melted. Serves 6.

Light Tomato Sauce

1   can (28 ounces) crushed tomatoes in tomato puree
1   tablespoon dried onion flakes
1   teaspoon Italian Herb Seasoning
1/2   teaspoon basil
1   teaspoon sugar
1   bay leaf
1   tablespoon oil
      salt and pepper to taste

In a saucepan, combine all the ingredients and simmer mixture for 10 minutes. Remove bay leaf.

Honey Baked Beans with Bacon, Onions & Cheese

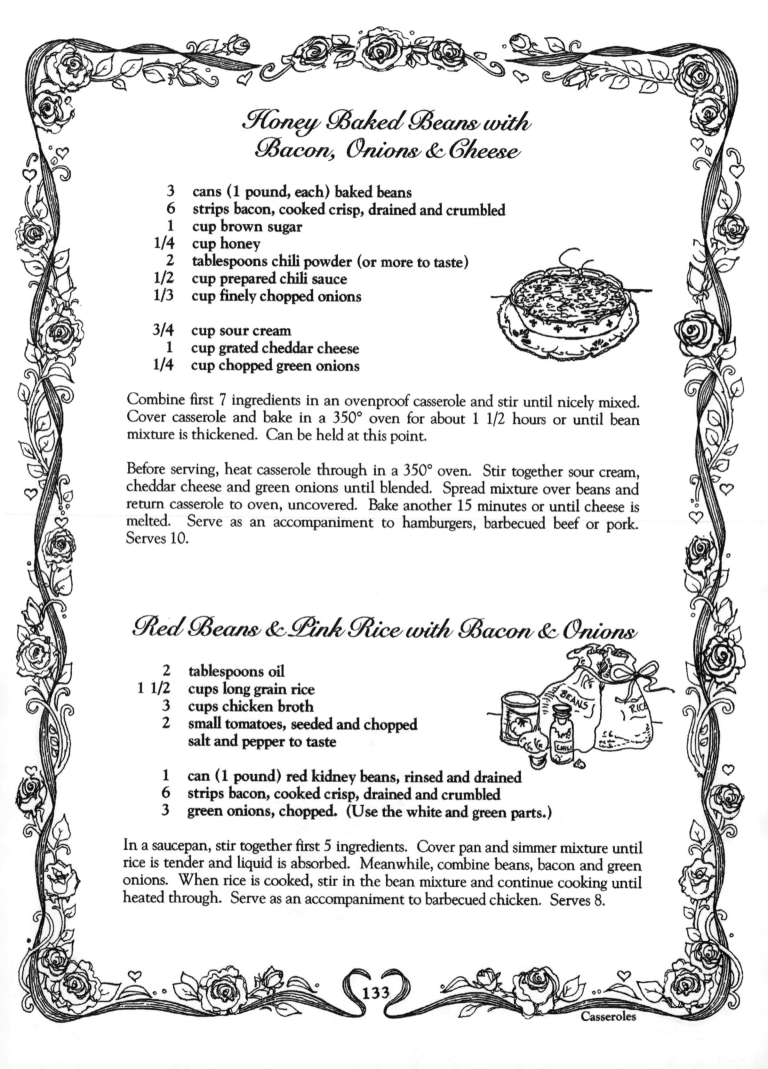

3	cans (1 pound, each) baked beans
6	strips bacon, cooked crisp, drained and crumbled
1	cup brown sugar
1/4	cup honey
2	tablespoons chili powder (or more to taste)
1/2	cup prepared chili sauce
1/3	cup finely chopped onions
3/4	cup sour cream
1	cup grated cheddar cheese
1/4	cup chopped green onions

Combine first 7 ingredients in an ovenproof casserole and stir until nicely mixed. Cover casserole and bake in a 350° oven for about 1 1/2 hours or until bean mixture is thickened. Can be held at this point.

Before serving, heat casserole through in a 350° oven. Stir together sour cream, cheddar cheese and green onions until blended. Spread mixture over beans and return casserole to oven, uncovered. Bake another 15 minutes or until cheese is melted. Serve as an accompaniment to hamburgers, barbecued beef or pork. Serves 10.

Red Beans & Pink Rice with Bacon & Onions

2	tablespoons oil
1 1/2	cups long grain rice
3	cups chicken broth
2	small tomatoes, seeded and chopped
	salt and pepper to taste
1	can (1 pound) red kidney beans, rinsed and drained
6	strips bacon, cooked crisp, drained and crumbled
3	green onions, chopped. (Use the white and green parts.)

In a saucepan, stir together first 5 ingredients. Cover pan and simmer mixture until rice is tender and liquid is absorbed. Meanwhile, combine beans, bacon and green onions. When rice is cooked, stir in the bean mixture and continue cooking until heated through. Serve as an accompaniment to barbecued chicken. Serves 8.

Tomatoes Stuffed with Turkey in Light Tomato Sauce

Using the ground turkey meat instead of beef reduces the number of calories and cholesterol. But it is still very delicious. This is a good dish to consider serving as a main course with rice. As an accompaniment to dinner, it will serve 8.

8	medium-sized firm tomatoes, 1 1/2 pounds
1/2	pound ground turkey, white meat
1/2	cup fresh bread crumbs (about 1 1/2 slices without crusts)
1	small onion, grated
1	egg, beaten
1	tablespoon chopped parsley
	pepper to taste

Cut l/4-inch off the tops of the tomatoes and scoop out pulp. Chop tomato pulp coarsely and set it aside for the sauce. Combine the remaining ingredients until blended and stuff tomatoes loosely with turkey mixture.

In an 10-inch round porcelain baker, place the tomatoes in one layer. Spoon Light Tomato Sauce over the top and bake in a 350° oven for about 30 to 40 minutes, or until meat is cooked through. Serves 4 as a main course.

Light Tomato Sauce:

1	teaspoon oil
	reserved chopped tomato pulp
1	can (1 pound) stewed tomatoes, chopped and drained. Reserve juice for another use.
1/4	teaspoon, each Italian Herb Seasoning and sweet basil flakes
1/8	teaspoon, each, garlic powder and onion powder
	pinch of cayenne pepper
	freshly ground black pepper to taste

Stir together all the ingredients until blended.

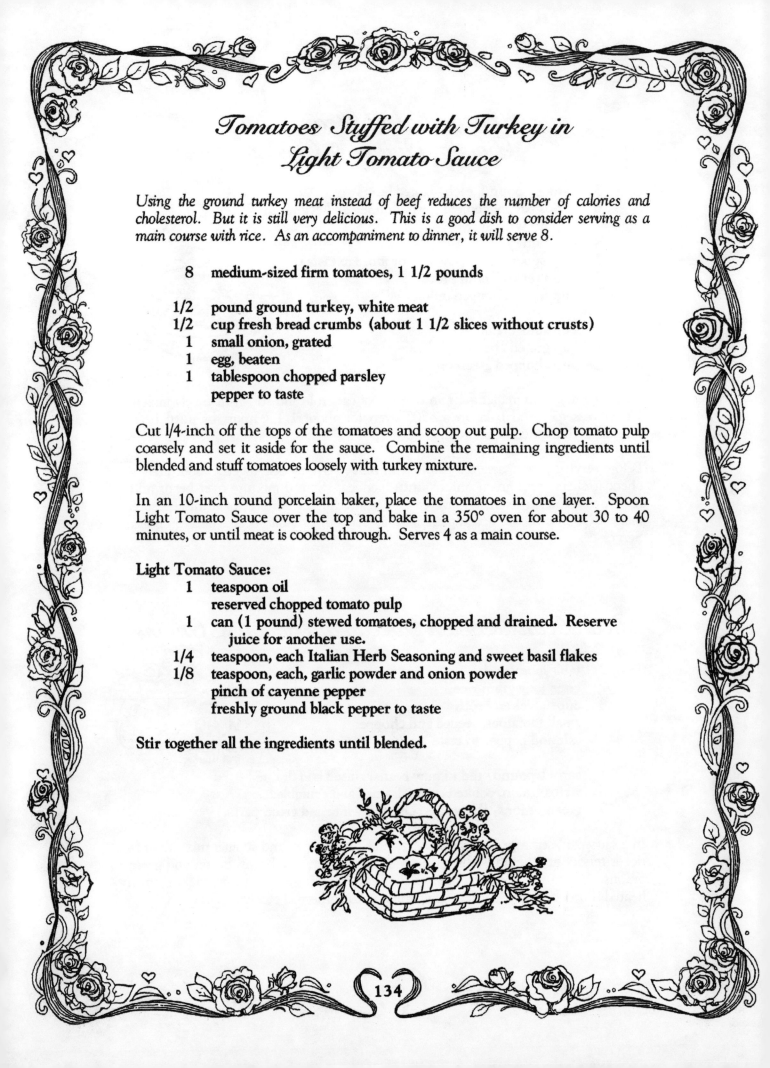

The Best Stuffed Tomatoes with Garlic & Herbs

I love stuffed tomatoes...as a first course or as an accompaniment to dinner. When we visited Italy, I ate one practically every day. These are very much like the ones we enjoyed, rather simple, pure flavors accented with a delicious sauce.

12   medium tomatoes (about 3 pounds). Cut a thin slice off the tops, scoop out the centers with a grapefruit knife and then a teaspoon. Reserve the tomato pulp.

Tomato & Rice Filling:

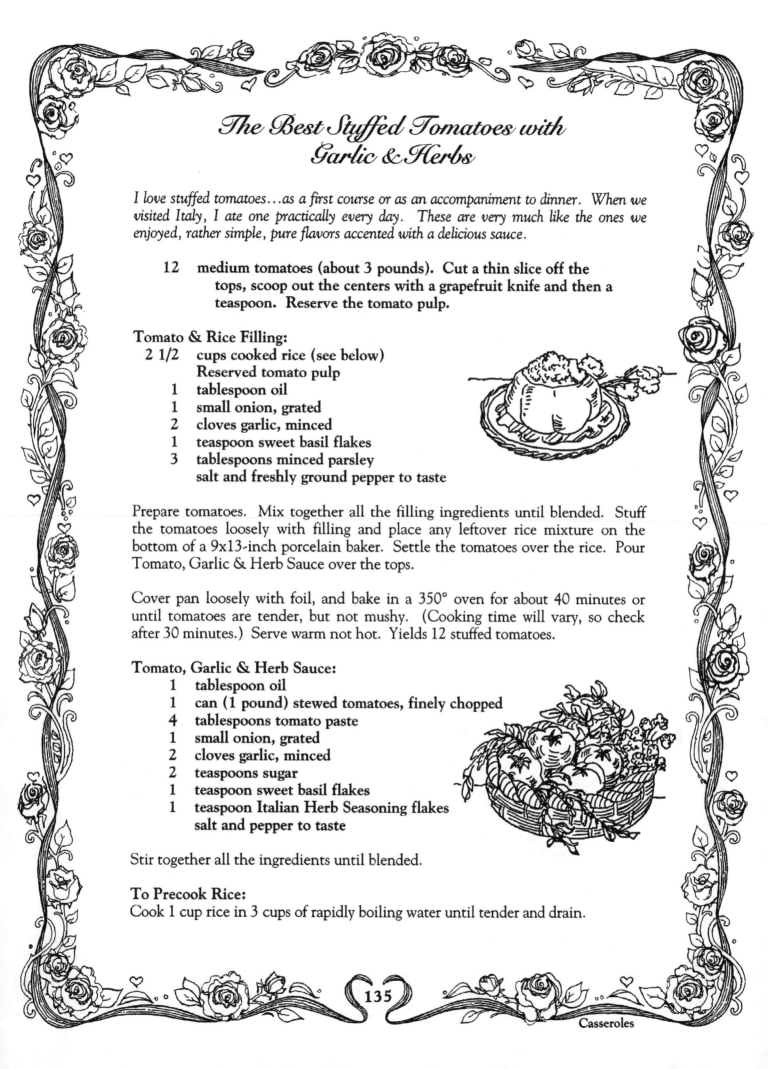

2 1/2 cups cooked rice (see below)
      Reserved tomato pulp
1 tablespoon oil
1 small onion, grated
2 cloves garlic, minced
1 teaspoon sweet basil flakes
3 tablespoons minced parsley
    salt and freshly ground pepper to taste

Prepare tomatoes. Mix together all the filling ingredients until blended. Stuff the tomatoes loosely with filling and place any leftover rice mixture on the bottom of a 9x13-inch porcelain baker. Settle the tomatoes over the rice. Pour Tomato, Garlic & Herb Sauce over the tops.

Cover pan loosely with foil, and bake in a 350° oven for about 40 minutes or until tomatoes are tender, but not mushy. (Cooking time will vary, so check after 30 minutes.) Serve warm not hot. Yields 12 stuffed tomatoes.

Tomato, Garlic & Herb Sauce:
1 tablespoon oil
1 can (1 pound) stewed tomatoes, finely chopped
4 tablespoons tomato paste
1 small onion, grated
2 cloves garlic, minced
2 teaspoons sugar
1 teaspoon sweet basil flakes
1 teaspoon Italian Herb Seasoning flakes
    salt and pepper to taste

Stir together all the ingredients until blended.

To Precook Rice:
Cook 1 cup rice in 3 cups of rapidly boiling water until tender and drain.

Casseroles

Quiche with Bacon, Onions & Swiss Cheese
(Classic Quiche Lorraine)

2   9-inch frozen pie shells (purchase the shallow shells)

1   large onion, finely chopped
2   tablespoons butter

1/4   pound bacon, cooked crisp, drained and crumbled
1   cup grated Swiss cheese

3   eggs
1 1/2 cups half and half
1/4   cup grated Parmesan cheese
       salt and pepper to taste

Bake frozen pie shells in a 400° oven for about 10 minutes or until lightly golden.

Meanwhile, sauté onion in butter until onions are soft. In another pan, cook the bacon until crisp. Then drain fat on paper towels and crumble.

Divide onion and bacon between the two pie shells. Beat together the eggs and cream for 2 minutes at medium speed. Beat in the cheese and seasonings. Divide egg mixture evenly between the 2 pie shells.

Place quiches on a cookie sheet and bake in a 350° oven for 40 to 45 minutes or until custard is set and top is golden. Each pie serves 4 to 6.

Tomato, Mushroom & Goat Cheese Salad

2   medium tomatoes, coarsely chopped
1/2   cup crumbled goat cheese
1/2   pound mushrooms, sliced
1/4   cup chopped green onions
2   tablespoons chopped red onions
2   tablespoons grated Parmesan cheese
1   teaspoon oil
1/4   cup rice vinegar
       pepper to taste

In a large bowl, toss together all the ingredients until nicely mixed. Cover bowl and refrigerate until ready to serve. Serves 8.

Note: - Can be prepared up to 4 hours before serving.

Clam Pie with Bacon & Green Onions

2   9-inch frozen pie shells (purchase the shallow shells, about 1-inch deep)

4   eggs
1/2   cup cream
1/2   teaspoon dried dill weed
4   tablespoons grated Parmesan cheese

1   package (8 ounces) cream cheese, cut into 1/2-inch dice
2   cans (7 ounces, each) minced clams, drained
1/2   cup finely chopped green onions
6   strips bacon, cooked crisp, drained and crumbled
    salt and pepper to taste

Bake frozen pie shells in a 400° oven for about 10 minutes or until lightly golden.

Beat eggs with cream, dill and grated cheese. Stir in cream cheese, clams, onions, bacon and seasonings. Divide mixture evenly between the 2 pie shells.

Place pies on a cookie sheet and bake in a 350° oven for 40 to 45 minutes or until custard is set. Each pie serves 4 to 6.

Note: -I do not recommend freezing for these pies.

Spiced Apples with Walnuts

3   large apples, cut in half, cored and do not peel

1/2   cup orange juice
3   tablespoons brown sugar
1/2   teaspoon cinnamon
3   sprinkles, each, ground nutmeg and ground cloves
1/2   cup coarsely cut walnuts

Place apples in a 10x3-inch porcelain baker and pour orange juice on top. Stir together brown sugar, cinnamon, nutmeg and cloves and sprinkle evenly over the fruit.

Bake apples in a 350° oven, basting every now and again, about 30 minutes. Sprinkle top with walnuts and bake another 10 minutes. Serve warm or at room temperature. Serves 6.

French Mushroom Onion Pies

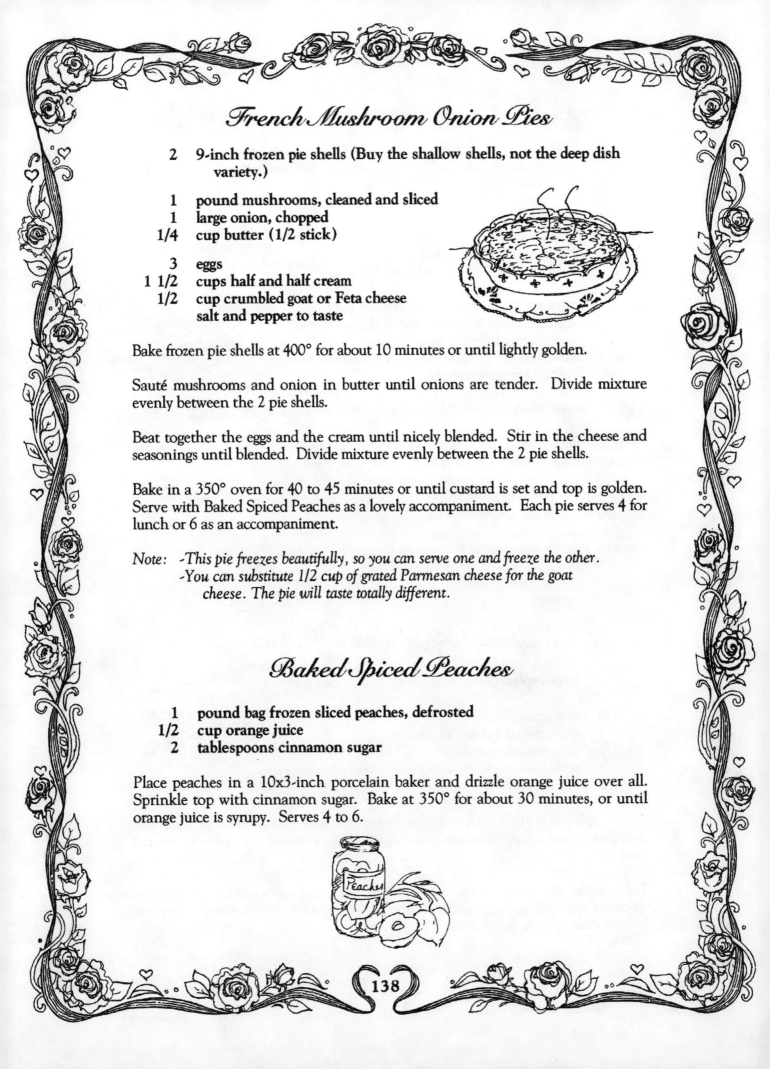

2　9-inch frozen pie shells (Buy the shallow shells, not the deep dish variety.)

1　pound mushrooms, cleaned and sliced
1　large onion, chopped
1/4　cup butter (1/2 stick)

3　eggs
1 1/2　cups half and half cream
1/2　cup crumbled goat or Feta cheese
　　salt and pepper to taste

Bake frozen pie shells at 400° for about 10 minutes or until lightly golden.

Sauté mushrooms and onion in butter until onions are tender. Divide mixture evenly between the 2 pie shells.

Beat together the eggs and the cream until nicely blended. Stir in the cheese and seasonings until blended. Divide mixture evenly between the 2 pie shells.

Bake in a 350° oven for 40 to 45 minutes or until custard is set and top is golden. Serve with Baked Spiced Peaches as a lovely accompaniment. Each pie serves 4 for lunch or 6 as an accompaniment.

Note:　-This pie freezes beautifully, so you can serve one and freeze the other.
*　　　　-You can substitute 1/2 cup of grated Parmesan cheese for the goat*
*　　　　　cheese. The pie will taste totally different.*

Baked Spiced Peaches

1　pound bag frozen sliced peaches, defrosted
1/2　cup orange juice
2　tablespoons cinnamon sugar

Place peaches in a 10x3-inch porcelain baker and drizzle orange juice over all. Sprinkle top with cinnamon sugar. Bake at 350° for about 30 minutes, or until orange juice is syrupy. Serves 4 to 6.

Cracker Pie with Bacon, Onions & Swiss Cheese

1 1/2	cups Ritz cracker crumbs (about 34 crackers) crumbled in processor
1/4	cup butter (1/2 stick), melted
3	eggs, beaten
1/4	cup milk
1/2	cup sour cream
1	cup Swiss cheese, grated
6	strips bacon, cooked crisp and crumbled
2	teaspoons dried onion flakes
1	tablespoon chopped parsley
	salt and pepper to taste

Combine cracker crumbs and melted butter and mix until blended. Pat mixture evenly on the bottom and sides of a 9-inch pie pan. Bake crust in a 350° oven for 8 minutes or until top is lightly browned. Set aside to cool.

Meanwhile, beat eggs with milk and sour cream until light. Stir in the remaining ingredients. Pour mixture into prepared crust and bake in a 350° oven about 40 minutes or until custard is set. Serves 4 for lunch.

Homey Cole Slaw with Apples & Raisins

Apples and raisins add a delicious sweetness to this cole slaw. This recipe is a nice change from the more-often-used crushed pineapple.

1/2	cup low-fat mayonnaise
1/2	cup low-fat sour cream
1	teaspoon sugar
2	apples, peeled, cored, grated and tossed with 1/4 cup lemon juice
1	small head of cabbage, about 1 pound, shredded
2	carrots, peeled and grated
1/3	cup yellow raisins
1/2	teaspoon celery seed
	salt to taste

Stir together first 3 ingredients until blended. Toss apples in lemon juice until nicely coated. In a large bowl, toss together all the ingredients until well mixed. Serves 6 to 8.

Casseroles

Mexican Tomato Chili Cheese Pies

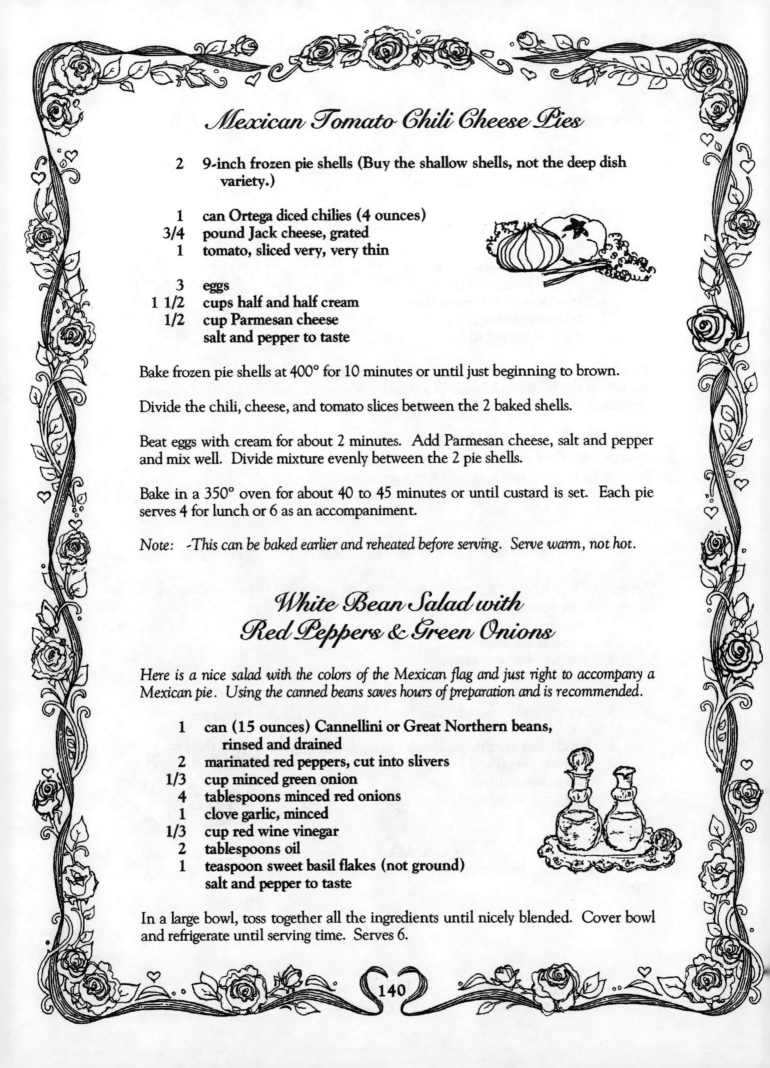

  2   9-inch frozen pie shells (Buy the shallow shells, not the deep dish
        variety.)

  1   can Ortega diced chilies (4 ounces)
3/4   pound Jack cheese, grated
  1   tomato, sliced very, very thin

  3   eggs
1 1/2   cups half and half cream
1/2   cup Parmesan cheese
        salt and pepper to taste

Bake frozen pie shells at 400° for 10 minutes or until just beginning to brown.

Divide the chili, cheese, and tomato slices between the 2 baked shells.

Beat eggs with cream for about 2 minutes. Add Parmesan cheese, salt and pepper and mix well. Divide mixture evenly between the 2 pie shells.

Bake in a 350° oven for about 40 to 45 minutes or until custard is set. Each pie serves 4 for lunch or 6 as an accompaniment.

Note: -This can be baked earlier and reheated before serving. Serve warm, not hot.

White Bean Salad with Red Peppers & Green Onions

Here is a nice salad with the colors of the Mexican flag and just right to accompany a Mexican pie. Using the canned beans saves hours of preparation and is recommended.

  1   can (15 ounces) Cannellini or Great Northern beans,
        rinsed and drained
  2   marinated red peppers, cut into slivers
1/3   cup minced green onion
  4   tablespoons minced red onions
  1   clove garlic, minced
1/3   cup red wine vinegar
  2   tablespoons oil
  1   teaspoon sweet basil flakes (not ground)
        salt and pepper to taste

In a large bowl, toss together all the ingredients until nicely blended. Cover bowl and refrigerate until serving time. Serves 6.

Hot & Spicy Cajun Cornmeal Beef Pie with Chiles and Cheese

Everybody loves this pie. Basically, it is two crusty layers of cornmeal with a spicy layer of beef and chiles sandwiched in-between. It is hot and spicy, but you can reduce the amount of red pepper, if you like it less hot. Cut into squares, this can also be served as an accompaniment to soup.

3/4	pound ground beef
1	medium onion, grated
4	cloves garlic, minced
3	whole green chiles (canned) coarsely chopped (4 ounces)
1	cup grated Cheddar cheese
1/8	teaspoon cayenne pepper, or more to taste
1	cup yellow cornmeal
2	eggs
1	cup milk
1 1/2	teaspoons baking soda
1/4	cup melted butter (1/2 stick)
	salt and pepper to taste

In a skillet, sauté together beef, onion and garlic until meat is crumbly and loses its pinkness. Drain beef mixture and toss with chiles, cheese, and cayenne pepper. In another bowl, beat together the remaining ingredients until blended.

In a greased 10-inch quiche pan, pour 1/2 the cornmeal batter. Sprinkle meat mixture evenly on top, and pour remaining batter over all. Bake in a 350° oven for about 25 minutes or until top is golden brown and batter is set. Serve warm. Serves 8.

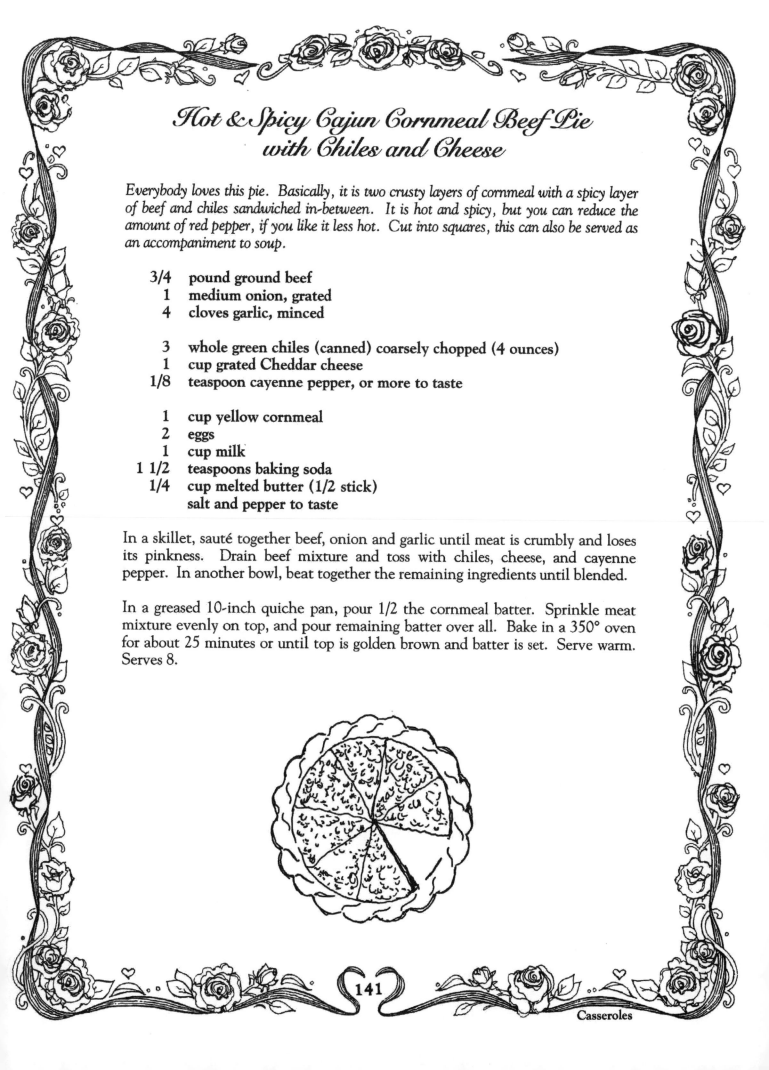

Eggplant, Red Pepper & Cheese Pie

There are few dishes that you can prepare for brunch or lunch that are more exciting and delicious than this one. The eggplant acts as the casing, saving hundreds of calories. The filling is a lovely blend of flavors.

1	small eggplant, (about 1 pound), cut into 1/4 inch thick slices. Lay eggplant slices into a 9x13-inch baking pan, drizzle with 1 tablespoon oil and cover pan tightly with foil. Bake in a 400° oven for 20 minutes or until eggplant is soft, but not mushy.

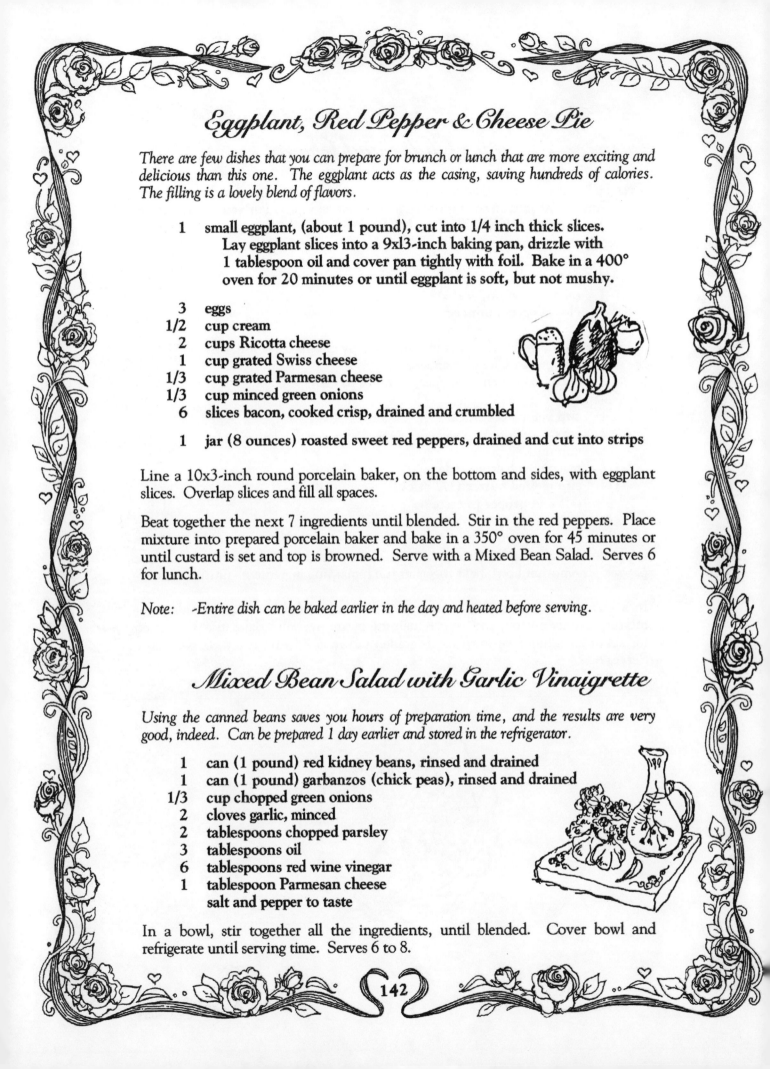

3	eggs
1/2	cup cream
2	cups Ricotta cheese
1	cup grated Swiss cheese
1/3	cup grated Parmesan cheese
1/3	cup minced green onions
6	slices bacon, cooked crisp, drained and crumbled
1	jar (8 ounces) roasted sweet red peppers, drained and cut into strips

Line a 10x3-inch round porcelain baker, on the bottom and sides, with eggplant slices. Overlap slices and fill all spaces.

Beat together the next 7 ingredients until blended. Stir in the red peppers. Place mixture into prepared porcelain baker and bake in a 350° oven for 45 minutes or until custard is set and top is browned. Serve with a Mixed Bean Salad. Serves 6 for lunch.

Note: -Entire dish can be baked earlier in the day and heated before serving.

Mixed Bean Salad with Garlic Vinaigrette

Using the canned beans saves you hours of preparation time, and the results are very good, indeed. Can be prepared 1 day earlier and stored in the refrigerator.

1	can (1 pound) red kidney beans, rinsed and drained
1	can (1 pound) garbanzos (chick peas), rinsed and drained
1/3	cup chopped green onions
2	cloves garlic, minced
2	tablespoons chopped parsley
3	tablespoons oil
6	tablespoons red wine vinegar
1	tablespoon Parmesan cheese
	salt and pepper to taste

In a bowl, stir together all the ingredients, until blended. Cover bowl and refrigerate until serving time. Serves 6 to 8.

Fish

and

Shellfish

Baked Tuna in Spicy Spanish Sauce with Currants & Pine Nuts

This is a delicious change from broiled or grilled tuna. The sauce can be prepared earlier in the day and stored in the refrigerator. Spoon sauce over the fish just before baking.

Spanish Sauce:
- 1 tablespoon olive oil
- 3 cloves garlic, minced
- 2 small onions, minced

- 1 can (1 pound) stewed tomatoes, drained and chopped
- 1 teaspoon sugar
- 4 tablespoons dried black currants
- 2 tablespoons lemon juice
- 3 shakes cayenne pepper
- salt and pepper to taste

- 6 tuna steaks, about 1-inch thick, about 2 pounds
- 1/4 cup toasted pine nuts

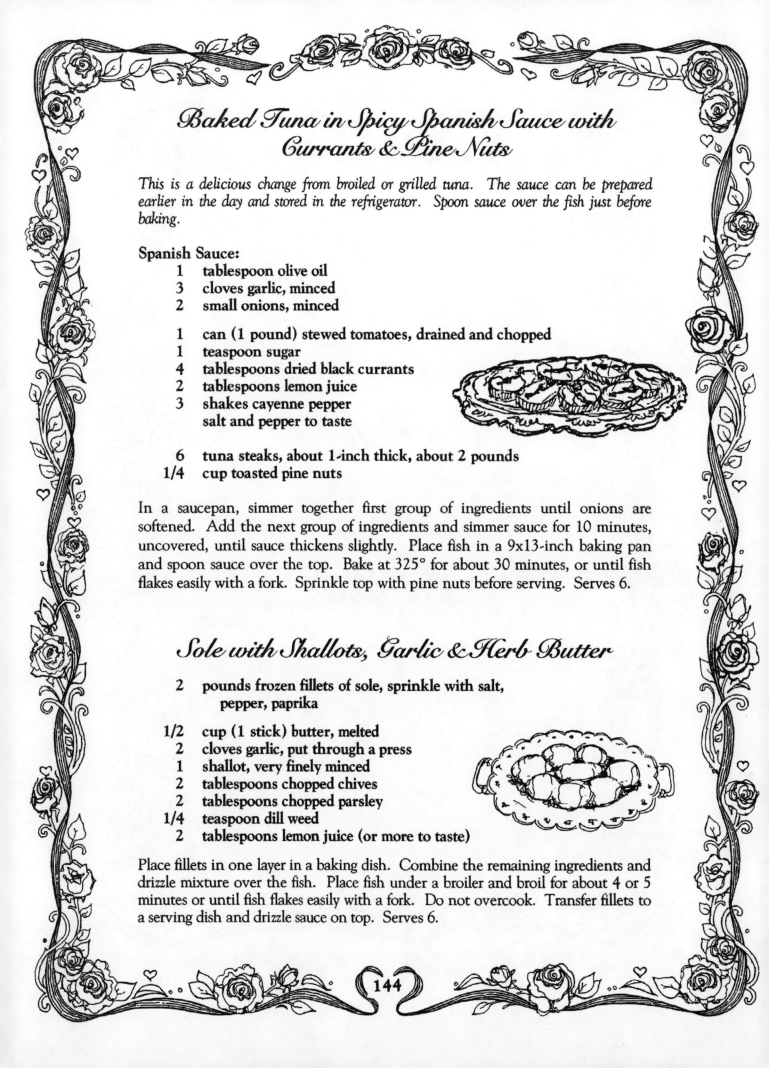

In a saucepan, simmer together first group of ingredients until onions are softened. Add the next group of ingredients and simmer sauce for 10 minutes, uncovered, until sauce thickens slightly. Place fish in a 9x13-inch baking pan and spoon sauce over the top. Bake at 325° for about 30 minutes, or until fish flakes easily with a fork. Sprinkle top with pine nuts before serving. Serves 6.

Sole with Shallots, Garlic & Herb Butter

- 2 pounds frozen fillets of sole, sprinkle with salt, pepper, paprika

- 1/2 cup (1 stick) butter, melted
- 2 cloves garlic, put through a press
- 1 shallot, very finely minced
- 2 tablespoons chopped chives
- 2 tablespoons chopped parsley
- 1/4 teaspoon dill weed
- 2 tablespoons lemon juice (or more to taste)

Place fillets in one layer in a baking dish. Combine the remaining ingredients and drizzle mixture over the fish. Place fish under a broiler and broil for about 4 or 5 minutes or until fish flakes easily with a fork. Do not overcook. Transfer fillets to a serving dish and drizzle sauce on top. Serves 6.

Whitefish with Lemon, Dill & Garlic Crumbs

These savory crumbs made with lemon, chives, garlic and dill are lovely over sole, red snapper, sea bass or shrimp.

Lemon, Dill & Garlic Crumbs:

1/4	cup butter
6	cloves garlic, minced
4	shallots, minced
1/4	cup dry white wine
1/2	cup chopped chives
2	tablespoons chopped parsley leaves
1/2	teaspoon dried dill weed
2	tablespoons lemon juice
1/2	cup fresh bread crumbs
2	pounds whitefish fillets, brushed with a little butter and sprinkled with salt and white pepper

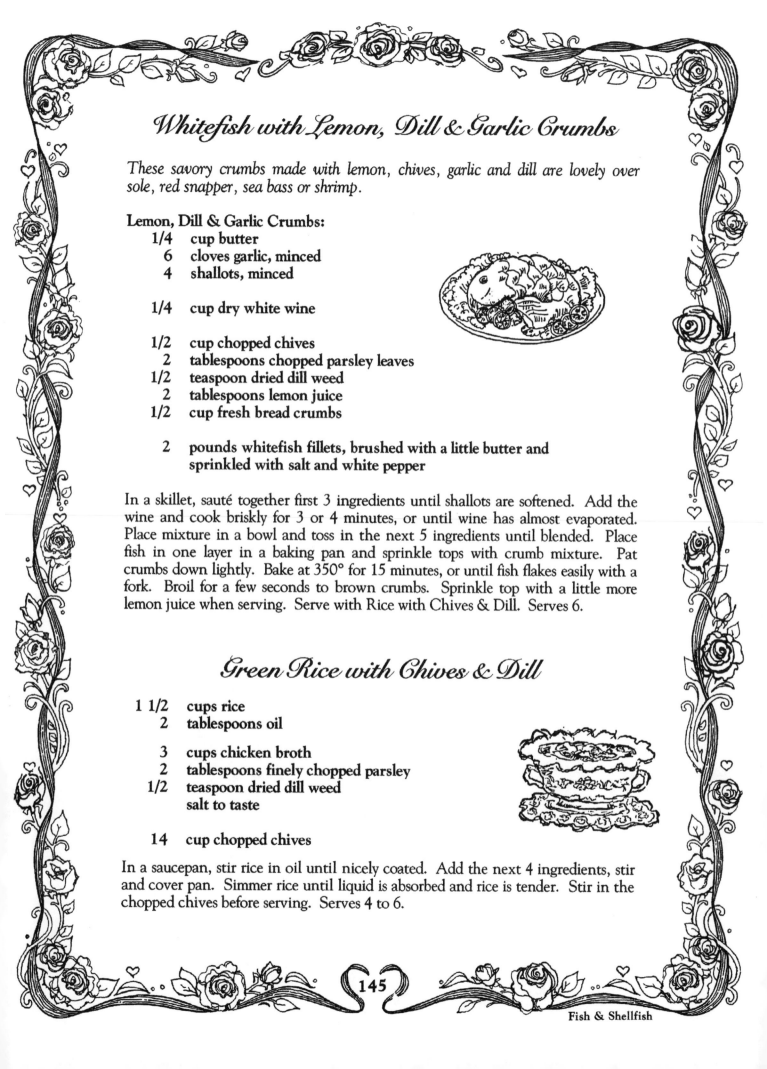

In a skillet, sauté together first 3 ingredients until shallots are softened. Add the wine and cook briskly for 3 or 4 minutes, or until wine has almost evaporated. Place mixture in a bowl and toss in the next 5 ingredients until blended. Place fish in one layer in a baking pan and sprinkle tops with crumb mixture. Pat crumbs down lightly. Bake at 350° for 15 minutes, or until fish flakes easily with a fork. Broil for a few seconds to brown crumbs. Sprinkle top with a little more lemon juice when serving. Serve with Rice with Chives & Dill. Serves 6.

Green Rice with Chives & Dill

1 1/2	cups rice
2	tablespoons oil
3	cups chicken broth
2	tablespoons finely chopped parsley
1/2	teaspoon dried dill weed
	salt to taste
14	cup chopped chives

In a saucepan, stir rice in oil until nicely coated. Add the next 4 ingredients, stir and cover pan. Simmer rice until liquid is absorbed and rice is tender. Stir in the chopped chives before serving. Serves 4 to 6.

Sea Bass with Sun-Dried Tomatoes & Peppers

As a general rule, buy sun-dried tomatoes that are packed in oil. They are far more flavorful and the little bit of oil can easily be drained. Sun-dried tomatoes packed in salt, must be rinsed and then stored in oil. They are too salty for my taste.

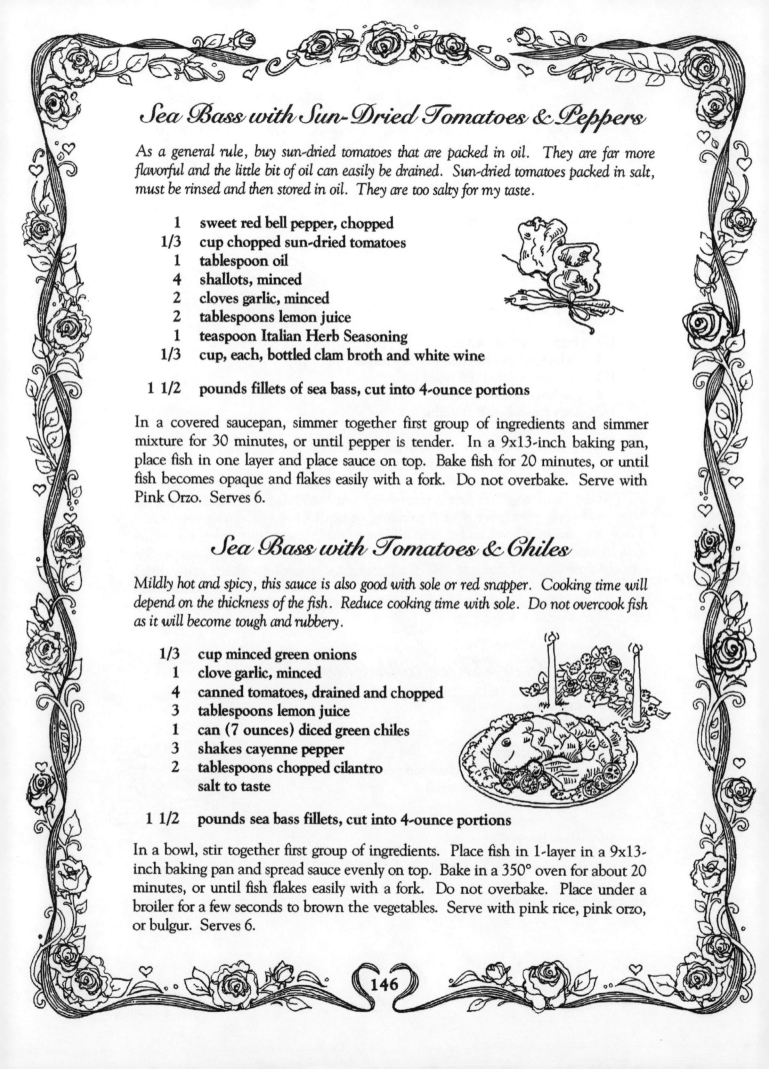

1	sweet red bell pepper, chopped
1/3	cup chopped sun-dried tomatoes
1	tablespoon oil
4	shallots, minced
2	cloves garlic, minced
2	tablespoons lemon juice
1	teaspoon Italian Herb Seasoning
1/3	cup, each, bottled clam broth and white wine

1 1/2	pounds fillets of sea bass, cut into 4-ounce portions

In a covered saucepan, simmer together first group of ingredients and simmer mixture for 30 minutes, or until pepper is tender. In a 9x13-inch baking pan, place fish in one layer and place sauce on top. Bake fish for 20 minutes, or until fish becomes opaque and flakes easily with a fork. Do not overbake. Serve with Pink Orzo. Serves 6.

Sea Bass with Tomatoes & Chiles

Mildly hot and spicy, this sauce is also good with sole or red snapper. Cooking time will depend on the thickness of the fish. Reduce cooking time with sole. Do not overcook fish as it will become tough and rubbery.

1/3	cup minced green onions
1	clove garlic, minced
4	canned tomatoes, drained and chopped
3	tablespoons lemon juice
1	can (7 ounces) diced green chiles
3	shakes cayenne pepper
2	tablespoons chopped cilantro
	salt to taste

1 1/2	pounds sea bass fillets, cut into 4-ounce portions

In a bowl, stir together first group of ingredients. Place fish in 1-layer in a 9x13-inch baking pan and spread sauce evenly on top. Bake in a 350° oven for about 20 minutes, or until fish flakes easily with a fork. Do not overbake. Place under a broiler for a few seconds to brown the vegetables. Serve with pink rice, pink orzo, or bulgur. Serves 6.

Sea Bass Valencia with Salsa Español

Salsa Español:

- 1 can (1 pound) stewed tomatoes, chopped. Do not drain.
- 2 tablespoons tomato paste
- 2 medium onions, chopped
- 1/2 yellow bell pepper, cut into strips
- 1/2 sweet red bell pepper, cut into strips
- 3 cloves garlic, minced
- 4 tablespoons lemon juice
- 4 tablespoons dry white wine
- 1 teaspoon turmeric
- 1/2 teaspoon ground cumin
- 1/4 teaspoon hot red pepper flakes
  salt and pepper to taste

- 2 pounds sea bass fillets

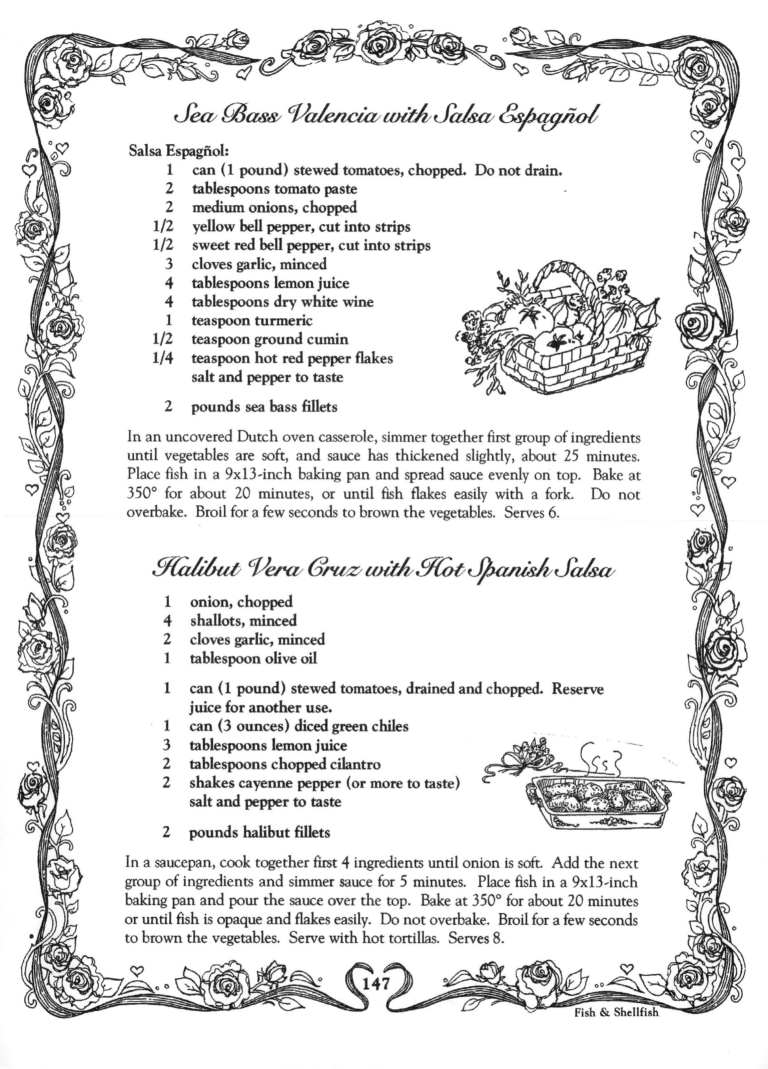

In an uncovered Dutch oven casserole, simmer together first group of ingredients until vegetables are soft, and sauce has thickened slightly, about 25 minutes. Place fish in a 9x13-inch baking pan and spread sauce evenly on top. Bake at 350° for about 20 minutes, or until fish flakes easily with a fork. Do not overbake. Broil for a few seconds to brown the vegetables. Serves 6.

Halibut Vera Cruz with Hot Spanish Salsa

- 1 onion, chopped
- 4 shallots, minced
- 2 cloves garlic, minced
- 1 tablespoon olive oil

- 1 can (1 pound) stewed tomatoes, drained and chopped. Reserve juice for another use.
- 1 can (3 ounces) diced green chiles
- 3 tablespoons lemon juice
- 2 tablespoons chopped cilantro
- 2 shakes cayenne pepper (or more to taste)
  salt and pepper to taste

- 2 pounds halibut fillets

In a saucepan, cook together first 4 ingredients until onion is soft. Add the next group of ingredients and simmer sauce for 5 minutes. Place fish in a 9x13-inch baking pan and pour the sauce over the top. Bake at 350° for about 20 minutes or until fish is opaque and flakes easily. Do not overbake. Broil for a few seconds to brown the vegetables. Serve with hot tortillas. Serves 8.

Fish & Shellfish

Halibut with Tomatoes, Garlic & Feta Cheese

This is a delicious dish in a Spanish mood. It is very low in fat and cholesterol. Cheese can be omitted, but it adds a good deal of taste for the small amount used.

1	medium onion, finely chopped
2	cloves garlic, minced
2	tablespoons lemon juice
1	can (1 pound) stewed tomatoes, chopped
1/4	teaspoon sweet basil flakes
1 1/2	pounds halibut fillets, cut into 6 serving pieces
2	tablespoons chopped black olives
1/2	cup (2 ounces) crumbled Feta cheese

In an uncovered saucepan, cook together first 5 ingredients until onion is soft, about 15 minutes. In an 8x12-inch baking pan, spread half the sauce. Place fish on top in one layer, and top with the remaining sauce. Sprinkle top with olives and Feta cheese. Bake at 350° for 25 minutes, or until fish flakes easily with a fork. Serve with wild rice or brown rice. Serves 6.

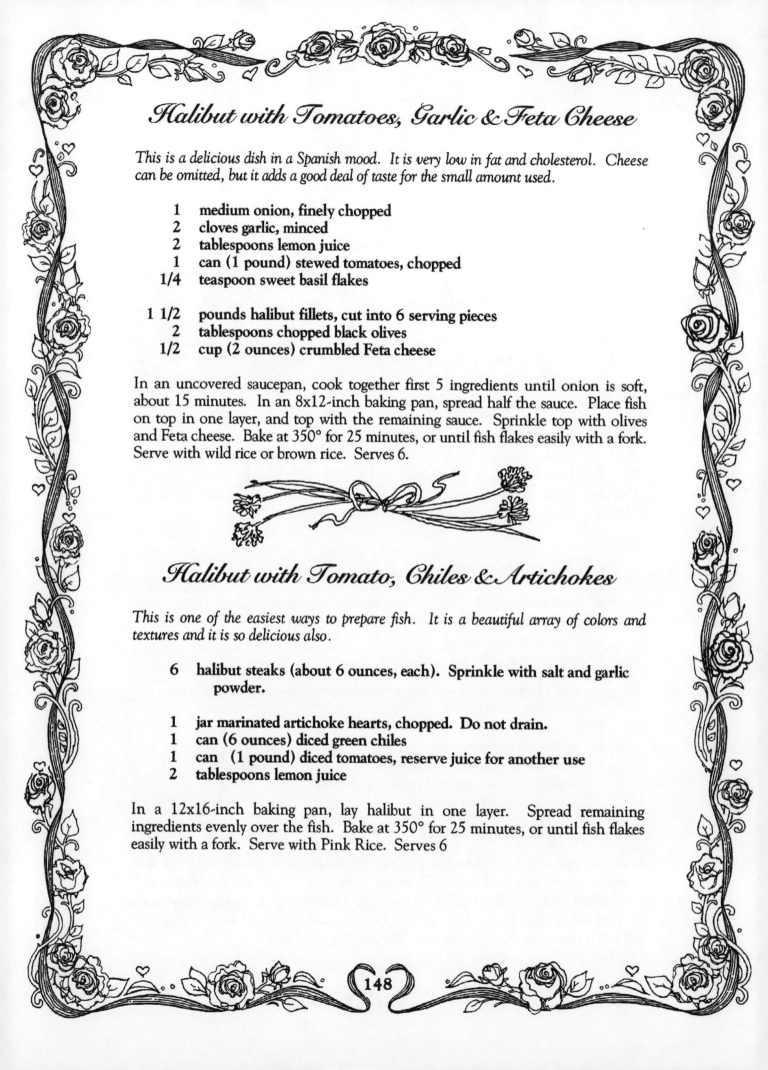

Halibut with Tomato, Chiles & Artichokes

This is one of the easiest ways to prepare fish. It is a beautiful array of colors and textures and it is so delicious also.

6	halibut steaks (about 6 ounces, each). Sprinkle with salt and garlic powder.
1	jar marinated artichoke hearts, chopped. Do not drain.
1	can (6 ounces) diced green chiles
1	can (1 pound) diced tomatoes, reserve juice for another use
2	tablespoons lemon juice

In a 12x16-inch baking pan, lay halibut in one layer. Spread remaining ingredients evenly over the fish. Bake at 350° for 25 minutes, or until fish flakes easily with a fork. Serve with Pink Rice. Serves 6

Batter Fried Fillets of Sole Parmesan

We have Veal Parmesan, Chicken Parmesan, so why not have a Sole Parmesan. Fish is becoming more and more popular, so a few new ways to serve it, adds interest to the meal.

Batter:

1	cup flour
2	eggs
1	cup milk
1/4	cup grated Parmesan cheese
	salt and pepper to taste

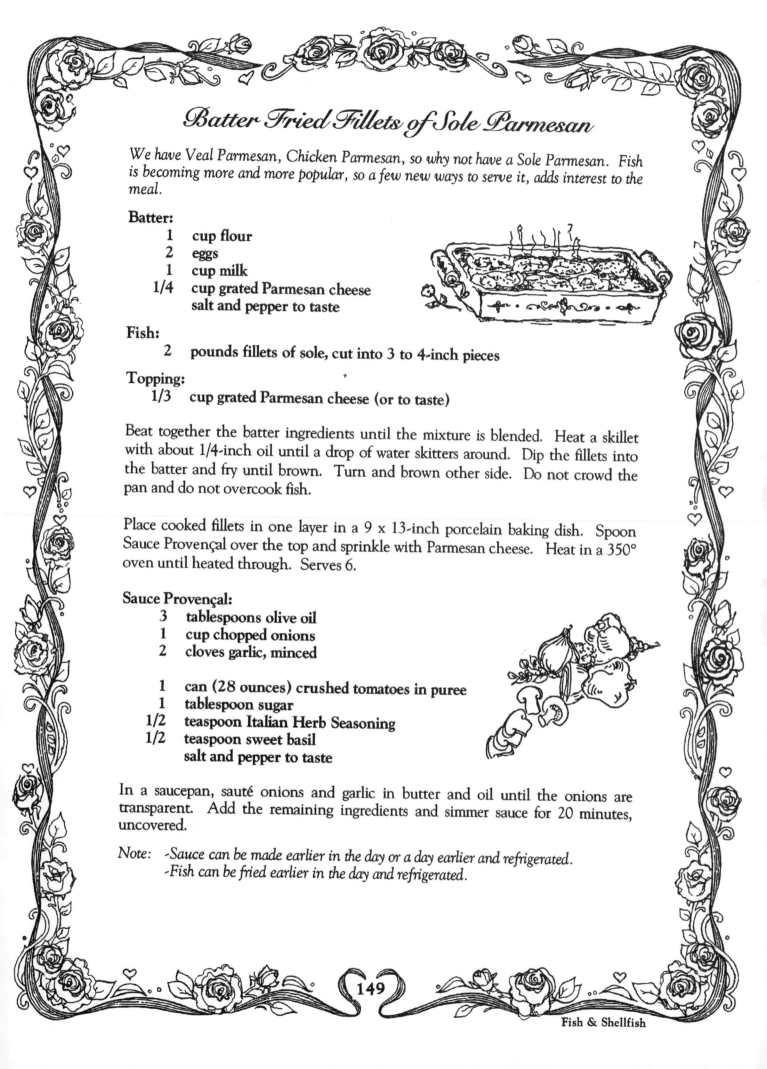

Fish:

2	pounds fillets of sole, cut into 3 to 4-inch pieces

Topping:

1/3	cup grated Parmesan cheese (or to taste)

Beat together the batter ingredients until the mixture is blended. Heat a skillet with about 1/4-inch oil until a drop of water skitters around. Dip the fillets into the batter and fry until brown. Turn and brown other side. Do not crowd the pan and do not overcook fish.

Place cooked fillets in one layer in a 9 x 13-inch porcelain baking dish. Spoon Sauce Provençal over the top and sprinkle with Parmesan cheese. Heat in a 350° oven until heated through. Serves 6.

Sauce Provençal:

3	tablespoons olive oil
1	cup chopped onions
2	cloves garlic, minced
1	can (28 ounces) crushed tomatoes in puree
1	tablespoon sugar
1/2	teaspoon Italian Herb Seasoning
1/2	teaspoon sweet basil
	salt and pepper to taste

In a saucepan, sauté onions and garlic in butter and oil until the onions are transparent. Add the remaining ingredients and simmer sauce for 20 minutes, uncovered.

Note: -Sauce can be made earlier in the day or a day earlier and refrigerated.
-Fish can be fried earlier in the day and refrigerated.

Butterfish with Tomato Lemon Vinaigrette

2   pounds fillets of butterfish (or sole or red snapper),
      sprinkled salt, pepper and lemon juice to taste.

2   tablespoons melted butter

1   can (1 pound) stewed tomatoes, finely chopped
3   green onions, finely chopped
2   tablespoons parsley, finely chopped
1/4   cup oil
2   tablespoons red wine vinegar
2   tablespoons lemon juice
      salt and pepper to taste

Place fish in one layer in a 12x16-inch baking pan and drizzle tops with the melted butter. Bake fish in a 350° oven for about 10 minutes or until it flakes with a fork.

Meanwhile combine the remaining ingredients in a saucepan and heat it for about 5 minutes. Pour sauce evenly over the fish and serve hot. Serve with a simple pilaf and buttered green vegetable. Serves 6 to 8.

Salmon Steaks with Dilled Cream Mayonnaise

6   center cut salmon steaks, cut into 1-inch thick slices

Lemon Butter Wash:
3   tablespoons butter, melted
3   tablespoons lemon juice
      salt and pepper to taste

Preheat broiler. Combine Lemon Butter Wash ingredients and brush salmon with the mixture. Place salmon on rack in broiler pan. Broil, about 6-inches from heat, about 6 minutes on each side, or until salmon is opaque and cooked through. Do not overcook. Brush salmon lightly with Dilled Cream Mayonnaise and serve remaining sauce on the side. Serves 6.

Dilled Cream Mayonnaise
1/2   cup mayonnaise
1/2   cup sour cream
4   tablespoons minced chives
2   tablespoons finely minced parsley
1   tablespoon dill weed
2   tablespoons lemon juice

In a jar with a tight-fitting lid, combine all the ingredients and stir to blend. Refrigerate until serving time. Yields 1 1/4 cups sauce.

Fillets of Sole Provençale with Tomatoes, Onions & Cheese

This little dish is amazingly low in calories and quite satisfying, considering its diet qualities. Flavor the fillets generously with pepper, garlic powder and paprika to enhance the taste.

2	pounds fillets of sole. Sprinkle generously with pepper, garlic powder and paprika.
1	can (1 pound) stewed tomatoes, drained and chopped. Reserve juice for another use.
1/2	cup chopped green onions
4	tablespoons chopped parsley
4	tablespoons grated Parmesan cheese
8	thin lemon slices

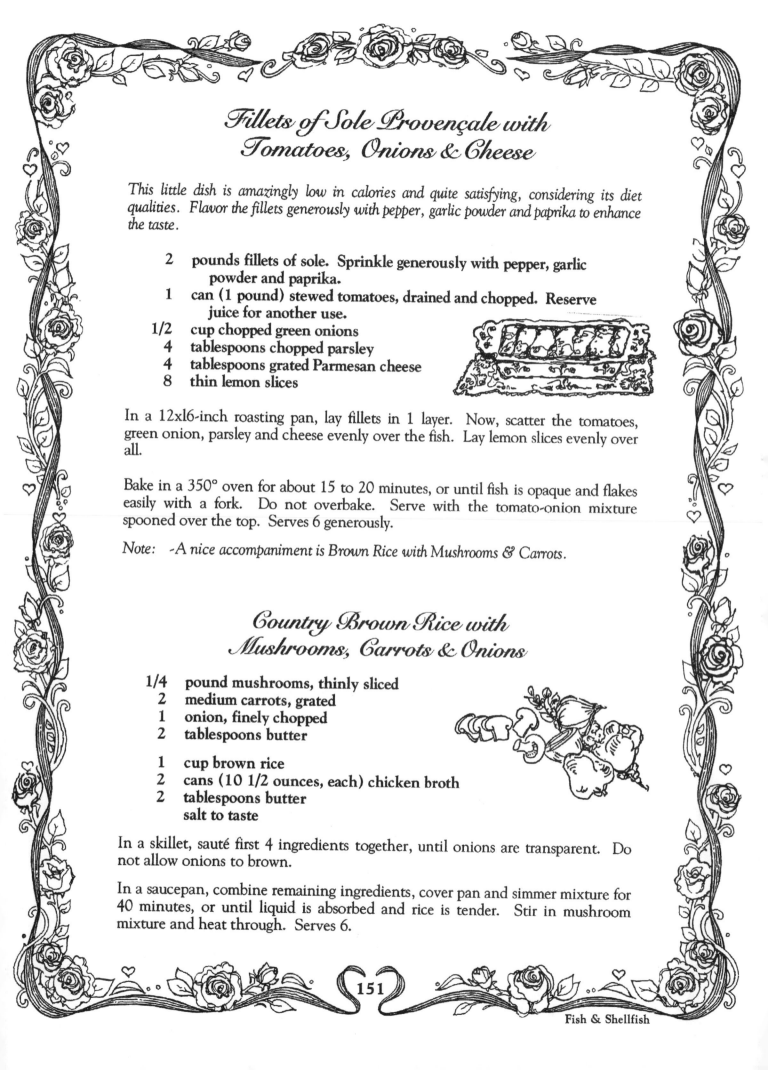

In a 12x16-inch roasting pan, lay fillets in 1 layer. Now, scatter the tomatoes, green onion, parsley and cheese evenly over the fish. Lay lemon slices evenly over all.

Bake in a 350° oven for about 15 to 20 minutes, or until fish is opaque and flakes easily with a fork. Do not overbake. Serve with the tomato-onion mixture spooned over the top. Serves 6 generously.

Note: -A nice accompaniment is Brown Rice with Mushrooms & Carrots.

Country Brown Rice with Mushrooms, Carrots & Onions

1/4	pound mushrooms, thinly sliced
2	medium carrots, grated
1	onion, finely chopped
2	tablespoons butter
1	cup brown rice
2	cans (10 1/2 ounces, each) chicken broth
2	tablespoons butter
	salt to taste

In a skillet, sauté first 4 ingredients together, until onions are transparent. Do not allow onions to brown.

In a saucepan, combine remaining ingredients, cover pan and simmer mixture for 40 minutes, or until liquid is absorbed and rice is tender. Stir in mushroom mixture and heat through. Serves 6.

Fillets of Sole in
Herbed Lemon Artichoke Sauce

This little dish is a poem of flavors, tangy and delicious. The sauce and fish can be prepared in minutes, making this is a good choice for a night when you are running late.

- 1 pound fillets of sole. Sprinkle with pepper, garlic powder and a pinch of paprika.
- 2 tablespoons melted butter

- 1 jar (8 ounces) marinated artichoke hearts, drained and chopped
- 2 shallots, minced
- 2 tablespoons minced green onions
- 1 clove garlic, minced
- 2 tablespoons minced parsley
- 1 tablespoon lemon juice
- 1 teaspoon sweet basil flakes
- salt and white pepper to taste

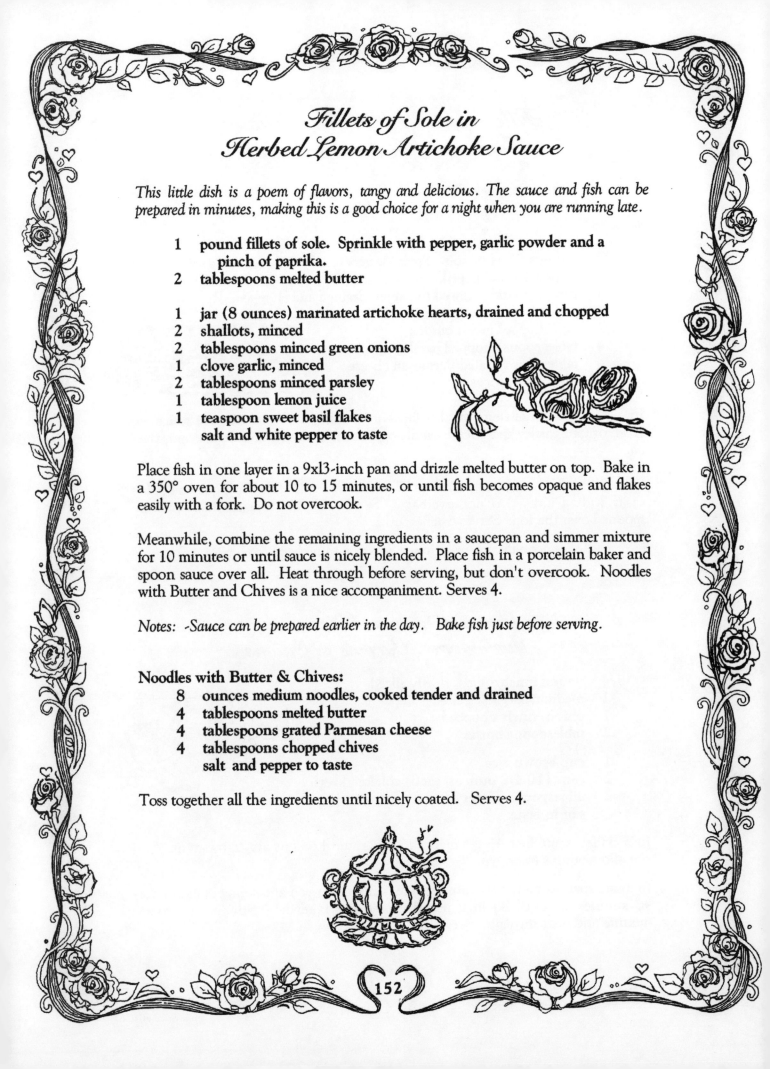

Place fish in one layer in a 9x13-inch pan and drizzle melted butter on top. Bake in a 350° oven for about 10 to 15 minutes, or until fish becomes opaque and flakes easily with a fork. Do not overcook.

Meanwhile, combine the remaining ingredients in a saucepan and simmer mixture for 10 minutes or until sauce is nicely blended. Place fish in a porcelain baker and spoon sauce over all. Heat through before serving, but don't overcook. Noodles with Butter and Chives is a nice accompaniment. Serves 4.

Notes: -Sauce can be prepared earlier in the day. Bake fish just before serving.

Noodles with Butter & Chives:
- 8 ounces medium noodles, cooked tender and drained
- 4 tablespoons melted butter
- 4 tablespoons grated Parmesan cheese
- 4 tablespoons chopped chives
- salt and pepper to taste

Toss together all the ingredients until nicely coated.   Serves 4.

Fillets of Sole with Lemon Dill Sauce

Lemon Dill Sauce is one of the nicest, delicate sauces to serve with fish or shellfish. It can be prepared with low-fat mayonnaise and sour cream.

- 2 pounds fillets of sole
- 6 tablespoons melted butter
- 4 tablespoons dry white wine
- salt and pepper to taste

Place fillets in one layer in a 12x16-inch roasting pan. Drizzle them with melted butter and sprinkle with white wine. Salt and pepper them to taste. Bake fillets in a 350° oven for about 15 minutes or until fish flakes easily with a fork. Do not overbake. Serve with Lemon Dill Sauce on the side. Serves 6.

Lemon Dill Sauce:
- 1/4 cup mayonnaise
- 1/4 cup sour cream
- 2 tablespoons lemon juice
- 2 tablespoons chopped chives
- 1 teaspoon sugar
- 1 teaspoon dried dill weed

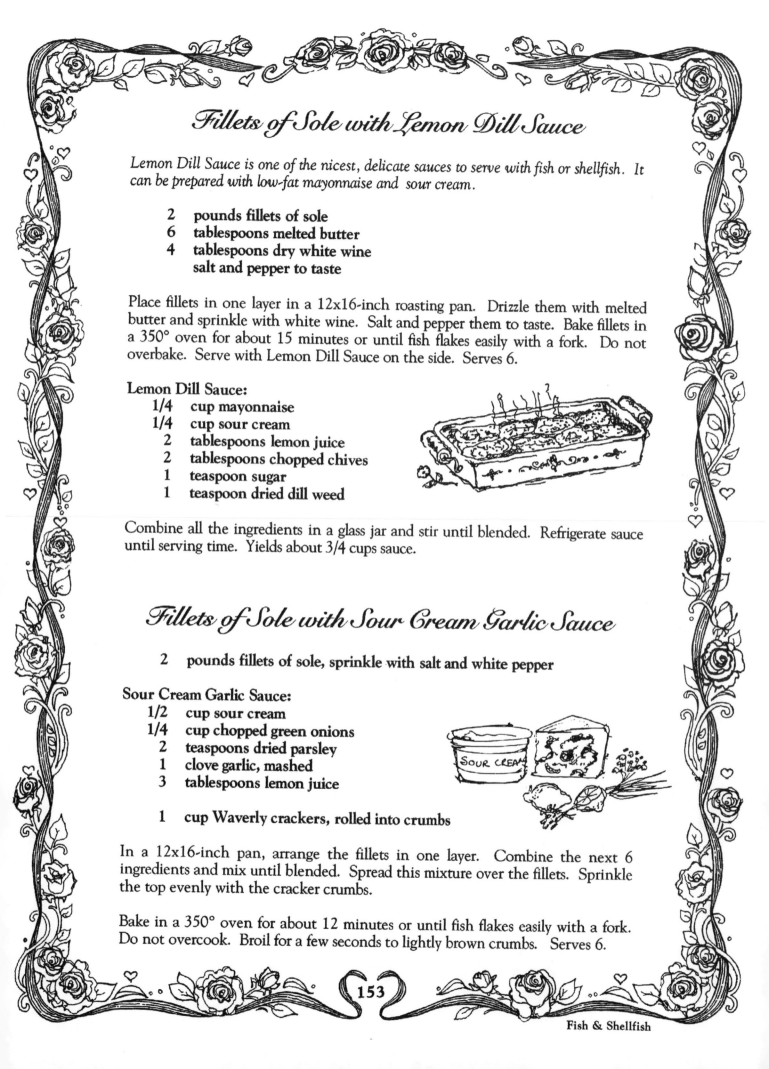

Combine all the ingredients in a glass jar and stir until blended. Refrigerate sauce until serving time. Yields about 3/4 cups sauce.

Fillets of Sole with Sour Cream Garlic Sauce

- 2 pounds fillets of sole, sprinkle with salt and white pepper

Sour Cream Garlic Sauce:
- 1/2 cup sour cream
- 1/4 cup chopped green onions
- 2 teaspoons dried parsley
- 1 clove garlic, mashed
- 3 tablespoons lemon juice

- 1 cup Waverly crackers, rolled into crumbs

In a 12x16-inch pan, arrange the fillets in one layer. Combine the next 6 ingredients and mix until blended. Spread this mixture over the fillets. Sprinkle the top evenly with the cracker crumbs.

Bake in a 350° oven for about 12 minutes or until fish flakes easily with a fork. Do not overcook. Broil for a few seconds to lightly brown crumbs. Serves 6.

Fish & Shellfish

Red Snapper in Spicy Artichoke Sauce

The Artichoke Sauce is also a fine accompaniment to fillets of sole or sea bass.

1	onion, chopped
4	shallots, minced
6	cloves garlic, minced
1	jar (6 1/2 ounces) marinated artichoke hearts, coarsely chopped
1/4	cup dry white wine
1/4	cup clam broth
4	canned tomatoes, drained and chopped
1	tablespoon tomato paste
1	teaspoon turmeric
1/2	teaspoon ground cumin
3	shakes cayenne pepper
2	pounds red snapper fillets, cut into 2-inch pieces

In a Dutch oven casserole, simmer together first group of ingredients until onion is soft and sauce is slightly thickened. Place fish in one layer in a 9x13-inch baking pan and spread sauce on top. Bake in a 350° oven for 20 minutes or until fish is opaque and flakes easily with a fork. Do not overbake. Serve with Pink Rice with Tomato & Chives. Serves 8.

Swordfish with Sun-Dried Tomatoes, Garlic & Red Peppers

8	1-inch thick swordfish steaks (about 6 ounces, each)
2	tablespoons olive oil
4	tablespoons lemon juice
3	sun-dried tomatoes packed in oil, drained and finely chopped
2	marinated red peppers, cut into thin strips
1/4	cup chopped green onions
2	cloves garlic, minced
1/2	tablespoon minced fresh, sweet basil or 1/2 teaspoon dried pepper to taste

Place fish in one layer in a 9x13-inch baking pan. Combine the remaining ingredients and spread evenly over the fish. Bake fish at 350° for 20 minutes, or until it flakes easily with a fork. Broil for a few seconds to brown vegetables. Serves 8.

Salmon Poached in Champagne with Sour Cream Dill Sauce

6   tablespoons butter
3   tablespoons lemon juice
1/2   cup Champagne
2   tablespoons chopped chives

6   slices salmon, about 1 inch thick

In a pan you will cook salmon, melt the butter. Add the lemon juice, Champagne and chives. Place salmon in butter mixture and baste. Cover and cook, on low heat, (#2 on my stove) about 30 minutes, basting now and again, until salmon is cooked through. Place salmon on a lovely platter and brush with a little Sour Cream Dill Sauce on the top. Serve additional sauce on the side. Serves 6

Note: -You can substitute dry white wine for the Champagne.

Sour Cream Dill Sauce:
1/2   cup sour cream
1   tablespoon Dijon-style mustard
2   tablespoons lemon juice
1   tablespoon chopped chives
2   tablespoons sugar
1   teaspoon dried dill weed

Combine all the ingredients in a glass jar and stir until they are blended. Refrigerate sauce until serving time. Makes about 3/4 cup sauce.

Swordfish with Tomatoes & Artichokes

6   swordfish steaks, about 1-inch thick (about 5 ounces, each)
2   cloves garlic, minced
4   tablespoons lemon juice
1   can (1 pound) stewed tomatoes, drained and chopped
1   jar (7 ounces) marinated artichoke hearts, chopped
1/3   cup minced green onions
1/2   teaspoon sweet basil flakes
1   tablespoon chopped parsley
      pinch of cayenne pepper
2   tablespoons grated Parmesan cheese

In a 9x13-inch pan, place the swordfish in one layer. Stir together the remaining ingredients and place evenly over the fish. Bake at 350° for about 20 minutes, or until fish is opaque and flakes easily with a fork. Broil for a few seconds to lightly brown vegetables (optional). Serve with brown rice or bulgur. Serves 6.

New Orleans-Style Hot & Spicy Shrimp

If you are stout of heart and enjoy hot, fiery dishes, this is a nice one to consider. This is very "hot" for me although blazing palates will find this mild. Increase the amount of cayenne, if you enjoy bringing tears to your eyes.

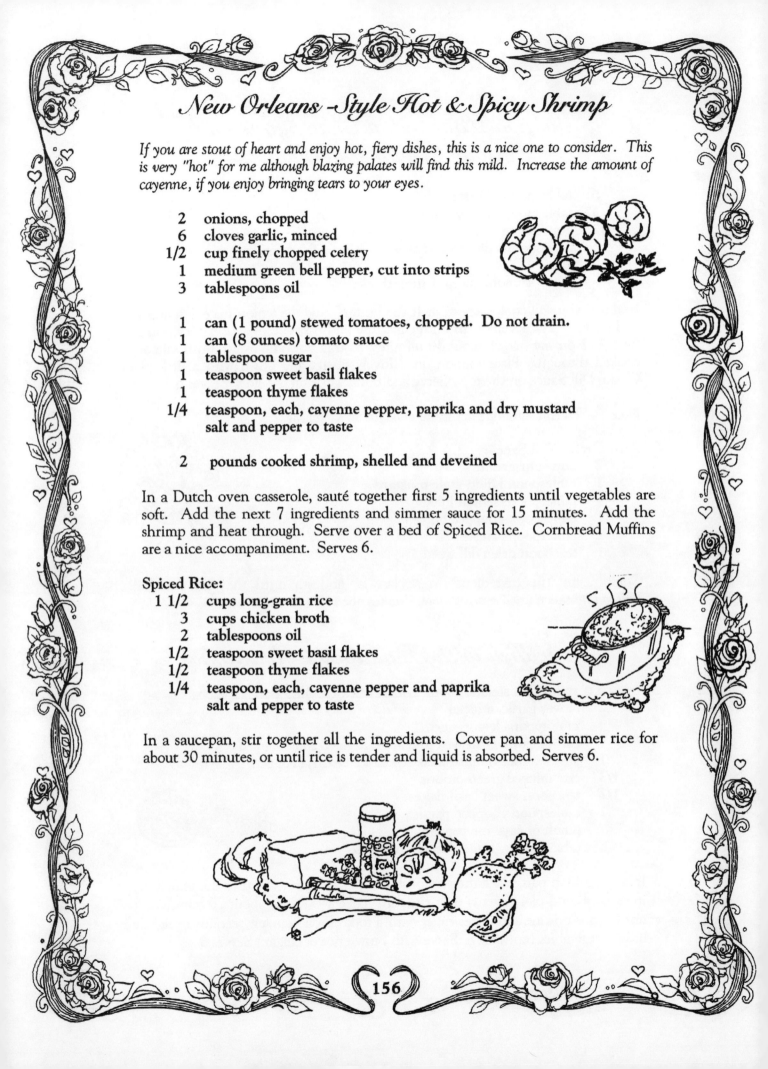

2	onions, chopped
6	cloves garlic, minced
1/2	cup finely chopped celery
1	medium green bell pepper, cut into strips
3	tablespoons oil

1	can (1 pound) stewed tomatoes, chopped. Do not drain.
1	can (8 ounces) tomato sauce
1	tablespoon sugar
1	teaspoon sweet basil flakes
1	teaspoon thyme flakes
1/4	teaspoon, each, cayenne pepper, paprika and dry mustard
	salt and pepper to taste

2	pounds cooked shrimp, shelled and deveined

In a Dutch oven casserole, sauté together first 5 ingredients until vegetables are soft. Add the next 7 ingredients and simmer sauce for 15 minutes. Add the shrimp and heat through. Serve over a bed of Spiced Rice. Cornbread Muffins are a nice accompaniment. Serves 6.

Spiced Rice:

1 1/2	cups long-grain rice
3	cups chicken broth
2	tablespoons oil
1/2	teaspoon sweet basil flakes
1/2	teaspoon thyme flakes
1/4	teaspoon, each, cayenne pepper and paprika
	salt and pepper to taste

In a saucepan, stir together all the ingredients. Cover pan and simmer rice for about 30 minutes, or until rice is tender and liquid is absorbed. Serves 6.

Red Hot Garlic Shrimp with Lemon & Herbs

This dish can be prepared in minutes and is a good choice on a night when you are running late. Sauce can be prepared earlier in the day, or even 1 day earlier, and heated before cooking the shrimp.

6   shallots, minced
6   cloves garlic, minced
6   tablespoons butter (3/4 stick)

1   teaspoon paprika
2   sprinkles cayenne pepper (or to taste)
1/2   teaspoon sweet basil flakes
1/2   teaspoon oregano flakes
3   tablespoons lemon juice
   salt and pepper to taste

1 1/2   pounds raw shrimp, shelled and deveined

In a large skillet, sauté shallots and garlic in butter until shallots are soft, but not browned. Add the next 6 ingredients and cook over low heat for 1 minute. Raise heat to medium, add shrimp, and cook, tossing and turning, until shrimp become opaque. (Please do not overcook, or shrimp will become tough and rubbery.) Serve on a bed of Lemon Rice with Chives & Cheese. Serves 6.

Lobster Italienne with Red Pepper & Basil

Lobster served with a delicate cream sauce, sparkled with red pepper and basil makes a fine combination. The sauce can also be served over cooked fillets of sole. It is not a lot of sauce. Just enough to coat the lobster and add its distinct flavor.

1   medium sweet red bell pepper, cut into strips
1/2   cup chopped green onions
2   cloves garlic, minced
2   shallots, minced
2   tablespoons butter

1/4   cup dry white wine

2   tablespoons chopped parsley
2   tablespoons lemon juice
1   teaspoon dried sweet basil flakes
1/2   cup cream
   salt and white pepper to taste
1   pound cooked lobster meat, cut into chunks

In a saucepan, sauté together first 5 ingredients until pepper is softened. Add the wine, and cook until wine has evaporated. Add the next 5 ingredients, and simmer sauce for 10 minutes. Add the cooked lobster meat and heat through. Serve with rice, sprinkled with chives and grated Parmesan cheese. Serves 4.

Fish & Shellfish

Shrimp with Emerald Garlic Butter

Emerald Garlic Butter:

2	tablespoons lemon juice
1/4	cup fresh egg bread crumbs, about 2 slices without crusts
1/2	cup butter (1 stick)
2	shallots, minced
4	cloves garlic, put through a press
2	tablespoons parsley, finely chopped
1/4	cup chopped chives
	salt and pepper to taste
2	pounds medium raw shrimp, peeled and deveined

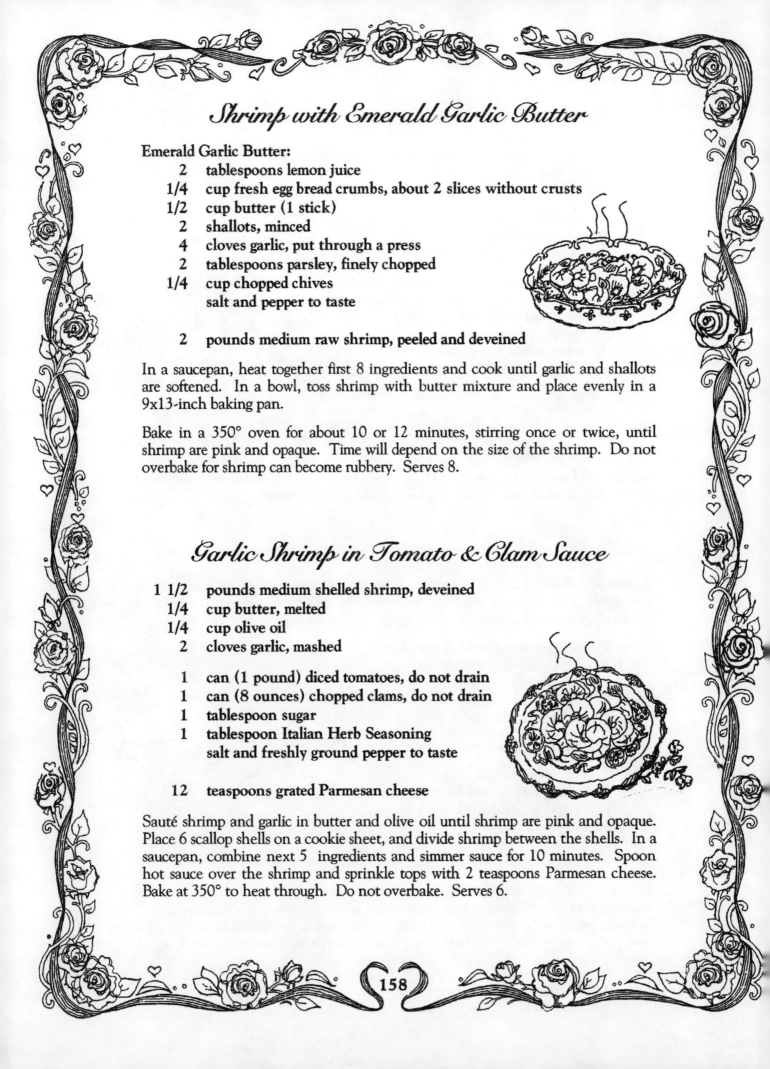

In a saucepan, heat together first 8 ingredients and cook until garlic and shallots are softened. In a bowl, toss shrimp with butter mixture and place evenly in a 9x13-inch baking pan.

Bake in a 350° oven for about 10 or 12 minutes, stirring once or twice, until shrimp are pink and opaque. Time will depend on the size of the shrimp. Do not overbake for shrimp can become rubbery. Serves 8.

Garlic Shrimp in Tomato & Clam Sauce

1 1/2	pounds medium shelled shrimp, deveined
1/4	cup butter, melted
1/4	cup olive oil
2	cloves garlic, mashed
1	can (1 pound) diced tomatoes, do not drain
1	can (8 ounces) chopped clams, do not drain
1	tablespoon sugar
1	tablespoon Italian Herb Seasoning
	salt and freshly ground pepper to taste
12	teaspoons grated Parmesan cheese

Sauté shrimp and garlic in butter and olive oil until shrimp are pink and opaque. Place 6 scallop shells on a cookie sheet, and divide shrimp between the shells. In a saucepan, combine next 5 ingredients and simmer sauce for 10 minutes. Spoon hot sauce over the shrimp and sprinkle tops with 2 teaspoons Parmesan cheese. Bake at 350° to heat through. Do not overbake. Serves 6.

Shrimp Jambalaya

This is a nice, easy shrimp dish that is bursting with flavor. The calories can be lowered by using firm-fleshed white fish like sole or halibut. This can be added to the stew base just before serving and cooked for 5 minutes, or until fish is opaque. Do not overcook. Stew base can be prepared earlier in the day and heated before serving. Add the shrimp or the fish just before serving.

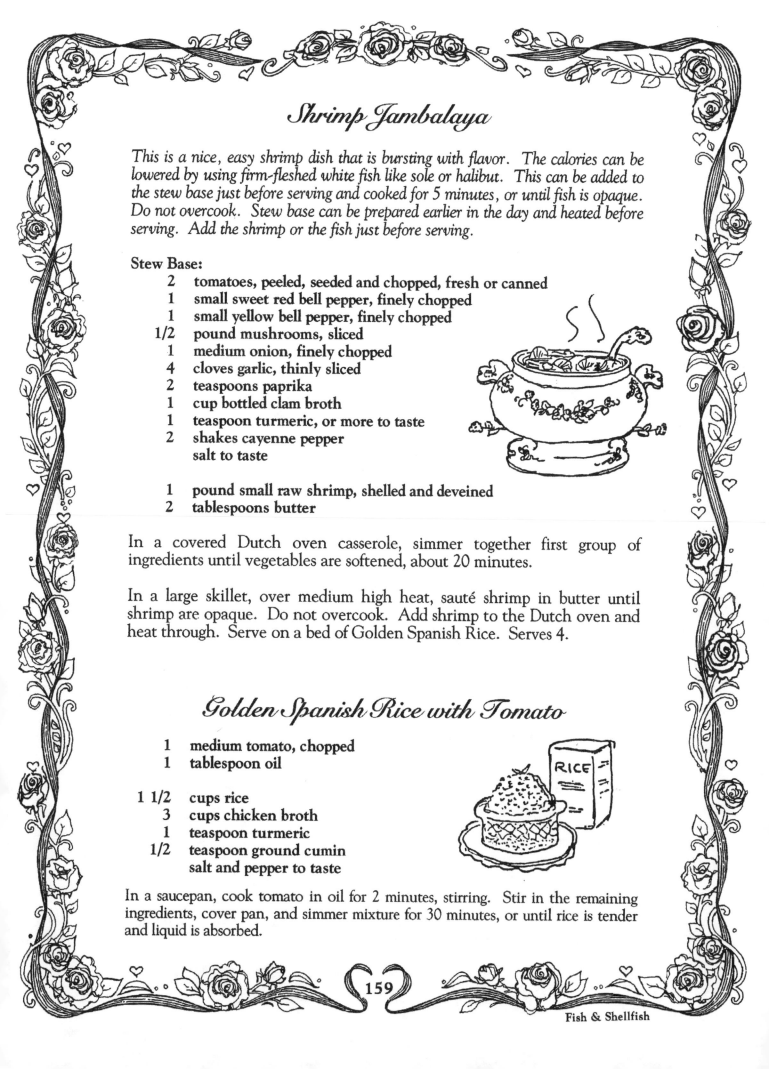

Stew Base:

2	tomatoes, peeled, seeded and chopped, fresh or canned
1	small sweet red bell pepper, finely chopped
1	small yellow bell pepper, finely chopped
1/2	pound mushrooms, sliced
1	medium onion, finely chopped
4	cloves garlic, thinly sliced
2	teaspoons paprika
1	cup bottled clam broth
1	teaspoon turmeric, or more to taste
2	shakes cayenne pepper
	salt to taste

1	pound small raw shrimp, shelled and deveined
2	tablespoons butter

In a covered Dutch oven casserole, simmer together first group of ingredients until vegetables are softened, about 20 minutes.

In a large skillet, over medium high heat, sauté shrimp in butter until shrimp are opaque. Do not overcook. Add shrimp to the Dutch oven and heat through. Serve on a bed of Golden Spanish Rice. Serves 4.

Golden Spanish Rice with Tomato

1	medium tomato, chopped
1	tablespoon oil

1 1/2	cups rice
3	cups chicken broth
1	teaspoon turmeric
1/2	teaspoon ground cumin
	salt and pepper to taste

In a saucepan, cook tomato in oil for 2 minutes, stirring. Stir in the remaining ingredients, cover pan, and simmer mixture for 30 minutes, or until rice is tender and liquid is absorbed.

Scampi with Shallots, Garlic & Lemon Sauce

Perhaps one of the easiest and best ways to prepare shrimp is to broil them for a few minutes in a rich garlic, butter and lemon sauce. Serve with a loaf of crusty Italian bread to dip in the delicious sauce.

1 1/2   pounds large shelled shrimp, peeled and deveined. (If you can leave the tails on, it's especially attractive.)

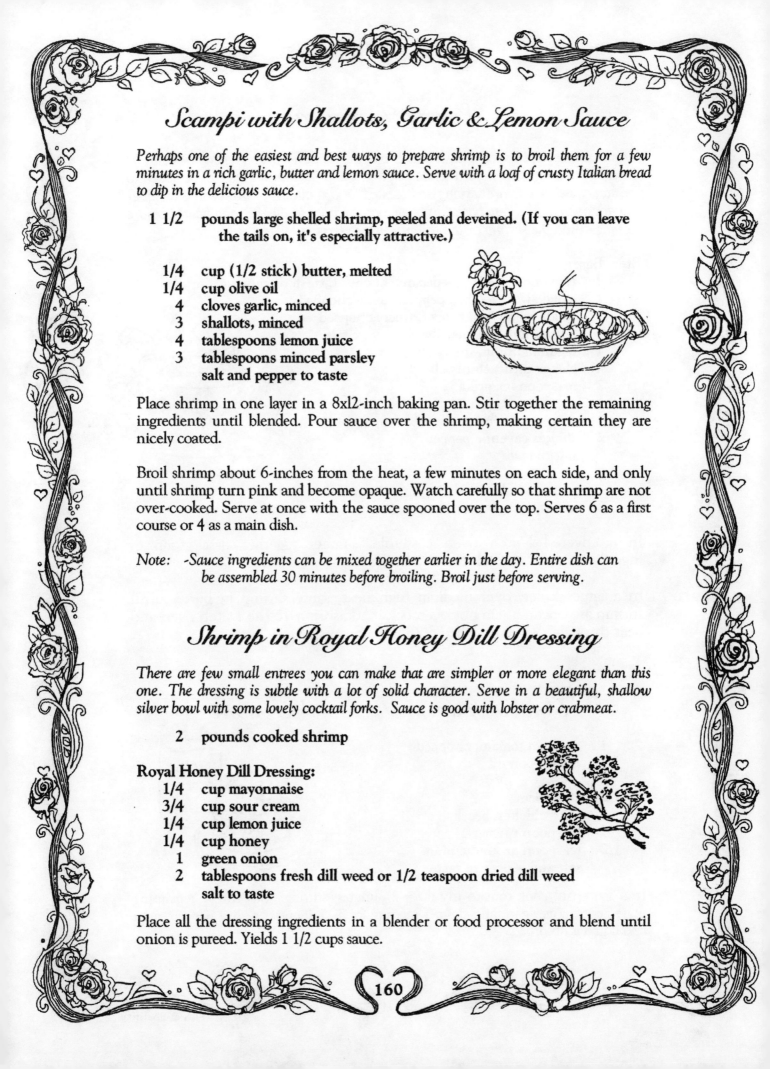

1/4   cup (1/2 stick) butter, melted
1/4   cup olive oil
4   cloves garlic, minced
3   shallots, minced
4   tablespoons lemon juice
3   tablespoons minced parsley
   salt and pepper to taste

Place shrimp in one layer in a 8x12-inch baking pan. Stir together the remaining ingredients until blended. Pour sauce over the shrimp, making certain they are nicely coated.

Broil shrimp about 6-inches from the heat, a few minutes on each side, and only until shrimp turn pink and become opaque. Watch carefully so that shrimp are not over-cooked. Serve at once with the sauce spooned over the top. Serves 6 as a first course or 4 as a main dish.

Note: -Sauce ingredients can be mixed together earlier in the day. Entire dish can be assembled 30 minutes before broiling. Broil just before serving.

Shrimp in Royal Honey Dill Dressing

There are few small entrees you can make that are simpler or more elegant than this one. The dressing is subtle with a lot of solid character. Serve in a beautiful, shallow silver bowl with some lovely cocktail forks. Sauce is good with lobster or crabmeat.

2   pounds cooked shrimp

Royal Honey Dill Dressing:
1/4   cup mayonnaise
3/4   cup sour cream
1/4   cup lemon juice
1/4   cup honey
1   green onion
2   tablespoons fresh dill weed or 1/2 teaspoon dried dill weed
   salt to taste

Place all the dressing ingredients in a blender or food processor and blend until onion is pureed. Yields 1 1/2 cups sauce.

Scampi with Yellow Rice & Tomatoes

This dish is a blaze of color...yellow rice, red tomatoes, green spinach...and is richly flavored with shallots and garlic.

3 tablespoons olive oil
2 pounds medium-size shrimp (about 20 per pound), peeled and deveined

Tomato & Spinach Sauce:
6 shallots, minced
3 cloves garlic, minced

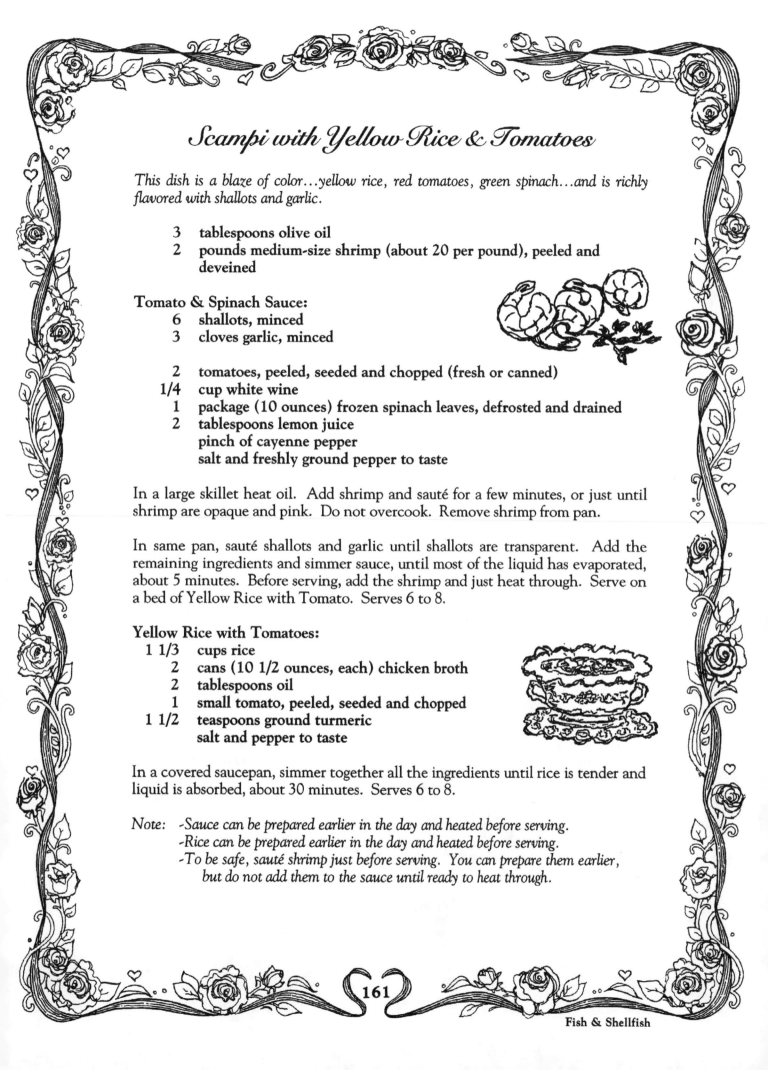

2 tomatoes, peeled, seeded and chopped (fresh or canned)
1/4 cup white wine
1 package (10 ounces) frozen spinach leaves, defrosted and drained
2 tablespoons lemon juice
pinch of cayenne pepper
salt and freshly ground pepper to taste

In a large skillet heat oil. Add shrimp and sauté for a few minutes, or just until shrimp are opaque and pink. Do not overcook. Remove shrimp from pan.

In same pan, sauté shallots and garlic until shallots are transparent. Add the remaining ingredients and simmer sauce, until most of the liquid has evaporated, about 5 minutes. Before serving, add the shrimp and just heat through. Serve on a bed of Yellow Rice with Tomato. Serves 6 to 8.

Yellow Rice with Tomatoes:
1 1/3 cups rice
2 cans (10 1/2 ounces, each) chicken broth
2 tablespoons oil
1 small tomato, peeled, seeded and chopped
1 1/2 teaspoons ground turmeric
salt and pepper to taste

In a covered saucepan, simmer together all the ingredients until rice is tender and liquid is absorbed, about 30 minutes. Serves 6 to 8.

Note: -Sauce can be prepared earlier in the day and heated before serving.
        -Rice can be prepared earlier in the day and heated before serving.
        -To be safe, sauté shrimp just before serving. You can prepare them earlier,
          but do not add them to the sauce until ready to heat through.

Easiest & Best American Fish Chowder

This lovely dish is not quite a stew, nor a soup. It lies somewhere in-between and it is filled with all manner of good things. The soup base is rich and flavorful, with just the mildest "bite."

Soup Base:

2	tablespoons oil
2	large onions, chopped
3	shallots, chopped
6	cloves garlic, minced
1	can (1 pound) stewed tomatoes, chopped. Do not drain.
3	cups tomato juice
1	tablespoon parsley flakes
1	teaspoon thyme flakes
1	teaspoon sweet basil flakes
2	teaspoons sugar
3	threads of saffron
1/2	teaspoon turmeric
1/4	teaspoon red pepper flakes
	salt and pepper to taste

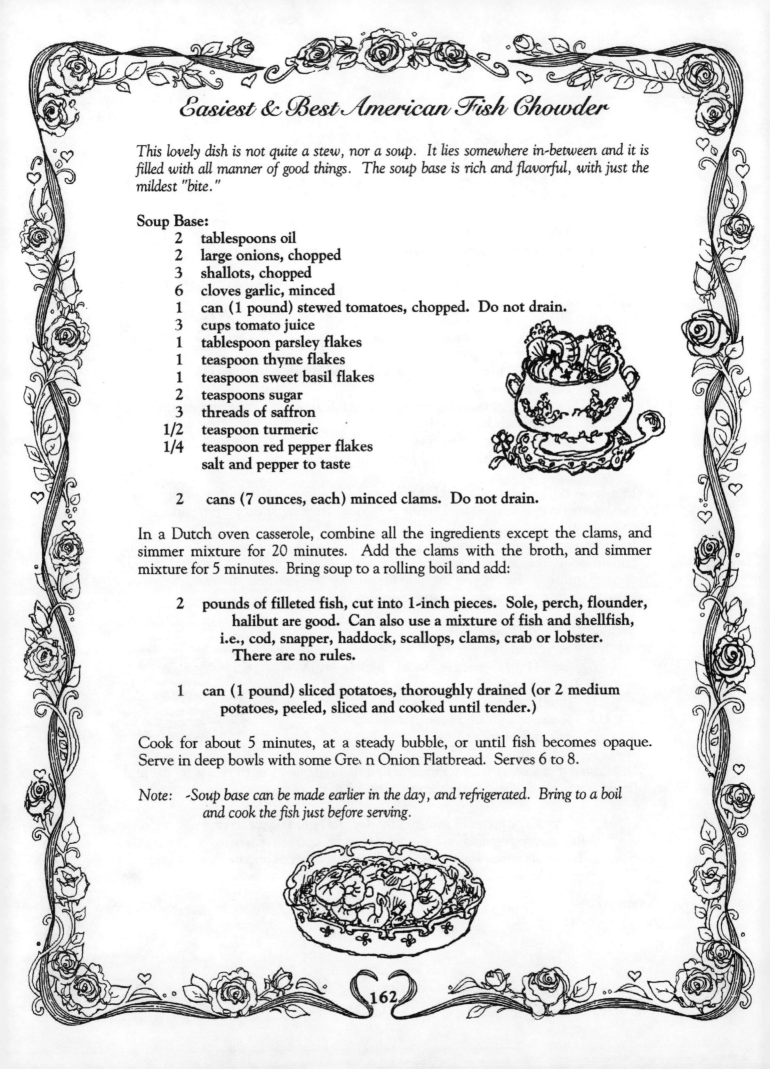

2   cans (7 ounces, each) minced clams. Do not drain.

In a Dutch oven casserole, combine all the ingredients except the clams, and simmer mixture for 20 minutes. Add the clams with the broth, and simmer mixture for 5 minutes. Bring soup to a rolling boil and add:

2   pounds of filleted fish, cut into 1-inch pieces. Sole, perch, flounder, halibut are good. Can also use a mixture of fish and shellfish, i.e., cod, snapper, haddock, scallops, clams, crab or lobster. There are no rules.

1   can (1 pound) sliced potatoes, thoroughly drained (or 2 medium potatoes, peeled, sliced and cooked until tender.)

Cook for about 5 minutes, at a steady bubble, or until fish becomes opaque. Serve in deep bowls with some Green Onion Flatbread. Serves 6 to 8.

Note: -Soup base can be made earlier in the day, and refrigerated. Bring to a boil and cook the fish just before serving.

Chili Horseradish Sauce for Fish or Shellfish

1 cup chili sauce
2 tablespoons, minced green onion
2 tablespoons, lemon juice
2 tablespoons prepared horseradish
   pinch of salt

In a glass jar, combine all the ingredients and stir to blend. Store in the refrigerator until serving time. Yields 1 1/4 cups sauce.

Cucumber Sauce for Cold Salmon or Shellfish

1/2 cup mayonnaise
1/2 cup sour cream
2   tablespoons lemon juice
1/4 cup finely chopped green onions
1/2 teaspoon dried dill weed
2   tablespoons finely chopped parsley
     salt and pepper to taste

1   cucumber, peeled, seeded and grated

Combine all the ingredients, except the cucumber, in a glass jar with a tight-fitting lid and stir until the mixture is throughly combined.

Salt the cucumber and let it drain in a strainer for 1 hour. Squeeze out the excess moisture. Add the cucumber to the dressing. Serve with cold poached salmon or shellfish. Yields 1 1/4 cups sauce.

Dilled Mustard Mayonnaise for Fish or Shellfish

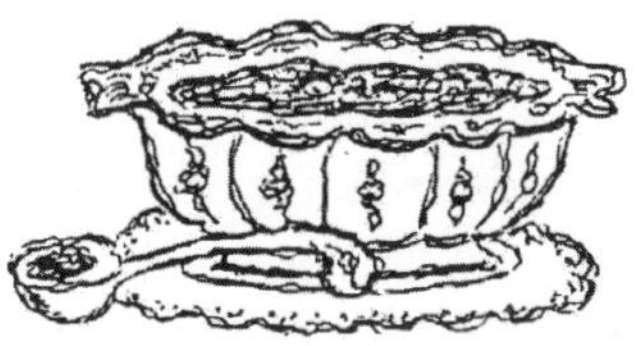

1/2 cup mayonnaise
2   tablespoons sour ream
1   tablespoon Dijon-style mustard
2   tablespoons sugar
3   tablespoons wine vinegar
1/2 teaspoon dill weed

Combine all the ingredients in a glass jar with a tight-fitting lid and stir until the mixture is thoroughly combined. Serve with cold poached fish or shellfish. Yields about 1 cup sauce.

Lobster with Tomatoes & Green Onions with Instant Cheese Sauce & Garlic Crumbs

This is an extremely simple dish. The Cheese sauce assembles in minutes and when you buy the lobster already cooked, then just brush with sauce, sprinkle the crumbs and heat and serve. You can substitute shrimp with equally good results.

1 1/2	pounds cooked lobster meat
2 or 3	finely chopped green onions
2	medium tomatoes, chopped
1/2	cup sour cream
	salt and pepper to taste
2	tablespoons lemon juice

In a bowl, combine all the ingredients and mix them until they are blended. Place mixture in a shallow baking dish and top with Instant Cheese Sauce and sprinkle with Garlic Cheese Crumbs. Heat in a 350° oven for about 15 minutes or until heated through. Serve with toast points. Lemon Rice with Peas & Parmesan and Spiced Peaches or Apricots are nice accompaniments. Serves 6 for lunch or 4 for dinner.

Instant Cheese Sauce:

1	cup sour cream
1	cup grated Gruyere cheese
2	tablespoons lemon juice

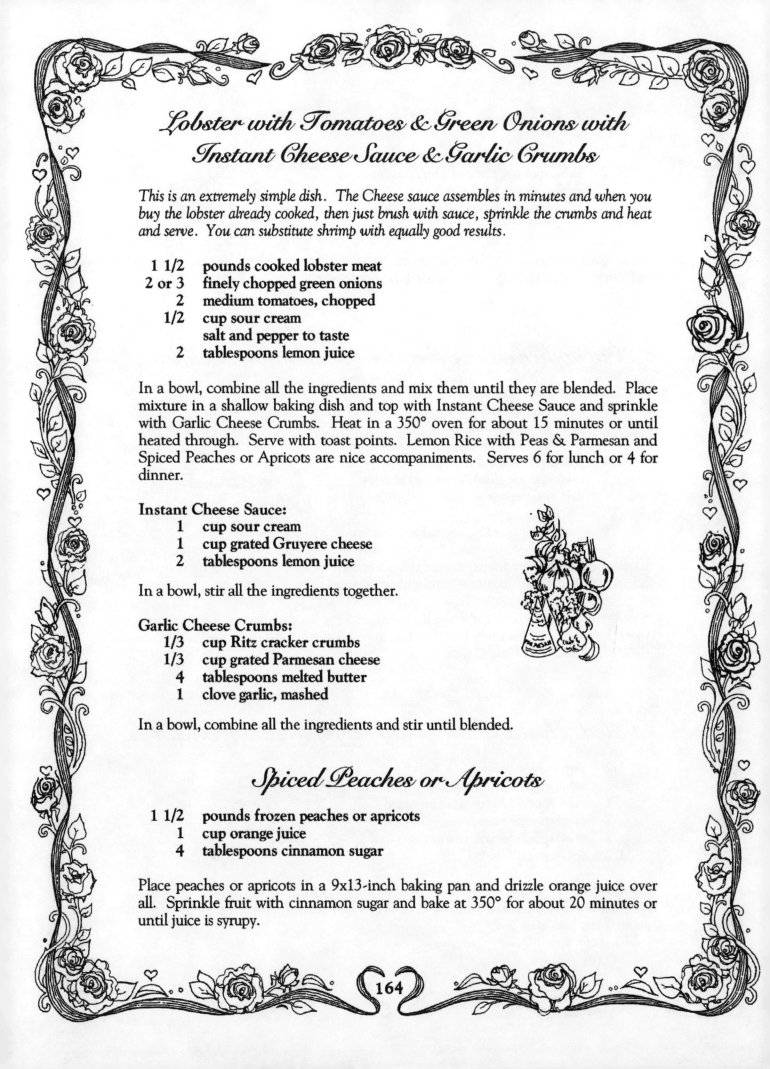

In a bowl, stir all the ingredients together.

Garlic Cheese Crumbs:

1/3	cup Ritz cracker crumbs
1/3	cup grated Parmesan cheese
4	tablespoons melted butter
1	clove garlic, mashed

In a bowl, combine all the ingredients and stir until blended.

Spiced Peaches or Apricots

1 1/2	pounds frozen peaches or apricots
1	cup orange juice
4	tablespoons cinnamon sugar

Place peaches or apricots in a 9x13-inch baking pan and drizzle orange juice over all. Sprinkle fruit with cinnamon sugar and bake at 350° for about 20 minutes or until juice is syrupy.

Poultry & Dressings

Chicken

Turkey

Rock Cornish Hens

Duck

Goose

Stuffings

Chicken Stroganov a la Russe

1 1/2	pounds boned chicken breasts, cut into bite-size pieces. Season with white pepper, garlic powder, paprika and dust with a little flour.
3	tablespoons butter
1/4	cup Cognac

Stroganov Sauce:
2	onions, finely chopped
2	tablespoons butter
1	pound mushrooms, thinly sliced
2	teaspoons sweet paprika
	salt to taste
1	cup sour cream

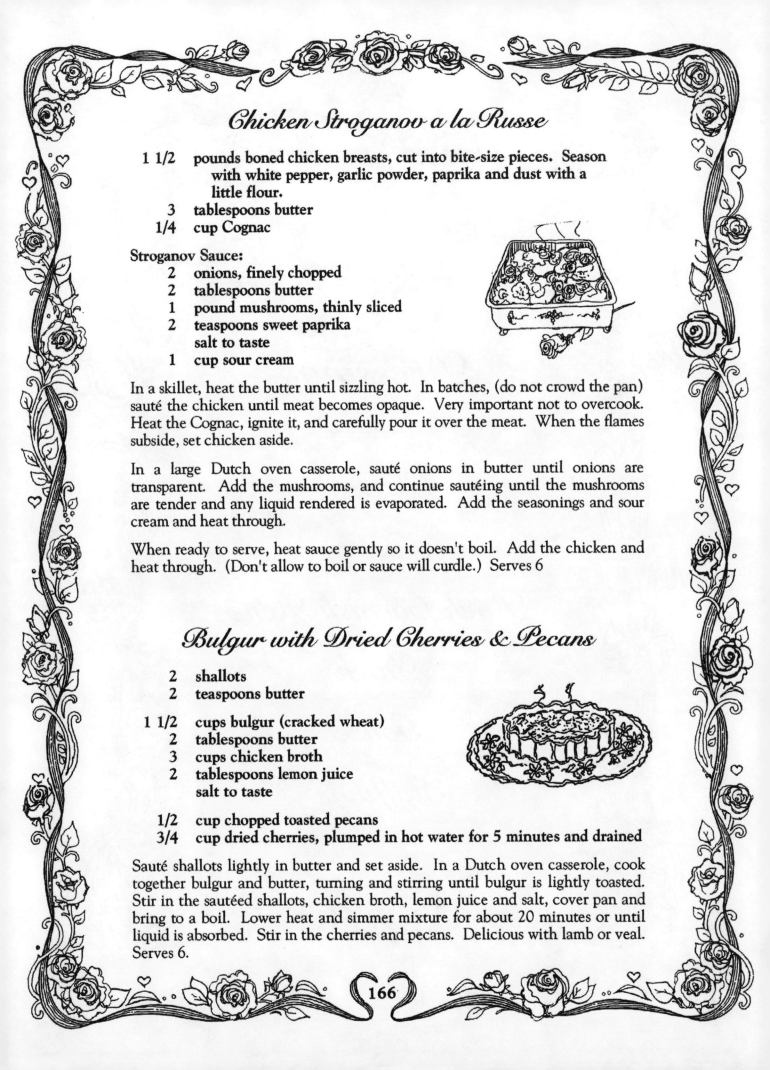

In a skillet, heat the butter until sizzling hot. In batches, (do not crowd the pan) sauté the chicken until meat becomes opaque. Very important not to overcook. Heat the Cognac, ignite it, and carefully pour it over the meat. When the flames subside, set chicken aside.

In a large Dutch oven casserole, sauté onions in butter until onions are transparent. Add the mushrooms, and continue sautéing until the mushrooms are tender and any liquid rendered is evaporated. Add the seasonings and sour cream and heat through.

When ready to serve, heat sauce gently so it doesn't boil. Add the chicken and heat through. (Don't allow to boil or sauce will curdle.) Serves 6

Bulgur with Dried Cherries & Pecans

2	shallots
2	teaspoons butter
1 1/2	cups bulgur (cracked wheat)
2	tablespoons butter
3	cups chicken broth
2	tablespoons lemon juice
	salt to taste
1/2	cup chopped toasted pecans
3/4	cup dried cherries, plumped in hot water for 5 minutes and drained

Sauté shallots lightly in butter and set aside. In a Dutch oven casserole, cook together bulgur and butter, turning and stirring until bulgur is lightly toasted. Stir in the sautéed shallots, chicken broth, lemon juice and salt, cover pan and bring to a boil. Lower heat and simmer mixture for about 20 minutes or until liquid is absorbed. Stir in the cherries and pecans. Delicious with lamb or veal. Serves 6.

Chicken in a Delicate Mushroom & Lemon Dill Sauce

This is one of the simplest, most elegant dishes you can serve for the most discriminating dinner party. Yet it is simple enough to prepare for family and friends some Sunday night, soon. The sauce is subtle and delicate with a good deal of depth and character. And it can be prepared, from beginning to end, in 30 minutes.

- 4 chicken breasts, boned and cut in halves. Sprinkle lightly with salt and garlic powder. Dust lightly with flour and brush lightly with 3 tablespoons melted butter.

Mushroom & Lemon Sauce:

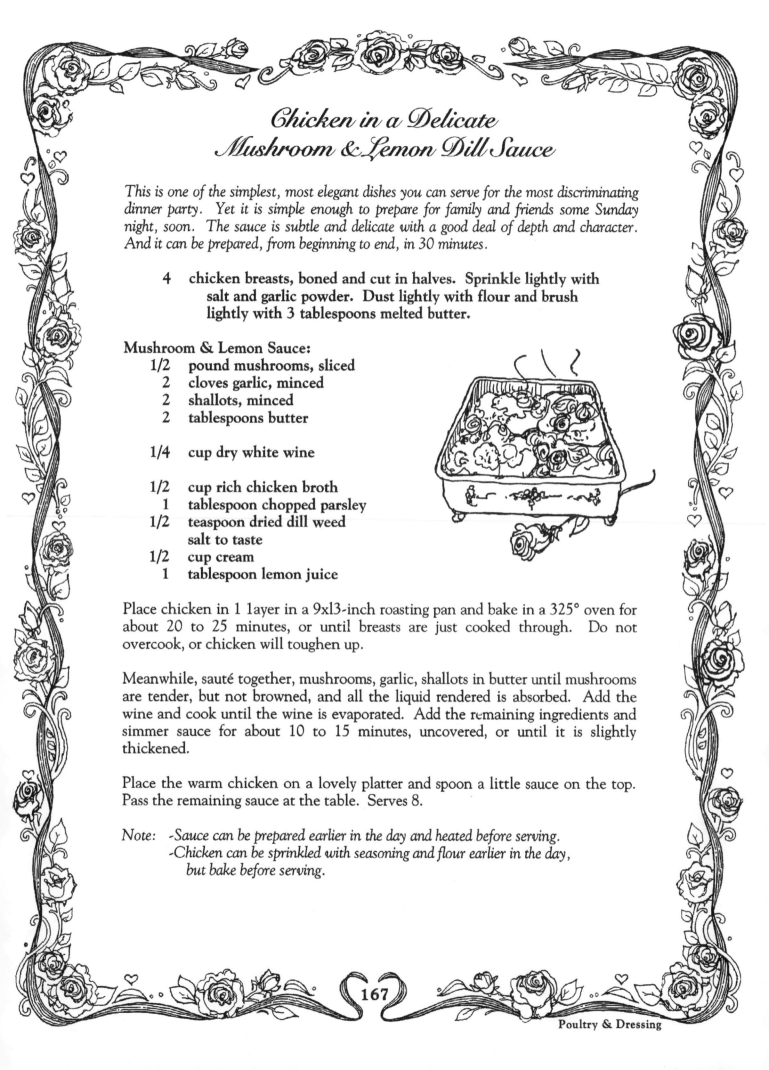

- 1/2 pound mushrooms, sliced
- 2 cloves garlic, minced
- 2 shallots, minced
- 2 tablespoons butter

- 1/4 cup dry white wine

- 1/2 cup rich chicken broth
- 1 tablespoon chopped parsley
- 1/2 teaspoon dried dill weed
  salt to taste
- 1/2 cup cream
- 1 tablespoon lemon juice

Place chicken in 1 layer in a 9x13-inch roasting pan and bake in a 325° oven for about 20 to 25 minutes, or until breasts are just cooked through. Do not overcook, or chicken will toughen up.

Meanwhile, sauté together, mushrooms, garlic, shallots in butter until mushrooms are tender, but not browned, and all the liquid rendered is absorbed. Add the wine and cook until the wine is evaporated. Add the remaining ingredients and simmer sauce for about 10 to 15 minutes, uncovered, or until it is slightly thickened.

Place the warm chicken on a lovely platter and spoon a little sauce on the top. Pass the remaining sauce at the table. Serves 8.

Note: -Sauce can be prepared earlier in the day and heated before serving.
-Chicken can be sprinkled with seasoning and flour earlier in the day, but bake before serving.

Oven-Fried Yogurt Chicken with Chiles & Cheese

If you are looking for an easy and unusual way to serve chicken, this is a good recipe to consider. The marinade is made with yogurt instead of butter and the lemon and chiles add a good deal of flavor.

1	can (7 ounces) diced green chiles
3/4	cup unflavored yogurt
	pinch of cayenne pepper
1/3	cup chopped chives
1	tablespoon lemon juice
12	chicken drumsticks or thighs, (about 3 pounds), sprinkled with salt and pepper
1 1/2	cups fresh lightly toasted bread crumbs

In a food processor, puree together first 5 ingredients. Brush mixture generously on the chicken and then coat chicken with crumbs. Place chicken on a greased 9x13-inch baking pan and bake at 400° for 30 minutes. Reduce heat to 350° and continue baking for 20 minutes, or until chicken is tender. Serve with Mexican Pink Rice. Serves 6.

Mexican Pink Rice

1 1/4	cups rice
2 1/2	cups chicken broth
2	medium tomatoes, seeded and chopped, fresh or canned
1	tablespoon oil
	salt to taste

In a Dutch oven casserole, stir together all the ingredients, cover pan and simmer mixture for 30 minutes, or until rice is tender and liquid is absorbed. Serves 6

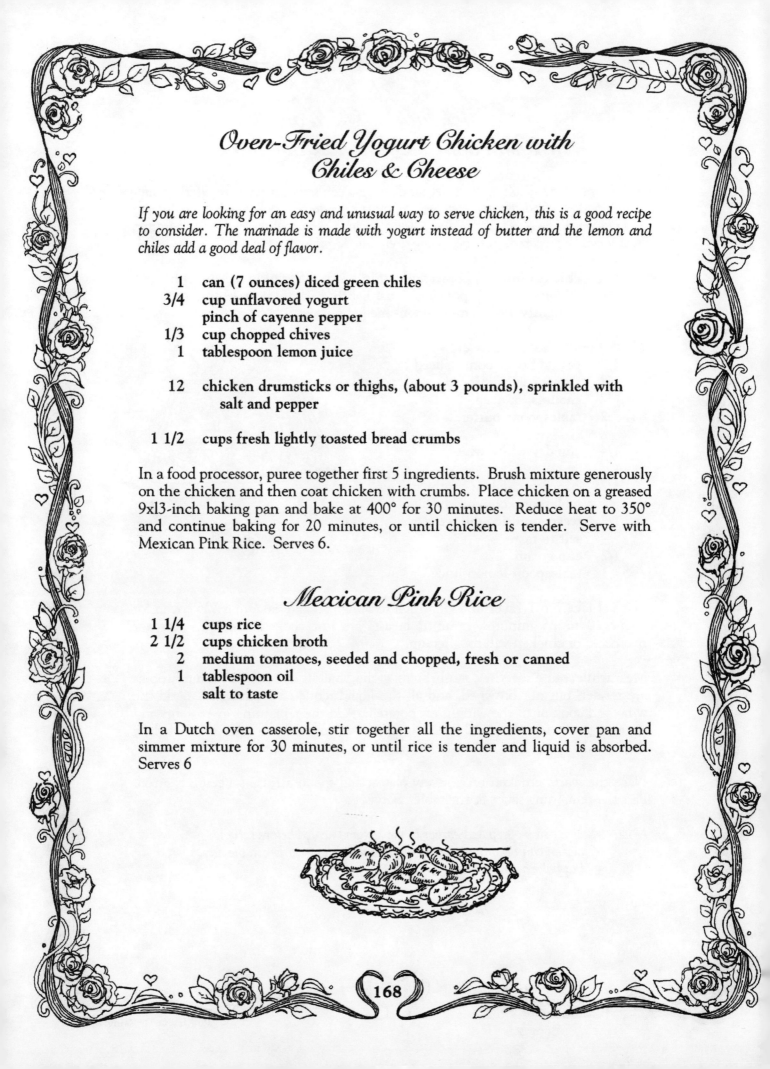

American Chicken Pad Thai

This is a fabulous dish to serve for an informal dinner with family and friends. I have detailed the instructions very carefully to assure success. In truth, after you make this dish once, you will be surprised that soaking the noodles takes the most time. The whole dish can be prepared in less than 15 minutes. Have to add that some Pad Thai lovers have said this was the best Pad Thai they ever had.

Prepare the Noodles (Step 1)

1   pound Thai rice noodles, medium-width

Place noodles in a large bowl and cover with hot tap water. Allow to stand for 30 minutes, or until noodles are limp. Place noodles in a colander to drain.

Prepare the Thai Sauce (Step 2)

1/2   cup butter
1   teaspoon minced garlic

1/3   cup sugar
1/3   cup ketchup
3   tablespoons Nampla (fish sauce)
1/4   teaspoon salt

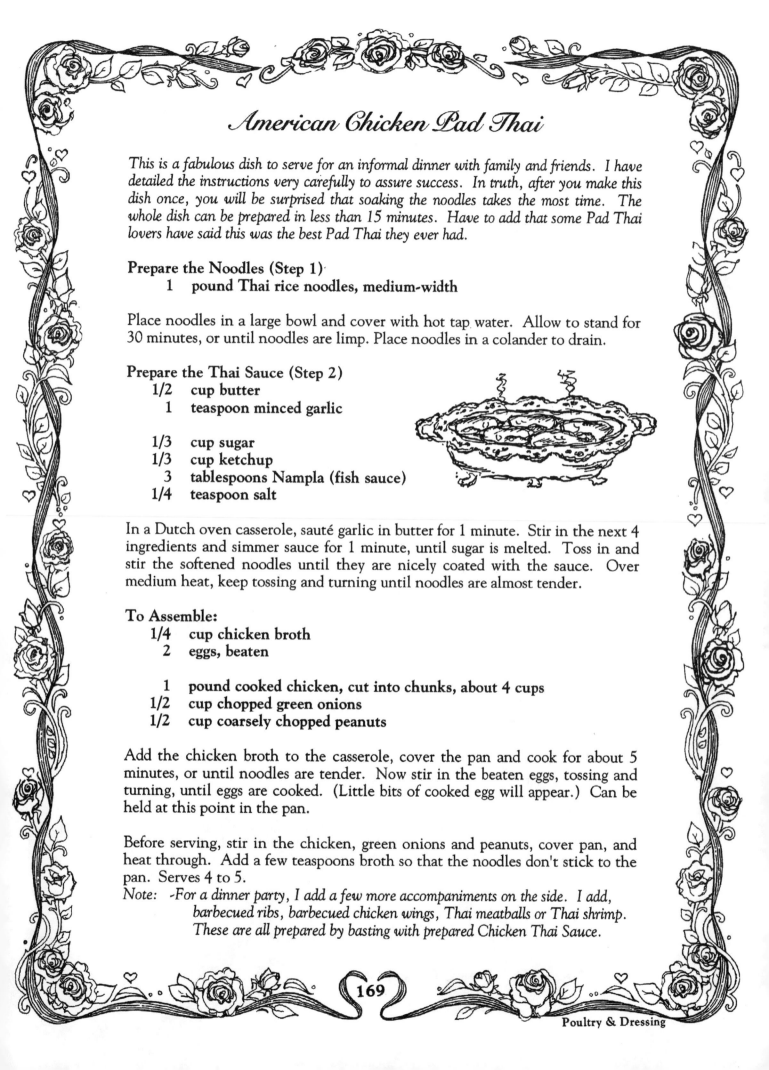

In a Dutch oven casserole, sauté garlic in butter for 1 minute. Stir in the next 4 ingredients and simmer sauce for 1 minute, until sugar is melted. Toss in and stir the softened noodles until they are nicely coated with the sauce. Over medium heat, keep tossing and turning until noodles are almost tender.

To Assemble:

1/4   cup chicken broth
2   eggs, beaten

1   pound cooked chicken, cut into chunks, about 4 cups
1/2   cup chopped green onions
1/2   cup coarsely chopped peanuts

Add the chicken broth to the casserole, cover the pan and cook for about 5 minutes, or until noodles are tender. Now stir in the beaten eggs, tossing and turning, until eggs are cooked. (Little bits of cooked egg will appear.) Can be held at this point in the pan.

Before serving, stir in the chicken, green onions and peanuts, cover pan, and heat through. Add a few teaspoons broth so that the noodles don't stick to the pan. Serves 4 to 5.

Note: -For a dinner party, I add a few more accompaniments on the side. I add, barbecued ribs, barbecued chicken wings, Thai meatballs or Thai shrimp. These are all prepared by basting with prepared Chicken Thai Sauce.

Chicken Creole in Hot Pepper Tomato Sauce

It is no small wonder that Creole cooking is so popular today. While this dish will not blister your palate, it is not for the faint of heart either. Of course, if you like it more peppery, add a pinch extra of cayenne. Go easy, though, to avoid a predominance of a single taste.

Sauce:
- 1 can (28-ounce) crushed tomatoes in tomato puree (reserve 2 tablespoons if preparing Pink Rice & Mushrooms)
- 6 tablespoons tomato paste
- 2 onions, chopped
- 1 red bell pepper, cut into strips
- 1 green bell pepper, cut into strips
- 6 cloves garlic, minced
- 2 tablespoons lemon juice
- 1/2 teaspoon each, paprika, sweet basil flakes and thyme flakes
- 1/8 teaspoon each, cayenne pepper and white pepper

- 3 chicken breasts, skinned, boned and halved. Sprinkle with garlic powder, onion powder and paprika.

In a Dutch oven casserole place all the sauce ingredients and simmer sauce for 30 minutes or until onions and peppers are softened.

In a 9x13-inch pan, place chicken breasts and bake at 350° for 15 minutes. Pour sauce over the breasts and bake for an additional 5 minutes, or until entire dish is heated through. Do not overcook at this point, or breasts will toughen up. Serve with Pink Rice and Mushrooms. Serves 6.

Pink Rice and Mushrooms:
- 1 cup rice
- 1 can (10 1/2 ounces) chicken broth
- 3/4 cup water
- 2 tablespoons tomato sauce
- pepper to taste

- 1/2 pound mushrooms
- 1 tablespoon oil

In a saucepan, stir together first 5 ingredients and simmer mixture for about 30 minutes, or until rice is tender and liquid is absorbed. Meanwhile, sauté mushrooms in oil until mushrooms are tender and liquid is evaporated. Toss mushrooms into rice, heat through and serve. Serves 6.

New Orleans Spicy & Hot Fried Chicken

As you probably know, I do not have a special fondness for peppery dishes that make your eyes tear and your breath come short. This chicken is "hot" but your palate will not get overpowered.

2   fryer chickens (about 2 1/2 pounds, each). Ask the butcher to cut each chicken into 10 pieces, (2 legs, 2 thighs, 2 wings, and 4 breast pieces.) Save the backs and necks for another use.

Pepper Seasoned Coating

2   eggs
2   tablespoons water

oil for frying

Roll the chicken pieces in the Pepper Seasoned Coating until they are nicely coated. Beat together the eggs with the water until blended.

Dip the coated chicken pieces in the egg mixture and sauté them in a little hot oil until they are golden brown on all sides. Place chicken pieces in a 12x16-inch roasting pan and bake for 25 to 30 minutes or until tender. Serves 8.

Pepper Seasoned Coating:
1/2   cup flour
1/2   cup grated Parmesan cheese
1 1/2   teaspoons garlic powder
1   teaspoon onion powder
1   tablespoon paprika
1/4   teaspoon cayenne pepper
salt to taste (I used 1/2 teaspoon.)

In a plastic container with a tight-fitting lid, combine all the ingredients and shake to blend. Unused coating mix can be store in the freezer.

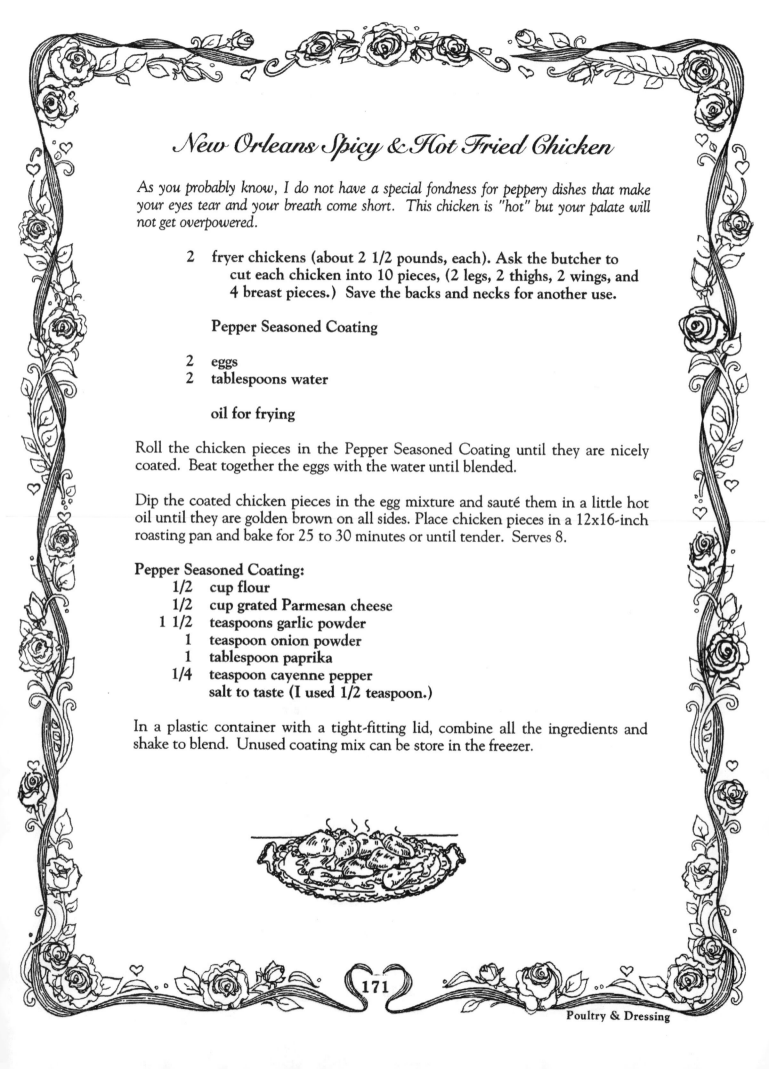

Chicken with Sweet Red Peppers, Garlic & Angel Hair Pasta

Tender, succulent chicken breasts, served with sautéed green and red peppers, strongly accented with garlic, all add to a wonderful dish for informal dinners. Serve this with Angel Hair Pasta with Fresh Tomatoes, Garlic & Basil.

6   boned chicken breast halves, sprinkled with paprika, pepper, and garlic powder. Brush with a little butter.

2   large sweet red peppers, seeded and cut into 1-inch slices
1   large green pepper, seeded and cut into 1-inch slices
4   cloves garlic, minced
1/2   cup chicken broth
1   tablespoon olive oil
    salt and pepper to taste

Bake chicken breasts in a 325° oven for about 25 minutes or until just cooked through. Do not overbake. Allow to cool and cut into large chunks. Place chicken in an oval porcelain baker.

In a covered Dutch oven casserole, simmer together remaining ingredients until vegetables are tender, about 15 minutes.

Place cooked peppers over the chicken and drizzle the pan juices evenly over all. Chicken can be held at this point. When ready to serve, sprinkle with a little grated Parmesan cheese and heat in a 325° oven until heated through. Do not overheat. Serves 6.

Angel Hair Pasta with Fresh Tomatoes, Garlic & Basil:
3   cloves garlic, minced
2   tablespoons olive oil

8   medium tomatoes, (about 2 pounds), peeled, seeded and chopped
1/2   teaspoon vinegar
1   teaspoon sugar
    salt and freshly ground pepper to taste

2   tablespoons chopped fresh basil

3/4   pound angel hair pasta, cooked al dente, tender but firm

In a saucepan, sauté garlic in oil for 1 minute, stirring. Add the next 5 ingredients and simmer mixture for about 10 minutes, or until some of the liquid has evaporated and sauce has thickened slightly. Add the basil and cook for 1 minute longer. Serve it over angel hair pasta and serves 6.

Sweet & Sour Country Chicken with Carrots & Raisins

Serve this succulent chicken dish with a crusty French bread to soak up the delicious gravy.

2   fryer chickens (about 2 1/2 pounds, each) cut up.
       Sprinkle with salt, pepper and garlic powder.

1   tablespoon oil
1   can (16 ounces) tomato sauce
1   carrot, grated
1   onion, finely chopped
1   cup sauerkraut, undrained
1/2 cup brown sugar
1/2 cup yellow raisins
       salt and pepper to taste

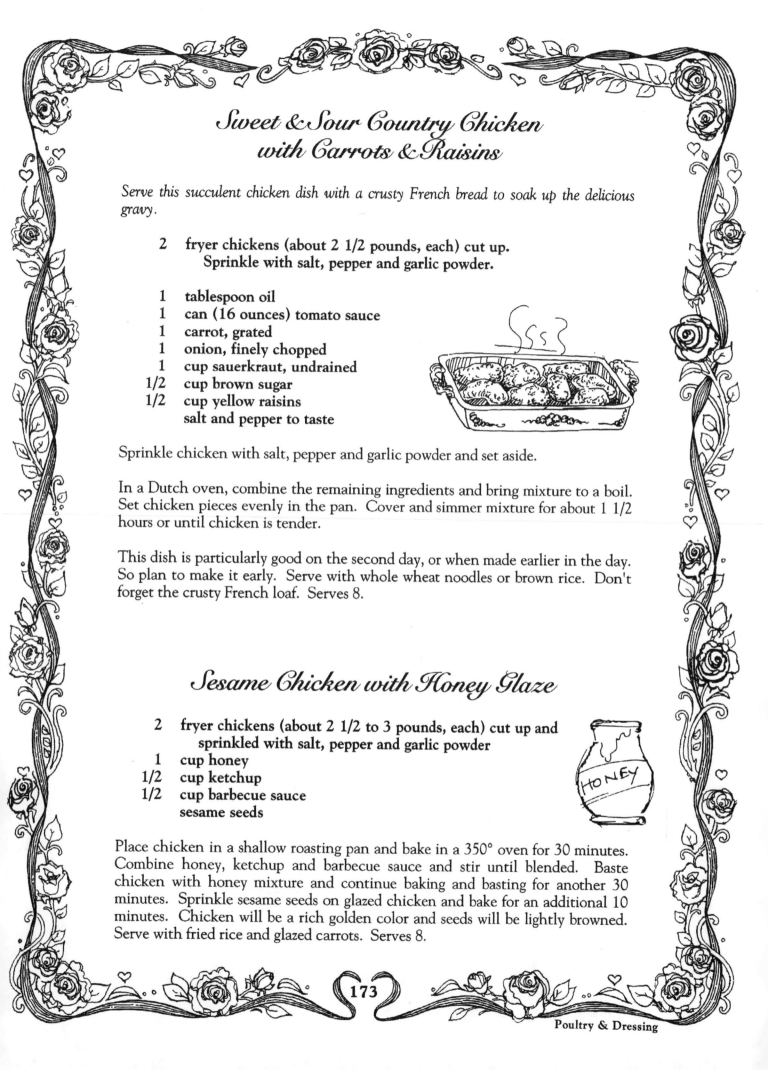

Sprinkle chicken with salt, pepper and garlic powder and set aside.

In a Dutch oven, combine the remaining ingredients and bring mixture to a boil. Set chicken pieces evenly in the pan. Cover and simmer mixture for about 1 1/2 hours or until chicken is tender.

This dish is particularly good on the second day, or when made earlier in the day. So plan to make it early. Serve with whole wheat noodles or brown rice. Don't forget the crusty French loaf. Serves 8.

Sesame Chicken with Honey Glaze

2   fryer chickens (about 2 1/2 to 3 pounds, each) cut up and
       sprinkled with salt, pepper and garlic powder
1   cup honey
1/2 cup ketchup
1/2 cup barbecue sauce
       sesame seeds

Place chicken in a shallow roasting pan and bake in a 350° oven for 30 minutes. Combine honey, ketchup and barbecue sauce and stir until blended. Baste chicken with honey mixture and continue baking and basting for another 30 minutes. Sprinkle sesame seeds on glazed chicken and bake for an additional 10 minutes. Chicken will be a rich golden color and seeds will be lightly browned. Serve with fried rice and glazed carrots. Serves 8.

Honey Buttermilk Chicken with Honey Pecan Glaze

Chicken on Sunday is an old American tradition. But serving it glazed with honey and pecans adds a new touch to an old favorite. Chicken can be prepared earlier in the day, but sprinkle pecans the last 10 minutes of reheating.

2	fryer chickens, cut up into serving pieces. Sprinkle with salt, pepper and garlic powder.

2	tablespoons honey
1	egg
1/2	cup buttermilk

1/2	cup cracker crumbs. (Use a savory cracker, like Ritz or Waverly.)

1/2	cup honey, heated
1/2	cup chopped pecans

Beat together honey, egg and buttermilk until blended. On a flat plate, place cracker crumbs. Dip chicken pieces into buttermilk mixture and then roll lightly into cracker crumbs. Place chicken pieces in 1 layer in a 12x16-inch baking pan.

Bake in a 350° oven for 40 minutes. Baste chicken lightly with warm honey and continue baking for 30 minutes. Now, baste with honey again and sprinkle chicken with chopped pecans. Bake for another 8 minutes or until pecans are lightly toasted. (Watch carefully so that pecans do not burn.)

Serve at once with warm Buttery Raisin Scones, buttered broccoli and Orange Honey Baked Apples. Wonderful! Serves 6 to 8.

Orange Honey Baked Apples:

6	baking apples, peeled, cored and sliced
1/4	cup honey
3/4	cup orange juice
1/2	grated orange (Use fruit, juice and peel.)
1/4	cup yellow raisins

3	tablespoons cinnamon sugar

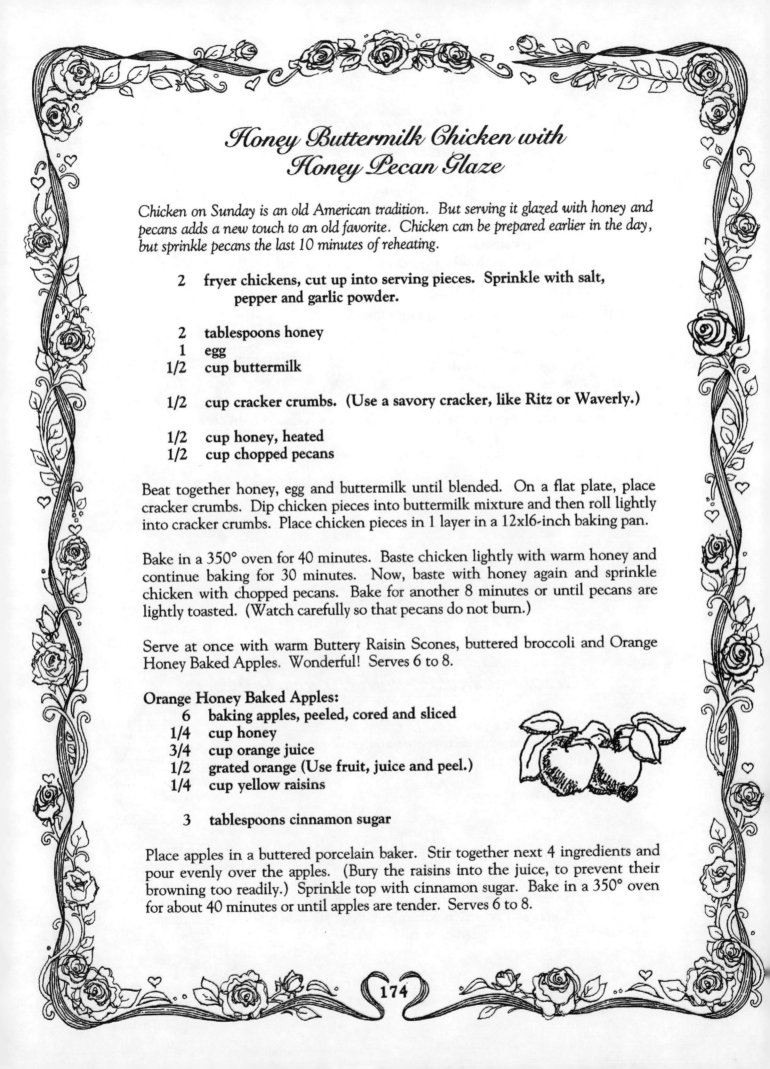

Place apples in a buttered porcelain baker. Stir together next 4 ingredients and pour evenly over the apples. (Bury the raisins into the juice, to prevent their browning too readily.) Sprinkle top with cinnamon sugar. Bake in a 350° oven for about 40 minutes or until apples are tender. Serves 6 to 8.

Black Raspberry Glazed Chicken with Wild Rice & Almond Stuffing

This is a grand dish to serve for a formal dinner party, yet simple enough to serve family and friends on an evening when preparation time is limited. Serve with additional wild rice as an accompaniment, or buttered vegetables and spiced apricots … DELICIOUS!

8   halved chicken breasts (about 6 to 8 ounces, each, after boning.)
        (Ask butcher to remove skin and bones and to gently flatten.)
        Sprinkle with salt, paprika and garlic.

Wild Rice & Almond Stuffing

Black Raspberry Honey Glaze

Place 1 part stuffing in center of each (half) breast. Roll and secure with a wooden toothpick. Dust stuffed breasts lightly with flour. Melt 1/2 cup butter (1 stick) in a 9x13-inch baking pan and roll stuffed breasts in melted butter. Bake in a 325° oven for 30 minutes.

Now, baste with Black Raspberry Honey Glaze and continue baking and basting until chicken is tender and highly glazed, about 30 minutes. (Baste 2 or 3 times during the final baking period.)

Serve with additional wild rice, a simple buttered vegetable, or spiced fruit. Carrots, glazed with raisins, is especially nice. Serves 8.

Wild Rice & Almond Stuffing:
Cook 1 package (7 ounces) Herb Seasoned Wild and Long Grain Rice according to the directions on the package, except substitute 2 cups chicken broth for the 2 cups water. When rice is tender, and all the liquid is absorbed, stir in 1/2 cup toasted slivered almonds.

Black Raspberry Honey Glaze:
    1/2   cup seedless black raspberry jam
    1/2   cup honey
      2   tablespoons frozen orange juice concentrate. Do not dilute.
      1   teaspoon finely grated orange peel

In a saucepan, heat all the ingredients together and stir until blended.

Note: -Entire dish can be prepared earlier in the day, but shorten baking time by 10 minutes. Continue baking and glazing just before ready to serve.

Chicken Normandy with Apples & Cream

Fruit is a marvelous accompaniment to chicken…and it always amazes me as to how many combinations are possible. This is a very simple dish to prepare, but the results are literally fit for a king.

- 2   fryers (2 1/2 to 3 pounds, each) cut into pieces. **Baste with butter and sprinkle with salt, pepper, garlic powder and a light sprinkle of onion powder.**

- 1/2   cup butter (1 stick)
- 2   tablespoons sugar
- 1/4   teaspoon cinnamon
- 6   medium apples, cored, peeled and cut into quarters. Sprinkle with lemon juice to keep apples from darkening.

- 1   cup apple juice
- 1/4   teaspoon poultry seasoning
     pinch of thyme

- 1   cup cream

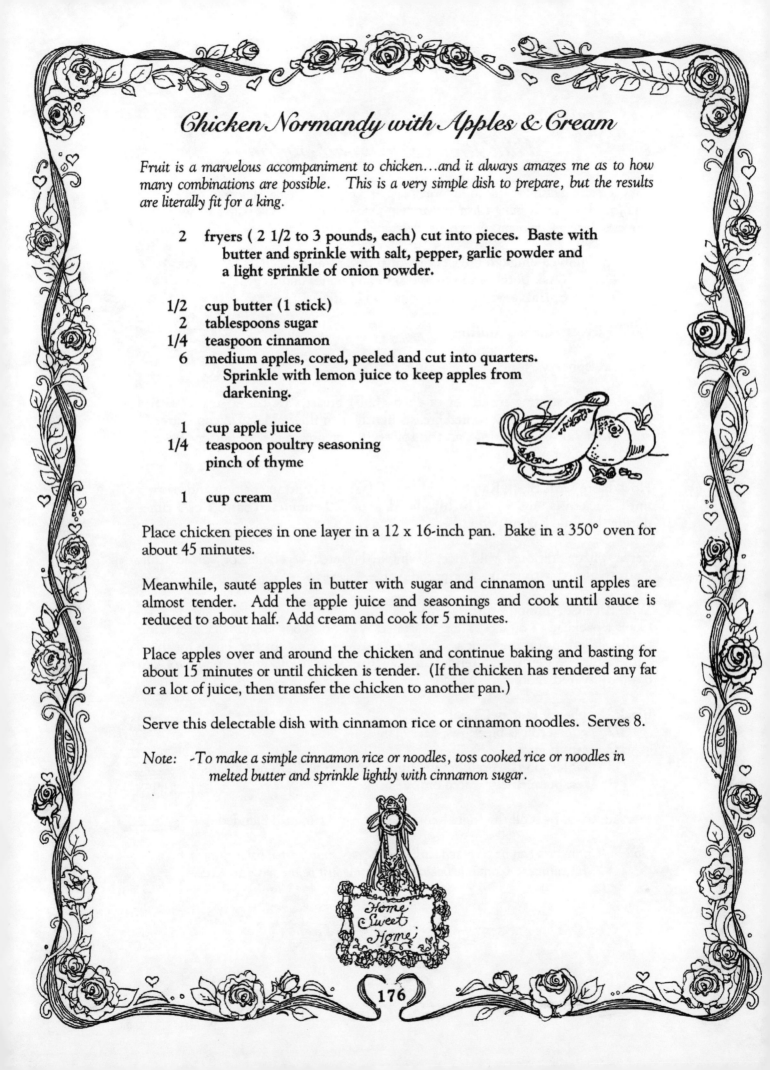

Place chicken pieces in one layer in a 12 x 16-inch pan. Bake in a 350° oven for about 45 minutes.

Meanwhile, sauté apples in butter with sugar and cinnamon until apples are almost tender. Add the apple juice and seasonings and cook until sauce is reduced to about half. Add cream and cook for 5 minutes.

Place apples over and around the chicken and continue baking and basting for about 15 minutes or until chicken is tender. (If the chicken has rendered any fat or a lot of juice, then transfer the chicken to another pan.)

Serve this delectable dish with cinnamon rice or cinnamon noodles. Serves 8.

Note: -To make a simple cinnamon rice or noodles, toss cooked rice or noodles in melted butter and sprinkle lightly with cinnamon sugar.

Honey-Glazed Roast Chicken with Old-Fashioned Fruit Pudding

This dish is the quintessence of Sunday family dinners. While it is so simple to prepare it adds a great deal of glamour and excitement to a plain roast chicken. The fruit pudding is a family favorite and I hope it will be for yours, too.

2   fryer chickens, cut into serving pieces (about 2 1/2 to 3 pounds, each). Sprinkle generously with salt, pepper and garlic powder.

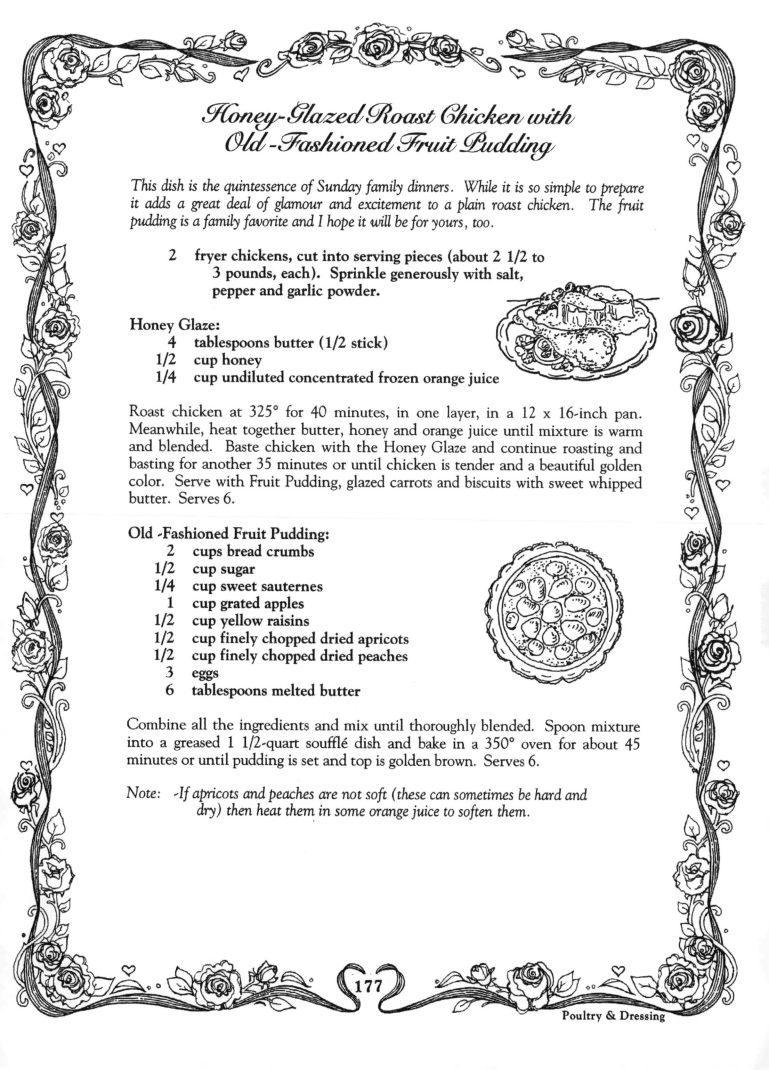

Honey Glaze:
- 4   tablespoons butter (1/2 stick)
- 1/2   cup honey
- 1/4   cup undiluted concentrated frozen orange juice

Roast chicken at 325° for 40 minutes, in one layer, in a 12 x 16-inch pan. Meanwhile, heat together butter, honey and orange juice until mixture is warm and blended. Baste chicken with the Honey Glaze and continue roasting and basting for another 35 minutes or until chicken is tender and a beautiful golden color. Serve with Fruit Pudding, glazed carrots and biscuits with sweet whipped butter. Serves 6.

Old-Fashioned Fruit Pudding:
- 2   cups bread crumbs
- 1/2   cup sugar
- 1/4   cup sweet sauternes
- 1   cup grated apples
- 1/2   cup yellow raisins
- 1/2   cup finely chopped dried apricots
- 1/2   cup finely chopped dried peaches
- 3   eggs
- 6   tablespoons melted butter

Combine all the ingredients and mix until thoroughly blended. Spoon mixture into a greased 1 1/2-quart soufflé dish and bake in a 350° oven for about 45 minutes or until pudding is set and top is golden brown. Serves 6.

Note: -If apricots and peaches are not soft (these can sometimes be hard and dry) then heat them in some orange juice to soften them.

Kung Pao Chicken with Peanuts

Kung Pao Chicken is one of my favorite Asian dishes. Restaurants usually prepare this dish very hot and spicy. I always order it "mild". Dried red chili peppers is the spice most often used. But Chinese Chili Sauce is a good substitute.

Chicken Mixture:

4	chicken breast halves (4 ounces, each) skinned, boned and cut into 1/2-inch cubes
3/4	cup peanuts
3/4	cup green onions, cut on the diagonal into 1/2-inch slices
3	cloves garlic minced
1/4	teaspoon Chinese Chili Sauce

Sauce:

3/4	cup rich chicken broth
1	tablespoon soy sauce
1	tablespoon hoisin sauce
1	tablespoon sesame oil
2	teaspoons rice vinegar
1	tablespoon cornstarch
2	tablespoons peanut oil

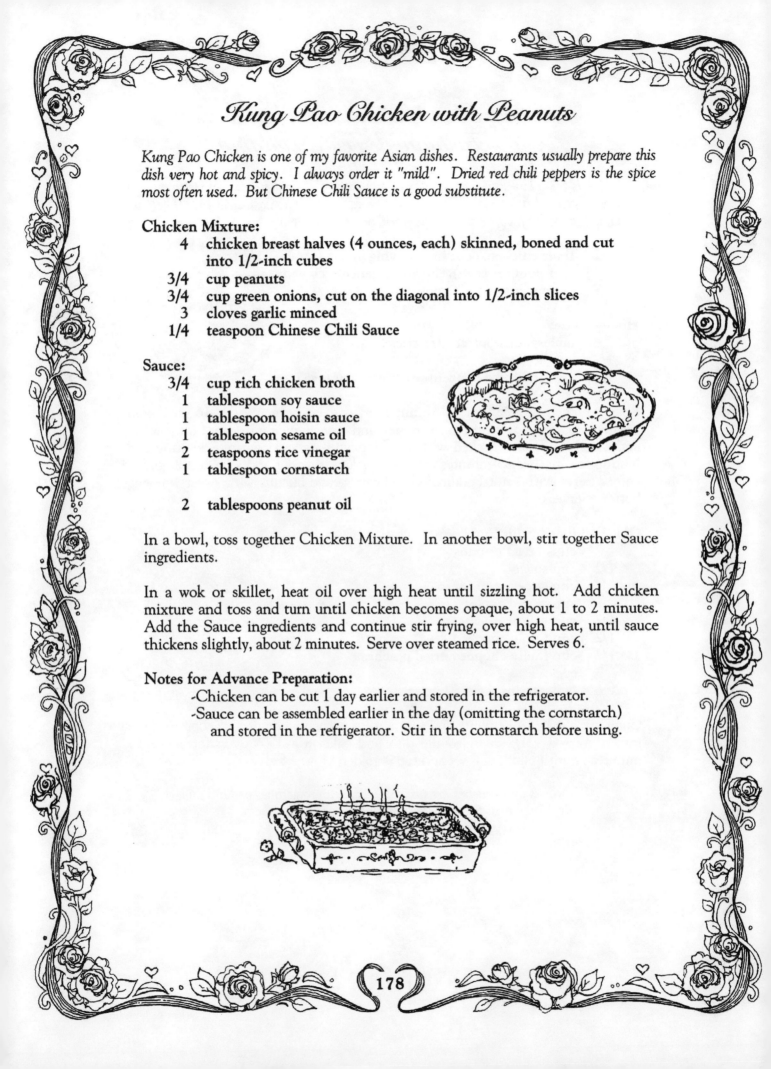

In a bowl, toss together Chicken Mixture. In another bowl, stir together Sauce ingredients.

In a wok or skillet, heat oil over high heat until sizzling hot. Add chicken mixture and toss and turn until chicken becomes opaque, about 1 to 2 minutes. Add the Sauce ingredients and continue stir frying, over high heat, until sauce thickens slightly, about 2 minutes. Serve over steamed rice. Serves 6.

Notes for Advance Preparation:
-Chicken can be cut 1 day earlier and stored in the refrigerator.
-Sauce can be assembled earlier in the day (omitting the cornstarch) and stored in the refrigerator. Stir in the cornstarch before using.

Roast Chicken with Cinnamon, Orange & Honey Glaze

2　fryer chickens (about 3 pounds each), cut into serving pieces.
　　Sprinkle with salt, pepper, garlic powder and paprika to taste.
4　tablespoons melted butter

Cinnamon, Orange & Honey Glaze:
　1　cup honey
1/2　cup orange juice
　1　tablespoon grated orange peel
1/2　teaspoon cinnamon
　　pinch of powdered cloves

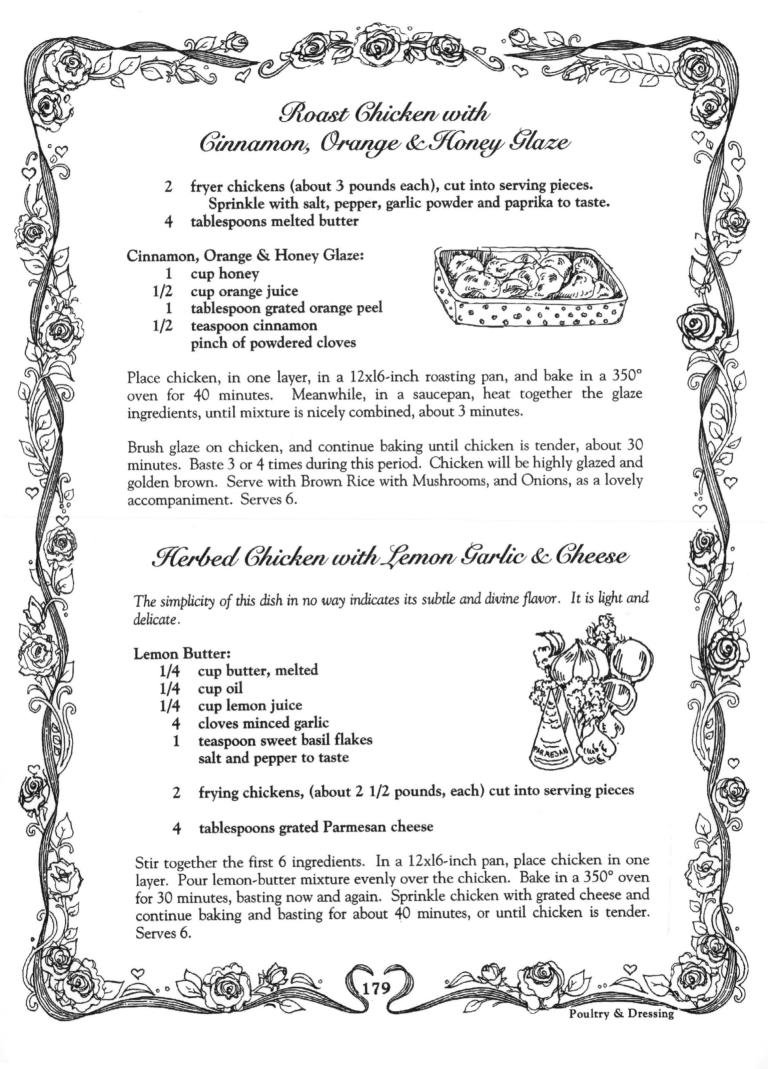

Place chicken, in one layer, in a 12x16-inch roasting pan, and bake in a 350° oven for 40 minutes.　Meanwhile, in a saucepan, heat together the glaze ingredients, until mixture is nicely combined, about 3 minutes.

Brush glaze on chicken, and continue baking until chicken is tender, about 30 minutes.　Baste 3 or 4 times during this period.　Chicken will be highly glazed and golden brown.　Serve with Brown Rice with Mushrooms, and Onions, as a lovely accompaniment.　Serves 6.

Herbed Chicken with Lemon Garlic & Cheese

The simplicity of this dish in no way indicates its subtle and divine flavor. It is light and delicate.

Lemon Butter:
1/4　cup butter, melted
1/4　cup oil
1/4　cup lemon juice
　4　cloves minced garlic
　1　teaspoon sweet basil flakes
　　salt and pepper to taste

2　frying chickens, (about 2 1/2 pounds, each) cut into serving pieces

4　tablespoons grated Parmesan cheese

Stir together the first 6 ingredients.　In a 12x16-inch pan, place chicken in one layer.　Pour lemon-butter mixture evenly over the chicken.　Bake in a 350° oven for 30 minutes, basting now and again.　Sprinkle chicken with grated cheese and continue baking and basting for about 40 minutes, or until chicken is tender.　Serves 6.

Chicken Curry with Apples and Raisins

2 tablespoons butter
2 onions, finely chopped
2 cloves garlic, minced

1/4 cup flour
1 tablespoon curry powder (or to taste)
    salt to taste

2 large apples, peeled, cored and grated
2 tablespoons brown sugar
1 cup yellow raisins, plumped overnight in orange juice
2 cans chicken broth (10 1/2 ounces, each)

1 cup low-fat sour cream
3 cups cooked chicken breasts, cut into chunks

Sauté onion and garlic in butter until onions are transparent. Add flour, curry powder and salt and cook for two minutes stirring all the while.

Add apples, brown sugar, raisins and chicken broth. Cook over low heat, stirring, until sauce thickens. (If sauce is too thick, add a little more broth).

Stir in sour cream and chicken and heat through. Do not allow to boil. Serves 6.

Cinnamon Rice with Raisins & Pine Nuts

1 cup rice
2 cups chicken broth
2 tablespoons butter
    salt to taste

2 onions, chopped
2 tablespoons butter
1 tablespoon sugar

1 cup yellow raisins
3/4 cup pine nuts
1/4 teaspoon cinnamon

In a saucepan, stir together first 4 ingredients. Cover pan and simmer rice, until liquid is absorbed and rice is tender, about 30 minutes. In a skillet, sauté onions in butter with sugar until onions are soft. Stir in raisins, pine nuts and cinnamon and cook and stir for 1 minute. Stir together cooked rice and onion mixture until well mixed. Place mixture into a 2-quart soufflé dish and cover tightly with foil.

At serving time, add a little broth, cover with foil and heat in a 325° oven until heated through, about 25 minutes. Serves 6.

Golden Plum-Glazed Chicken Teriyaki

2   fryer chickens (about 2 1/2 pounds, each) cut into serving pieces.
      Baste with a Teriyaki Marinade. Sprinkle chicken with pepper
      and garlic powder.

Place chicken in one layer in a 12x16-inch baking pan and bake at 325° for 40 minutes. Baste with Hot Plum Glaze 2 or 3 times during the remainder of the baking, about 40 minutes or until chicken is tender and golden. Serves 8.

Teriyaki Marinade:
1/2   cup soy sauce
2   tablespoons brown sugar

Stir together all the ingredients until mixture is blended and sugar is dissolved.

Hot Plum Glaze:
1   cup plum jam
2   tablespoons vinegar
2   tablespoons soy sauce
1/2   cup chili sauce
1   tablespoon brown sugar
       pinch of cayenne pepper

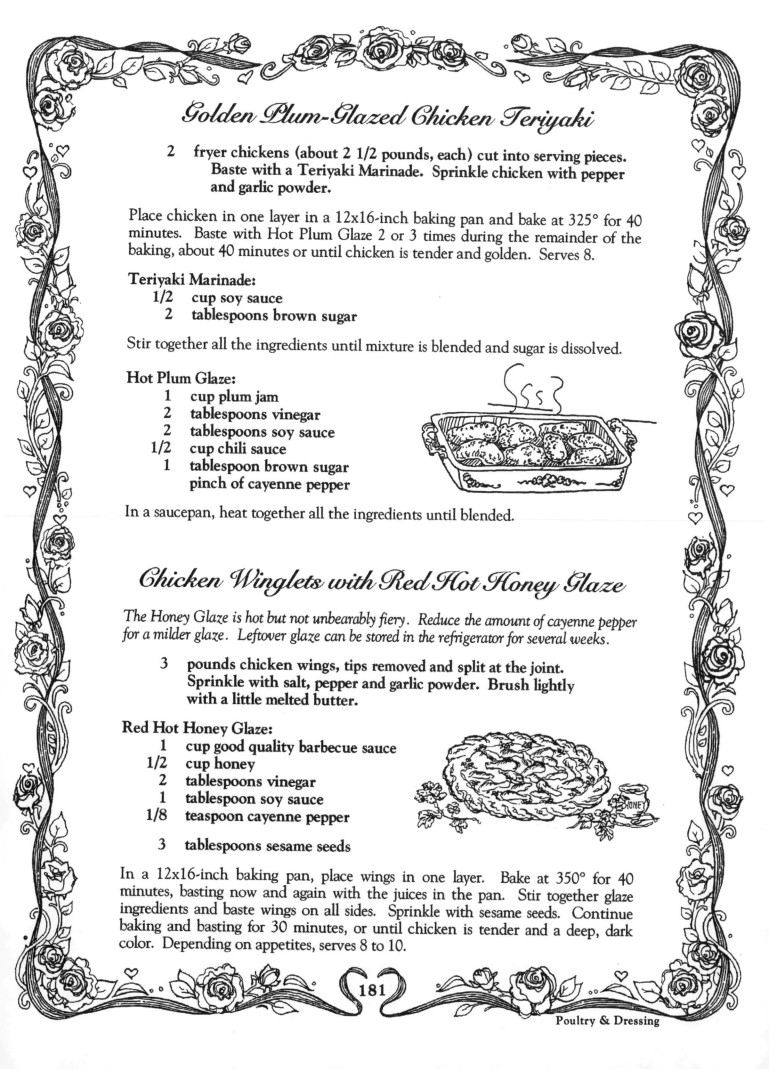

In a saucepan, heat together all the ingredients until blended.

Chicken Winglets with Red Hot Honey Glaze

The Honey Glaze is hot but not unbearably fiery. Reduce the amount of cayenne pepper for a milder glaze. Leftover glaze can be stored in the refrigerator for several weeks.

3   pounds chicken wings, tips removed and split at the joint.
       Sprinkle with salt, pepper and garlic powder. Brush lightly
       with a little melted butter.

Red Hot Honey Glaze:
1   cup good quality barbecue sauce
1/2   cup honey
2   tablespoons vinegar
1   tablespoon soy sauce
1/8   teaspoon cayenne pepper

3   tablespoons sesame seeds

In a 12x16-inch baking pan, place wings in one layer. Bake at 350° for 40 minutes, basting now and again with the juices in the pan. Stir together glaze ingredients and baste wings on all sides. Sprinkle with sesame seeds. Continue baking and basting for 30 minutes, or until chicken is tender and a deep, dark color. Depending on appetites, serves 8 to 10.

Easiest & Best Roast Chicken

When you serve chicken with another main course, it usually means a big family dinner, where you are trying to please different palates. This is a very easy way to prepare chicken, and easily one of the best. Unused Basting Mixture produces the finest tasting chicken and turkey and can be stored for 2 weeks in the refrigerator.

　　　2　fryer chickens (about 3 pounds, each), cut into serving pieces

Basting Mixture:
　1/2　cup butter (1 stick)
　　1　teaspoon garlic powder
　　1　teaspoon onion powder
　　2　teaspoons paprika

To Make Gravy:
　1/2　cup chicken broth

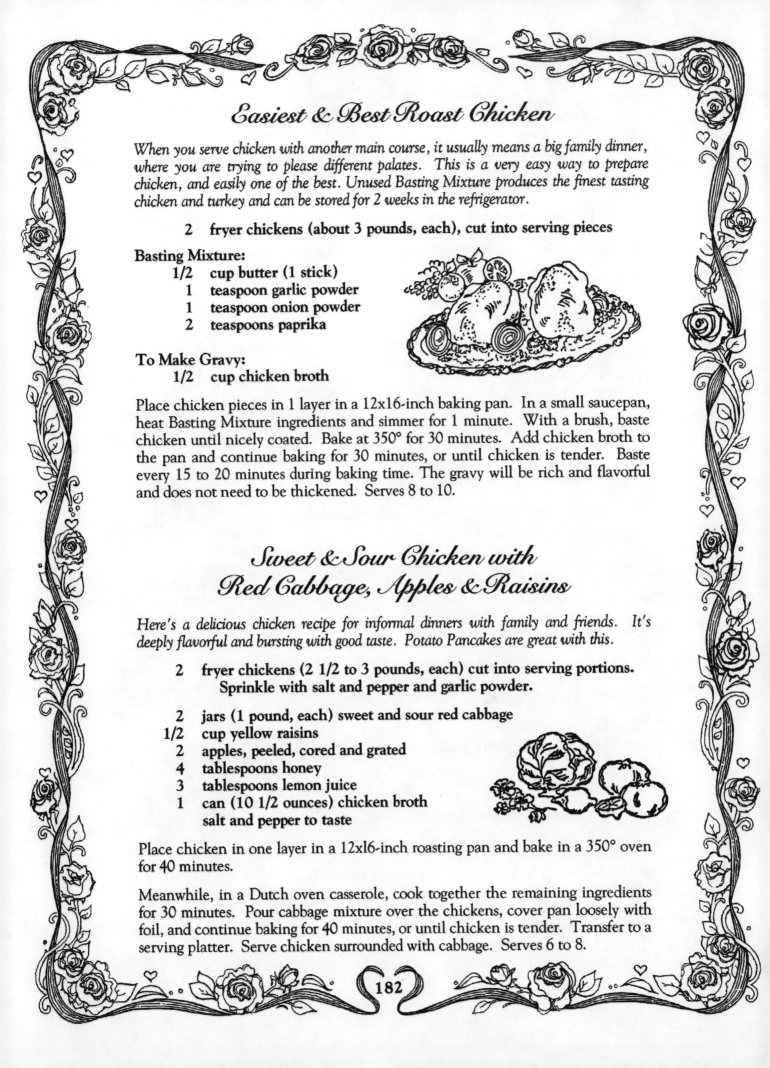

Place chicken pieces in 1 layer in a 12x16-inch baking pan. In a small saucepan, heat Basting Mixture ingredients and simmer for 1 minute. With a brush, baste chicken until nicely coated. Bake at 350° for 30 minutes. Add chicken broth to the pan and continue baking for 30 minutes, or until chicken is tender. Baste every 15 to 20 minutes during baking time. The gravy will be rich and flavorful and does not need to be thickened. Serves 8 to 10.

Sweet & Sour Chicken with
Red Cabbage, Apples & Raisins

Here's a delicious chicken recipe for informal dinners with family and friends. It's deeply flavorful and bursting with good taste. Potato Pancakes are great with this.

　　2　fryer chickens (2 1/2 to 3 pounds, each) cut into serving portions.
　　　　Sprinkle with salt and pepper and garlic powder.

　　2　jars (1 pound, each) sweet and sour red cabbage
　1/2　cup yellow raisins
　　2　apples, peeled, cored and grated
　　4　tablespoons honey
　　3　tablespoons lemon juice
　　1　can (10 1/2 ounces) chicken broth
　　　salt and pepper to taste

Place chicken in one layer in a 12x16-inch roasting pan and bake in a 350° oven for 40 minutes.

Meanwhile, in a Dutch oven casserole, cook together the remaining ingredients for 30 minutes. Pour cabbage mixture over the chickens, cover pan loosely with foil, and continue baking for 40 minutes, or until chicken is tender. Transfer to a serving platter. Serve chicken surrounded with cabbage. Serves 6 to 8.

Russian Honey Chicken with Apricots & Cherries

This is a nice homey dish, elevated with dried apricots and cherries. Dried cranberries can be substituted, but they are a little harder to find.

2   fryer chicken (about 3 pounds, each) cut into serving pieces and sprinkled with salt, pepper, garlic and onion powder

1 1/2	cups chicken broth
2	medium onions, thinly sliced
4	cloves garlic, minced
8	dried apricots, halved
1/2	cup dried cherries
2	tablespoons honey
2	tablespoons vinegar
	salt and pepper to taste

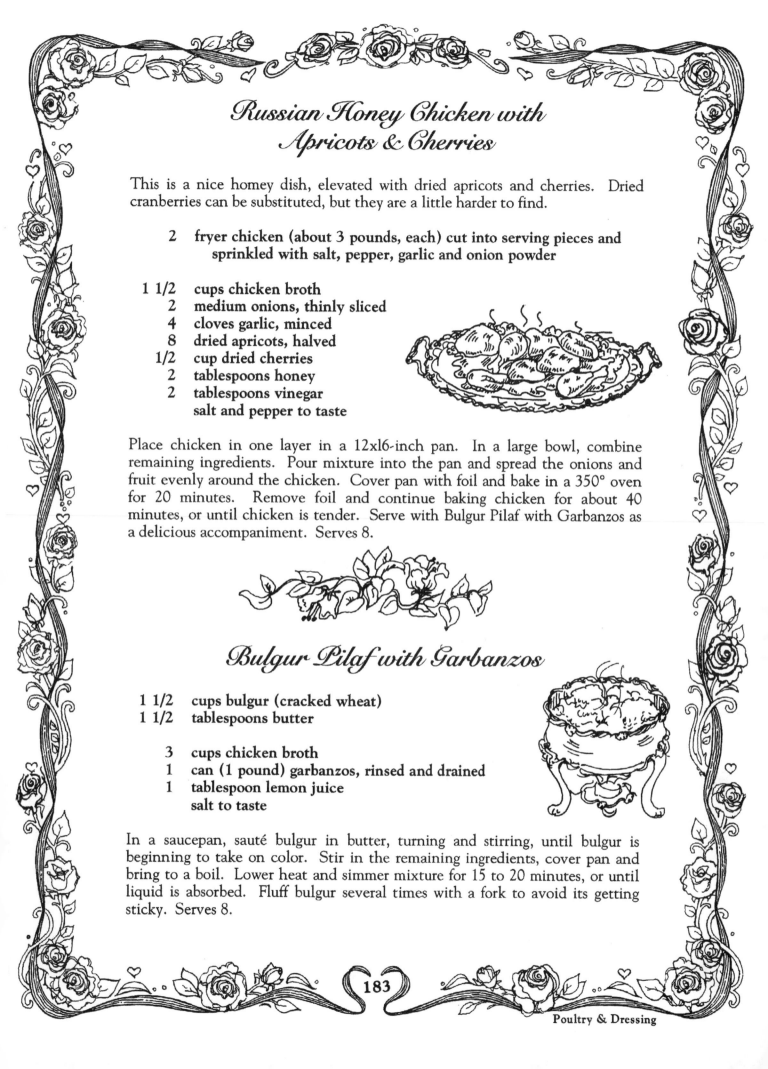

Place chicken in one layer in a 12x16-inch pan. In a large bowl, combine remaining ingredients. Pour mixture into the pan and spread the onions and fruit evenly around the chicken. Cover pan with foil and bake in a 350° oven for 20 minutes. Remove foil and continue baking chicken for about 40 minutes, or until chicken is tender. Serve with Bulgur Pilaf with Garbanzos as a delicious accompaniment. Serves 8.

Bulgur Pilaf with Garbanzos

1 1/2	cups bulgur (cracked wheat)
1 1/2	tablespoons butter
3	cups chicken broth
1	can (1 pound) garbanzos, rinsed and drained
1	tablespoon lemon juice
	salt to taste

In a saucepan, sauté bulgur in butter, turning and stirring, until bulgur is beginning to take on color. Stir in the remaining ingredients, cover pan and bring to a boil. Lower heat and simmer mixture for 15 to 20 minutes, or until liquid is absorbed. Fluff bulgur several times with a fork to avoid its getting sticky. Serves 8.

Chicken with Orange Currant Glaze

1 fryer chicken (about 2 1/2 to 3 pounds) cut up.
    Sprinkle with salt and garlic powder.
1/4 cup butter, melted

1/2 cup currant jelly
1/4 cup frozen orange juice, undiluted
1 tablespoon Dijon-style mustard
1 clove garlic, put through a press
1/4 cup butter, melted
2 tablespoons ketchup
1 tablespoon grated orange peel

Place chicken in a baking dish and baste with the melted butter. Cook chicken in a 350° oven for about 40 minutes.

Meanwhile, place the remaining ingredients in a saucepan and heat until jelly is melted and mixture is blended. Baste chicken with jelly mixture and continue baking and basting for another 40 minutes. Chicken will be a deep golden color.

Serve with Brown Rice with Raisins and Almonds as a lovely accompaniment. Serves 4.

Brown Rice with Raisins & Almonds

1 1/2 cups brown rice
3 cans (10 1/2 ounces, each) chicken broth
4 tablespoons butter
    salt and pepper to taste

1/2 cup toasted slivered almonds
1/2 cup golden raisins, plumped in hot water and drained

Combine rice, broth, butter and seasonings in a medium-sized saucepan. Bring to a boil, stir and cover. Reduce heat and simmer rice for about 40 minutes or until rice is tender and liquid is absorbed. Stir in almonds and raisins.

Baked Chicken Breasts with Tomato Artichoke Sauce

This dish is especially easy to prepare and it has good, deep, solid character. The sauce is light and full of flavor. Everybody loved it and welcomed the subtle balance of tomato and artichokes.

4   boned chicken breasts, skinned, boned and cut into halves (about 4 ounces, each.) Sprinkle with garlic powder and paprika.

1   can (1 pound) stewed tomatoes, chopped. Do not drain.
1   jar (6 ounces) marinated artichokes, drained and chopped
1   clove minced garlic
1   teaspoon sugar
1   tablespoon lemon juice
     salt and pepper to taste

In a 9x13-inch pan, place the chicken breasts in one layer. Bake in a 350° oven for about 20 minutes or until breasts are cooked through. Do not overbake.

Meanwhile, in a saucepan, heat together the remaining ingredients and simmer mixture for 10 minutes. Pour sauce over the chicken breasts and bake for another 5 minutes. Serve with angel hair pasta, cooked al dente, and spoon a little sauce on top. Serves 8.

Note: -Sauce can be prepared earlier in the day and heated at serving time. However, bake chicken breasts just before serving to make certain they are not overcooked.
       -Angel hair pasta is delicious with this dish. 8-ounces of pasta will produce about 4 cups cooked pasta.

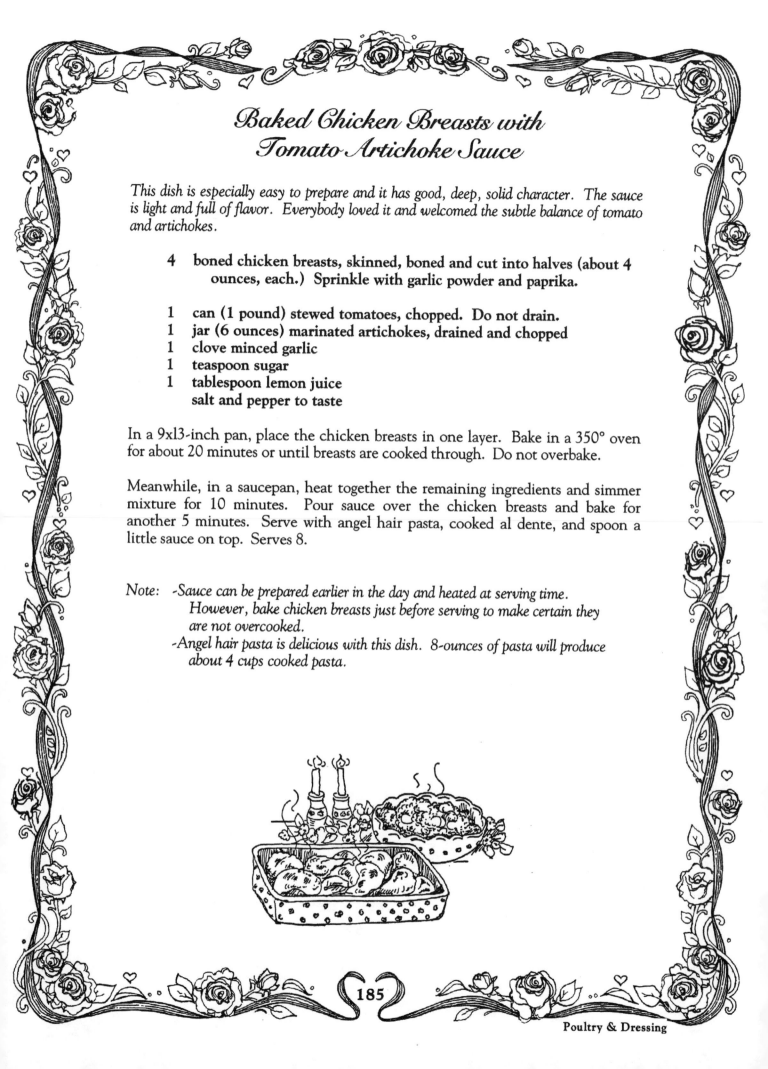

185

Chicken with Tomatoes, Peppers & Onions

2   fryer chickens (about 3 pounds, each) cut up. Sprinkle
       with salt and pepper. Brush chicken with 1/4 cup
       melted butter.

Tomato, Pepper and Onion Sauce:
   2   shallots, minced
1/4   cup melted butter
   2   onions, finely chopped
   1   green pepper, chopped
   1   can (1 pound) stewed tomatoes, chopped
         Use the juice, too.
   1   teaspoon Italian Herb Seasoning
   2   cloves garlic, put through a press
        salt and pepper to taste

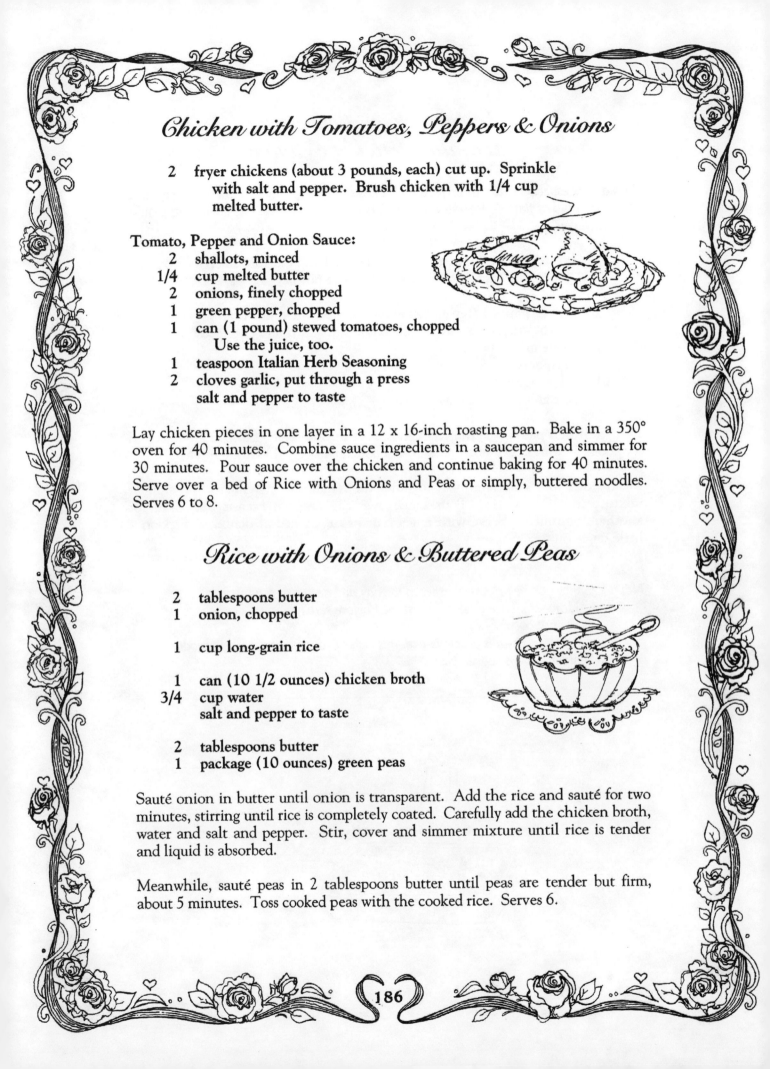

Lay chicken pieces in one layer in a 12 x 16-inch roasting pan. Bake in a 350° oven for 40 minutes. Combine sauce ingredients in a saucepan and simmer for 30 minutes. Pour sauce over the chicken and continue baking for 40 minutes. Serve over a bed of Rice with Onions and Peas or simply, buttered noodles. Serves 6 to 8.

Rice with Onions & Buttered Peas

2   tablespoons butter
1   onion, chopped

1   cup long-grain rice

1   can (10 1/2 ounces) chicken broth
3/4   cup water
     salt and pepper to taste

2   tablespoons butter
1   package (10 ounces) green peas

Sauté onion in butter until onion is transparent. Add the rice and sauté for two minutes, stirring until rice is completely coated. Carefully add the chicken broth, water and salt and pepper. Stir, cover and simmer mixture until rice is tender and liquid is absorbed.

Meanwhile, sauté peas in 2 tablespoons butter until peas are tender but firm, about 5 minutes. Toss cooked peas with the cooked rice. Serves 6.

Roast Turkey with
Apple & Chestnut Raisin Bread Stuffing

This is glorious stuffing, filled with all manner of good things ... apples, chestnuts, cinnamon, raisin bread. I prefer to make stuffing in a separate pan, and thereby, avoid the problem of harmful bacteria forming. If you prefer to stuff the turkey, then stuff it just before baking. Figure about 3/4-cup stuffing for each pound of turkey.

1 turkey (about 15 to 16 pounds), ready to cook, but not butter basted

Basting Mixture:
- 1 cup melted butter
- 1 tablespoon paprika
- 1 teaspoon salt
- 1/4 teaspoon pepper
- 2 teaspoons garlic powder
- 2 teaspoons onion powder
- 1 teaspoon poultry seasoning

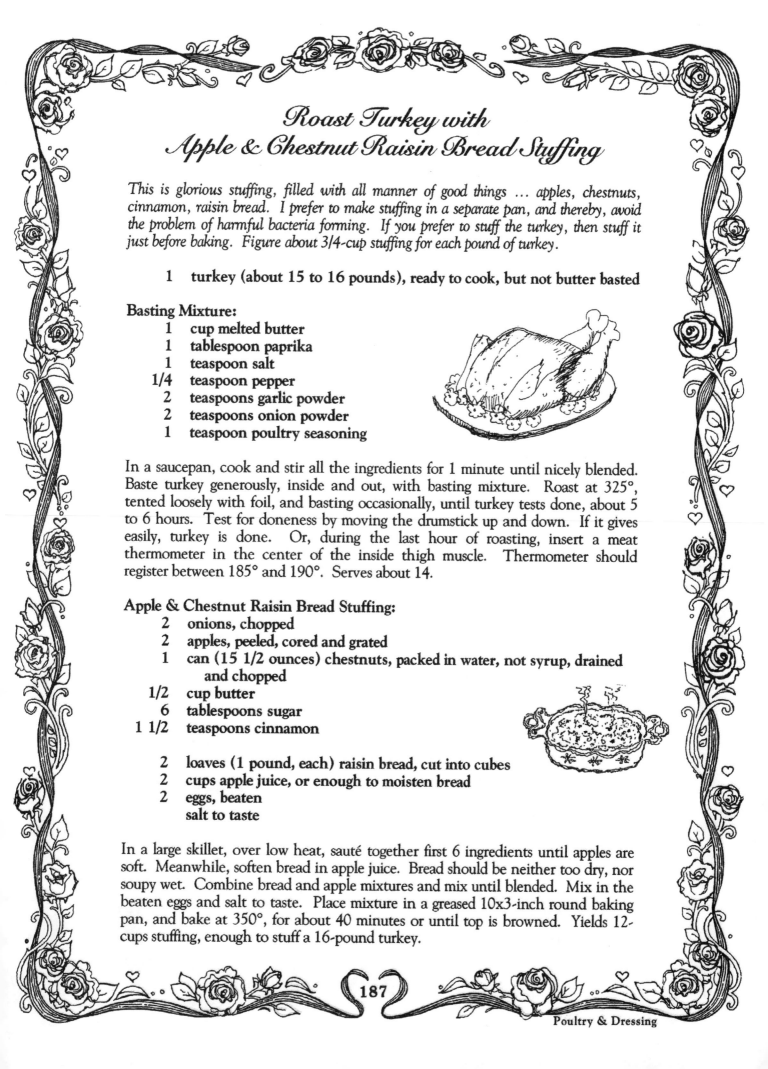

In a saucepan, cook and stir all the ingredients for 1 minute until nicely blended. Baste turkey generously, inside and out, with basting mixture. Roast at 325°, tented loosely with foil, and basting occasionally, until turkey tests done, about 5 to 6 hours. Test for doneness by moving the drumstick up and down. If it gives easily, turkey is done. Or, during the last hour of roasting, insert a meat thermometer in the center of the inside thigh muscle. Thermometer should register between 185° and 190°. Serves about 14.

Apple & Chestnut Raisin Bread Stuffing:
- 2 onions, chopped
- 2 apples, peeled, cored and grated
- 1 can (15 1/2 ounces) chestnuts, packed in water, not syrup, drained and chopped
- 1/2 cup butter
- 6 tablespoons sugar
- 1 1/2 teaspoons cinnamon

- 2 loaves (1 pound, each) raisin bread, cut into cubes
- 2 cups apple juice, or enough to moisten bread
- 2 eggs, beaten
-    salt to taste

In a large skillet, over low heat, sauté together first 6 ingredients until apples are soft. Meanwhile, soften bread in apple juice. Bread should be neither too dry, nor soupy wet. Combine bread and apple mixtures and mix until blended. Mix in the beaten eggs and salt to taste. Place mixture in a greased 10x3-inch round baking pan, and bake at 350°, for about 40 minutes or until top is browned. Yields 12-cups stuffing, enough to stuff a 16-pound turkey.

Curried Turkey with Peanuts & Raisins

This is a variation of my favorite curry. Using leftover turkey is especially helpful around holiday time. Cooked chicken is equally good. Serve this with Ginger Rice and Green Onions.

1	large onion, chopped
2	cloves garlic, put through a press
4	tablespoons butter

1	tablespoon flour
1	tablespoon curry powder
	salt and pepper to taste

1	apple, peeled, cored and grated
1	tablespoon brown sugar
1	can (10 1/2 ounces) chicken broth

1/2	cup cream
1/2	cup sour cream
1/2	cup yellow raisins
1/2	cup peanuts
3	cups cooked turkey

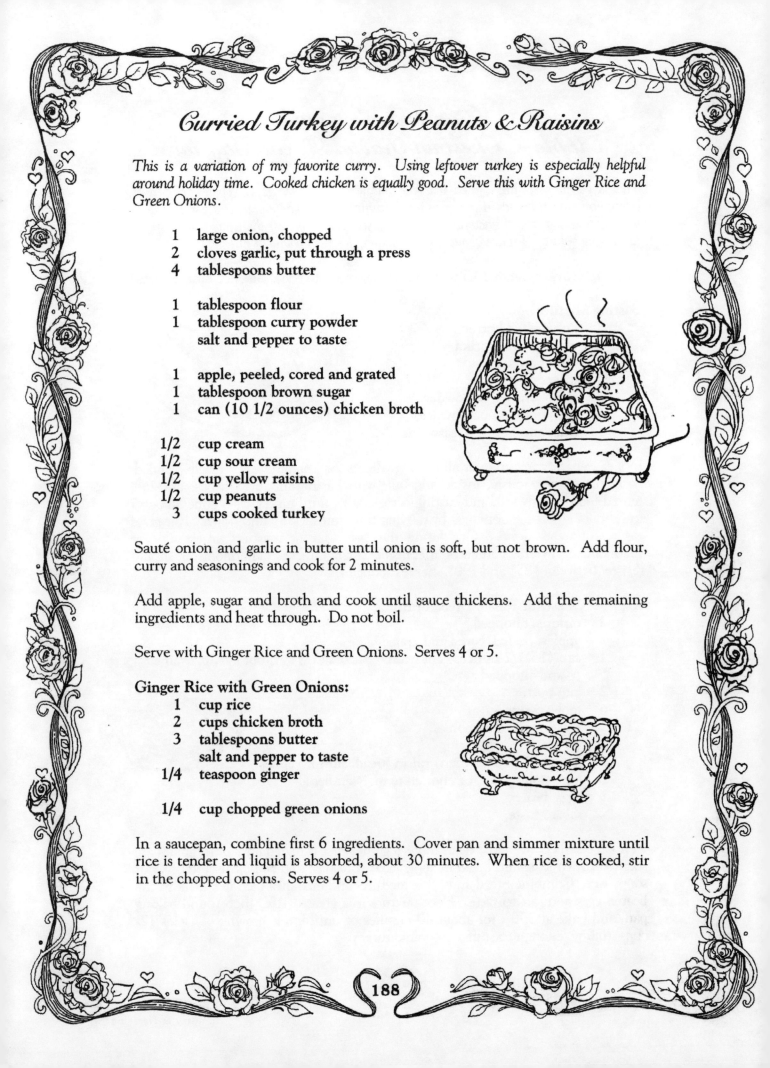

Sauté onion and garlic in butter until onion is soft, but not brown. Add flour, curry and seasonings and cook for 2 minutes.

Add apple, sugar and broth and cook until sauce thickens. Add the remaining ingredients and heat through. Do not boil.

Serve with Ginger Rice and Green Onions. Serves 4 or 5.

Ginger Rice with Green Onions:

1	cup rice
2	cups chicken broth
3	tablespoons butter
	salt and pepper to taste
1/4	teaspoon ginger
1/4	cup chopped green onions

In a saucepan, combine first 6 ingredients. Cover pan and simmer mixture until rice is tender and liquid is absorbed, about 30 minutes. When rice is cooked, stir in the chopped onions. Serves 4 or 5.

Roasted Turkey Breast Roll

To assure that the turkey does not turn out dry and tasteless, do not overbake it. Most meat thermometers recommend poultry temperatures at 185° or 190°, but that is too high for the delicate breast. I have found that by removing it from the oven at 170° or 175°, it is juicy, succulent and delicious. As our family prefers the white meat, I always make an extra breast in addition to the big bird during the holidays.

> 1   boned turkey breast, rolled and tied (3 to 4 pounds net weight)
> 1/4   cup chicken broth

In a 9x13-inch baking pan, place turkey and broth.

Basting Mixture:
> 1/2   cup butter (1 stick)
> 1   teaspoon garlic powder
> 1   teaspoon onion powder
> 2   teaspoons paprika

In a small saucepan, heat Basting Mixture ingredients and simmer for 1 minute. Brush turkey on all sides with Basting Mixture. Insert a meat thermometer in the thickest part of the roast, and bake at 350° until thermometer register 170°. Allow to stand for 5 minutes, and then cut into slices. The gravy is a rich and delicious broth and does not need to be thickened. Serves 8.

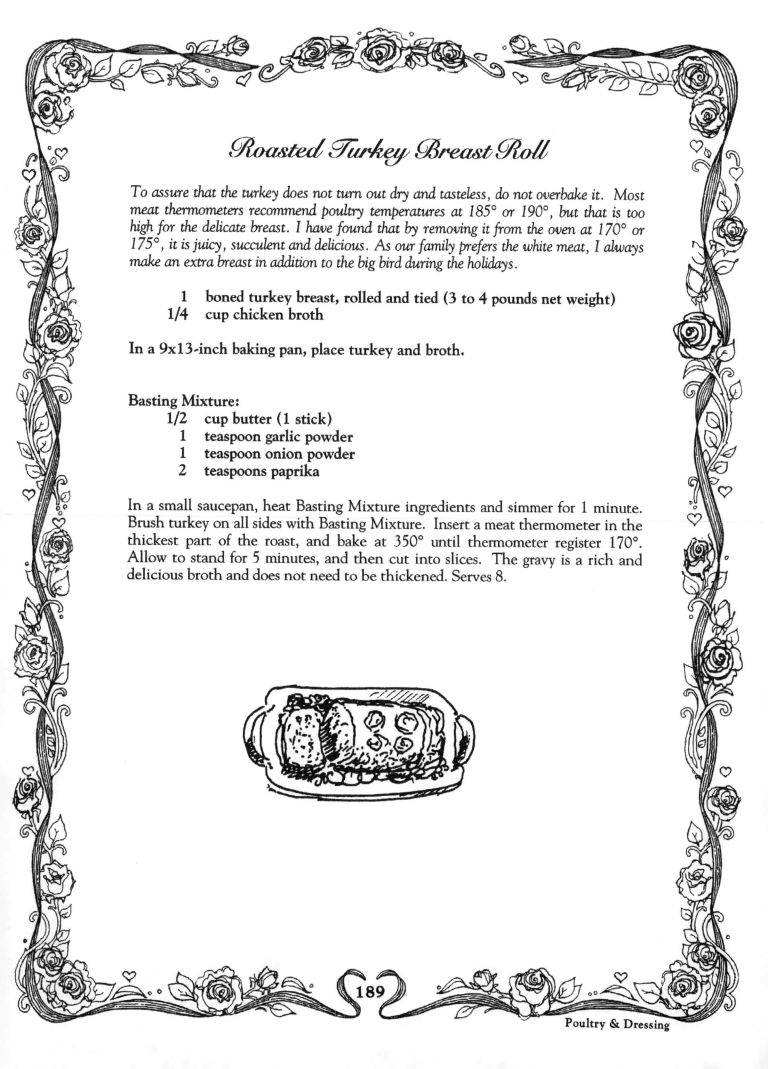

Maple Cinnamon Glazed Rock Cornish Hens with Spiced Apple & Raisin Stuffing

This is a delicious stuffing for these succulent little hens. It is spicy and fruity and a lovely blend of flavors. The stuffing can be assembled in advance, but stuff the hens just before baking.

- 4   Rock Cornish Hens (about 1 to 1 1/4 pounds, each). Sprinkle generously with paprika, garlic powder and a little salt.
- 1/4   cup melted butter

Stuff hen cavities 3/4 full with Spiced Apple & Raisin Stuffing and skewer openings with wooden picks or metal skewers. Place hens in a roasting pan and bake in a 325° oven for 45 minutes, basting with a little melted butter and pan juices.

Now start basting with Maple Cinnamon Glaze, every 10 minutes, for about 30 minutes, or until hens are a rich, golden color. (Total cooking time is about 1 hour 15 minutes.)

To serve, remove skewers and place hens on a bed of Brown Rice with Onions and Mushrooms. Delicious! Serves 4.

Spiced Apple & Raisin Stuffing:
- 2   medium apples, peeled, cored and grated
- 1/4   cup orange juice
- 1/2   cup yellow raisins
- 1/4   cup honey
- 2   teaspoons pumpkin pie spice
- 1/2   cup chopped walnuts or pecans
- 1/4   cup butter (1/2 stick)

- 1   cup fresh bread crumbs

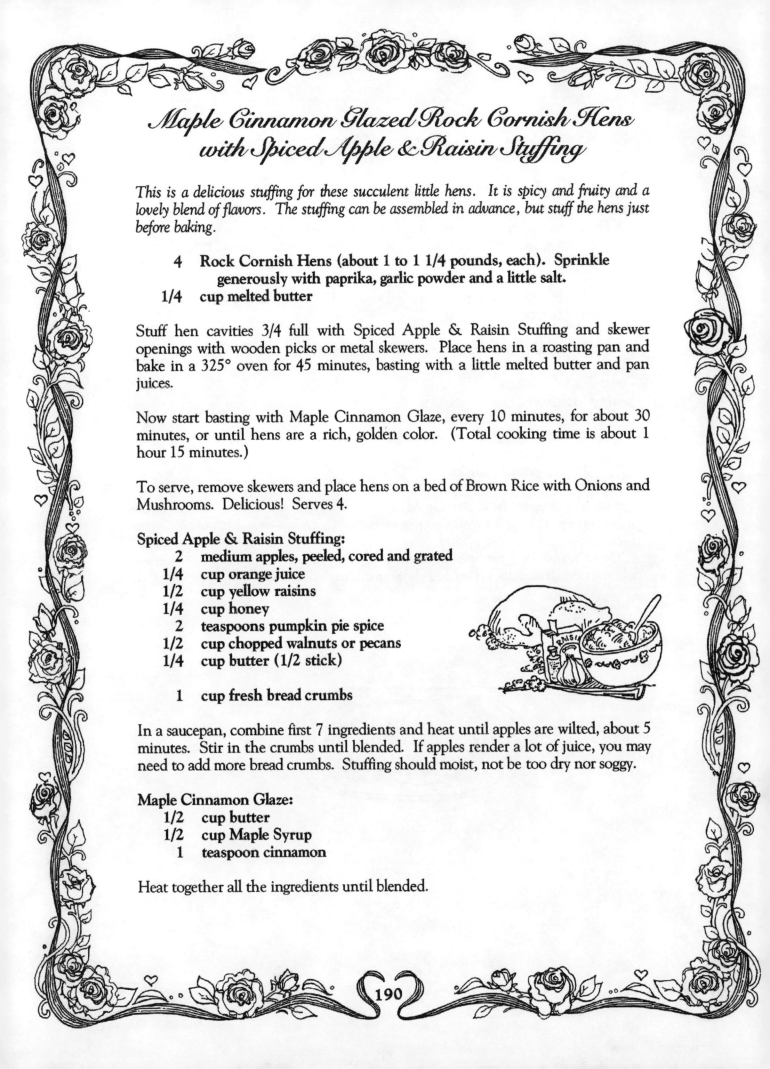

In a saucepan, combine first 7 ingredients and heat until apples are wilted, about 5 minutes. Stir in the crumbs until blended. If apples render a lot of juice, you may need to add more bread crumbs. Stuffing should moist, not be too dry nor soggy.

Maple Cinnamon Glaze:
- 1/2   cup butter
- 1/2   cup Maple Syrup
- 1   teaspoon cinnamon

Heat together all the ingredients until blended.

Stuffed Rock Cornish Hens with Sour Cherry Butter Glaze

6   Rock Cornish hens, sprinkled with salt, pepper, garlic powder and paprika. Brush generously with melted butter.

1   package (8 ounces) herb seasoning stuffing mix
1/4   teaspoon paprika
1/4   teaspoon poultry seasoning
1/4   cup melted butter (1/2 stick)

1   onion, very finely chopped
1/4   cup very finely chopped celery
1/4   cup butter (1/2 stick)

1   can (10 1/2 ounces) chicken broth

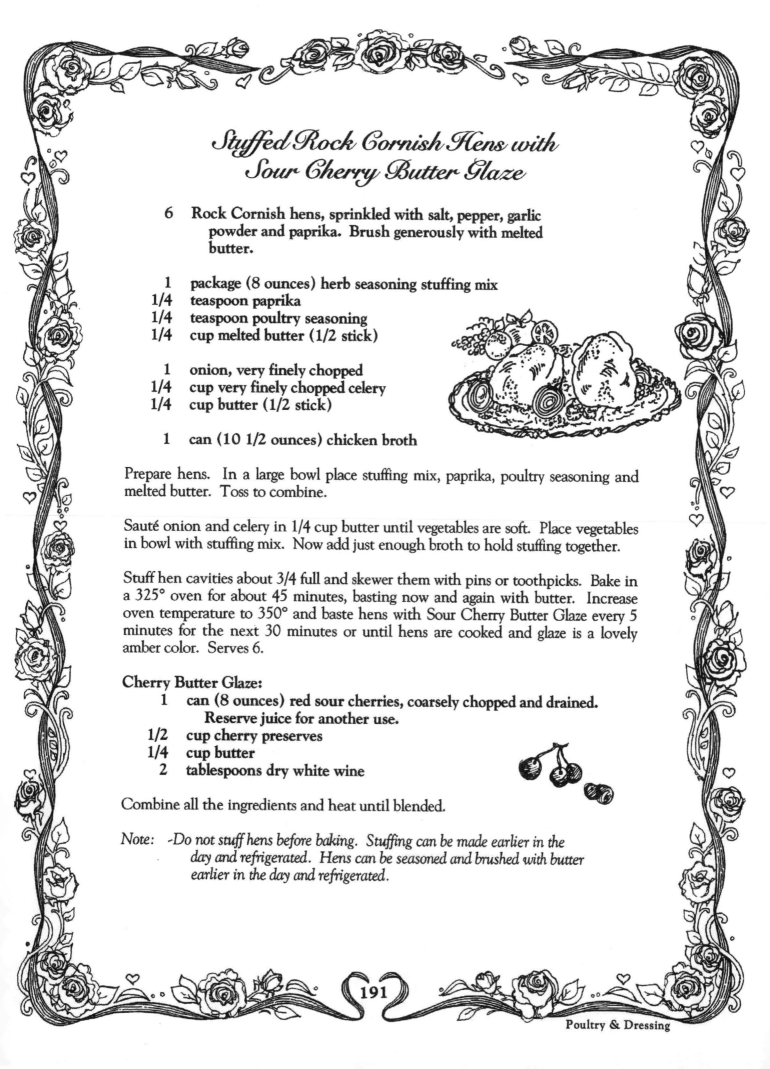

Prepare hens. In a large bowl place stuffing mix, paprika, poultry seasoning and melted butter. Toss to combine.

Sauté onion and celery in 1/4 cup butter until vegetables are soft. Place vegetables in bowl with stuffing mix. Now add just enough broth to hold stuffing together.

Stuff hen cavities about 3/4 full and skewer them with pins or toothpicks. Bake in a 325° oven for about 45 minutes, basting now and again with butter. Increase oven temperature to 350° and baste hens with Sour Cherry Butter Glaze every 5 minutes for the next 30 minutes or until hens are cooked and glaze is a lovely amber color. Serves 6.

Cherry Butter Glaze:
1   can (8 ounces) red sour cherries, coarsely chopped and drained. Reserve juice for another use.
1/2   cup cherry preserves
1/4   cup butter
2   tablespoons dry white wine

Combine all the ingredients and heat until blended.

Note: -Do not stuff hens before baking. Stuffing can be made earlier in the day and refrigerated. Hens can be seasoned and brushed with butter earlier in the day and refrigerated.

Honeyed Duck with Glazed Peaches & Peach Brandy

This is a variation of an old favorite, Duck a l'Orange. Somehow, people shy away from serving duck, these days. "It's kinda' fatty" they complain, "and there's hardly any meat on the bones." All true. But it does have a unique and delicious flavor. Roasting it in quarters helps to drain the fat and crisp the skin. Serve it with the Glazed Peaches and a casual dinner will feel like a party.

1 duck (about 4 to 5 pounds), cut into quarters and
      sprinkled with salt and garlic powder

1 can (1 pound 12 ounces) peach halves in syrup, drained

1/2 cup peach jam
2 tablespoons peach brandy or Cognac
1/2 cup honey
1/2 teaspoon cinnamon
1 tablespoon lemon juice

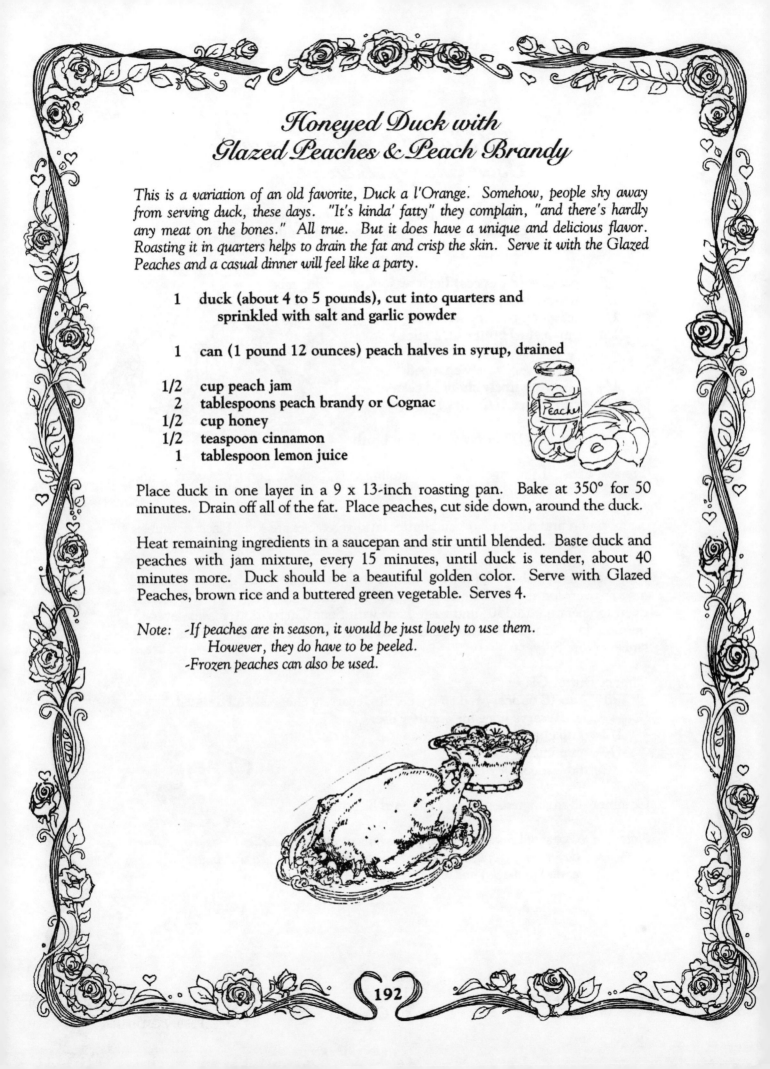

Place duck in one layer in a 9 x 13-inch roasting pan. Bake at 350° for 50 minutes. Drain off all of the fat. Place peaches, cut side down, around the duck.

Heat remaining ingredients in a saucepan and stir until blended. Baste duck and peaches with jam mixture, every 15 minutes, until duck is tender, about 40 minutes more. Duck should be a beautiful golden color. Serve with Glazed Peaches, brown rice and a buttered green vegetable. Serves 4.

Note: -If peaches are in season, it would be just lovely to use them.
        However, they do have to be peeled.
     -Frozen peaches can also be used.

Honey Plum-Glazed Goose with Apricot, Chestnut & Wild Rice Stuffing

This is an exciting change from the usual roast turkey or ham traditionally served at Christmas dinner. Chestnuts are wonderful with the stuffing, but, in absence of these, 1 cup toasted pecans can be substituted. I prefer preparing the stuffing separately, as I have said so many times before. To reheat rice, sprinkle it with 2 tablespoons broth before reheating. Cover pan and use a low heat setting.

1   goose, about 12 pounds (fresh or frozen). If frozen, allow to
     defrost in the refrigerator overnight. Prick the skin on the
     back of the goose in 5 or 6 places to allow the fat to drip
     out. Cut a lemon in half and rub it on the goose, inside
     and out. Sprinkle with salt to taste. Place a meat
     thermometer in the middle of the upper thigh, not
     touching the bone. Place 1/2 sliced orange and 1/2 sliced apple
     in cavity. Tie the legs together.

Honey Plum Basting Mixture:
1/2   cup plum jam
3   tablespoons honey
2   tablespoons melted butter
4   cloves minced garlic
1/2   cup dry white wine

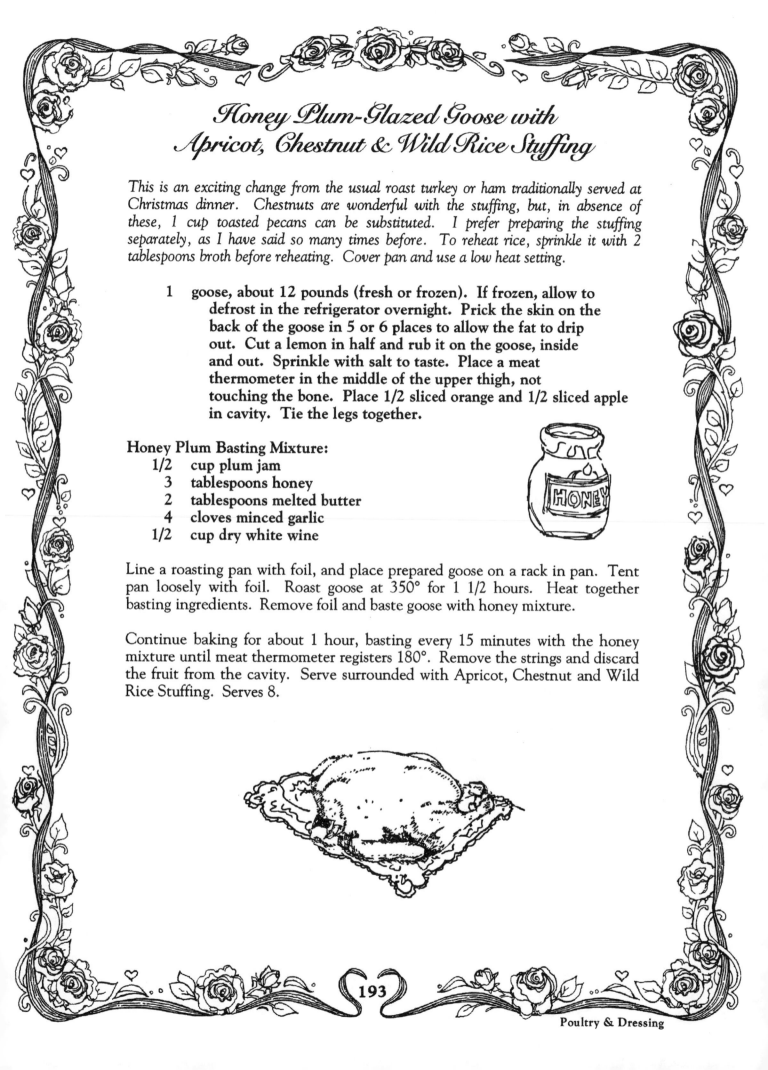

Line a roasting pan with foil, and place prepared goose on a rack in pan. Tent pan loosely with foil. Roast goose at 350° for 1 1/2 hours. Heat together basting ingredients. Remove foil and baste goose with honey mixture.

Continue baking for about 1 hour, basting every 15 minutes with the honey mixture until meat thermometer registers 180°. Remove the strings and discard the fruit from the cavity. Serve surrounded with Apricot, Chestnut and Wild Rice Stuffing. Serves 8.

Royal Herbed Cornbread Stuffing with Chestnuts, Apples & Raisins

2   stalks celery, chopped
1   onion, chopped
2   cloves garlic, minced
4   shallots, chopped
1   apple, peeled, cored and grated
1/2   cup butter

1   can (15 ounces) chestnuts, drained and chopped
1/2   cup yellow raisins
2   tablespoons chopped parsley
1   package (8-ounces) herbed cornbread stuffing

2   eggs, beaten
     chicken broth, about 1/2 to 3/4 cup
1/2   teaspoon dried sage flakes
     salt and pepper to taste

In a large skillet, sauté together first 6 ingredients until vegetables are soft. Toss mixture in a large bowl with chestnuts, raisins, parsley and stuffing.

Stir in the eggs and some of the chicken broth, until stuffing is moist, but not soggy. Stir in seasonings.

Place stuffing in a 10-inch round porcelain baker and bake in a 350° oven for about 30 minutes or until stuffing is set and lightly browned. Serves 8.

Note: -The above stuffing can be further glamorized with the addition of several dried fruits and nuts. Add any combination of the following:

6   pitted prunes, soaked in orange juice, and chopped
1/2   cup black currants, soaked in orange juice
1/2   cup yellow raisins, soaked in orange juice
6   dried apricot halves, soaked in orange juice
1/3   cup walnuts, coarsely chopped
1/3   cup pecans, coarsely chopped

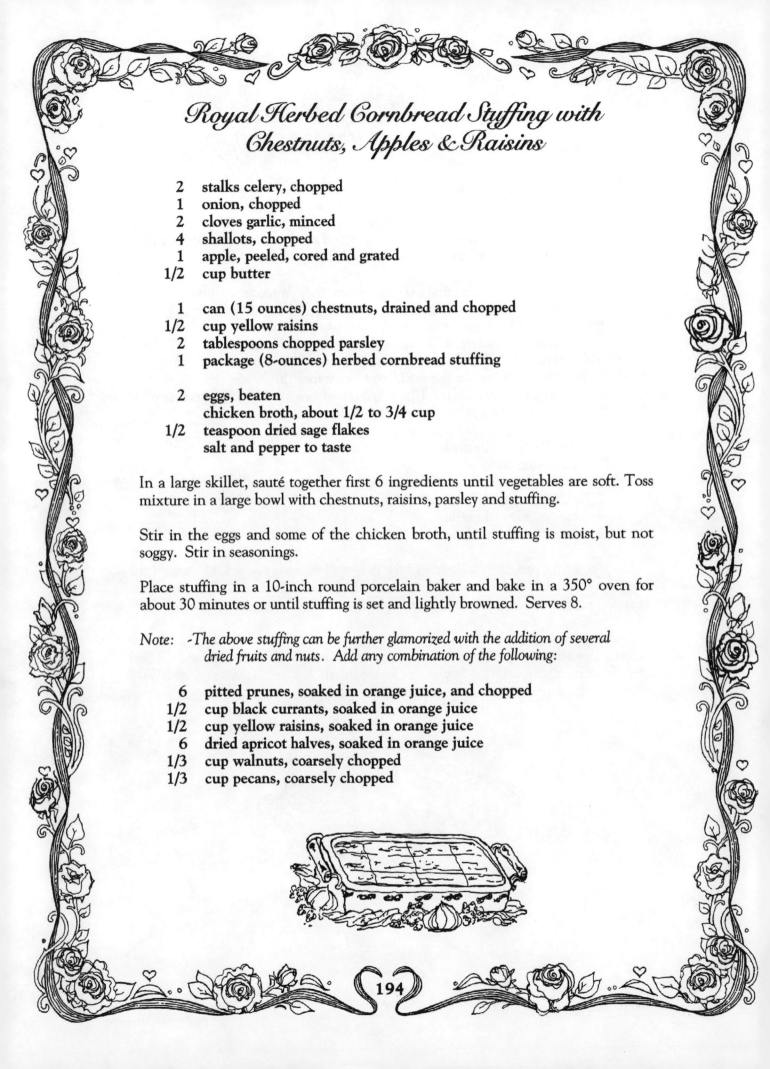

Old-Fashioned Bread Stuffing

This is enough stuffing to fill an 18-pound turkey. I prefer baking the stuffing separately to avoid any problem of contamination. However, a stuffed turkey does look beautiful, so use good care in handling.

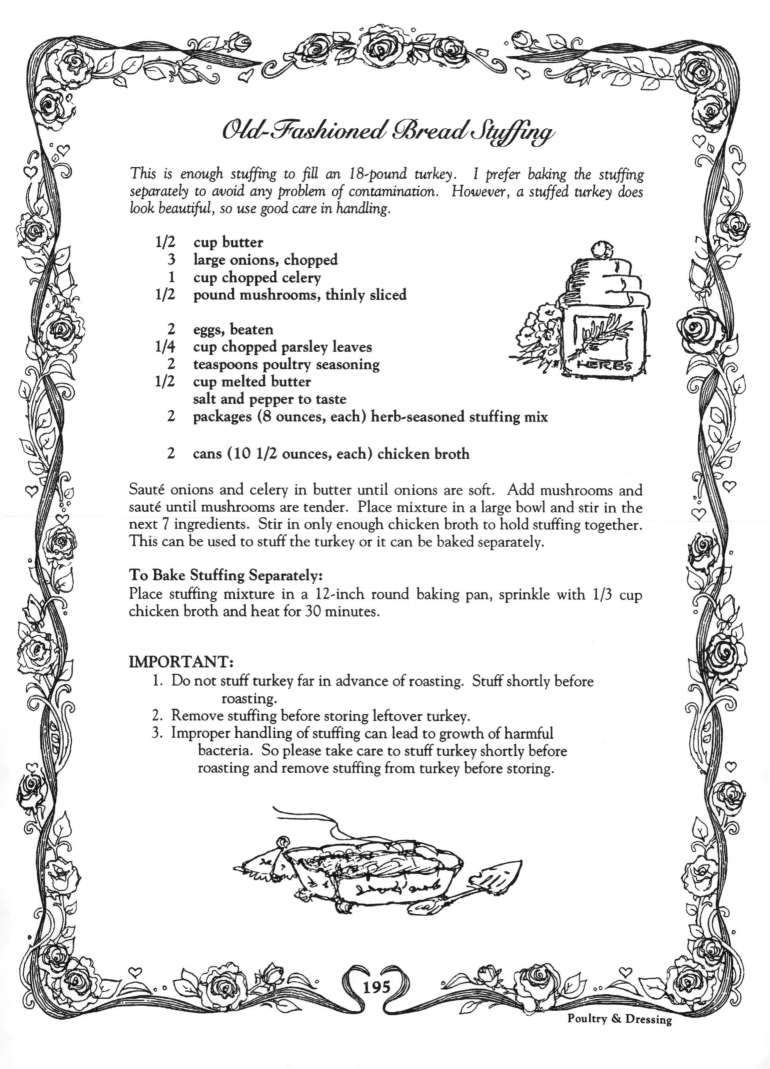

1/2	cup butter
3	large onions, chopped
1	cup chopped celery
1/2	pound mushrooms, thinly sliced
2	eggs, beaten
1/4	cup chopped parsley leaves
2	teaspoons poultry seasoning
1/2	cup melted butter
	salt and pepper to taste
2	packages (8 ounces, each) herb-seasoned stuffing mix
2	cans (10 1/2 ounces, each) chicken broth

Sauté onions and celery in butter until onions are soft. Add mushrooms and sauté until mushrooms are tender. Place mixture in a large bowl and stir in the next 7 ingredients. Stir in only enough chicken broth to hold stuffing together. This can be used to stuff the turkey or it can be baked separately.

To Bake Stuffing Separately:
Place stuffing mixture in a 12-inch round baking pan, sprinkle with 1/3 cup chicken broth and heat for 30 minutes.

IMPORTANT:
1. Do not stuff turkey far in advance of roasting. Stuff shortly before roasting.
2. Remove stuffing before storing leftover turkey.
3. Improper handling of stuffing can lead to growth of harmful bacteria. So please take care to stuff turkey shortly before roasting and remove stuffing from turkey before storing.

Old-Fashioned Soda Cracker Stuffing with Onions, Carrots & Mushrooms

This is another marvelous stuffing filled with flavor and goodness. This stuffing can be prepared exactly the same, substituting bread cubes for the soda crackers. The combination of vegetables, garlic and herbs is truly wonderful. Stuffing can be baked separately in a 10x3-inch round baking pan. Bake for 40 to 45 minutes, or until top is lightly browned.

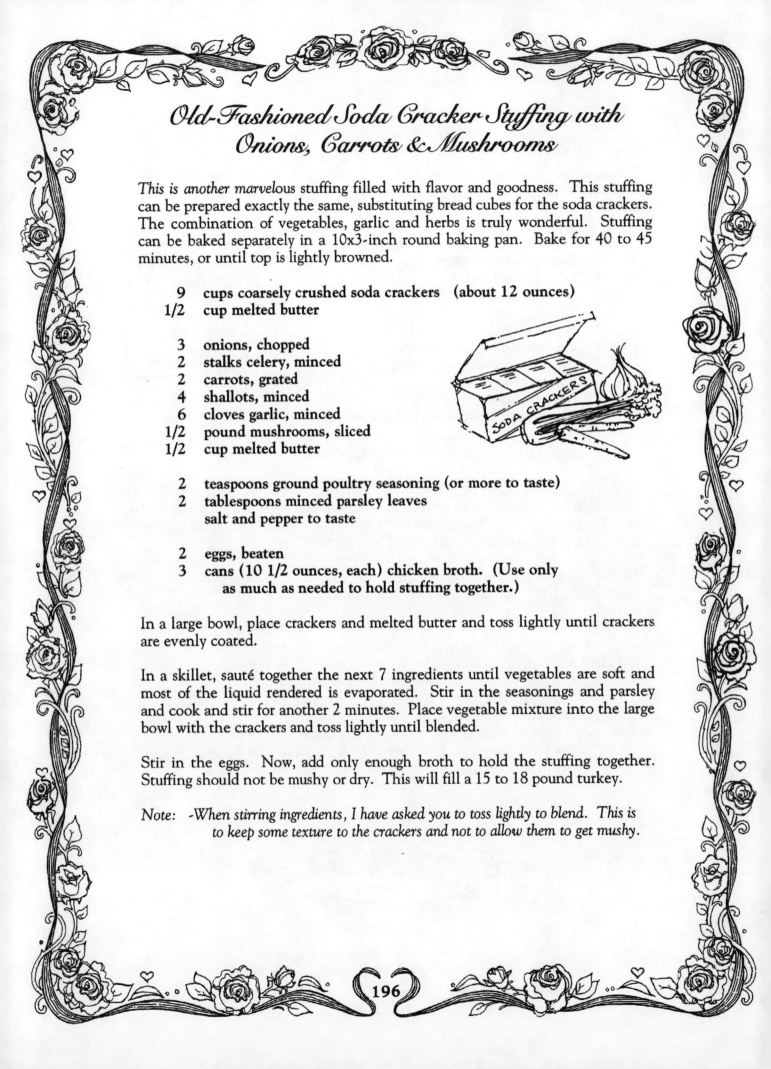

9	cups coarsely crushed soda crackers (about 12 ounces)
1/2	cup melted butter
3	onions, chopped
2	stalks celery, minced
2	carrots, grated
4	shallots, minced
6	cloves garlic, minced
1/2	pound mushrooms, sliced
1/2	cup melted butter
2	teaspoons ground poultry seasoning (or more to taste)
2	tablespoons minced parsley leaves
	salt and pepper to taste
2	eggs, beaten
3	cans (10 1/2 ounces, each) chicken broth. (Use only as much as needed to hold stuffing together.)

In a large bowl, place crackers and melted butter and toss lightly until crackers are evenly coated.

In a skillet, sauté together the next 7 ingredients until vegetables are soft and most of the liquid rendered is evaporated. Stir in the seasonings and parsley and cook and stir for another 2 minutes. Place vegetable mixture into the large bowl with the crackers and toss lightly until blended.

Stir in the eggs. Now, add only enough broth to hold the stuffing together. Stuffing should not be mushy or dry. This will fill a 15 to 18 pound turkey.

Note: -When stirring ingredients, I have asked you to toss lightly to blend. This is to keep some texture to the crackers and not to allow them to get mushy.

Apricot, Chestnut & Wild Rice Stuffing

Granted they are expensive, using canned chestnuts makes this delicious stuffing easy to prepare. Not only is it time-saving, but also peeling roasted chestnuts is really hard on your fingers. Chestnuts can be substituted with 1 cup chopped pecans. Stuffing can be prepared earlier in the day and placed in a heat and serve casserole. Sprinkle with 1 tablespoon water, cover tightly with foil and reheat in a 350° oven until heated through, about 25 minutes.

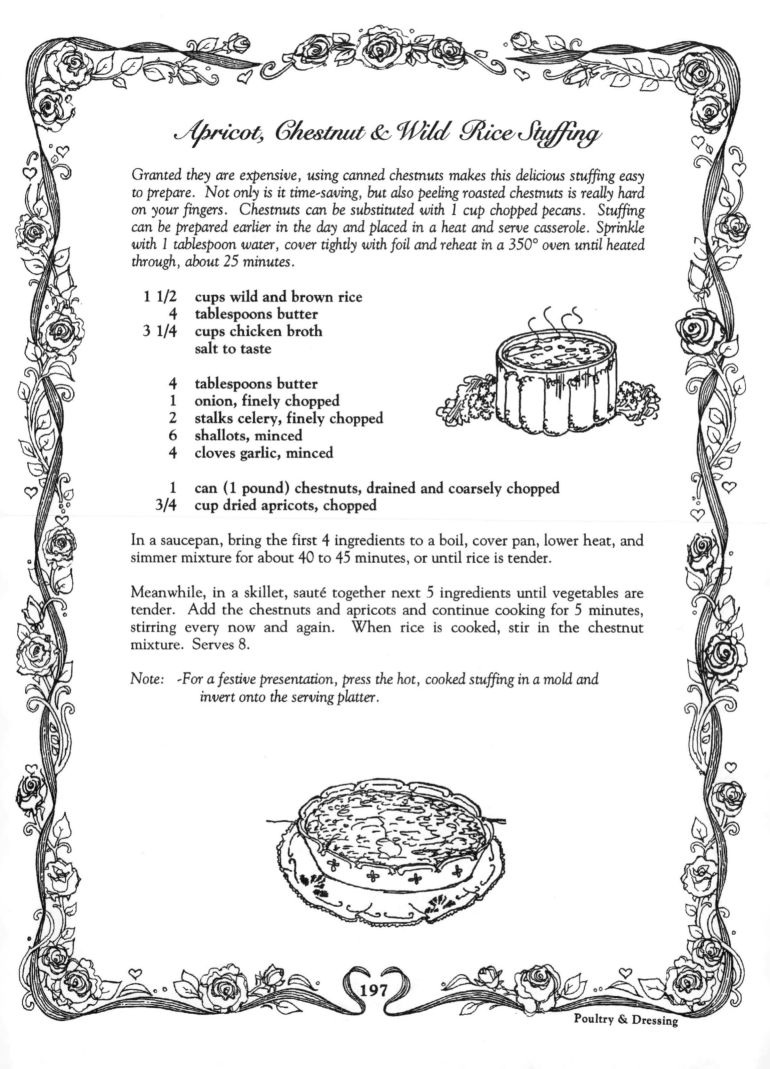

1 1/2	cups wild and brown rice
4	tablespoons butter
3 1/4	cups chicken broth
	salt to taste
4	tablespoons butter
1	onion, finely chopped
2	stalks celery, finely chopped
6	shallots, minced
4	cloves garlic, minced
1	can (1 pound) chestnuts, drained and coarsely chopped
3/4	cup dried apricots, chopped

In a saucepan, bring the first 4 ingredients to a boil, cover pan, lower heat, and simmer mixture for about 40 to 45 minutes, or until rice is tender.

Meanwhile, in a skillet, sauté together next 5 ingredients until vegetables are tender. Add the chestnuts and apricots and continue cooking for 5 minutes, stirring every now and again. When rice is cooked, stir in the chestnut mixture. Serves 8.

Note: -For a festive presentation, press the hot, cooked stuffing in a mold and invert onto the serving platter.

Raisin Cornbread Stuffing with Apricots

This delicious stuffing, much like a fluffy pudding, is a grand accompaniment to roast ham, chicken or turkey. Dried fruits can be varied...figs, currants, dates can be substituted.

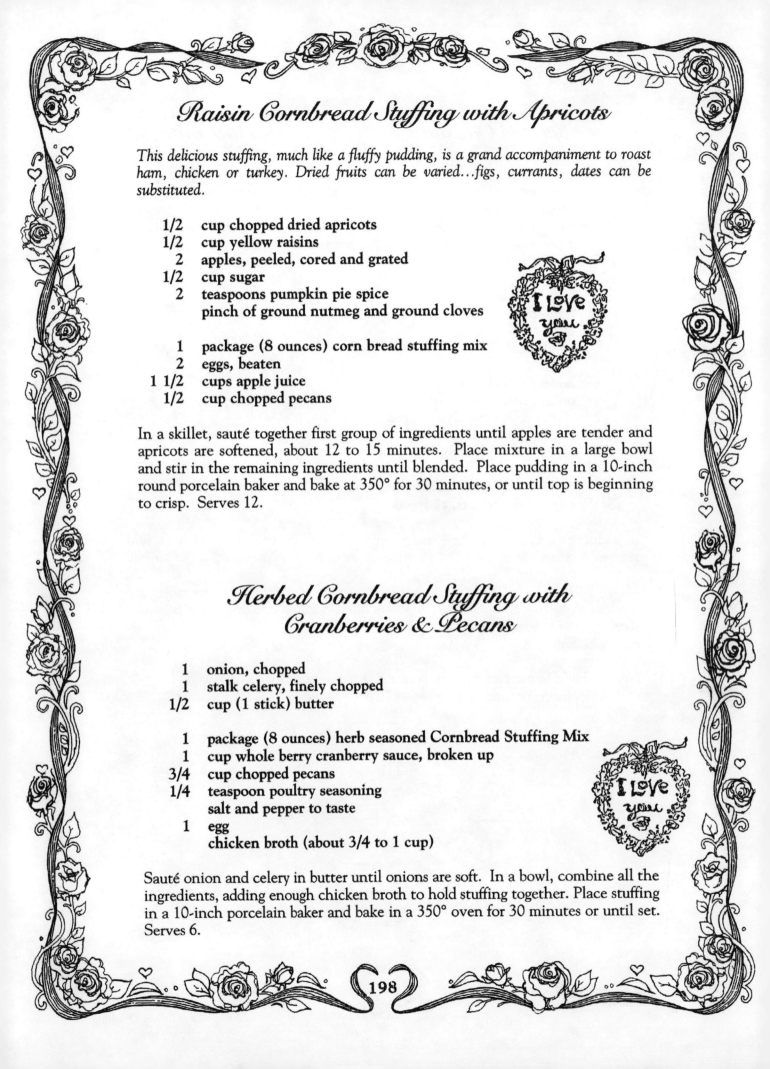

1/2	cup chopped dried apricots
1/2	cup yellow raisins
2	apples, peeled, cored and grated
1/2	cup sugar
2	teaspoons pumpkin pie spice
	pinch of ground nutmeg and ground cloves
1	package (8 ounces) corn bread stuffing mix
2	eggs, beaten
1 1/2	cups apple juice
1/2	cup chopped pecans

In a skillet, sauté together first group of ingredients until apples are tender and apricots are softened, about 12 to 15 minutes. Place mixture in a large bowl and stir in the remaining ingredients until blended. Place pudding in a 10-inch round porcelain baker and bake at 350° for 30 minutes, or until top is beginning to crisp. Serves 12.

Herbed Cornbread Stuffing with Cranberries & Pecans

1	onion, chopped
1	stalk celery, finely chopped
1/2	cup (1 stick) butter
1	package (8 ounces) herb seasoned Cornbread Stuffing Mix
1	cup whole berry cranberry sauce, broken up
3/4	cup chopped pecans
1/4	teaspoon poultry seasoning
	salt and pepper to taste
1	egg
	chicken broth (about 3/4 to 1 cup)

Sauté onion and celery in butter until onions are soft. In a bowl, combine all the ingredients, adding enough chicken broth to hold stuffing together. Place stuffing in a 10-inch porcelain baker and bake in a 350° oven for 30 minutes or until set. Serves 6.

Meats

Beef

Lamb

Pork

Veal

Barbecued Brisket & Honey Barbecue Sauce

Brisket is a very flavorful cut of meat. It is especially good braised in this very tasty barbecue sauce. Use the sauce on chicken or pork or other barbecued meats.

1   brisket of beef, about 4 pounds, trimmed of fat. Sprinkle with salt, pepper, paprika and lots of garlic powder.

Barbecue Sauce:
1   large onion, minced
3/4   cup good quality barbecue sauce
1/4   cup honey
1/2   cup dark brown sugar
1   can (10 1/2 ounces) beef broth
2   tablespoons dark molasses

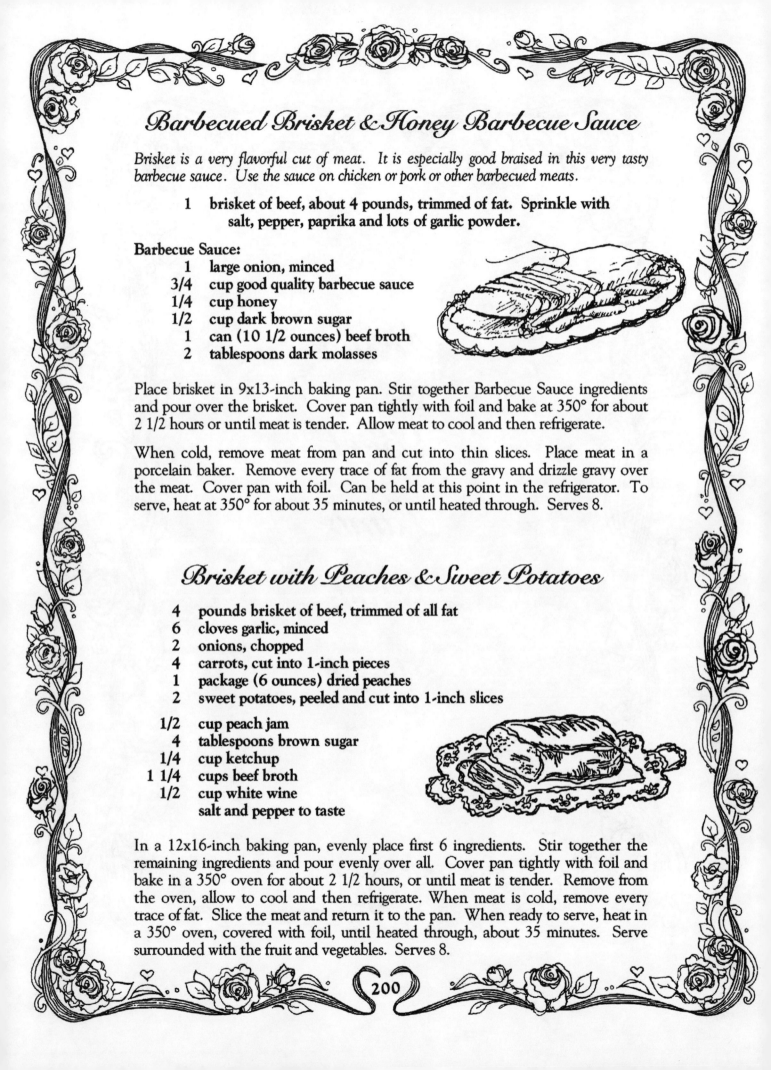

Place brisket in 9x13-inch baking pan. Stir together Barbecue Sauce ingredients and pour over the brisket. Cover pan tightly with foil and bake at 350° for about 2 1/2 hours or until meat is tender. Allow meat to cool and then refrigerate.

When cold, remove meat from pan and cut into thin slices. Place meat in a porcelain baker. Remove every trace of fat from the gravy and drizzle gravy over the meat. Cover pan with foil. Can be held at this point in the refrigerator. To serve, heat at 350° for about 35 minutes, or until heated through. Serves 8.

Brisket with Peaches & Sweet Potatoes

4   pounds brisket of beef, trimmed of all fat
6   cloves garlic, minced
2   onions, chopped
4   carrots, cut into 1-inch pieces
1   package (6 ounces) dried peaches
2   sweet potatoes, peeled and cut into 1-inch slices

1/2   cup peach jam
4   tablespoons brown sugar
1/4   cup ketchup
1 1/4 cups beef broth
1/2   cup white wine
       salt and pepper to taste

In a 12x16-inch baking pan, evenly place first 6 ingredients. Stir together the remaining ingredients and pour evenly over all. Cover pan tightly with foil and bake in a 350° oven for about 2 1/2 hours, or until meat is tender. Remove from the oven, allow to cool and then refrigerate. When meat is cold, remove every trace of fat. Slice the meat and return it to the pan. When ready to serve, heat in a 350° oven, covered with foil, until heated through, about 35 minutes. Serve surrounded with the fruit and vegetables. Serves 8.

Minute Chile Meat Loaf

If you are a fan of meatloaf, you will enjoy this one. Don't think for a moment that anything that can be put together so quickly simply can't be good. If I must admit, I served this for a Sunday night dinner with the family and they all loved it so much. I must confess I loved it too. It is important to handle the meat gently. With two forks, toss and turn the meat lightly until all the ingredients are nicely mixed. Don't stir the ingredients or press them down. Allow the air to be incorporated as you toss and turn the meat. You'll be surprised how light and delicious the meatloaf will be. I have listed the names of the seasonings I used, so that this can easily be duplicated.

2 1/2	pounds lean ground beef (chuck is good)
1	envelope Lipton's Onion Soup
1	envelope Lawry's Chile Seasonings
1/4	teaspoon Lawry's Coarse Grind Garlic Powder
2	cups dried bread crumbs
3	eggs, beaten
	salt to taste

   1   can (1 pound) diced tomatoes. Do not drain.

In a large bowl, place the first 7 ingredients. Toss and turn the mixture until it is nicely blended. Place meat evenly in a 9x13-inch baking pan, leaving a 1-inch border along the edges. Fill the edges with the tomato dice and juice.

Bake at 350° for 50 minutes to 1 hour or until meat loses it's pinkness. Cut into slices and serve 6 to 8.

To Make Dried Bread Crumbs:
   8   slices day old egg bread, crusts removed

Place bread slices on a cookie sheet and toast in a 350° oven until bread is crisp. Time will vary depending on the thickness of the slice. Place bread in a processor and pulse until you have fine crumbs. Freeze unused crumbs in a plastic bag and use as a coating on chicken or fish.

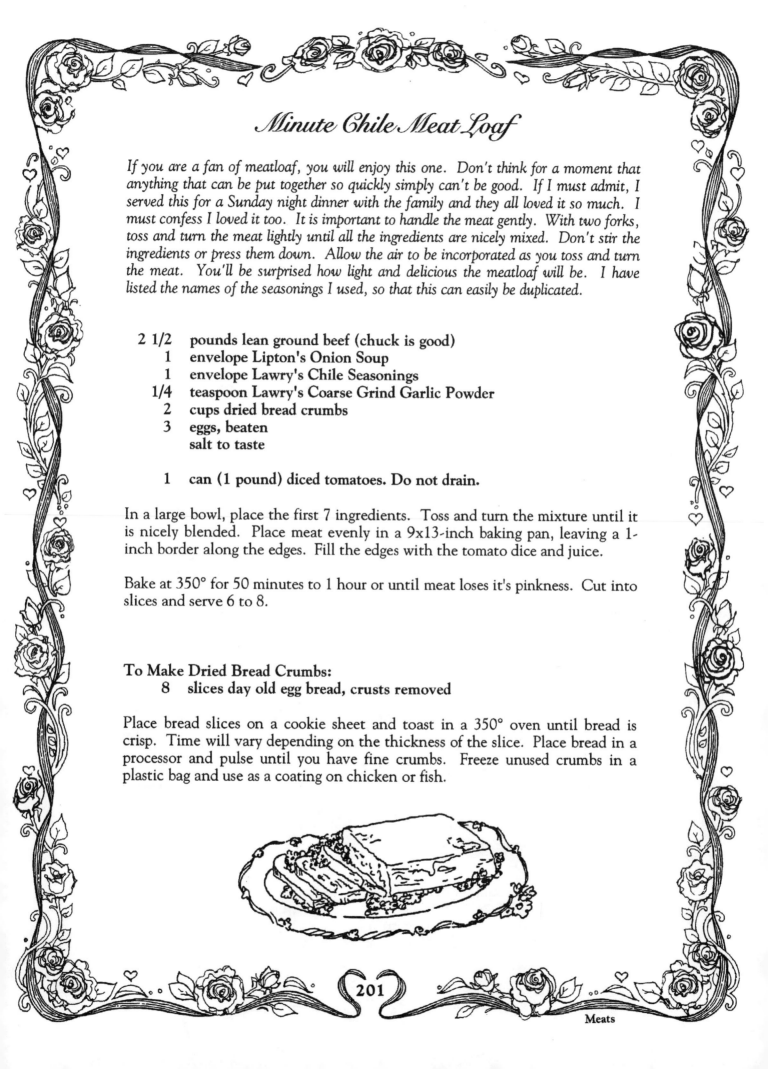

Farmhouse Sweet & Sour Pot Roast with Apples & Raisins

This sweet and sour pot roast in a German or Austrian mood is the essence of simplicity and a triumph of taste. It assembles easily and produces a fine tasting pot roast. Garlic Mashed Potatoes are getting more and more popular today. Hope you enjoy them, too.

1	brisket of beef, about 4 pounds, trimmed of all fat and sprinkled with salt, pepper and garlic powder
1	jar (1 pound) sweet sour red cabbage
1/2	cup brown sugar
1/4	cup vinegar
1/2	cup dry white wine
1	onion, chopped
1/2	cup yellow raisins
1	apple, peeled, cored and grated
	salt and pepper to taste

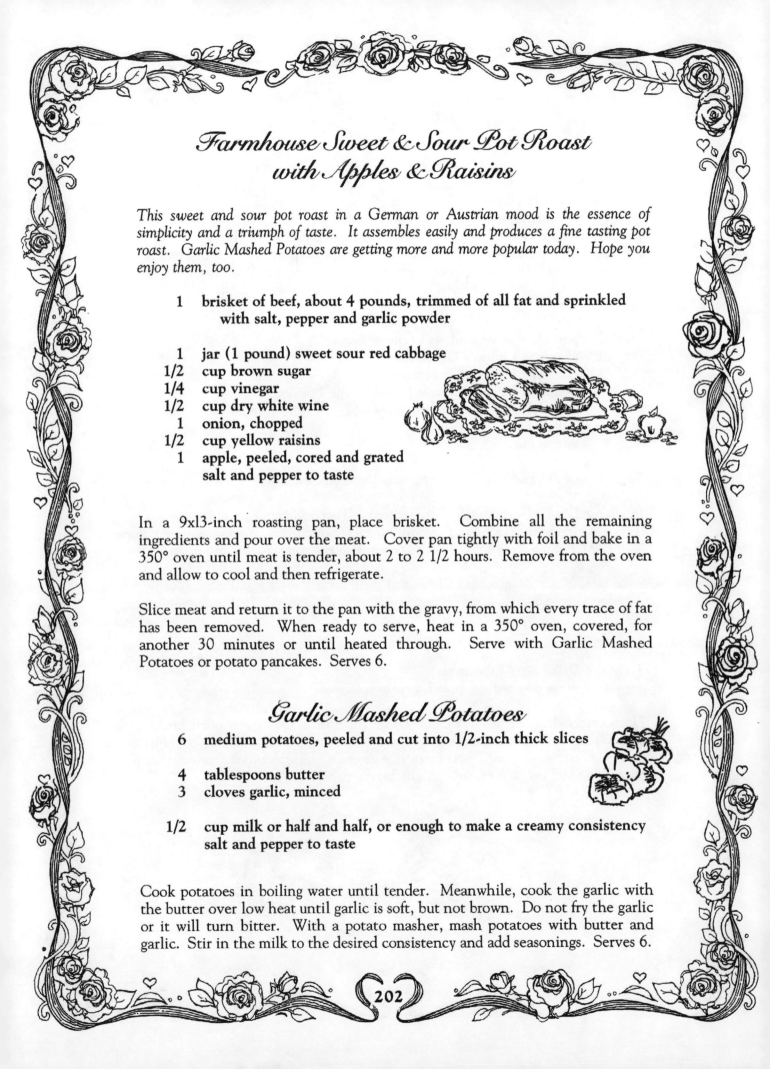

In a 9x13-inch roasting pan, place brisket. Combine all the remaining ingredients and pour over the meat. Cover pan tightly with foil and bake in a 350° oven until meat is tender, about 2 to 2 1/2 hours. Remove from the oven and allow to cool and then refrigerate.

Slice meat and return it to the pan with the gravy, from which every trace of fat has been removed. When ready to serve, heat in a 350° oven, covered, for another 30 minutes or until heated through. Serve with Garlic Mashed Potatoes or potato pancakes. Serves 6.

Garlic Mashed Potatoes

6	medium potatoes, peeled and cut into 1/2-inch thick slices
4	tablespoons butter
3	cloves garlic, minced
1/2	cup milk or half and half, or enough to make a creamy consistency
	salt and pepper to taste

Cook potatoes in boiling water until tender. Meanwhile, cook the garlic with the butter over low heat until garlic is soft, but not brown. Do not fry the garlic or it will turn bitter. With a potato masher, mash potatoes with butter and garlic. Stir in the milk to the desired consistency and add seasonings. Serves 6.

Family Night Meat Loaf with Diced Tomatoes

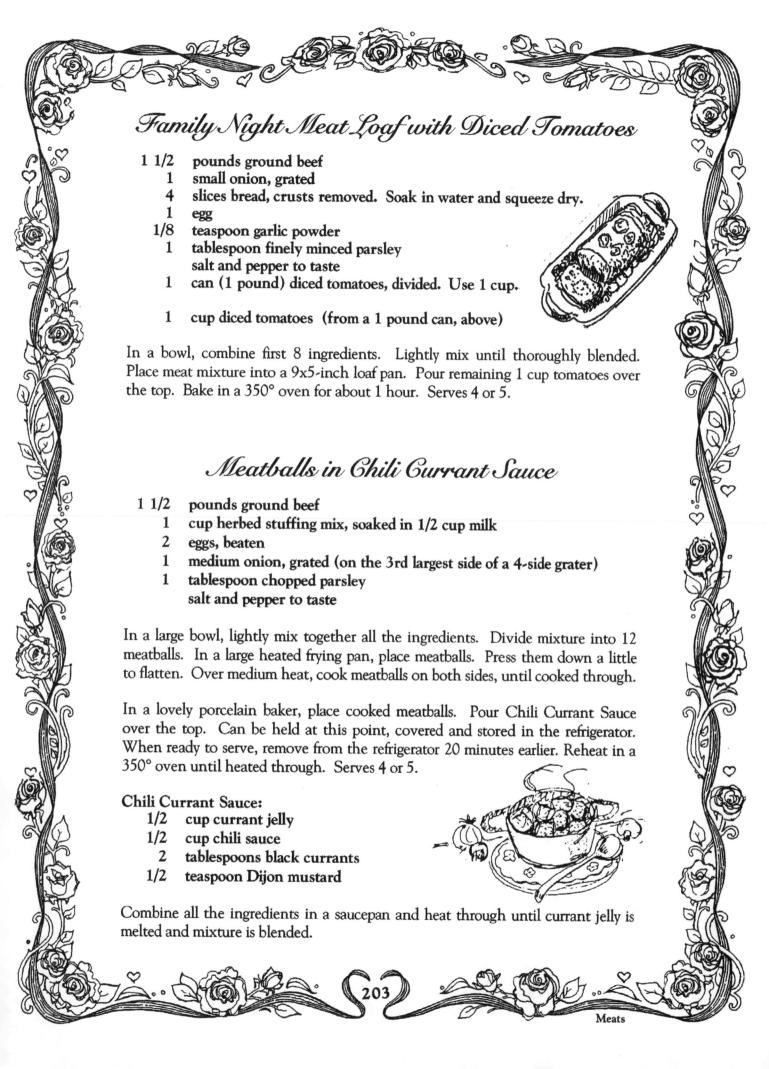

1 1/2	pounds ground beef
1	small onion, grated
4	slices bread, crusts removed. Soak in water and squeeze dry.
1	egg
1/8	teaspoon garlic powder
1	tablespoon finely minced parsley
	salt and pepper to taste
1	can (1 pound) diced tomatoes, divided. Use 1 cup.
1	cup diced tomatoes (from a 1 pound can, above)

In a bowl, combine first 8 ingredients. Lightly mix until thoroughly blended. Place meat mixture into a 9x5-inch loaf pan. Pour remaining 1 cup tomatoes over the top. Bake in a 350° oven for about 1 hour. Serves 4 or 5.

Meatballs in Chili Currant Sauce

1 1/2	pounds ground beef
1	cup herbed stuffing mix, soaked in 1/2 cup milk
2	eggs, beaten
1	medium onion, grated (on the 3rd largest side of a 4-side grater)
1	tablespoon chopped parsley
	salt and pepper to taste

In a large bowl, lightly mix together all the ingredients. Divide mixture into 12 meatballs. In a large heated frying pan, place meatballs. Press them down a little to flatten. Over medium heat, cook meatballs on both sides, until cooked through.

In a lovely porcelain baker, place cooked meatballs. Pour Chili Currant Sauce over the top. Can be held at this point, covered and stored in the refrigerator. When ready to serve, remove from the refrigerator 20 minutes earlier. Reheat in a 350° oven until heated through. Serves 4 or 5.

Chili Currant Sauce:
1/2	cup currant jelly
1/2	cup chili sauce
2	tablespoons black currants
1/2	teaspoon Dijon mustard

Combine all the ingredients in a saucepan and heat through until currant jelly is melted and mixture is blended.

Old-Fashioned Hungarian Goulash with Spaetzel & Sweet & Sour Red Cabbage

This lovely goulash is an upscaled version of the traditional Hungarian stew. Usually made with a tougher cut of beef, cooking time was markedly longer. Using sirloin steak, not only decreases cooking time to minutes, but the beef is tender and succulent and I do believe, more delightful served this way.

2   pounds sirloin steak cut into very thin slices and then into 1x1-inch squares. Toss with 2 tablespoons Dijon mustard.
3   tablespoons butter

2   onions, chopped
2   cloves garlic, minced
1   carrot, grated (not traditional, but very good)
2   tablespoons brown sugar
2   tablespoons butter
1/4   cup dry white wine

1/4   cup tomato sauce
1   can (10 1/2 ounces) beef broth
1/2   teaspoon Bovril, beef-seasoned stock base
2   tablespoons paprika
    salt and pepper to taste

1 1/2   cups sour cream

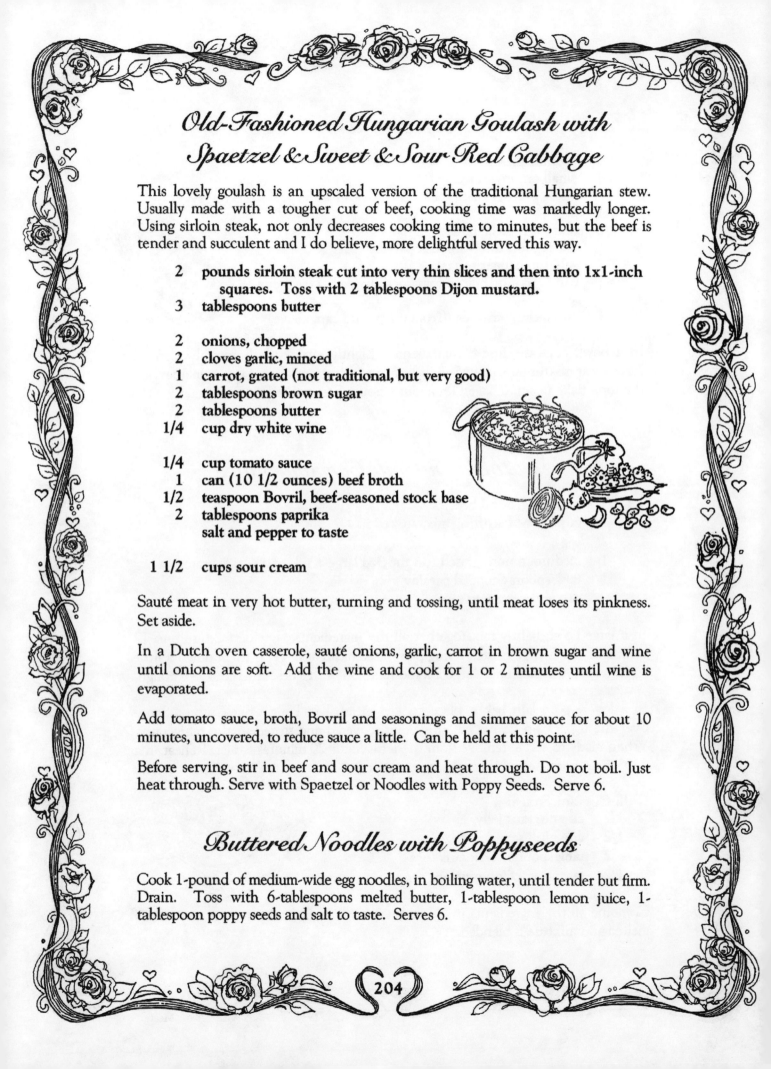

Sauté meat in very hot butter, turning and tossing, until meat loses its pinkness. Set aside.

In a Dutch oven casserole, sauté onions, garlic, carrot in brown sugar and wine until onions are soft. Add the wine and cook for 1 or 2 minutes until wine is evaporated.

Add tomato sauce, broth, Bovril and seasonings and simmer sauce for about 10 minutes, uncovered, to reduce sauce a little. Can be held at this point.

Before serving, stir in beef and sour cream and heat through. Do not boil. Just heat through. Serve with Spaetzel or Noodles with Poppy Seeds. Serve 6.

Buttered Noodles with Poppyseeds

Cook 1-pound of medium-wide egg noodles, in boiling water, until tender but firm. Drain. Toss with 6-tablespoons melted butter, 1-tablespoon lemon juice, 1-tablespoon poppy seeds and salt to taste. Serves 6.

Easiest & Best Hungarian Spaetzel

Spaetzel are little Hungarian noodles that are a pleasant accompaniment to soups or stews. They can be served as a starch, very much like rice or potatoes. They can be served "natural," tossed in butter or with an infinite variety of sauces or gravies.

The recipe I am sharing today is made foolproof with the addition of a little baking powder. The Spaetzel are exceedingly light and the onion powder imparts a very delicate flavor.

Spaetzel are excellent served with stews or soups. As these are made in a minute in a mixer, you can depend on them when you are really pressed for time. Once you try these little balls of noodles, you will enjoy using them often. The shapes are very irregular, so don't think anything went wrong.

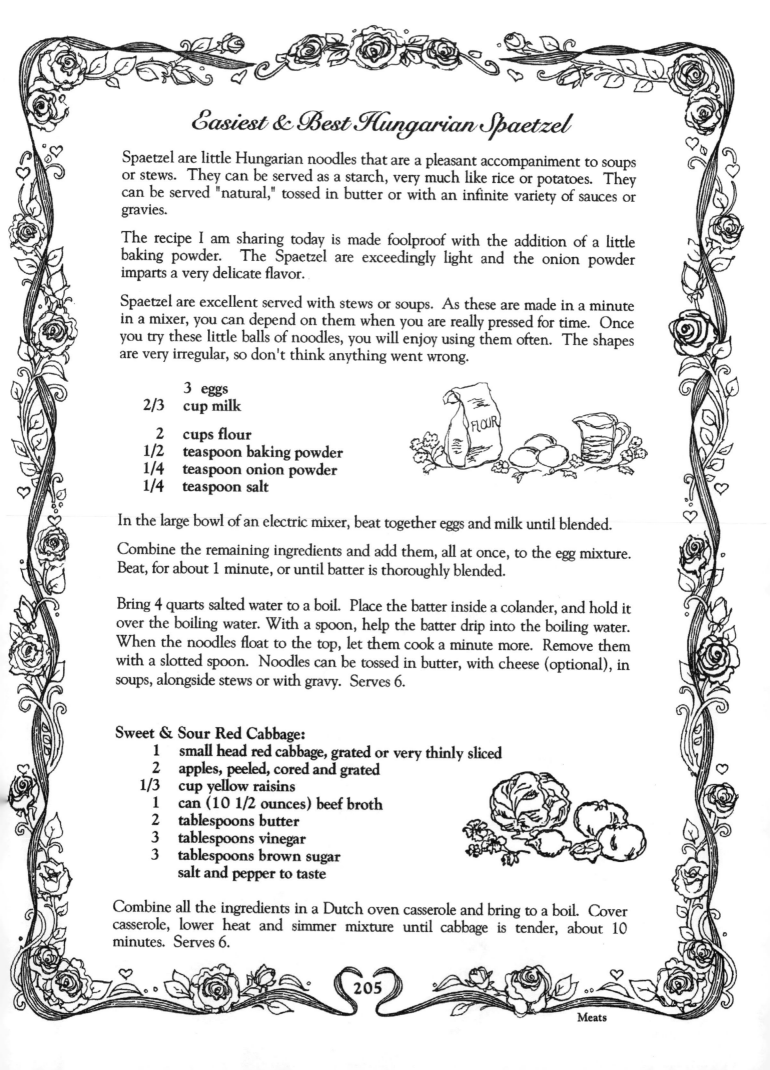

	3	eggs
2/3	cup milk
	2	cups flour
1/2	teaspoon baking powder
1/4	teaspoon onion powder
1/4	teaspoon salt

In the large bowl of an electric mixer, beat together eggs and milk until blended.

Combine the remaining ingredients and add them, all at once, to the egg mixture. Beat, for about 1 minute, or until batter is thoroughly blended.

Bring 4 quarts salted water to a boil. Place the batter inside a colander, and hold it over the boiling water. With a spoon, help the batter drip into the boiling water. When the noodles float to the top, let them cook a minute more. Remove them with a slotted spoon. Noodles can be tossed in butter, with cheese (optional), in soups, alongside stews or with gravy. Serves 6.

Sweet & Sour Red Cabbage:
- 1   small head red cabbage, grated or very thinly sliced
- 2   apples, peeled, cored and grated
- 1/3   cup yellow raisins
- 1   can (10 1/2 ounces) beef broth
- 2   tablespoons butter
- 3   tablespoons vinegar
- 3   tablespoons brown sugar
  - salt and pepper to taste

Combine all the ingredients in a Dutch oven casserole and bring to a boil. Cover casserole, lower heat and simmer mixture until cabbage is tender, about 10 minutes. Serves 6.

Meats

Butterflied Roast Leg of Lamb with Lemon, Garlic & Yogurt

1 leg of lamb, about 5 pounds, (ask the butcher to bone and butterfly it.) Sprinkle with salt and pepper.

1 cup unflavored yogurt
1 onion, finely chopped
1/4 cup oil
4 tablespoons lemon juice
3 cloves garlic, minced
1/2 teaspoon dried dill weed

In a ceramic or plastic bowl, place the leg of lamb. Combine the remaining ingredients and spread it on all sides of the lamb. Cover the bowl with plastic wrap and refrigerate it for several hours or overnight.

Lay the boned lamb in a 9x13-inch roasting pan, and spread some of the yogurt marinade on the cut side of the lamb. Roast the lamb, skin side down, in a 350° oven for about 1 1/2 hours or until a meat thermometer, inserted in the fleshiest part of the lamb, registers 150° for medium-rare and 160° for medium.

Remove any trace of the fat from the juices, slice the lamb and drizzle the natural juices over the lamb. Serve with rice seasoned with lemon and dill. Cucumber salad is a nice accompaniment. Serves 6 to 8.

Note: -*When I last made the lamb, I roasted it in the following manner. It was a bit unconventional, but the results were so excellent, that I will share them with you. To avoid the last minute reheating, I started the lamb about 3 hours before serving. I roasted it at 350° for 1 hour, reduced the oven temperature to 150° and continued roasting for 2 hours. Somewhere, in between, I defatted the natural juices, and at serving time, the lamb was pink and juicy and perfect for serving. Carve it at the table, and serve with pride.*
   -*Whichever method you choose, be certain to check your meat temperature for the degree of doneness.*

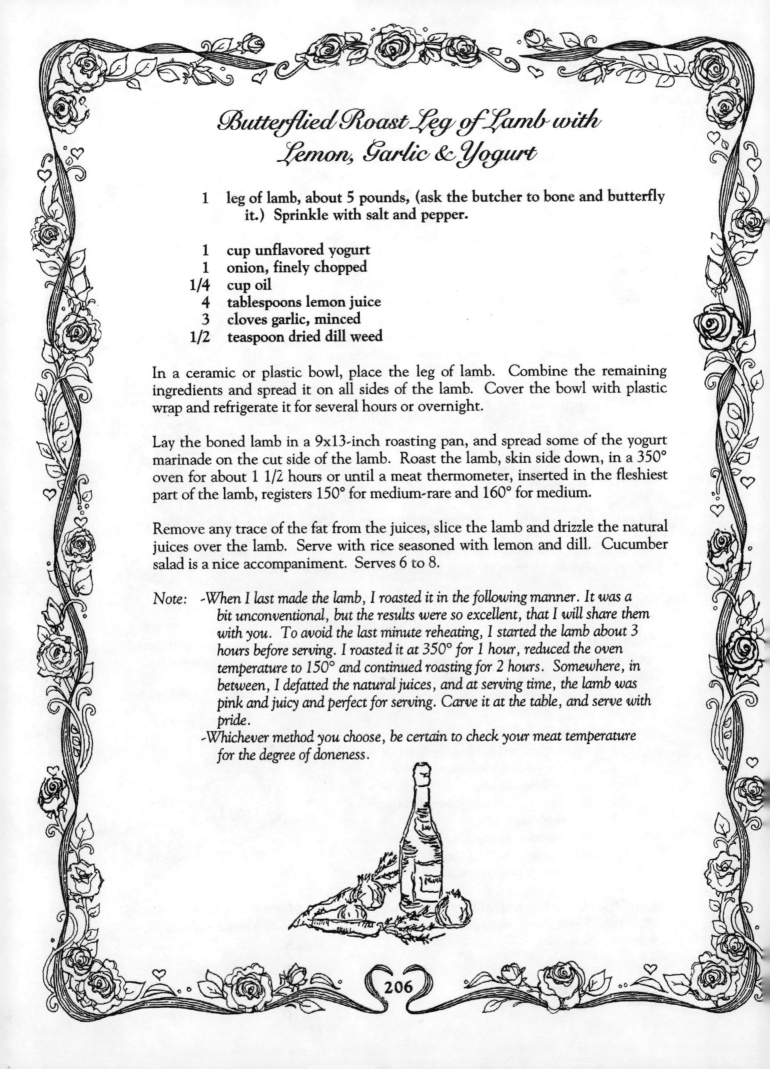

Crown Roast of Lamb with Bulgur, Lamb, Lemon & Chive Stuffing

This stuffing is so delicious, I can make a meal of it. The lamb is faintly sparkled with shallots, lemon and chives. The bulgur adds an interesting texture. The best way to make certain not to overcook the lamb is to remove it from the oven at 140° to 145° (rare), for it does continue to cook for several minutes and it will be a perfect medium rare when serving. Timing is extremely important with this recipe, for it is a real pity if the lamb is overcooked.

Bulgur & Lamb Stuffing:

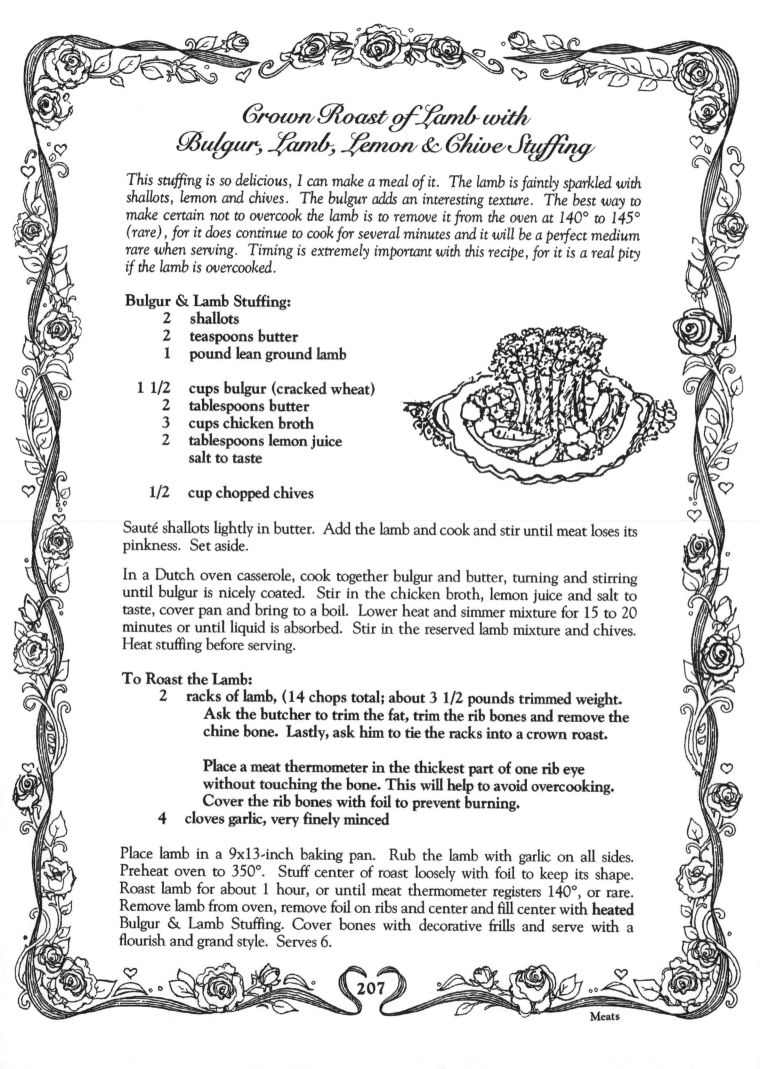

2	shallots
2	teaspoons butter
1	pound lean ground lamb
1 1/2	cups bulgur (cracked wheat)
2	tablespoons butter
3	cups chicken broth
2	tablespoons lemon juice
	salt to taste
1/2	cup chopped chives

Sauté shallots lightly in butter. Add the lamb and cook and stir until meat loses its pinkness. Set aside.

In a Dutch oven casserole, cook together bulgur and butter, turning and stirring until bulgur is nicely coated. Stir in the chicken broth, lemon juice and salt to taste, cover pan and bring to a boil. Lower heat and simmer mixture for 15 to 20 minutes or until liquid is absorbed. Stir in the reserved lamb mixture and chives. Heat stuffing before serving.

To Roast the Lamb:

2   racks of lamb, (14 chops total; about 3 1/2 pounds trimmed weight. Ask the butcher to trim the fat, trim the rib bones and remove the chine bone. Lastly, ask him to tie the racks into a crown roast.

Place a meat thermometer in the thickest part of one rib eye without touching the bone. This will help to avoid overcooking. Cover the rib bones with foil to prevent burning.

4   cloves garlic, very finely minced

Place lamb in a 9x13-inch baking pan. Rub the lamb with garlic on all sides. Preheat oven to 350°. Stuff center of roast loosely with foil to keep its shape. Roast lamb for about 1 hour, or until meat thermometer registers 140°, or rare. Remove lamb from oven, remove foil on ribs and center and fill center with **heated** Bulgur & Lamb Stuffing. Cover bones with decorative frills and serve with a flourish and grand style. Serves 6.

Greek-Styled Lamb Shanks in a Tomato-Garlic Wine Sauce

This is an adaptation of the classic Italian Osso Bucco. The lamb gives the sauce a totally different character and flavor. Orzo, a rice-shaped pasta, is an especially good accompaniment. Orzo comes in 3 sizes, small, medium and large. Use the large-sized orzo because it is more dramatic. If you use the smaller-sized orzo, reduce the amount of broth to 3 cups.

6	lamb shanks (about 3/4 pound, each) trimmed of any visible fat. Sprinkle with salt, pepper and a faint dusting of flour.
6	medium onions, thinly sliced
2	cans (1 pound each) stewed tomatoes, chopped. Discard seeds.
1	can (6 ounces) tomato paste
1	cup dry white wine
1	can (10 1/2 ounces) beef broth
3	carrots, finely grated
1	tablespoon sugar
3	tablespoons olive oil
6	cloves garlic, minced
1/2	teaspoon each, oregano, basil and thyme flakes salt and pepper to taste

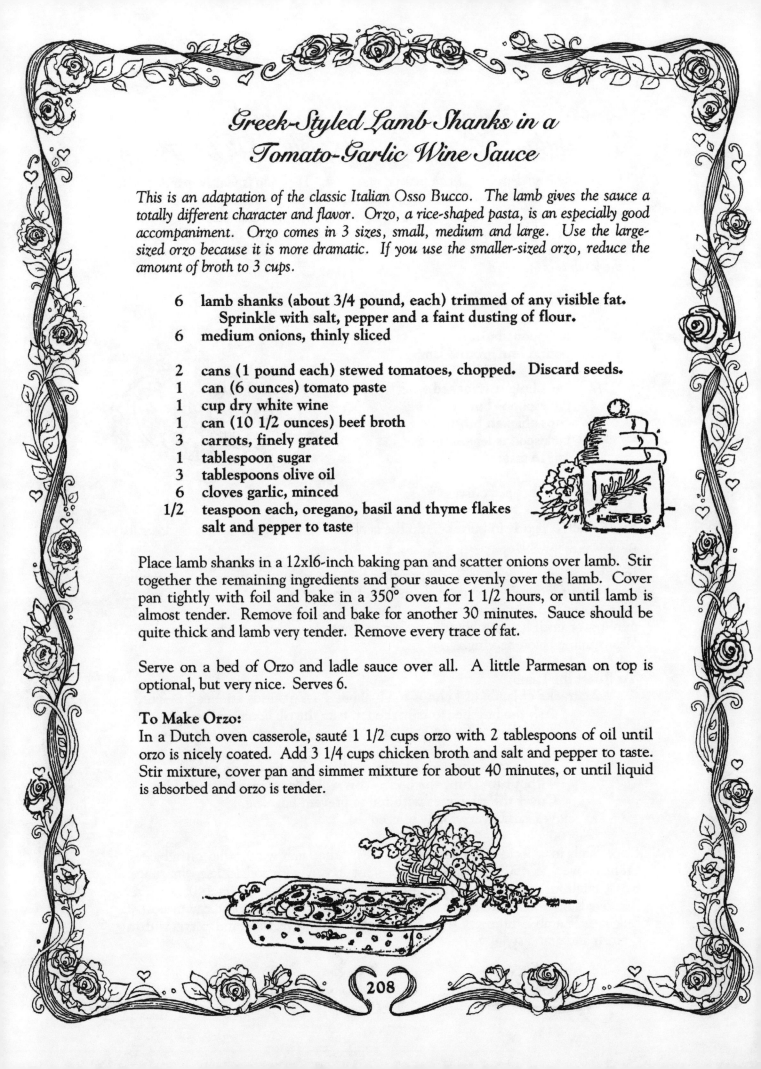

Place lamb shanks in a 12x16-inch baking pan and scatter onions over lamb. Stir together the remaining ingredients and pour sauce evenly over the lamb. Cover pan tightly with foil and bake in a 350° oven for 1 1/2 hours, or until lamb is almost tender. Remove foil and bake for another 30 minutes. Sauce should be quite thick and lamb very tender. Remove every trace of fat.

Serve on a bed of Orzo and ladle sauce over all. A little Parmesan on top is optional, but very nice. Serves 6.

To Make Orzo:
In a Dutch oven casserole, sauté 1 1/2 cups orzo with 2 tablespoons of oil until orzo is nicely coated. Add 3 1/4 cups chicken broth and salt and pepper to taste. Stir mixture, cover pan and simmer mixture for about 40 minutes, or until liquid is absorbed and orzo is tender.

Rack of Lamb with Garlic & Herbs

1   rack of lamb, (7 chops total; about 2 pounds. Ask the butcher to trim the fat and rib bones, and remove the chine bone. Place a meat thermometer in the thickest part of one rib eye without touching the bone. This will help to avoid overcooking. Cover the rib bones with foil to prevent burning.

2   cloves garlic, very finely minced

1/3   cup bread crumbs
2   cloves garlic, put through a press
1   teaspoon chopped parsley
1/4   teaspoon dried thyme flakes
     salt and pepper to taste

2   tablespoons butter, melted

Place lamb, fat side up (bones make a natural rack for lamb), in a 9x13-inch roasting pan. Rub the lamb with garlic. Roast lamb in a 350° oven for 35 minutes.

Meanwhile, combine crumbs, garlic, parsley, thyme, salt and pepper and mix until blended. Remove lamb from oven and allow it to rest for about 5 minutes. Baste lamb with butter and sprinkle crumb mixture on top of lamb ... careful not to burn your fingers. Return lamb to oven and continue roasting until thermometer registers 140° for rare or 160° for medium. Recipe can be doubled. Serves 2 or 3.

Rack of Lamb with Orange Lemon Glaze

1   rack of lamb, (7 chops total; about 2 pounds. Ask the butcher to trim the fat and rib bones, and remove the chine bone. Place a meat thermometer in the thickest part of one rib eye without touching the bone. This will help to avoid overcooking. Cover the rib bones with foil to prevent burning.

2   cloves garlic, very finely minced

1/4   cup orange marmalade
2   ounces (1/3 can) orange juice concentrate
2   tablespoons lemon juice
4   tablespoons (1/2 stick) butter

Place lamb, fat side up (bones make a natural rack for lamb), in a 9x13-inch roasting pan. Rub the lamb with garlic. Roast lamb in a 350° oven for 35 minutes.

Meanwhile, heat together the marmalade, orange juice concentrate, lemon juice and butter. Simmer mixture for a few minutes until blended. Baste lamb generously with this mixture. Continue roasting and basting until meat thermometer registers 140° for rare or 160° for medium. Remove aluminum foil and serve with pride. Recipe can be doubled. Serves 2 or 3.

Cassoulet of Lamb Shanks and Beans

Though very country and heady with garlic, this is still a very exciting dish and very satisfying. Purchase small lamb shanks as they are tender and less fat. They also are good as an individual portion. Serve it with some crusty French bread.

1	pound Great Northern dried white beans, washed and picked over for any foreign particles
2	quarts water
6	small lamb shanks (about 12 ounces, each) trimmed of visible fat
2	onions, chopped
6	cloves garlic, minced
2	tablespoons olive oil
1	can (1 pound) stewed tomatoes, chopped. Do not drain.
1	can (10 1/2 ounces beef broth)
2	tablespoons tomato paste
1	teaspoon sugar
1/2	cup dry red wine
1	teaspoon thyme flakes
	salt and pepper to taste

In a Dutch oven casserole, bring beans and water to a boil. Boil vigorously for 5 minutes, remove from heat and allow to stand for 1 hour. Drain beans in a colander and discard liquid.

In the same Dutch oven casserole, brown lamb shanks, onions and garlic in oil for about 10 minutes, tossing and turning. Add the beans and the remaining ingredients, cover casserole and simmer mixture for about 1 1/2 to 2 hours or until beans and meat are tender. Serve with a crusty French bread and a green salad. Serves 6.

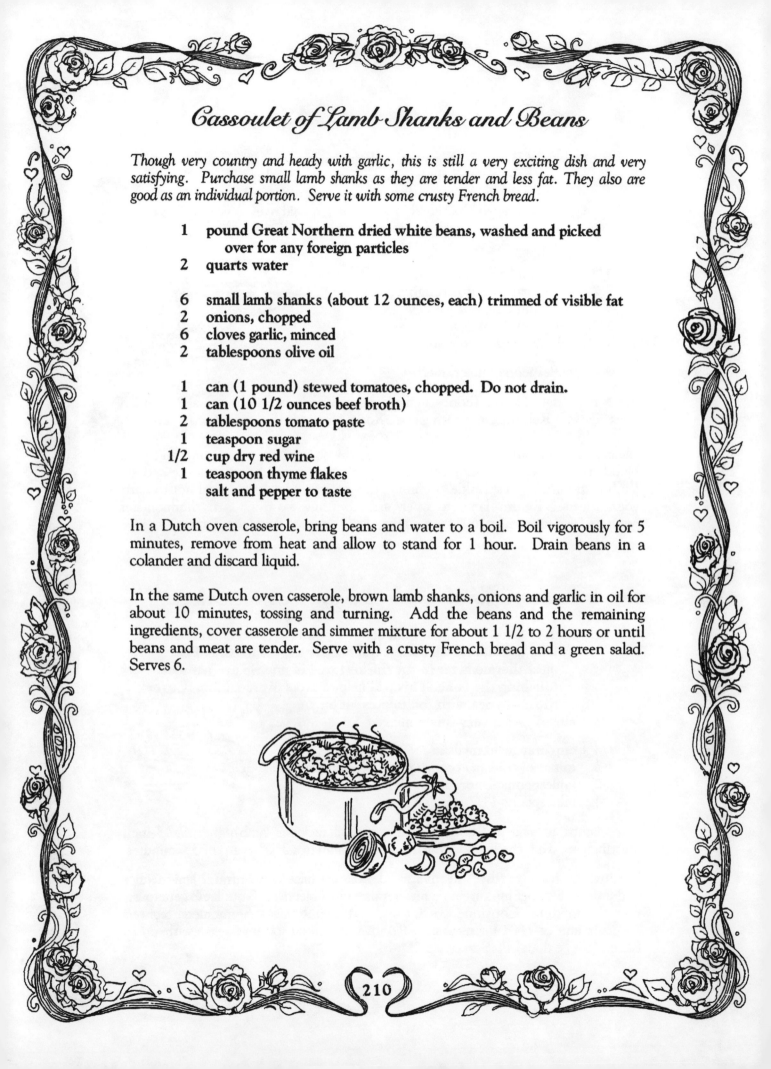

Dilled Lamb with
Yogurt, Lemon & Garlic Sauce

Lamb is so nice around the Easter holidays. Marinated in a mixture of yogurt and lemon juice and then cooked with tomatoes and dill is a special delight.

3	pounds boneless lamb, cut from the leg and into 3/4-inch cubes
2	tablespoons lemon juice
2	tablespoons oil
1/4	cup yogurt
2	onions, chopped
6	cloves garlic, minced
1	can (1 pound) stewed tomatoes, chopped. Do not drain.
1	can (10 1/2 ounces) chicken broth
1/2	teaspoon dried dill weed
	salt and pepper to taste

In a large bowl, toss together lamb, lemon juice, oil and yogurt. Allow to stand at room temperature for 2 hours, turning and tossing every now and again. (Refrigerate, if marinating for a longer period.)

In a 9x13-inch pan, toss together meat and the remaining ingredients until blended. Cover pan tightly with foil and bake in a 350° oven for about 1 1/2 hours or until lamb is tender.

Transfer to a porcelain casserole and remove every trace of fat. Heat through before serving. Serve with Brown Rice with Mushrooms and Onions as a hearty accompaniment. Serves 6 to 8.

Brown Rice with Mushrooms & Onions

1 1/2	cups brown rice
2	tablespoons oil
3	cups chicken broth
	salt and pepper to taste
1/4	pound mushrooms
1	small onion, chopped
2	tablespoons butter

In a covered saucepan, simmer together first 4 ingredients until rice is tender and liquid is absorbed, about 35 minutes. Meanwhile, sauté mushrooms and onions in butter until onions are soft. When rice is cooked, stir in the mushrooms and onions. Can be made earlier in day and heated before serving. Serves 6 to 8.

Teriyaki Pork Roast with Apple Jelly Glaze

Teriyaki marinade can be purchased at most supermarkets. If you have any trouble finding it, you can make it by stirring together 1/2 cup soy sauce and 2 tablespoons brown sugar. Pork can be prepared earlier in the day and reheated at serving time.

2   pork tenderloins (about 1 1/2 pounds, each.) Sprinkle with pepper and garlic powder to taste.

Apple Jelly Glaze:
- 1/2 cup apple jelly
- 1/4 cup apple juice
- 1/4 cup teriyaki marinade
- 1 tablespoon lemon juice
- 1 teaspoon ground ginger
- salt and pepper to taste

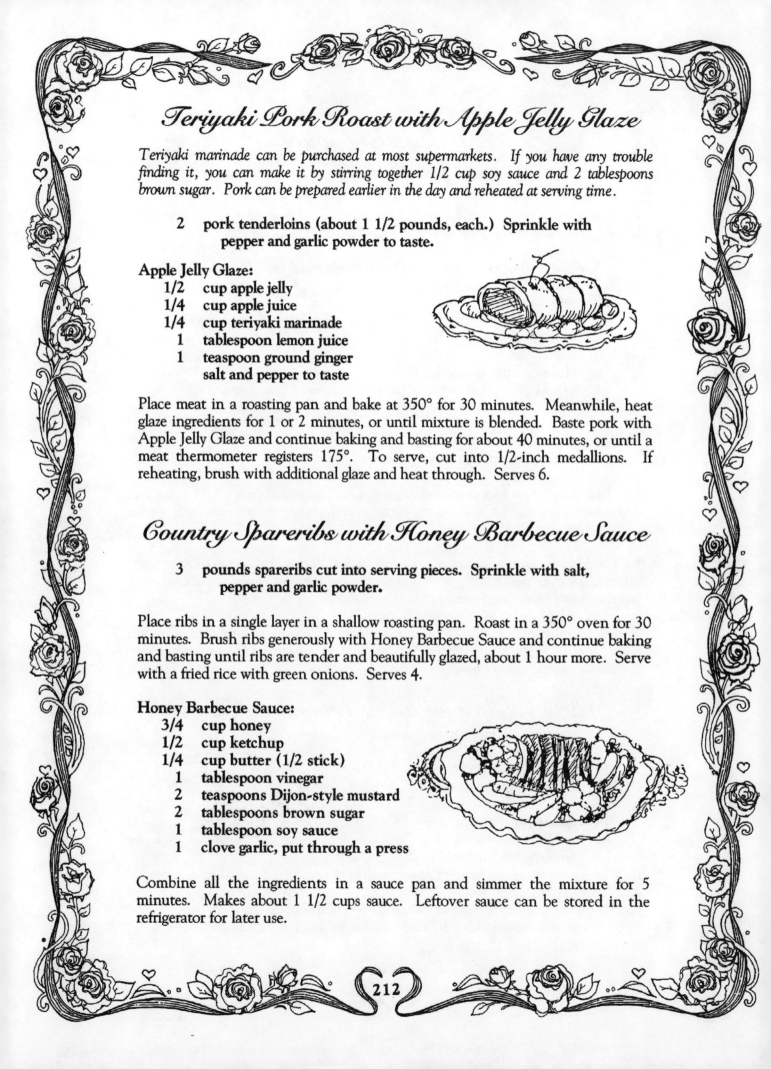

Place meat in a roasting pan and bake at 350° for 30 minutes. Meanwhile, heat glaze ingredients for 1 or 2 minutes, or until mixture is blended. Baste pork with Apple Jelly Glaze and continue baking and basting for about 40 minutes, or until a meat thermometer registers 175°. To serve, cut into 1/2-inch medallions. If reheating, brush with additional glaze and heat through. Serves 6.

Country Spareribs with Honey Barbecue Sauce

3   pounds spareribs cut into serving pieces. Sprinkle with salt, pepper and garlic powder.

Place ribs in a single layer in a shallow roasting pan. Roast in a 350° oven for 30 minutes. Brush ribs generously with Honey Barbecue Sauce and continue baking and basting until ribs are tender and beautifully glazed, about 1 hour more. Serve with a fried rice with green onions. Serves 4.

Honey Barbecue Sauce:
- 3/4 cup honey
- 1/2 cup ketchup
- 1/4 cup butter (1/2 stick)
- 1 tablespoon vinegar
- 2 teaspoons Dijon-style mustard
- 2 tablespoons brown sugar
- 1 tablespoon soy sauce
- 1 clove garlic, put through a press

Combine all the ingredients in a sauce pan and simmer the mixture for 5 minutes. Makes about 1 1/2 cups sauce. Leftover sauce can be stored in the refrigerator for later use.

Plum-Glazed Barbecued Spareribs

This is a lovely barbecue sauce and, also, good as a glaze for chicken.

> 4 pounds pork spareribs, cut into 2-rib pieces and sprinkled with
> salt and garlic powder to taste

In a covered Dutch oven casserole, cook ribs in 2-inches of simmering water for 30 minutes. Drain and discard water.

Place partially cooked ribs in a roasting pan and baste on all sides with Plum Barbecue Glaze. Bake in a 350° oven for 30 minutes, basting 3 or 4 times with the barbecue sauce until the ribs are nicely glazed and tender. Serves 6.

Plum Barbecue Glaze:
- 1 cup plum jam
- 1/4 cup honey
- 3/4 cup ketchup
- 1/4 cup vinegar
- 2 tablespoons lemon juice
- pinch of cayenne pepper
- salt and pepper to taste

In a saucepan, simmer together all the ingredients for 2 or 3 minutes, or until sauce is nicely blended. Yields about 2 1/4 cups sauce.

Apricot Glazed Canadian Bacon

> 2 pounds Canadian bacon or boneless ham round (ready to eat)

- 1/2 cup apricot jam
- 1/4 cup honey
- 1 tablespoon prepared mustard

Combine apricot jam, honey and mustard and heat until blended. Spread mixture over bacon or ham. Bake in a 375° oven for about 30 minutes or until meat is glazed. Cool. Slice thinly, reshape and place in a porcelain baker. Can be prepared a day earlier and reheated at time of serving. Serve garnished with Glazed Brandied Apricots. Serves 8.

Glazed Brandied Apricots:
- 12 dried apricots
- 1/4 cup orange juice
- 2 tablespoons sugar
- 1 tablespoon Apricot Brandy

In a saucepan, simmer together all the ingredients for 5 minutes, or until apricots

Meats

Roast Tenderloin of Pork with Apple Jelly

Pork tenderloin is a succulent, tender and flavorful cut of meat. For my taste, it is most delicious when glazed with different fruit flavors. Here are two of them.

> 2   tenderloins of pork, (about 1 1/2 pounds each), sprinkle with salt, pepper and garlic powder
>
> **Lawry's Teriyaki Marinade**

Place the tenderloins of pork in a shallow roasting pan. Roast in a 350° oven for about 30 minutes, basting frequently with Teriyaki Marinade. Then baste every 15 minutes with Apple Jelly Sauce until meat is tender and meat thermometer registers 175°, about another 40 minutes. Serve with rice or with oriental noodles. Serves 8.

Apple Jelly Sauce:
> 1   cup apple juice
> 1   apple, peeled, cored and grated
> 1/2   cup apple jelly

Combine all the ingredients and cook for a few minutes until heated through and apple jelly is softened and blended. Use to baste the pork.

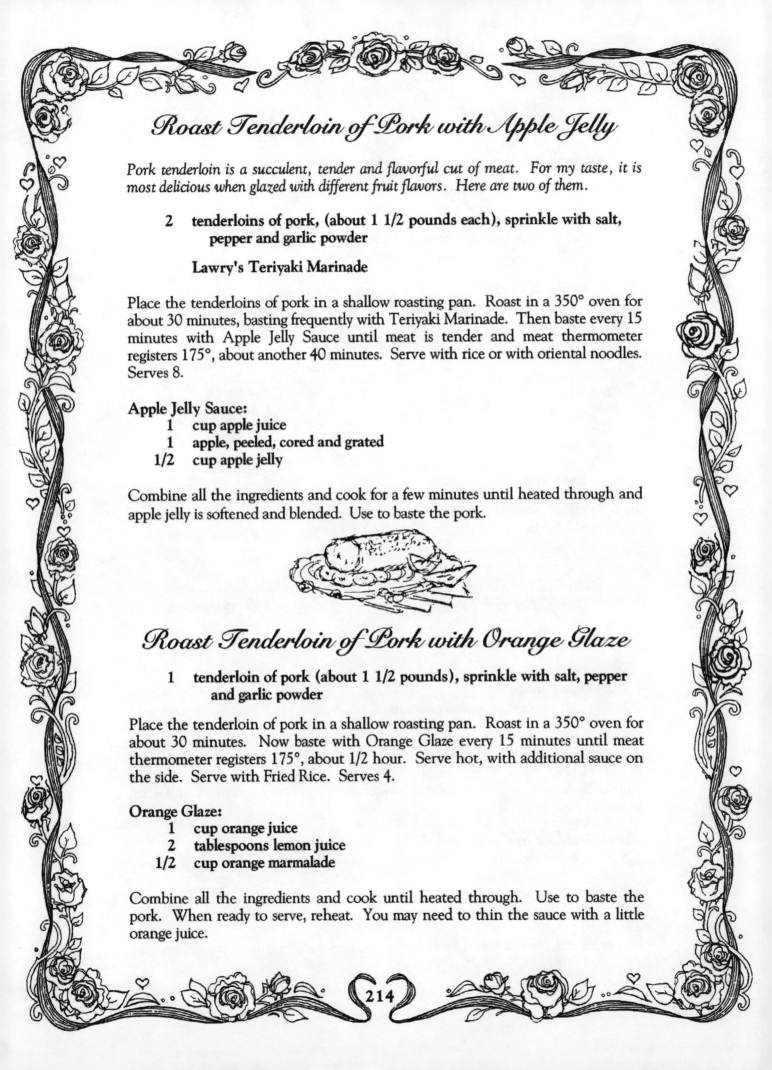

Roast Tenderloin of Pork with Orange Glaze

> 1   tenderloin of pork (about 1 1/2 pounds), sprinkle with salt, pepper and garlic powder

Place the tenderloin of pork in a shallow roasting pan. Roast in a 350° oven for about 30 minutes. Now baste with Orange Glaze every 15 minutes until meat thermometer registers 175°, about 1/2 hour. Serve hot, with additional sauce on the side. Serve with Fried Rice. Serves 4.

Orange Glaze:
> 1   cup orange juice
> 2   tablespoons lemon juice
> 1/2   cup orange marmalade

Combine all the ingredients and cook until heated through. Use to baste the pork. When ready to serve, reheat. You may need to thin the sauce with a little orange juice.

Pork Dumplings & Apricot Peanut Sauce

Both the Pork Dumplings and the Apricot Peanut Sauce can be prepared in advance, making this a great dish to serve for an Asian dinner. Dumplings can be frozen in double thicknesses of plastic wrap and foil. To serve, defrost and heat in a 350° oven until heated through. Apricot Peanut Sauce can be prepared 1 week in advance. Pork can be substituted with ground beef or ground turkey.

Pork Dumplings:

1	pound lean ground pork
4	cloves finely minced garlic
1/3	cup finely minced green onions
2	tablespoons soy sauce (or teriyaki marinade)
1	egg, beaten
2	slices fresh bread, sprinkled with water and squeezed dry
1/4	teaspoon ground ginger
	salt and pepper to taste

flaked coconut for coating dumplings

In a large bowl, mix together first group of ingredients until blended. Shape meat mixture into 1/2-inch balls, roll lightly in coconut flakes and flatten slightly. Place dumplings in a non-stick skillet and cook until bottoms are browned, about 2 minutes. Turn and brown other side. Serve with Apricot Peanut Sauce on the side for dipping. Yields 36 dumplings.

Apricot Peanut Sauce:

1/2	cup apricot jam
1	tablespoon brown sugar
2	tablespoons lemon juice
1	teaspoon soy sauce
2	tablespoons very finely chopped peanuts

In a small saucepan, heat together all the ingredients until sugar is dissolved. Serve sauce warm, not hot. Yields about 3/4 cup sauce.

Notes for Advance Preparation:

-Pork Dumplings can be made 1 day earlier and refrigerated or 1 week earlier and stored in the freezer.

-Apricot Peanut Sauce can be prepared 1 week earlier and stored in the refrigerator.

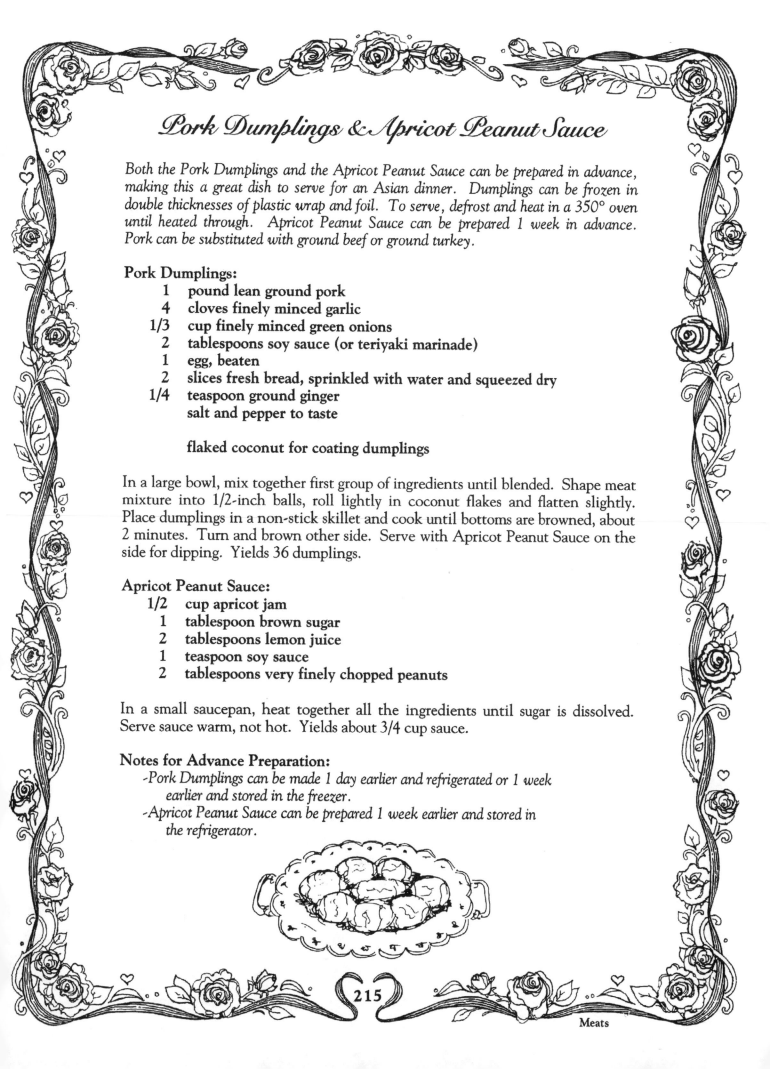

Meats

Sweet & Sour Barbecued Loin of Pork with Baked Apples & Raisins

1   loin of pork roast, about 4 to 5 pounds. Ask butcher to remove the chine bone and any excess fat. Sprinkle with salt and pepper and garlic powder to taste. Brush top with 2 tablespoons Dijon mustard. Place meat thermometer into the thickest part of the meat, making certain it rests in the center and does not touch the bone.

Place roast in a shallow baking pan, bone side down, and bake in a 325° oven for about 2 1/2 hours, or until meat thermometer registers 160°. Now, brush Sweet & Sour Barbecue Sauce over the roast, and continue baking and basting until pork is tender and meat thermometer registers 175°. Serve with Baked Apples & Raisins. Serves 6.

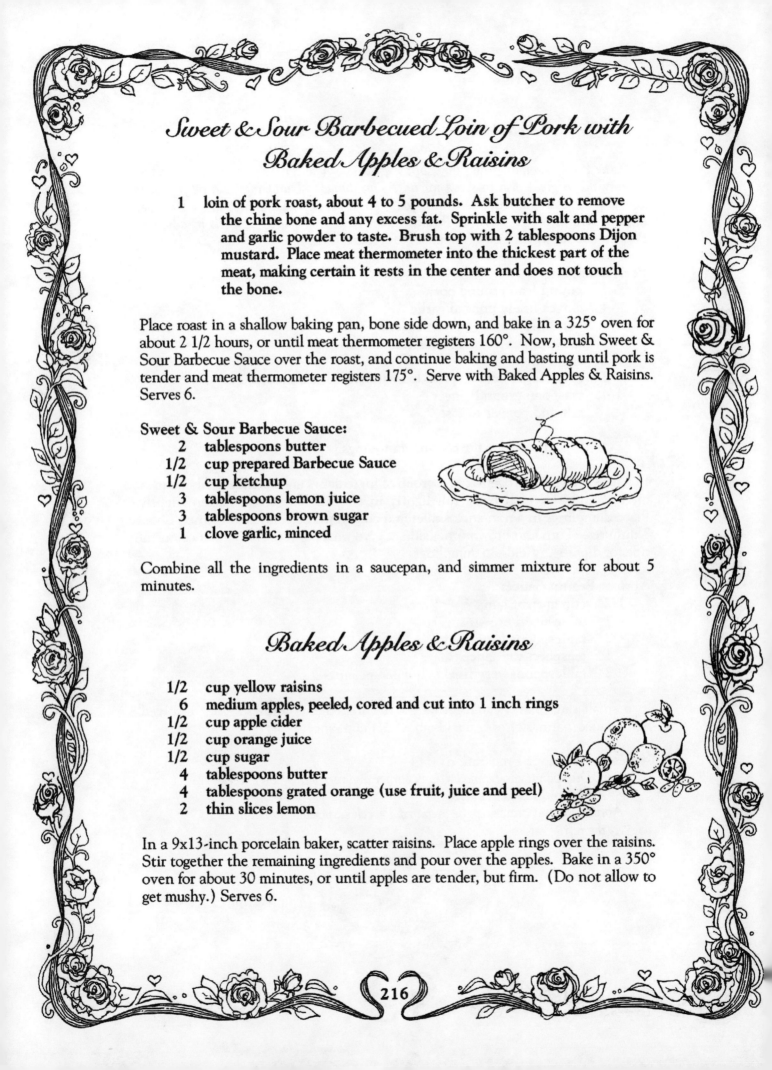

Sweet & Sour Barbecue Sauce:

2   tablespoons butter
1/2 cup prepared Barbecue Sauce
1/2 cup ketchup
3   tablespoons lemon juice
3   tablespoons brown sugar
1   clove garlic, minced

Combine all the ingredients in a saucepan, and simmer mixture for about 5 minutes.

Baked Apples & Raisins

1/2 cup yellow raisins
6   medium apples, peeled, cored and cut into 1 inch rings
1/2 cup apple cider
1/2 cup orange juice
1/2 cup sugar
4   tablespoons butter
4   tablespoons grated orange (use fruit, juice and peel)
2   thin slices lemon

In a 9x13-inch porcelain baker, scatter raisins. Place apple rings over the raisins. Stir together the remaining ingredients and pour over the apples. Bake in a 350° oven for about 30 minutes, or until apples are tender, but firm. (Do not allow to get mushy.) Serves 6.

Honey Baked Ham
with Glazed Cinnamon Apple Rings

This is a traditional recipe for baked ham, sparkled with brown sugar, mustard and cloves. The apple rings are a nice accompaniment.

1 ready-to-eat ham, about 12 pounds, with bone in. With a sharp knife, remove the skin and fat, leaving a thin layer of fat to keep meat moist while baking. Score surface of ham in a diamond pattern, without cutting into the meat.

3 tablespoons Dijon mustard
   whole cloves
1 cup brown sugar
1/2 cup honey

1 1/2 cups apple juice

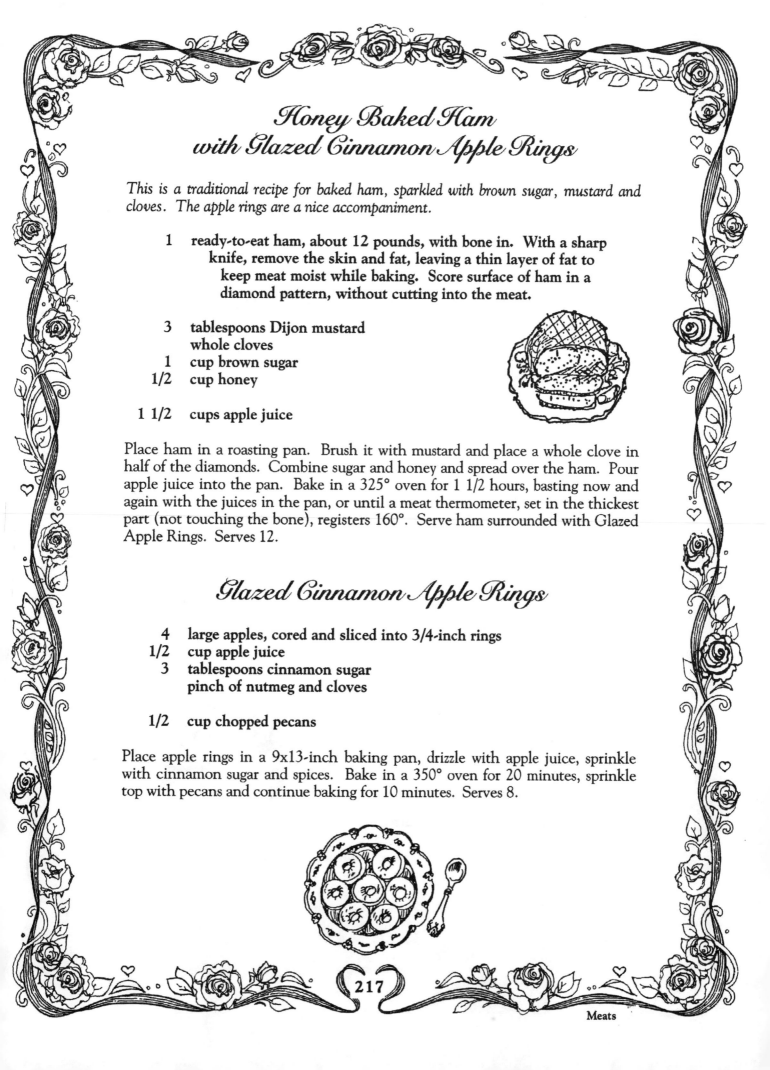

Place ham in a roasting pan. Brush it with mustard and place a whole clove in half of the diamonds. Combine sugar and honey and spread over the ham. Pour apple juice into the pan. Bake in a 325° oven for 1 1/2 hours, basting now and again with the juices in the pan, or until a meat thermometer, set in the thickest part (not touching the bone), registers 160°. Serve ham surrounded with Glazed Apple Rings. Serves 12.

Glazed Cinnamon Apple Rings

4 large apples, cored and sliced into 3/4-inch rings
1/2 cup apple juice
3 tablespoons cinnamon sugar
   pinch of nutmeg and cloves

1/2 cup chopped pecans

Place apple rings in a 9x13-inch baking pan, drizzle with apple juice, sprinkle with cinnamon sugar and spices. Bake in a 350° oven for 20 minutes, sprinkle top with pecans and continue baking for 10 minutes. Serves 8.

Meats

Honey-Baked Ham with
Apple & Pecan Cornbread Pudding

This is a grand way to serve ham, accompanied with a deeply fragrant apple and pecan pudding. The pudding is basically a stuffing baked in a separate pan. The stuffing is also good served with chicken or turkey.

1	canned ham (about 5 pounds). Score top of ham in a diamond pattern with the tip of a knife. Do not cut deep into the meat. Place 1 clove in every other diamond.
1/2	cup honey
1/4	cup apple cider
1	teaspoon Dijon mustard
1/2	cup brown sugar

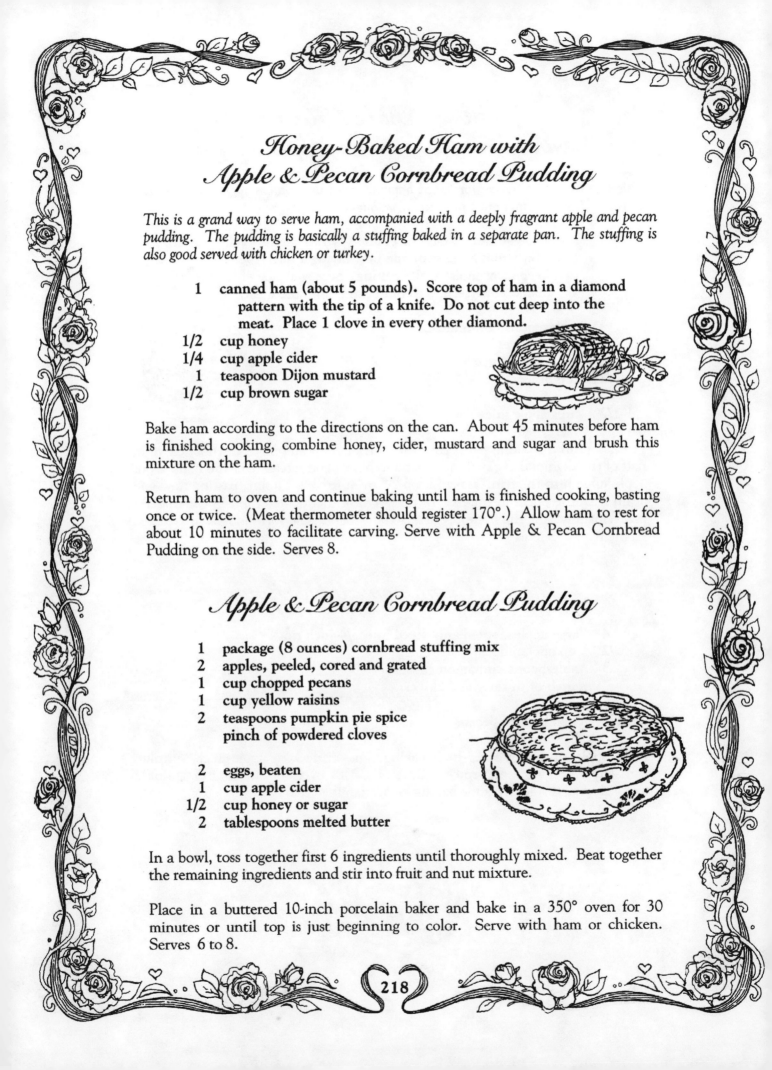

Bake ham according to the directions on the can. About 45 minutes before ham is finished cooking, combine honey, cider, mustard and sugar and brush this mixture on the ham.

Return ham to oven and continue baking until ham is finished cooking, basting once or twice. (Meat thermometer should register 170°.) Allow ham to rest for about 10 minutes to facilitate carving. Serve with Apple & Pecan Cornbread Pudding on the side. Serves 8.

Apple & Pecan Cornbread Pudding

1	package (8 ounces) cornbread stuffing mix
2	apples, peeled, cored and grated
1	cup chopped pecans
1	cup yellow raisins
2	teaspoons pumpkin pie spice
	pinch of powdered cloves
2	eggs, beaten
1	cup apple cider
1/2	cup honey or sugar
2	tablespoons melted butter

In a bowl, toss together first 6 ingredients until thoroughly mixed. Beat together the remaining ingredients and stir into fruit and nut mixture.

Place in a buttered 10-inch porcelain baker and bake in a 350° oven for 30 minutes or until top is just beginning to color. Serve with ham or chicken. Serves 6 to 8.

Easiest & Best Osso Bucco alla Milanese

It is such fun to pick the succulent meat off the bones and to scoop out every morsel of delicious marrow. Sauce does not need to be thickened. Traditionally served with Risotto alla Milanese, I like to add a little tomato to the rice. It adds a wonderful flavor.

3	veal shanks (also called shinbones) about 6 pounds. Ask butcher to saw them into 3-inch pieces. Sprinkle them with salt and pepper and dust them lightly with flour.
3	medium onions, cut into fourths
2	cans (1 pound, each) diced tomatoes. Do not drain.
1	can (6 ounces) tomato paste
1	cup dry white wine
2	teaspoons beef stock base
1	carrot, grated
1	teaspoon sugar
2	tablespoons olive oil
6	cloves garlic, minced
1 1/2	teaspoons Italian Herb Seasoning
	salt and freshly ground pepper to taste

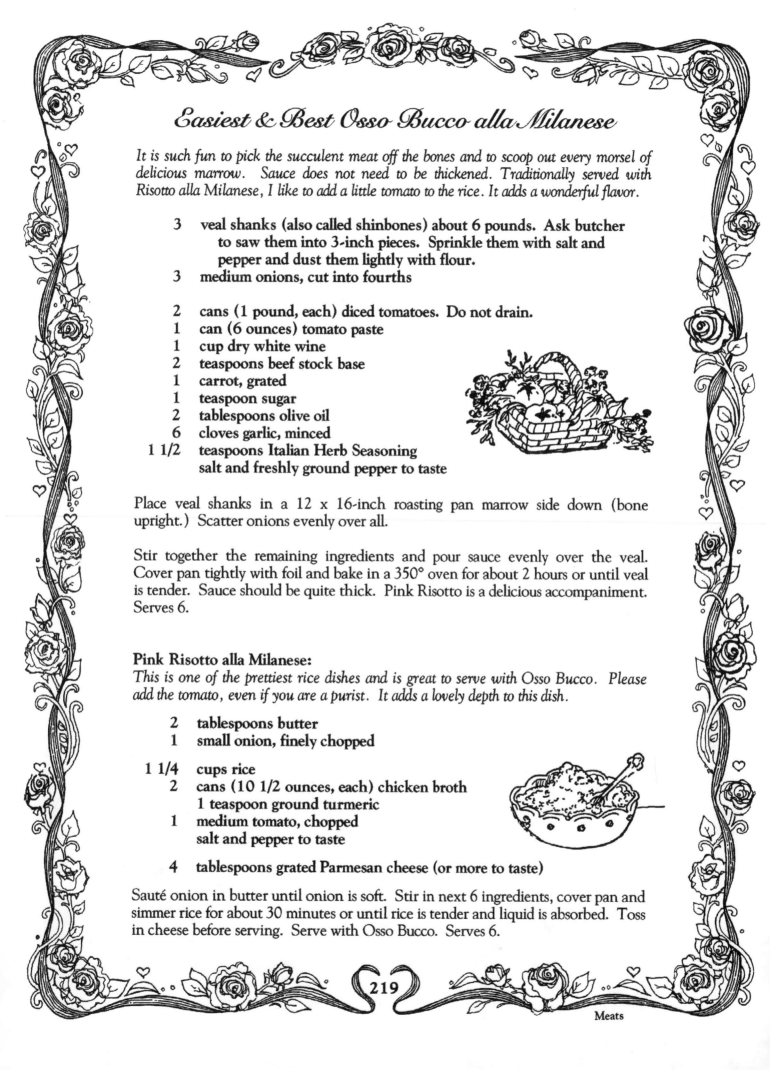

Place veal shanks in a 12 x 16-inch roasting pan marrow side down (bone upright.) Scatter onions evenly over all.

Stir together the remaining ingredients and pour sauce evenly over the veal. Cover pan tightly with foil and bake in a 350° oven for about 2 hours or until veal is tender. Sauce should be quite thick. Pink Risotto is a delicious accompaniment. Serves 6.

Pink Risotto alla Milanese:
This is one of the prettiest rice dishes and is great to serve with Osso Bucco. Please add the tomato, even if you are a purist. It adds a lovely depth to this dish.

2	tablespoons butter
1	small onion, finely chopped
1 1/4	cups rice
2	cans (10 1/2 ounces, each) chicken broth
	1 teaspoon ground turmeric
1	medium tomato, chopped
	salt and pepper to taste
4	tablespoons grated Parmesan cheese (or more to taste)

Sauté onion in butter until onion is soft. Stir in next 6 ingredients, cover pan and simmer rice for about 30 minutes or until rice is tender and liquid is absorbed. Toss in cheese before serving. Serve with Osso Bucco. Serves 6.

Meats

Herb Stuffed Breast of Veal in Currant Wine Sauce

A delicious herb stuffing sparkles the breast of veal and the Currant Wine Sauce is the perfect balance. This is truly delicious and a marvelous choice for dinner with family and friends. Veal can be served immediately after baking, but it is a little more difficult to slice. By allowing it to chill, it cuts into the most attractive slices.

1   breast of veal (about 6 to 7 pounds), boned and trimmed of any fat. This will yield about 5 pounds, net weight. Sprinkle with garlic powder on both sides.

2   onions, finely chopped
2   carrots, grated

2   stalks celery, finely chopped
6   cloves garlic, minced
1/2   cup (1 stick) butter

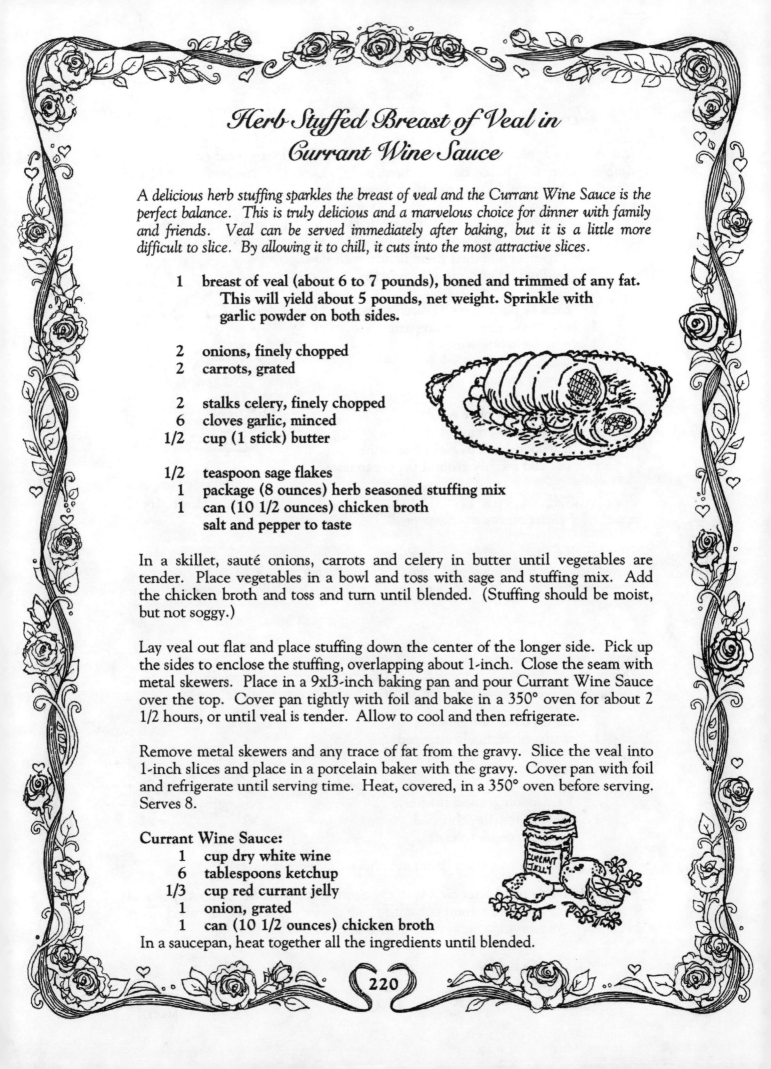

1/2   teaspoon sage flakes
1   package (8 ounces) herb seasoned stuffing mix
1   can (10 1/2 ounces) chicken broth
salt and pepper to taste

In a skillet, sauté onions, carrots and celery in butter until vegetables are tender. Place vegetables in a bowl and toss with sage and stuffing mix. Add the chicken broth and toss and turn until blended. (Stuffing should be moist, but not soggy.)

Lay veal out flat and place stuffing down the center of the longer side. Pick up the sides to enclose the stuffing, overlapping about 1-inch. Close the seam with metal skewers. Place in a 9x13-inch baking pan and pour Currant Wine Sauce over the top. Cover pan tightly with foil and bake in a 350° oven for about 2 1/2 hours, or until veal is tender. Allow to cool and then refrigerate.

Remove metal skewers and any trace of fat from the gravy. Slice the veal into 1-inch slices and place in a porcelain baker with the gravy. Cover pan with foil and refrigerate until serving time. Heat, covered, in a 350° oven before serving. Serves 8.

Currant Wine Sauce:
1   cup dry white wine
6   tablespoons ketchup
1/3   cup red currant jelly
1   onion, grated
1   can (10 1/2 ounces) chicken broth
In a saucepan, heat together all the ingredients until blended.

Veal Meatloaf with Brandied Apple Rings

Meat loaf can be elevated quite a few notches, with the addition of apples and cream. The Herbed Rice is a lovely accompaniment.

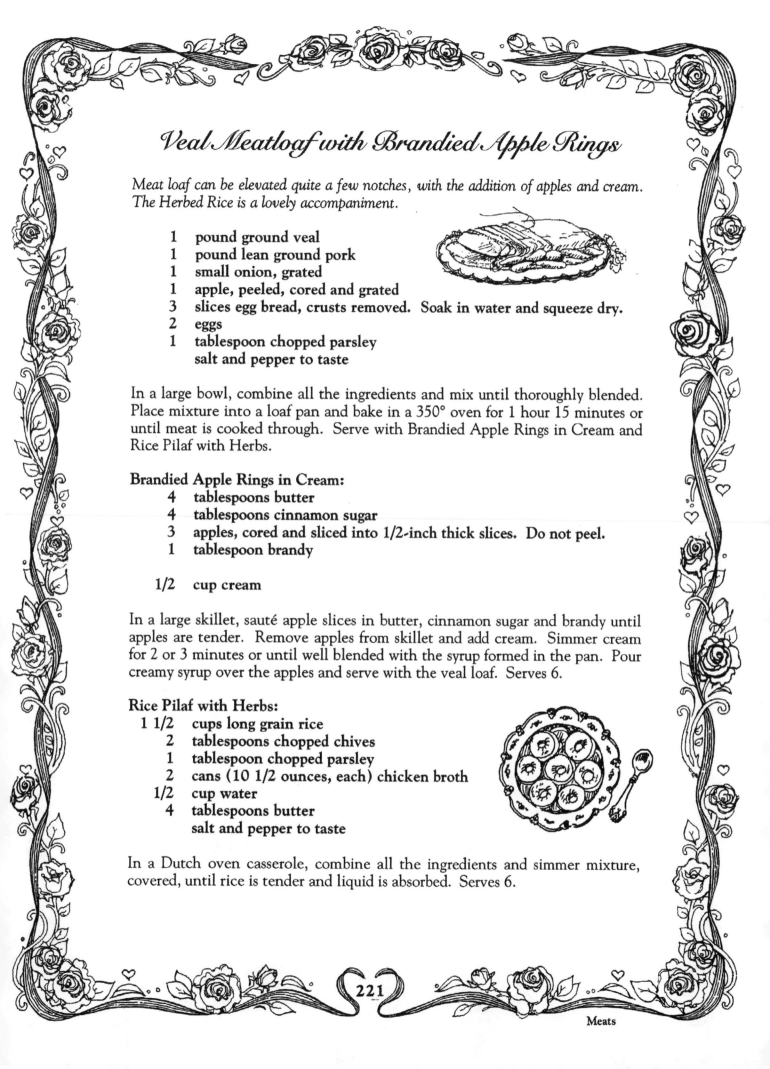

- 1 pound ground veal
- 1 pound lean ground pork
- 1 small onion, grated
- 1 apple, peeled, cored and grated
- 3 slices egg bread, crusts removed. Soak in water and squeeze dry.
- 2 eggs
- 1 tablespoon chopped parsley
- salt and pepper to taste

In a large bowl, combine all the ingredients and mix until thoroughly blended. Place mixture into a loaf pan and bake in a 350° oven for 1 hour 15 minutes or until meat is cooked through. Serve with Brandied Apple Rings in Cream and Rice Pilaf with Herbs.

Brandied Apple Rings in Cream:
- 4 tablespoons butter
- 4 tablespoons cinnamon sugar
- 3 apples, cored and sliced into 1/2-inch thick slices. Do not peel.
- 1 tablespoon brandy

- 1/2 cup cream

In a large skillet, sauté apple slices in butter, cinnamon sugar and brandy until apples are tender. Remove apples from skillet and add cream. Simmer cream for 2 or 3 minutes or until well blended with the syrup formed in the pan. Pour creamy syrup over the apples and serve with the veal loaf. Serves 6.

Rice Pilaf with Herbs:
- 1 1/2 cups long grain rice
- 2 tablespoons chopped chives
- 1 tablespoon chopped parsley
- 2 cans (10 1/2 ounces, each) chicken broth
- 1/2 cup water
- 4 tablespoons butter
- salt and pepper to taste

In a Dutch oven casserole, combine all the ingredients and simmer mixture, covered, until rice is tender and liquid is absorbed. Serves 6.

Meats

Pate of Veal & Red Peppers with Herbed Tomato Sauce

Veal and peppers are a wonderful blend of flavors. This elegant pate is much too grand to call "meat loaf." It is nice for an informal dinner and the sauce, so easy and delicious, can be served with many other dishes. If you are using the sauce for another purpose, it must be simmered for 20 minutes.

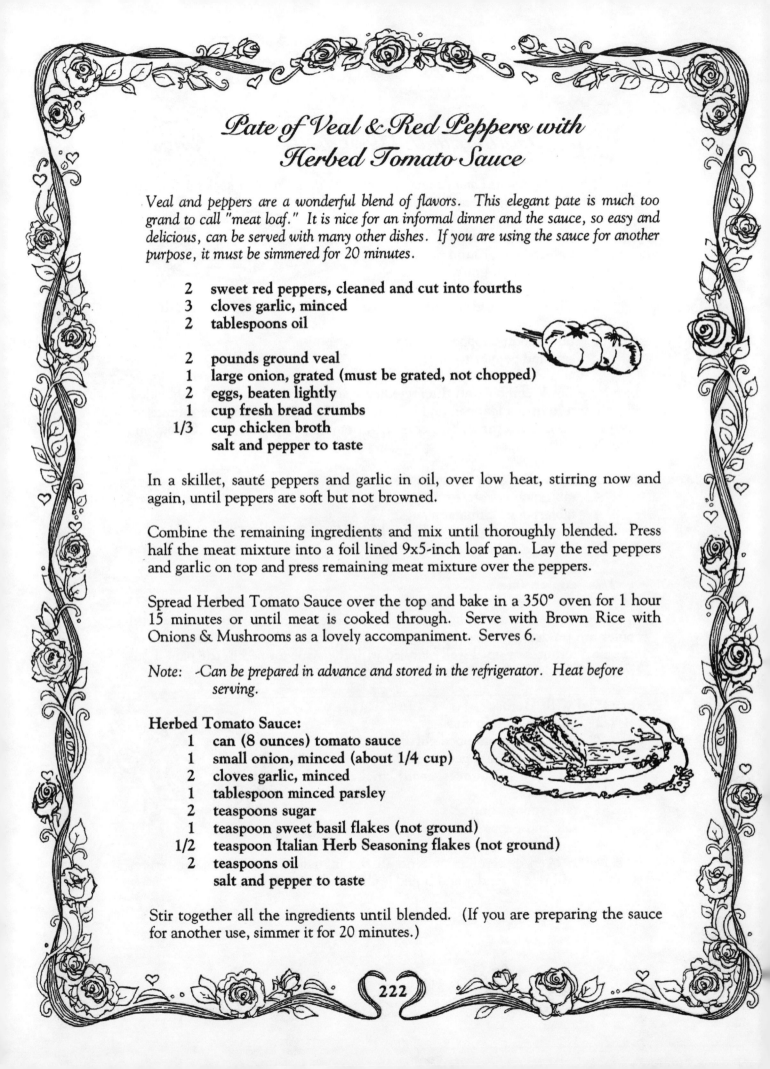

2	sweet red peppers, cleaned and cut into fourths
3	cloves garlic, minced
2	tablespoons oil
2	pounds ground veal
1	large onion, grated (must be grated, not chopped)
2	eggs, beaten lightly
1	cup fresh bread crumbs
1/3	cup chicken broth
	salt and pepper to taste

In a skillet, sauté peppers and garlic in oil, over low heat, stirring now and again, until peppers are soft but not browned.

Combine the remaining ingredients and mix until thoroughly blended. Press half the meat mixture into a foil lined 9x5-inch loaf pan. Lay the red peppers and garlic on top and press remaining meat mixture over the peppers.

Spread Herbed Tomato Sauce over the top and bake in a 350° oven for 1 hour 15 minutes or until meat is cooked through. Serve with Brown Rice with Onions & Mushrooms as a lovely accompaniment. Serves 6.

Note: -Can be prepared in advance and stored in the refrigerator. Heat before serving.

Herbed Tomato Sauce:

1	can (8 ounces) tomato sauce
1	small onion, minced (about 1/4 cup)
2	cloves garlic, minced
1	tablespoon minced parsley
2	teaspoons sugar
1	teaspoon sweet basil flakes (not ground)
1/2	teaspoon Italian Herb Seasoning flakes (not ground)
2	teaspoons oil
	salt and pepper to taste

Stir together all the ingredients until blended. (If you are preparing the sauce for another use, simmer it for 20 minutes.)

Rice

Noodles

Grains

Pastas

Lemon Rice with Peas & Parmesan Cheese

This is a nice dish to serve with Osso Bucco. It is especially attractive flecked with peas and sparkled with Parmesan.

1	small onion, finely chopped
4	tablespoons butter
1 1/2	cups rice
2	cans (10 1/2 ounces, each) chicken broth
1/2	cup water
2	tablespoons lemon juice
	salt to taste
1	package (10 ounces) frozen peas, cooked in 1/4 cup water for 5 minutes, and drained
4	tablespoons grated Parmesan cheese

In a Dutch oven casserole sauté onion in butter until onion is soft. Add the rice and sauté for 2 minutes, stirring and turning. Carefully stir in the broth (it will splatter for a few seconds), water, lemon juice and salt. Cover pan and simmer rice for about 30 minutes, or until rice is tender and liquid is absorbed. Stir in cooked peas and heat through. Just before serving, toss with grated Parmesan cheese. Serves 6.

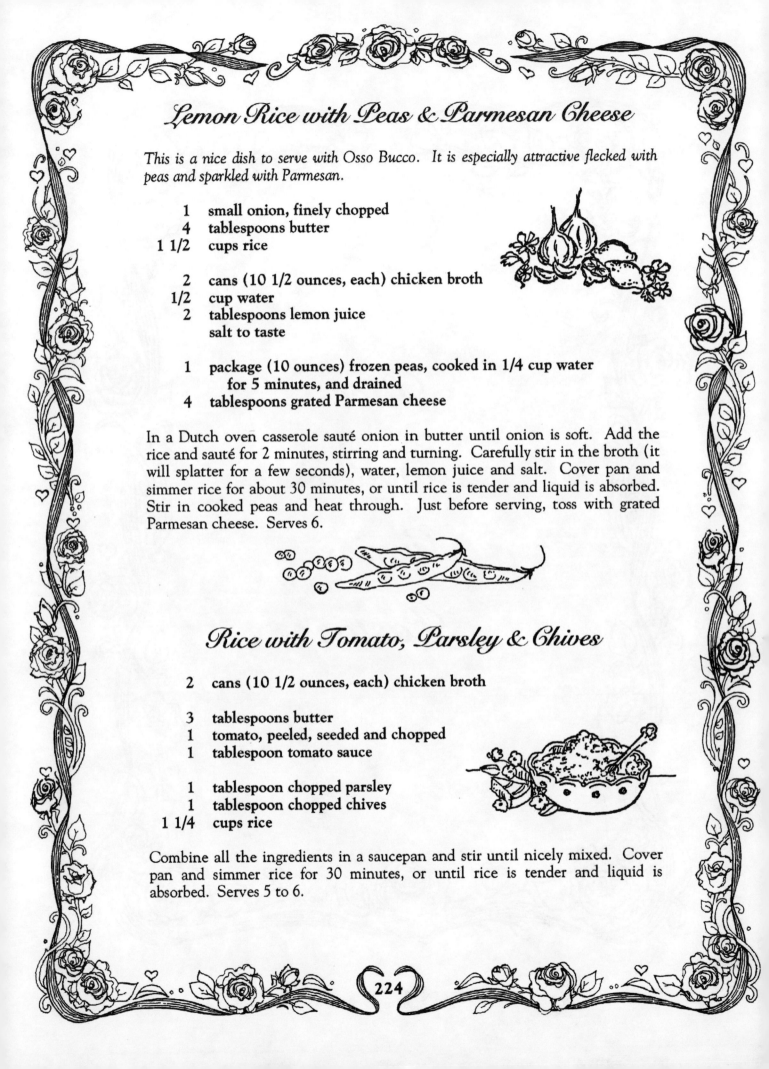

Rice with Tomato, Parsley & Chives

2	cans (10 1/2 ounces, each) chicken broth
3	tablespoons butter
1	tomato, peeled, seeded and chopped
1	tablespoon tomato sauce
1	tablespoon chopped parsley
1	tablespoon chopped chives
1 1/4	cups rice

Combine all the ingredients in a saucepan and stir until nicely mixed. Cover pan and simmer rice for 30 minutes, or until rice is tender and liquid is absorbed. Serves 5 to 6.

Pink Rice with Chili Beans

This is a nice dish to consider for a barbecue or a backyard picnic. It is a great accompaniment to broiled meats.

2	cups rice
4	cups chicken broth (homemade or canned)
4	tablespoons butter
1	tablespoon tomato sauce (from below)
	salt and pepper to taste

1	onion, chopped
2	shallots, minced
3	cloves garlic, minced
3	tablespoons butter

1	can (1 pound) stewed tomatoes, chopped. Do not drain.
1	can (8 ounces) tomato sauce. (Use 1 tablespoon for the rice above.)
2	cans (1 pound, each) kidney beans, rinsed and drained
2	tablespoons chili powder, or to taste
	salt and pepper to taste

In a Dutch oven casserole, place first 5 ingredients, cover pan and simmer mixture until rice is tender and liquid is absorbed, about 35 minutes.

Meanwhile, in a saucepan, sauté onion, shallots and garlic in butter until onion is soft, but not browned. Add the remaining ingredients and simmer mixture for 20 minutes, uncovered or until kidney beans are softened and mixture is thickened.

Add the bean mixture to the rice and toss and turn until everything is nicely blended. Serves 10 to 12.

Note: -Casserole can be prepared earlier in the day and stored in the refrigerator. Reheat over low heat, stirring now and again to prevent rice from sticking to the bottom of the pan.

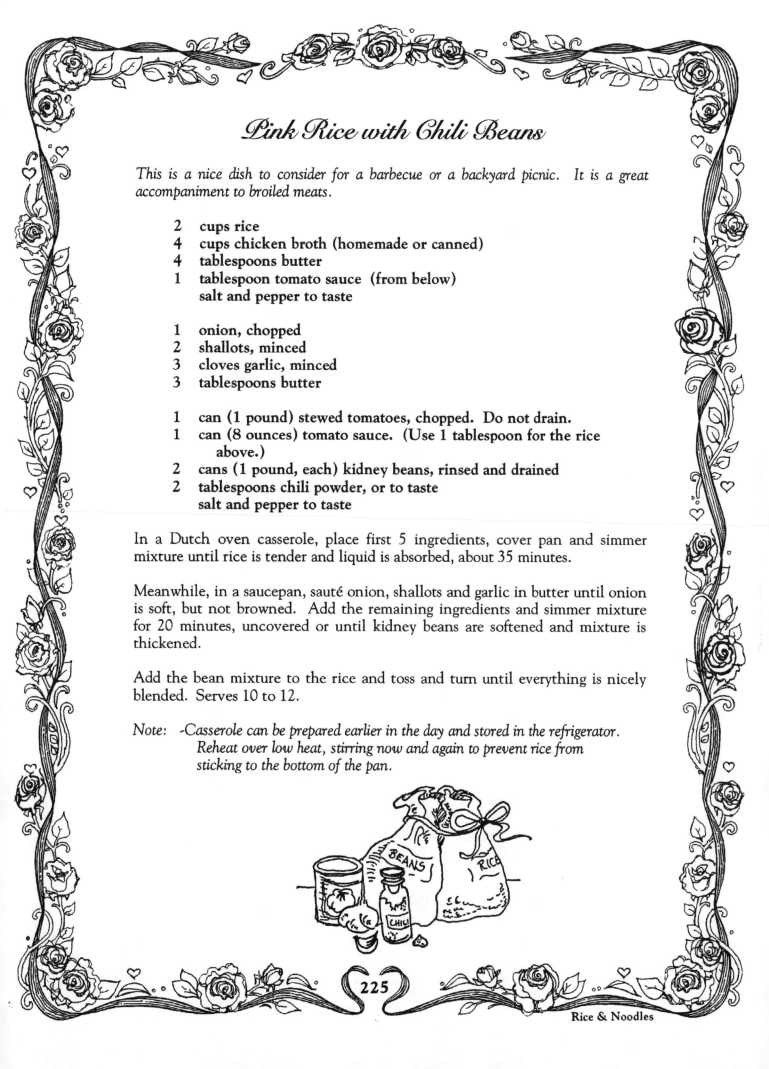

Vegetable Fried Rice

This is not the traditional fried rice, but it is very good, indeed. It is a gorgeous array of colors and presents beautifully. Everybody loves it because it is light and very flavorful. This can be made in advance and heated at serving time.

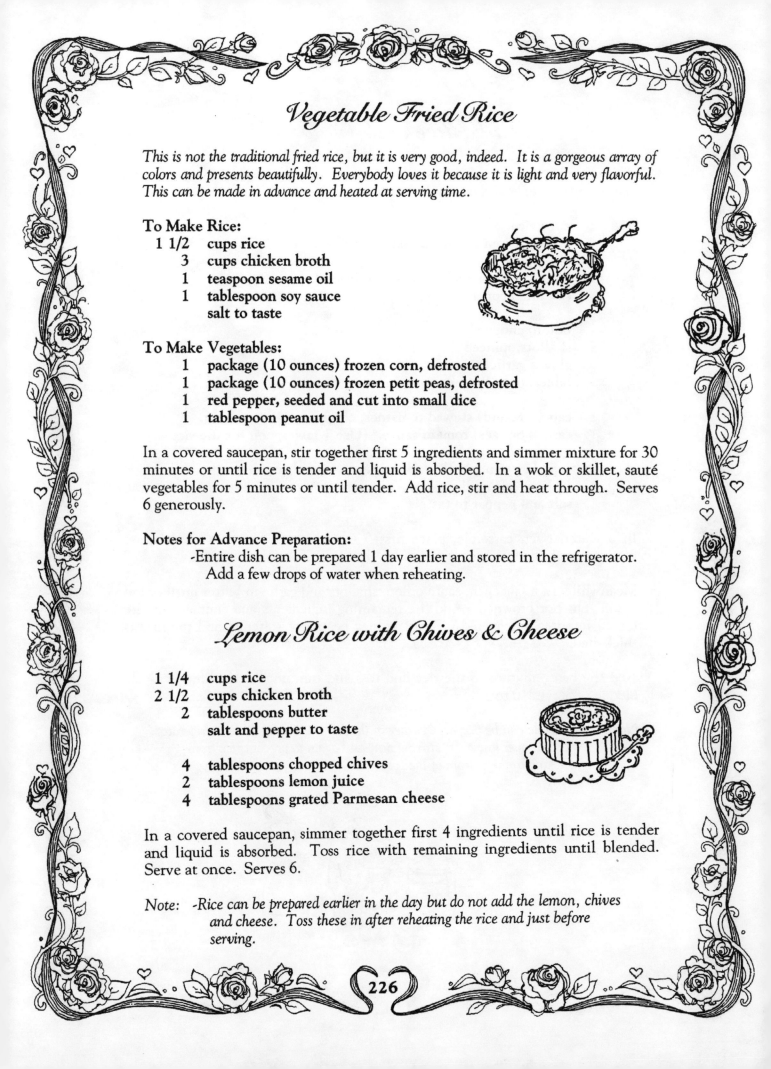

To Make Rice:
1 1/2	cups rice
3	cups chicken broth
1	teaspoon sesame oil
1	tablespoon soy sauce
	salt to taste

To Make Vegetables:
1	package (10 ounces) frozen corn, defrosted
1	package (10 ounces) frozen petit peas, defrosted
1	red pepper, seeded and cut into small dice
1	tablespoon peanut oil

In a covered saucepan, stir together first 5 ingredients and simmer mixture for 30 minutes or until rice is tender and liquid is absorbed. In a wok or skillet, sauté vegetables for 5 minutes or until tender. Add rice, stir and heat through. Serves 6 generously.

Notes for Advance Preparation:
　　-Entire dish can be prepared 1 day earlier and stored in the refrigerator. Add a few drops of water when reheating.

Lemon Rice with Chives & Cheese

1 1/4	cups rice
2 1/2	cups chicken broth
2	tablespoons butter
	salt and pepper to taste
4	tablespoons chopped chives
2	tablespoons lemon juice
4	tablespoons grated Parmesan cheese

In a covered saucepan, simmer together first 4 ingredients until rice is tender and liquid is absorbed. Toss rice with remaining ingredients until blended. Serve at once. Serves 6.

Note: -Rice can be prepared earlier in the day but do not add the lemon, chives and cheese. Toss these in after reheating the rice and just before serving.

Oven-Baked Rice & Vermicelli with Onions & Mushrooms

1   cup rice
1   cup vermicelli (fideos) crushed into 1-inch pieces
4   tablespoons butter

3   cans (10 1/2 ounces, each) chicken broth
     salt and pepper to taste

1   onion, chopped
1/2   pound mushrooms, sliced
3   tablespoons butter

In a skillet, saute rice and vermicelli in butter until vermicelli is just beginning to color. Spoon mixture into a round baking pan, 8x3-inches. Add chicken broth and seasonings, cover pan tightly and bake in a 350° oven for about 40 minutes or until rice is tender and liquid is absorbed.

Meanwhile, in a skillet, saute mushrooms and onion in butter until onions are soft. Stir mushroom mixture into rice and continue baking, covered, until heated through. To serve, garnish top with finely chopped green onions. Serves 6.

Brown Rice & Lentil Casserole with Carrots & Onions

What a nice family dish to serve on a frosty night when the weather is storming outside. It is a hearty, satisfying dish that is especially good with pot roast or potted chicken.

1   onion, chopped
1   carrot, grated
4   tablespoons butter

1/2   cup brown rice
1/2   cup lentils, washed and drained
1   can (10 1/2 ounces) chicken broth
1   can (10 1/2 ounces) water
2   teaspoons chicken seasoned stock base
     salt and pepper to taste

In a Dutch oven casserole, saute onion and carrot in butter until onions are transparent. Add the remaining ingredients, cover and bring mixture to a boil. Lower heat and simmer for about 40 or 45 minutes or until rice and lentils are tender and liquid is absorbed. Serves 4 to 5.
Note: - Casserole can be made earlier in the day and heated before serving.

Rice & Noodles

Timbales of Rice & Carrots

1   cup cooked long-grain rice
1/2 pound carrots, cooked in water with a pinch of sugar until tender and drained. Reserve 1 carrot for garnish and coarsely chop the remaining carrots in a food processor. (Can be mashed with a fork.) Slice reserved carrot decoratively.

2   eggs, beaten
3/4 cup cream
2   tablespoons chopped chives
      salt and white pepper to taste

Place rice and carrots in a bowl. Beat together the remaining ingredients until blended and add to rice and carrot mixture. Stir until blended. Butter 6 muffin molds and sprinkle with dry bread crumbs until nicely coated.

Divide mixture between the molds. Place pan in a larger pan with simmering water and bake in a 400° oven for about 40 to 45 minutes or until timbale is set. Remove muffin pan from water and allow to set for 10 minutes before unmolding. Decorate top with carrot slices. Serves 6.

Green Rice with Lemon & Herbs

1   small onion, finely chopped
2   tablespoons butter

1   tablespoon lemon juice
1   cup long-grain rice
1   can (10-1/2 ounces) chicken broth
3/4 cup water
2   tablespoons finely chopped chives
      salt and pepper to taste

In a saucepan, sauté onion in butter until onion is transparent. Stir in the remaining ingredients, cover pan and simmer rice until liquid is absorbed and rice is tender. Serves 6.

Casserole of Wild Rice with Apples & Chives

Wild rice, faintly sweetened with apple and sparkled with chives is a nice accompaniment to beef. This can be prepared earlier in the day and heated before serving.

1 cup wild rice
1 cup long-grain brown rice
4 cups chicken broth
2 tablespoons butter
   salt and pepper to taste

1 apple, peeled, cored and grated
1 tablespoon butter

3 tablespoons chopped chives

In a covered saucepan, place first group of ingredients, and simmer mixture for about 40 to 45 minutes, or until rice is tender. In a skillet, sauté apple in butter until apple is tender. When rice is cooked, fluff it up with a fork and stir in the apple and chives. Serves 12.

Golden Mexican Rice with Tomato & Chiles

1 medium tomato, chopped
1 can (4 ounces) diced green chiles
1 tablespoon oil

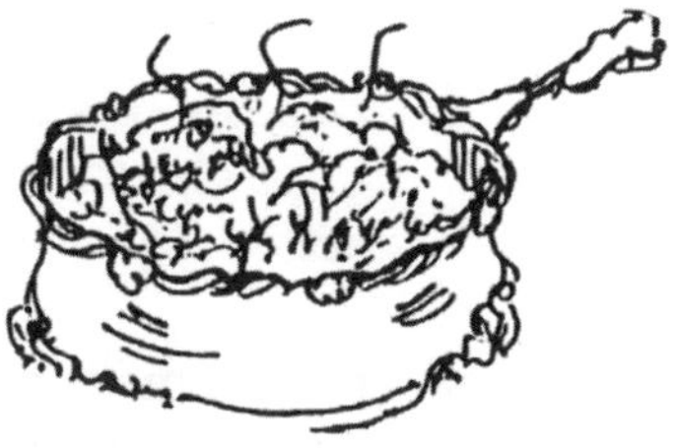

1 1/2 cups rice
3 cups chicken broth
1 teaspoon turmeric
1/2 teaspoon ground cumin
   salt and pepper to taste

In a saucepan, cook tomato and chiles in oil for 2 minutes, stirring. Stir in the remaining ingredients, cover pan, and simmer mixture for 30 minutes, or until rice is tender and liquid is absorbed. This is excellent to serve with Chili con Carne or Red Hot Lentil Chili. Serves 8.

Casserole of Brown Rice with Cabbage & Onions

This is an unusual combination but it is very delicious, and a lovely accompaniment to roast goose or pork. Add a little leftover meat, and it does well for a light supper.

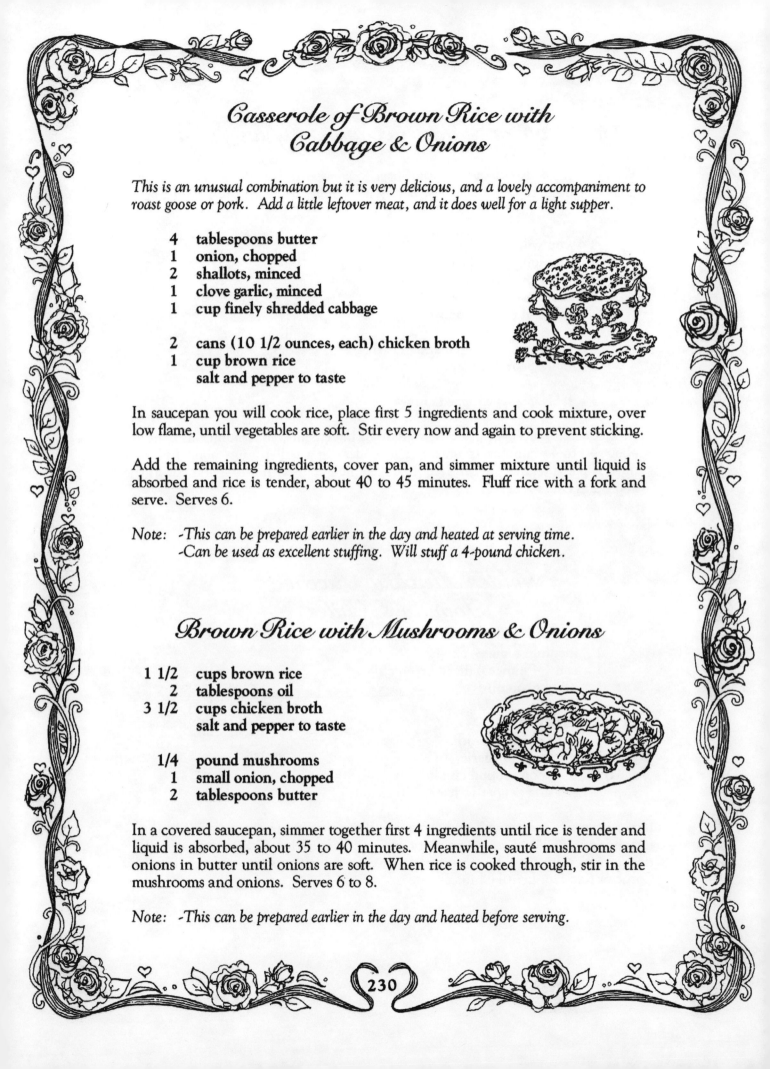

4   tablespoons butter
1   onion, chopped
2   shallots, minced
1   clove garlic, minced
1   cup finely shredded cabbage

2   cans (10 1/2 ounces, each) chicken broth
1   cup brown rice
    salt and pepper to taste

In saucepan you will cook rice, place first 5 ingredients and cook mixture, over low flame, until vegetables are soft. Stir every now and again to prevent sticking.

Add the remaining ingredients, cover pan, and simmer mixture until liquid is absorbed and rice is tender, about 40 to 45 minutes. Fluff rice with a fork and serve. Serves 6.

Note: -This can be prepared earlier in the day and heated at serving time.
      -Can be used as excellent stuffing. Will stuff a 4-pound chicken.

Brown Rice with Mushrooms & Onions

1 1/2   cups brown rice
2   tablespoons oil
3 1/2   cups chicken broth
        salt and pepper to taste

1/4   pound mushrooms
1   small onion, chopped
2   tablespoons butter

In a covered saucepan, simmer together first 4 ingredients until rice is tender and liquid is absorbed, about 35 to 40 minutes. Meanwhile, sauté mushrooms and onions in butter until onions are soft. When rice is cooked through, stir in the mushrooms and onions. Serves 6 to 8.

Note: -This can be prepared earlier in the day and heated before serving.

Curried Rice with Mushrooms & Peas

1	cup rice
2	cups chicken broth
1	tablespoon oil
2	teaspoons curry powder
	salt and pepper to taste
1/2	pound mushrooms, sliced
1	tablespoon butter
1	package (10 ounces) frozen petit peas

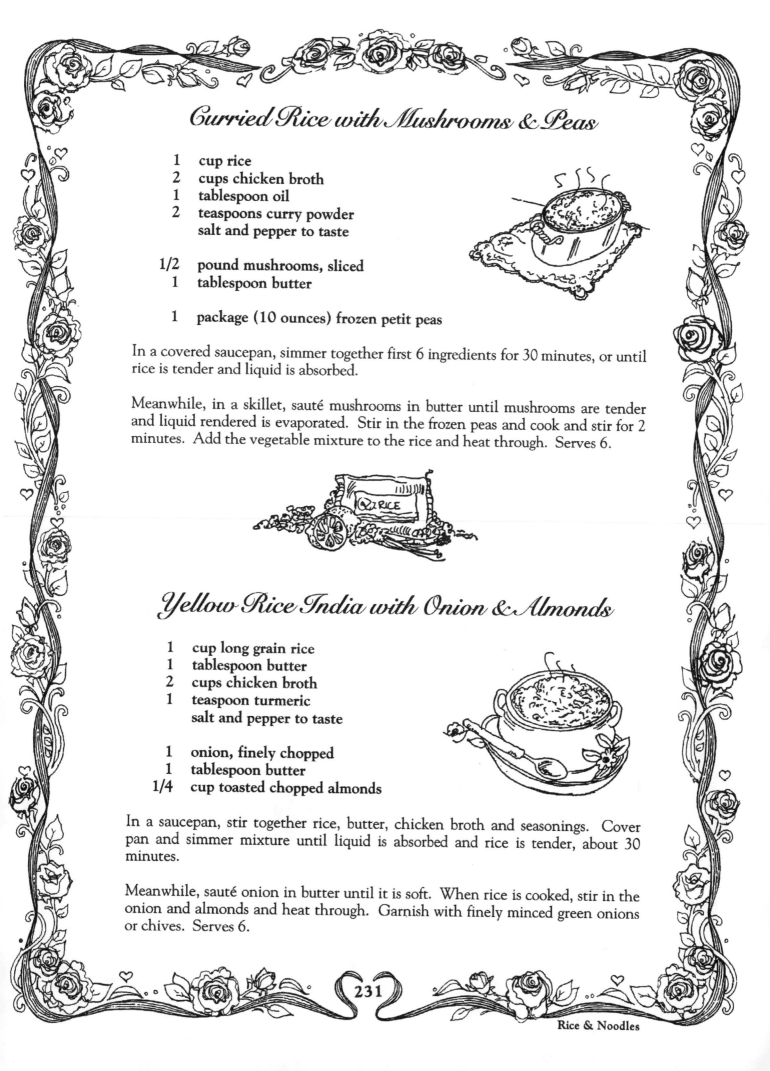

In a covered saucepan, simmer together first 6 ingredients for 30 minutes, or until rice is tender and liquid is absorbed.

Meanwhile, in a skillet, sauté mushrooms in butter until mushrooms are tender and liquid rendered is evaporated. Stir in the frozen peas and cook and stir for 2 minutes. Add the vegetable mixture to the rice and heat through. Serves 6.

Yellow Rice India with Onion & Almonds

1	cup long grain rice
1	tablespoon butter
2	cups chicken broth
1	teaspoon turmeric
	salt and pepper to taste
1	onion, finely chopped
1	tablespoon butter
1/4	cup toasted chopped almonds

In a saucepan, stir together rice, butter, chicken broth and seasonings. Cover pan and simmer mixture until liquid is absorbed and rice is tender, about 30 minutes.

Meanwhile, sauté onion in butter until it is soft. When rice is cooked, stir in the onion and almonds and heat through. Garnish with finely minced green onions or chives. Serves 6.

Noodle Pudding with Apples & Raisins

This is my favorite noodle pudding with the additional flavor of apple and orange. It is truly delicious. There is a cute story attached to this pudding. I made it for a charity luncheon and our speaker was an amazing party planner who had arranged parties for the crown heads of Europe. In the middle of his talk, as he is describing a special party with many famous people, he stopped and said, "By the way, who made this amazing noodle pudding. It is the best I have ever eaten." Hope you enjoy it, too.

4	large apples, peeled, cored and grated
1/4	cup orange juice
1	tablespoon grated orange peel
4	tablespoons cinnamon sugar
1/2	cup yellow raisins
1	package (8 ounces) medium noodles, cooked and drained
1/3	cup melted butter
4	eggs, beaten
3/4	cup sugar
2	cups sour cream
1	teaspoon vanilla
	salt to taste

In a saucepan, cook together first 5 ingredients until apples are soft, about 20 minutes. In a 9x13-inch pan, toss together noodles and butter. Toss in apple mixture. Beat together the remaining ingredients until blended and pour evenly over the noodles. (Ease the noodles, here and there, so that the egg mixture is even.) Bake at 350° for about 1 hour or until top is golden and custard is set. Cut into squares to serve. Serves 12.

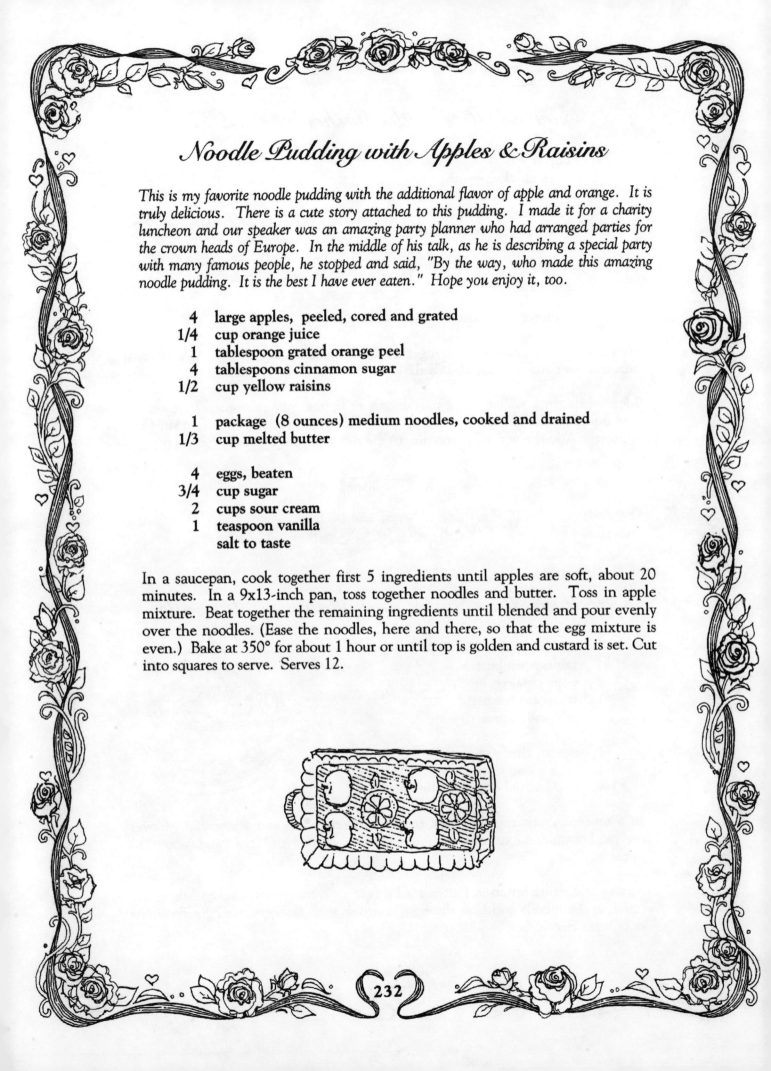

The Best Noodle Pudding with Sour Cream & Raisins

8   ounces (1/2 pound) medium noodles, cooked and drained
1/2 cup butter (1 stick)

1   cup yellow raisins, soaked in boiling water for 5 minutes
       and drained

4   eggs
1   pint (2 cups) sour cream (regular or low-fat)
1/2 cup milk
1   teaspoon vanilla
1   cup sugar
1/2 teaspoon salt

2   tablespoons cinnamon sugar

In a 9x13-inch pan, melt the butter. Add the cooked and drained noodles and toss them in the butter until they are completely coated. Toss in the drained raisins until evenly distributed. Spread noodles evenly in pan.

Beat together the eggs, sour cream, milk, vanilla, sugar and salt until the mixture is well blended.

Pour the egg mixture evenly over the noodles and sprinkle top with cinnamon sugar. Bake in a 350° oven for 1 hour. Cut into squares and serve warm. Yields 12 generous servings.

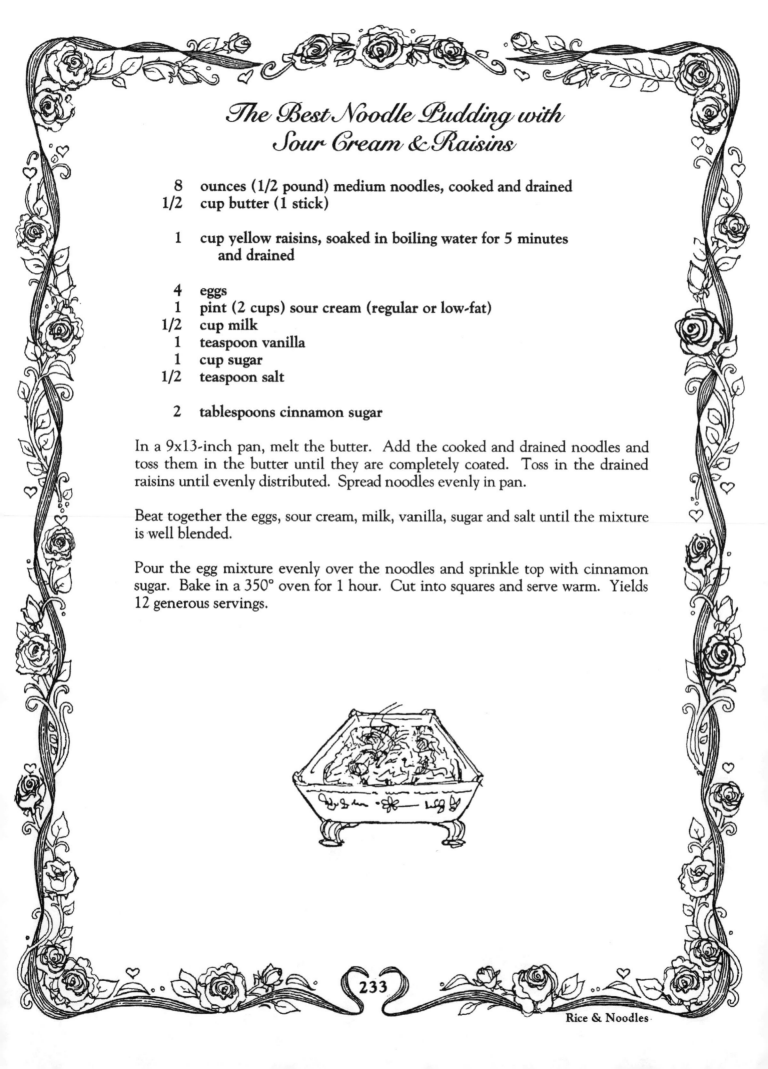

Noodle Pudding with Sweet Red Peppers & Cheese

This is a beautiful dish to serve on a buffet for a lovely luncheon. It is also a grand accompaniment to dinner with a simple roast of veal. Roast chicken is very good, too.

1/2	pound medium noodles, cooked in boiling water and 1 tablespoon oil, until tender but firm and drained.
1	jar (15 ounces) sweet red peppers, drained and chopped (or pimientos)

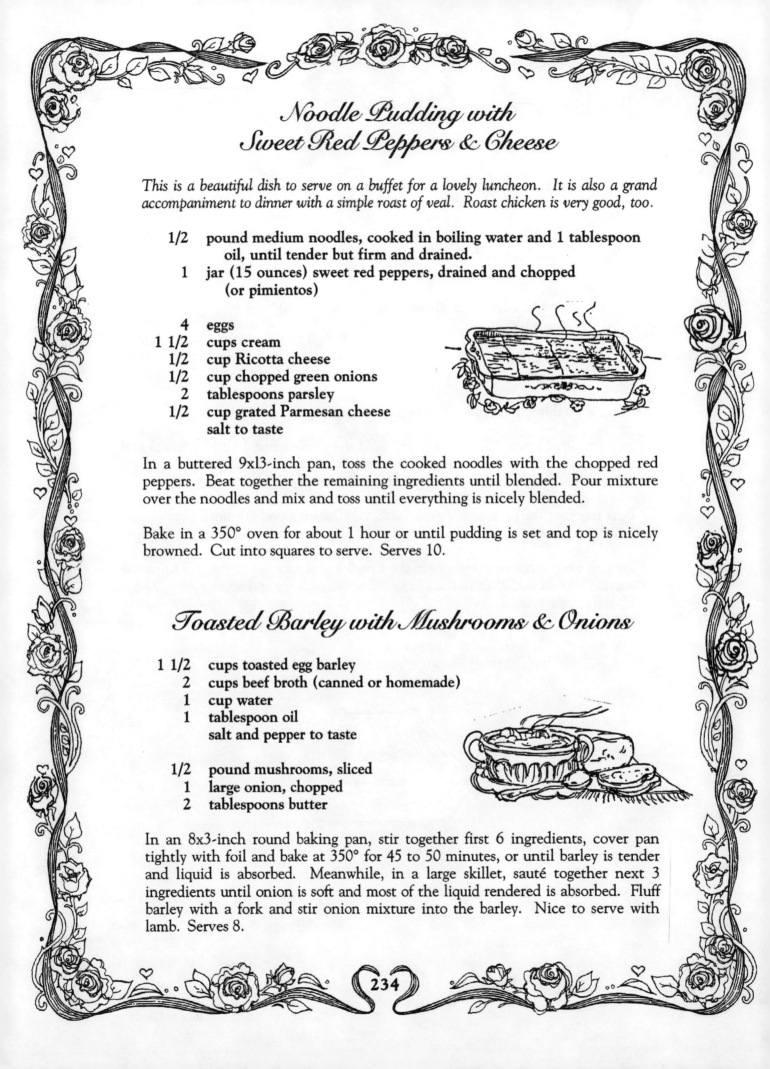

4	eggs
1 1/2	cups cream
1/2	cup Ricotta cheese
1/2	cup chopped green onions
2	tablespoons parsley
1/2	cup grated Parmesan cheese
	salt to taste

In a buttered 9x13-inch pan, toss the cooked noodles with the chopped red peppers. Beat together the remaining ingredients until blended. Pour mixture over the noodles and mix and toss until everything is nicely blended.

Bake in a 350° oven for about 1 hour or until pudding is set and top is nicely browned. Cut into squares to serve. Serves 10.

Toasted Barley with Mushrooms & Onions

1 1/2	cups toasted egg barley
2	cups beef broth (canned or homemade)
1	cup water
1	tablespoon oil
	salt and pepper to taste

1/2	pound mushrooms, sliced
1	large onion, chopped
2	tablespoons butter

In an 8x3-inch round baking pan, stir together first 6 ingredients, cover pan tightly with foil and bake at 350° for 45 to 50 minutes, or until barley is tender and liquid is absorbed. Meanwhile, in a large skillet, sauté together next 3 ingredients until onion is soft and most of the liquid rendered is absorbed. Fluff barley with a fork and stir onion mixture into the barley. Nice to serve with lamb. Serves 8.

Toasted Vermicelli in Chicken Broth

Vermicelli, also known as fideos, is a very thin pasta, sold in coils. Often it is fried before cooking, but I prefer to toast it in the oven for several reasons. Mainly, it is easier to control the toasting and fideos browns more evenly. Also, I prefer adding the oil to the broth.

8 ounces toasted vermicelli coils. Crunch the coils to break them up a little.

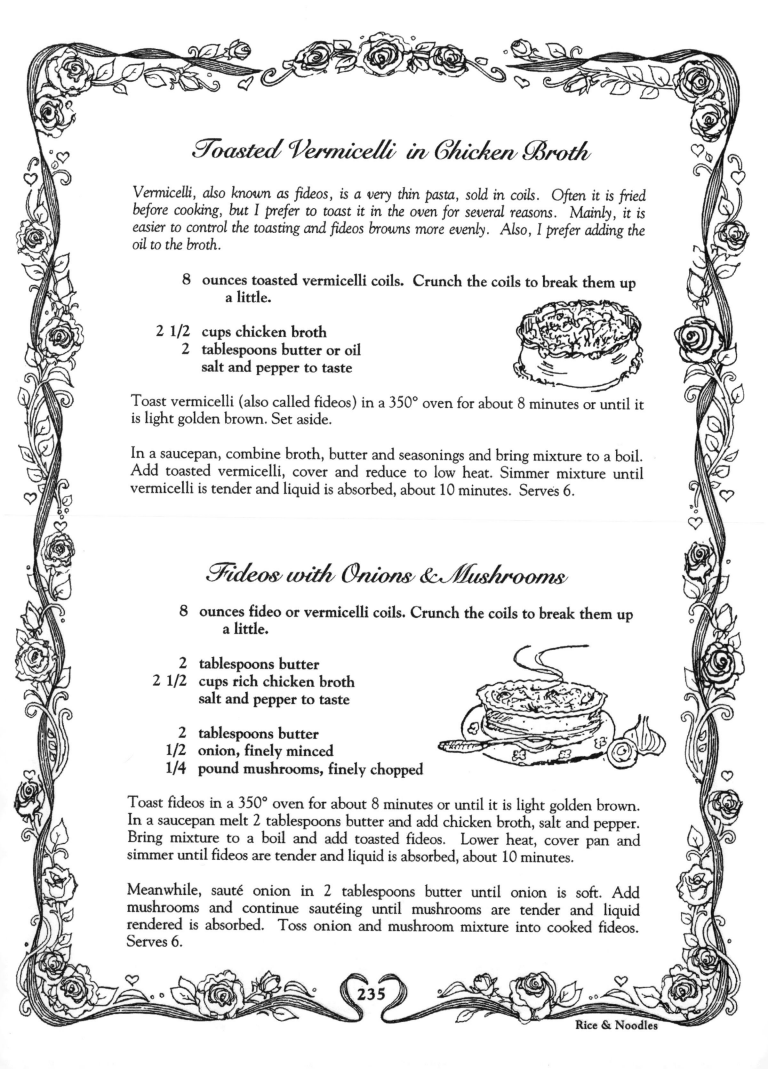

2 1/2 cups chicken broth
2 tablespoons butter or oil
salt and pepper to taste

Toast vermicelli (also called fideos) in a 350° oven for about 8 minutes or until it is light golden brown. Set aside.

In a saucepan, combine broth, butter and seasonings and bring mixture to a boil. Add toasted vermicelli, cover and reduce to low heat. Simmer mixture until vermicelli is tender and liquid is absorbed, about 10 minutes. Serves 6.

Fideos with Onions & Mushrooms

8 ounces fideo or vermicelli coils. Crunch the coils to break them up a little.

2 tablespoons butter
2 1/2 cups rich chicken broth
salt and pepper to taste

2 tablespoons butter
1/2 onion, finely minced
1/4 pound mushrooms, finely chopped

Toast fideos in a 350° oven for about 8 minutes or until it is light golden brown. In a saucepan melt 2 tablespoons butter and add chicken broth, salt and pepper. Bring mixture to a boil and add toasted fideos. Lower heat, cover pan and simmer until fideos are tender and liquid is absorbed, about 10 minutes.

Meanwhile, sauté onion in 2 tablespoons butter until onion is soft. Add mushrooms and continue sautéing until mushrooms are tender and liquid rendered is absorbed. Toss onion and mushroom mixture into cooked fideos. Serves 6.

235

Ramekins of Noodles with Red Peppers & Cheese

This is a truly delicious and glamorous accompaniment to roast chicken or veal. It is an especially good choice for dinner in an Italian mood.

- 1 package (8 ounces) fine egg noodles, cooked until firm-tender and drained
- 1 jar (8 ounces) roasted sweet red peppers, drained and chopped

- 3 eggs
- 1 cup cottage cheese
- 1 cup sour cream
- 1/4 cup grated Parmesan cheese
- 1/4 cup chopped chives
- 2 tablespoons chopped parsley
- pinch cayenne
- salt and pepper to taste

Toss together noodles and red peppers until combined. Beat together the remaining ingredients and stir with noodle mixture until nicely blended. Divide between 8 heavily greased 8-ounce ramekins and place in a pan with 1-inch boiling water.

Bake in a 350° oven for about 30 minutes, or until eggs are set and a knife, inserted in center, comes out clean. Serve it in the ramekins. Or, you can gently loosen ramekins, by running a knife around the edge and invert onto a buttered porcelain baker. Sprinkle tops with Cheese Chive Crumbs and heat through before serving. Serves 8.

Cheese & Chive Crumbs:
Stir together 1 tablespoon grated Parmesan cheese, 1 tablespoon chopped chives and 1 tablespoon cracker crumbs, until blended.

Note: -Can be prepared earlier in the day and stored in the refrigerator. Heat before serving.
-This can be baked in a 9x13-inch baking pan, and cut into squares to serve. Bake at 350° for 45 minutes, or until top is very lightly browned.

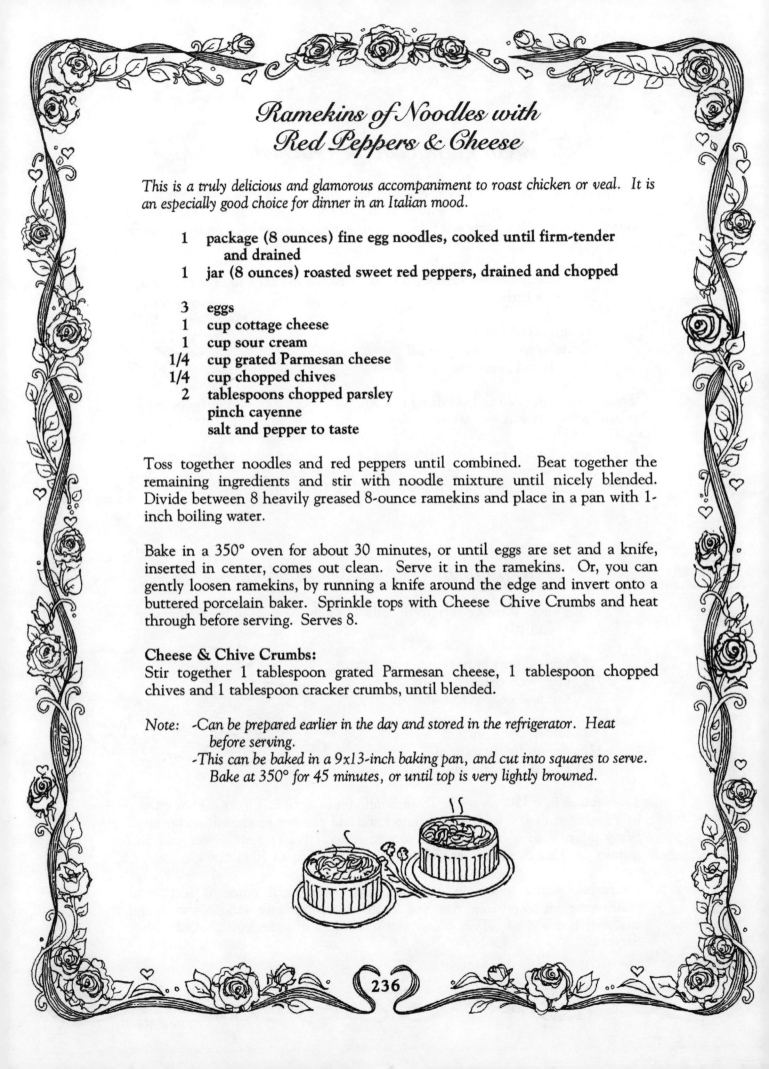

Easiest & Best Barbecued Baked Beans

I have prepared this so many times for backyard picnics and barbecues and the response is always so great. It is amazingly easy to assemble and it can be prepared a day in advance and stored in the refrigerator. Make certain you have a pan with a tight-fitting lid that will safely go into the oven. Aluminum foil can be used as a cover, but it is a bit of a bother to remove and reseal when you check that the sauce doesn't run low. The following recipe works perfectly for me, without the need to add any more broth. I do not add salt or pepper. I have added the names of the national products I use, so that you can duplicate this recipe exactly. I hope you enjoy this dish as much as so many of our friends have.

3 cans (15 ounces, each) Navy Beans packed in water, rinsed and drained
1 large onion, minced
3/4 cup barbecue sauce. (I used Chris' & Pitt's Original BBQ Sauce)
3/4 cup dark brown sugar
1/4 cup dark molasses (Brer Rabbit Dark Molasses)
1 tablespoon Bovril (concentrated Beef-flavored Bouillon)
3/4 cup canned beef broth (I use Campbell's). Do not dilute.

In an oven-proof Dutch oven or covered casserole, add all the ingredients and stir until nicely mixed. Cover pan and bake in a 325° oven for 1 1/2 hours or until the sauce has thickened. Check after 1 hour and if sauce looks dry, add a little broth. (Normally, this is not necessary.) This should serve 8 to 10, but allow for extras. Enjoy!

Red Beans, Pink Rice & Green Onions

This casserole is beautiful and delicious too. Pink rice, red beans, green onions add color and excitement to this dish.

2 tablespoons oil
1 1/2 cups long-grain rice
3 cups chicken broth
2 small tomatoes, peeled, seeded and chopped
1 can (1 pound) red kidney beans, rinsed and drained
    salt and pepper to taste

3 green onions, finely chopped. (Use the green part of the onion.)

In a saucepan, stir together first 7 ingredients. Cover pan and simmer mixture for 30 minutes or until rice is tender and liquid is absorbed. When rice is cooked, stir in the green onions. Serve as an accompaniment to dinner in a Mexican mood. Serves 8.

Kasha with Mushrooms & Onions

Your guests will love this flavorful kasha. It is a perfect accompaniment to the Chicken Stroganov. I recommend that you prepare an extra amount as I have found that most people tend to have seconds.

1	cup kasha (also known as cracked-wheat bulgur)
1	tablespoon oil

1 1/4	cups chicken broth
3/4	cup water
	salt and pepper to taste

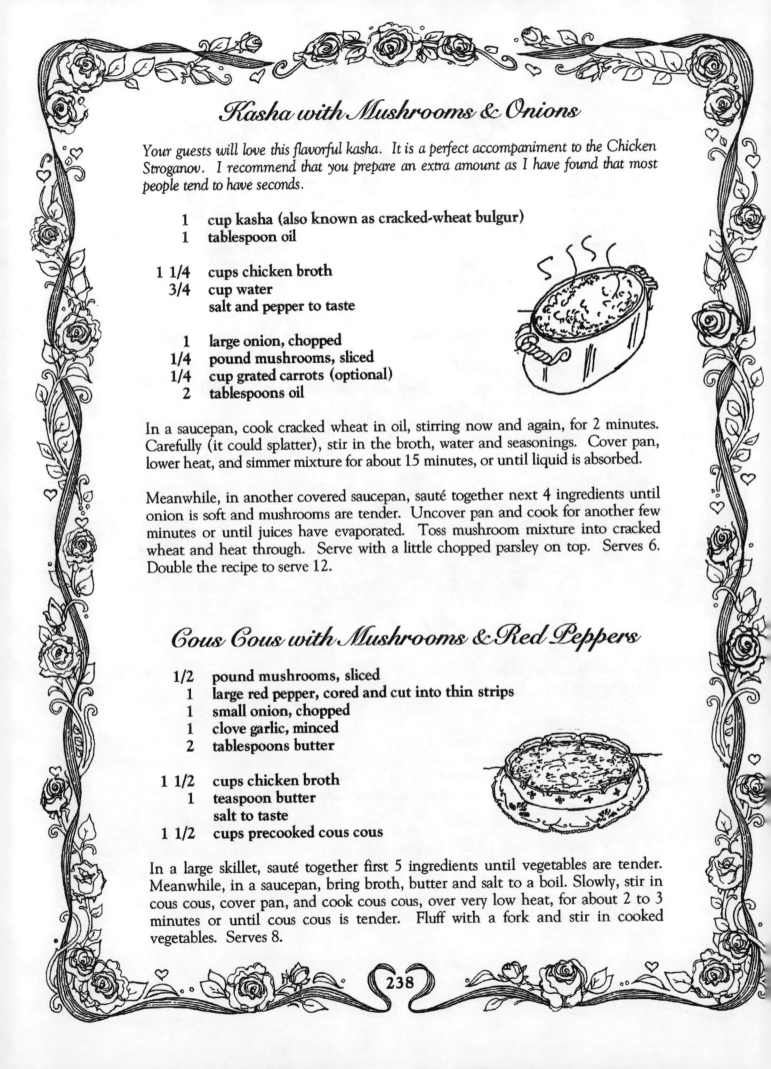

1	large onion, chopped
1/4	pound mushrooms, sliced
1/4	cup grated carrots (optional)
2	tablespoons oil

In a saucepan, cook cracked wheat in oil, stirring now and again, for 2 minutes. Carefully (it could splatter), stir in the broth, water and seasonings. Cover pan, lower heat, and simmer mixture for about 15 minutes, or until liquid is absorbed.

Meanwhile, in another covered saucepan, sauté together next 4 ingredients until onion is soft and mushrooms are tender. Uncover pan and cook for another few minutes or until juices have evaporated. Toss mushroom mixture into cracked wheat and heat through. Serve with a little chopped parsley on top. Serves 6. Double the recipe to serve 12.

Cous Cous with Mushrooms & Red Peppers

1/2	pound mushrooms, sliced
1	large red pepper, cored and cut into thin strips
1	small onion, chopped
1	clove garlic, minced
2	tablespoons butter

1 1/2	cups chicken broth
1	teaspoon butter
	salt to taste
1 1/2	cups precooked cous cous

In a large skillet, sauté together first 5 ingredients until vegetables are tender. Meanwhile, in a saucepan, bring broth, butter and salt to a boil. Slowly, stir in cous cous, cover pan, and cook cous cous, over very low heat, for about 2 to 3 minutes or until cous cous is tender. Fluff with a fork and stir in cooked vegetables. Serves 8.

Bulgur with Dried Cherries & Pecans

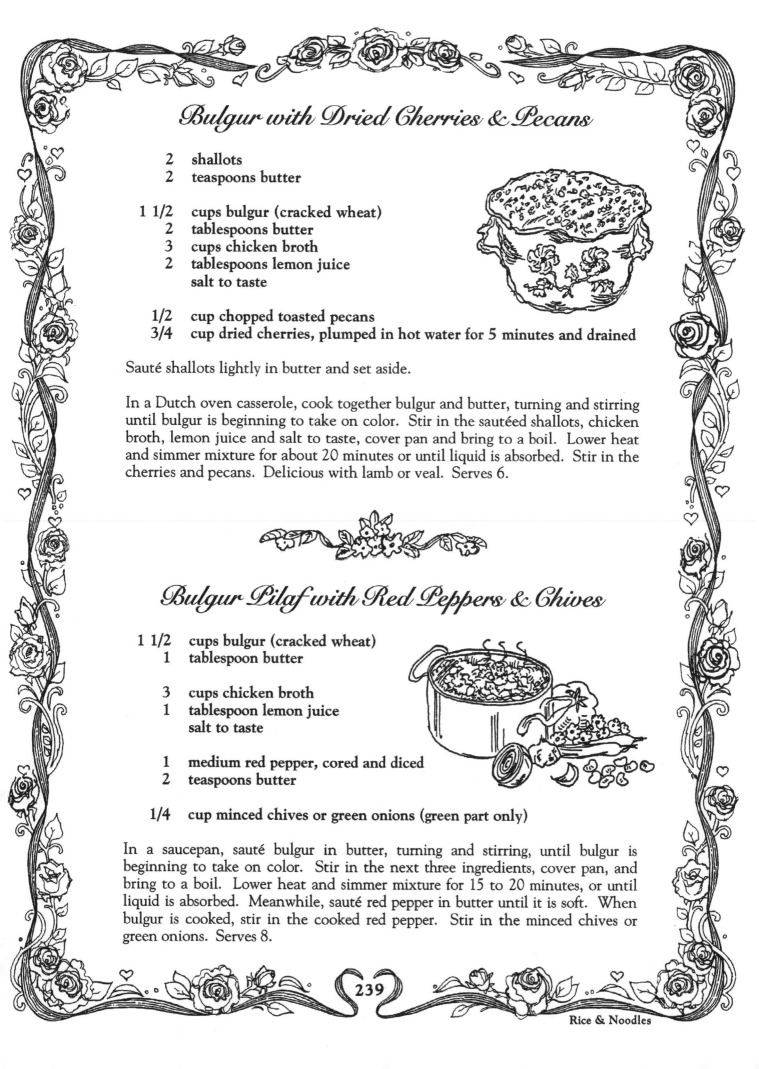

2	shallots
2	teaspoons butter
1 1/2	cups bulgur (cracked wheat)
2	tablespoons butter
3	cups chicken broth
2	tablespoons lemon juice
	salt to taste
1/2	cup chopped toasted pecans
3/4	cup dried cherries, plumped in hot water for 5 minutes and drained

Sauté shallots lightly in butter and set aside.

In a Dutch oven casserole, cook together bulgur and butter, turning and stirring until bulgur is beginning to take on color. Stir in the sautéed shallots, chicken broth, lemon juice and salt to taste, cover pan and bring to a boil. Lower heat and simmer mixture for about 20 minutes or until liquid is absorbed. Stir in the cherries and pecans. Delicious with lamb or veal. Serves 6.

Bulgur Pilaf with Red Peppers & Chives

1 1/2	cups bulgur (cracked wheat)
1	tablespoon butter
3	cups chicken broth
1	tablespoon lemon juice
	salt to taste
1	medium red pepper, cored and diced
2	teaspoons butter
1/4	cup minced chives or green onions (green part only)

In a saucepan, sauté bulgur in butter, turning and stirring, until bulgur is beginning to take on color. Stir in the next three ingredients, cover pan, and bring to a boil. Lower heat and simmer mixture for 15 to 20 minutes, or until liquid is absorbed. Meanwhile, sauté red pepper in butter until it is soft. When bulgur is cooked, stir in the cooked red pepper. Stir in the minced chives or green onions. Serves 8.

Rice & Noodles

Bulgur with Ground Lamb

2   shallots
2   teaspoons butter
1   pound lean ground lamb

1 1/2   cups bulgur (cracked wheat)
2   tablespoons butter

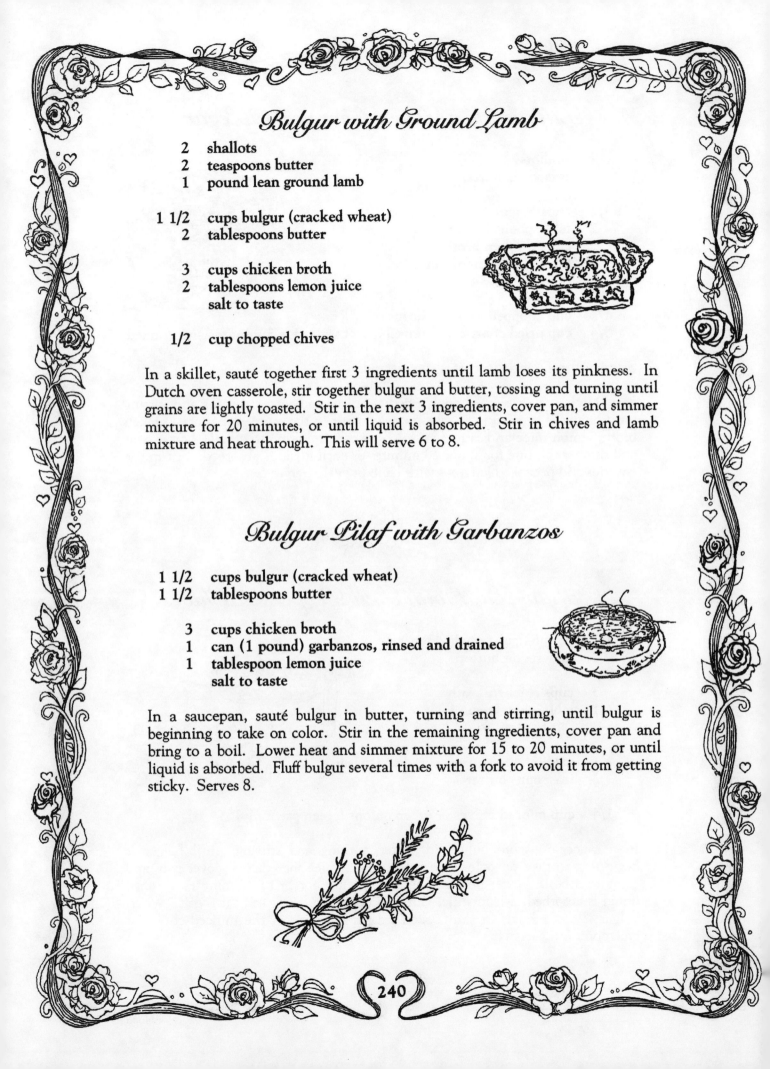

3   cups chicken broth
2   tablespoons lemon juice
     salt to taste

1/2   cup chopped chives

In a skillet, sauté together first 3 ingredients until lamb loses its pinkness. In Dutch oven casserole, stir together bulgur and butter, tossing and turning until grains are lightly toasted. Stir in the next 3 ingredients, cover pan, and simmer mixture for 20 minutes, or until liquid is absorbed. Stir in chives and lamb mixture and heat through. This will serve 6 to 8.

Bulgur Pilaf with Garbanzos

1 1/2   cups bulgur (cracked wheat)
1 1/2   tablespoons butter

3   cups chicken broth
1   can (1 pound) garbanzos, rinsed and drained
1   tablespoon lemon juice
     salt to taste

In a saucepan, sauté bulgur in butter, turning and stirring, until bulgur is beginning to take on color. Stir in the remaining ingredients, cover pan and bring to a boil. Lower heat and simmer mixture for 15 to 20 minutes, or until liquid is absorbed. Fluff bulgur several times with a fork to avoid it from getting sticky. Serves 8.

Kasha with Dried Cherries & Pecans

Your guests will love this very flavorful kasha. It is a perfect accompaniment to the Chicken Stroganov. I recommend your preparing an extra amount as I have found that most people tend to have seconds.

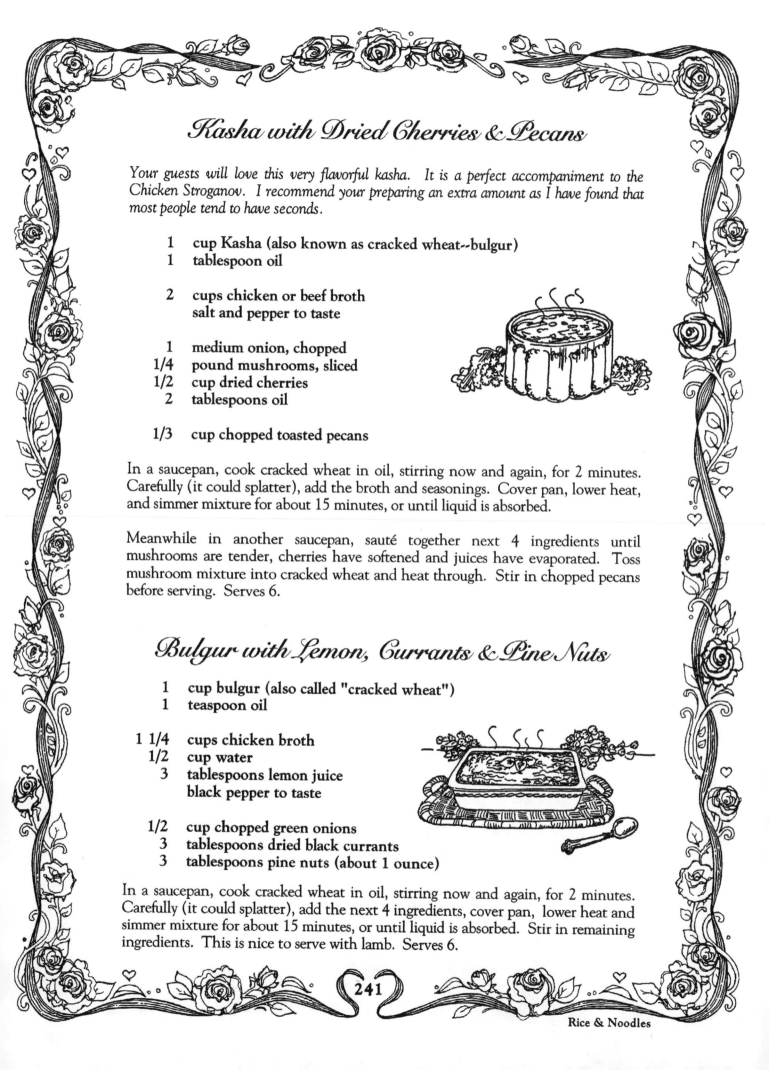

1	cup Kasha (also known as cracked wheat--bulgur)
1	tablespoon oil
2	cups chicken or beef broth
	salt and pepper to taste
1	medium onion, chopped
1/4	pound mushrooms, sliced
1/2	cup dried cherries
2	tablespoons oil
1/3	cup chopped toasted pecans

In a saucepan, cook cracked wheat in oil, stirring now and again, for 2 minutes. Carefully (it could splatter), add the broth and seasonings. Cover pan, lower heat, and simmer mixture for about 15 minutes, or until liquid is absorbed.

Meanwhile in another saucepan, sauté together next 4 ingredients until mushrooms are tender, cherries have softened and juices have evaporated. Toss mushroom mixture into cracked wheat and heat through. Stir in chopped pecans before serving. Serves 6.

Bulgur with Lemon, Currants & Pine Nuts

1	cup bulgur (also called "cracked wheat")
1	teaspoon oil
1 1/4	cups chicken broth
1/2	cup water
3	tablespoons lemon juice
	black pepper to taste
1/2	cup chopped green onions
3	tablespoons dried black currants
3	tablespoons pine nuts (about 1 ounce)

In a saucepan, cook cracked wheat in oil, stirring now and again, for 2 minutes. Carefully (it could splatter), add the next 4 ingredients, cover pan, lower heat and simmer mixture for about 15 minutes, or until liquid is absorbed. Stir in remaining ingredients. This is nice to serve with lamb. Serves 6.

Bulgur with Apricots, Raisins & Pine Nuts

1	large onion, chopped
6	cloves garlic, coarsely chopped
1	tablespoon olive oil
2	cups bulgur (cracked wheat)
4	cups chicken broth
1	teaspoon turmeric
	pepper to taste
1/4	cup chopped dried apricots
1/4	cup yellow raisins
2	cups boiling water

Topping:
1/4   cup toasted pine nuts.

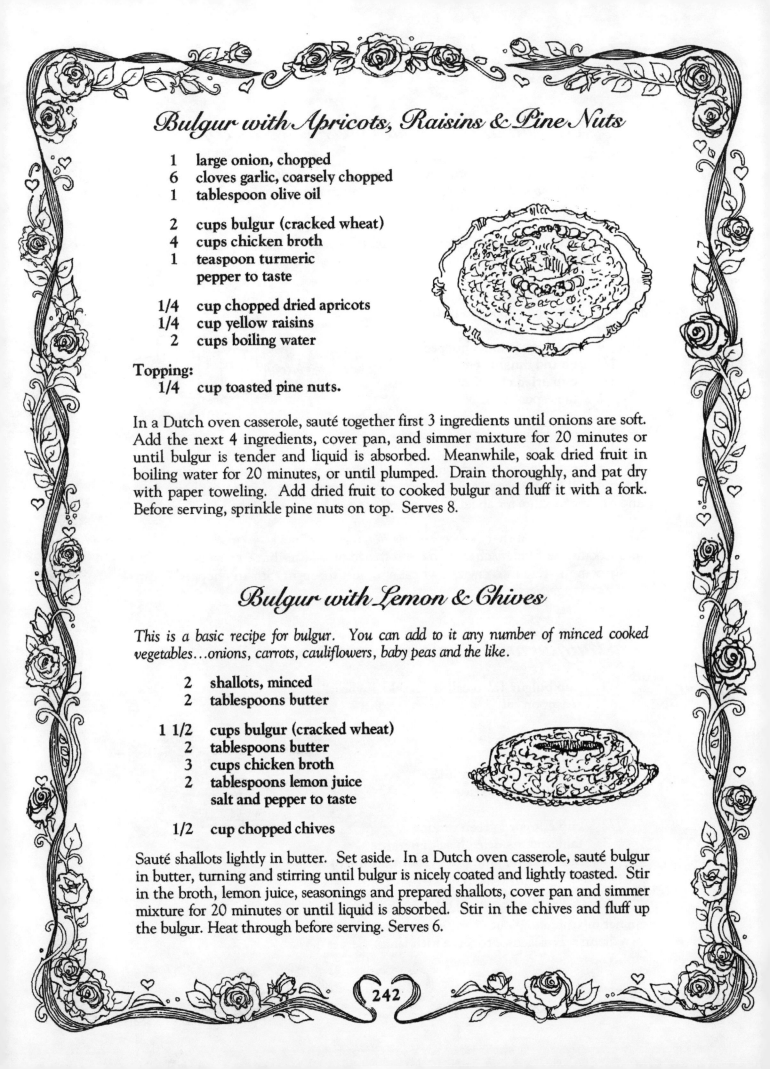

In a Dutch oven casserole, sauté together first 3 ingredients until onions are soft. Add the next 4 ingredients, cover pan, and simmer mixture for 20 minutes or until bulgur is tender and liquid is absorbed. Meanwhile, soak dried fruit in boiling water for 20 minutes, or until plumped. Drain thoroughly, and pat dry with paper toweling. Add dried fruit to cooked bulgur and fluff it with a fork. Before serving, sprinkle pine nuts on top. Serves 8.

Bulgur with Lemon & Chives

This is a basic recipe for bulgur. You can add to it any number of minced cooked vegetables...onions, carrots, cauliflowers, baby peas and the like.

2	shallots, minced
2	tablespoons butter
1 1/2	cups bulgur (cracked wheat)
2	tablespoons butter
3	cups chicken broth
2	tablespoons lemon juice
	salt and pepper to taste
1/2	cup chopped chives

Sauté shallots lightly in butter. Set aside. In a Dutch oven casserole, sauté bulgur in butter, turning and stirring until bulgur is nicely coated and lightly toasted. Stir in the broth, lemon juice, seasonings and prepared shallots, cover pan and simmer mixture for 20 minutes or until liquid is absorbed. Stir in the chives and fluff up the bulgur. Heat through before serving. Serves 6.

Garbanzos with Tomatoes & Onion Curry

Garbanzos make an excellent side-dish. My Mom served these in so many ways…with tomatoes, onions.. in spinach, rice and more. The combinations are endless. Here, they are flavored with tomatoes and onions and spiced with curry and cumin.

- 2 tablespoons butter
- 1 onion, finely chopped
- 4 cloves garlic, minced

- 1 can (1 pound) stewed tomatoes, chopped. Do not drain.
- 2 cans (15 ounces, each) garbanzos, rinsed and drained
- 2 teaspoons ground curry powder (or more to taste)
- 1 teaspoon ground cumin powder
  salt to taste

In a covered saucepan, sauté onion and garlic in butter until onion is transparent. Add the remaining ingredients and simmer mixture for 30 minutes. Serves 6.

Red Lentils with Tomatoes & Fried Onions

This is a most delicious accompaniment to dinner in an Indian mood. It is beautiful to behold and the fried onions add the nicest flavor.

- 1 onion, coarsely chopped
- 4 cloves garlic, minced
- 2 tablespoons butter

- 1 cup red lentils, rinsed and picked over for foreign particles
- 2 cups chicken broth
- 1 can (1 pound) stewed tomatoes, drained and chopped
- 1 teaspoon ground turmeric or more to taste
- 1/2 teaspoon ground cumin
  salt and pepper to taste

- 1 can (6 ounces) French's Fried Onions

In a saucepan, sauté onion and garlic in butter until onion is beginning to take on color. Stir in next group of ingredients, cover pan, and simmer mixture for 45 minutes, or until lentils are tender and most of the liquid is absorbed. When ready to serve heat through and sprinkle with Fried Onions to taste. Serves 6.

Toasted Orzo with Mushrooms & Onions

Orzo comes in 3 sizes, small, medium or large. I prefer the large size for it's dramatic appearance. Serving it with mushrooms and onions is truly wonderful.

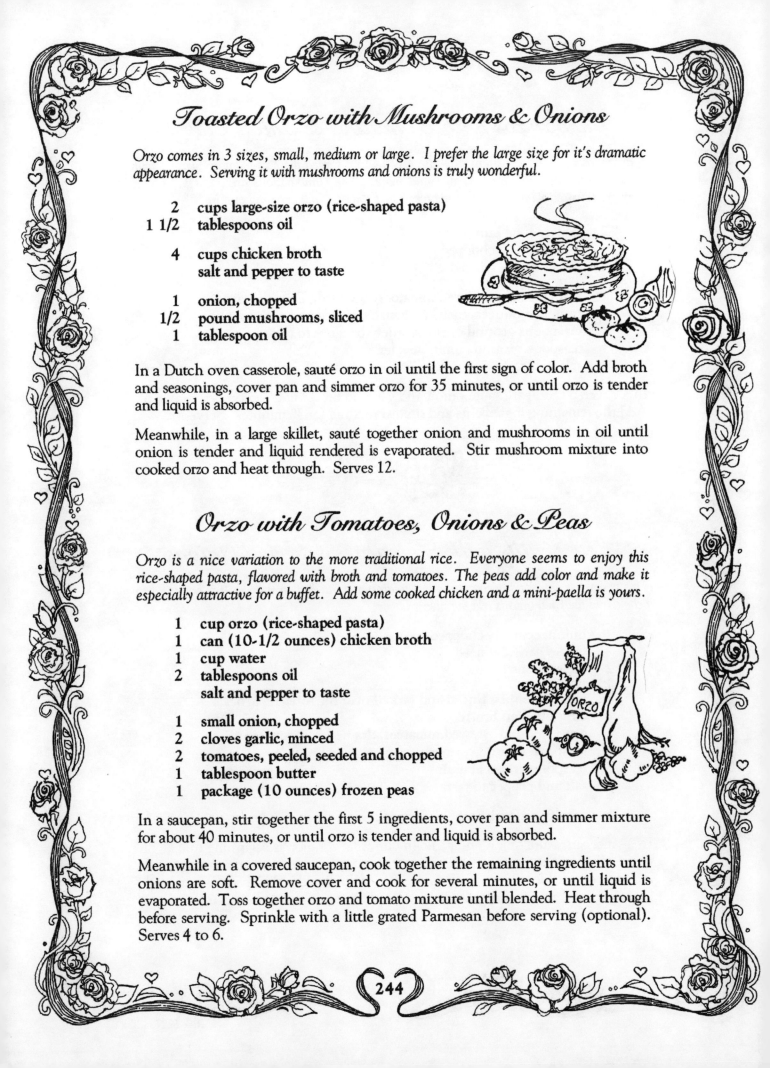

2	cups large-size orzo (rice-shaped pasta)
1 1/2	tablespoons oil
4	cups chicken broth
	salt and pepper to taste
1	onion, chopped
1/2	pound mushrooms, sliced
1	tablespoon oil

In a Dutch oven casserole, sauté orzo in oil until the first sign of color. Add broth and seasonings, cover pan and simmer orzo for 35 minutes, or until orzo is tender and liquid is absorbed.

Meanwhile, in a large skillet, sauté together onion and mushrooms in oil until onion is tender and liquid rendered is evaporated. Stir mushroom mixture into cooked orzo and heat through. Serves 12.

Orzo with Tomatoes, Onions & Peas

Orzo is a nice variation to the more traditional rice. Everyone seems to enjoy this rice-shaped pasta, flavored with broth and tomatoes. The peas add color and make it especially attractive for a buffet. Add some cooked chicken and a mini-paella is yours.

1	cup orzo (rice-shaped pasta)
1	can (10-1/2 ounces) chicken broth
1	cup water
2	tablespoons oil
	salt and pepper to taste
1	small onion, chopped
2	cloves garlic, minced
2	tomatoes, peeled, seeded and chopped
1	tablespoon butter
1	package (10 ounces) frozen peas

In a saucepan, stir together the first 5 ingredients, cover pan and simmer mixture for about 40 minutes, or until orzo is tender and liquid is absorbed.

Meanwhile in a covered saucepan, cook together the remaining ingredients until onions are soft. Remove cover and cook for several minutes, or until liquid is evaporated. Toss together orzo and tomato mixture until blended. Heat through before serving. Sprinkle with a little grated Parmesan before serving (optional). Serves 4 to 6.

Spaghetti alla Bolognese

This rich and flavorful spaghetti sauce is one of the best-loved sauces in all of Italy. It is a good basic sauce to be used over eggplant and any number of pastas.

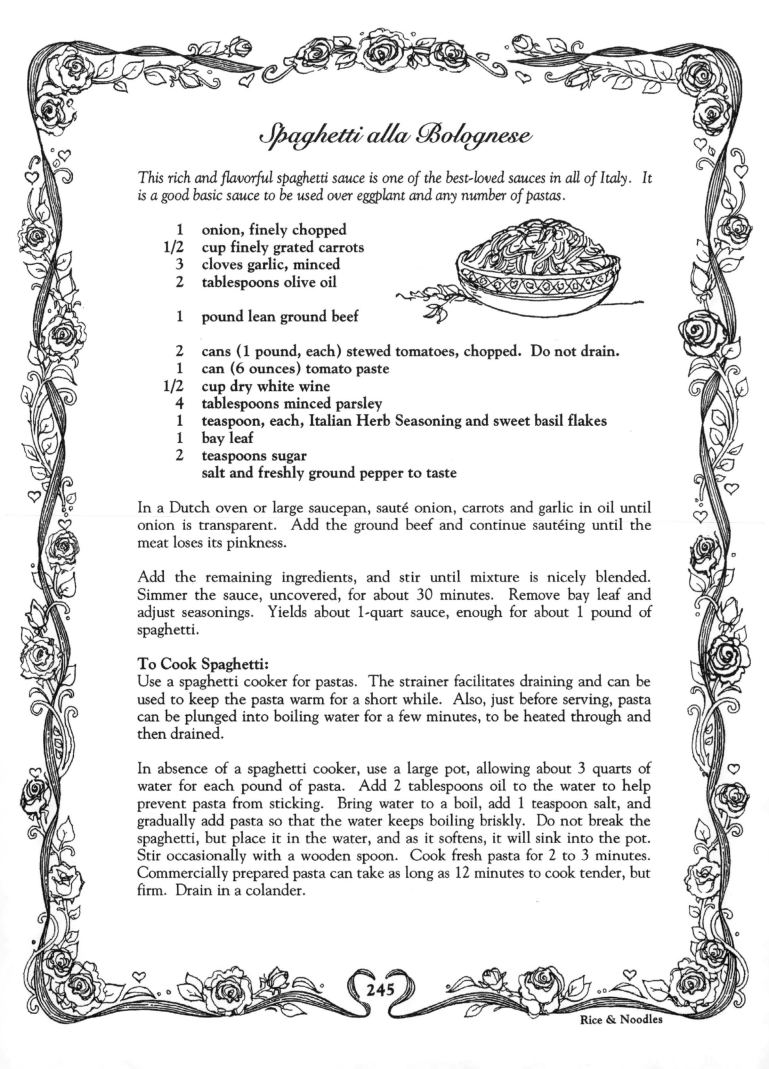

1	onion, finely chopped
1/2	cup finely grated carrots
3	cloves garlic, minced
2	tablespoons olive oil
1	pound lean ground beef
2	cans (1 pound, each) stewed tomatoes, chopped. Do not drain.
1	can (6 ounces) tomato paste
1/2	cup dry white wine
4	tablespoons minced parsley
1	teaspoon, each, Italian Herb Seasoning and sweet basil flakes
1	bay leaf
2	teaspoons sugar
	salt and freshly ground pepper to taste

In a Dutch oven or large saucepan, sauté onion, carrots and garlic in oil until onion is transparent. Add the ground beef and continue sautéing until the meat loses its pinkness.

Add the remaining ingredients, and stir until mixture is nicely blended. Simmer the sauce, uncovered, for about 30 minutes. Remove bay leaf and adjust seasonings. Yields about 1-quart sauce, enough for about 1 pound of spaghetti.

To Cook Spaghetti:
Use a spaghetti cooker for pastas. The strainer facilitates draining and can be used to keep the pasta warm for a short while. Also, just before serving, pasta can be plunged into boiling water for a few minutes, to be heated through and then drained.

In absence of a spaghetti cooker, use a large pot, allowing about 3 quarts of water for each pound of pasta. Add 2 tablespoons oil to the water to help prevent pasta from sticking. Bring water to a boil, add 1 teaspoon salt, and gradually add pasta so that the water keeps boiling briskly. Do not break the spaghetti, but place it in the water, and as it softens, it will sink into the pot. Stir occasionally with a wooden spoon. Cook fresh pasta for 2 to 3 minutes. Commercially prepared pasta can take as long as 12 minutes to cook tender, but firm. Drain in a colander.

Fettuccini alla Romano with Onions, Pepper & Cheese

Let me say, right at the start, that while I am not overly fond of green bell peppers (or they are not overly fond of me), but I do love yellow and red peppers. This sauce should be fresh and flavorful, and not simmered for hours... 20 to 30 minutes is about all I recommend.

2	onions, chopped
1	yellow bell pepper, cut into strips
1	red bell pepper, cut into strips
4	cloves garlic, minced
1/2	pound mushrooms, sliced
4	tablespoons oil

1/4	cup dry red wine
1	can (1 pound 12 ounces) crushed tomatoes in puree
2	cans (8 ounces, each) tomato sauce
1	teaspoon sweet basil flakes
1	teaspoon Italian Herb Seasoning
2	teaspoons sugar
	pinch of cayenne pepper
	salt and pepper to taste

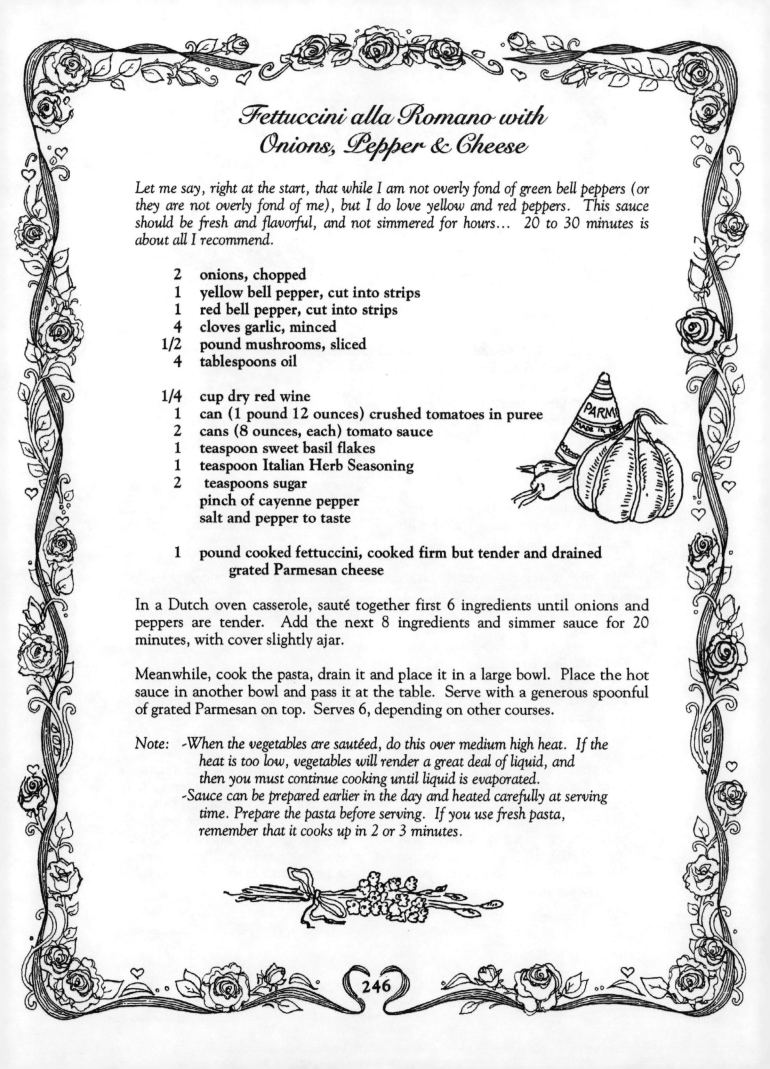

1	pound cooked fettuccini, cooked firm but tender and drained
	grated Parmesan cheese

In a Dutch oven casserole, sauté together first 6 ingredients until onions and peppers are tender. Add the next 8 ingredients and simmer sauce for 20 minutes, with cover slightly ajar.

Meanwhile, cook the pasta, drain it and place it in a large bowl. Place the hot sauce in another bowl and pass it at the table. Serve with a generous spoonful of grated Parmesan on top. Serves 6, depending on other courses.

Note: -When the vegetables are sautéed, do this over medium high heat. If the heat is too low, vegetables will render a great deal of liquid, and then you must continue cooking until liquid is evaporated.
-Sauce can be prepared earlier in the day and heated carefully at serving time. Prepare the pasta before serving. If you use fresh pasta, remember that it cooks up in 2 or 3 minutes.

Fresh Linguini with Basil & Sun-Dried Tomato Sauce

1   pound fresh linguini, cooked in 4 quarts boiling water until al dente
     and drained. Fresh linguini cooks in minutes, so watch the time
     carefully.

Basil & Sun-Dried Tomato Sauce:
8   shallots, minced
8   cloves garlic, minced
2   tablespoons olive oil

4   sun-dried tomatoes (packed in oil) drained and chopped
1   can (1 pound 12 ounces) crushed tomatoes in puree
1   teaspoon dried basil flakes
     pinch of cayenne pepper

Sauté shallots and garlic in olive oil until shallots are transparent. Add the
remaining ingredients and simmer sauce for 10 minutes. Serve sauce over
linguini. A teaspoon of grated cheese is nice, but optional. Serves 6 to 8.

*Note: -Sauce can be prepared earlier in the day and stored in the refrigerator.
         Heat before serving.*

Angel Hair Pasta with Fresh Tomatoes, Garlic & Basil

3   cloves garlic, minced
2   tablespoons olive oil

8   medium tomatoes, (about 2 pounds), peeled, seeded and chopped
1/2 teaspoon vinegar
1   teaspoon sugar
     salt and freshly ground pepper to taste

2   tablespoons chopped fresh basil or 1 teaspoon dried basil flakes

1   pound angel hair pasta, cooked al dente, tender but firm

In a saucepan, sauté garlic in oil for 1 minute, stirring. Add the next 5
ingredients and simmer mixture for about 10 minutes, or until some of the
liquid has evaporated and sauce has thickened slightly. Add the basil and cook
for 1 minute longer. Serve it over angel hair pasta and serves 6.

247

Baked Ziti with Ricotta & Mozzarella in Instant Tomato Sauce

This is a very abbreviated version of a classic dish. The sauce is truly delicious and no one will guess it took 5 minutes to prepare. It is a good basic sauce for pasta, chicken or veal.

1/2   pound ziti pasta (tube pasta), cooked in boiling water until tender (al dente), and drained thoroughly

Cheese Mixture:
- 1   pound low fat Ricotta cheese
- 4   ounces grated Mozzarella cheese
- 1   egg
- 1/2   cup grated Parmesan cheese

Instant Tomato Sauce:
- 1   can (1 pound 12 ounces) crushed tomatoes in puree
- 2   teaspoons oil
- 2   tablespoons minced dried onions
- 1/2   teaspoon coarse grind garlic powder
- 1   teaspoon sugar
- 1   teaspoon Italian Herb Seasoning flakes
- 1   teaspoon sweet basil flakes
-     salt and pepper to taste
- 1   sprinkle cayenne pepper

Have everything ready before you assemble the dish. Prepare ziti and set aside to drain in a colander, shaking occasionally to remove all water. Stir together Cheese Mixture and set aside. Place Instant Tomato Sauce ingredients in a saucepan and heat for 5 minutes.

In a 9x13-inch porcelain baker, place half the ziti. Spoon Cheese Mixture over the top and cover evenly with remaining ziti. Pour sauce evenly over all and sprinkle with additional grated Parmesan cheese. Bake at 350° for 30 minutes or until piping hot. Serves 6.

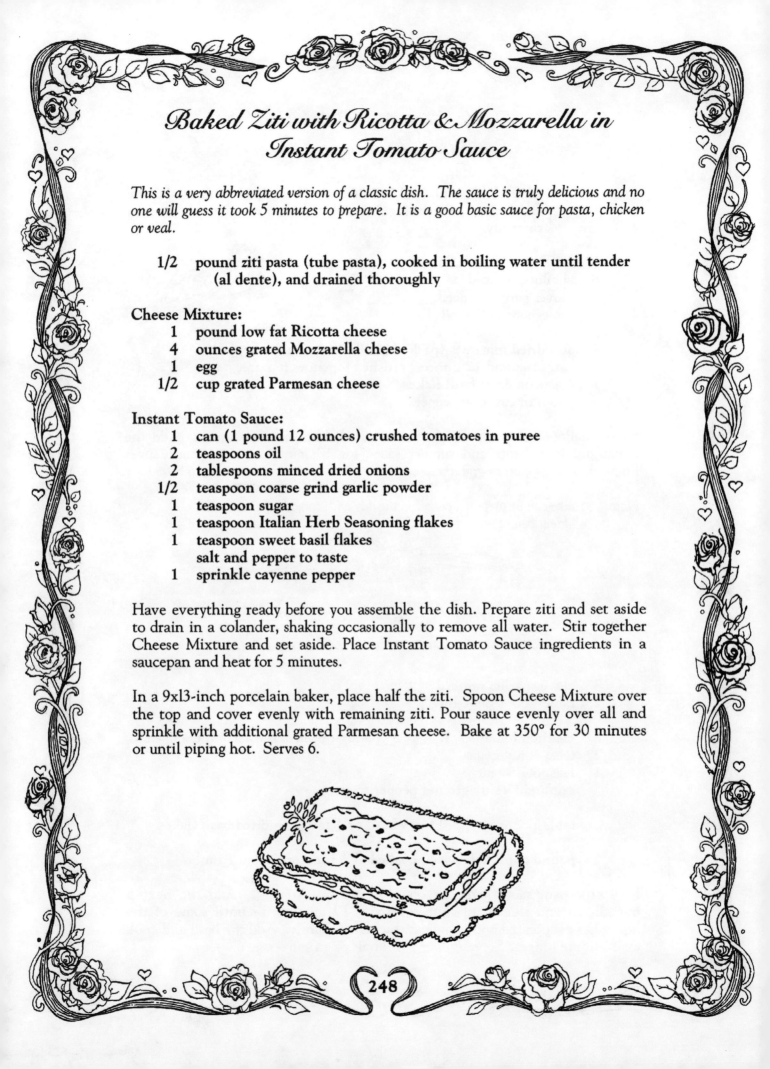

Vegetables

Artichokes
Asparagus
Brussels Sprouts
Cauliflower
Cabbage
Carrots
Corn
Chestnut Pudding
Eggplant
Green Beans
Mushrooms
Onions
Peas
Stuffed Peppers
Potatoes
Sweet Potatoes
Spinach
Stuffed Tomatoes
Zucchini

Mini-Soufflé with Artichokes, Spinach & Cheese

1   jar (15 ounces) marinated artichoke hearts, drained and cut into
        fourths. Place in 1 layer in a greased 12-inch oval au gratin
        dish.

5   eggs
1   cup half and half
1   package (8 ounces) cream cheese, at room temperature and
        cut into 8 pieces
1   cup grated Swiss cheese
1/2 cup grated Parmesan cheese
1   package (10 ounces) frozen chopped spinach, defrosted and
        drained
1/3 cup chopped green onions
    salt and pepper to taste

Prepare artichokes. In a food processor, blend the eggs, cream and cheeses until blended. Stir in the remaining ingredients. Pour egg mixture over the artichokes, and bake in a 350° oven for about 25 minutes, or until top is browned and soufflé is puffed. Serve at once. Serves 6.

Artichokes with Mushrooms & Cheese Crumb Topping

1/2 pound mushrooms, sliced
1   onion, minced
2   shallots, minced
4   cloves garlic, minced
3   tablespoons butter

1/4 cup cream
1   tablespoon lemon juice
1   jar (15 ounces) marinated artichoke hearts, drained

Sauté together first 5 ingredients until mushrooms are softened. Add the cream and lemon juice and cook for 2 minutes. In a 10-inch oval porcelain baker, stir together mushroom mixture and artichokes and sprinkle top with Cheese Crumb Topping. Bake in a 350° oven for 25 minutes or until crumbs are browned. Serves 6.

Cheese Crumb Topping:
Toss together until blended 2 tablespoons fresh breadcrumbs, 2 tablespoons grated Parmesan cheese and 1 tablespoon melted butter.

Asparagus in Lemon Cheese Sauce

2   pounds asparagus washed to remove every trace of sand. Snap or cut off the twiggy bottoms. (I like to run a vegetable peeler over the remaining bottoms, to assure tender stalks, but this is optional.) Asparagus should be tied into bundles and <u>steamed</u> upright. Boiling may leave the tips too soft. They can also be cooked (vertically) in 1-inch boiling water. Cook asparagus for about 8 to 10 minutes, or until tender but firm, and drain.

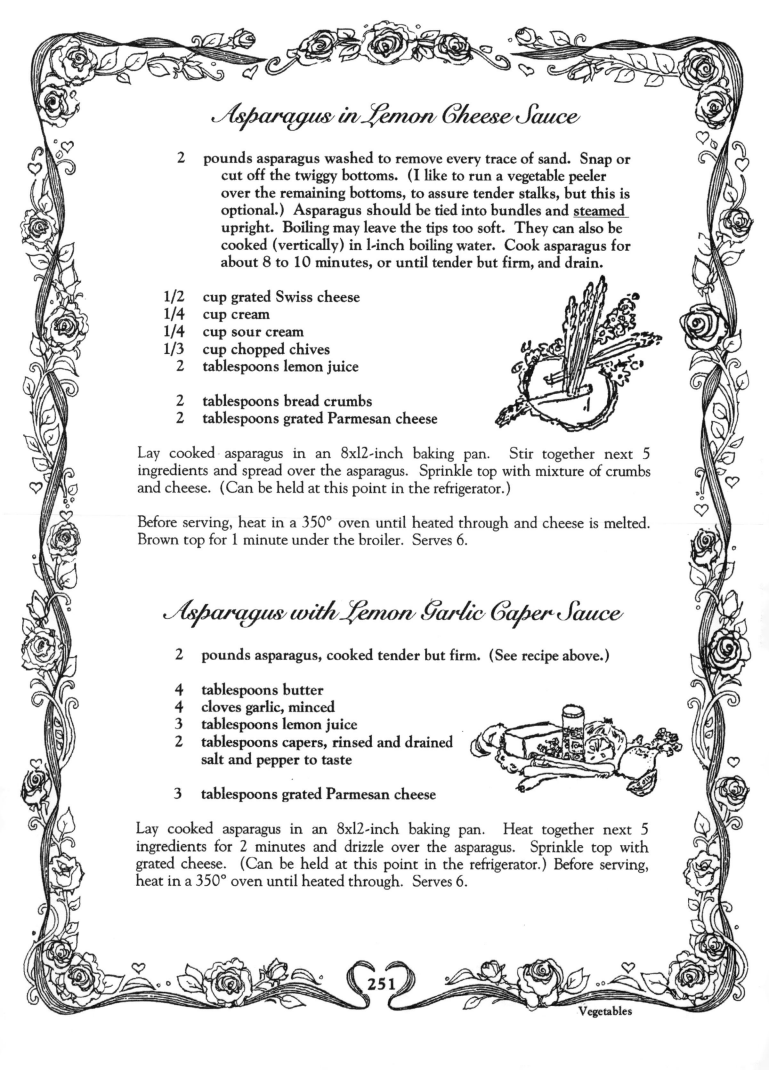

1/2   cup grated Swiss cheese
1/4   cup cream
1/4   cup sour cream
1/3   cup chopped chives
2   tablespoons lemon juice

2   tablespoons bread crumbs
2   tablespoons grated Parmesan cheese

Lay cooked asparagus in an 8x12-inch baking pan. Stir together next 5 ingredients and spread over the asparagus. Sprinkle top with mixture of crumbs and cheese. (Can be held at this point in the refrigerator.)

Before serving, heat in a 350° oven until heated through and cheese is melted. Brown top for 1 minute under the broiler. Serves 6.

Asparagus with Lemon Garlic Caper Sauce

2   pounds asparagus, cooked tender but firm. (See recipe above.)

4   tablespoons butter
4   cloves garlic, minced
3   tablespoons lemon juice
2   tablespoons capers, rinsed and drained
    salt and pepper to taste

3   tablespoons grated Parmesan cheese

Lay cooked asparagus in an 8x12-inch baking pan. Heat together next 5 ingredients for 2 minutes and drizzle over the asparagus. Sprinkle top with grated cheese. (Can be held at this point in the refrigerator.) Before serving, heat in a 350° oven until heated through. Serves 6.

Brussels Sprouts with Mushrooms, Shallots & Garlic

2   packages (10 ounces, each) frozen Brussels sprouts
1/2   cup chicken broth
1/4   teaspoon dill weed

1/4   pound, mushrooms, thinly sliced
3   shallots, finely minced
3   cloves garlic,, minced
2   tablespoons butter

2   tablespoons chopped chives
       salt and pepper to taste

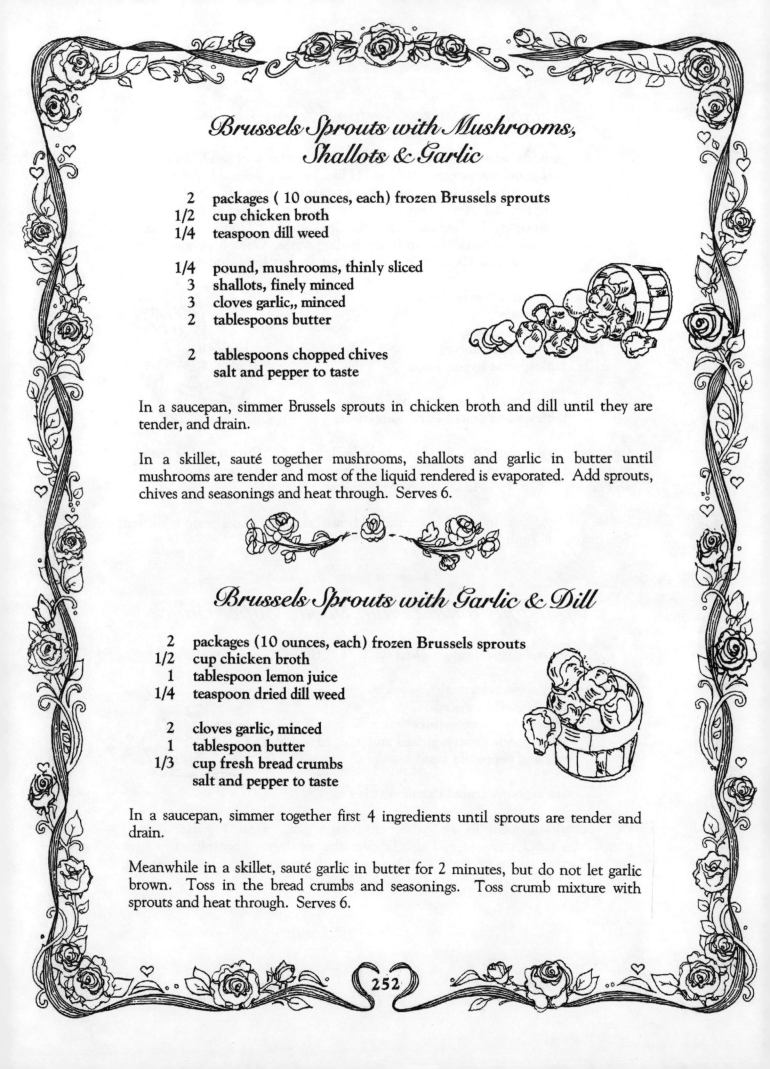

In a saucepan, simmer Brussels sprouts in chicken broth and dill until they are tender, and drain.

In a skillet, sauté together mushrooms, shallots and garlic in butter until mushrooms are tender and most of the liquid rendered is evaporated. Add sprouts, chives and seasonings and heat through. Serves 6.

Brussels Sprouts with Garlic & Dill

2   packages (10 ounces, each) frozen Brussels sprouts
1/2   cup chicken broth
1   tablespoon lemon juice
1/4   teaspoon dried dill weed

2   cloves garlic, minced
1   tablespoon butter
1/3   cup fresh bread crumbs
       salt and pepper to taste

In a saucepan, simmer together first 4 ingredients until sprouts are tender and drain.

Meanwhile in a skillet, sauté garlic in butter for 2 minutes, but do not let garlic brown. Toss in the bread crumbs and seasonings. Toss crumb mixture with sprouts and heat through. Serves 6.

Cauliflower & Cheese Onion Frittata

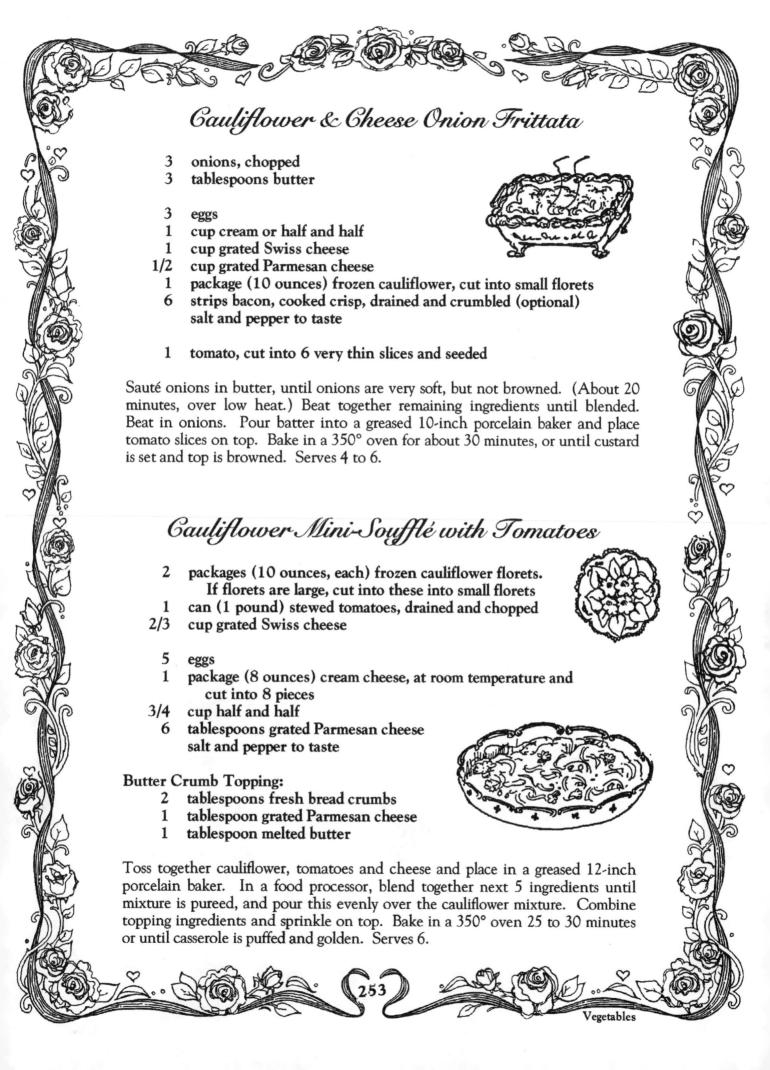

3 onions, chopped
3 tablespoons butter

3 eggs
1 cup cream or half and half
1 cup grated Swiss cheese
1/2 cup grated Parmesan cheese
1 package (10 ounces) frozen cauliflower, cut into small florets
6 strips bacon, cooked crisp, drained and crumbled (optional)
    salt and pepper to taste

1 tomato, cut into 6 very thin slices and seeded

Sauté onions in butter, until onions are very soft, but not browned. (About 20 minutes, over low heat.) Beat together remaining ingredients until blended. Beat in onions. Pour batter into a greased 10-inch porcelain baker and place tomato slices on top. Bake in a 350° oven for about 30 minutes, or until custard is set and top is browned. Serves 4 to 6.

Cauliflower Mini-Soufflé with Tomatoes

2 packages (10 ounces, each) frozen cauliflower florets.
    If florets are large, cut into these into small florets
1 can (1 pound) stewed tomatoes, drained and chopped
2/3 cup grated Swiss cheese

5 eggs
1 package (8 ounces) cream cheese, at room temperature and
    cut into 8 pieces
3/4 cup half and half
6 tablespoons grated Parmesan cheese
    salt and pepper to taste

Butter Crumb Topping:
2 tablespoons fresh bread crumbs
1 tablespoon grated Parmesan cheese
1 tablespoon melted butter

Toss together cauliflower, tomatoes and cheese and place in a greased 12-inch porcelain baker. In a food processor, blend together next 5 ingredients until mixture is pureed, and pour this evenly over the cauliflower mixture. Combine topping ingredients and sprinkle on top. Bake in a 350° oven 25 to 30 minutes or until casserole is puffed and golden. Serves 6.

Cabbage with Apples & Raisins

Even if cabbage is not your preferred vegetable, you will enjoy this delicious combination of cabbage, apples, raisins in a lemony cream sauce. Sprinkle top with buttered crumbs just before serving.

1	onion, chopped
2	tablespoons sugar
2	tablespoons butter
1/2	cup chicken broth
1	small cabbage (about 1 pound), grated
1	apple, peeled and grated
1/2	cup yellow raisins
1/2	cup cream
2	teaspoons lemon juice
	salt and pepper to taste
	buttered crumbs

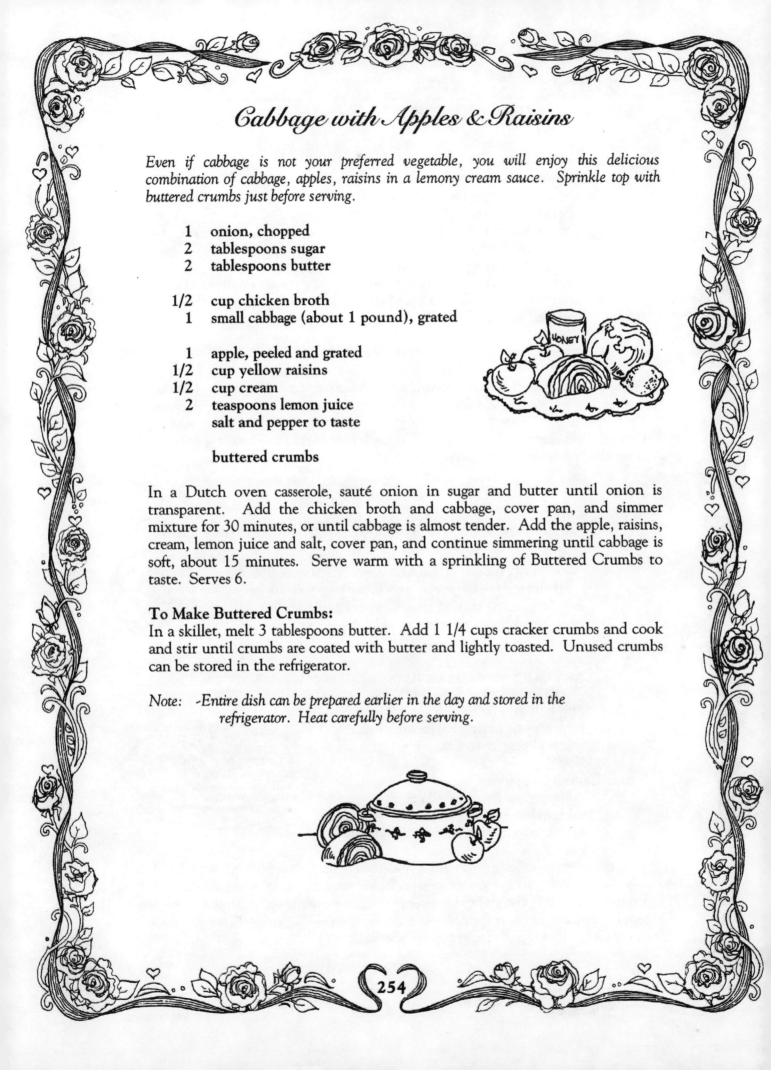

In a Dutch oven casserole, sauté onion in sugar and butter until onion is transparent. Add the chicken broth and cabbage, cover pan, and simmer mixture for 30 minutes, or until cabbage is almost tender. Add the apple, raisins, cream, lemon juice and salt, cover pan, and continue simmering until cabbage is soft, about 15 minutes. Serve warm with a sprinkling of Buttered Crumbs to taste. Serves 6.

To Make Buttered Crumbs:
In a skillet, melt 3 tablespoons butter. Add 1 1/4 cups cracker crumbs and cook and stir until crumbs are coated with butter and lightly toasted. Unused crumbs can be stored in the refrigerator.

Note: -Entire dish can be prepared earlier in the day and stored in the refrigerator. Heat carefully before serving.

Molded Ramekins with Carrots, Onions & Cream

1   pound carrots, cleaned and cut into 1 inch slices
1   onion, chopped
2   tablespoons butter

3   eggs
1/2   cup cream
     salt to taste
     pinch of nutmeg

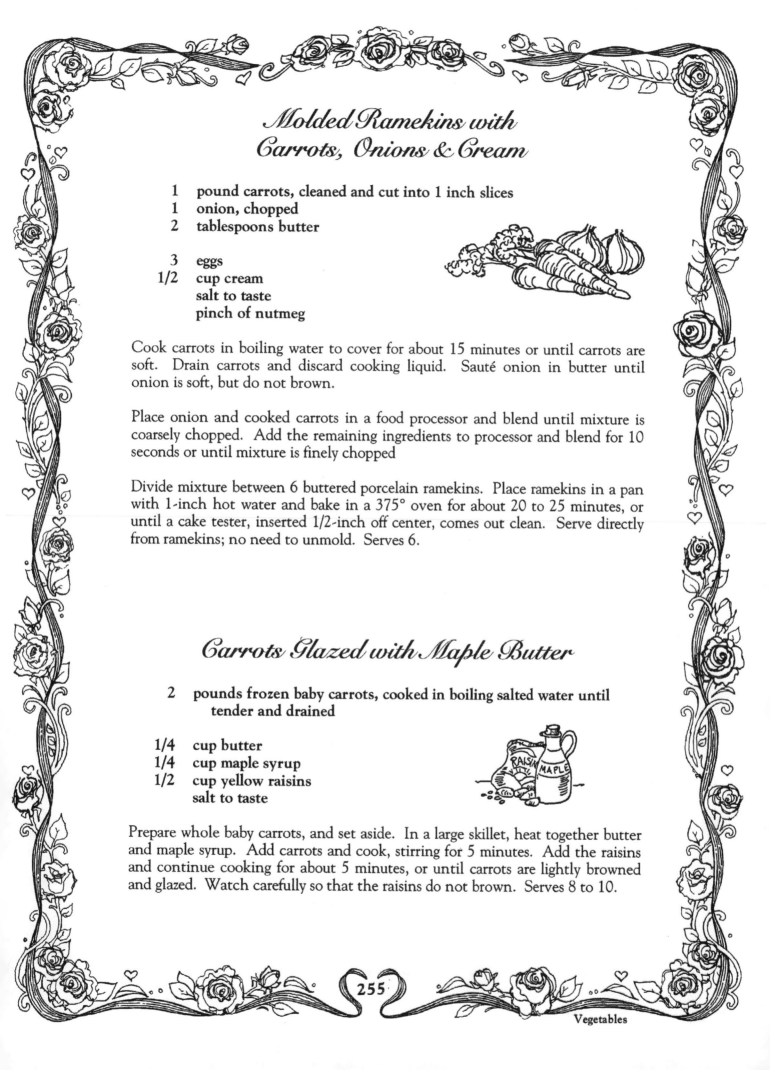

Cook carrots in boiling water to cover for about 15 minutes or until carrots are soft. Drain carrots and discard cooking liquid. Sauté onion in butter until onion is soft, but do not brown.

Place onion and cooked carrots in a food processor and blend until mixture is coarsely chopped. Add the remaining ingredients to processor and blend for 10 seconds or until mixture is finely chopped

Divide mixture between 6 buttered porcelain ramekins. Place ramekins in a pan with 1-inch hot water and bake in a 375° oven for about 20 to 25 minutes, or until a cake tester, inserted 1/2-inch off center, comes out clean. Serve directly from ramekins; no need to unmold. Serves 6.

Carrots Glazed with Maple Butter

2   pounds frozen baby carrots, cooked in boiling salted water until
     tender and drained

1/4   cup butter
1/4   cup maple syrup
1/2   cup yellow raisins
     salt to taste

Prepare whole baby carrots, and set aside. In a large skillet, heat together butter and maple syrup. Add carrots and cook, stirring for 5 minutes. Add the raisins and continue cooking for about 5 minutes, or until carrots are lightly browned and glazed. Watch carefully so that the raisins do not brown. Serves 8 to 10.

Vegetables

Cauliflower Casserole with Tomatoes, Chiles & Cheese

This is a nice vegetarian casserole that is filled with all manner of good things ... eggs, vegetables, cheese. It is exceptionally easy to prepare as it can be assembled in literally minutes.

1/4	cup chopped chives
2	packages (10 ounces, each) frozen cauliflower, cut into florets
2	tomatoes, peeled, seeded and diced
1	can (3 1/2 ounces) diced green chiles
1 1/2	cups grated Swiss cheese
3	eggs
1	cup half and half
1/2	cup grated Parmesan cheese
3	tablespoons cracker crumbs
3	tablespoons grated Parmesan cheese

Toss together first 5 ingredients until nicely mixed and place in a greased 9x13-inch porcelain baker. Beat together eggs, half-and-half, and grated Parmesan until blended. Pour this over the vegetables in the pan and spread evenly. Sprinkle top with cracker crumbs and Parmesan cheese.

Bake casserole in a 350° oven for about 45 to 50 minutes, or until custard is set and topping is browned. Cut into squares to serve. Serves 6 for lunch, or 12 as an accompaniment to lunch or dinner.

Note: -*If you are assembling this earlier in the day, follow this plan. Place vegetables in the porcelain baker and refrigerate. Eggs can be beaten with half-and-half and cheese, earlier in the day, and stored in the refrigerator. Have crumbs and cheese ready. Just before baking, pour egg mixture over the vegetables, sprinkle crumbs on top, and bake as described above.*

New Orleans Corn & Red Pepper Sauté

(Maque Choux)

Corn, combined with red pepper, green onions and tomatoes is one of the most beautiful dishes to serve. The colors excite the palate. It promises and delivers good taste and enjoyment.

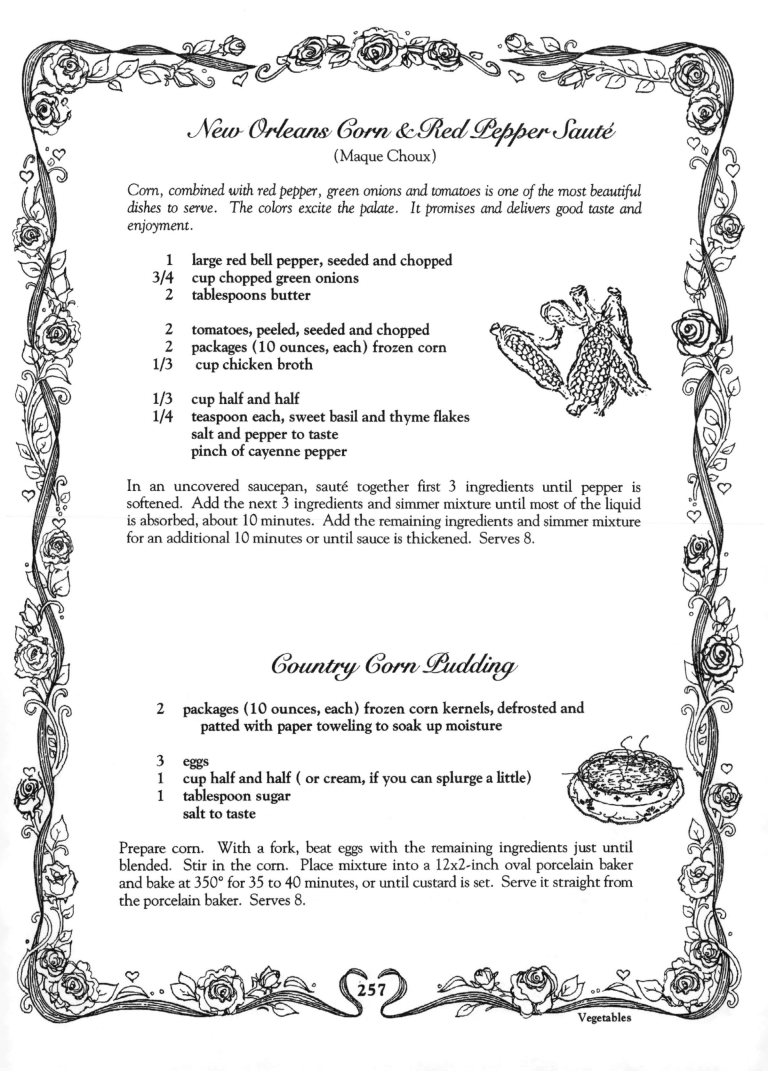

1	large red bell pepper, seeded and chopped
3/4	cup chopped green onions
2	tablespoons butter
2	tomatoes, peeled, seeded and chopped
2	packages (10 ounces, each) frozen corn
1/3	cup chicken broth
1/3	cup half and half
1/4	teaspoon each, sweet basil and thyme flakes
	salt and pepper to taste
	pinch of cayenne pepper

In an uncovered saucepan, sauté together first 3 ingredients until pepper is softened. Add the next 3 ingredients and simmer mixture until most of the liquid is absorbed, about 10 minutes. Add the remaining ingredients and simmer mixture for an additional 10 minutes or until sauce is thickened. Serves 8.

Country Corn Pudding

2	packages (10 ounces, each) frozen corn kernels, defrosted and patted with paper toweling to soak up moisture
3	eggs
1	cup half and half (or cream, if you can splurge a little)
1	tablespoon sugar
	salt to taste

Prepare corn. With a fork, beat eggs with the remaining ingredients just until blended. Stir in the corn. Place mixture into a 12x2-inch oval porcelain baker and bake at 350° for 35 to 40 minutes, or until custard is set. Serve it straight from the porcelain baker. Serves 8.

Vegetables

Chestnut Pudding with Raisins & Prunes

This recipe can also double as a stuffing for roast capon or Cornish hens. I prefer to bake this separately and serve it in a silver platter.

1	onion, chopped
2	medium carrots, grated
4	tablespoons butter
1	can (15 1/2 ounces) chestnuts, drained and coarsely chopped
1/2	cup chopped prunes
1/4	cup yellow raisins
1	package (8 ounces) herb-seasoned stuffing mix
2	eggs, beaten
	salt and pepper to taste
3/4	cup chicken broth (Use only enough to hold stuffing together.)

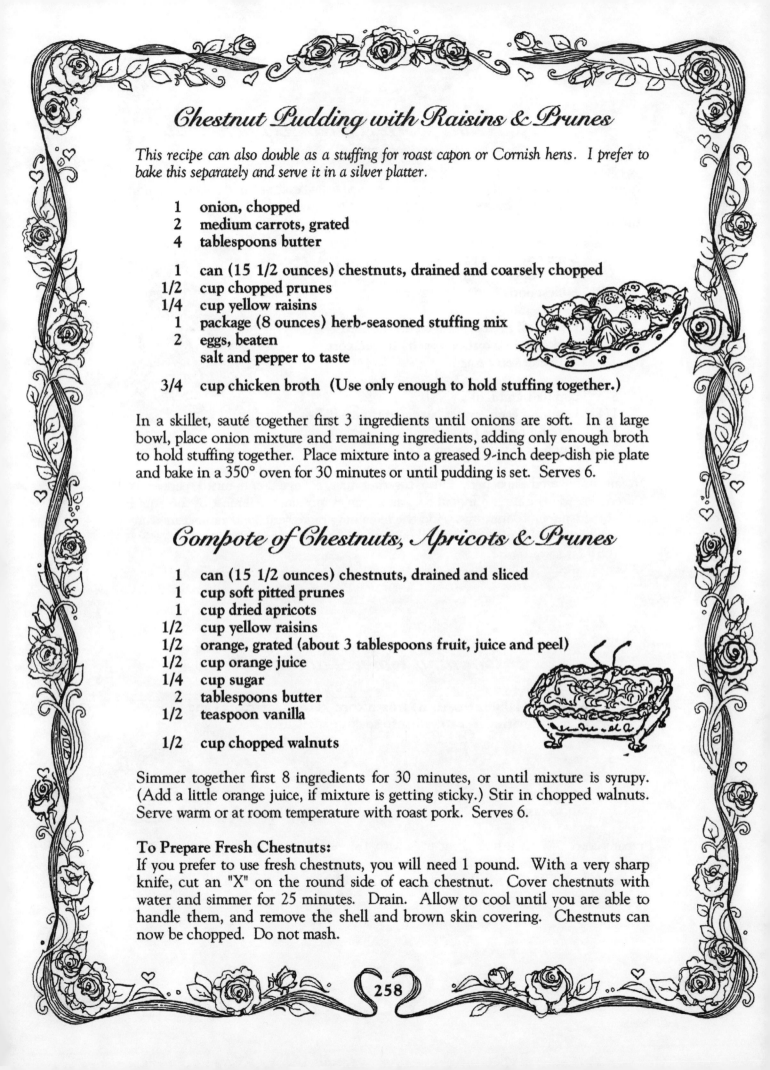

In a skillet, sauté together first 3 ingredients until onions are soft. In a large bowl, place onion mixture and remaining ingredients, adding only enough broth to hold stuffing together. Place mixture into a greased 9-inch deep-dish pie plate and bake in a 350° oven for 30 minutes or until pudding is set. Serves 6.

Compote of Chestnuts, Apricots & Prunes

1	can (15 1/2 ounces) chestnuts, drained and sliced
1	cup soft pitted prunes
1	cup dried apricots
1/2	cup yellow raisins
1/2	orange, grated (about 3 tablespoons fruit, juice and peel)
1/2	cup orange juice
1/4	cup sugar
2	tablespoons butter
1/2	teaspoon vanilla
1/2	cup chopped walnuts

Simmer together first 8 ingredients for 30 minutes, or until mixture is syrupy. (Add a little orange juice, if mixture is getting sticky.) Stir in chopped walnuts. Serve warm or at room temperature with roast pork. Serves 6.

To Prepare Fresh Chestnuts:
If you prefer to use fresh chestnuts, you will need 1 pound. With a very sharp knife, cut an "X" on the round side of each chestnut. Cover chestnuts with water and simmer for 25 minutes. Drain. Allow to cool until you are able to handle them, and remove the shell and brown skin covering. Chestnuts can now be chopped. Do not mash.

Eggplant Dumplings with Onions & Cheese

This is a lovely vegetarian dish filled with so many good things, that are good for you, too. Serve these dumplings with a spoonful of Light Tomato Sauce.

1	small eggplant, about 3/4 pound, peeled and cut into 1/4-inch slices
1	tablespoon oil

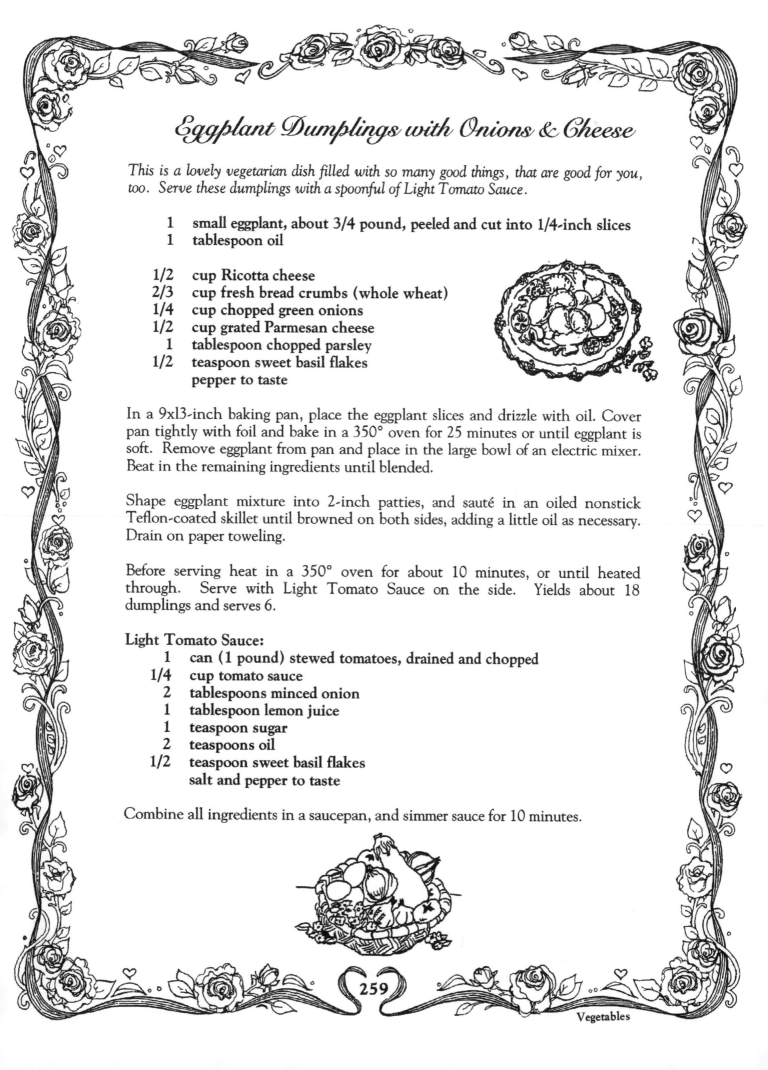

1/2	cup Ricotta cheese
2/3	cup fresh bread crumbs (whole wheat)
1/4	cup chopped green onions
1/2	cup grated Parmesan cheese
1	tablespoon chopped parsley
1/2	teaspoon sweet basil flakes
	pepper to taste

In a 9x13-inch baking pan, place the eggplant slices and drizzle with oil. Cover pan tightly with foil and bake in a 350° oven for 25 minutes or until eggplant is soft. Remove eggplant from pan and place in the large bowl of an electric mixer. Beat in the remaining ingredients until blended.

Shape eggplant mixture into 2-inch patties, and sauté in an oiled nonstick Teflon-coated skillet until browned on both sides, adding a little oil as necessary. Drain on paper toweling.

Before serving heat in a 350° oven for about 10 minutes, or until heated through. Serve with Light Tomato Sauce on the side. Yields about 18 dumplings and serves 6.

Light Tomato Sauce:

1	can (1 pound) stewed tomatoes, drained and chopped
1/4	cup tomato sauce
2	tablespoons minced onion
1	tablespoon lemon juice
1	teaspoon sugar
2	teaspoons oil
1/2	teaspoon sweet basil flakes
	salt and pepper to taste

Combine all ingredients in a saucepan, and simmer sauce for 10 minutes.

Vegetables

Green Beans with Tomatoes, Onions, & Chiles

This is a delicious dish to serve with barbecued or roasted meats or poultry. Make certain that the vegetables stay crisp and tender, but not too raw. You can overdo "crisp" vegetables.

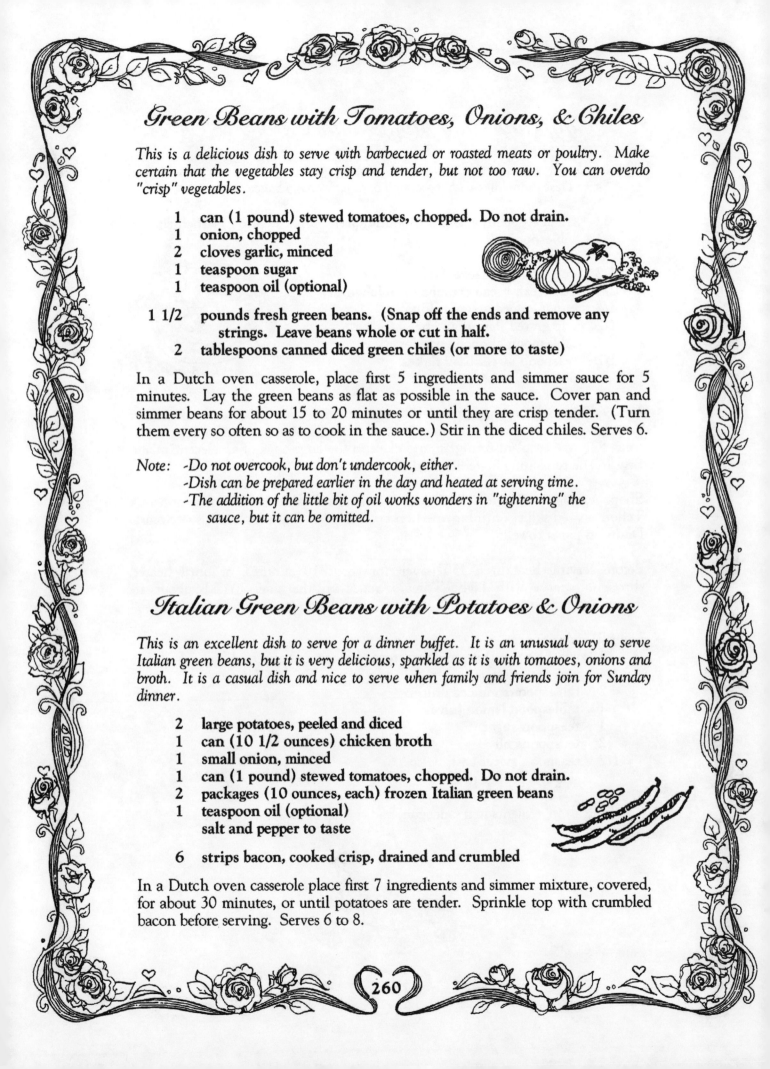

1   can (1 pound) stewed tomatoes, chopped. Do not drain.
1   onion, chopped
2   cloves garlic, minced
1   teaspoon sugar
1   teaspoon oil (optional)

1 1/2   pounds fresh green beans. (Snap off the ends and remove any strings. Leave beans whole or cut in half.
2   tablespoons canned diced green chiles (or more to taste)

In a Dutch oven casserole, place first 5 ingredients and simmer sauce for 5 minutes. Lay the green beans as flat as possible in the sauce. Cover pan and simmer beans for about 15 to 20 minutes or until they are crisp tender. (Turn them every so often so as to cook in the sauce.) Stir in the diced chiles. Serves 6.

Note: -Do not overcook, but don't undercook, either.
        -Dish can be prepared earlier in the day and heated at serving time.
        -The addition of the little bit of oil works wonders in "tightening" the
          sauce, but it can be omitted.

Italian Green Beans with Potatoes & Onions

This is an excellent dish to serve for a dinner buffet. It is an unusual way to serve Italian green beans, but it is very delicious, sparkled as it is with tomatoes, onions and broth. It is a casual dish and nice to serve when family and friends join for Sunday dinner.

2   large potatoes, peeled and diced
1   can (10 1/2 ounces) chicken broth
1   small onion, minced
1   can (1 pound) stewed tomatoes, chopped. Do not drain.
2   packages (10 ounces, each) frozen Italian green beans
1   teaspoon oil (optional)
     salt and pepper to taste

6   strips bacon, cooked crisp, drained and crumbled

In a Dutch oven casserole place first 7 ingredients and simmer mixture, covered, for about 30 minutes, or until potatoes are tender. Sprinkle top with crumbled bacon before serving. Serves 6 to 8.

Mushrooms with Tomatoes, Onions & Garlic

1   pound mushrooms, thinly sliced
2   tablespoons butter
2   cloves garlic, finely minced

2   canned tomatoes, drained and finely chopped
2   green onions, finely chopped
2   tablespoons chopped parsley
1   tablespoon lemon juice
     salt and pepper to taste

In a saucepan, sauté mushrooms and garlic in butter until mushrooms are tender. Add the remaining ingredients and simmer mixture until juices have evaporated and sauce has thickened. When ready to serve, a sprinkling of grated Parmesan is lovely but optional. Serves 6.

Glazed Onions with Cinnamon & Raisins

1   pound frozen baby white onions, cooked in chicken broth for about 20 minutes or until tender and drained.

2   tablespoons sugar
1/4   teaspoon cinnamon
2   tablespoons butter

1/3   cup yellow raisins
     salt to taste

Prepare small white onions, and set aside. In a large skillet, heat together sugar, cinnamon and butter. Add onions and cook, stirring, for about 5 minutes. Add the raisins and salt to taste and continue cooking for about 5 minutes, or until onions are lightly browned and glazed. Watch so that the raisins do not brown. They will plump up. Serves 8.

Roasted Red Onions

6   medium red onions, peeled, cut into thin slices, separate into rings
1/2   cup chicken broth
2   tablespoons oil
2   tablespoons vinegar
1   teaspoon dried sage flakes
     salt and pepper to taste

In a 9x13-inch baking pan place the onions. Stir together the remaining ingredients and pour evenly over the onions. Toss and turn onions until they are evenly coated. Cover pan with foil and bake at 350° for about 45 minutes, or until onions are soft. Remove foil and broil onions, 6 inches from the heat, turning and tossing until onions are flecked with brown. Serves 12.

Vegetables

French Peas with Butter & Shallots

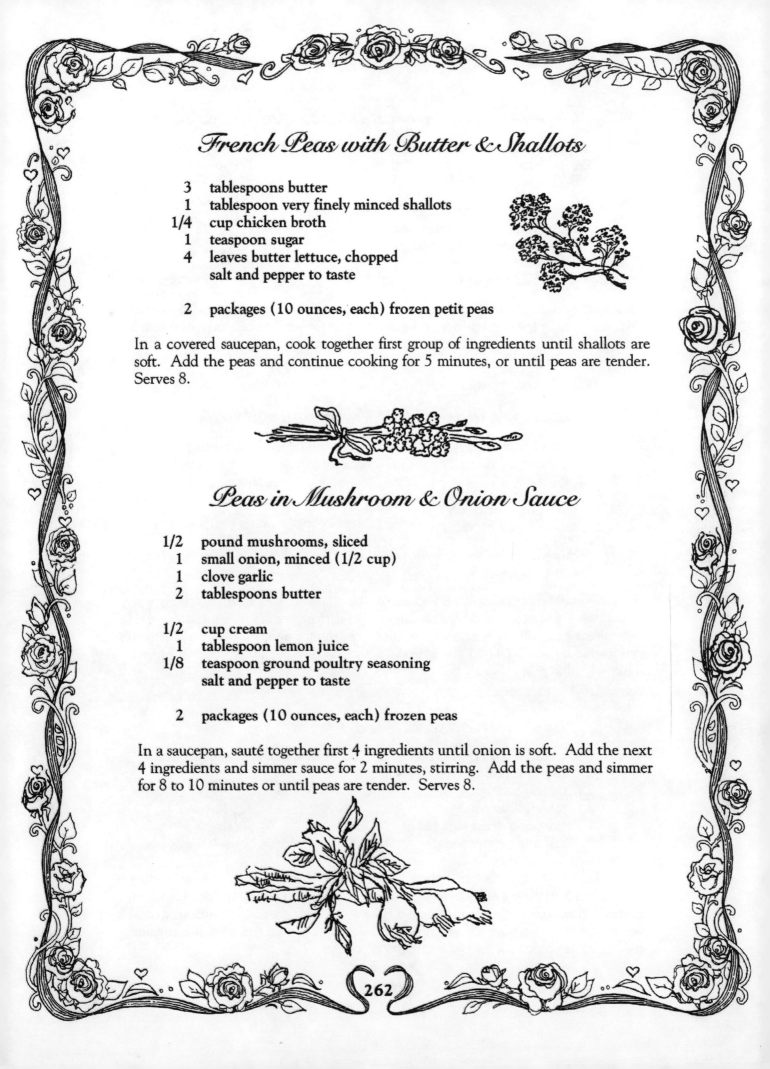

3 tablespoons butter
1 tablespoon very finely minced shallots
1/4 cup chicken broth
1 teaspoon sugar
4 leaves butter lettuce, chopped
   salt and pepper to taste

2 packages (10 ounces, each) frozen petit peas

In a covered saucepan, cook together first group of ingredients until shallots are soft. Add the peas and continue cooking for 5 minutes, or until peas are tender. Serves 8.

Peas in Mushroom & Onion Sauce

1/2 pound mushrooms, sliced
1 small onion, minced (1/2 cup)
1 clove garlic
2 tablespoons butter

1/2 cup cream
1 tablespoon lemon juice
1/8 teaspoon ground poultry seasoning
   salt and pepper to taste

2 packages (10 ounces, each) frozen peas

In a saucepan, sauté together first 4 ingredients until onion is soft. Add the next 4 ingredients and simmer sauce for 2 minutes, stirring. Add the peas and simmer for 8 to 10 minutes or until peas are tender. Serves 8.

Italian-Style Stuffed Red Peppers
with Beef & Rice

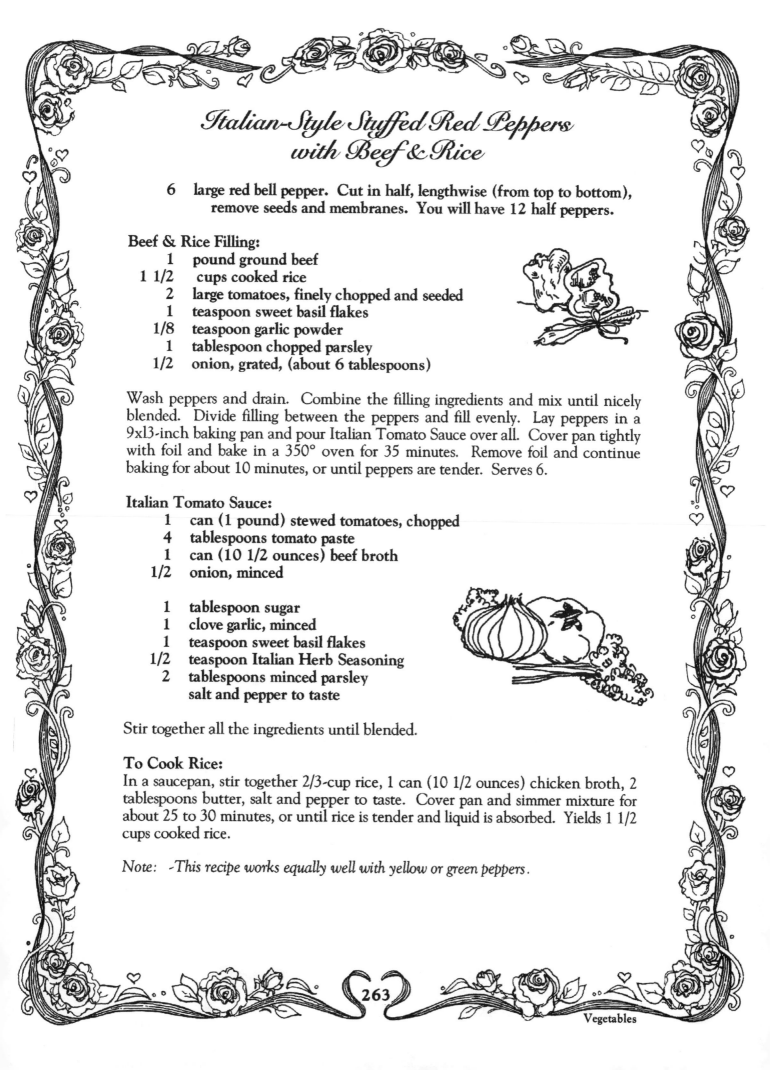

6   large red bell pepper. Cut in half, lengthwise (from top to bottom), remove seeds and membranes. You will have 12 half peppers.

Beef & Rice Filling:

1   pound ground beef
1 1/2   cups cooked rice
2   large tomatoes, finely chopped and seeded
1   teaspoon sweet basil flakes
1/8   teaspoon garlic powder
1   tablespoon chopped parsley
1/2   onion, grated, (about 6 tablespoons)

Wash peppers and drain. Combine the filling ingredients and mix until nicely blended. Divide filling between the peppers and fill evenly. Lay peppers in a 9x13-inch baking pan and pour Italian Tomato Sauce over all. Cover pan tightly with foil and bake in a 350° oven for 35 minutes. Remove foil and continue baking for about 10 minutes, or until peppers are tender. Serves 6.

Italian Tomato Sauce:

1   can (1 pound) stewed tomatoes, chopped
4   tablespoons tomato paste
1   can (10 1/2 ounces) beef broth
1/2   onion, minced

1   tablespoon sugar
1   clove garlic, minced
1   teaspoon sweet basil flakes
1/2   teaspoon Italian Herb Seasoning
2   tablespoons minced parsley
   salt and pepper to taste

Stir together all the ingredients until blended.

To Cook Rice:

In a saucepan, stir together 2/3-cup rice, 1 can (10 1/2 ounces) chicken broth, 2 tablespoons butter, salt and pepper to taste. Cover pan and simmer mixture for about 25 to 30 minutes, or until rice is tender and liquid is absorbed. Yields 1 1/2 cups cooked rice.

Note: -This recipe works equally well with yellow or green peppers.

Large Potato Pancake with Orange Applesauce

If you find that you do not have enough time to prepare individual potato pancakes, this can be made in a 9x13-inch baking pan and cut into squares to serve. It can be prepared earlier in the day, chilled and cut into squares. Reheat in a 400° oven until hot and crisped. Recipe for individual pancakes follows.

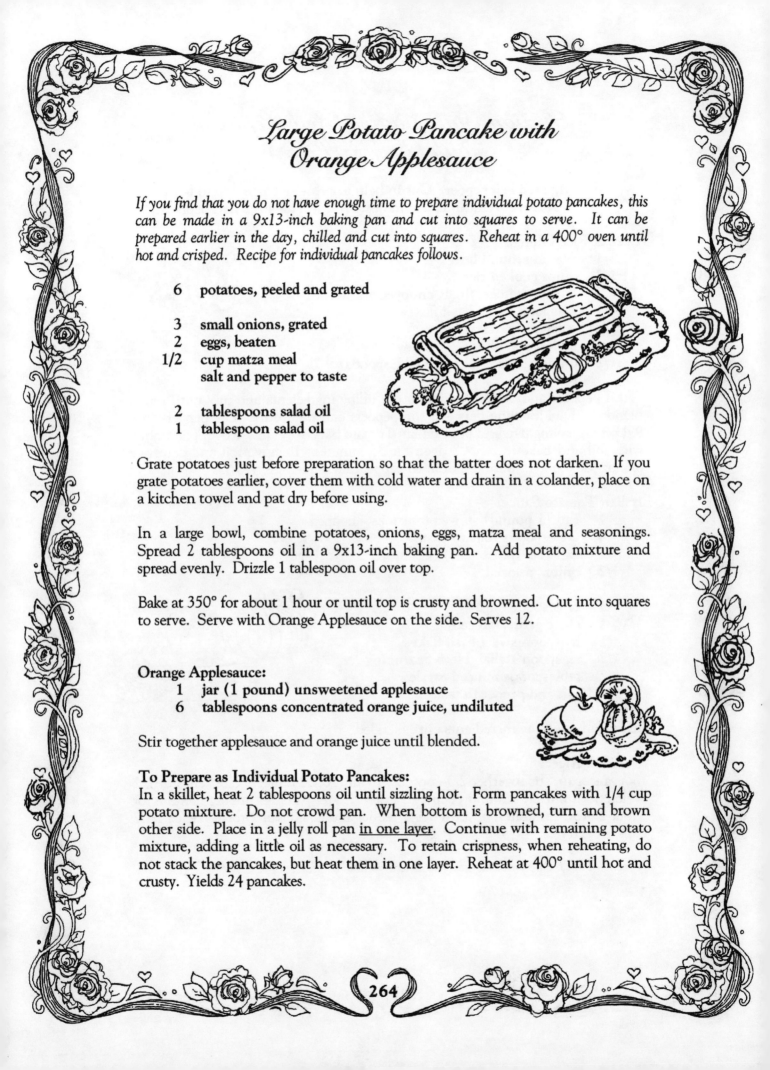

6	potatoes, peeled and grated
3	small onions, grated
2	eggs, beaten
1/2	cup matza meal
	salt and pepper to taste
2	tablespoons salad oil
1	tablespoon salad oil

Grate potatoes just before preparation so that the batter does not darken. If you grate potatoes earlier, cover them with cold water and drain in a colander, place on a kitchen towel and pat dry before using.

In a large bowl, combine potatoes, onions, eggs, matza meal and seasonings. Spread 2 tablespoons oil in a 9x13-inch baking pan. Add potato mixture and spread evenly. Drizzle 1 tablespoon oil over top.

Bake at 350° for about 1 hour or until top is crusty and browned. Cut into squares to serve. Serve with Orange Applesauce on the side. Serves 12.

Orange Applesauce:
1   jar (1 pound) unsweetened applesauce
6   tablespoons concentrated orange juice, undiluted

Stir together applesauce and orange juice until blended.

To Prepare as Individual Potato Pancakes:
In a skillet, heat 2 tablespoons oil until sizzling hot. Form pancakes with 1/4 cup potato mixture. Do not crowd pan. When bottom is browned, turn and brown other side. Place in a jelly roll pan <u>in one layer</u>. Continue with remaining potato mixture, adding a little oil as necessary. To retain crispness, when reheating, do not stack the pancakes, but heat them in one layer. Reheat at 400° until hot and crusty. Yields 24 pancakes.

Yellow Potatoes with Mushrooms & Onions

These potatoes are an attractive addition to an Indian buffet. They are exceedingly delicious and I know you will love the taste.

4	medium potatoes, peeled and cut into 3/4-inch dice
1	cup chicken broth
1	teaspoon ground turmeric
1/2	teaspoon ground cumin
	salt and pepper to taste
2	onions, chopped
4	cloves garlic, minced
2	tablespoons butter
1/2	pound mushrooms, sliced

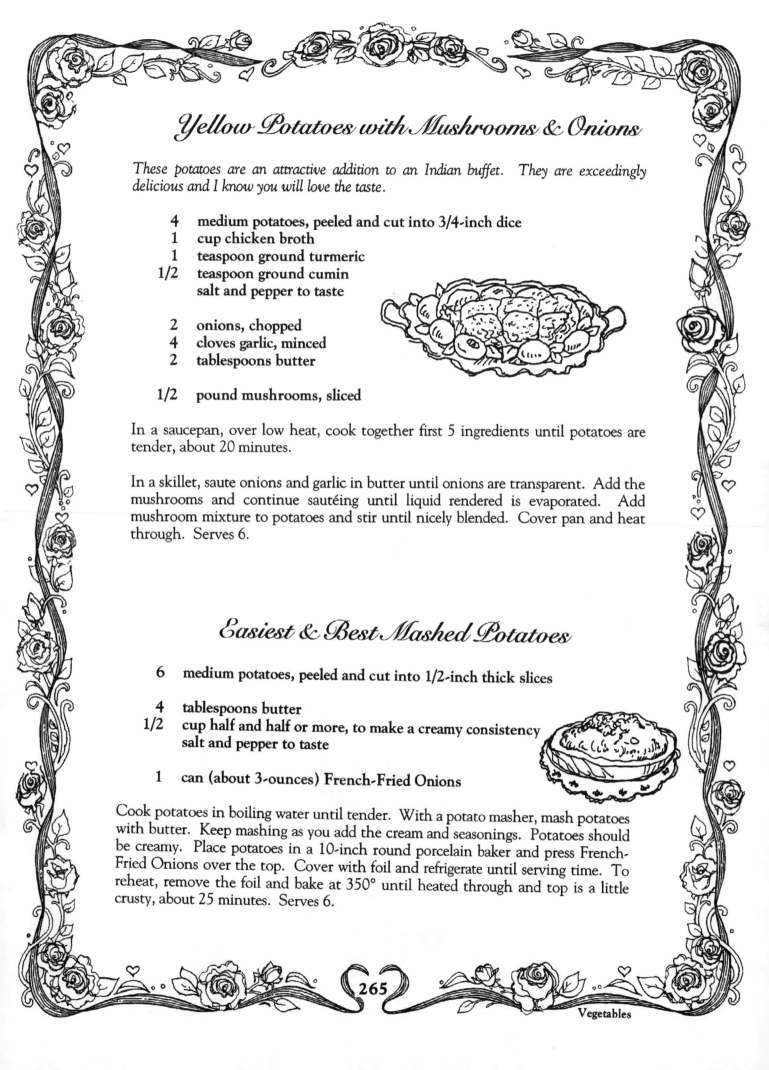

In a saucepan, over low heat, cook together first 5 ingredients until potatoes are tender, about 20 minutes.

In a skillet, saute onions and garlic in butter until onions are transparent. Add the mushrooms and continue sautéing until liquid rendered is evaporated. Add mushroom mixture to potatoes and stir until nicely blended. Cover pan and heat through. Serves 6.

Easiest & Best Mashed Potatoes

6	medium potatoes, peeled and cut into 1/2-inch thick slices
4	tablespoons butter
1/2	cup half and half or more, to make a creamy consistency
	salt and pepper to taste
1	can (about 3-ounces) French-Fried Onions

Cook potatoes in boiling water until tender. With a potato masher, mash potatoes with butter. Keep mashing as you add the cream and seasonings. Potatoes should be creamy. Place potatoes in a 10-inch round porcelain baker and press French-Fried Onions over the top. Cover with foil and refrigerate until serving time. To reheat, remove the foil and bake at 350° until heated through and top is a little crusty, about 25 minutes. Serves 6.

Vegetables

Classic Brown Sugar Glazed Sweet Potatoes

Potatoes can be prepared 1 day earlier and stored in the refrigerator. Bring to room temperature before heating. This is the classic recipe...the simplest and easily one of the best. But there are a few alternatives, which are found at the bottom of the page.

Basic Recipe:

3 pounds sweet potatoes or yams, tubbed and scrubbed
    pinch of salt

1/2 cup brown sugar
1/3 cup melted butter

2 tablespoons sifted brown sugar

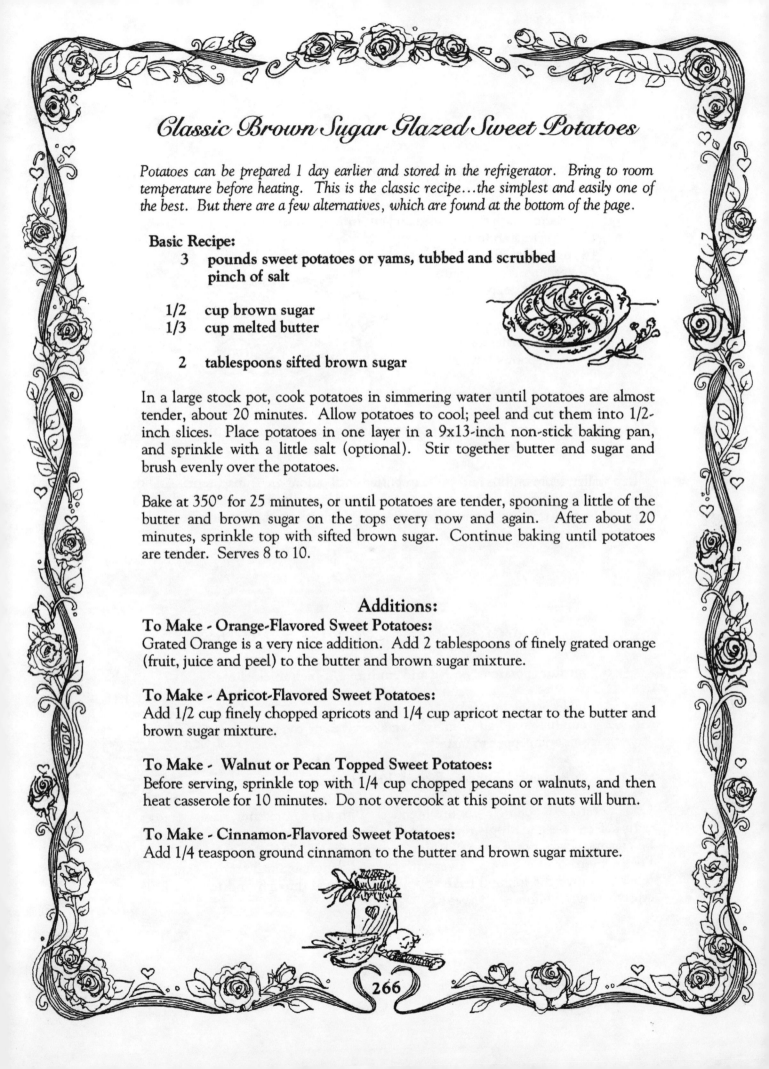

In a large stock pot, cook potatoes in simmering water until potatoes are almost tender, about 20 minutes. Allow potatoes to cool; peel and cut them into 1/2-inch slices. Place potatoes in one layer in a 9x13-inch non-stick baking pan, and sprinkle with a little salt (optional). Stir together butter and sugar and brush evenly over the potatoes.

Bake at 350° for 25 minutes, or until potatoes are tender, spooning a little of the butter and brown sugar on the tops every now and again. After about 20 minutes, sprinkle top with sifted brown sugar. Continue baking until potatoes are tender. Serves 8 to 10.

Additions:

To Make - Orange-Flavored Sweet Potatoes:
Grated Orange is a very nice addition. Add 2 tablespoons of finely grated orange (fruit, juice and peel) to the butter and brown sugar mixture.

To Make - Apricot-Flavored Sweet Potatoes:
Add 1/2 cup finely chopped apricots and 1/4 cup apricot nectar to the butter and brown sugar mixture.

To Make - Walnut or Pecan Topped Sweet Potatoes:
Before serving, sprinkle top with 1/4 cup chopped pecans or walnuts, and then heat casserole for 10 minutes. Do not overcook at this point or nuts will burn.

To Make - Cinnamon-Flavored Sweet Potatoes:
Add 1/4 teaspoon ground cinnamon to the butter and brown sugar mixture.

Sweet Potato Pancake with Orange & Apples

If you are looking for a new and delicious way to prepare sweet potatoes, please don't wait for a holiday, but make this casserole soon. Grated sweet potatoes, flavored with orange and apples and sparkled with cinnamon is truly fit for a king.

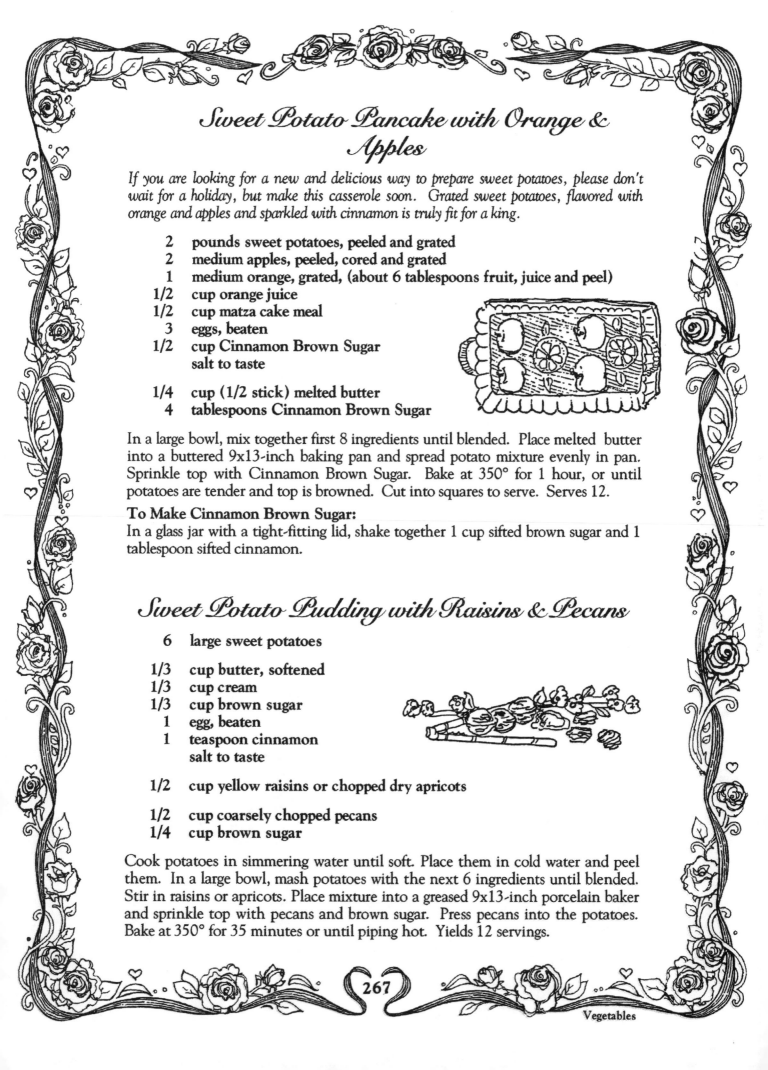

2	pounds sweet potatoes, peeled and grated
2	medium apples, peeled, cored and grated
1	medium orange, grated, (about 6 tablespoons fruit, juice and peel)
1/2	cup orange juice
1/2	cup matza cake meal
3	eggs, beaten
1/2	cup Cinnamon Brown Sugar
	salt to taste
1/4	cup (1/2 stick) melted butter
4	tablespoons Cinnamon Brown Sugar

In a large bowl, mix together first 8 ingredients until blended. Place melted butter into a buttered 9x13-inch baking pan and spread potato mixture evenly in pan. Sprinkle top with Cinnamon Brown Sugar. Bake at 350° for 1 hour, or until potatoes are tender and top is browned. Cut into squares to serve. Serves 12.

To Make Cinnamon Brown Sugar:
In a glass jar with a tight-fitting lid, shake together 1 cup sifted brown sugar and 1 tablespoon sifted cinnamon.

Sweet Potato Pudding with Raisins & Pecans

6	large sweet potatoes
1/3	cup butter, softened
1/3	cup cream
1/3	cup brown sugar
1	egg, beaten
1	teaspoon cinnamon
	salt to taste
1/2	cup yellow raisins or chopped dry apricots
1/2	cup coarsely chopped pecans
1/4	cup brown sugar

Cook potatoes in simmering water until soft. Place them in cold water and peel them. In a large bowl, mash potatoes with the next 6 ingredients until blended. Stir in raisins or apricots. Place mixture into a greased 9x13-inch porcelain baker and sprinkle top with pecans and brown sugar. Press pecans into the potatoes. Bake at 350° for 35 minutes or until piping hot. Yields 12 servings.

Orange-Glazed Sweet Potatoes

This is a variation of my favorite apple recipe. It is especially nice because it does not contain butter and the orange juice and cinnamon add a great flavor. This can be prepared in advance and heated before serving.

6	large sweet potatoes, peeled and cut into 1/4-inch slices
	pinch of salt
2 1/2	cups orange juice
1	tablespoon grated orange zest (orange part of the peel)
1	teaspoon vanilla
1/4	cup cinnamon sugar

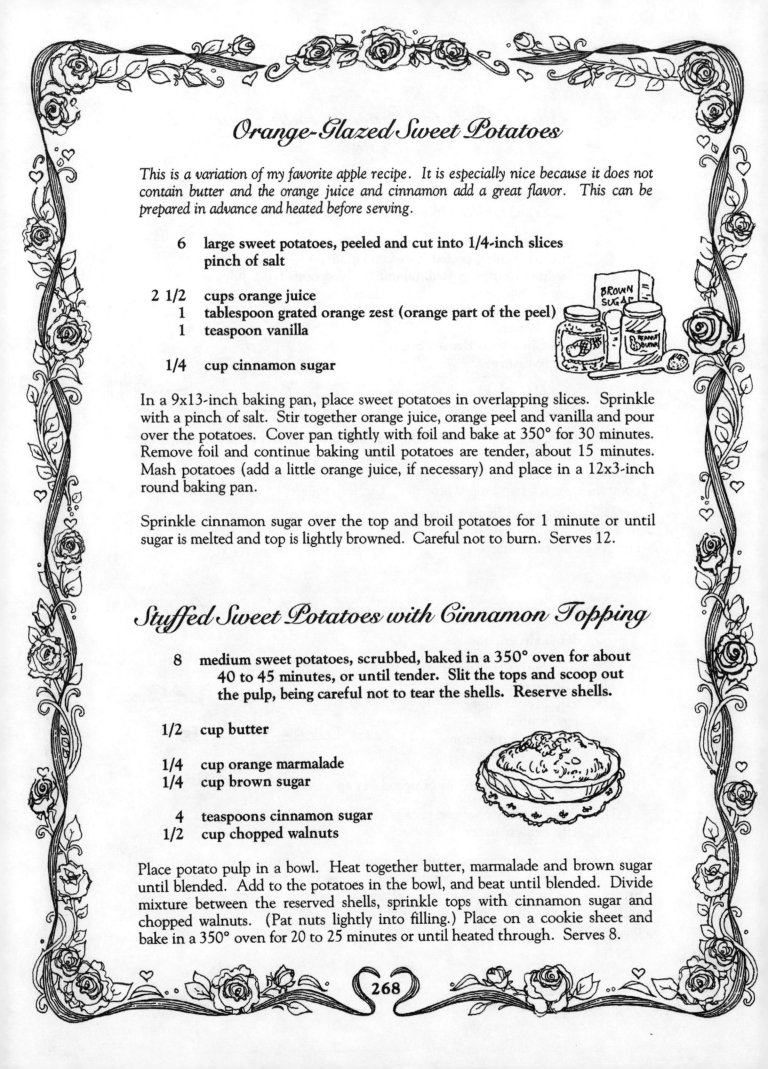

In a 9x13-inch baking pan, place sweet potatoes in overlapping slices. Sprinkle with a pinch of salt. Stir together orange juice, orange peel and vanilla and pour over the potatoes. Cover pan tightly with foil and bake at 350° for 30 minutes. Remove foil and continue baking until potatoes are tender, about 15 minutes. Mash potatoes (add a little orange juice, if necessary) and place in a 12x3-inch round baking pan.

Sprinkle cinnamon sugar over the top and broil potatoes for 1 minute or until sugar is melted and top is lightly browned. Careful not to burn. Serves 12.

Stuffed Sweet Potatoes with Cinnamon Topping

8	medium sweet potatoes, scrubbed, baked in a 350° oven for about 40 to 45 minutes, or until tender. Slit the tops and scoop out the pulp, being careful not to tear the shells. Reserve shells.
1/2	cup butter
1/4	cup orange marmalade
1/4	cup brown sugar
4	teaspoons cinnamon sugar
1/2	cup chopped walnuts

Place potato pulp in a bowl. Heat together butter, marmalade and brown sugar until blended. Add to the potatoes in the bowl, and beat until blended. Divide mixture between the reserved shells, sprinkle tops with cinnamon sugar and chopped walnuts. (Pat nuts lightly into filling.) Place on a cookie sheet and bake in a 350° oven for 20 to 25 minutes or until heated through. Serves 8.

Spinach & Red Pepper Dumplings with Onions & Cheese

Vegetable dumplings are versatile. They can be served as a main course, small entree or hors d'oeuvre. As an hors d'oeuvre, they should be shaped into smaller patties.

1	package (10 ounces) frozen chopped spinach, defrosted and thoroughly drained
3	tablespoons roasted sweet red pepper strips or pimientos
2	eggs
2/3	cup fresh whole wheat bread crumbs
1/2	cup grated Parmesan cheese
3	tablespoons minced green onion
	salt and pepper to taste (remember cheese is salty)

In a large bowl, stir together all the ingredients until mixture is blended. Shape spinach mixture into 2-inch patties and sauté in an oiled Teflon skillet until browned on both sides, adding a little oil as necessary. (These can also be baked in a 9x13-inch oiled Teflon baking pan, about 10 minutes on each side.) Drain on paper toweling.

Before serving, heat in a 350° oven for about 10 minutes, or until heated through. Serve with a spoonful of Red Pepper Sauce. Yields 12 to 14 dumplings. Serves 4 to 6.

Red Pepper Sauce:

1/4	cup cream
1/4	cup sour cream
2	tablespoons red pepper strips
2	tablespoons chopped chives
1	teaspoon lemon juice
	pinch of cayenne
	salt to taste

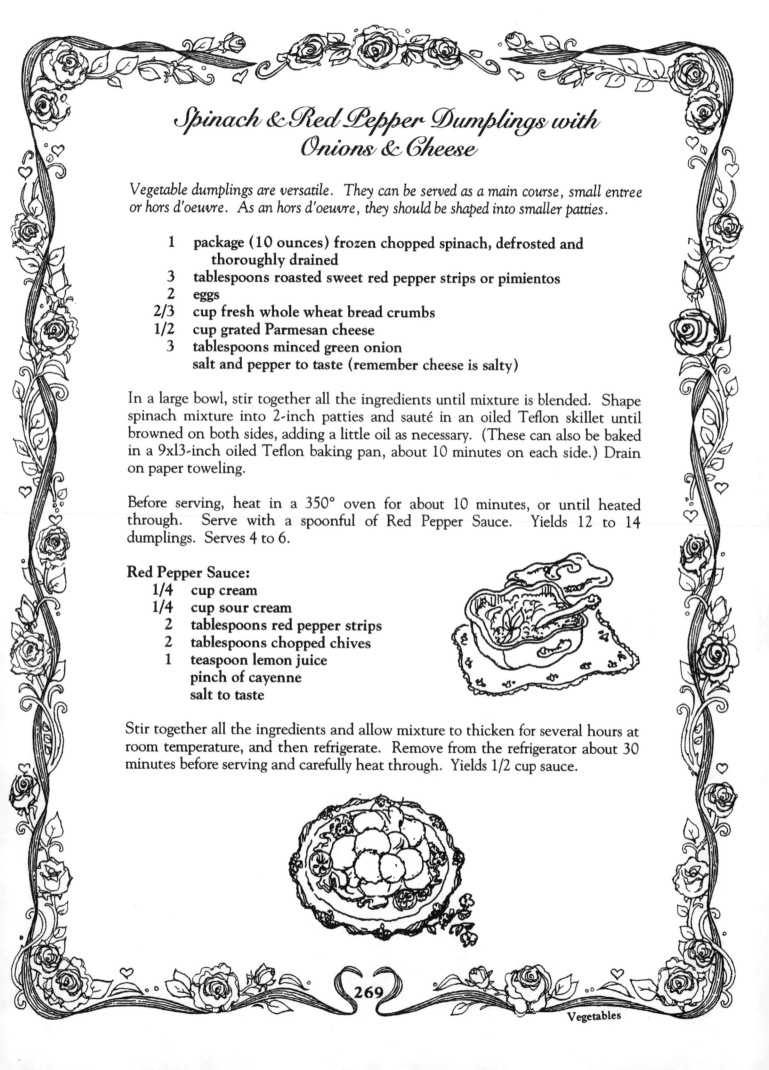

Stir together all the ingredients and allow mixture to thicken for several hours at room temperature, and then refrigerate. Remove from the refrigerator about 30 minutes before serving and carefully heat through. Yields 1/2 cup sauce.

Molded Ramekins with Spinach, Noodles & Cheese

1   package (6 ounces) fine egg noodles, cooked until tender
      and drained
1   package (10 ounces) frozen chopped spinach, defrosted
      and pressed in a strainer to drain
3   eggs
1   pint cottage cheese
1   cup cream
3/4   cup grated Parmesan cheese
1/4   cup chopped chives
      salt and pepper to taste

In a large bowl, stir together all the ingredients. Divide mixture between 8 buttered porcelain ramekins. Sprinkle tops with a little additional grated Parmesan cheese. Place ramekins in a pan with 1-inch hot water and bake in a 375° oven for about 25 minutes, or until a cake tester, inserted 1/2-inch off center, comes out clean. Serve directly from ramekins. Serves 8.

Note: -The ramekins are best freshly baked, but they can be prepared earlier in the
         day and heated at serving time.
       -If you feel you must unmold the ramekins, then they must be heavily
         buttered and dusted with breadcrumbs.

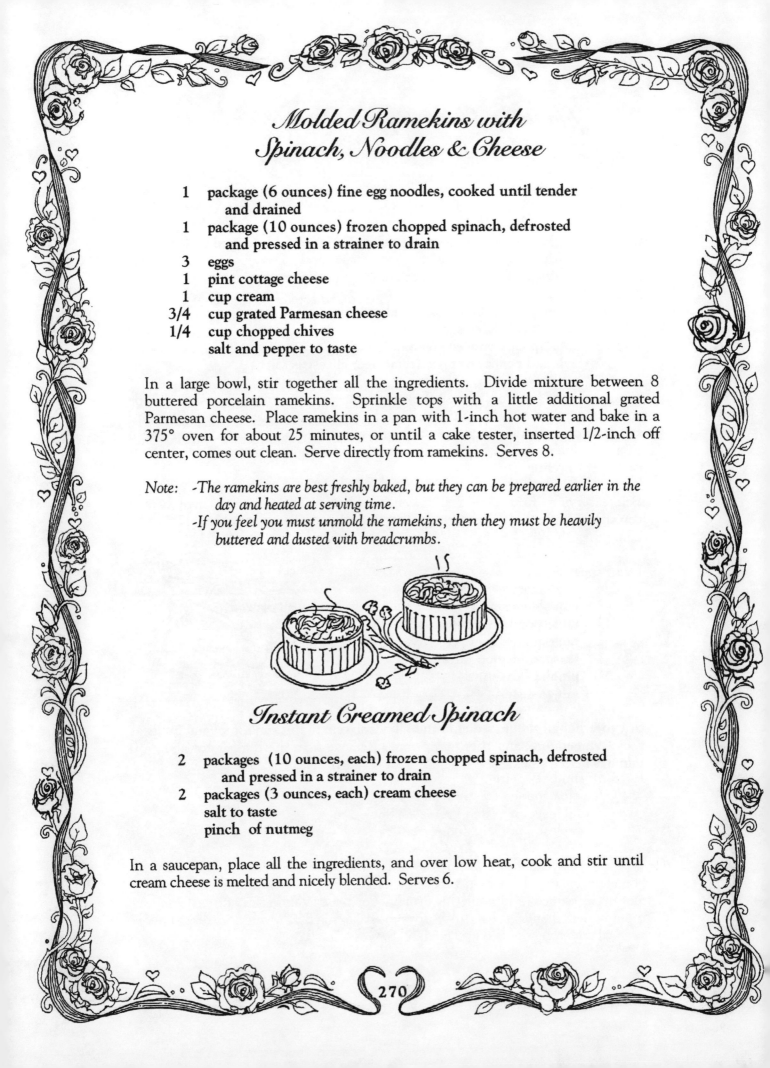

Instant Creamed Spinach

2   packages (10 ounces, each) frozen chopped spinach, defrosted
      and pressed in a strainer to drain
2   packages (3 ounces, each) cream cheese
      salt to taste
      pinch of nutmeg

In a saucepan, place all the ingredients, and over low heat, cook and stir until cream cheese is melted and nicely blended. Serves 6.

Old-Fashioned Tomatoes Stuffed with Rice, Tomatoes & Garlic

I love stuffed tomatoes...as a first course or as an accompaniment to dinner. When we visited Italy, I ate one practically every day. These are very much like the ones we enjoyed, simple, pure flavored and with a delicious sauce.

12   medium tomatoes (about 3 pounds). Cut a 1/2-inch slice from the top. Scoop out the centers with a grapefruit knife or a teaspoon. Reserve tomato pulp.

Tomato & Rice Filling:
2 1/2   cups cooked rice (see below)
       Reserved tomato pulp, chopped, (discard seeds)
1   tablespoon oil
1   small onion, grated
1   teaspoon dried sweet basil flakes
3   tablespoons minced parsley
2   cloves garlic, minced
    salt and freshly ground pepper to taste

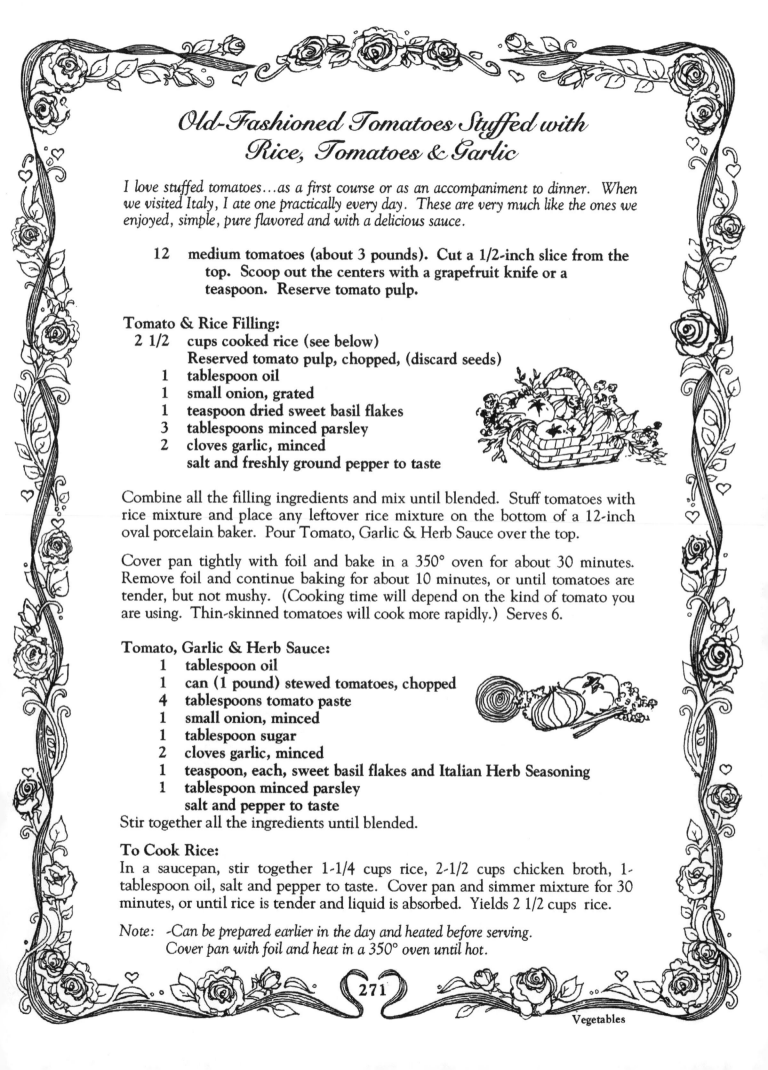

Combine all the filling ingredients and mix until blended. Stuff tomatoes with rice mixture and place any leftover rice mixture on the bottom of a 12-inch oval porcelain baker. Pour Tomato, Garlic & Herb Sauce over the top.

Cover pan tightly with foil and bake in a 350° oven for about 30 minutes. Remove foil and continue baking for about 10 minutes, or until tomatoes are tender, but not mushy. (Cooking time will depend on the kind of tomato you are using. Thin-skinned tomatoes will cook more rapidly.) Serves 6.

Tomato, Garlic & Herb Sauce:
1   tablespoon oil
1   can (1 pound) stewed tomatoes, chopped
4   tablespoons tomato paste
1   small onion, minced
1   tablespoon sugar
2   cloves garlic, minced
1   teaspoon, each, sweet basil flakes and Italian Herb Seasoning
1   tablespoon minced parsley
    salt and pepper to taste
Stir together all the ingredients until blended.

To Cook Rice:
In a saucepan, stir together 1-1/4 cups rice, 2-1/2 cups chicken broth, 1-tablespoon oil, salt and pepper to taste. Cover pan and simmer mixture for 30 minutes, or until rice is tender and liquid is absorbed. Yields 2 1/2 cups rice.

Note: -Can be prepared earlier in the day and heated before serving.
    Cover pan with foil and heat in a 350° oven until hot.

Vegetables

Zucchini Casserole with Cheese, Onions & Garlic

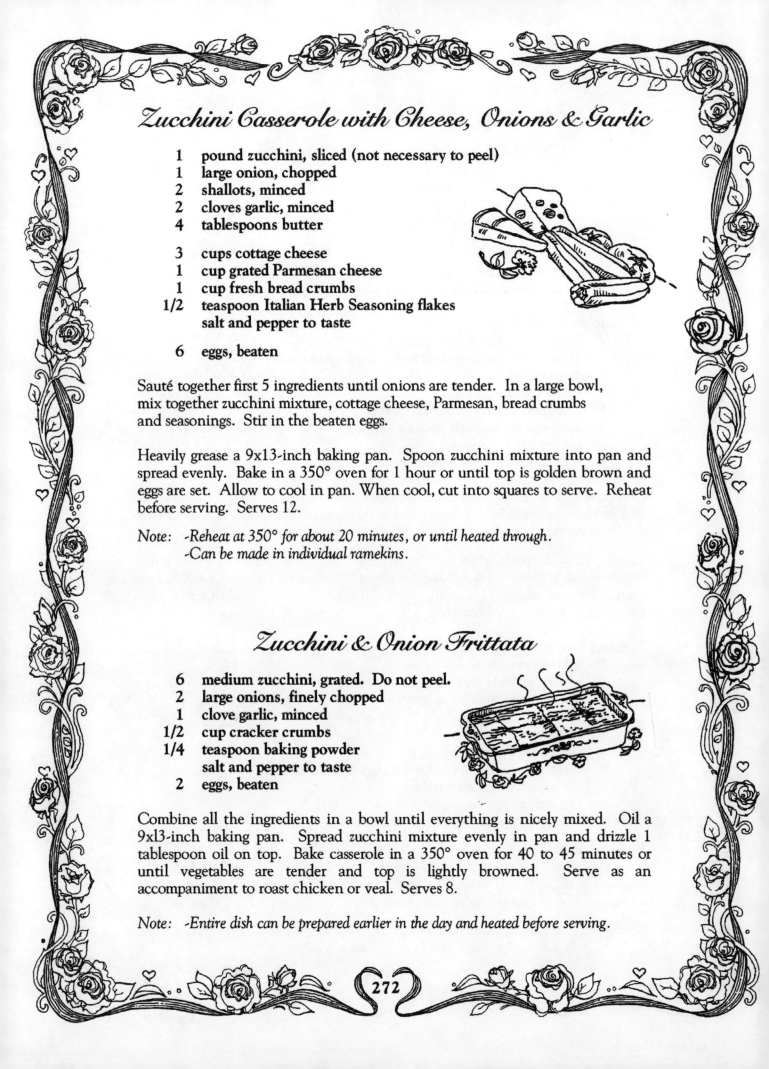

1	pound zucchini, sliced (not necessary to peel)
1	large onion, chopped
2	shallots, minced
2	cloves garlic, minced
4	tablespoons butter
3	cups cottage cheese
1	cup grated Parmesan cheese
1	cup fresh bread crumbs
1/2	teaspoon Italian Herb Seasoning flakes
	salt and pepper to taste
6	eggs, beaten

Sauté together first 5 ingredients until onions are tender. In a large bowl, mix together zucchini mixture, cottage cheese, Parmesan, bread crumbs and seasonings. Stir in the beaten eggs.

Heavily grease a 9x13-inch baking pan. Spoon zucchini mixture into pan and spread evenly. Bake in a 350° oven for 1 hour or until top is golden brown and eggs are set. Allow to cool in pan. When cool, cut into squares to serve. Reheat before serving. Serves 12.

Note: -Reheat at 350° for about 20 minutes, or until heated through.
        -Can be made in individual ramekins.

Zucchini & Onion Frittata

6	medium zucchini, grated. Do not peel.
2	large onions, finely chopped
1	clove garlic, minced
1/2	cup cracker crumbs
1/4	teaspoon baking powder
	salt and pepper to taste
2	eggs, beaten

Combine all the ingredients in a bowl until everything is nicely mixed. Oil a 9x13-inch baking pan. Spread zucchini mixture evenly in pan and drizzle 1 tablespoon oil on top. Bake casserole in a 350° oven for 40 to 45 minutes or until vegetables are tender and top is lightly browned. Serve as an accompaniment to roast chicken or veal. Serves 8.

Note: -Entire dish can be prepared earlier in the day and heated before serving.

Desserts

Cakes & Tortes

Candy

Cheesecake

Cookies

Fruit

Ice Cream & Ices

Pies, Tarts & Cobblers

Puddings

Soufflés

Strudels & Danish

Chocolate Decadence with Fudge Glaze

Deep, dark, delicious and totally decadent, is this moist chocolate cake, sparkled with the flavor of apricot and chocolate and beautiful with its dark, shiny chocolate glaze. Save this recipe for the special moments, as this is what chocolate dreams are made of.

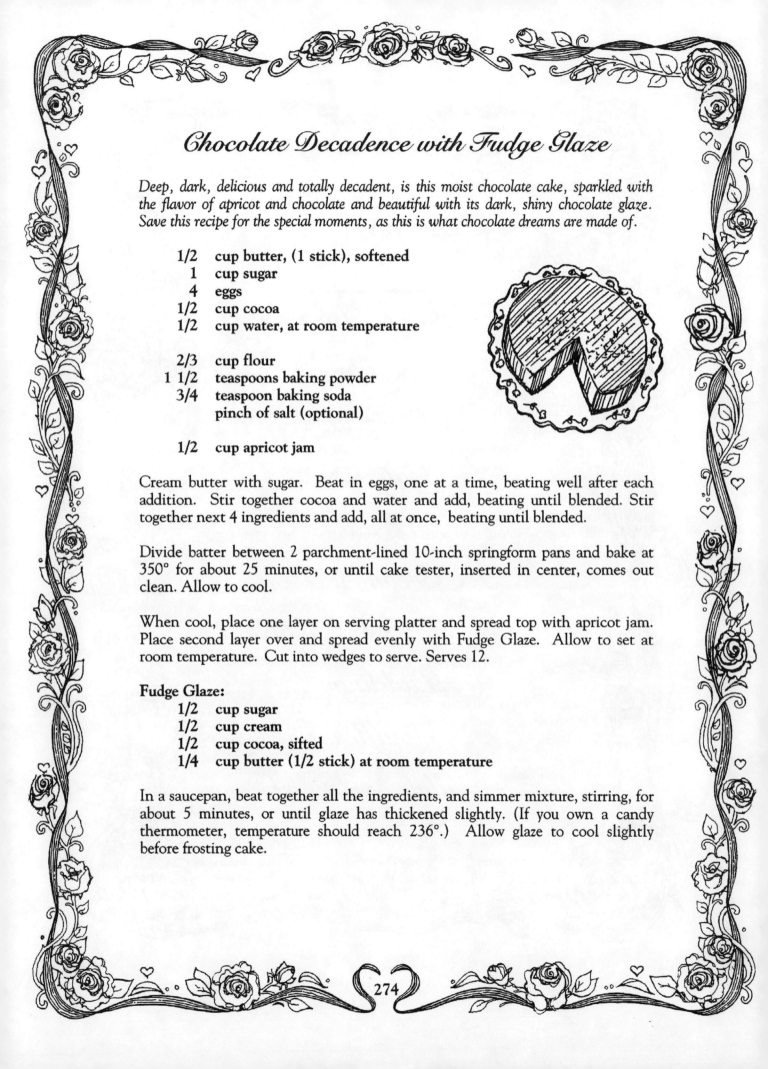

1/2	cup butter, (1 stick), softened
1	cup sugar
4	eggs
1/2	cup cocoa
1/2	cup water, at room temperature
2/3	cup flour
1 1/2	teaspoons baking powder
3/4	teaspoon baking soda
	pinch of salt (optional)
1/2	cup apricot jam

Cream butter with sugar. Beat in eggs, one at a time, beating well after each addition. Stir together cocoa and water and add, beating until blended. Stir together next 4 ingredients and add, all at once, beating until blended.

Divide batter between 2 parchment-lined 10-inch springform pans and bake at 350° for about 25 minutes, or until cake tester, inserted in center, comes out clean. Allow to cool.

When cool, place one layer on serving platter and spread top with apricot jam. Place second layer over and spread evenly with Fudge Glaze. Allow to set at room temperature. Cut into wedges to serve. Serves 12.

Fudge Glaze:

1/2	cup sugar
1/2	cup cream
1/2	cup cocoa, sifted
1/4	cup butter (1/2 stick) at room temperature

In a saucepan, beat together all the ingredients, and simmer mixture, stirring, for about 5 minutes, or until glaze has thickened slightly. (If you own a candy thermometer, temperature should reach 236°.) Allow glaze to cool slightly before frosting cake.

Fantastic Spiced Orange Cake with Orange Glaze

This is a very flavorful, super marvelous cake, flavored with orange and yogurt and spices. The walnuts and currants add a great balance of texture.

3	eggs
1	cup sugar
3/4	cup oil
1/2	cup unflavored yogurt
1	medium orange, cut into 8 pieces, about 6 tablespoons

2 1/2	cups flour
2	teaspoons baking powder
1	teaspoon baking soda
1 12	teaspoons pumpkin pie spice
1	cup chopped walnuts
1/2	cup dried currants

In the bowl of a food processor, place first 5 ingredients and blend until orange is very finely chopped, but not pureed.

In the large bowl of an electric mixer, stir together the remaining ingredients. Add the orange mixture and beat until blended. Do not overbeat. Spread batter into a greased 10-inch tube pan and bake in a 350° oven for about 40 to 45 minutes, or until a cake tester, inserted in center, comes out clean. Allow to cool in pan.

When cool, drizzle top with Orange Glaze, allowing some to drip down the sides. Serves 10.

Orange Glaze:

1	tablespoon orange juice
1/2	cup sifted powdered sugar
2	teaspoons grated orange peel

Stir together orange juice and sugar until blended. Stir in the orange peel until blended.

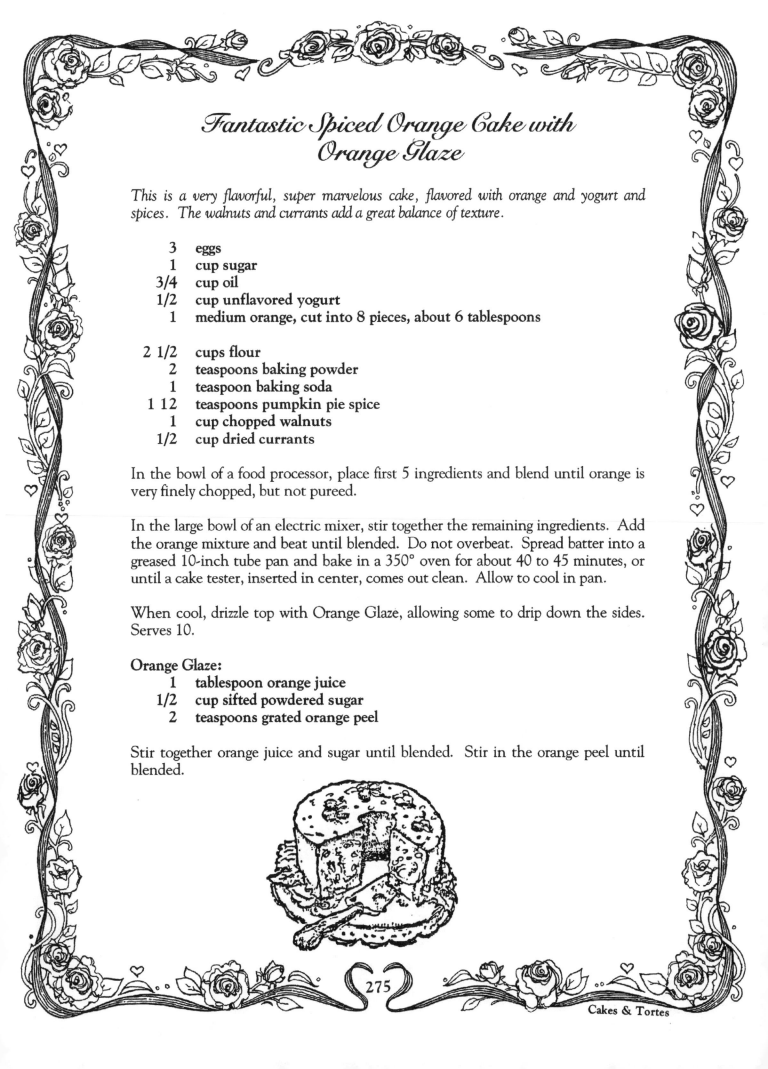

275

Imperial Chocolate Torte
with Apricot & Chocolate Buttercream

This dark, dense chocolate cake is combined with the flavor of apricot. The cake is highly textured and the smooth chocolate buttercream adds the perfect balance. This is a grand finale for a dinner party. This is another torte that can be made in a matter of minutes.

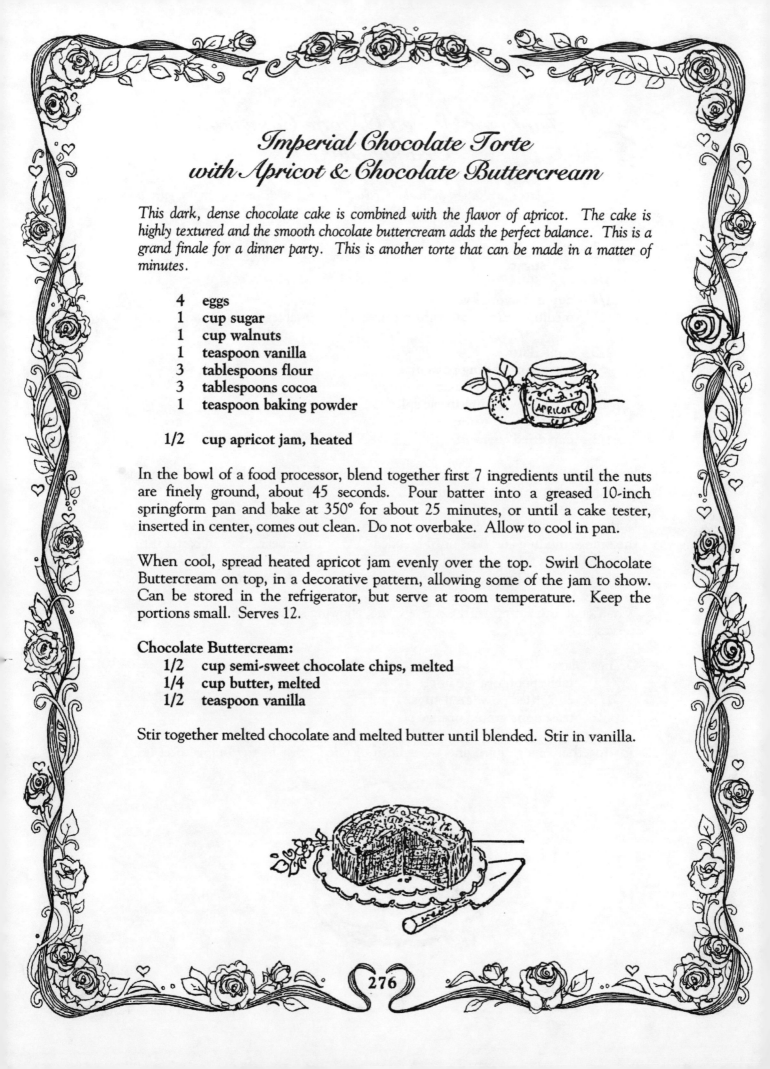

4	eggs
1	cup sugar
1	cup walnuts
1	teaspoon vanilla
3	tablespoons flour
3	tablespoons cocoa
1	teaspoon baking powder
1/2	cup apricot jam, heated

In the bowl of a food processor, blend together first 7 ingredients until the nuts are finely ground, about 45 seconds. Pour batter into a greased 10-inch springform pan and bake at 350° for about 25 minutes, or until a cake tester, inserted in center, comes out clean. Do not overbake. Allow to cool in pan.

When cool, spread heated apricot jam evenly over the top. Swirl Chocolate Buttercream on top, in a decorative pattern, allowing some of the jam to show. Can be stored in the refrigerator, but serve at room temperature. Keep the portions small. Serves 12.

Chocolate Buttercream:
1/2	cup semi-sweet chocolate chips, melted
1/4	cup butter, melted
1/2	teaspoon vanilla

Stir together melted chocolate and melted butter until blended. Stir in vanilla.

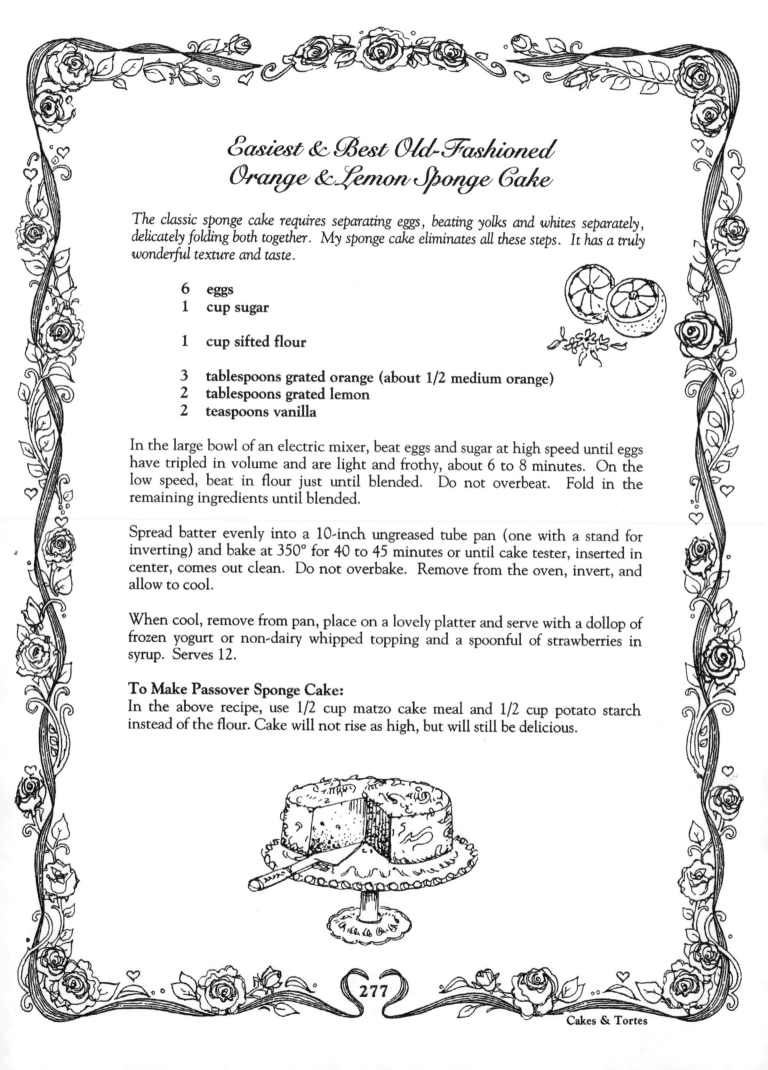

Easiest & Best Old-Fashioned
Orange & Lemon Sponge Cake

The classic sponge cake requires separating eggs, beating yolks and whites separately, delicately folding both together. My sponge cake eliminates all these steps. It has a truly wonderful texture and taste.

6	eggs
1	cup sugar
1	cup sifted flour
3	tablespoons grated orange (about 1/2 medium orange)
2	tablespoons grated lemon
2	teaspoons vanilla

In the large bowl of an electric mixer, beat eggs and sugar at high speed until eggs have tripled in volume and are light and frothy, about 6 to 8 minutes. On the low speed, beat in flour just until blended. Do not overbeat. Fold in the remaining ingredients until blended.

Spread batter evenly into a 10-inch ungreased tube pan (one with a stand for inverting) and bake at 350° for 40 to 45 minutes or until cake tester, inserted in center, comes out clean. Do not overbake. Remove from the oven, invert, and allow to cool.

When cool, remove from pan, place on a lovely platter and serve with a dollop of frozen yogurt or non-dairy whipped topping and a spoonful of strawberries in syrup. Serves 12.

To Make Passover Sponge Cake:
In the above recipe, use 1/2 cup matzo cake meal and 1/2 cup potato starch instead of the flour. Cake will not rise as high, but will still be delicious.

Cakes & Tortes

Easiest & Best
Walnut & Raspberry Torte with Lemon Glaze

This marvelous nut cake, accented with raspberry jam and complemented with lemon is a beautiful balance of flavors. Best of all, it can be prepared in minutes in a food processor. The results will truly amaze you.

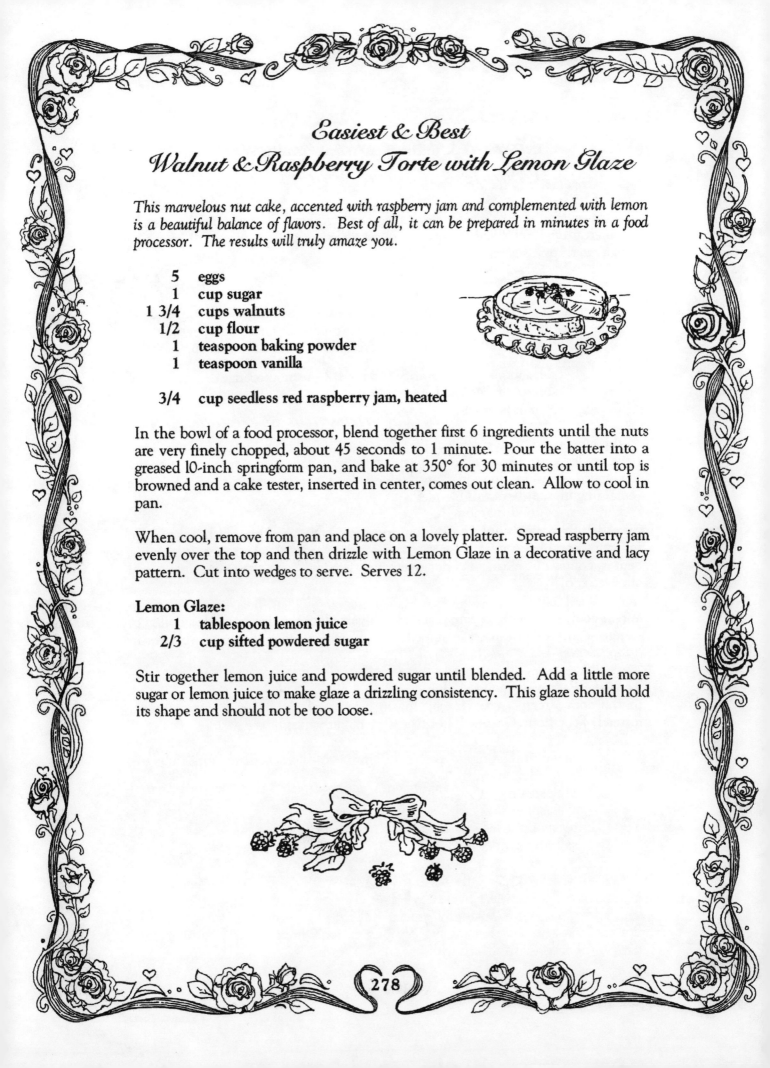

5	eggs
1	cup sugar
1 3/4	cups walnuts
1/2	cup flour
1	teaspoon baking powder
1	teaspoon vanilla
3/4	cup seedless red raspberry jam, heated

In the bowl of a food processor, blend together first 6 ingredients until the nuts are very finely chopped, about 45 seconds to 1 minute. Pour the batter into a greased 10-inch springform pan, and bake at 350° for 30 minutes or until top is browned and a cake tester, inserted in center, comes out clean. Allow to cool in pan.

When cool, remove from pan and place on a lovely platter. Spread raspberry jam evenly over the top and then drizzle with Lemon Glaze in a decorative and lacy pattern. Cut into wedges to serve. Serves 12.

Lemon Glaze:
1	tablespoon lemon juice
2/3	cup sifted powdered sugar

Stir together lemon juice and powdered sugar until blended. Add a little more sugar or lemon juice to make glaze a drizzling consistency. This glaze should hold its shape and should not be too loose.

Viennese Apple & Orange Pecan Torte
with Orange Peel Glaze

This little gem was fashioned after a delicious cake we enjoyed in Vienna. It is a rather dense cake, very moist and fruity. Not the least of its virtues is the fact that it can be prepared in minutes in the food processor...including chopping the fruit and nuts. The Orange Peel Glaze adds a little bite, which is a lovely balance.

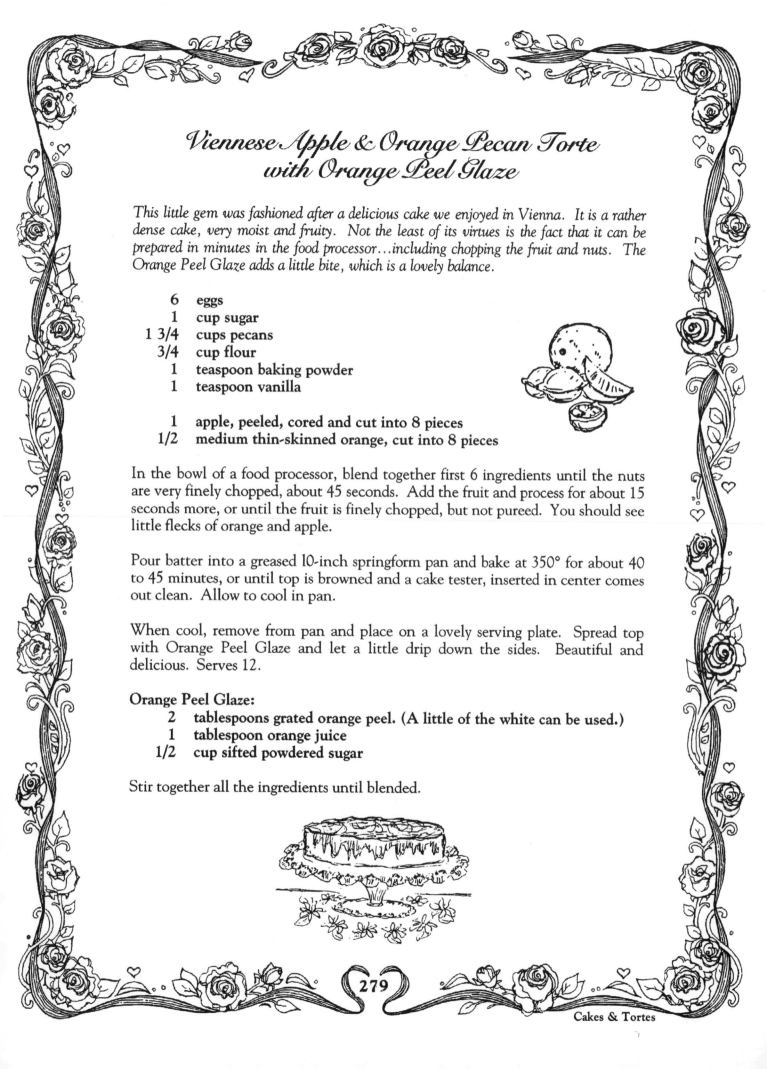

6	eggs
1	cup sugar
1 3/4	cups pecans
3/4	cup flour
1	teaspoon baking powder
1	teaspoon vanilla
1	apple, peeled, cored and cut into 8 pieces
1/2	medium thin-skinned orange, cut into 8 pieces

In the bowl of a food processor, blend together first 6 ingredients until the nuts are very finely chopped, about 45 seconds. Add the fruit and process for about 15 seconds more, or until the fruit is finely chopped, but not pureed. You should see little flecks of orange and apple.

Pour batter into a greased 10-inch springform pan and bake at 350° for about 40 to 45 minutes, or until top is browned and a cake tester, inserted in center comes out clean. Allow to cool in pan.

When cool, remove from pan and place on a lovely serving plate. Spread top with Orange Peel Glaze and let a little drip down the sides. Beautiful and delicious. Serves 12.

Orange Peel Glaze:

2	tablespoons grated orange peel. (A little of the white can be used.)
1	tablespoon orange juice
1/2	cup sifted powdered sugar

Stir together all the ingredients until blended.

Cakes & Tortes

Chocolate Fudge Torte with Chocolate Glaze

This is one of the easiest and best cakes that you can prepare. It is a moist and tender chocolate cake. Don't be misled by its simplicity. It is a fine tasting torte, takes minutes to assemble, can be made ahead and, not the least of its virtues, it freezes beautifully.

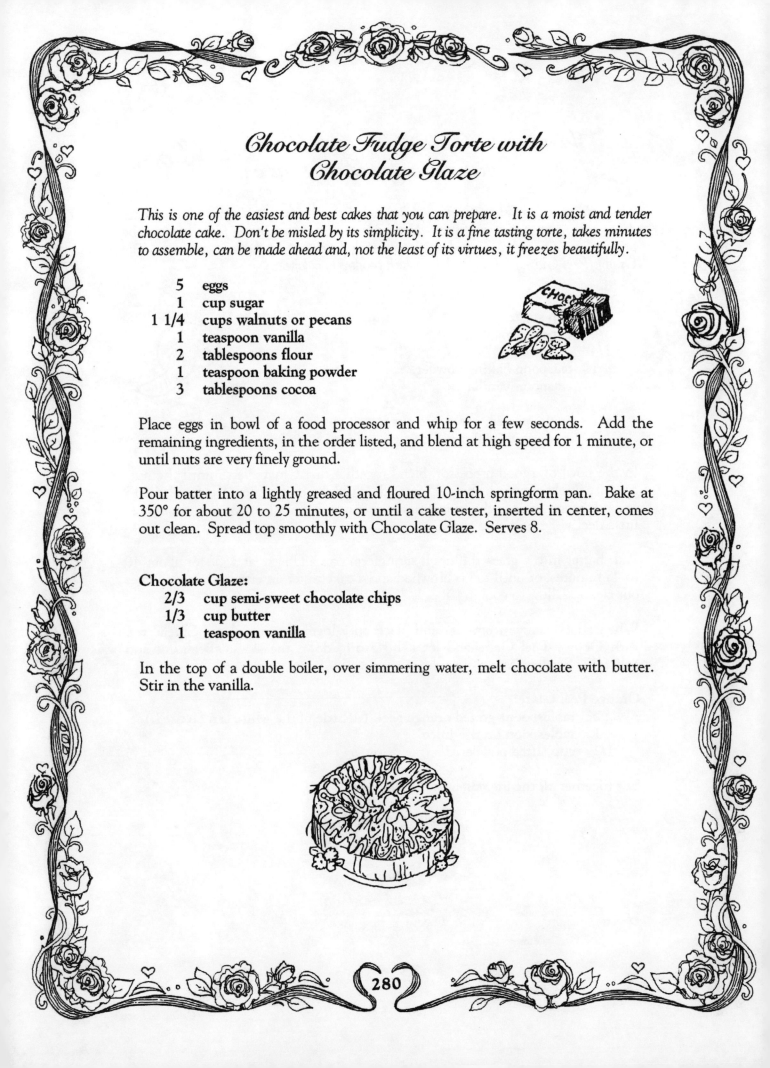

5	eggs
1	cup sugar
1 1/4	cups walnuts or pecans
1	teaspoon vanilla
2	tablespoons flour
1	teaspoon baking powder
3	tablespoons cocoa

Place eggs in bowl of a food processor and whip for a few seconds. Add the remaining ingredients, in the order listed, and blend at high speed for 1 minute, or until nuts are very finely ground.

Pour batter into a lightly greased and floured 10-inch springform pan. Bake at 350° for about 20 to 25 minutes, or until a cake tester, inserted in center, comes out clean. Spread top smoothly with Chocolate Glaze. Serves 8.

Chocolate Glaze:

2/3	cup semi-sweet chocolate chips
1/3	cup butter
1	teaspoon vanilla

In the top of a double boiler, over simmering water, melt chocolate with butter. Stir in the vanilla.

Chocolate Torte with Apricot & Cocoa Buttercream

These few simple cupboard ingredients, produce the finest tasting chocolate cake. This is one of my favorites. The first amount of nuts acts like the flour in the cake. The second amount of nuts is for texture. The Cocoa Buttercream, for some reason, is the perfect balance of flavors, for my taste. It is a low cake, so don't think anything went wrong.

4	eggs
1	cup sugar
3	tablespoons flour
1 1/4	cups chopped walnuts
2	tablespoons cocoa
1	teaspoon baking powder
1	teaspoon vanilla

1/3	cup chopped walnuts
1/2	cup apricot jam

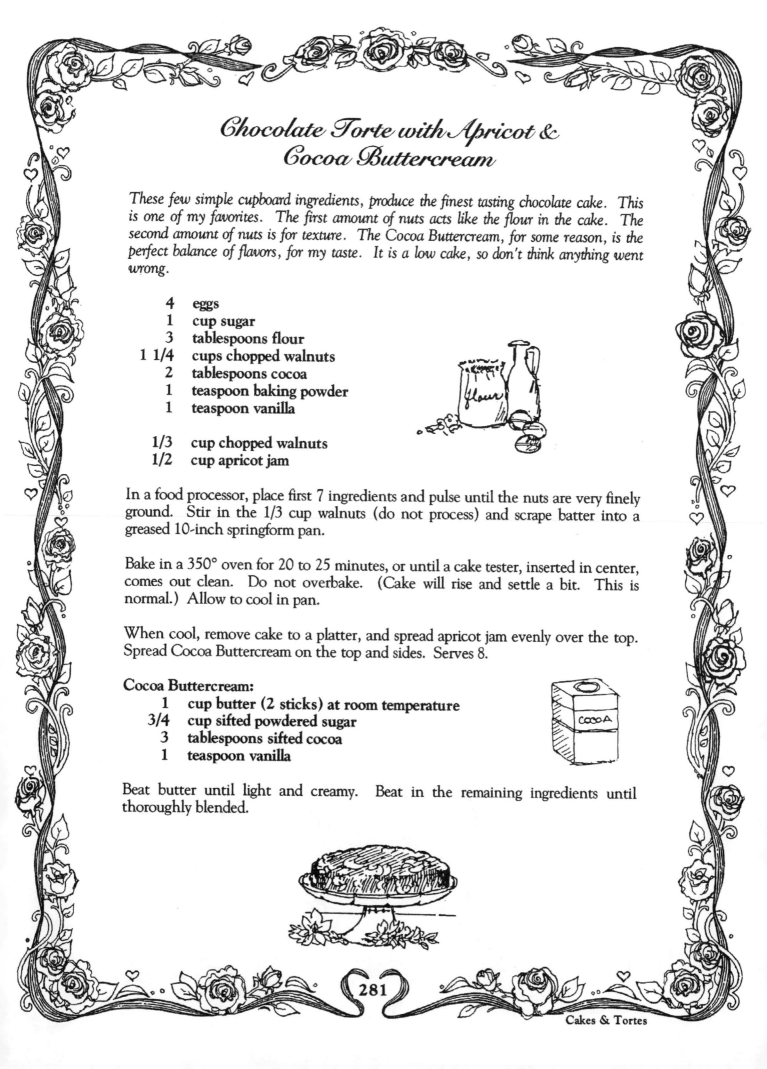

In a food processor, place first 7 ingredients and pulse until the nuts are very finely ground. Stir in the 1/3 cup walnuts (do not process) and scrape batter into a greased 10-inch springform pan.

Bake in a 350° oven for 20 to 25 minutes, or until a cake tester, inserted in center, comes out clean. Do not overbake. (Cake will rise and settle a bit. This is normal.) Allow to cool in pan.

When cool, remove cake to a platter, and spread apricot jam evenly over the top. Spread Cocoa Buttercream on the top and sides. Serves 8.

Cocoa Buttercream:

1	cup butter (2 sticks) at room temperature
3/4	cup sifted powdered sugar
3	tablespoons sifted cocoa
1	teaspoon vanilla

Beat butter until light and creamy. Beat in the remaining ingredients until thoroughly blended.

Pecan Torte with Raspberry & Lemon Glaze

This is one of my very best nut cakes and one of the very best, too. Raspberry jam is wonderful with this and the Lemon Glaze adds just the right tartness.

5	eggs
1 1/2	cups pecans
1	cup sugar
1	teaspoon vanilla
4	tablespoons flour
1	teaspoon baking powder
1/2	cup seedless red raspberry jam, heated

Place first 6 ingredients in a food processor and blend for 1 minute, or until pecans are very finely ground. Pour batter into a greased 10-inch springform pan and bake in a 350° oven for about 30 minutes, or until top is lightly browned, and a cake tester, inserted in center, comes out clean. Do not overbake.

Allow to cool in pan. When cool, spread top with raspberry jam (heating makes it easier to spread). Drizzle top with Lemon Glaze, in a lacy pattern, and allow some of the jam to show. Serves 8.

Lemon Glaze:

1	tablespoon lemon juice
1/2	cup sifted powdered sugar

Stir together lemon juice and powdered sugar until blended. Add a little lemon juice or powdered sugar to make glaze a drizzling consistency.

Note: -Cake can be baked and glazed 1 day earlier. To store, place 4 or 5 toothpicks on cake and cover loosely with plastic wrap. Remove toothpicks and plastic wrap (of course) to serve.

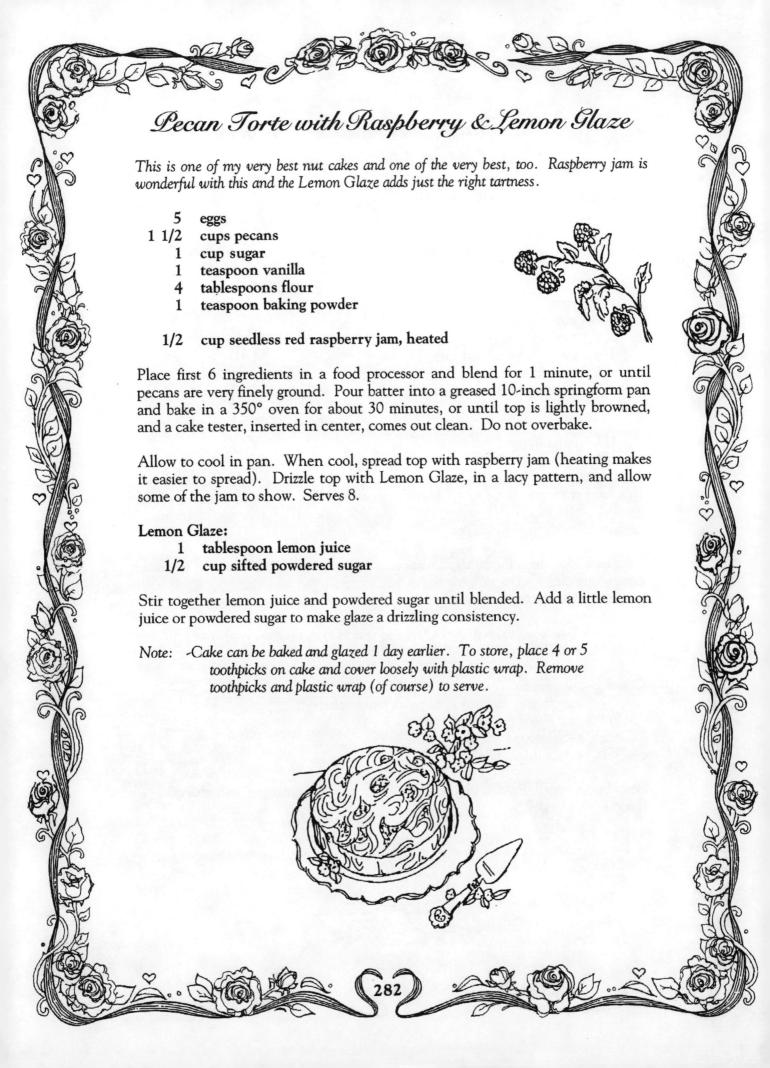

Cranberry, Orange & Lemon Tea Cake with Orange Lemon Wash

This is a tart, fruity cake, very chunky and simply delicious. When cranberries are in season, buy extras, for they freeze well. And, then, you can enjoy this lovely cake, at other times during the year.

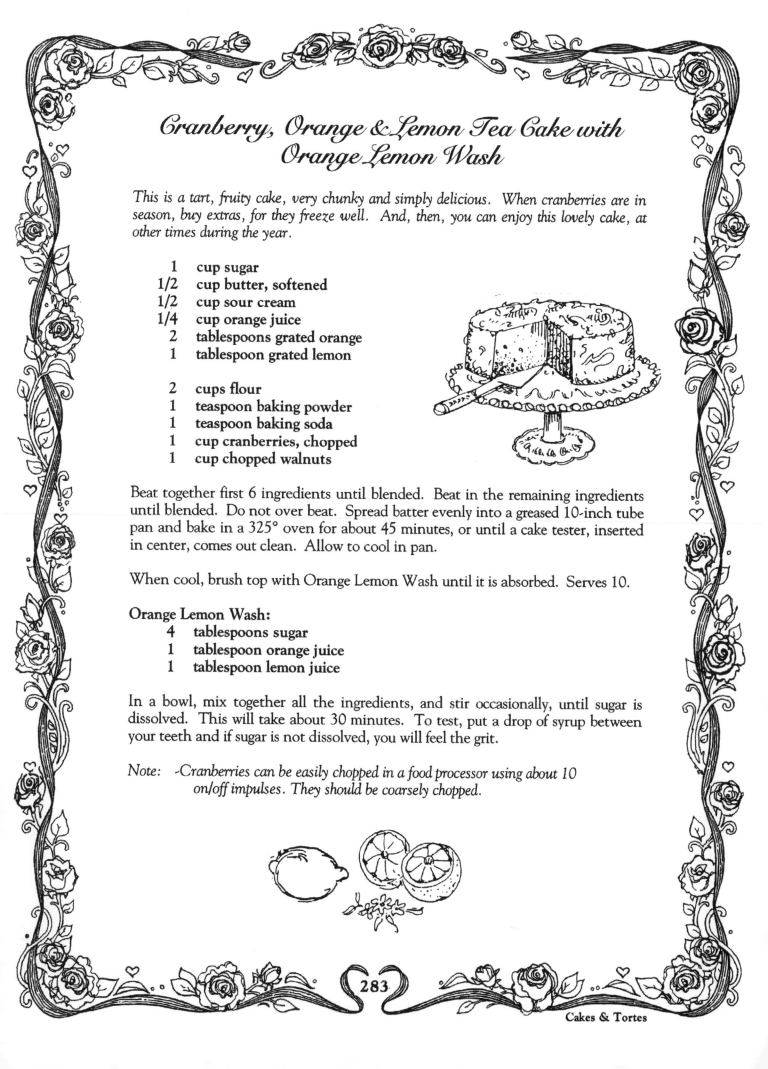

1	cup sugar
1/2	cup butter, softened
1/2	cup sour cream
1/4	cup orange juice
2	tablespoons grated orange
1	tablespoon grated lemon
2	cups flour
1	teaspoon baking powder
1	teaspoon baking soda
1	cup cranberries, chopped
1	cup chopped walnuts

Beat together first 6 ingredients until blended. Beat in the remaining ingredients until blended. Do not over beat. Spread batter evenly into a greased 10-inch tube pan and bake in a 325° oven for about 45 minutes, or until a cake tester, inserted in center, comes out clean. Allow to cool in pan.

When cool, brush top with Orange Lemon Wash until it is absorbed. Serves 10.

Orange Lemon Wash:
4	tablespoons sugar
1	tablespoon orange juice
1	tablespoon lemon juice

In a bowl, mix together all the ingredients, and stir occasionally, until sugar is dissolved. This will take about 30 minutes. To test, put a drop of syrup between your teeth and if sugar is not dissolved, you will feel the grit.

Note: Cranberries can be easily chopped in a food processor using about 10 on/off impulses. They should be coarsely chopped.

California Carrot Cake with Pineapple, Coconut & Walnuts

Some carrot cakes have pineapple or coconut or walnuts for additional excitement and interest. This carrot cake has all of these and it is very good, indeed. Cream Cheese Frosting is really the best frosting for this cake. This recipe produces 2 good-sized cakes. Use one and freeze the other.

4	eggs
1 1/4	cups oil
2	cups sugar
2	teaspoons vanilla
2	cups flour
2	teaspoons baking powder
1	teaspoon baking soda
1/4	teaspoon salt
2 1/2	teaspoons cinnamon
2 1/2	cups grated carrots
1	can (8 ounces) crushed pineapple, drained
1/2	cup coconut flakes
1	cup chopped walnuts

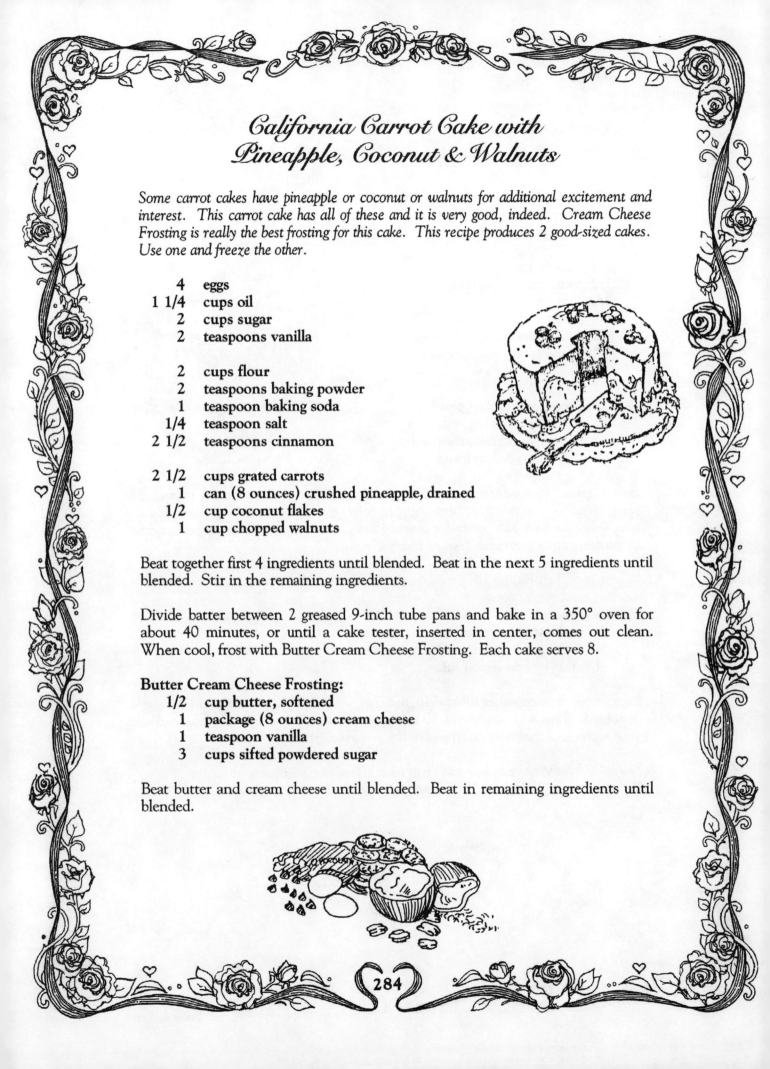

Beat together first 4 ingredients until blended. Beat in the next 5 ingredients until blended. Stir in the remaining ingredients.

Divide batter between 2 greased 9-inch tube pans and bake in a 350° oven for about 40 minutes, or until a cake tester, inserted in center, comes out clean. When cool, frost with Butter Cream Cheese Frosting. Each cake serves 8.

Butter Cream Cheese Frosting:

1/2	cup butter, softened
1	package (8 ounces) cream cheese
1	teaspoon vanilla
3	cups sifted powdered sugar

Beat butter and cream cheese until blended. Beat in remaining ingredients until blended.

Farmhouse Carrot Cake with Pineapple & Buttermilk Glaze

This is an old-fashioned cake with a very special touch. After baking, a delightful glaze made with buttermilk and honey and flavored with lemon is poured on top. This makes the cake exceedingly moist and it will last for days in the refrigerator.

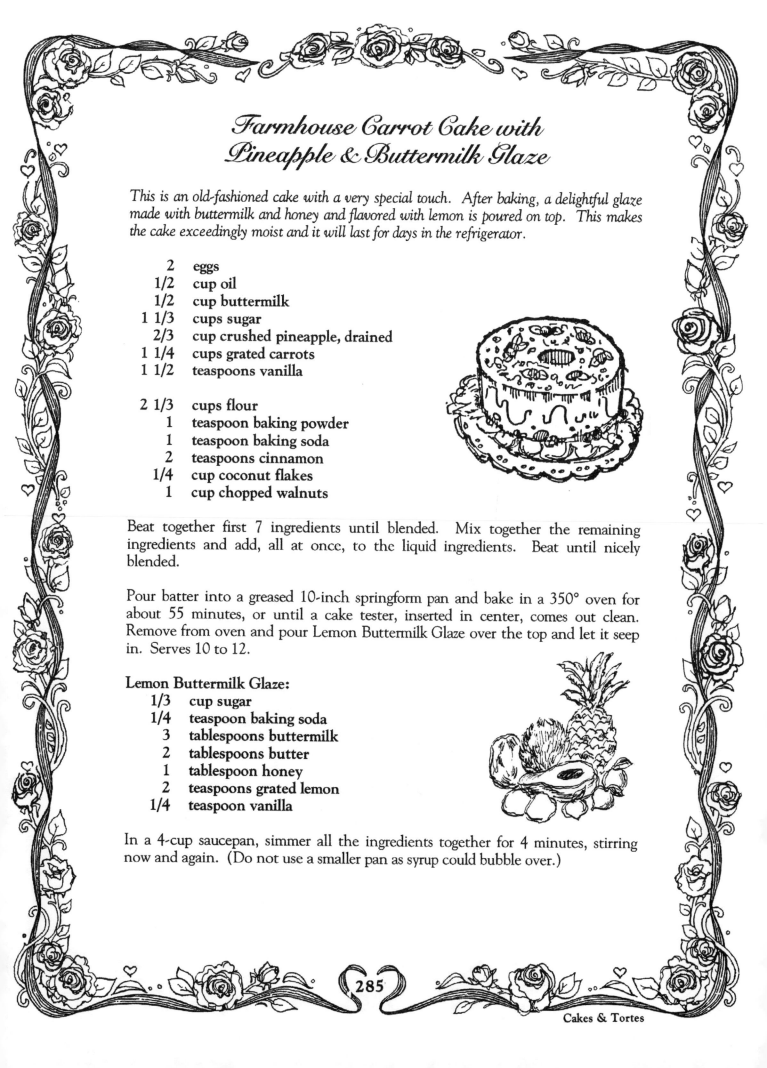

2	eggs
1/2	cup oil
1/2	cup buttermilk
1 1/3	cups sugar
2/3	cup crushed pineapple, drained
1 1/4	cups grated carrots
1 1/2	teaspoons vanilla
2 1/3	cups flour
1	teaspoon baking powder
1	teaspoon baking soda
2	teaspoons cinnamon
1/4	cup coconut flakes
1	cup chopped walnuts

Beat together first 7 ingredients until blended. Mix together the remaining ingredients and add, all at once, to the liquid ingredients. Beat until nicely blended.

Pour batter into a greased 10-inch springform pan and bake in a 350° oven for about 55 minutes, or until a cake tester, inserted in center, comes out clean. Remove from oven and pour Lemon Buttermilk Glaze over the top and let it seep in. Serves 10 to 12.

Lemon Buttermilk Glaze:

1/3	cup sugar
1/4	teaspoon baking soda
3	tablespoons buttermilk
2	tablespoons butter
1	tablespoon honey
2	teaspoons grated lemon
1/4	teaspoon vanilla

In a 4-cup saucepan, simmer all the ingredients together for 4 minutes, stirring now and again. (Do not use a smaller pan as syrup could bubble over.)

Cakes & Tortes

Easiest and Best Apple Cake with Orange & Pecans & Creamy Glaze

This little gem is truly a wonder. Place a few ingredients in your food processor and Voila! a fruity, nutty torte that is just bursting with moistness and flavor.

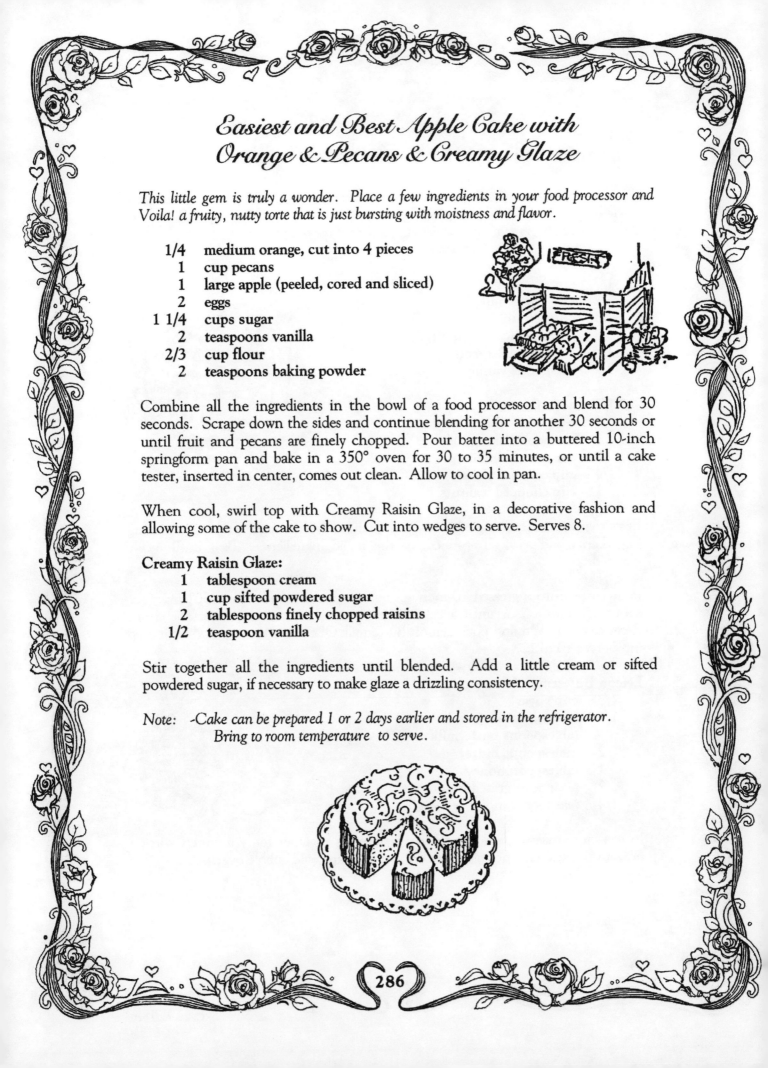

1/4	medium orange, cut into 4 pieces
1	cup pecans
1	large apple (peeled, cored and sliced)
2	eggs
1 1/4	cups sugar
2	teaspoons vanilla
2/3	cup flour
2	teaspoons baking powder

Combine all the ingredients in the bowl of a food processor and blend for 30 seconds. Scrape down the sides and continue blending for another 30 seconds or until fruit and pecans are finely chopped. Pour batter into a buttered 10-inch springform pan and bake in a 350° oven for 30 to 35 minutes, or until a cake tester, inserted in center, comes out clean. Allow to cool in pan.

When cool, swirl top with Creamy Raisin Glaze, in a decorative fashion and allowing some of the cake to show. Cut into wedges to serve. Serves 8.

Creamy Raisin Glaze:

1	tablespoon cream
1	cup sifted powdered sugar
2	tablespoons finely chopped raisins
1/2	teaspoon vanilla

Stir together all the ingredients until blended. Add a little cream or sifted powdered sugar, if necessary to make glaze a drizzling consistency.

Note: -Cake can be prepared 1 or 2 days earlier and stored in the refrigerator.
Bring to room temperature to serve.

286

Fresh Apple Sour Cream Cake with Buttermilk Glaze

Fresh apples, sour cream, cinnamon, raisins and walnuts all add to make this cake rich and flavorful. The Buttermilk Glaze adds the perfect tartness.

1 1/3	cups sugar
2/3	cup butter
3	eggs
1/2	cup sour cream
2	cups flour
2	teaspoons cinnamon
1	teaspoon baking powder
1/2	teaspoon baking soda
2	apples, peeled, cored and grated
2	cups chopped walnuts
3/4	cup yellow raisins
1	teaspoon vanilla

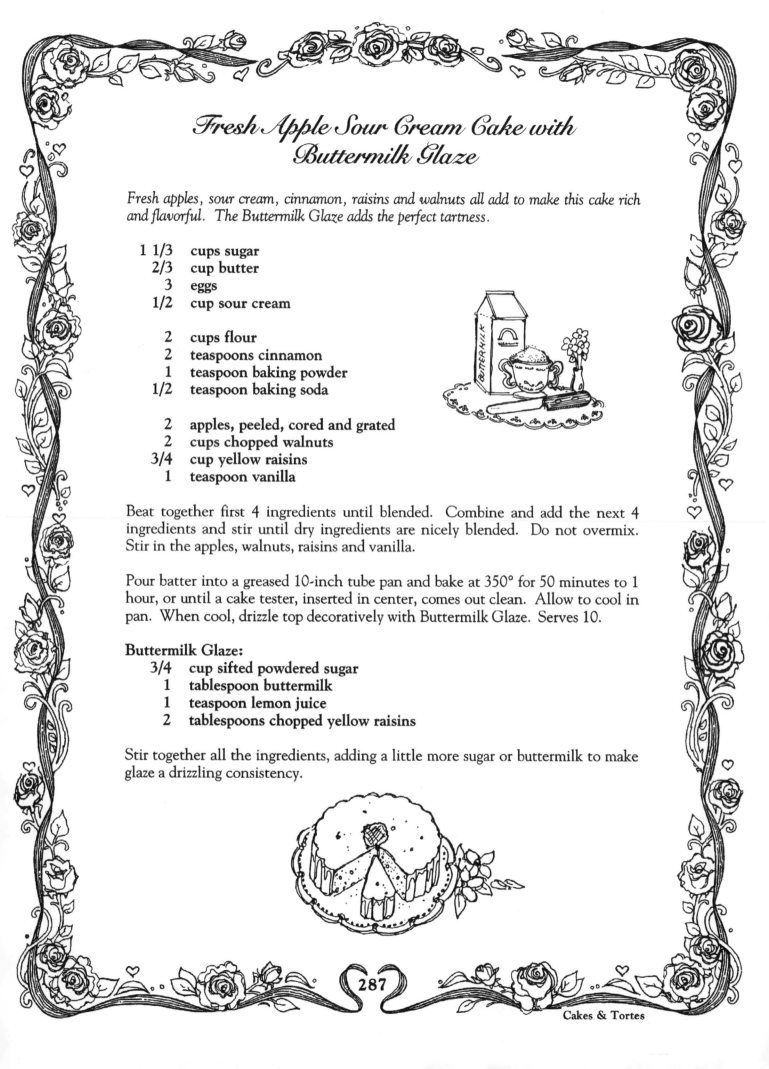

Beat together first 4 ingredients until blended. Combine and add the next 4 ingredients and stir until dry ingredients are nicely blended. Do not overmix. Stir in the apples, walnuts, raisins and vanilla.

Pour batter into a greased 10-inch tube pan and bake at 350° for 50 minutes to 1 hour, or until a cake tester, inserted in center, comes out clean. Allow to cool in pan. When cool, drizzle top decoratively with Buttermilk Glaze. Serves 10.

Buttermilk Glaze:

3/4	cup sifted powdered sugar
1	tablespoon buttermilk
1	teaspoon lemon juice
2	tablespoons chopped yellow raisins

Stir together all the ingredients, adding a little more sugar or buttermilk to make glaze a drizzling consistency.

Cakes & Tortes

Fantasy Cake with Chocolate, Coconut, & Walnuts

This cake is beautiful, delicious, easy to prepare, and a wonderful combination of tastes and textures. And starting with a cake mix will save you a great deal of time.

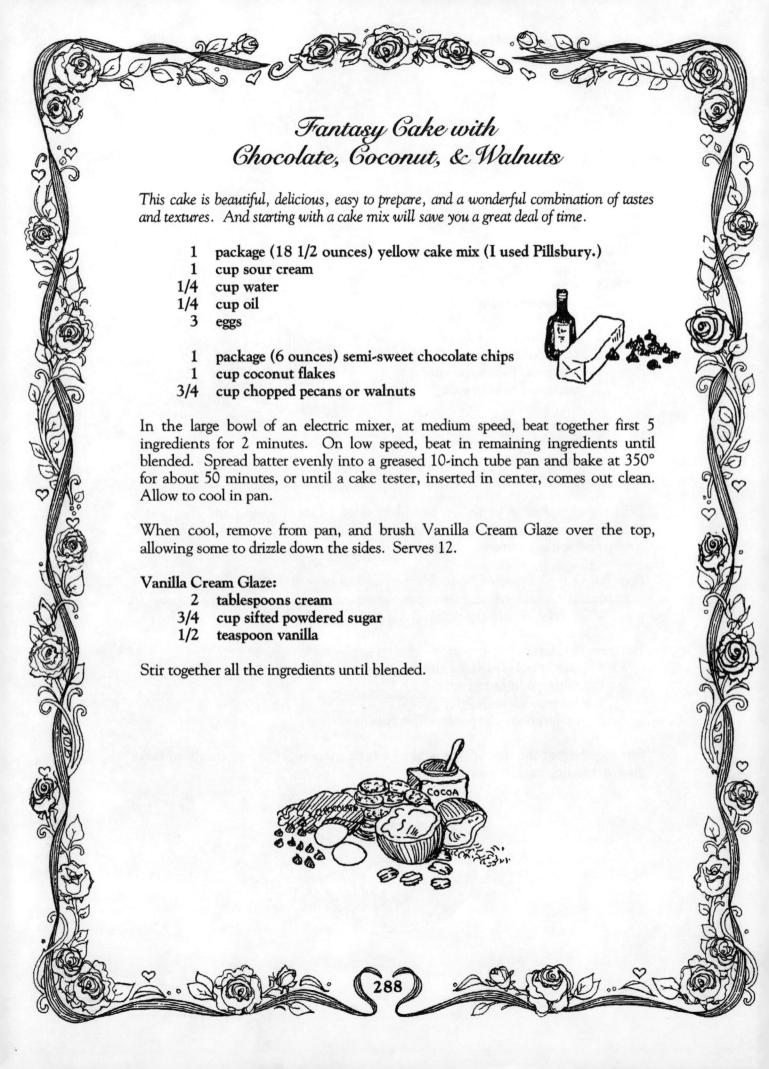

- 1   package (18 1/2 ounces) yellow cake mix (I used Pillsbury.)
- 1   cup sour cream
- 1/4   cup water
- 1/4   cup oil
- 3   eggs

- 1   package (6 ounces) semi-sweet chocolate chips
- 1   cup coconut flakes
- 3/4   cup chopped pecans or walnuts

In the large bowl of an electric mixer, at medium speed, beat together first 5 ingredients for 2 minutes. On low speed, beat in remaining ingredients until blended. Spread batter evenly into a greased 10-inch tube pan and bake at 350° for about 50 minutes, or until a cake tester, inserted in center, comes out clean. Allow to cool in pan.

When cool, remove from pan, and brush Vanilla Cream Glaze over the top, allowing some to drizzle down the sides. Serves 12.

Vanilla Cream Glaze:
- 2   tablespoons cream
- 3/4   cup sifted powdered sugar
- 1/2   teaspoon vanilla

Stir together all the ingredients until blended.

Black Cherry & Almond Cake
with Streusel Oat Topping

A hearty country cake with a streusel topping made with flour and oats, that is crunchy and delicious.

1/2	cup butter
1	cup sugar
2	eggs
2/3	cup sour cream
1	cup pitted black cherries (or Bing cherries), fresh or frozen
1	cup flour
1/2	cup whole wheat flour
1/2	cup quick-cooking oats
2	teaspoons baking powder
1	teaspoon baking soda
1	cup chopped toasted almonds

Beat together first 5 ingredients until blended. Combine and add the remaining ingredients and stir until nicely blended. Do not overmix.

Place batter into a greased 10-inch springform pan and sprinkle top with Streusel Oat Topping. Bake in a 350° oven for about 40 minutes, or until a cake tester, inserted in center, comes out clean. Allow to cool in pan. When cool, remove from pan and cut into wedges to serve. Serves 10.

Streusel Oat Topping:

1/4	cup butter
1/4	cup sugar
1/4	cup flour
1/4	cup quick-cooking oats
1/2	teaspoon cinnamon
	pinch of baking powder

Mix together all the ingredients until mixture is crumbly.

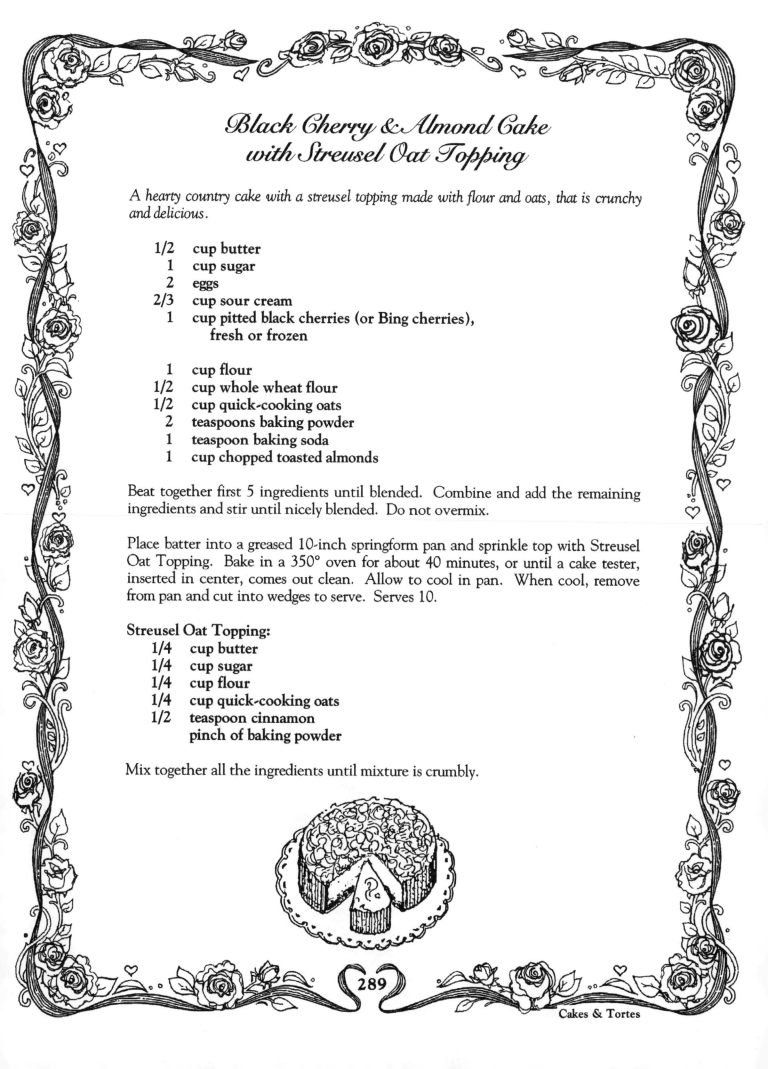

Cakes & Tortes

Greek Honey Nut Cake

This is a very unusual and interesting dessert that is especially nice for a dinner in a Greek mood. It is very different, but it does produce a marvelous dessert, that I am certain you will enjoy.

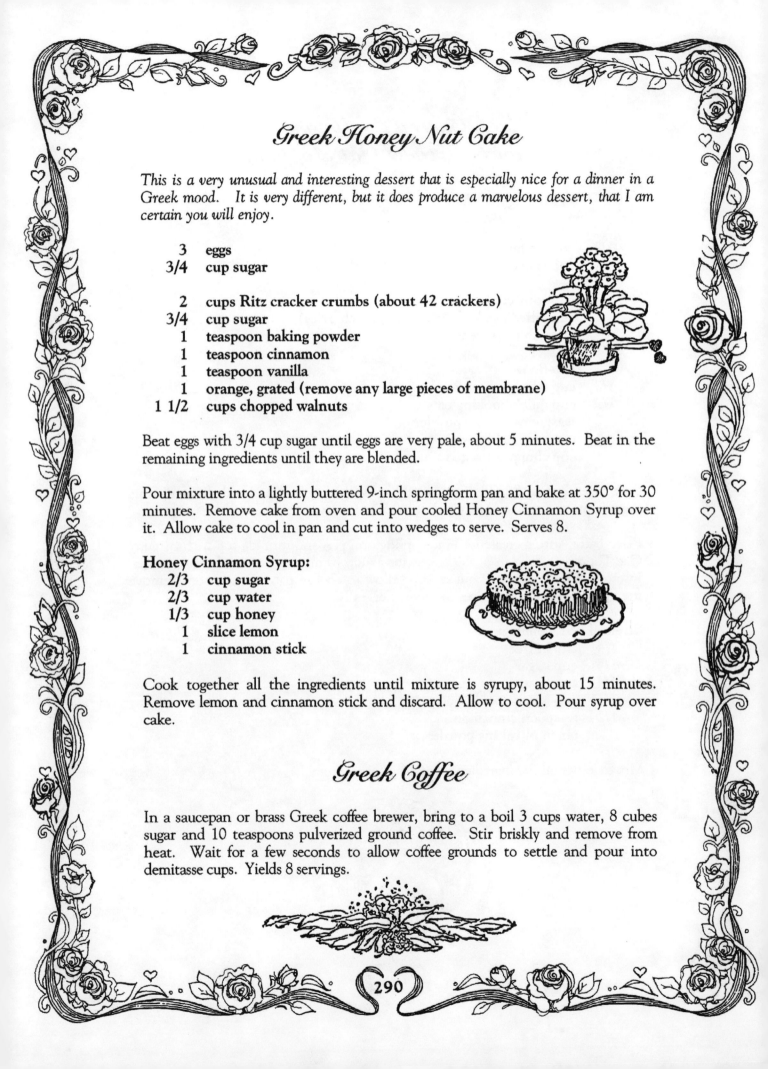

3	eggs
3/4	cup sugar
2	cups Ritz cracker crumbs (about 42 crackers)
3/4	cup sugar
1	teaspoon baking powder
1	teaspoon cinnamon
1	teaspoon vanilla
1	orange, grated (remove any large pieces of membrane)
1 1/2	cups chopped walnuts

Beat eggs with 3/4 cup sugar until eggs are very pale, about 5 minutes. Beat in the remaining ingredients until they are blended.

Pour mixture into a lightly buttered 9-inch springform pan and bake at 350° for 30 minutes. Remove cake from oven and pour cooled Honey Cinnamon Syrup over it. Allow cake to cool in pan and cut into wedges to serve. Serves 8.

Honey Cinnamon Syrup:

2/3	cup sugar
2/3	cup water
1/3	cup honey
1	slice lemon
1	cinnamon stick

Cook together all the ingredients until mixture is syrupy, about 15 minutes. Remove lemon and cinnamon stick and discard. Allow to cool. Pour syrup over cake.

Greek Coffee

In a saucepan or brass Greek coffee brewer, bring to a boil 3 cups water, 8 cubes sugar and 10 teaspoons pulverized ground coffee. Stir briskly and remove from heat. Wait for a few seconds to allow coffee grounds to settle and pour into demitasse cups. Yields 8 servings.

The Ultimate Scone Cakebread with Apricots and Walnuts

If you like the taste of dried apricots and the texture of scones made into a breakfast bread, I do believe you will love this recipe. It is dense, flavorful and the walnuts add a bit of crunch. Actually, it is not a bread, nor a cake, nor a scone, but can be served as any one of these. When you make it, you will see why.

3	cups flour
1/2	cup sugar
1	tablespoon baking powder
1/2	cup butter (1 stick), cut into the thinnest slices
1	cup chopped dried apricots
1	cup chopped walnuts
1	egg, beaten
3/4	cup milk
1/2	cup sour cream
1	teaspoon vanilla
1	tablespoon sugar

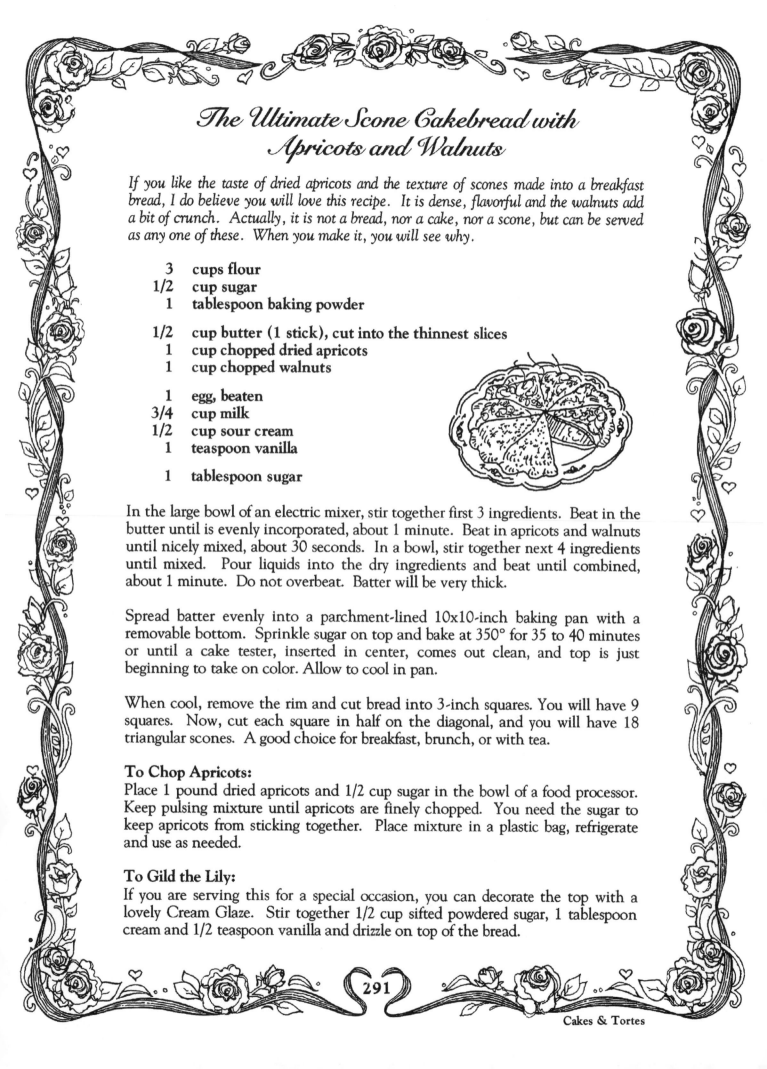

In the large bowl of an electric mixer, stir together first 3 ingredients. Beat in the butter until is evenly incorporated, about 1 minute. Beat in apricots and walnuts until nicely mixed, about 30 seconds. In a bowl, stir together next 4 ingredients until mixed. Pour liquids into the dry ingredients and beat until combined, about 1 minute. Do not overbeat. Batter will be very thick.

Spread batter evenly into a parchment-lined 10x10-inch baking pan with a removable bottom. Sprinkle sugar on top and bake at 350° for 35 to 40 minutes or until a cake tester, inserted in center, comes out clean, and top is just beginning to take on color. Allow to cool in pan.

When cool, remove the rim and cut bread into 3-inch squares. You will have 9 squares. Now, cut each square in half on the diagonal, and you will have 18 triangular scones. A good choice for breakfast, brunch, or with tea.

To Chop Apricots:
Place 1 pound dried apricots and 1/2 cup sugar in the bowl of a food processor. Keep pulsing mixture until apricots are finely chopped. You need the sugar to keep apricots from sticking together. Place mixture in a plastic bag, refrigerate and use as needed.

To Gild the Lily:
If you are serving this for a special occasion, you can decorate the top with a lovely Cream Glaze. Stir together 1/2 cup sifted powdered sugar, 1 tablespoon cream and 1/2 teaspoon vanilla and drizzle on top of the bread.

Cakes & Tortes

Applesauce Cake with Cloves

This is a very spicy cake, strong with the fragrance of cloves. It is a nice ending to a curry dinner. Cake can be prepared and glazed 1 day before serving.

1/2	cup butter	
1	cup sugar	
1	egg	
1/4	cup sour cream	
1	cup applesauce	

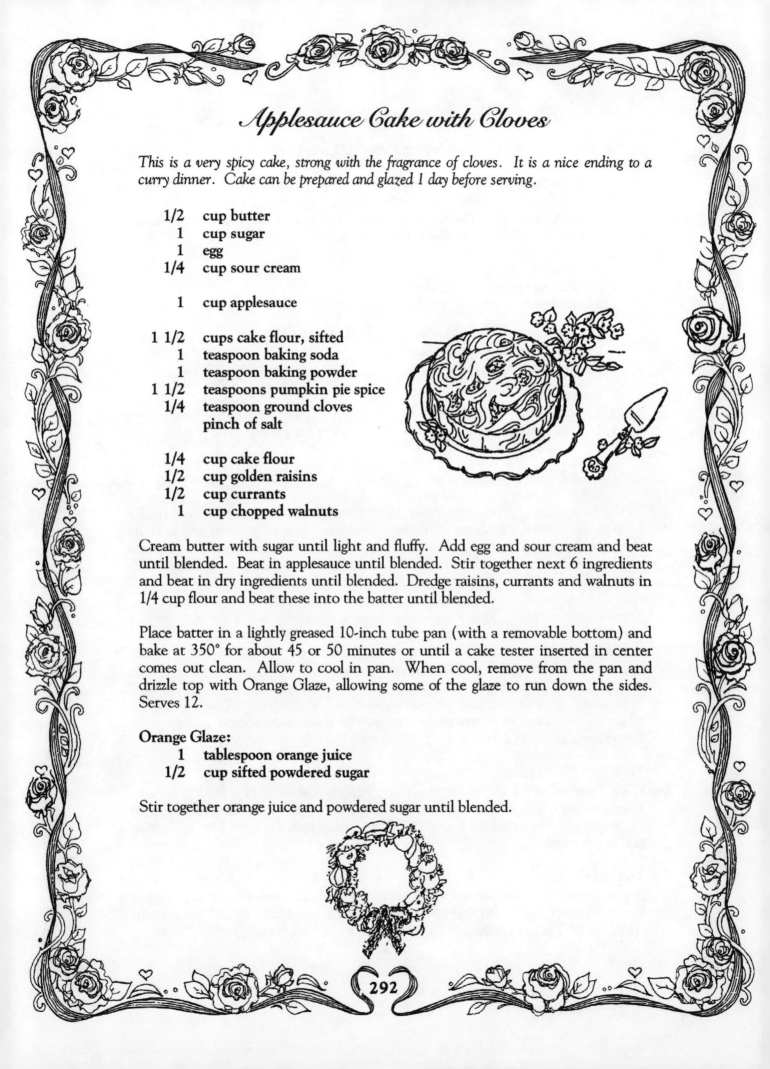

1 1/2   cups cake flour, sifted
1   teaspoon baking soda
1   teaspoon baking powder
1 1/2   teaspoons pumpkin pie spice
1/4   teaspoon ground cloves
pinch of salt

1/4   cup cake flour
1/2   cup golden raisins
1/2   cup currants
1   cup chopped walnuts

Cream butter with sugar until light and fluffy. Add egg and sour cream and beat until blended. Beat in applesauce until blended. Stir together next 6 ingredients and beat in dry ingredients until blended. Dredge raisins, currants and walnuts in 1/4 cup flour and beat these into the batter until blended.

Place batter in a lightly greased 10-inch tube pan (with a removable bottom) and bake at 350° for about 45 or 50 minutes or until a cake tester inserted in center comes out clean. Allow to cool in pan. When cool, remove from the pan and drizzle top with Orange Glaze, allowing some of the glaze to run down the sides. Serves 12.

Orange Glaze:
1   tablespoon orange juice
1/2   cup sifted powdered sugar

Stir together orange juice and powdered sugar until blended.

Thanksgiving Orange Pumpkin Apple Cake

This is a great cake to serve with hot spicy cider. It is moist, fruity and sparkled with spices. It is an especially fine choice as a gift from your kitchen during holiday times. For gift giving, I would suggest you bake this in 4 mini-loaf foil pans, 6x3x2-inches, for about 40 minutes.

1/2	cup butter, softened
1 1/4	cups sugar
2	eggs
1/2	orange grated (3 tablespoons fruit, juice and peel)
2	small apples, peeled, cored and grated
1	cup canned pumpkin puree
2	cups flour
2	teaspoons baking powder
1/2	teaspoon baking soda
3	teaspoons pumpkin pie spice
1/4	cup chopped walnuts (for the top)

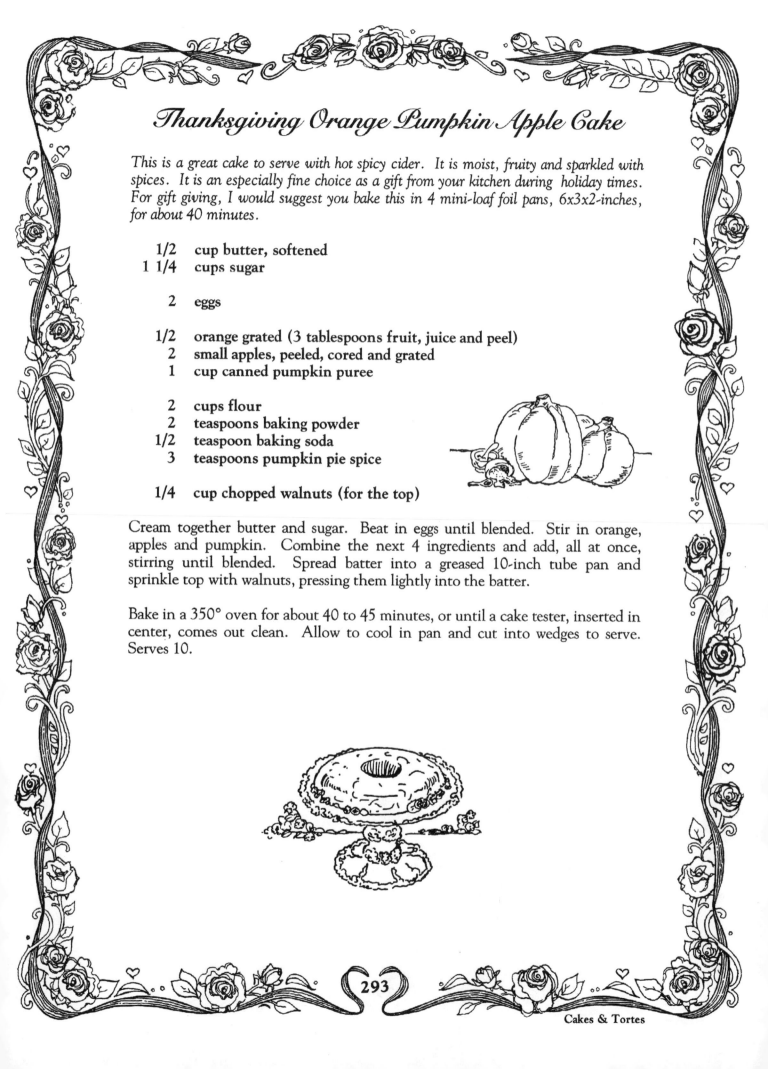

Cream together butter and sugar. Beat in eggs until blended. Stir in orange, apples and pumpkin. Combine the next 4 ingredients and add, all at once, stirring until blended. Spread batter into a greased 10-inch tube pan and sprinkle top with walnuts, pressing them lightly into the batter.

Bake in a 350° oven for about 40 to 45 minutes, or until a cake tester, inserted in center, comes out clean. Allow to cool in pan and cut into wedges to serve. Serves 10.

Nut Lover's Greatest Walnut Cake with Raspberries & Lemon Drizzle

If nut cakes are your fancy, this is a little "treasure" you will enjoy often. The nut crust is like an old-fashioned cookie crust, topped with raspberry jam and covered with a tender nut layer. The Lemon Drizzle adds the perfect tartness.

Nut Cookie Crust:

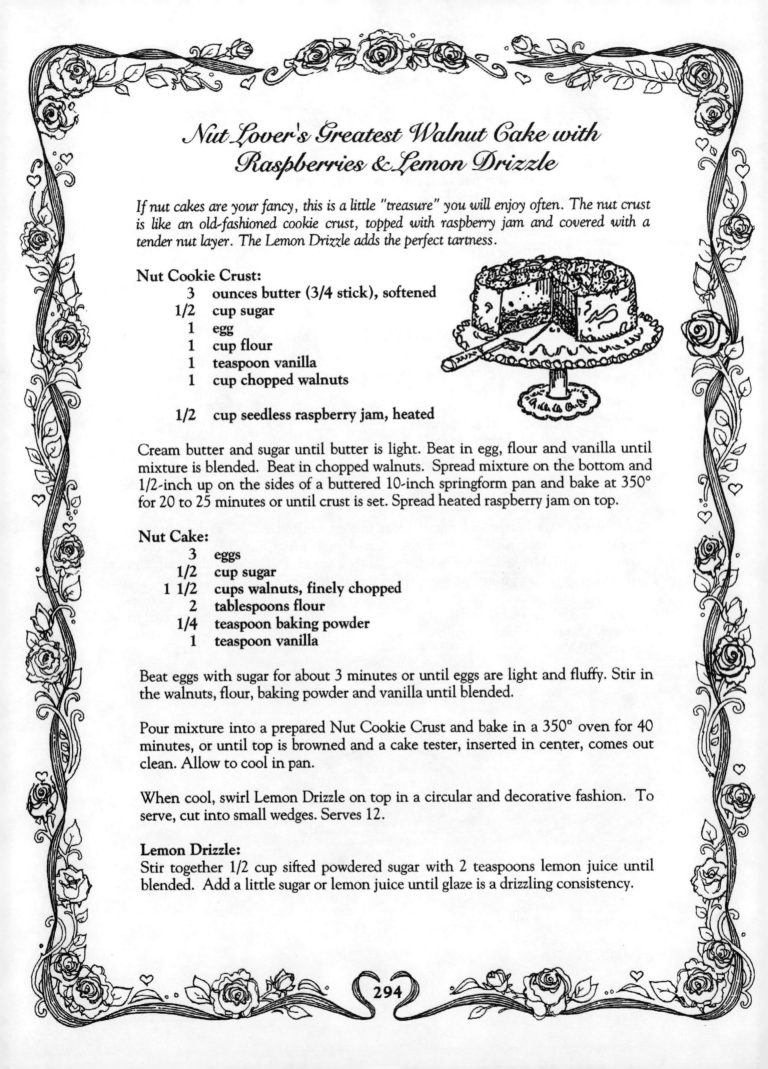

3	ounces butter (3/4 stick), softened
1/2	cup sugar
1	egg
1	cup flour
1	teaspoon vanilla
1	cup chopped walnuts
1/2	cup seedless raspberry jam, heated

Cream butter and sugar until butter is light. Beat in egg, flour and vanilla until mixture is blended. Beat in chopped walnuts. Spread mixture on the bottom and 1/2-inch up on the sides of a buttered 10-inch springform pan and bake at 350° for 20 to 25 minutes or until crust is set. Spread heated raspberry jam on top.

Nut Cake:

3	eggs
1/2	cup sugar
1 1/2	cups walnuts, finely chopped
2	tablespoons flour
1/4	teaspoon baking powder
1	teaspoon vanilla

Beat eggs with sugar for about 3 minutes or until eggs are light and fluffy. Stir in the walnuts, flour, baking powder and vanilla until blended.

Pour mixture into a prepared Nut Cookie Crust and bake in a 350° oven for 40 minutes, or until top is browned and a cake tester, inserted in center, comes out clean. Allow to cool in pan.

When cool, swirl Lemon Drizzle on top in a circular and decorative fashion. To serve, cut into small wedges. Serves 12.

Lemon Drizzle:
Stir together 1/2 cup sifted powdered sugar with 2 teaspoons lemon juice until blended. Add a little sugar or lemon juice until glaze is a drizzling consistency.

Easiest & Best Apricot Nut Torte with Whipped Crème Fraiche

Perhaps one of the easiest and most delicious desserts (if you love apricots and walnuts) is this marvelous chewy torte. It is tart and fruity and the frosting is the perfect accompaniment. Pecans can be substituted for the walnuts.

3	egg whites
1/2	cup sugar

3/4	cup dried apricots
1/2	cup sugar

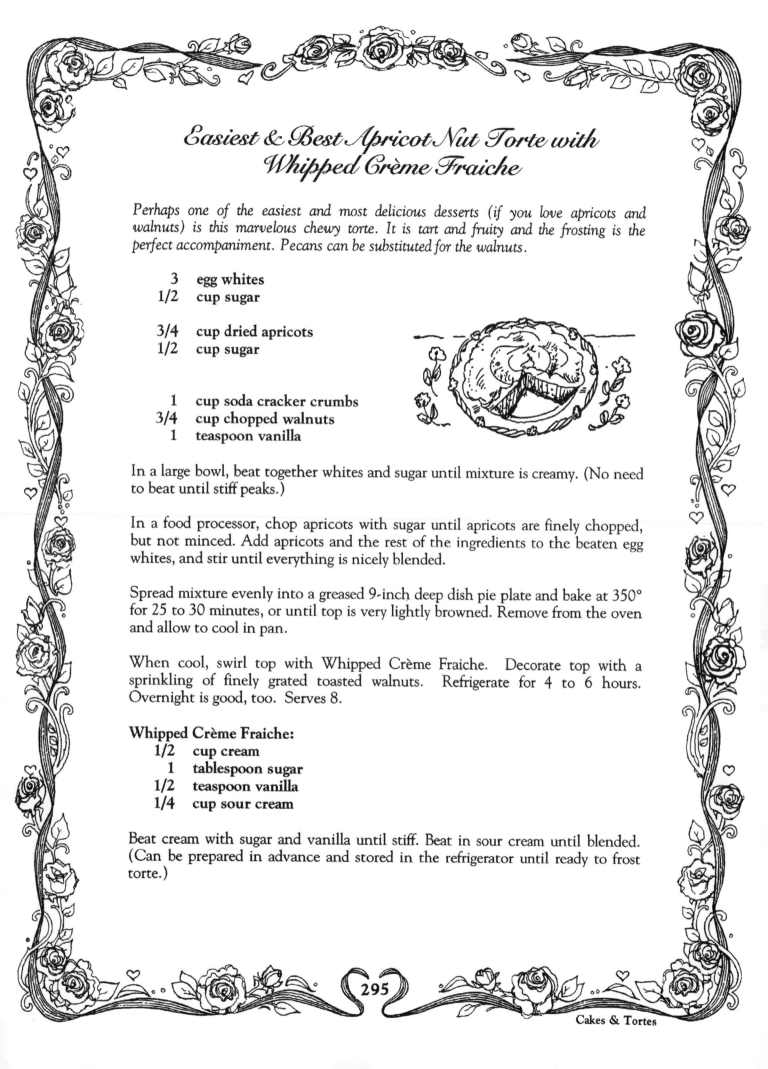

1	cup soda cracker crumbs
3/4	cup chopped walnuts
1	teaspoon vanilla

In a large bowl, beat together whites and sugar until mixture is creamy. (No need to beat until stiff peaks.)

In a food processor, chop apricots with sugar until apricots are finely chopped, but not minced. Add apricots and the rest of the ingredients to the beaten egg whites, and stir until everything is nicely blended.

Spread mixture evenly into a greased 9-inch deep dish pie plate and bake at 350° for 25 to 30 minutes, or until top is very lightly browned. Remove from the oven and allow to cool in pan.

When cool, swirl top with Whipped Crème Fraiche. Decorate top with a sprinkling of finely grated toasted walnuts. Refrigerate for 4 to 6 hours. Overnight is good, too. Serves 8.

Whipped Crème Fraiche:

1/2	cup cream
1	tablespoon sugar
1/2	teaspoon vanilla
1/4	cup sour cream

Beat cream with sugar and vanilla until stiff. Beat in sour cream until blended. (Can be prepared in advance and stored in the refrigerator until ready to frost torte.)

Pineapple Coconut Cake with Pineapple Cream Glaze

This cake is really moist and delicious. The flavors of pineapple and coconut work so well together. It is amazingly simple to prepare, starting as it does, with a cake mix. Enjoy.

1	package (18 1/2 ounces) white cake mix
1	cup crushed pineapple, do not drain
1/2	cup sour cream
1/4	cup oil
3	eggs
1	cup coconut flakes

In the large bowl of an electric mixer, at medium speed, beat together first 5 ingredients for 2 minutes. On low speed, beat in remaining ingredient until blended. Spread batter evenly into a greased 10-inch tube pan and bake at 350° for about 50 minutes, or until a cake tester, inserted in center, comes out clean. Allow to cool in pan.

When cool, remove from pan, and brush Pineapple Cream Glaze over the top, allowing some to drizzle down the sides. Serves 12.

Pineapple Cream Glaze:

1	tablespoon cream
1	tablespoon crushed pineapple
2	tablespoons coconut flakes
1	cup sifted powdered sugar

Stir together all the ingredients until blended.

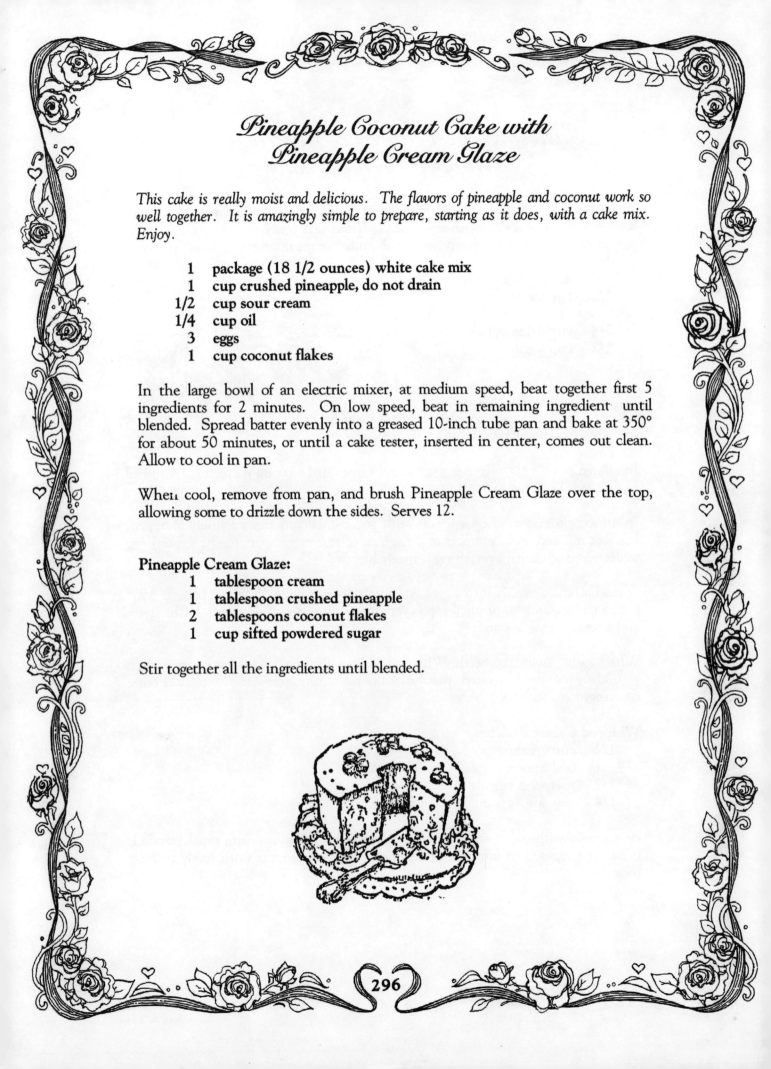

Banana Fudge Devil's Cake

This little treasure whips up in literally seconds and elevates a simple cake mix to gastronomical heights. Everybody loves this cake. It is moist, delicious and has a very fine texture.

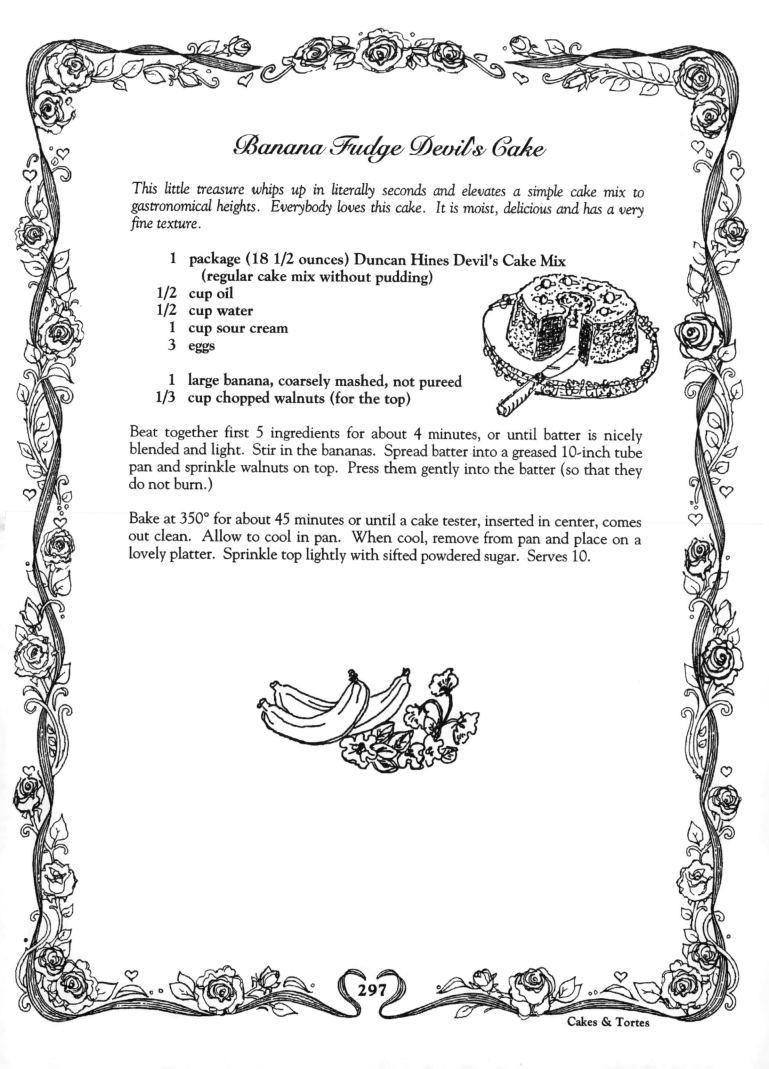

- 1 package (18 1/2 ounces) Duncan Hines Devil's Cake Mix
  (regular cake mix without pudding)
- 1/2 cup oil
- 1/2 cup water
- 1 cup sour cream
- 3 eggs

- 1 large banana, coarsely mashed, not pureed
- 1/3 cup chopped walnuts (for the top)

Beat together first 5 ingredients for about 4 minutes, or until batter is nicely blended and light. Stir in the bananas. Spread batter into a greased 10-inch tube pan and sprinkle walnuts on top. Press them gently into the batter (so that they do not burn.)

Bake at 350° for about 45 minutes or until a cake tester, inserted in center, comes out clean. Allow to cool in pan. When cool, remove from pan and place on a lovely platter. Sprinkle top lightly with sifted powdered sugar. Serves 10.

Cakes & Tortes

Candied Pecans

This is one of the best recipes for Candied Pecans. The original was given to me by a tennis friend, many years ago. I made a few changes, but she should get the credit.

1	egg white
1	teaspoon water
1/2	teaspoon vanilla
1/2	cup sugar
1/2	teaspoon cinnamon
1	pound pecan halves

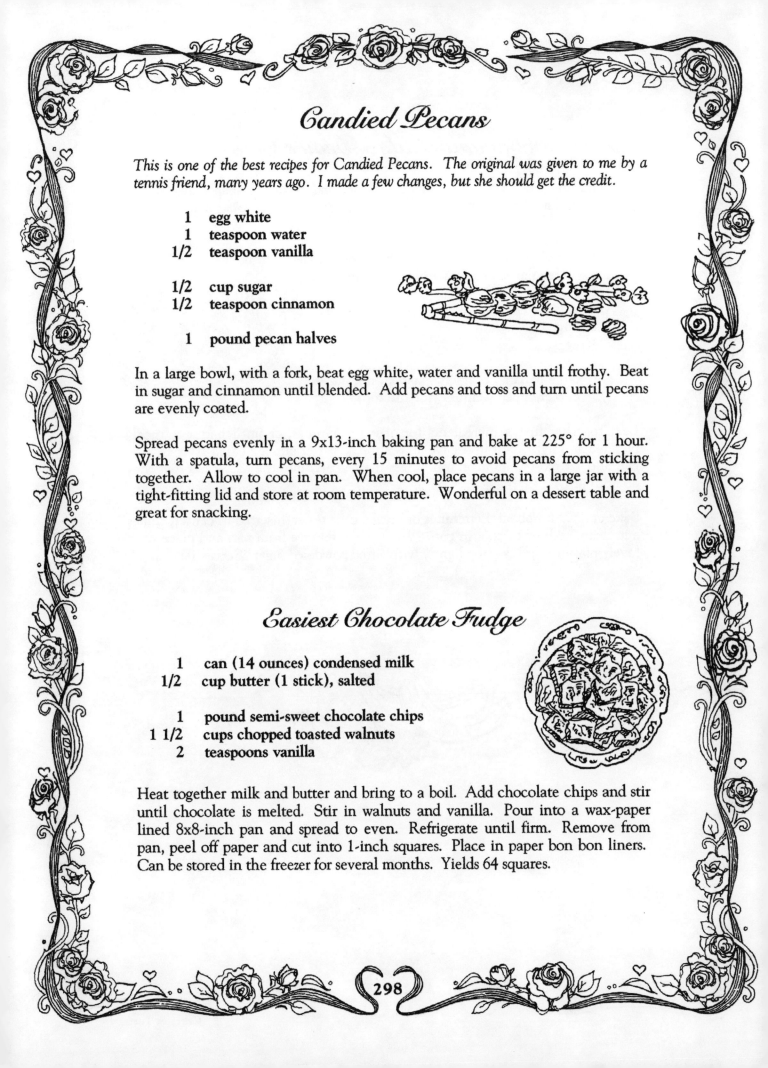

In a large bowl, with a fork, beat egg white, water and vanilla until frothy. Beat in sugar and cinnamon until blended. Add pecans and toss and turn until pecans are evenly coated.

Spread pecans evenly in a 9x13-inch baking pan and bake at 225° for 1 hour. With a spatula, turn pecans, every 15 minutes to avoid pecans from sticking together. Allow to cool in pan. When cool, place pecans in a large jar with a tight-fitting lid and store at room temperature. Wonderful on a dessert table and great for snacking.

Easiest Chocolate Fudge

1	can (14 ounces) condensed milk
1/2	cup butter (1 stick), salted
1	pound semi-sweet chocolate chips
1 1/2	cups chopped toasted walnuts
2	teaspoons vanilla

Heat together milk and butter and bring to a boil. Add chocolate chips and stir until chocolate is melted. Stir in walnuts and vanilla. Pour into a wax-paper lined 8x8-inch pan and spread to even. Refrigerate until firm. Remove from pan, peel off paper and cut into 1-inch squares. Place in paper bon bon liners. Can be stored in the freezer for several months. Yields 64 squares.

Crustless Cheesecake Pudding with Raspberry & Apricot Sauce

This pudding was an absolute rage at a recent dessert meeting. The texture is as smooth as velvet and the marriage of flavors simply divine. It is exceptionally easy to prepare, can be made a day earlier and will truly add a wonderful flair to dessert. I call this a "crustless cheesecake." In Italy it is called a "Budino."

Please use ingredients at room temperature for smoother texture.

1	pound cream cheese (2 8-ounce packages)
1/2	cup sour cream
3	eggs
1/3	cup sugar
3	tablespoons finely grated lemon, (thin-skinned). Use fruit, juice and peel.

Beat together all the ingredients until nicely blended. Place mixture into a buttered 10-inch round porcelain baker. Place the porcelain baker into a larger baking pan and pour in hot water to reach 1-inch up the side. Bake at 350° for 30 to 35 minutes or until pudding is set. Remove pudding from hot water bath, allow to cool, cover loosely with waxed paper and refrigerate until completely chilled.

To serve, spoon into pretty dessert bowls and top with a teaspoon of Raspberry & Apricot Sauce. Serves 8.

Raspberry & Apricot Sauce:

1	package (10 ounces) frozen raspberries in syrup
8	dried apricots, finely chopped
1	thin slice lemon

In a saucepan, simmer together all the ingredients until apricots are soft, about 10 minutes. Remove the lemon slice and place sauce in a bowl. Cover and refrigerate until serving time.

Note: -Pudding and sauce can be prepared a day earlier and stored, covered, in the refrigerator.

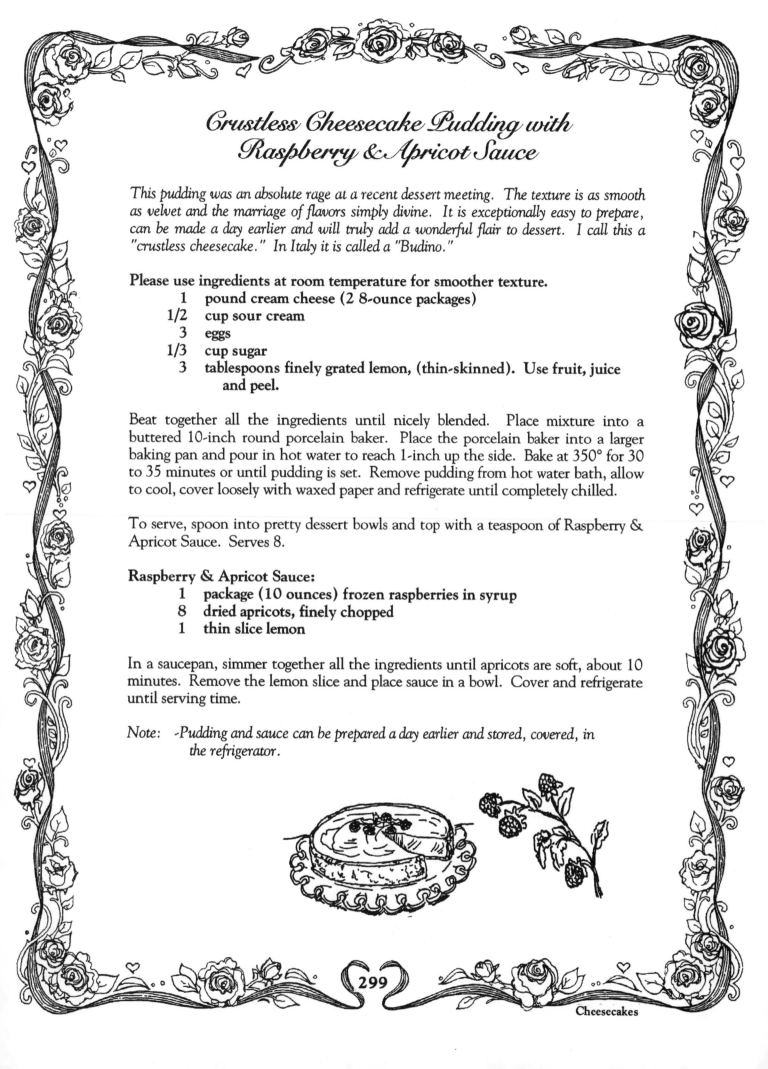

Cheesecakes

Easiest & Best
Imperial Velvet Chocolate Cheesecake

The texture of this cheesecake is as smooth as velvet. And one bite into this chocolate velvet is sheer ecstasy. The Almond Macaroon Crust adds just the right crunch.

1/2	cup cream
8	ounces semi-sweet chocolate chips
3	packages (8 ounces, each) cream cheese, at room temperature
1	cup sugar
3	eggs
1	cup sour cream
2	teaspoons vanilla

In a small saucepan heat the cream to boiling point. Remove the pan from the heat and add the chocolate chips, stirring until chocolate is melted. Set aside.

In the large bowl of an electric mixer, beat cream cheese until it is light (about 1 minute.) Beat in sugar, eggs, sour cream and vanilla until blended. Beat in the melted chocolate. Pour mixture into prepared crust and bake in a 325° oven for 55 minutes. (Top will appear soft in the middle, but it will firm up in the refrigerator.)

Allow to cool, and then refrigerate for 6 hours, or until thoroughly chilled. Overnight is good too. Decorate top with a thin layer of Vanilla Crème Fraiche and sprinkle top lightly with grated chocolate. Serves 10 to 12.

Vanilla Crème Fraiche:
Stir together until blended, 1/3 cup cream, 1/3 cup sour cream, 1 tablespoon sugar and 1 teaspoon vanilla until blended. Allow mixture to stand at room temperature for about 3 hours, or until it is thickened. Refrigerate until ready to use.

Almond Macaroon Crust:
Stir together 2 cups macaroon cookie crumbs, 1/3 cup melted butter and 1/3 cup finely chopped almonds, until blended. Pat mixture on the bottom of a 10-inch springform pan.

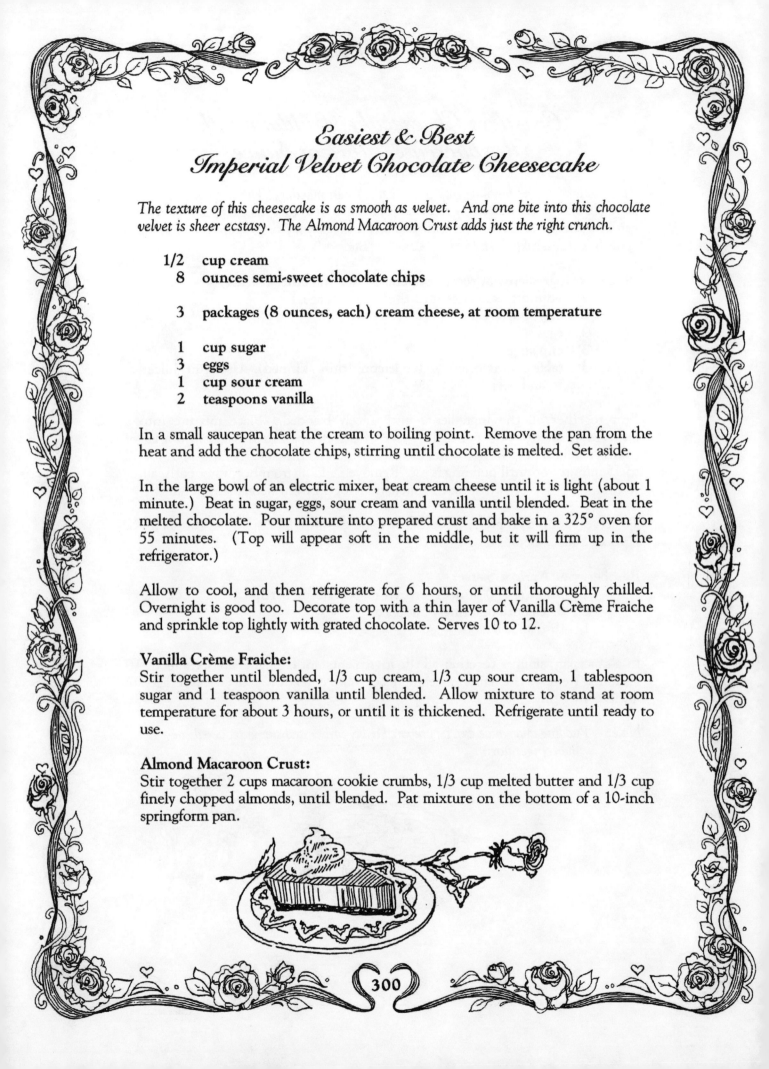

Cheesecake on Butter Cookie Crust & Glazed Strawberries

Butter Cookie Crust:
- 1 cup flour
- 1/4 cup sugar
- 1/2 cup butter, softened

- 1 egg yolk
- 1 tablespoon water
- 1 tablespoon grated lemon peel

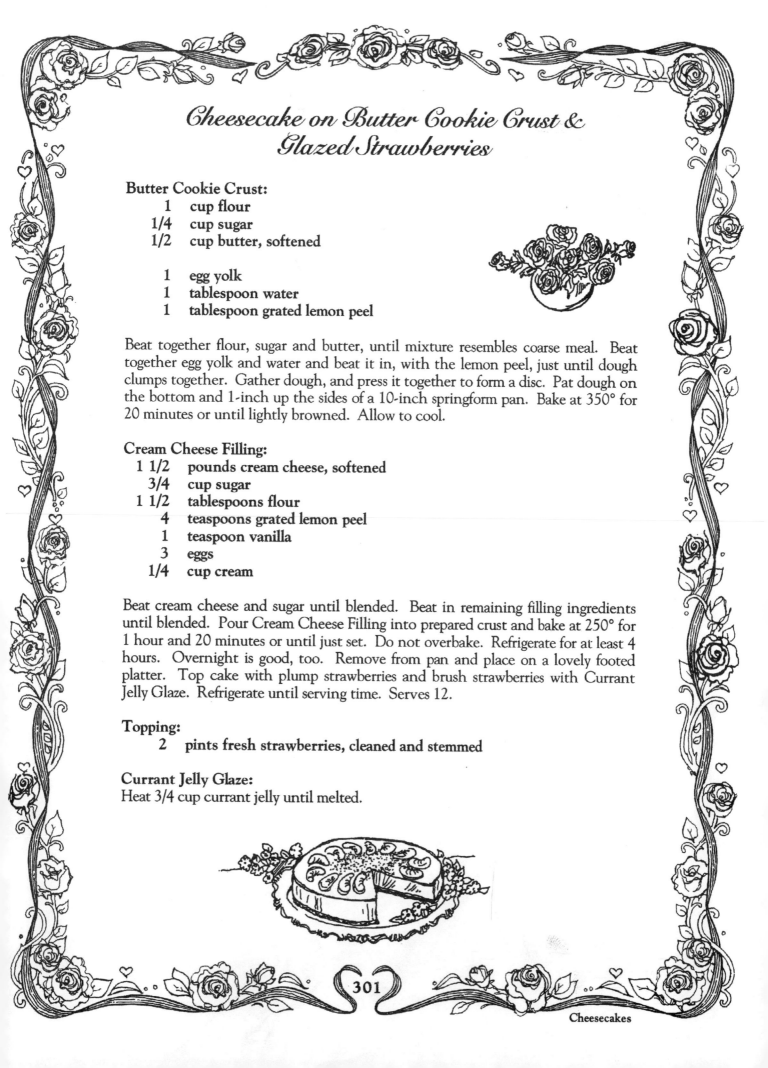

Beat together flour, sugar and butter, until mixture resembles coarse meal. Beat together egg yolk and water and beat it in, with the lemon peel, just until dough clumps together. Gather dough, and press it together to form a disc. Pat dough on the bottom and 1-inch up the sides of a 10-inch springform pan. Bake at 350° for 20 minutes or until lightly browned. Allow to cool.

Cream Cheese Filling:
- 1 1/2 pounds cream cheese, softened
- 3/4 cup sugar
- 1 1/2 tablespoons flour
- 4 teaspoons grated lemon peel
- 1 teaspoon vanilla
- 3 eggs
- 1/4 cup cream

Beat cream cheese and sugar until blended. Beat in remaining filling ingredients until blended. Pour Cream Cheese Filling into prepared crust and bake at 250° for 1 hour and 20 minutes or until just set. Do not overbake. Refrigerate for at least 4 hours. Overnight is good, too. Remove from pan and place on a lovely footed platter. Top cake with plump strawberries and brush strawberries with Currant Jelly Glaze. Refrigerate until serving time. Serves 12.

Topping:
- 2 pints fresh strawberries, cleaned and stemmed

Currant Jelly Glaze:
Heat 3/4 cup currant jelly until melted.

Cheesecakes

Lemon Vanilla Cheesecake with Raspberry Syrup

Lemon and vanilla are a wonderful pair in this creamy cheesecake. A word of caution. Cream cheese is now being made with ingredients that make it more spreadable. It is not the best for cheesecakes. It sometimes makes them grainy and not the usual velvety texture. Try to find a cheese store that sells the old-fashioned cream cheese in bulk. If not available, then underbake the cheesecake by 10 minutes and let it firm up in the refrigerator.

Crust:

1 1/4	cups graham cracker crumbs
2	ounces butter, (1/2 stick), melted
1/2	cup coarsely chopped walnuts
2	tablespoons cinnamon sugar

Filling:

1 1/2	pounds cream cheese, softened
1	cup sugar
3	eggs
2	cups sour cream
2	teaspoons vanilla
3	tablespoons lemon juice
2	teaspoons grated lemon zest

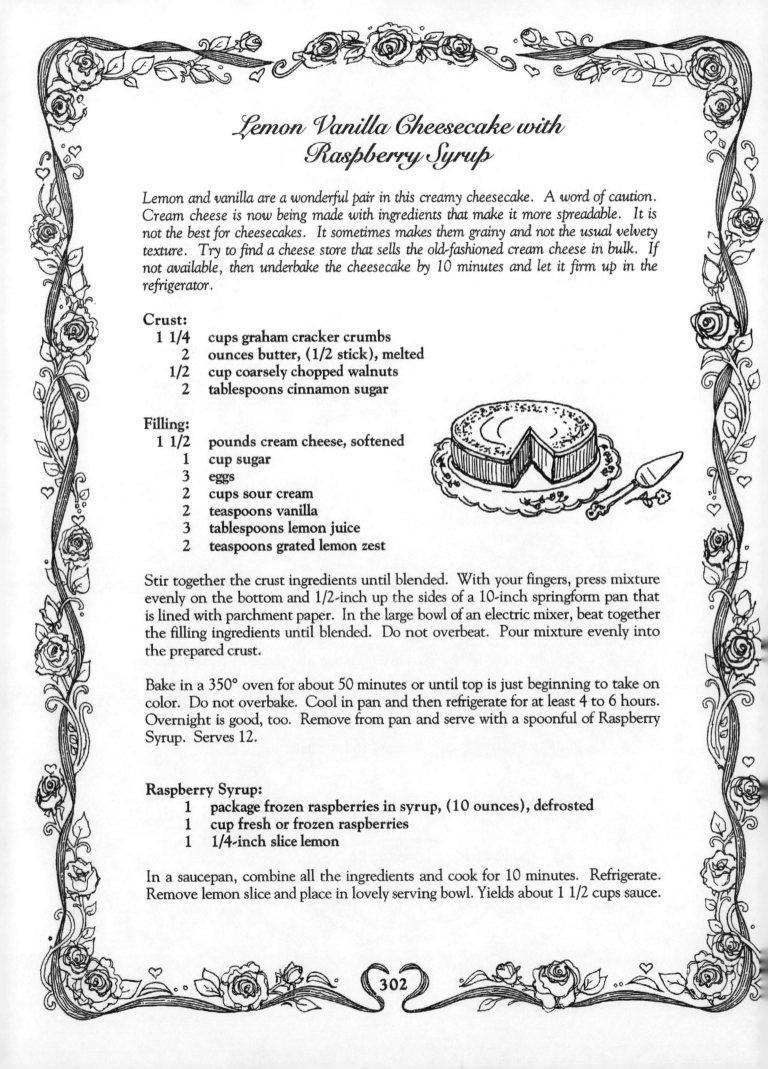

Stir together the crust ingredients until blended. With your fingers, press mixture evenly on the bottom and 1/2-inch up the sides of a 10-inch springform pan that is lined with parchment paper. In the large bowl of an electric mixer, beat together the filling ingredients until blended. Do not overbeat. Pour mixture evenly into the prepared crust.

Bake in a 350° oven for about 50 minutes or until top is just beginning to take on color. Do not overbake. Cool in pan and then refrigerate for at least 4 to 6 hours. Overnight is good, too. Remove from pan and serve with a spoonful of Raspberry Syrup. Serves 12.

Raspberry Syrup:

1	package frozen raspberries in syrup, (10 ounces), defrosted
1	cup fresh or frozen raspberries
1	1/4-inch slice lemon

In a saucepan, combine all the ingredients and cook for 10 minutes. Refrigerate. Remove lemon slice and place in lovely serving bowl. Yields about 1 1/2 cups sauce.

Whoopie Pie Primer

Whoopie Pies are basically cookie-size little firm sponge cakes. I call these cookie cakes. They are not crisp as a cookie nor are they as soft as a cake. They fall in between.

Kids love Whoopie Pies, and why not? They are delicious, they are rich and very sweet. I have tasted a lot of them, but these recipes are my very own version. I love the texture of my little cakes, and the Whoopie Frosting is delicious and tempered down a lot. But it is still rich and sweet, but not as much.

Important! I have used a Whoopie Pan with 20 molds. Each mold is 2-inches wide. It is absolutely the best size, for my taste, because the cakes are smaller, and they do not have to be cut in half. But I have made the classic size. They are 3-inches wide and this recipe will only make 12 pies. The smaller size will produce 30 pies.

The little cakes are firm, moist and so delicious, they can be eaten alone. But, of course, the frosting does elevate it to memorable heights.

There are many adaptations you can make with these 2 basic recipes. It isn't necessary to alter the basic recipes but you can make many additions to it. Similarly, small changes to the frosting will also change the taste and character of these little cakes. The possibilities are many. Have some fun with these. Whoopies are a rage now and have become the children's favorite.

Add One of the Following to Vanilla Cake Batter or Frosting
- 1/2 cup miniature chocolate chips
- 1/2 cup chopped raisins
- 1/2 cup chopped apricots
- 1/2 cup plumped currants
- 1/2 cup finely chopped pecans or walnuts
- 2 tablespoons finely grated orange zest
- 2 tablespoons finely grated lemon zest

Add One of the Following to Chocolate Cake Batter or Frosting
- 1/2 cup miniature chocolate chips
- 1/2 cup chopped white chocolate chips
- 1/2 cup finely chopped pecans or walnuts

Cookies

Chocolate Whoopie Pies

Chocolate Cookie Cakes:
- 1/2 cup butter, (1 stick) softened
- 1 1/4 cups sugar

- 1 egg
- 1 cup sour cream, at room temperature
- 1 teaspoon vanilla

- 1 3/4 cups flour
- 1/3 cup sifted unsweetened cocoa
- 1 teaspoon baking powder
- 1 teaspoon baking soda

Preheat oven to 350°. Grease the 20 molds of the Whoopie pan.

In the large bowl of an electric mixer, beat together butter and sugar until blended. Beat in the next 3 ingredients and beat until batter is light and fluffy, about 2 minutes. Stir together the dry ingredients, and add, all at once, and beat until blended. Do not overbeat at this point.

Half fill each mold (about 1 1/2 teaspoons) and bake for 8 to 9 minutes, or until a cake tester, inserted in center, comes out clean. Allow to cool for 5 minutes and then remove cakes from the pan onto brown paper to finish cooling. Repeat with remaining batter.

Spread half of the cake bottoms with 1 scant tablespoon frosting and top with the remaining cakes, bottoms down. Press gently so that the frosting reaches the edge of the cakes. Store cakes in a large plastic container. After 1 day, refrigerate. Yields 30 pies.

Chocolate Whoopie Frosting:
- 1/2 cup butter, softened
- 2 cups sifted powdered sugar
- 2 tablespoons sifted cocoa
- 1 teaspoon vanilla
- 3 1/2 ounces Marshmallow Cream (1/2 of a 7 ounce jar)

Beat together all the ingredients until mixture is light and fluffy, about 3 minutes. Refrigerate bowl for 30 minutes, so that the frosting will be a little firm. It is easier to spread and better holds its shape.

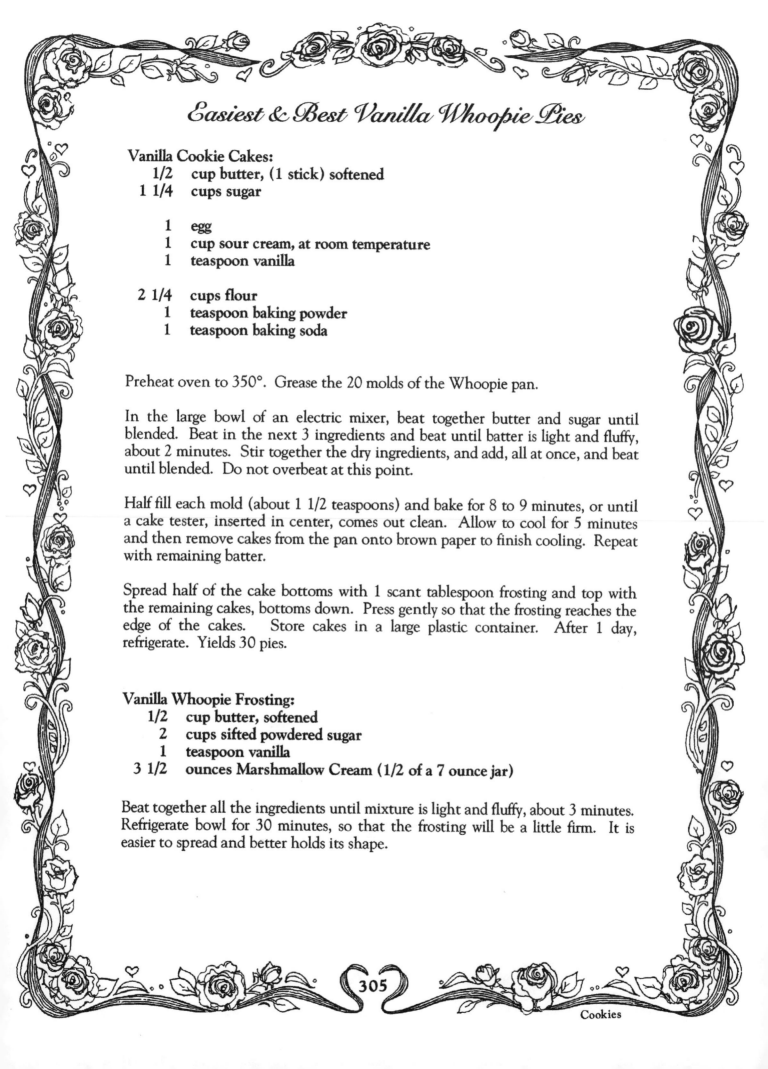

Easiest & Best Vanilla Whoopie Pies

Vanilla Cookie Cakes:

1/2	cup butter, (1 stick) softened
1 1/4	cups sugar
1	egg
1	cup sour cream, at room temperature
1	teaspoon vanilla
2 1/4	cups flour
1	teaspoon baking powder
1	teaspoon baking soda

Preheat oven to 350°. Grease the 20 molds of the Whoopie pan.

In the large bowl of an electric mixer, beat together butter and sugar until blended. Beat in the next 3 ingredients and beat until batter is light and fluffy, about 2 minutes. Stir together the dry ingredients, and add, all at once, and beat until blended. Do not overbeat at this point.

Half fill each mold (about 1 1/2 teaspoons) and bake for 8 to 9 minutes, or until a cake tester, inserted in center, comes out clean. Allow to cool for 5 minutes and then remove cakes from the pan onto brown paper to finish cooling. Repeat with remaining batter.

Spread half of the cake bottoms with 1 scant tablespoon frosting and top with the remaining cakes, bottoms down. Press gently so that the frosting reaches the edge of the cakes.   Store cakes in a large plastic container. After 1 day, refrigerate. Yields 30 pies.

Vanilla Whoopie Frosting:

1/2	cup butter, softened
2	cups sifted powdered sugar
1	teaspoon vanilla
3 1/2	ounces Marshmallow Cream (1/2 of a 7 ounce jar)

Beat together all the ingredients until mixture is light and fluffy, about 3 minutes. Refrigerate bowl for 30 minutes, so that the frosting will be a little firm. It is easier to spread and better holds its shape.

Cookies

Easiest & Best Date Nut Chewies

This homey cookie will always get you compliments. Somehow, every one loves the texture and taste of these simple-to-prepare cookies. I hope you agree.

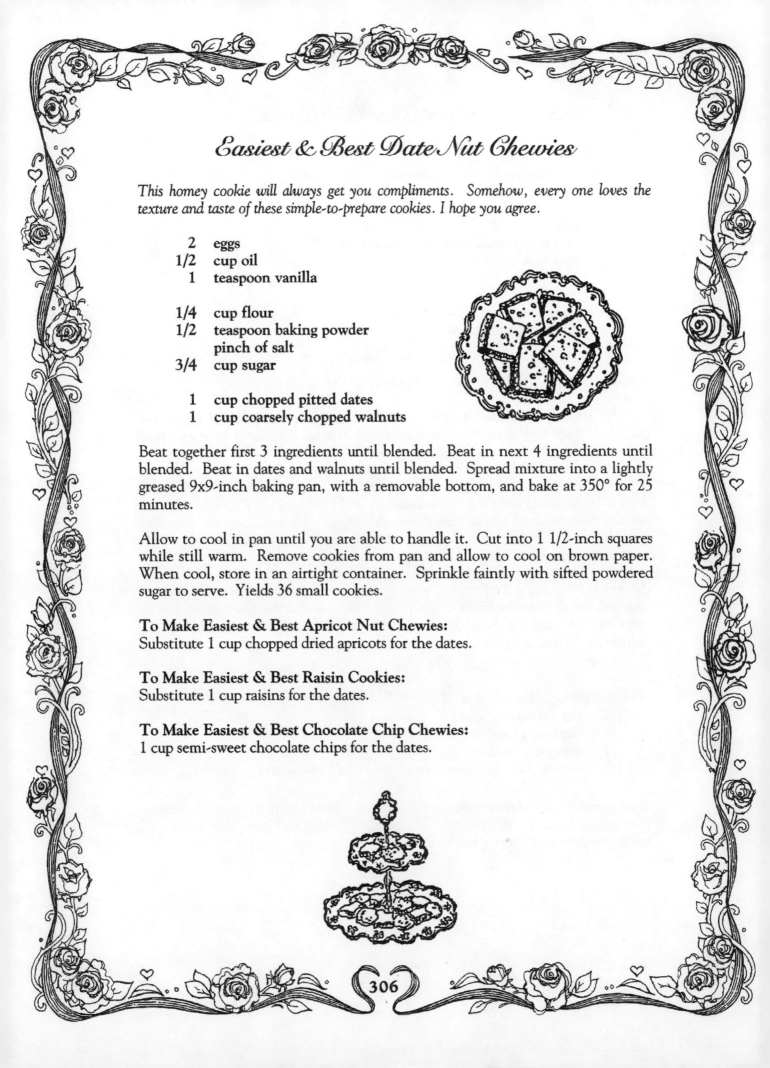

2	eggs
1/2	cup oil
1	teaspoon vanilla
1/4	cup flour
1/2	teaspoon baking powder
	pinch of salt
3/4	cup sugar
1	cup chopped pitted dates
1	cup coarsely chopped walnuts

Beat together first 3 ingredients until blended. Beat in next 4 ingredients until blended. Beat in dates and walnuts until blended. Spread mixture into a lightly greased 9x9-inch baking pan, with a removable bottom, and bake at 350° for 25 minutes.

Allow to cool in pan until you are able to handle it. Cut into 1 1/2-inch squares while still warm. Remove cookies from pan and allow to cool on brown paper. When cool, store in an airtight container. Sprinkle faintly with sifted powdered sugar to serve. Yields 36 small cookies.

To Make Easiest & Best Apricot Nut Chewies:
Substitute 1 cup chopped dried apricots for the dates.

To Make Easiest & Best Raisin Cookies:
Substitute 1 cup raisins for the dates.

To Make Easiest & Best Chocolate Chip Chewies:
1 cup semi-sweet chocolate chips for the dates.

Best Apricot Walnut Squares on Lemon Cookie Crust

A chewy apricot/nut topping on a lemon cookie crust makes this a truly marvelous cookie. The balance of sweet and tart, with the texture of fruits and nuts, is divine. The cookie crust is sparkled with lemon. Of course, you can tell, these are one of my very favorite cookies.

Crust:

2	cups flour
1/2	cup sugar
3/4	cup butter
2	tablespoons grated lemon (about 1/2 of a whole lemon)

Filling:

1	cup sugar
1/3	cup brown sugar
1	package (6 ounces) dried apricots
3	eggs
2	teaspoons vanilla
3	tablespoons flour
1 1/2	teaspoons baking powder
1	cup chopped walnuts

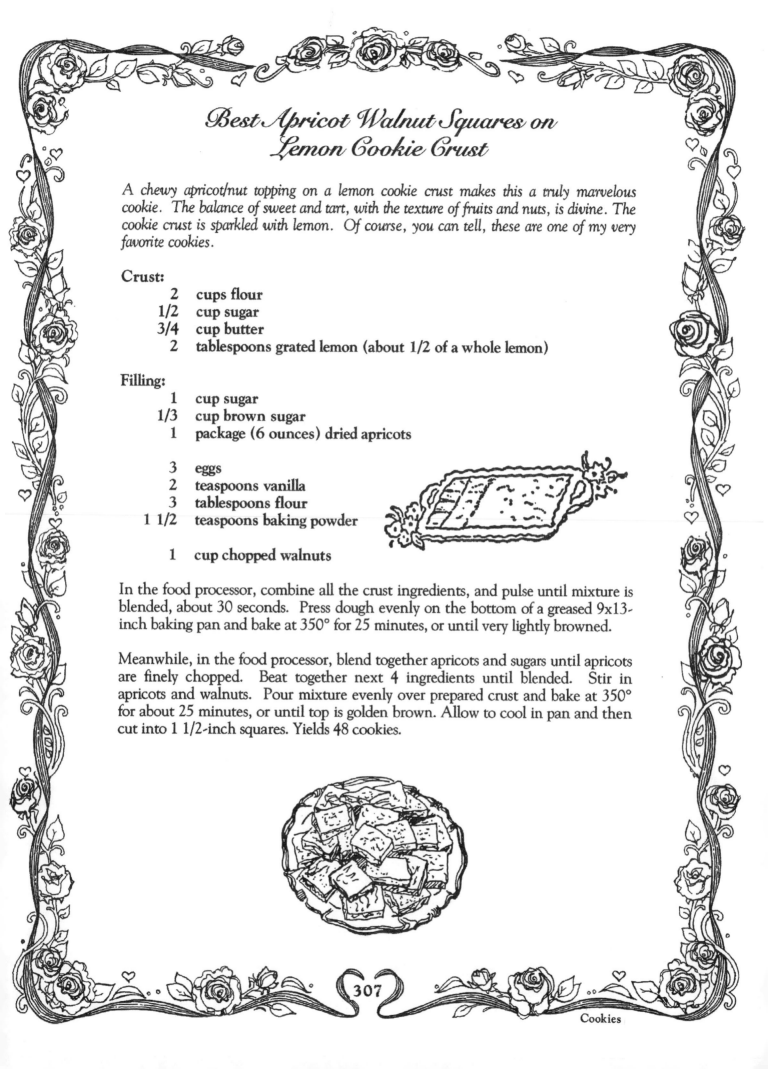

In the food processor, combine all the crust ingredients, and pulse until mixture is blended, about 30 seconds. Press dough evenly on the bottom of a greased 9x13-inch baking pan and bake at 350° for 25 minutes, or until very lightly browned.

Meanwhile, in the food processor, blend together apricots and sugars until apricots are finely chopped. Beat together next 4 ingredients until blended. Stir in apricots and walnuts. Pour mixture evenly over prepared crust and bake at 350° for about 25 minutes, or until top is golden brown. Allow to cool in pan and then cut into 1 1/2-inch squares. Yields 48 cookies.

Brownies

To make the perfect brownie for your taste, will require a few trials. In my oven, I bake brownies for 28 minutes. It is hard to test with a cake tester, but if you do use one, it should come out with a few moist crumbs clinging to it. It is a less than satisfactory test, but as each oven bakes with a slightly different character, please keep in mind that the longer you bake brownies, the crisper they become. Alternatively, the less you bake brownies, the more moist they are.

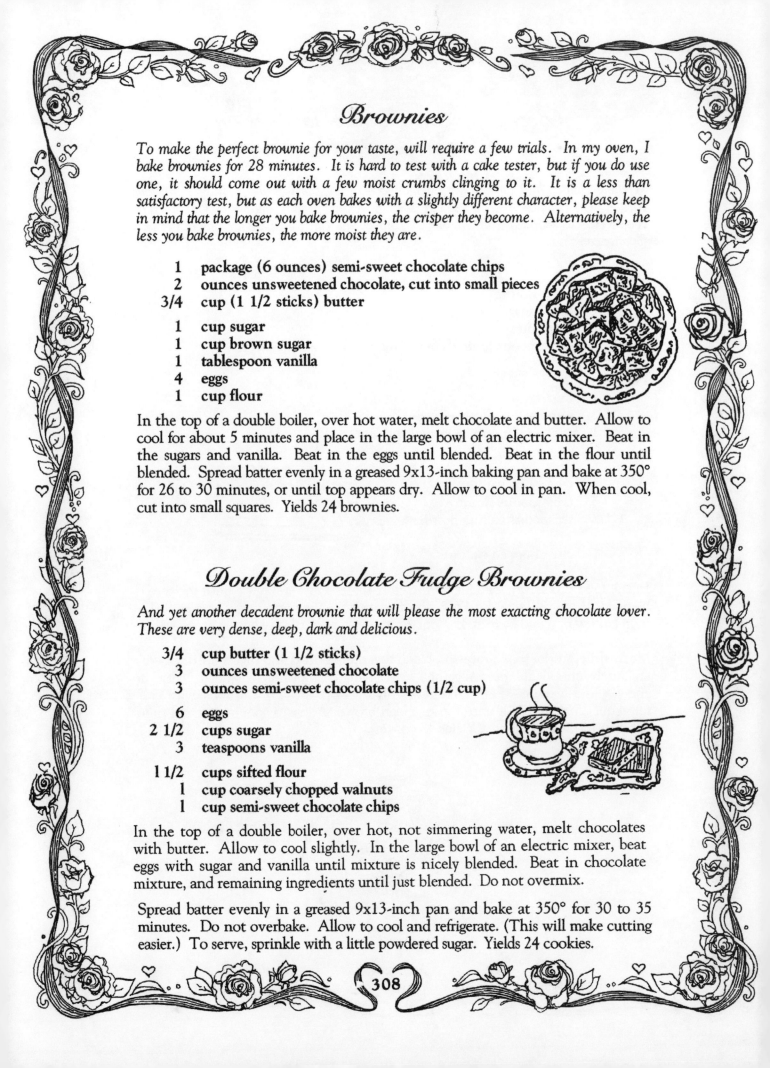

1	package (6 ounces) semi-sweet chocolate chips
2	ounces unsweetened chocolate, cut into small pieces
3/4	cup (1 1/2 sticks) butter
1	cup sugar
1	cup brown sugar
1	tablespoon vanilla
4	eggs
1	cup flour

In the top of a double boiler, over hot water, melt chocolate and butter. Allow to cool for about 5 minutes and place in the large bowl of an electric mixer. Beat in the sugars and vanilla. Beat in the eggs until blended. Beat in the flour until blended. Spread batter evenly in a greased 9x13-inch baking pan and bake at 350° for 26 to 30 minutes, or until top appears dry. Allow to cool in pan. When cool, cut into small squares. Yields 24 brownies.

Double Chocolate Fudge Brownies

And yet another decadent brownie that will please the most exacting chocolate lover. These are very dense, deep, dark and delicious.

3/4	cup butter (1 1/2 sticks)
3	ounces unsweetened chocolate
3	ounces semi-sweet chocolate chips (1/2 cup)
6	eggs
2 1/2	cups sugar
3	teaspoons vanilla
1 1/2	cups sifted flour
1	cup coarsely chopped walnuts
1	cup semi-sweet chocolate chips

In the top of a double boiler, over hot, not simmering water, melt chocolates with butter. Allow to cool slightly. In the large bowl of an electric mixer, beat eggs with sugar and vanilla until mixture is nicely blended. Beat in chocolate mixture, and remaining ingredients until just blended. Do not overmix.

Spread batter evenly in a greased 9x13-inch pan and bake at 350° for 30 to 35 minutes. Do not overbake. Allow to cool and refrigerate. (This will make cutting easier.) To serve, sprinkle with a little powdered sugar. Yields 24 cookies.

Velvet Brownies with Walnuts & Chocolate Buttercream

This is a super velvety brownie, that I know you will love. The only addition is chopped walnuts. Chocolate chips, dates, raisins, or even grated white chocolate can be added. The brownie base is truly delicious.

3/4	cup butter (1 1/2 sticks)
4	ounces unsweetened chocolate
1	teaspoon instant coffee
4	eggs
2	cups sugar
1	teaspoon vanilla
1	cup flour
1/4	teaspoon salt
1	cup chopped walnuts

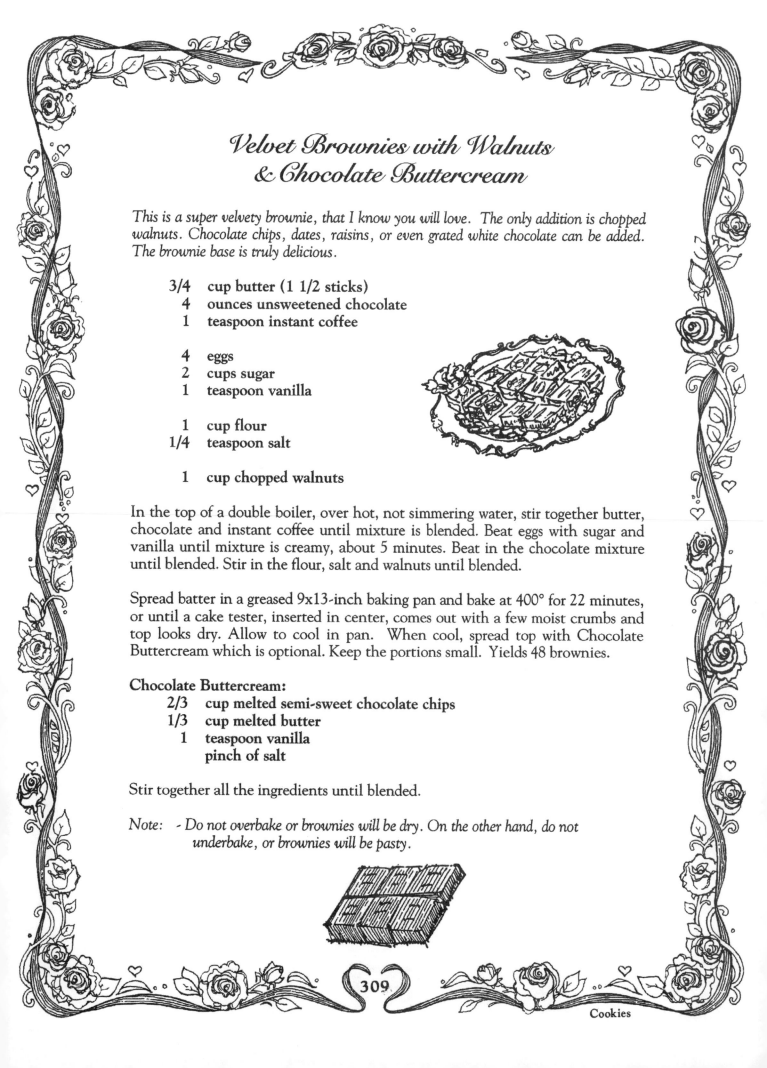

In the top of a double boiler, over hot, not simmering water, stir together butter, chocolate and instant coffee until mixture is blended. Beat eggs with sugar and vanilla until mixture is creamy, about 5 minutes. Beat in the chocolate mixture until blended. Stir in the flour, salt and walnuts until blended.

Spread batter in a greased 9x13-inch baking pan and bake at 400° for 22 minutes, or until a cake tester, inserted in center, comes out with a few moist crumbs and top looks dry. Allow to cool in pan. When cool, spread top with Chocolate Buttercream which is optional. Keep the portions small. Yields 48 brownies.

Chocolate Buttercream:

2/3	cup melted semi-sweet chocolate chips
1/3	cup melted butter
1	teaspoon vanilla
	pinch of salt

Stir together all the ingredients until blended.

Note: - Do not overbake or brownies will be dry. On the other hand, do not underbake, or brownies will be pasty.

Chewy Chocolate Chip Macaroons

This is an incredibly easy and very delicious cookie that is chewy AND crunchy. It assembles in seconds and bakes in minutes.

- 3   cups coconut meal (from the health food stores)
- 1   teaspoon vanilla
- 1   can (14 ounces) sweetened condensed milk
- 1   package (6 ounces) semi-sweet chocolate chips

Combine all the ingredients and stir until they are blended. Drop batter by the teaspoonful on a generously greased cookie sheet. Bake for 12 minutes at 350° or until lightly browned. Remove from cookie pan immediately and place cookies on a brown paper bag to cool. Yields about 48 cookies.

To Make Basic Macaroons:
Delete chocolate chips and proceed as above.

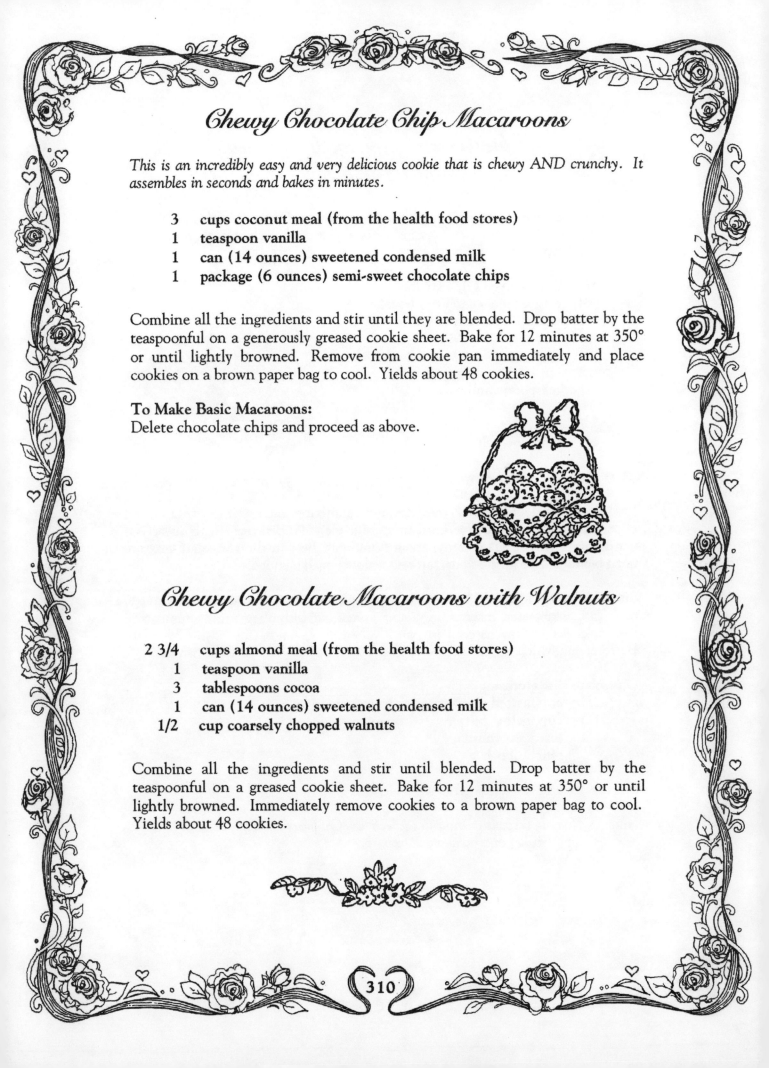

Chewy Chocolate Macaroons with Walnuts

- 2 3/4   cups almond meal (from the health food stores)
- 1   teaspoon vanilla
- 3   tablespoons cocoa
- 1   can (14 ounces) sweetened condensed milk
- 1/2   cup coarsely chopped walnuts

Combine all the ingredients and stir until blended. Drop batter by the teaspoonful on a greased cookie sheet. Bake for 12 minutes at 350° or until lightly browned. Immediately remove cookies to a brown paper bag to cool. Yields about 48 cookies.

Cranberry Pecan Bar Cake with Orange Glaze

I love cranberries. I love pecans. Put them together in this very easy-to-prepare cake and you have a small treasure you will use often. This produces a low cake so don't think anything went wrong.

3/4	cup butter (1 1/2 sticks) melted
2	eggs
3/4	cup sugar
1	cup flour
3/4	teaspoon baking powder
3	tablespoons grated orange (use fruit, juice and peel)
2	cups fresh or frozen cranberries
1	cup coarsely chopped pecans

In the large bowl of an electric mixer, beat together butter, eggs and sugar until nicely blended. Beat in flour and baking powder until blended. Stir in remaining ingredients until blended.

Spread batter evenly in a 10-inch springform pan and bake at 325° for about 40 minutes, or until top is browned and a tester, inserted in center, comes out clean. Allow to cool in pan. When cool brush top with Orange Glaze. Serves 8.

Orange Glaze:
1/2	cup sifted powdered sugar
1	tablespoon orange juice

In a small bowl, stir together sugar and orange juice until blended. Brush mixture on top of cooled cake.

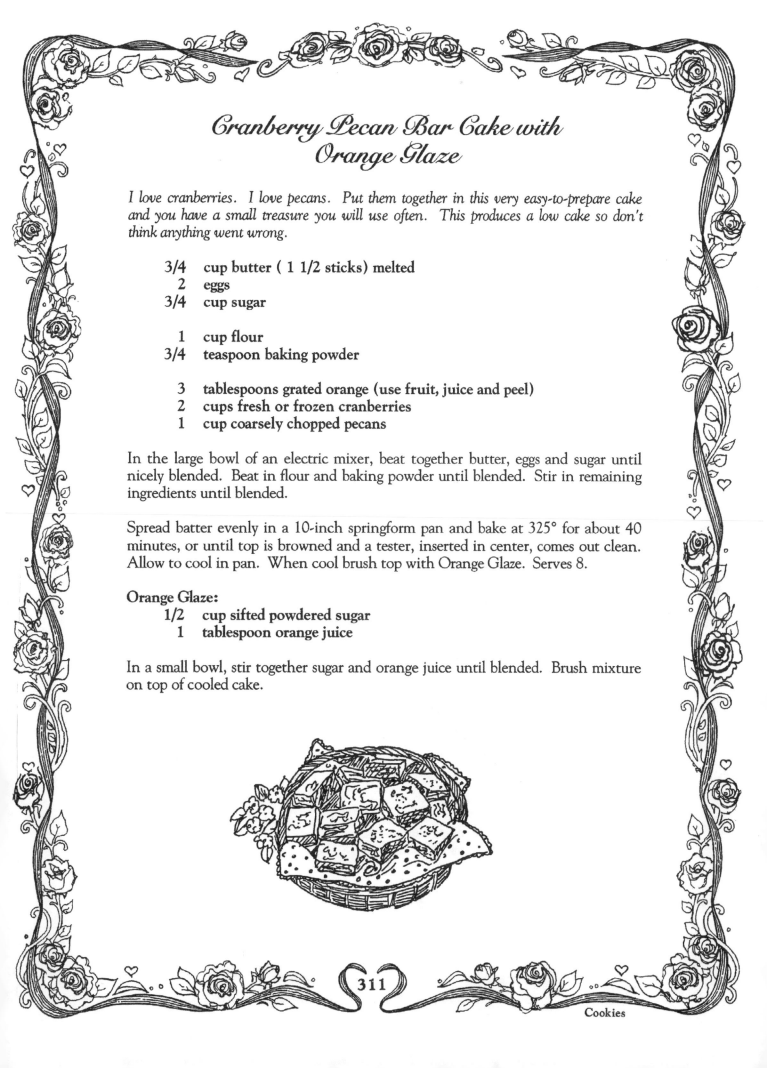

Oatmeal & Raisin Bar Cookies

This chewy cookie, full of oats and raisins, can be prepared and baked in minutes. It is very good with milk and for snacking after school. It tastes very much like the classic oatmeal raisin cookie, but far less sweet. If you add 2 teaspoons of cinnamon to the batter, the cookie takes on a totally different character.

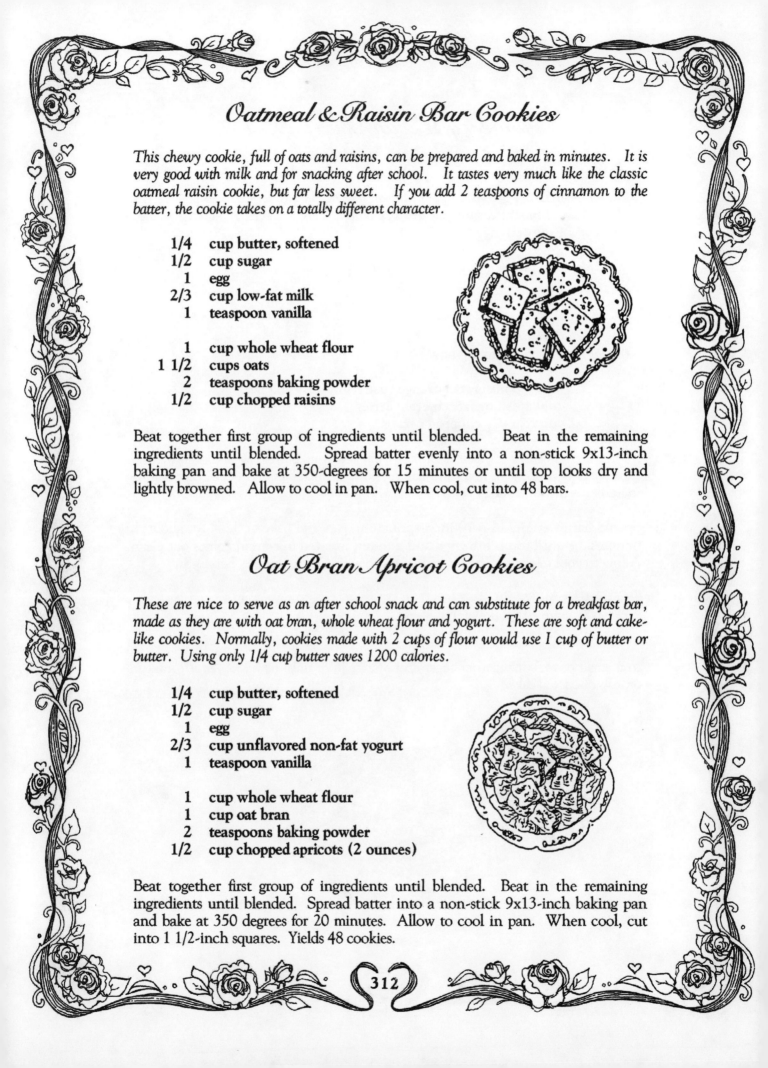

1/4	cup butter, softened
1/2	cup sugar
1	egg
2/3	cup low-fat milk
1	teaspoon vanilla
1	cup whole wheat flour
1 1/2	cups oats
2	teaspoons baking powder
1/2	cup chopped raisins

Beat together first group of ingredients until blended. Beat in the remaining ingredients until blended. Spread batter evenly into a non-stick 9x13-inch baking pan and bake at 350-degrees for 15 minutes or until top looks dry and lightly browned. Allow to cool in pan. When cool, cut into 48 bars.

Oat Bran Apricot Cookies

These are nice to serve as an after school snack and can substitute for a breakfast bar, made as they are with oat bran, whole wheat flour and yogurt. These are soft and cake-like cookies. Normally, cookies made with 2 cups of flour would use 1 cup of butter or butter. Using only 1/4 cup butter saves 1200 calories.

1/4	cup butter, softened
1/2	cup sugar
1	egg
2/3	cup unflavored non-fat yogurt
1	teaspoon vanilla
1	cup whole wheat flour
1	cup oat bran
2	teaspoons baking powder
1/2	cup chopped apricots (2 ounces)

Beat together first group of ingredients until blended. Beat in the remaining ingredients until blended. Spread batter into a non-stick 9x13-inch baking pan and bake at 350 degrees for 20 minutes. Allow to cool in pan. When cool, cut into 1 1/2-inch squares. Yields 48 cookies.

Butter Pecan Balls

To avoid breakage, small delicate baked goods are much easier to cool on brown paper, than on a rack. Brown paper is inexpensive and can be purchased in rolls.

1	cup butter (2 sticks)
1/2	cup sugar
2	teaspoons vanilla
2	cups cake flour
1 1/2	cups finely chopped pecans

sifted powdered sugar for dusting

Cream together butter and sugar. Beat in vanilla. Beat in flour until blended. Beat in pecans until blended. Shape dough into 3/4-inch balls and place on a lightly greased cookie sheet. Bake at 350° for about 12 to 14 minutes, or until cookies are set and just beginning to take on color. Do not brown. Allow cookies to cool on brown paper and roll in sifted powdered sugar when cool. Yields about 5 dozen cookies.

Butter Almond Cookies

Chinese almond cookies are traditionally made with lard. These flaky Butter Almond Cookies are a delicious substitute.

1/2	cup butter (1 stick), melted and cooled
1	cup flour
1/4	cup sifted powdered sugar
1/4	cup almond meal (finely grated almonds.) Use a nut grater to finely grate or purchase almond meal in health food stores.
1	teaspoon almond extract

whole blanched almonds

In a bowl, stir together first 5 ingredients until mixture is blended. With floured hands, roll 1 heaping tablespoon of dough into a ball and flatten it slightly. Place on a greased cookie sheet and press an almond into the center. Bake at 350° for 13 to 15 minutes or until cookies are set and lightly browned. Yields about 16 cookies.

Red Raspberry Butter Cookies with Coconut Meringue Topping

There are several variations for this great cookie. It can be prepared with apricot jam which is wonderful...almonds or pecans can be substituted for the walnuts.

Butter Cookie Crust:
1 1/2	cups flour
1/2	cup sifted powdered sugar
3/4	cup butter, cut into 12 pieces
2	tablespoons grated lemon peel
2	egg yolks

Filling:
1 1/4	cups seedless red raspberry jam
1	cup chopped walnuts

Topping:
2	egg whites
1/2	cup sugar
1/2	cup coconut flakes

In the large bowl of an electric mixer, beat together all the crust ingredients until mixture resembles coarse meal. Pat mixture on the bottom and 1-inch up the sides of a buttered 9x13-inch baking pan and bake in a 350° oven for 15 minutes. Spread raspberry jam evenly over the crust and sprinkle walnuts on top.

Beat egg whites with sugar until stiff. Beat in the coconut flakes until blended. Spread mixture evenly over the nuts and bake at 350° for about 25 minutes or until meringue is golden brown. To serve, cut into 1 1/2-inch squares. Yields 4 dozen cookies.

Petite Butter Crescents

These are very small, petite cookies that are nice to serve with frozen yogurt or ice cream. These can be shaped into crescents, into flat little wafers or small rings.

1/2	cup butter (1 stick), softened
1/4	cup sifted powdered sugar
1/2	teaspoon vanilla
1	cup flour, sifted
1/3	cup very finely chopped walnuts or pecans

Cream together butter, sugar and vanilla. Beat in flour until blended. Beat in nuts until blended. Shape 1 teaspoon of dough into tiny crescents. Place on a lightly greased cookie sheet and bake at 350° until dough is set and just beginning to take on color. Do not allow cookies to get brown. Allow to cool and sprinkle with sifted powdered sugar. Yields about 40 cookies.

Pecan Bars on Cookie Crust

Cookie Crust:

1 1/2	cups flour
1/3	cup sugar
1/2	cup butter (1 stick)

In the large bowl of an electric mixer, beat together all the ingredients until; mixture resembles coarse meal. Pat mixture into a lightly greased 9x13-inch pan and bake at 350° for 15 minutes, or until crust is just beginning to take on color.

Pecan Filling:

6	tablespoons butter, melted
1 1/2	cups brown sugar
2	eggs
2	teaspoons vanilla
3/4	cup flour
1	teaspoon baking powder
1	teaspoon cinnamon
1/4	teaspoon salt
2	cups chopped pecans

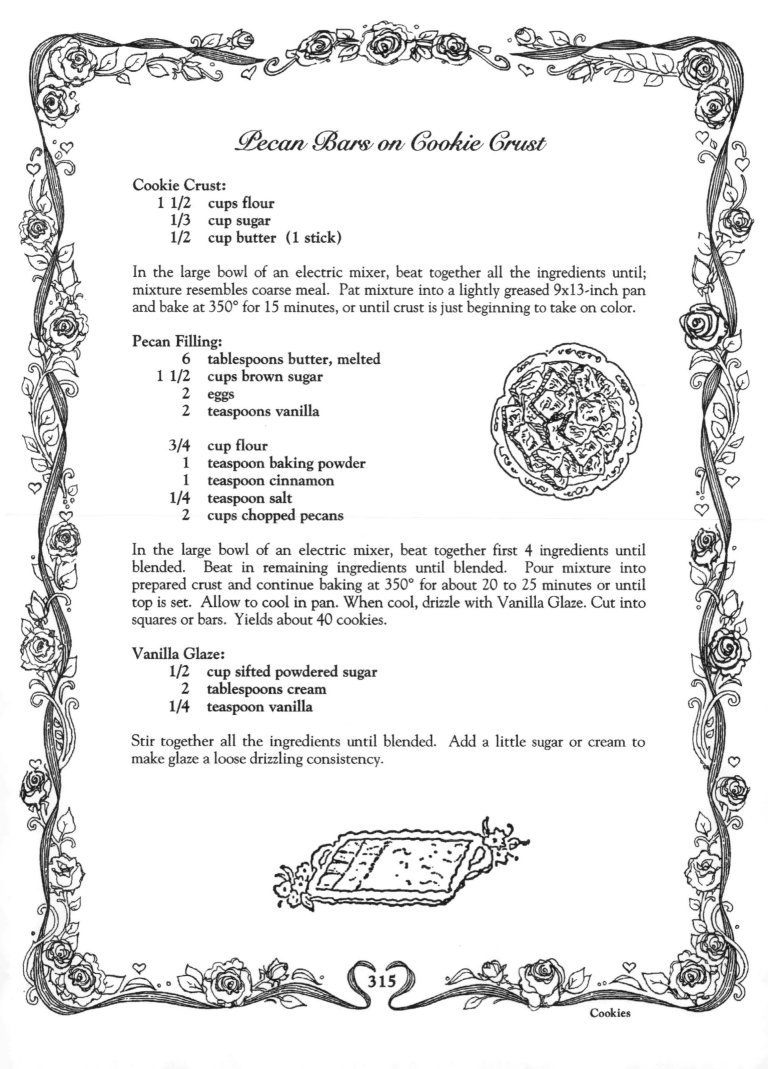

In the large bowl of an electric mixer, beat together first 4 ingredients until blended. Beat in remaining ingredients until blended. Pour mixture into prepared crust and continue baking at 350° for about 20 to 25 minutes or until top is set. Allow to cool in pan. When cool, drizzle with Vanilla Glaze. Cut into squares or bars. Yields about 40 cookies.

Vanilla Glaze:

1/2	cup sifted powdered sugar
2	tablespoons cream
1/4	teaspoon vanilla

Stir together all the ingredients until blended. Add a little sugar or cream to make glaze a loose drizzling consistency.

Mom's Greek Butter Cookies

This simple little butter cookie is one I grew up on. Mom would make these into balls, or flatten them into discs or into three-cornered hats. Often, she would make them without nuts. They are a poem of flavor and texture and one of my favorites.

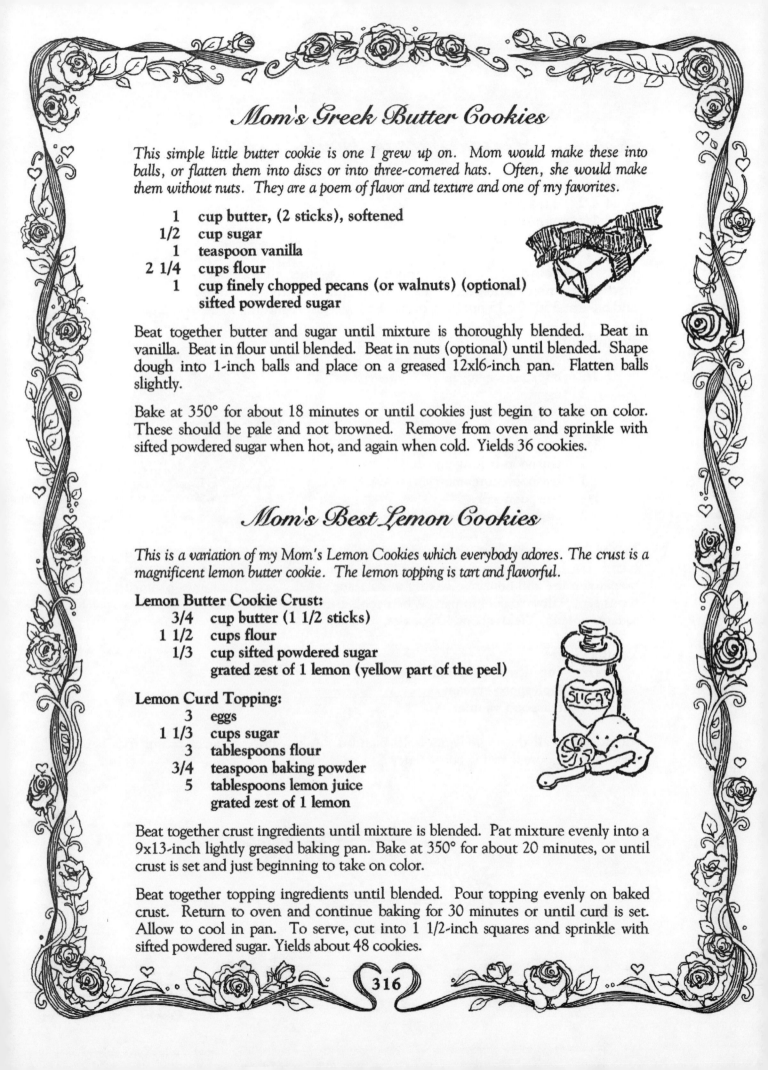

1	cup butter, (2 sticks), softened
1/2	cup sugar
1	teaspoon vanilla
2 1/4	cups flour
1	cup finely chopped pecans (or walnuts) (optional)
	sifted powdered sugar

Beat together butter and sugar until mixture is thoroughly blended. Beat in vanilla. Beat in flour until blended. Beat in nuts (optional) until blended. Shape dough into 1-inch balls and place on a greased 12x16-inch pan. Flatten balls slightly.

Bake at 350° for about 18 minutes or until cookies just begin to take on color. These should be pale and not browned. Remove from oven and sprinkle with sifted powdered sugar when hot, and again when cold. Yields 36 cookies.

Mom's Best Lemon Cookies

This is a variation of my Mom's Lemon Cookies which everybody adores. The crust is a magnificent lemon butter cookie. The lemon topping is tart and flavorful.

Lemon Butter Cookie Crust:

3/4	cup butter (1 1/2 sticks)
1 1/2	cups flour
1/3	cup sifted powdered sugar
	grated zest of 1 lemon (yellow part of the peel)

Lemon Curd Topping:

3	eggs
1 1/3	cups sugar
3	tablespoons flour
3/4	teaspoon baking powder
5	tablespoons lemon juice
	grated zest of 1 lemon

Beat together crust ingredients until mixture is blended. Pat mixture evenly into a 9x13-inch lightly greased baking pan. Bake at 350° for about 20 minutes, or until crust is set and just beginning to take on color.

Beat together topping ingredients until blended. Pour topping evenly on baked crust. Return to oven and continue baking for 30 minutes or until curd is set. Allow to cool in pan. To serve, cut into 1 1/2-inch squares and sprinkle with sifted powdered sugar. Yields about 48 cookies.

Hungarian Walnut & Apricot Squares on Lemon Shortbread Cookie Crust

This is an adaptation of a delicious cookie my mother-in-law made often. She used apricot jam, but raspberry jam works very well too. It is important to heat the jam as it will spread easily and will avoid tearing the crust. The Lemon Glaze is the perfect accent.

Lemon Shortbread Cookie Crust:

2	cups flour
1	cup sugar
1	cup cold butter (2 sticks), cut into 8 pieces
1	tablespoon grated lemon zest
1/2	cup apricot jam or raspberry jam, heated

In the large bowl of an electric mixer, beat together first 3 ingredients until mixture resembles fine meal. Toss in the lemon peel until blended. Pat dough on the bottom and 1-inch up the sides of a greased 9x13-inch baking pan and bake at 350° for 20 minutes, or until crust is just beginning to take on color.

Spread warmed jam evenly on crust. Pour Walnut Filling over the jam and smooth to spread evenly . Return pan to 350° oven and bake for another 30 minutes, or until a cake tester, inserted in center comes out clean. Allow to cool in pan. Drizzle top with Lemon Glaze. Cut into small squares. Yields 24 squares.

Walnut Filling:

4	eggs
2	cups brown sugar
1/4	cup flour
2	teaspoons vanilla
1	teaspoon baking powder
2	cups chopped walnuts

Beat together first 5 ingredients until nicely blended. Beat in the walnuts until blended.

Lemon Glaze:
Stir together 1 1/2 tablespoons lemon juice and 3/4 cup sifted powdered sugar. Add a little lemon juice or sugar to make glaze a drizzling consistency.

Little Chocolate Chip Goldies

To make these into "Blondies", substitute butterscotch chips for the chocolate chips. Both versions are memorable.

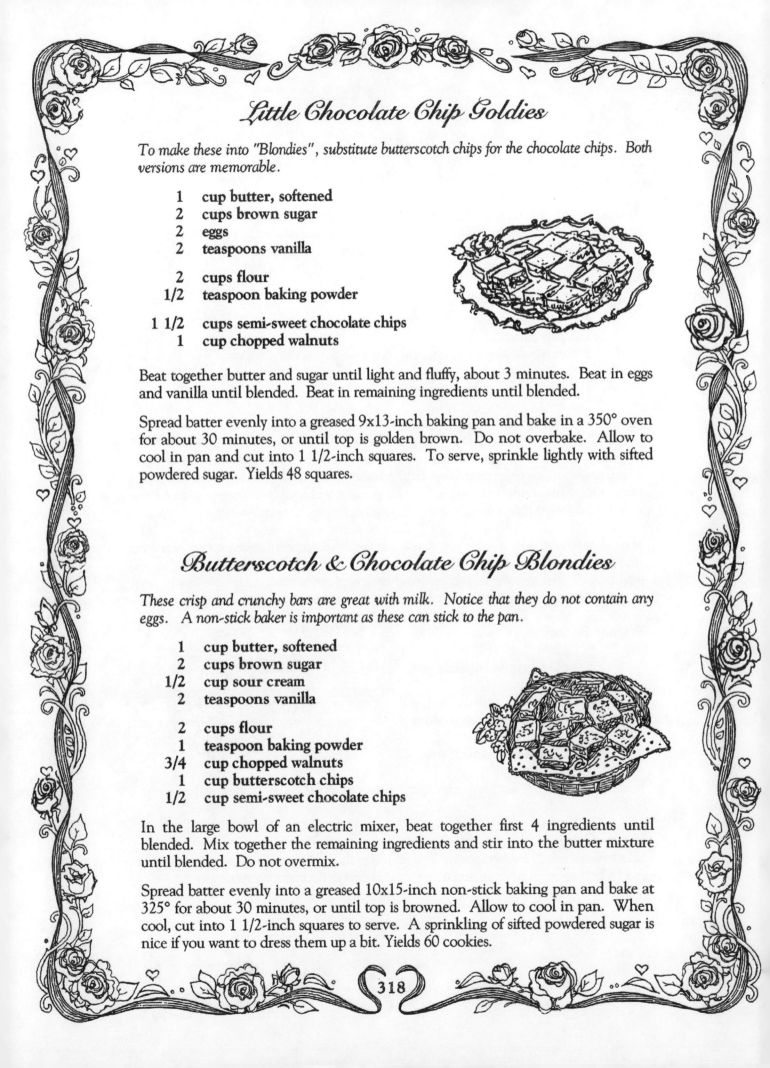

1	cup butter, softened
2	cups brown sugar
2	eggs
2	teaspoons vanilla
2	cups flour
1/2	teaspoon baking powder
1 1/2	cups semi-sweet chocolate chips
1	cup chopped walnuts

Beat together butter and sugar until light and fluffy, about 3 minutes. Beat in eggs and vanilla until blended. Beat in remaining ingredients until blended.

Spread batter evenly into a greased 9x13-inch baking pan and bake in a 350° oven for about 30 minutes, or until top is golden brown. Do not overbake. Allow to cool in pan and cut into 1 1/2-inch squares. To serve, sprinkle lightly with sifted powdered sugar. Yields 48 squares.

Butterscotch & Chocolate Chip Blondies

These crisp and crunchy bars are great with milk. Notice that they do not contain any eggs. A non-stick baker is important as these can stick to the pan.

1	cup butter, softened
2	cups brown sugar
1/2	cup sour cream
2	teaspoons vanilla
2	cups flour
1	teaspoon baking powder
3/4	cup chopped walnuts
1	cup butterscotch chips
1/2	cup semi-sweet chocolate chips

In the large bowl of an electric mixer, beat together first 4 ingredients until blended. Mix together the remaining ingredients and stir into the butter mixture until blended. Do not overmix.

Spread batter evenly into a greased 10x15-inch non-stick baking pan and bake at 325° for about 30 minutes, or until top is browned. Allow to cool in pan. When cool, cut into 1 1/2-inch squares to serve. A sprinkling of sifted powdered sugar is nice if you want to dress them up a bit. Yields 60 cookies.

Easiest & Best Apricot Nut Bars

This is an easy cookie that is tart and crunchy. Whenever I make it, everyone asks for the recipe. It is intensely "apricot" and for the apricot lover.

1	package (6 ounces) dried apricots
1/2	cup of sugar
1	cup butter, softened
1/2	cup sugar
1	cup brown sugar
2	teaspoons vanilla
2 1/4	cups flour
1/2	teaspoon baking powder
1/2	teaspoon baking soda
1	cup chopped walnuts

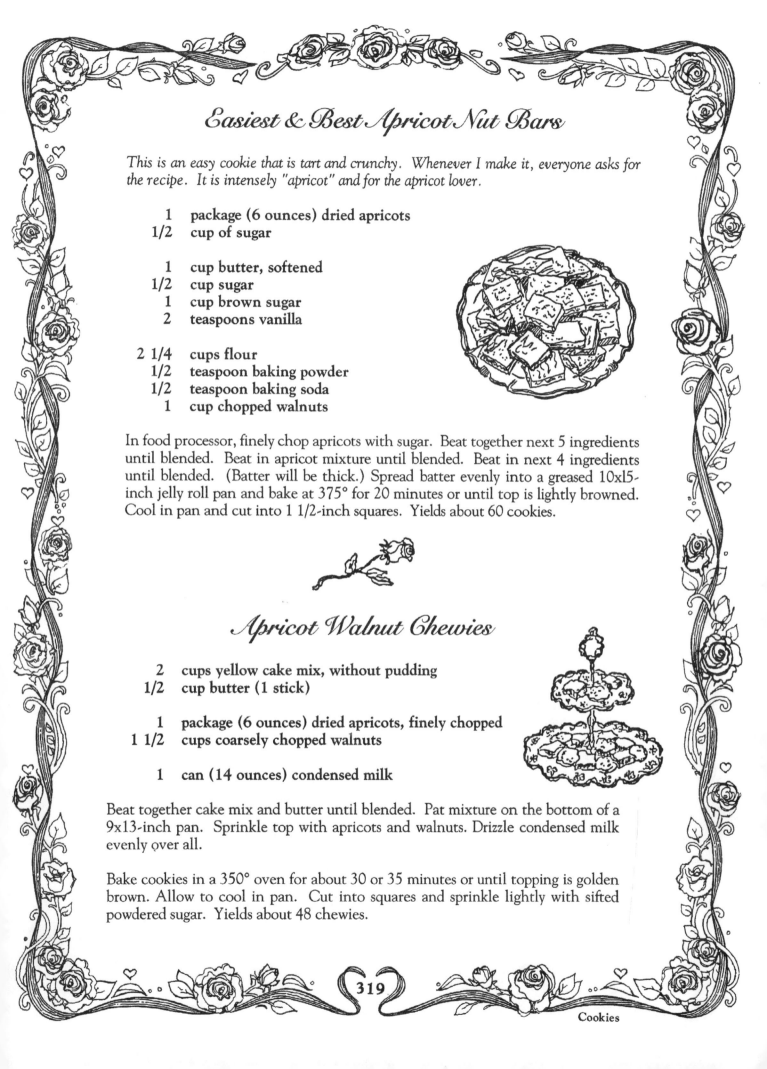

In food processor, finely chop apricots with sugar. Beat together next 5 ingredients until blended. Beat in apricot mixture until blended. Beat in next 4 ingredients until blended. (Batter will be thick.) Spread batter evenly into a greased 10x15-inch jelly roll pan and bake at 375° for 20 minutes or until top is lightly browned. Cool in pan and cut into 1 1/2-inch squares. Yields about 60 cookies.

Apricot Walnut Chewies

2	cups yellow cake mix, without pudding
1/2	cup butter (1 stick)
1	package (6 ounces) dried apricots, finely chopped
1 1/2	cups coarsely chopped walnuts
1	can (14 ounces) condensed milk

Beat together cake mix and butter until blended. Pat mixture on the bottom of a 9x13-inch pan. Sprinkle top with apricots and walnuts. Drizzle condensed milk evenly over all.

Bake cookies in a 350° oven for about 30 or 35 minutes or until topping is golden brown. Allow to cool in pan. Cut into squares and sprinkle lightly with sifted powdered sugar. Yields about 48 chewies.

Cookies

Compote of Mixed Berries & Peaches

I am offering this recipe with frozen fruit as fresh berries may be difficult to find at certain times of the year. If you use fresh berries add a few minutes to cooking time.

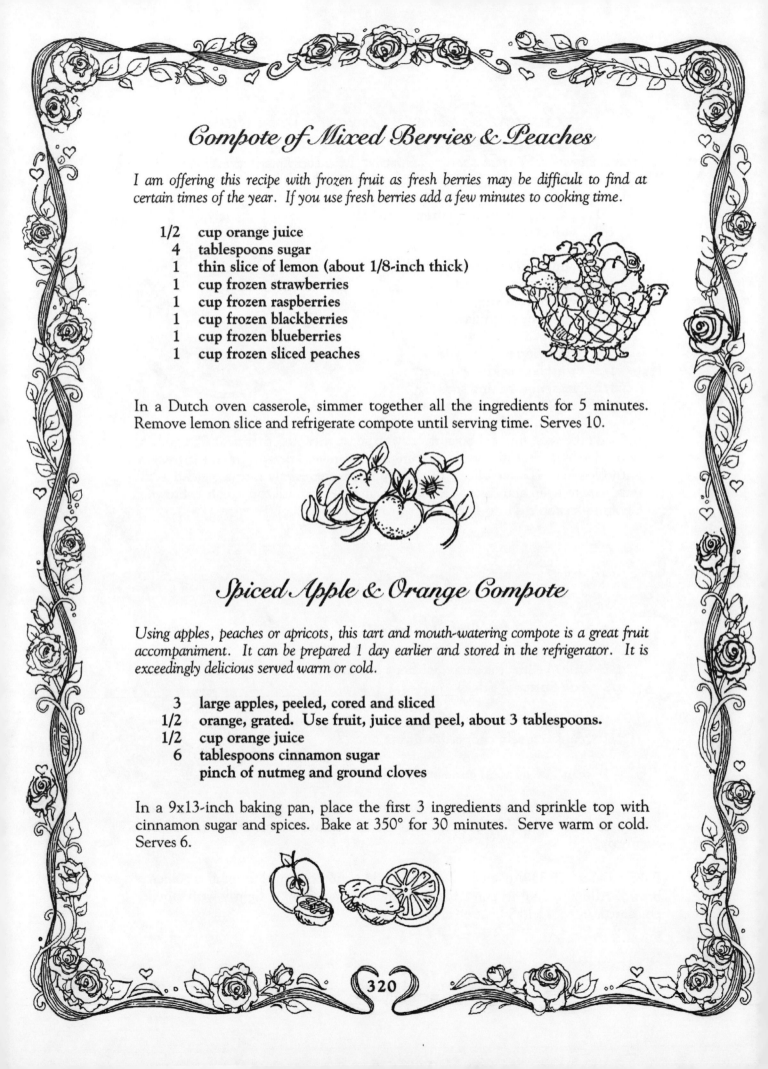

1/2	cup orange juice
4	tablespoons sugar
1	thin slice of lemon (about 1/8-inch thick)
1	cup frozen strawberries
1	cup frozen raspberries
1	cup frozen blackberries
1	cup frozen blueberries
1	cup frozen sliced peaches

In a Dutch oven casserole, simmer together all the ingredients for 5 minutes. Remove lemon slice and refrigerate compote until serving time. Serves 10.

Spiced Apple & Orange Compote

Using apples, peaches or apricots, this tart and mouth-watering compote is a great fruit accompaniment. It can be prepared 1 day earlier and stored in the refrigerator. It is exceedingly delicious served warm or cold.

3	large apples, peeled, cored and sliced
1/2	orange, grated. Use fruit, juice and peel, about 3 tablespoons.
1/2	cup orange juice
6	tablespoons cinnamon sugar
	pinch of nutmeg and ground cloves

In a 9x13-inch baking pan, place the first 3 ingredients and sprinkle top with cinnamon sugar and spices. Bake at 350° for 30 minutes. Serve warm or cold. Serves 6.

Compote of Apples & Cranberries

Apples with cranberries make a nice winter compote. This one is fruity and on the tart side, and a lovely accompaniment to lamb. This can be served slightly chilled or at room temperature.

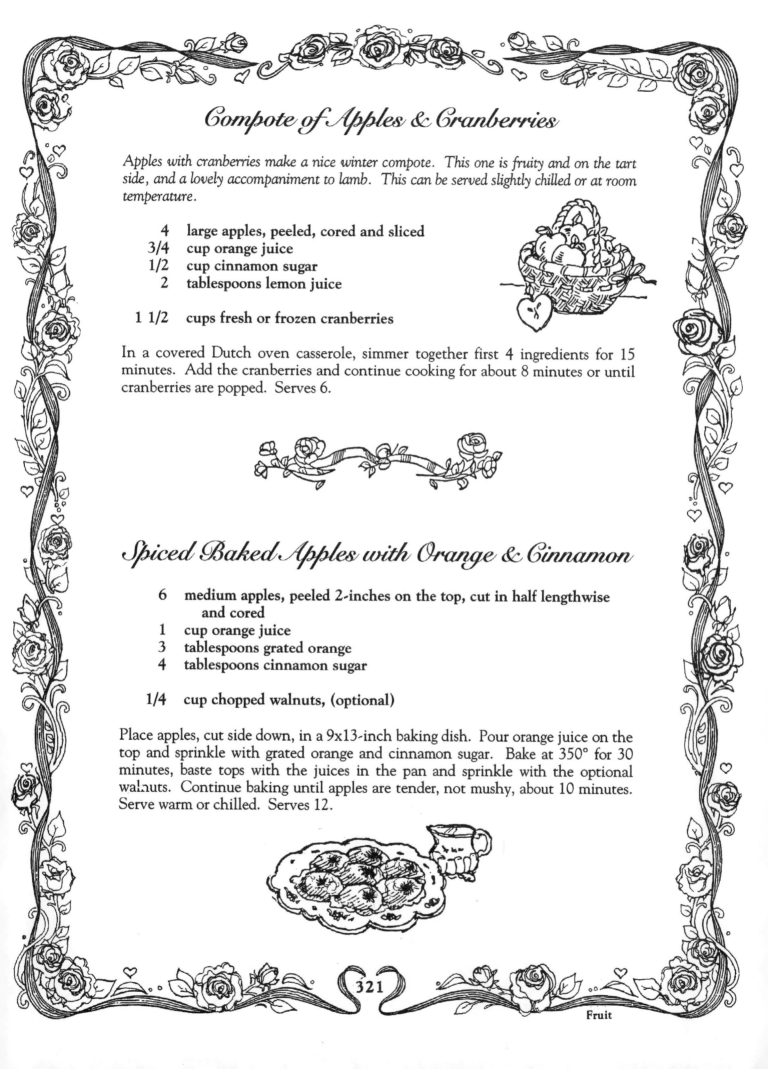

- 4 large apples, peeled, cored and sliced
- 3/4 cup orange juice
- 1/2 cup cinnamon sugar
- 2 tablespoons lemon juice

- 1 1/2 cups fresh or frozen cranberries

In a covered Dutch oven casserole, simmer together first 4 ingredients for 15 minutes. Add the cranberries and continue cooking for about 8 minutes or until cranberries are popped. Serves 6.

Spiced Baked Apples with Orange & Cinnamon

- 6 medium apples, peeled 2-inches on the top, cut in half lengthwise and cored
- 1 cup orange juice
- 3 tablespoons grated orange
- 4 tablespoons cinnamon sugar

- 1/4 cup chopped walnuts, (optional)

Place apples, cut side down, in a 9x13-inch baking dish. Pour orange juice on the top and sprinkle with grated orange and cinnamon sugar. Bake at 350° for 30 minutes, baste tops with the juices in the pan and sprinkle with the optional walnuts. Continue baking until apples are tender, not mushy, about 10 minutes. Serve warm or chilled. Serves 12.

Fruit

Spiced Peaches with Walnuts

This very versatile, tart and spicy fruit is nice to serve with chicken or veal. It is also great to serve as a topping for ice cream or non-fat yogurt. It is attractive and colorful on a buffet. Can be prepared earlier in the day and heated before serving. Apples or apricots can be substituted for the peaches. Can be served warm or cold.

8	peaches, (about 2 pounds) peeled, pitted and cut in half
1/2	cup orange juice
2	tablespoons sugar
1/2	teaspoon cinnamon
3	sprinkles, each, ground nutmeg and ground cloves
1/2	cup coarsely cut walnuts

Place peaches in one layer in a shallow baker and pour orange juice on top. Stir together sugar, cinnamon, nutmeg and cloves and sprinkle evenly over the fruit.

Bake peaches in a 350° oven, basting every now and again, about 20 minutes. Sprinkle top with walnuts and bake another 10 minutes. Serve warm or at room temperature. Serves 8.

To Make Spiced Apples with Walnuts:
Substitute 2 pounds apples, peeled, cored and sliced, for the peaches. Total baking time is 45 minutes. Sprinkle with walnuts after 35 minutes. and then bake 10 minutes longer.

To Make Spiced Apricots with Walnuts:
Substitute 2 pounds apricots, peeled, halved and stoned, for the peaches. Baking time is the same as for the peaches.

Glazed Cinnamon Apple Rings

4	large apples, cored and sliced into 3/4-inch rings
1/2	cup apple juice
3	tablespoons cinnamon sugar
	pinch of nutmeg and cloves
1/2	cup chopped pecans

Place apple rings in a 9x13-inch baking pan, drizzle with apple juice, sprinkle with cinnamon sugar and spices. Bake in a 350° oven for 20 minutes, sprinkle top with pecans and continue baking for 10 minutes. Serves 8.

Warm Compote of Spiced Mixed Fruit

This is a delicious fruit salad that can take the place of a vegetable. It is great to serve with Stuffed Breast of Veal. This is actually very simple to prepare...simmer the fruit in orange juice, add a couple of slices of lemon for balance, and sparkle with a little cinnamon. It can be prepared 1 day earlier, stored in the refrigerator and heated before serving.

2	packages (1 pound, each) mixed dried fruits - a combination of dried apricots, peaches, apples, pears and prunes. (Make certain that the prunes are pitted.)
1 1/2	cups orange juice
2	thin slices of lemon
4	tablespoons cinnamon sugar

In a covered Dutch oven casserole, simmer together dried fruits, orange juice, lemon and cinnamon sugar, until fruits are tender, about 10 minutes.

Can be held at this point, covered, in the refrigerator. Before serving, add a little orange juice if casserole appears dry. Warm over low heat, covered, until heated through. Serve warm, not hot. Serves 8 generously.

Glazed Brandied Apricots

This is not quite a jam, but can be used as such. Delicious with buttered toast, French toast, waffles or pancakes.

1	**cup** dried apricots
3/4	cup orange juice
6	tablespoons sugar
1	tablespoon Apricot Brandy

In a saucepan, simmer together all the ingredients for 5 minutes, or until apricots are softened and mixture is syrupy.

Orange Applesauce

Serve this incredible applesauce with Potato Pancakes, regular pancakes or over ice cream. It is a real treat, especially if you love applesauce.

1	jar (1 pound) unsweetened applesauce
4 to 6	tablespoons concentrated orange juice, undiluted

Stir together applesauce and concentrated orange juice until blended. Start with 4 tablespoons and add more to taste. Yields about 2 1/4 cups.

fruit

Lemon Gelati with Raspberry Sauce
(Lemon Iced Cream with Raspberry Sauce)

- 1   pint whipping cream or half and half
- 4   tablespoons lemon juice
- 1/2   lemon, finely grated. Remove any large pieces of membranes.
- 1   cup sugar

In a bowl, place all the ingredients and stir until the sugar is dissolved, about 1 minute. Divide the mixture between 12 paper-lined muffin cups and place in the freezer until firm. When frozen firm, store in double plastic bags.

Remove from the freezer about 5 minutes before serving. To serve, remove the paper liners and place iced cream in a lovely stemmed glass or pretty glass dessert dish. Spoon a little Raspberry Sauce on top. Serves 12.

Raspberry Sauce:
- 1   package (10 ounces) frozen raspberries in syrup, thawed
- 1   tablespoon lemon juice

Stir ingredients together until blended.

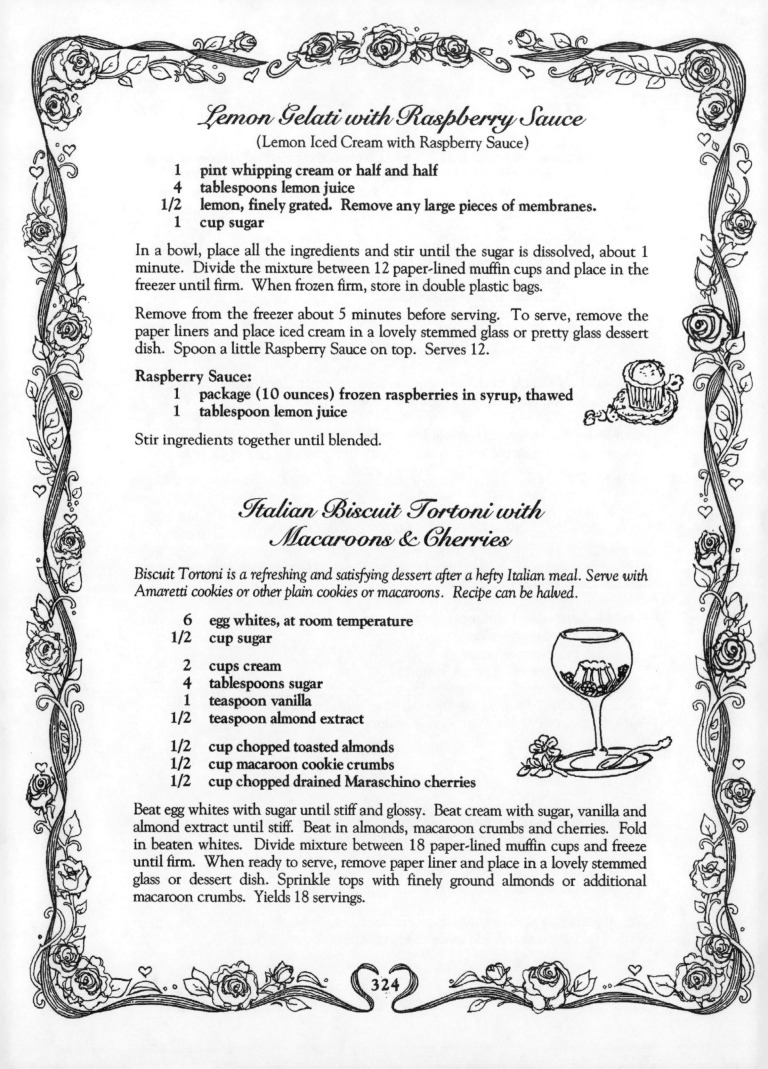

Italian Biscuit Tortoni with Macaroons & Cherries

Biscuit Tortoni is a refreshing and satisfying dessert after a hefty Italian meal. Serve with Amaretti cookies or other plain cookies or macaroons. Recipe can be halved.

- 6   egg whites, at room temperature
- 1/2   cup sugar

- 2   cups cream
- 4   tablespoons sugar
- 1   teaspoon vanilla
- 1/2   teaspoon almond extract

- 1/2   cup chopped toasted almonds
- 1/2   cup macaroon cookie crumbs
- 1/2   cup chopped drained Maraschino cherries

Beat egg whites with sugar until stiff and glossy. Beat cream with sugar, vanilla and almond extract until stiff. Beat in almonds, macaroon crumbs and cherries. Fold in beaten whites. Divide mixture between 18 paper-lined muffin cups and freeze until firm. When ready to serve, remove paper liner and place in a lovely stemmed glass or dessert dish. Sprinkle tops with finely ground almonds or additional macaroon crumbs. Yields 18 servings.

Iced Lemon Cream Cake with Raspberry Sauce

There is no iced dessert that is easier or more beautiful than this one. My original recipe was made with only heavy cream. This one is made a little lighter with half and half. It is a great dessert after a hefty meal.

2   packages (12 count, each) lady fingers, split in half. The lady fingers used to line the sides of the pan should be cut in half again. This is a low dessert.

1   cup whipping cream
1   cup half and half
4   tablespoons lemon juice
1/2 lemon, finely grated. Remove any large pieces of membrane.
1   cup sugar

Line an 8-inch springform pan with parchment paper. Now, line the bottom and sides of the pan with lady fingers, holding them in place with a smidgen of butter.

In a bowl, place the remaining ingredients and stir until sugar is dissolved, about 1 minute. Pour this into the prepared pan, cover with plastic wrap and freeze until firm. Remove from freezer, and using the parchment paper to help you, slide dessert onto a serving platter. To serve, cut into thin wedges and spoon a little Raspberry Sauce on top. Serves 10 to 12.

Raspberry Sauce:
1   package (10 ounces) frozen raspberries in syrup, defrosted
1   tablespoon lemon juice

Simply stir ingredients together until dissolved. Store in the refrigerator until ready to serve.

Note: -Lemon Cream can be divided between 12 paper-lined muffin cups and frozen until firm. To serve, remove the paper liners and place in a lovely stemmed glass. Spoon a little Raspberry Sauce on top.

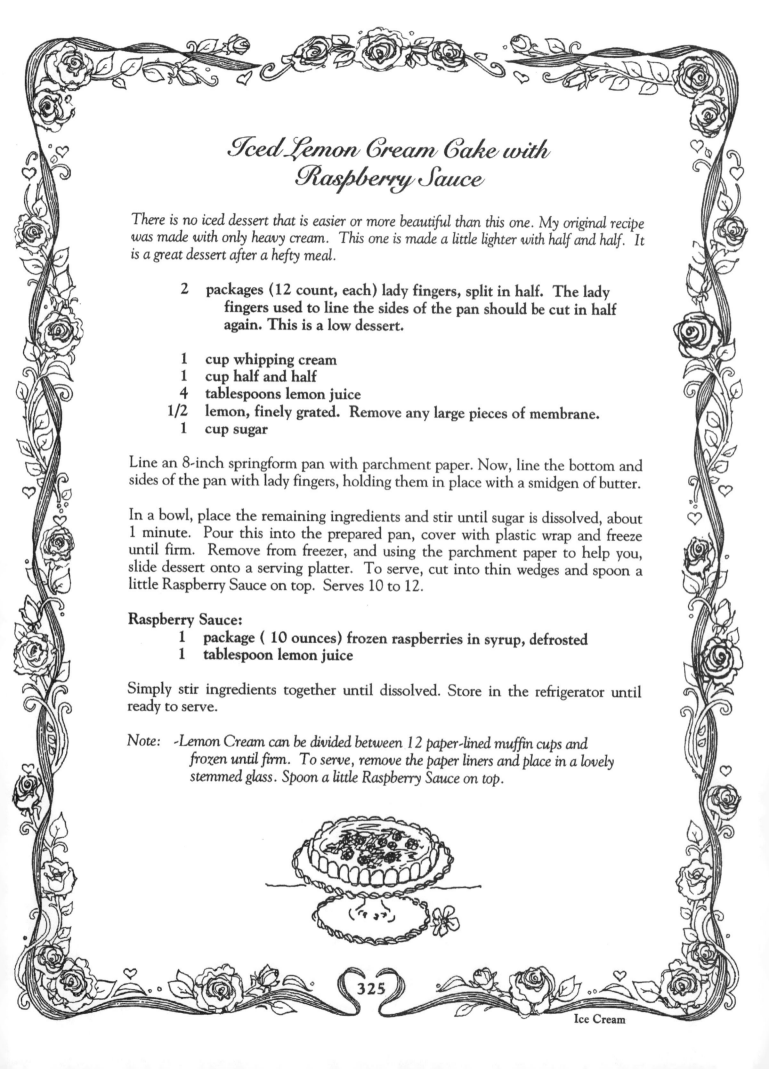

Ice Cream

Tartufo alla Tre Scalini Caffe

This delightful chocolate iced cream dessert is the famous specialty of the Caffe Tre Scalini in Rome. It holds so many fond memories for our family, as it was the first taste we sampled in Rome. It was 8 o'clock in the evening when our plane arrived and we raced by taxi to Tre Scalini. The Piazza was filled with barkers and vendors, fire eaters and jugglers. Young women walked around the edge of the Piazza and young men flirted and carried on. The evening was filled with unbelievable life and energy. And we sat and ate Tartufos and watched the gorgeous people of Rome pass by. We have been back to Tre Scalini many times since, and yes! you can go home again. The magic of our first visit has never diminished.

The original recipe for the chocolate ice cream is a zealously guarded secret, but using a very excellent quality chocolate ice cream produces a fine Tartuffo. Keep the cherries in the center as a surprise.

24	glacéed cherries
2	tablespoons rum (optional). Omit the rum for the youngsters.
12	large scoops of chocolate ice cream
1 1/2	cups semi-sweet chocolate chips
1/3	cup butter
3/4	cup toasted slivered almonds

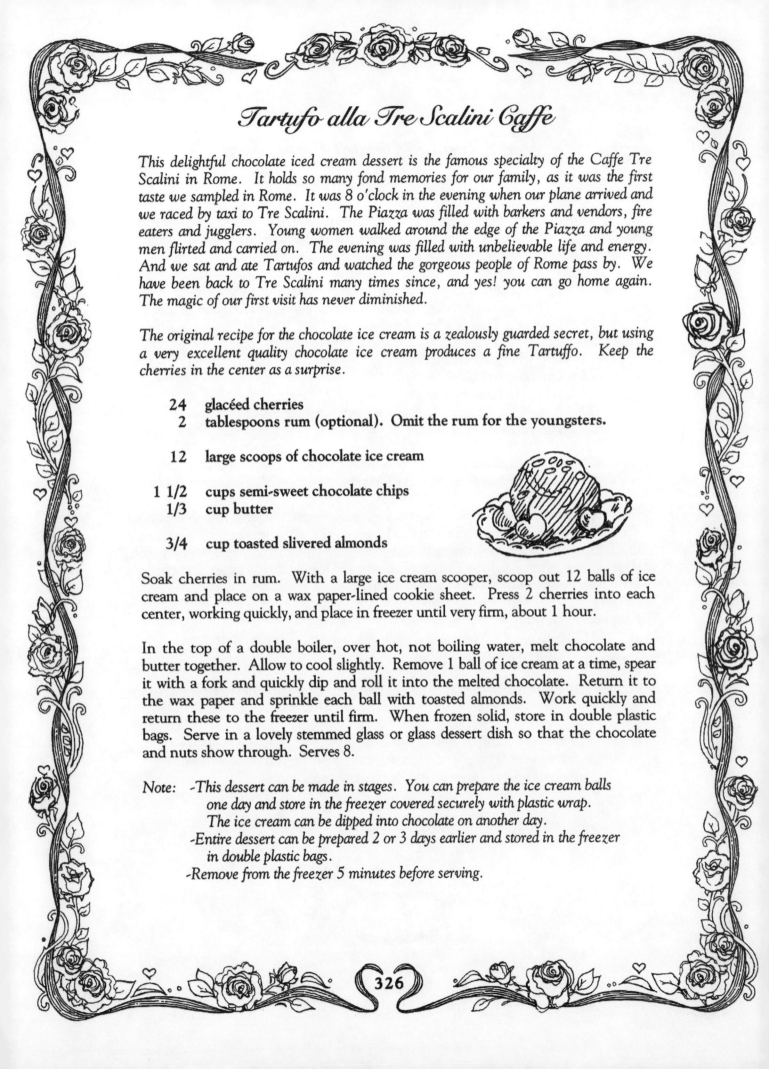

Soak cherries in rum. With a large ice cream scooper, scoop out 12 balls of ice cream and place on a wax paper-lined cookie sheet. Press 2 cherries into each center, working quickly, and place in freezer until very firm, about 1 hour.

In the top of a double boiler, over hot, not boiling water, melt chocolate and butter together. Allow to cool slightly. Remove 1 ball of ice cream at a time, spear it with a fork and quickly dip and roll it into the melted chocolate. Return it to the wax paper and sprinkle each ball with toasted almonds. Work quickly and return these to the freezer until firm. When frozen solid, store in double plastic bags. Serve in a lovely stemmed glass or glass dessert dish so that the chocolate and nuts show through. Serves 8.

Note: -This dessert can be made in stages. You can prepare the ice cream balls
one day and store in the freezer covered securely with plastic wrap.
The ice cream can be dipped into chocolate on another day.
-Entire dessert can be prepared 2 or 3 days earlier and stored in the freezer
in double plastic bags.
-Remove from the freezer 5 minutes before serving.

Chocolate Chip Cookie Pie

This is a variation of the classic chocolate chip cookie made into a pie. This is rich, so keep the portions small.

1 9-inch deep-dish frozen pie shell. Place shell on a cookie sheet and bake at 350° for 7 minutes or until crust is set.

Filling:

2 eggs
1/2 cup melted butter (1 stick)
1/2 cup sour cream
1/2 cup flour
3/4 cup brown sugar, packed
1/4 cup sugar
1 teaspoon vanilla

1 cup semi-sweet chocolate chips
1 cup coarsely chopped walnuts

Prepare pie shell and leave it on the cookie sheet. Beat together first 7 filling ingredients until blended. Stir in chocolate and nuts. Pour mixture into prepared pie shell and bake at 325° for about 1 hour or until top is browned. If the edges start to darken place a sheet of aluminum foil loosely over the top. Serve warm. Serves 10.

Chocolate Chip & Pecan Pie

Children love this pie…children of all ages, that is. This is a homey pie, easy to prepare and great for family dinners.

3 eggs
1/2 cup sugar

2 cups vanilla wafer crumbs
1/2 cup sugar
1 teaspoon baking powder
1 teaspoon vanilla
1 cup coarsely chopped pecans
1 cup semi-sweet chocolate chips

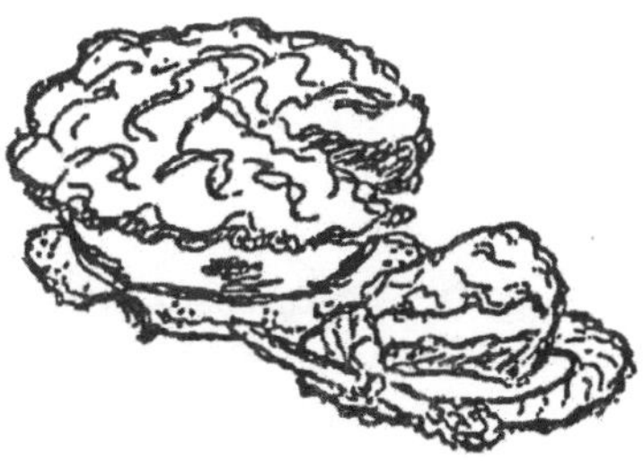

Beat eggs with sugar until light and fluffy, about 5 minutes. Fold in the remaining ingredients until blended. Pour batter into a buttered 9-inch pie plate and bake at 350° for 30 minutes. Frost with rosettes of Chocolate Chip Cream and sprinkle top with a teaspoon of finely chopped chocolate. Refrigerate overnight. Serves 8.

Chocolate Chip Cream:

3/4 cup cream
1 tablespoon sugar
3 tablespoons finely chopped chocolate chips

Beat cream with sugar until stiff. Beat in chocolate chips.

Chocolate Chip & Pecan Meringue Pie

This recipe is so versatile. It can be made with any number of different dried fruits. Several are listed below. Pie should be prepared 1 day earlier and stored in the refrigerator, overnight, to allow meringue to soften. The chocolate chips, used to decorate the pie, can be chopped in a food processor.

3   egg whites
     pinch of salt
1   cup sugar

1   cup crushed Ritz crackers   (about 22 crackers)
3/4   cup chopped pecans
3/4   cup semi-sweet chocolate chips

In the large bowl of an electric mixer, beat egg whites with salt until foamy. Slowly add the sugar and continue beating until whites are stiff, but not dry. On low speed, beat in the remaining ingredients. Place mixture into a greased 9-inch pie plate and bake at 350° for 25 to 30 minutes, or until top is lightly browned. Allow to cool in pan.

When cool, frost with Whipped Cream Vanilla and decorate with finely chopped chocolate chips on top. Cover pan with plastic wrap and refrigerate overnight. Serves 10.

Whipped Cream Vanilla:
1   cup heavy cream
1   tablespoon sugar
1   teaspoon vanilla

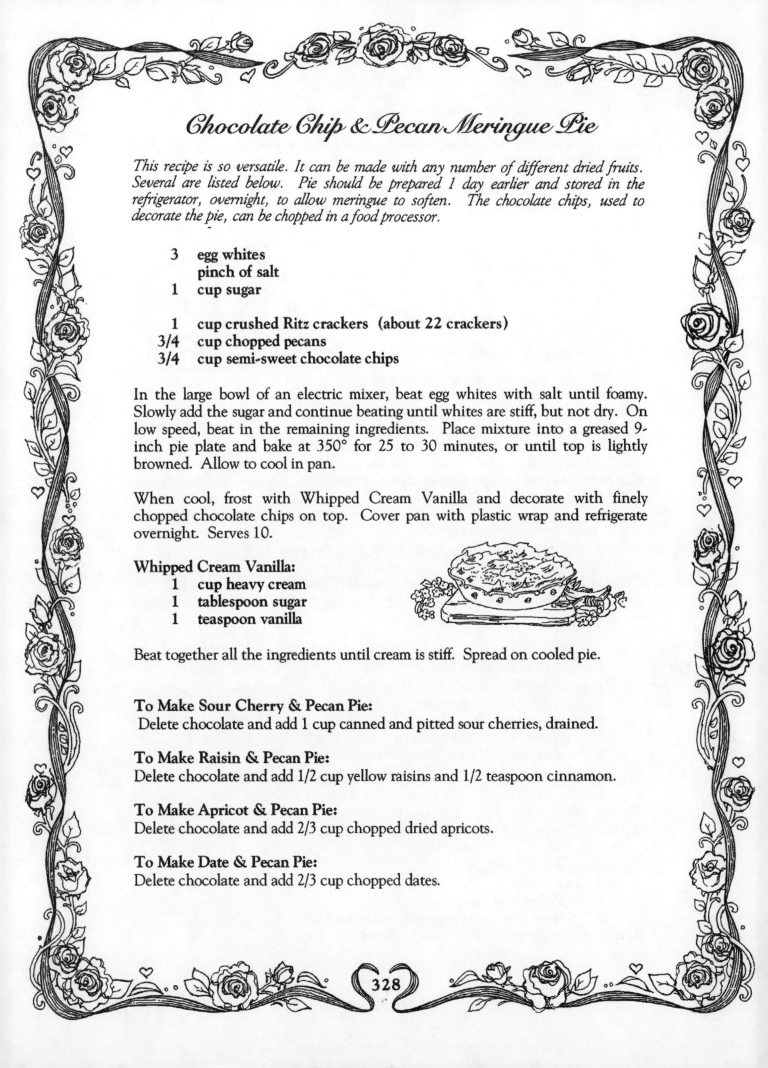

Beat together all the ingredients until cream is stiff. Spread on cooled pie.

To Make Sour Cherry & Pecan Pie:
Delete chocolate and add 1 cup canned and pitted sour cherries, drained.

To Make Raisin & Pecan Pie:
Delete chocolate and add 1/2 cup yellow raisins and 1/2 teaspoon cinnamon.

To Make Apricot & Pecan Pie:
Delete chocolate and add 2/3 cup chopped dried apricots.

To Make Date & Pecan Pie:
Delete chocolate and add 2/3 cup chopped dates.

Easiest & Best Almond & Raspberry Tart

The flavors of almond and raspberry are an elegant harmony. It is one of my preferred combinations…as this is one of my preferred tarts. It is on the order of a Linzer Tart, but very different, in that this dough is fine and delicate and fragrant with almonds

1	package (8 ounces) almond paste, crumbled
3/4	cup butter (1 1/2 sticks), softened
1/2	cup sifted powdered sugar
1	teaspoon almond extract
2	eggs, at room temperature
1	cup flour
1/2	teaspoon baking powder
1	teaspoon grated lemon peeled
1	cup raspberry jam

In the bowl of an electric mixer, beat together first 4 ingredients until mixture is thoroughly blended, and light and fluffy. Beat in the eggs until blended. Beat in the flour, baking powder and lemon peel until blended. (At this point, do not overbeat.)

Spread 2/3 of the batter on the bottom of a greased and parchment-lined 10-inch springform pan and spread the jam evenly over the top. Drop rounded teaspoons of the remaining batter over the jam, dotting them in a decorative fashion, resembling petals. Bake in a 350° oven for 30 to 35 minutes, or until top is golden brown. Allow to cool in pan.

When cool, sprinkle top with sifted powdered sugar and cut into wedges to serve. Serves 8 to 10.

Note: -This can be prepared 1 day earlier and stored at room temperature, covered with plastic wrap.

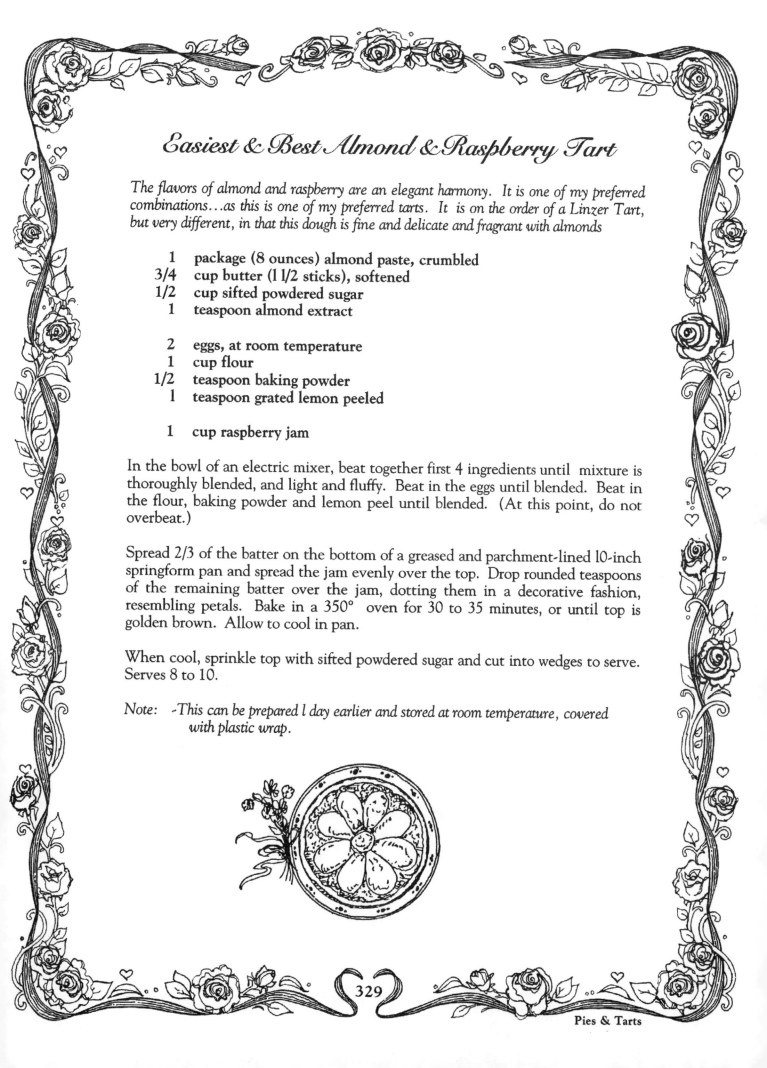

Almond Macaroon & Raspberry Tart
with Lemon Cookie Crust

This divine dessert is one of the finest tasting tarts. The Lemon Cookie Crust is the perfect balance for the Almond Macaroon Topping and the raspberry jam adds the perfect blend of balance. If piping is not your thing, then spoon the Almond Macaroon on top, in a decorative flower shape.

Lemon Butter Cookie Crust:

1 1/4	cups flour
1/2	cup sugar
1	teaspoon baking powder
1/2	cup butter (1 stick), slightly softened
1	tablespoon lemon peel
1	egg, beaten
3/4	cup raspberry jam, heated

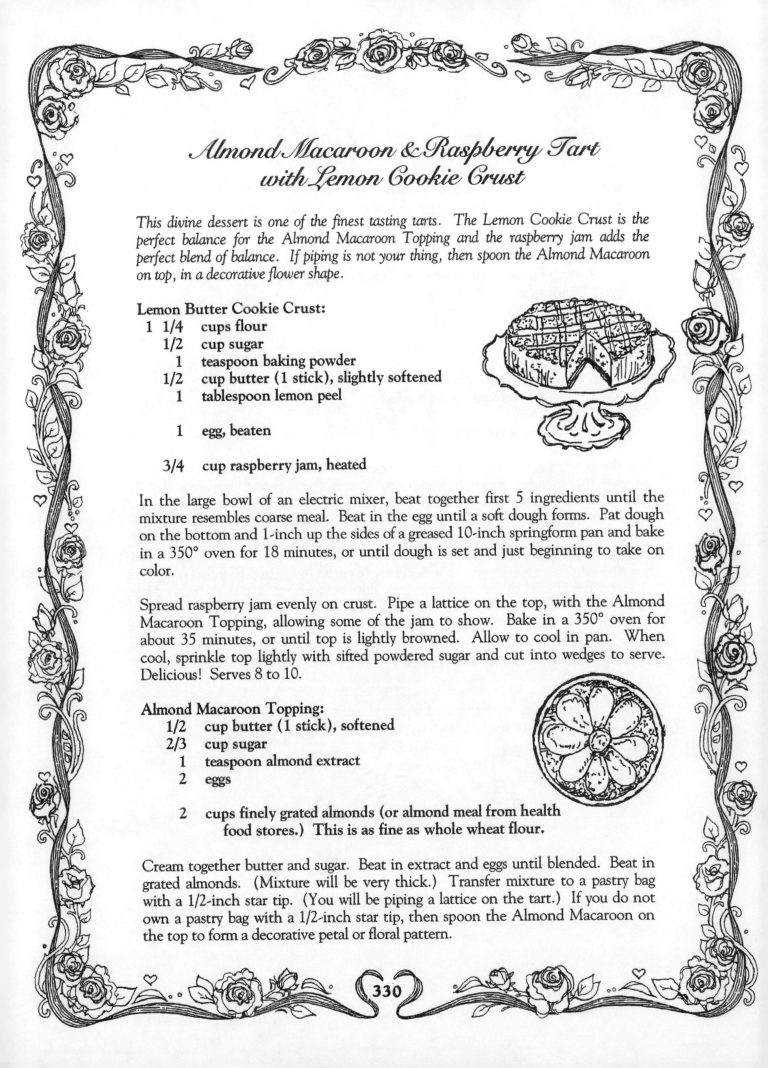

In the large bowl of an electric mixer, beat together first 5 ingredients until the mixture resembles coarse meal. Beat in the egg until a soft dough forms. Pat dough on the bottom and 1-inch up the sides of a greased 10-inch springform pan and bake in a 350° oven for 18 minutes, or until dough is set and just beginning to take on color.

Spread raspberry jam evenly on crust. Pipe a lattice on the top, with the Almond Macaroon Topping, allowing some of the jam to show. Bake in a 350° oven for about 35 minutes, or until top is lightly browned. Allow to cool in pan. When cool, sprinkle top lightly with sifted powdered sugar and cut into wedges to serve. Delicious! Serves 8 to 10.

Almond Macaroon Topping:

1/2	cup butter (1 stick), softened
2/3	cup sugar
1	teaspoon almond extract
2	eggs
2	cups finely grated almonds (or almond meal from health food stores.) This is as fine as whole wheat flour.

Cream together butter and sugar. Beat in extract and eggs until blended. Beat in grated almonds. (Mixture will be very thick.) Transfer mixture to a pastry bag with a 1/2-inch star tip. (You will be piping a lattice on the tart.) If you do not own a pastry bag with a 1/2-inch star tip, then spoon the Almond Macaroon on the top to form a decorative petal or floral pattern.

Bonnie Apple Pie in Apricot Cookie Crust

This is a lovely pie to serve at tea. It is a low pie, very delicate and delicious. In absence of a heart-shaped pan, use a 10-inch springform pan, lined with parchment paper. Instructions remain the same. The Cream Glaze adds a very nice touch, but it can be omitted. Sprinkle top with a little sifted powdered sugar if omitting the glaze.

Butter Cookie Crust:
1	cup butter
2	cups flour
1/3	cup sugar
1	beaten egg
1	tablespoon water
1/2	cup apricot jam

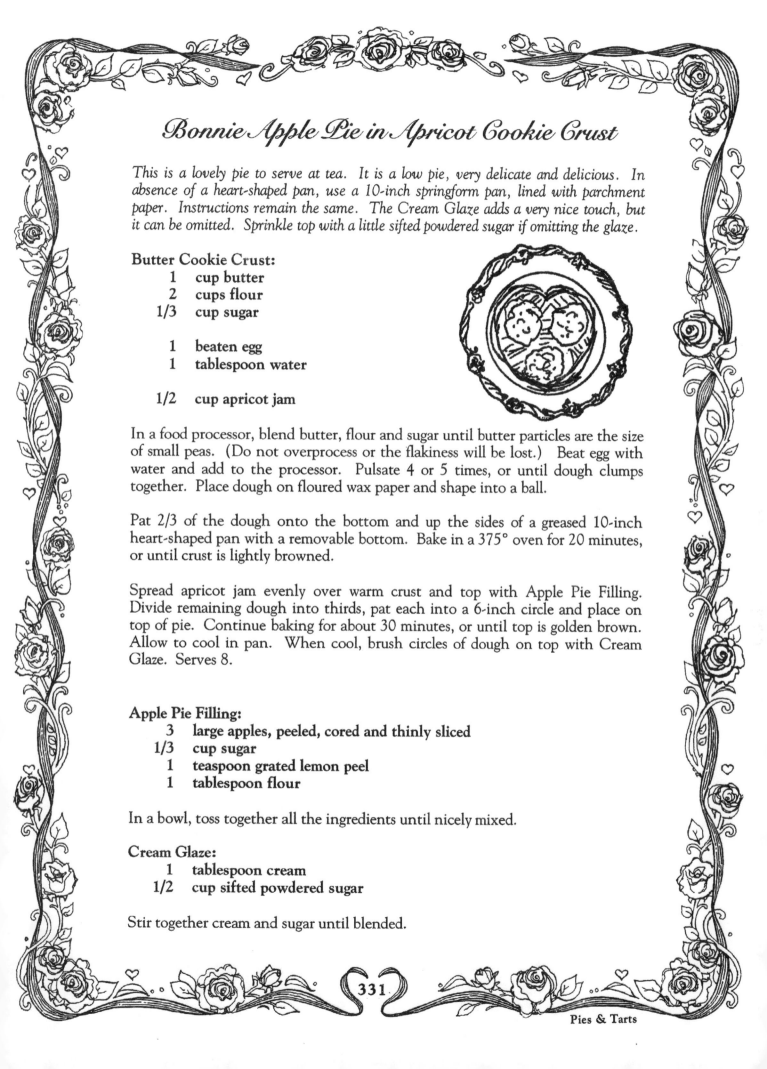

In a food processor, blend butter, flour and sugar until butter particles are the size of small peas. (Do not overprocess or the flakiness will be lost.) Beat egg with water and add to the processor. Pulsate 4 or 5 times, or until dough clumps together. Place dough on floured wax paper and shape into a ball.

Pat 2/3 of the dough onto the bottom and up the sides of a greased 10-inch heart-shaped pan with a removable bottom. Bake in a 375° oven for 20 minutes, or until crust is lightly browned.

Spread apricot jam evenly over warm crust and top with Apple Pie Filling. Divide remaining dough into thirds, pat each into a 6-inch circle and place on top of pie. Continue baking for about 30 minutes, or until top is golden brown. Allow to cool in pan. When cool, brush circles of dough on top with Cream Glaze. Serves 8.

Apple Pie Filling:
3	large apples, peeled, cored and thinly sliced
1/3	cup sugar
1	teaspoon grated lemon peel
1	tablespoon flour

In a bowl, toss together all the ingredients until nicely mixed.

Cream Glaze:
1	tablespoon cream
1/2	cup sifted powdered sugar

Stir together cream and sugar until blended.

The Best Apple & Rhubarb Pie
in a Flaky Pastry Crust

Apples and rhubarb are paired in this ultra-delicious pie. Very fruity and tart, it also serves beautifully, with large petals of flaky pastry allowing the apples and rhubarb to show through. It is further simplified with the use of a softer dough that can be pressed into the pan, avoiding the need to refrigerate or roll the pastry. This can be made in a 10-inch tart pan with a removable bottom.

Flaky Pastry:
- 1 cup butter (2 sticks)
- 2 cups flour
- 1/4 cup sugar

- 1 egg
- 2 tablespoons water (plus a few drops, if necessary, to hold dough together)
- 1 teaspoon cinnamon sugar

In a food processor, blend butter, flour and sugar until butter particles are the size of small peas. (Do not overprocess or the flakiness will be lost.) Lightly beat together the egg and water until blended. Add to the butter mixture and pulsate 4 or 5 times, or just until dough clumps together (adding a few drops of water, if necessary.) Place dough on floured wax paper and shape into a disc.

Pat 2/3 of the dough onto the bottom and up the sides of a greased 10-inch heart-shaped pan with a removable bottom. Bake in a 375° oven for 20 minutes, or until crust is lightly browned. Place Apple & Rhubarb Filling evenly over the crust. Divide remaining dough into three parts. With floured hands, pat each part into a 5-inch circle and place on top of pie. Sprinkle top with 1 teaspoon cinnamon sugar. Continue baking for about 30 minutes, or until top is golden brown. Serves 10.

Apple & Rhubarb Filling:
- 1 1/2 cups frozen rhubarb
- 1/4 cup orange juice
- 1/4 cup sugar
- 1 tablespoon lemon juice

- 3 large apples, peeled, cored and thinly sliced
- 1/3 cup sugar
- 3 tablespoons flour

In a saucepan, simmer together first 4 ingredients for 5 minutes. Place mixture in a large bowl, add the remaining ingredients and toss and stir until mixed.

Thanksgiving Southern Pecan Pie

This is a terrific, classic pecan pie. If you are pressed for time, the prepared pie crust works well. However, if you prefer making your own great crust, recipe follows.

1	frozen 10-inch deep dish pie shell. Place on a cookie sheet and bake at 350° for 7 minutes or until dough looks set.
4	eggs
1 1/4	cups dark brown sugar
1/2	cup light corn syrup
1/3	cup melted butter
2	teaspoons vanilla
1/4	teaspoon salt
2	cups coarsely chopped pecans

Prepare pie crust and keep it on the cookie sheet. Beat together next 6 ingredients until nicely blended. Stir in the pecans. Pour mixture evenly into prepared crust and bake at 350° for about 40 minutes or until pie is set. Serves 10.

Flaky Cookie Pie Crust:

3/4	cup butter (1 1/2 sticks)
1 1/2	cups flour
3	tablespoons sugar
1	egg yolk
2	tablespoons water

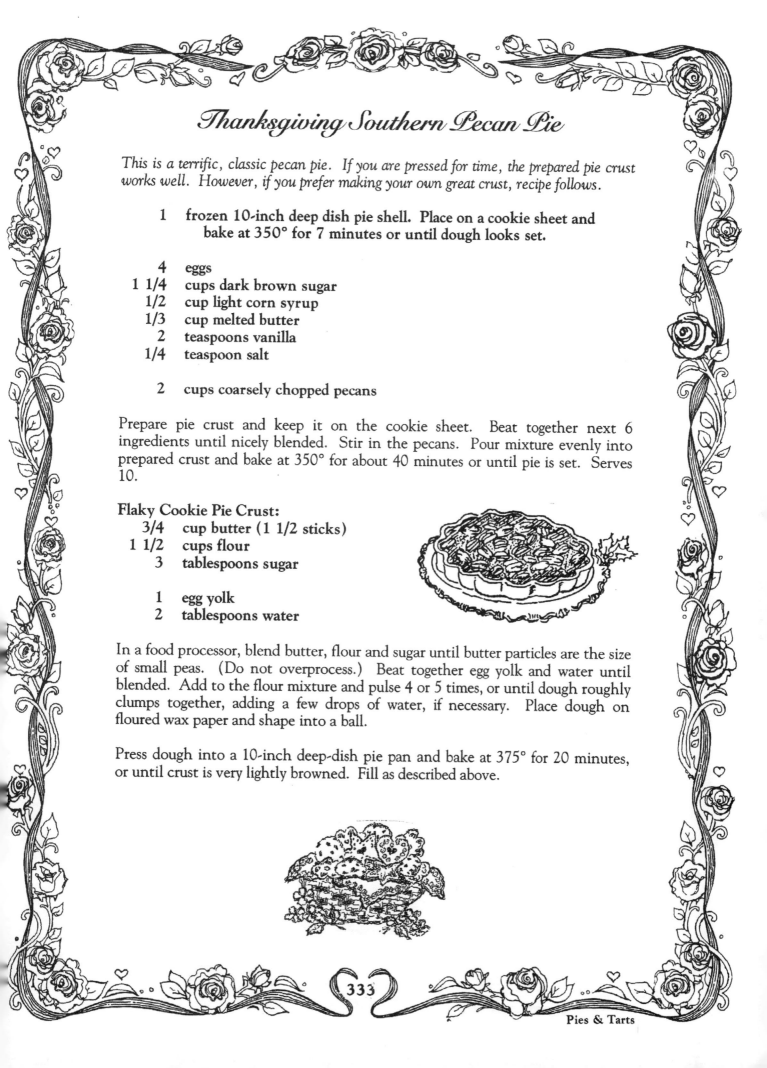

In a food processor, blend butter, flour and sugar until butter particles are the size of small peas. (Do not overprocess.) Beat together egg yolk and water until blended. Add to the flour mixture and pulse 4 or 5 times, or until dough roughly clumps together, adding a few drops of water, if necessary. Place dough on floured wax paper and shape into a ball.

Press dough into a 10-inch deep-dish pie pan and bake at 375° for 20 minutes, or until crust is very lightly browned. Fill as described above.

Thanksgiving Apple & Cranberry Pie in a Butter Cookie Crust

Apples and cranberries are wonderful together. My favorite pan, of course, is a 10-inch heart-shaped pan. A 10-inch springform pan or tart pan with a removable bottom works well, also. The crust is marvelously flaky. It is a soft dough and can easily be pressed into the pan, avoiding the need to refrigerate and then roll out the pastry.

Butter Cookie Crust:

1	cup butter (2 sticks)
2	cups flour
1/2	cup sugar
1	egg
2	tablespoons water
1	teaspoon cinnamon sugar

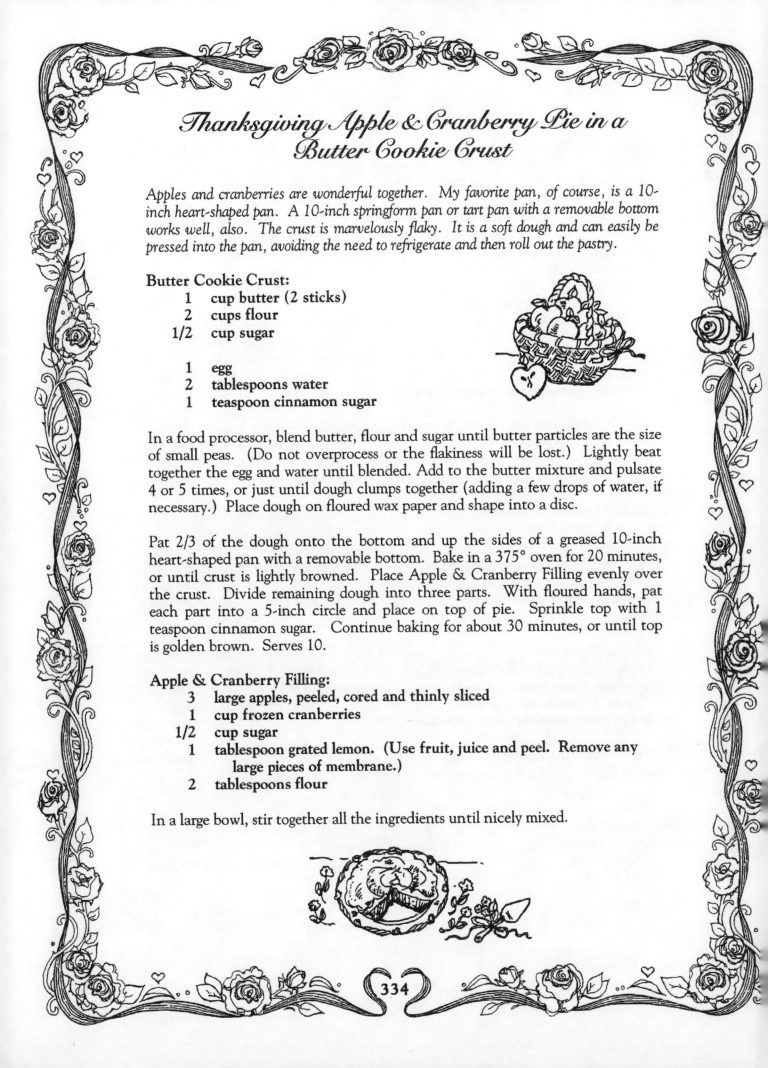

In a food processor, blend butter, flour and sugar until butter particles are the size of small peas. (Do not overprocess or the flakiness will be lost.) Lightly beat together the egg and water until blended. Add to the butter mixture and pulsate 4 or 5 times, or just until dough clumps together (adding a few drops of water, if necessary.) Place dough on floured wax paper and shape into a disc.

Pat 2/3 of the dough onto the bottom and up the sides of a greased 10-inch heart-shaped pan with a removable bottom. Bake in a 375° oven for 20 minutes, or until crust is lightly browned. Place Apple & Cranberry Filling evenly over the crust. Divide remaining dough into three parts. With floured hands, pat each part into a 5-inch circle and place on top of pie. Sprinkle top with 1 teaspoon cinnamon sugar. Continue baking for about 30 minutes, or until top is golden brown. Serves 10.

Apple & Cranberry Filling:

3	large apples, peeled, cored and thinly sliced
1	cup frozen cranberries
1/2	cup sugar
1	tablespoon grated lemon. (Use fruit, juice and peel. Remove any large pieces of membrane.)
2	tablespoons flour

In a large bowl, stir together all the ingredients until nicely mixed.

Chocolate Chip & Pecan Pie with Crème de Chocolat

This is a quick and easy dessert that you can prepare some evening when you are running late. It is not the traditional pecan pie, so don't think anything went wrong. It is very delicious and I know you will use it often.

2	tablespoons butter
1	cup coconut macaroon cookie crumbs
2	eggs
3/4	cup sugar
1/2	cup butter, (1 stick), softened
1/2	cup flour
3	tablespoons cocoa
1	cup (6 ounces) semi-sweet chocolate chips
1	cup chopped pecans
1/2	cup coconut flakes
2	teaspoons vanilla

Spread the 2 tablespoons butter on the bottom and sides of a 10-inch pie pan. Press macaroon crumbs evenly on the bottom and sides. Set aside.

Beat eggs, sugar, butter, flour and cocoa until blended. Stir in the remaining ingredients until blended. Spread mixture evenly into prepared pan and bake at 350° for 30 minutes, or until a cake tester, inserted in center, comes out clean. Allow to cool.

When cool, spread Crème de Chocolat on top and decorate top with a sprinkle of chopped chocolate chips. Serves 8.

Crème de Chocolat:

3/4	cup cream
1	tablespoon sugar
1	tablespoon Crème de Cacao Liqueur
2	tablespoons chopped semi-sweet chocolate chips

Beat cream with sugar until stiff. Beat in liqueur and chocolate chips until blended.

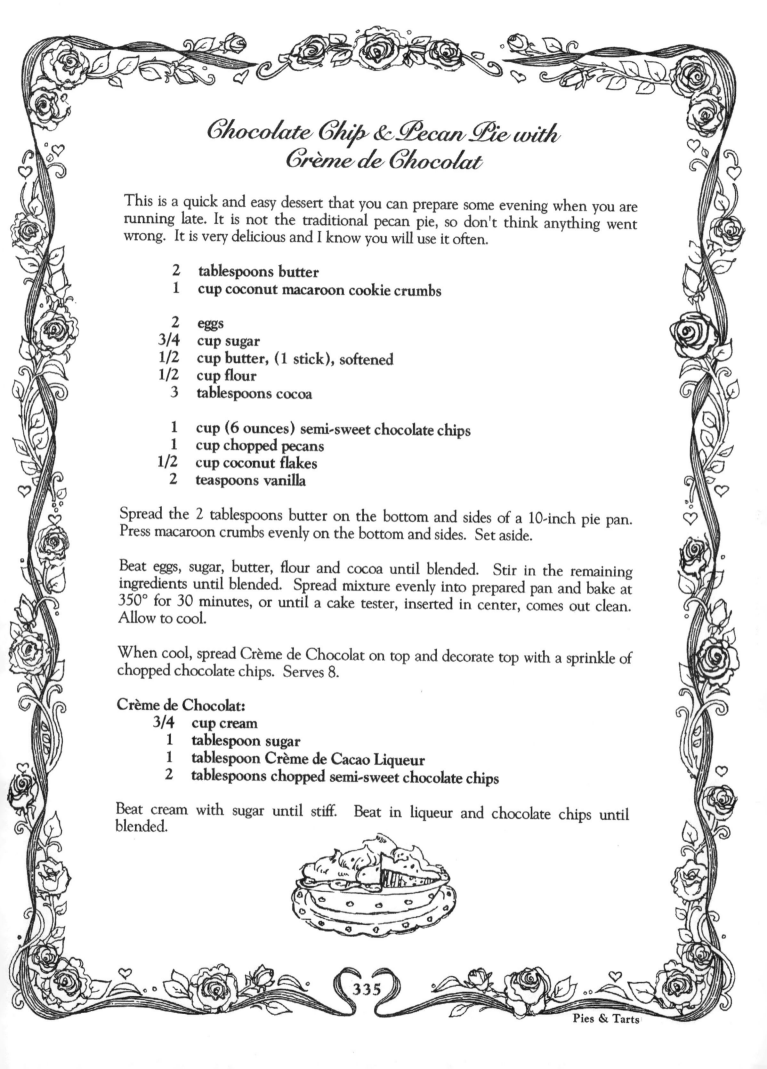

Flaky Pastry Peach & Cranberry Pie

Peaches and cranberries are paired in this ultra-delicious pie. Very fruity and tart, it also serves beautifully, with large petals of flaky pastry surrounded by peaches and cranberries. It is further simplified with the preparation of a softer dough that can be pressed into the pan, avoiding the need to refrigerate or roll the pastry. This is a sister of the Apple Cranberry Pie, but is so delicious, it merits it's own page.

Flaky Pastry:

1	cup butter (2 sticks)
2	cups flour
1/4	cup sugar
1	egg
1	tablespoon water
1	teaspoon cinnamon sugar

In a food processor, blend butter, flour and sugar until butter particles are the size of small peas. (Do not overprocess or the flakiness will be lost.) Lightly beat together the egg and water until blended. Add to the butter mixture and pulsate 4 or 5 times, or until dough clumps together. Place dough on floured wax paper and shape into a ball.

Pat 2/3 of the dough onto the bottom and up the sides of a greased 10-inch heart-shaped pan with a removable bottom. Bake in a 375° oven for 20 minutes, or until crust is lightly browned. Place Peach & Cranberry Filling evenly over the crust. Divide remaining dough into thirds, pat each into a 5-inch circle and place on top of pie. Sprinkle top with 1 teaspoon cinnamon sugar. Continue baking for about 30 minutes, or until top is golden brown. Serves 8.

Peach & Cranberry Filling:

1	pound sliced frozen peaches
1	cup frozen cranberries, picked over. Do not defrost.
1/2	cup sugar
2	tablespoons flour
1/2	small orange, grated (optional)

In a bowl, toss together all the ingredients until nicely mixed.

Strawberry & Rhubarb Cobbler with Oat Streusel Topping

This simple little cobbler will surprise you. It is so delicious and a wonderful blend of sweet and sour, balanced with a crunchy streusel topping. Using the frozen fruit allows you to make this dessert at any time during the year.

Fruit Mixture:

1	bag (20 ounces) frozen rhubarb, partially defrosted
1	package (12 ounces) frozen strawberries, partially defrosted
1/2	cup sugar
2	tablespoons lemon juice
3	tablespoons flour

In a large bowl, toss together fruit mixture until nicely blended and spread it evenly into a 9x13-inch porcelain baker.

Oat Streusel Topping:

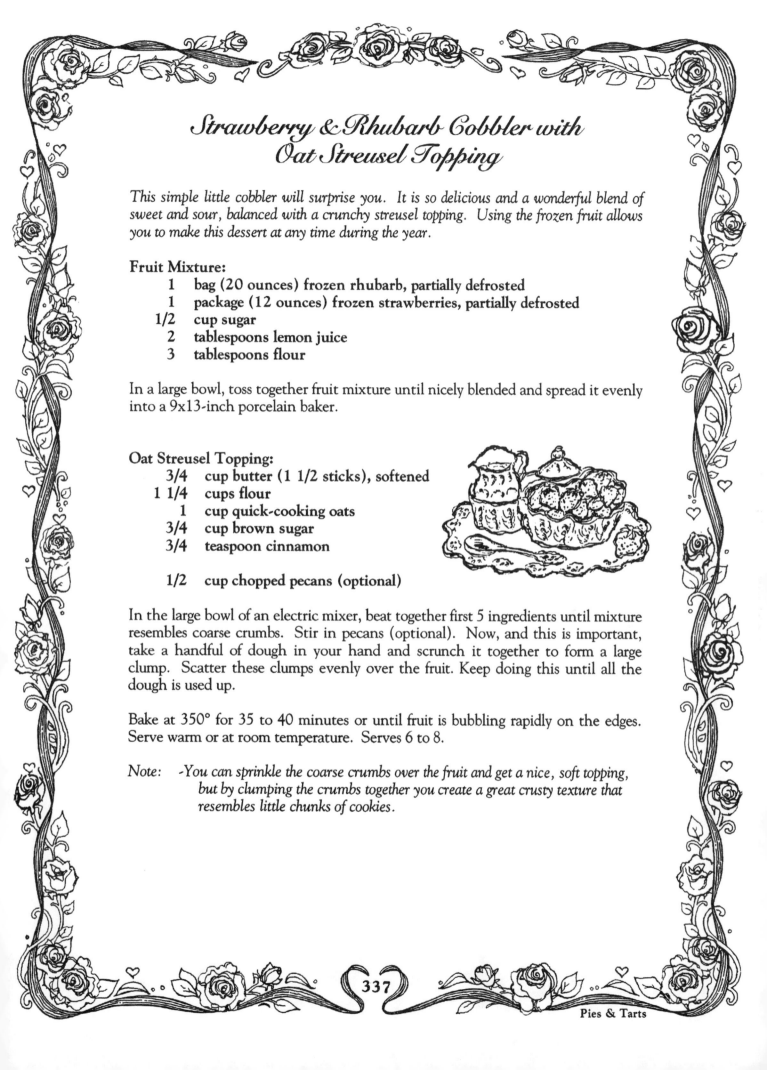

3/4	cup butter (1 1/2 sticks), softened
1 1/4	cups flour
1	cup quick-cooking oats
3/4	cup brown sugar
3/4	teaspoon cinnamon
1/2	cup chopped pecans (optional)

In the large bowl of an electric mixer, beat together first 5 ingredients until mixture resembles coarse crumbs. Stir in pecans (optional). Now, and this is important, take a handful of dough in your hand and scrunch it together to form a large clump. Scatter these clumps evenly over the fruit. Keep doing this until all the dough is used up.

Bake at 350° for 35 to 40 minutes or until fruit is bubbling rapidly on the edges. Serve warm or at room temperature. Serves 6 to 8.

Note: -You can sprinkle the coarse crumbs over the fruit and get a nice, soft topping, but by clumping the crumbs together you create a great crusty texture that resembles little chunks of cookies.

Pear Cobbler with Cinnamon, Orange & Pecans

This is one of the most delicious desserts, filled with lots of fruit, flavored with orange and cinnamon and topped with crunchy pecans. It is the essence of simplicity to prepare and wonderful for family dinners.

4	Bartlett pears, peeled, cored and sliced (about 1 1/2 pounds)
1/2	cup sugar
2	teaspoons cinnamon
2	eggs
1/2	cup oil
1	cup sugar
1	cup flour
1	teaspoon baking powder
2	tablespoons grated orange peel
1	cup chopped pecans
2	tablespoons cinnamon sugar

In a 9 x 13-inch baking pan, toss together pears, sugar and cinnamon, until fruit is evenly coated. Spread fruit evenly in pan.

Beat together next 5 ingredients until blended. Beat in the orange peel. Dribble batter over the pears, covering them evenly. Sprinkle top with pecans and cinnamon sugar. Pat the pecans lightly into the batter.

Bake in a 350° oven for 30 minutes, or until top is nicely browned. Allow to cool in pan. Cut into squares to serve and top with a little cream (optional) if you like. Serves 8.

Note: -Can be served warm or at room temperature.
      -Apples or peaches can be substituted.
      -Enjoy!

Peach & Cranberry Cobbler

I must have made this cobbler hundreds of times with different fruits, and different combination of fruits. I even made it with canned pie fillings. The reason that everything worked so well is how the Streusel Topping is handled. Be certain to make large clumps of dough to sprinkle on top. This will form a crustier topping.

Fruit Mixture:

1	pound sliced frozen peaches, slightly defrosted
1	cup frozen cranberries, slightly defrosted
1/3	cup sugar
1/2	orange, grated (optional, but delicious)
2	tablespoons flour

Streusel Topping:

1/2	cup butter
1	cup flour
1/2	cup brown sugar
1/2	teaspoon cinnamon
1/2	cup chopped pecans (optional)

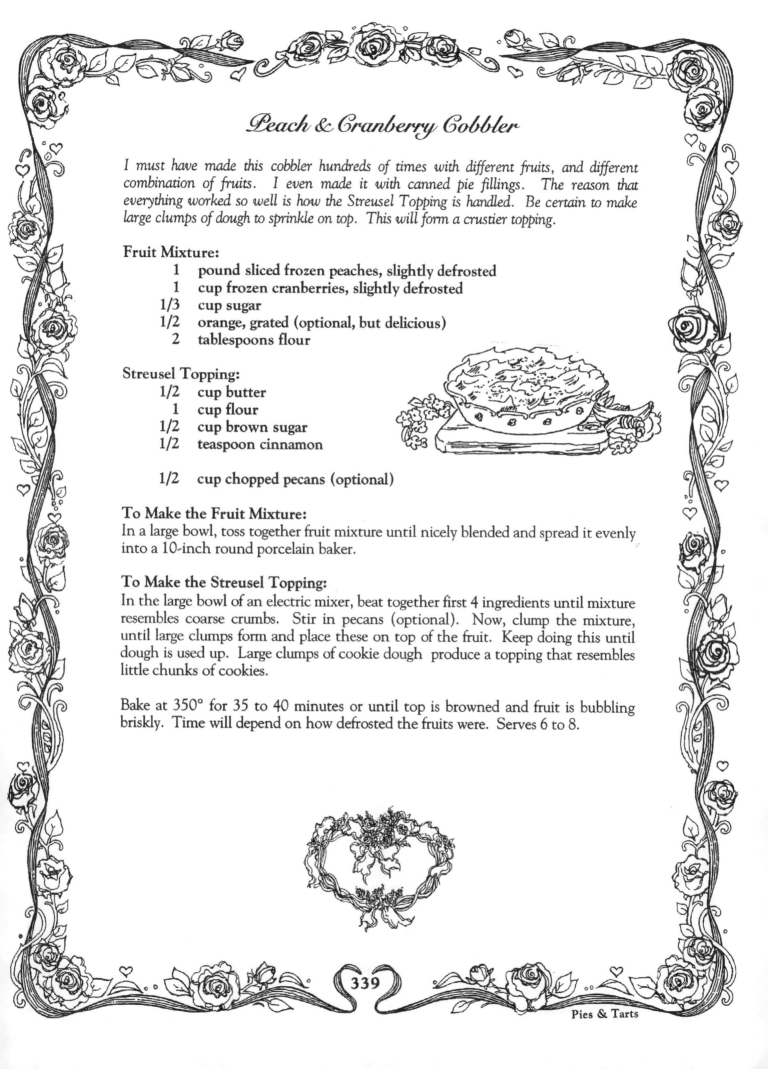

To Make the Fruit Mixture:
In a large bowl, toss together fruit mixture until nicely blended and spread it evenly into a 10-inch round porcelain baker.

To Make the Streusel Topping:
In the large bowl of an electric mixer, beat together first 4 ingredients until mixture resembles coarse crumbs. Stir in pecans (optional). Now, clump the mixture, until large clumps form and place these on top of the fruit. Keep doing this until dough is used up. Large clumps of cookie dough produce a topping that resembles little chunks of cookies.

Bake at 350° for 35 to 40 minutes or until top is browned and fruit is bubbling briskly. Time will depend on how defrosted the fruits were. Serves 6 to 8.

Bing Cherry & Pecan Bread Pudding

Bread puddings are becoming more and more popular lately and it is easy to see why. First, they are amazingly simple to prepare, they are not temperamental prima donnas, they keep and store easily, they are easy to serve, they are incredibly versatile and above all, they are very delicious. They can be savory or sweet, can be served as a main course at lunch or at dessert any time. Needless to add, I love bread puddings.

8	slices egg bread, crusts removed, torn into 1-inch pieces, about 8 cups.
3	cups pitted Bing cherries, fresh or frozen; pat dry. If frozen, defrost. and pat dry.
1	cup chopped pecans
4	eggs
1	cup milk
1	cup sugar
2	teaspoons vanilla
3	tablespoons Cinnamon Sugar

In a large bowl, place bread, cherries and pecans and set aside.

Beat together eggs, milk, sugar and vanilla until nicely blended. Pour over the bread mixture and toss and stir until bread absorbs the egg mixture. There may be a little extra egg around the edges, but that's o.k.

Spread mixture evenly into a buttered 10-inch round porcelain baker and sprinkle top with Cinnamon Sugar.

Bake at 350° for 50-55 minutes or until edges are browned. Serve warm or at room temperature. A little vanilla ice cream on top is nice, but optional. Keep the portions small, and serve 8 to 10.

Note: -Bing cherries can be purchased frozen. The one's I have used were so very good, large, plump and they tasted as if they were freshly picked.

Creamy Rice Pudding with Strawberry Sauce

This is perfectly lovely dessert for a spicy Indian Dinner. It can be prepared 1 day earlier and stored in the refrigerator. Make certain the rice is thoroughly cooked and soft because it will not soften further at this low baking temperature.

1/3	cup long-grain rice
3/4	cup water
2	cups milk (low-fat can be used)
1/2	cup sugar
1/4	cup white rum
	pinch of salt
3	eggs
1	cup sour cream (low-fat can be used)

In a covered saucepan, cook together rice and water for 25 minutes, or until rice is very soft and liquid is absorbed. Stir in the next 4 ingredients and heat, stirring, until sugar is dissolved.

In a large bowl, whisk eggs with sour cream until blended. Whisk in rice mixture until blended. Pour mixture into a 10x2-inch round porcelain baker and bake at 300° for 1 hour and 10 minutes. Remove from oven and allow to cool. (A little lip will have formed around the edge and it will hold the Strawberry Sauce.) When cool, refrigerate until serving time. Before serving, spread Strawberry Sauce over the top, and spoon into small dessert bowls at the table. Serves 8.

Strawberry Sauce:
Stir together 1 package (10 ounces) frozen strawberries in syrup with 1 tablespoon frozen concentrated orange juice (undiluted). Place in a glass bowl and store in the refrigerator until serving time. Yields 1 1/4 cups sauce.

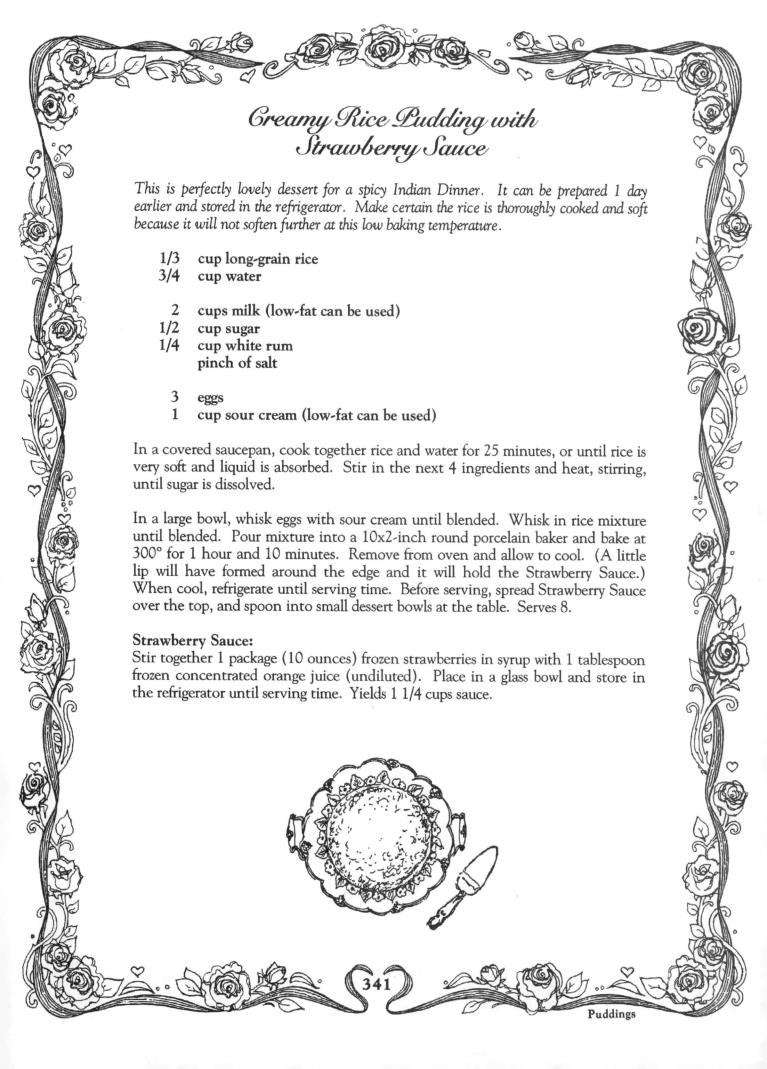

Cinnamon Matzo Brei Pudding with Apples, Raisins & Pecans

This is like one of my noodle puddings, but made with matzos. I have not given it to you before because it is a little more work, but it is truly delicious and worth the little extra effort of preparing the fruit.

2	apples, peeled, cored and cut into very thin slices
1/2	orange, grated. (Use fruit, juice, and peel, about 4 tablespoons.)
1	cup yellow raisins
1	cup sugar
1/2	teaspoon cinnamon
2	tablespoons lemon juice
2	tablespoons butter
1	teaspoon vanilla
6	whole matzos, soaked in hot water (about 5 minutes), squeezed dry and crumbled
6	eggs
1/4	cup whole pecans, broken into 1/2-inch pieces
3	tablespoons cinnamon sugar to sprinkle on top

In a skillet, sauté together first 8 ingredients until apples are soft. Meanwhile, soak the matzos, squeeze them dry and crumble them.

In a large bowl, beat 6 eggs until nicely mixed. Stir in the crumbled matzos until nicely mixed. Stir in the apple mixture and the pecans until nicely mixed. Do not over mix.

Spread mixture in a heavily-buttered (about 3 tablespoons) 9x13-inch baking pan. Sprinkle cinnamon sugar on top and bake at 350° for about 1 hour or until top is browned. Cut into squares and serve warm. A little drizzle of maple syrup is wonderful, but the choice is yours. Serves 12.

Note: -Bread puddings are difficult to test with a cake tester. So to make certain the pudding is cooked through, you only have the top as a guide. I have found that when the edges are well-browned, the pudding has been baked through.

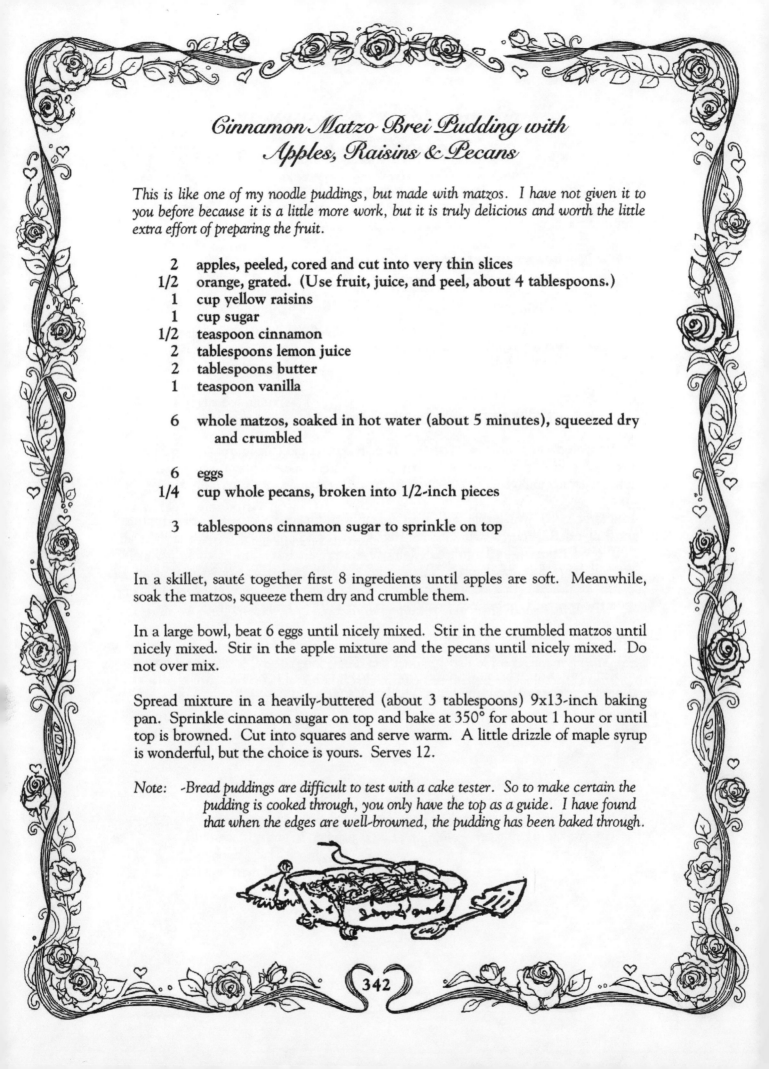

Strawberry Cheesecake Bread Pudding

Well, not exactly a cheesecake, but the taste is close. If you love the taste of cheesecakes, as I do, you will truly enjoy this combination.

8	slices day-old egg bread, crusts removed, torn into 1-inch pieces, about 8 cups.
4	eggs
1	package (8 ounces) cream cheese, softened
1/2	lemon, grated (about 2 tablespoons) use fruit, juice and peel
3/4	cup sugar
1	cup half-and-half
1	container (10 ounces) frozen strawberries in syrup, thawed

In a large bowl, place bread pieces. In a mixer, beat together eggs and cream cheese until blended. Beat in lemon, sugar and cream until blended. Pour mixture over the bread and toss and turn until blended, and most of the egg mixture is absorbed. Add strawberries to the bowl, and with a large spoon, stir it into the pudding. Do not overmix. Just toss it around so that it will be dispersed, but not heavily mixed. You should see streaks of strawberries throughout the pudding.

Spread pudding evenly into a lightly greased 9x13-inch pan, and allow to rest in the refrigerator for 30 minutes. Bake at 350° for about 55 minutes or until eggs are set and top is browned. This does not need a sauce. It is delicious as is... but if you like, a dollop of Lemon Crème France on top is nice.

Lemon Crème Fraiche:

1/2	cup cream
1/2	cup sour cream
2	tablespoons lemon juice
1	tablespoon sugar

In a glass bowl, stir together all the ingredients until nicely blended. Allow to stand at room temperature for 1 hour, and then refrigerate until ready to use. Leftover sauce can be used as a dip with sliced fruit.

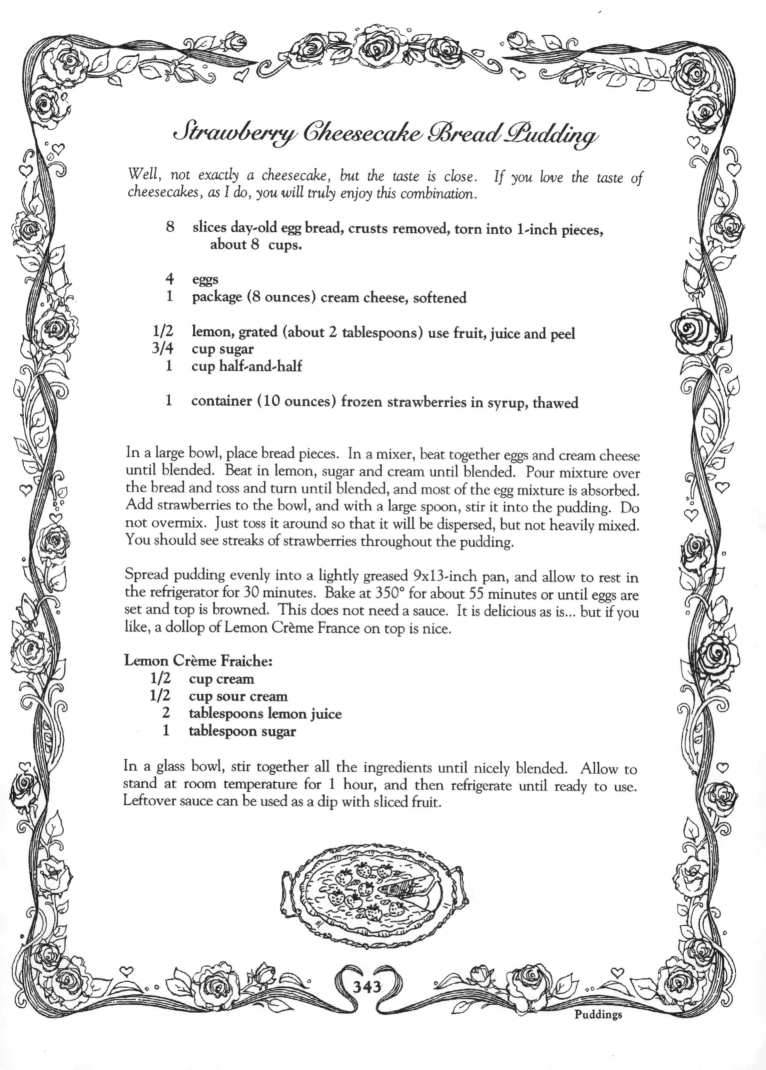

Family Chocolate Bread Pudding
with Crème Vanilla

This is a nice economical dessert that is prepared and enjoyed by all. It is homey and informal, yet when prepared in individual ramekins, it can be quite elegant. The Crème Vanilla will surprise you. It is easy and very delicious.

8	thick slices day-old egg bread, remove crusts and tear into pieces
1/2	cup semi-sweet chocolate mini-chips
2 1/2	cups half and half or milk
1/3	cup sifted cocoa
1	cup sugar
4	eggs
1	tablespoon vanilla
1	tablespoon rum (optional)

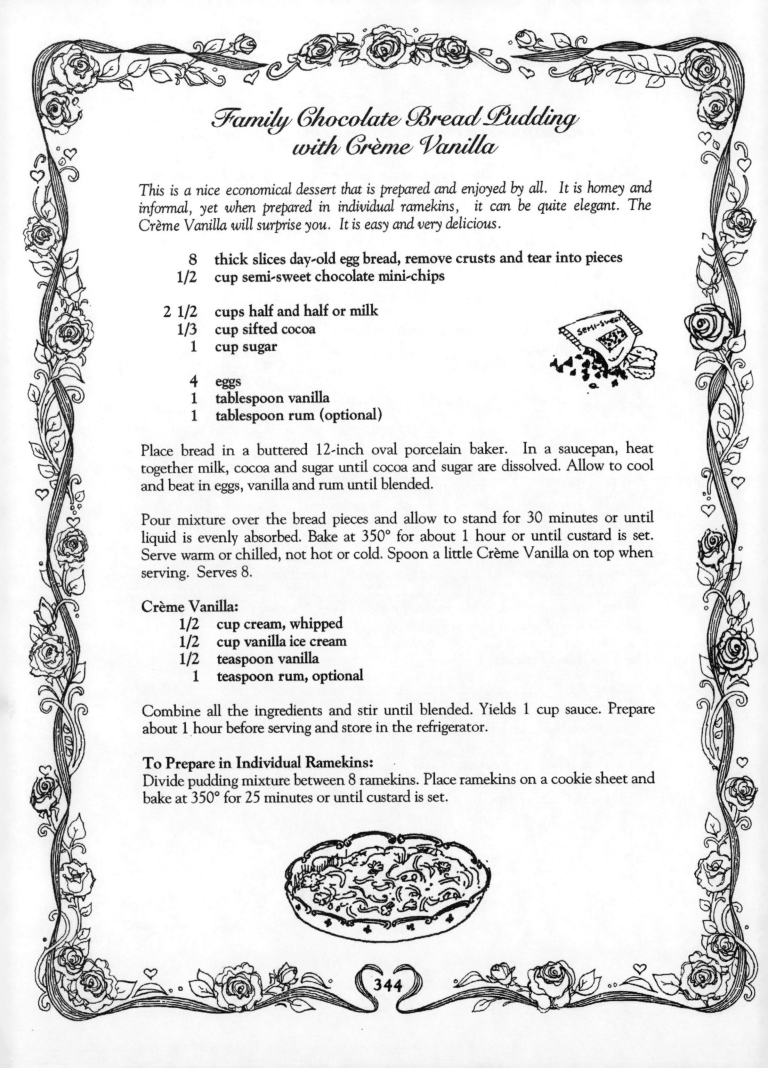

Place bread in a buttered 12-inch oval porcelain baker. In a saucepan, heat together milk, cocoa and sugar until cocoa and sugar are dissolved. Allow to cool and beat in eggs, vanilla and rum until blended.

Pour mixture over the bread pieces and allow to stand for 30 minutes or until liquid is evenly absorbed. Bake at 350° for about 1 hour or until custard is set. Serve warm or chilled, not hot or cold. Spoon a little Crème Vanilla on top when serving. Serves 8.

Crème Vanilla:

1/2	cup cream, whipped
1/2	cup vanilla ice cream
1/2	teaspoon vanilla
1	teaspoon rum, optional

Combine all the ingredients and stir until blended. Yields 1 cup sauce. Prepare about 1 hour before serving and store in the refrigerator.

To Prepare in Individual Ramekins:
Divide pudding mixture between 8 ramekins. Place ramekins on a cookie sheet and bake at 350° for 25 minutes or until custard is set.

New Orleans Bread Pudding with Apricots, Pecans & Bourbon Street Sauce

4	eggs
3/4	cup sugar
2	teaspoons vanilla
4	tablespoons melted butter
3	cups half-and-half or milk
12	slices toasted raisin bread, crusts removed. Tear into 1-inch pieces.
1	cup chopped dried apricots
1/2	cup chopped pecans
1	tablespoon cinnamon sugar

In a large bowl, beat together first 5 ingredients until blended. Toss in bread and allow to stand until bread is evenly absorbed. Stir in apricots and pecans. Place mixture into a buttered 9x13-inch baking pan and sprinkle top with cinnamon sugar. Bake at 350° for about 1 hour or until pudding is set and golden brown. To serve, cut into squares and serve with a spoonful of Bourbon Street Sauce on top. Whipped Creme Fraiche Vanilla is also very delicious. Serve 10.

Bourbon Street Sauce:

1	cup sugar
1/2	cup butter
2	tablespoons water
1	egg, well beaten
1/4	cup Bourbon whiskey

In the top of a double boiler, over hot water, beat together first 3 ingredients until sugar is melted. Stir in beaten egg and Bourbon and cook and stir until sauce is slightly thickened and mixture reaches 170° on a candy thermometer. Do not overcook. Yields about 1 1/4 cups sauce.

Bourbon Street Crème Fraiche Vanilla:

3/4	cup cream, whipped
2	tablespoons sugar
1	teaspoon vanilla
1/2	cup sour cream
2	teaspoons Bourbon

Beat cream with sugar and vanilla until stiff. Beat in sour cream and Bourbon until blended.

Soufflé au Chocolat with Crème Vanilla

This is one of my best inventions, and I hope you serve it often. In this recipe, the very complicated soufflé is amazingly simple and easy to prepare for a company dinner. Soufflé can be assembled earlier in the day, refrigerated and baked before serving. To assemble the soufflé, please make certain all ingredients are at room temperature.

1 1/2	cups semi-sweet chocolate chips
1	cup cream
5	eggs, at room temperature
8	ounces cream cheese, cut into 8 pieces, at room temperature
	pinch of salt
1	teaspoon vanilla or 1 tablespoon rum

Place chocolate chips in food processor bowl. Heat cream to boiling point and pour into the processor. Blend for 1 minute, or until chocolate is melted. Beat in eggs, one at a time, while processor continues running. Continue blending, adding the remaining ingredients, until cream cheese is completely blended.

Divide mixture between 6 buttered and lightly sugared ramekins. (Can be held, at this point, in the refrigerator.) Remove from the refrigerator 10 minutes before baking. Place ramekins on a cookie sheet, and bake at 375° for about 20 minutes, or until puffed and golden. Serve immediately with a spoonful of Crème Vanilla. This is easier to serve and requires less baking time. Serves 6.

Crème Vanilla:

1/2	cup whipping cream
2	teaspoons sugar
1/2	teaspoon vanilla
1/2	cup vanilla ice cream, softened

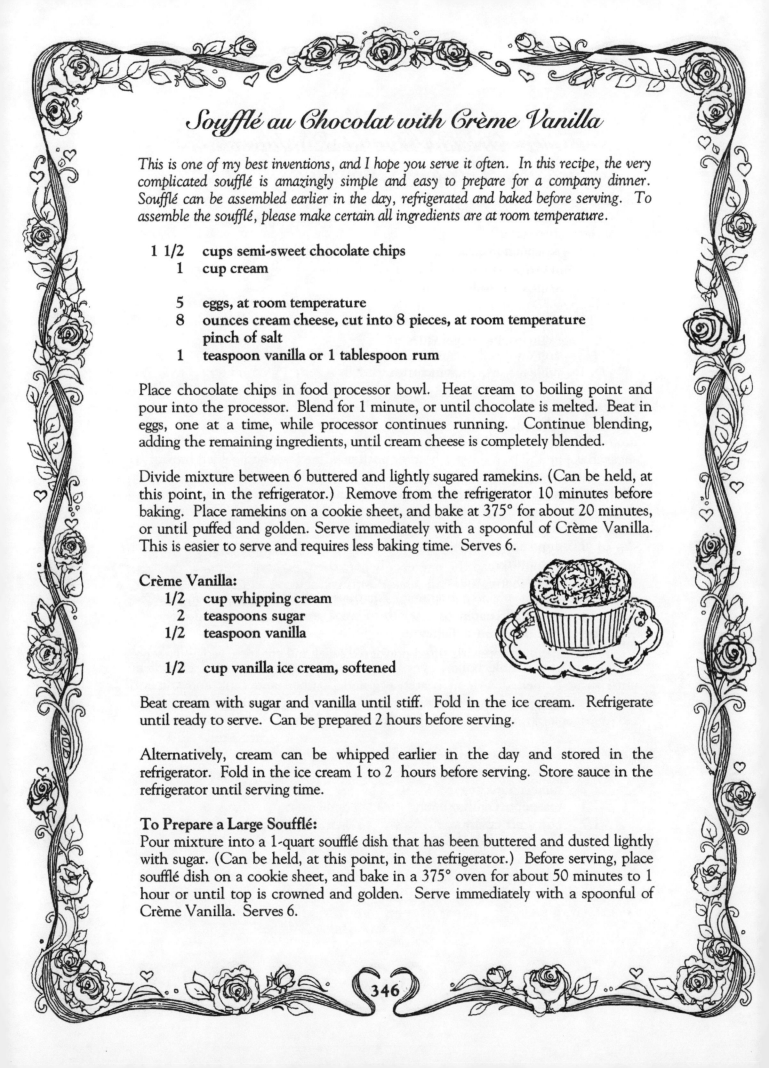

Beat cream with sugar and vanilla until stiff. Fold in the ice cream. Refrigerate until ready to serve. Can be prepared 2 hours before serving.

Alternatively, cream can be whipped earlier in the day and stored in the refrigerator. Fold in the ice cream 1 to 2 hours before serving. Store sauce in the refrigerator until serving time.

To Prepare a Large Soufflé:
Pour mixture into a 1-quart soufflé dish that has been buttered and dusted lightly with sugar. (Can be held, at this point, in the refrigerator.) Before serving, place soufflé dish on a cookie sheet, and bake in a 375° oven for about 50 minutes to 1 hour or until top is crowned and golden. Serve immediately with a spoonful of Crème Vanilla. Serves 6.

2-Minute Soufflé au Grand Marnier with Raspberries & Crème Fraiche

You will feel like a wizard when you serve this soufflé to company. No one will guess that it took minutes to prepare. It is amazing to consider that this majestic soufflé takes 2 minutes to assemble, and that it can also be assembled in advance. It is a little treasure that I hope you will keep handy. I don't have to remind you that soufflés require a good deal of earlier and last minute preparation time; separating eggs, making a white sauce, beating whites separately, folding whites in at the last minute, etc. so they are not good choices for a carefree company dinner. This little gem can be assembled earlier in the day, refrigerated and baked before serving. You cannot bake this in advance, for, like all soufflés, it will fall.

5	eggs, at room temperature
1	package (8 ounces) cream cheese, softened and cut into 8 pieces
3/4	cup cream, at room temperature
1/4	cup Grand Marnier liqueur
1/2	cup sugar

In a food processor, place all the ingredients and blend for 2 minutes. That's all there is to it.

Divide mixture between 6 buttered and lightly sugared 8-ounce ramekins. (Can be held, at this point, in the refrigerator.) Remove from the refrigerator 10 minutes before baking. Place ramekins on a cookie sheet, and bake at 375° for about 20 minutes, or until puffed and golden. Serve immediately with a spoonful of Raspberries & Crème Fraiche. This is easier to serve and requires less baking time. Serves 6.

Raspberries & Crème Fraiche:

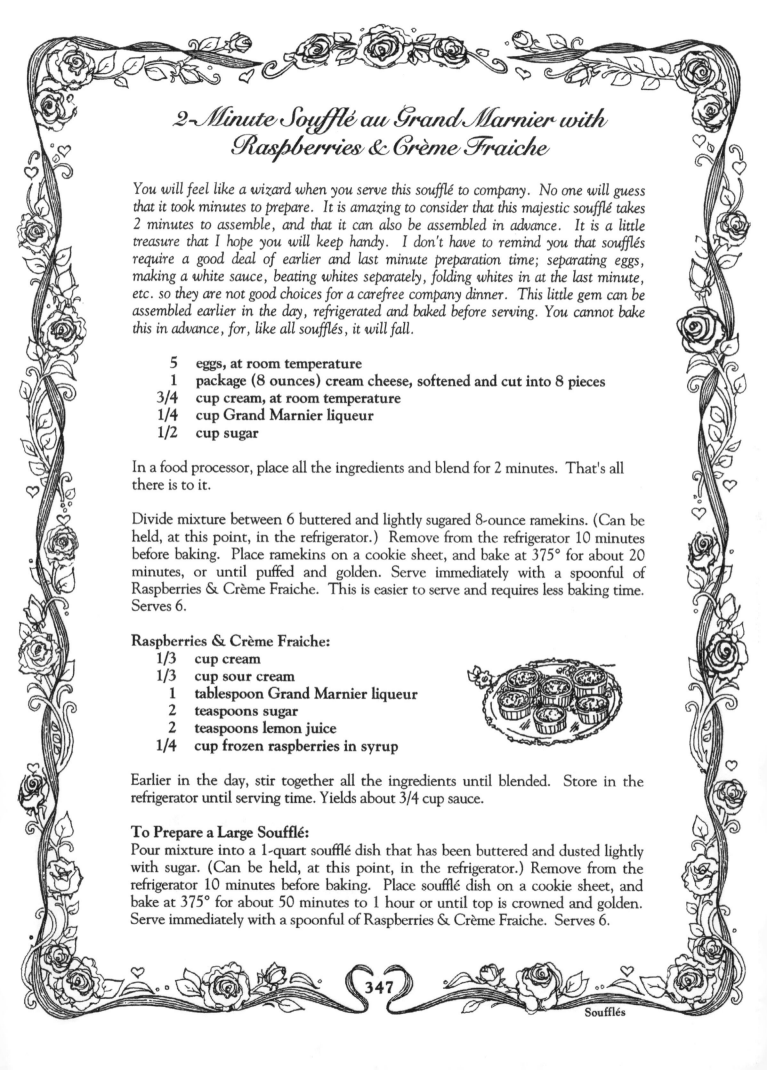

1/3	cup cream
1/3	cup sour cream
1	tablespoon Grand Marnier liqueur
2	teaspoons sugar
2	teaspoons lemon juice
1/4	cup frozen raspberries in syrup

Earlier in the day, stir together all the ingredients until blended. Store in the refrigerator until serving time. Yields about 3/4 cup sauce.

To Prepare a Large Soufflé:
Pour mixture into a 1-quart soufflé dish that has been buttered and dusted lightly with sugar. (Can be held, at this point, in the refrigerator.) Remove from the refrigerator 10 minutes before baking. Place soufflé dish on a cookie sheet, and bake at 375° for about 50 minutes to 1 hour or until top is crowned and golden. Serve immediately with a spoonful of Raspberries & Crème Fraiche. Serves 6.

Soufflé au Cappuccino with Crème de Kahlua

This dessert is very impressive and coffee lovers will find it delectable. When you consider that it assembles in minutes, can be assembled in advance and popped into the oven before serving, you won't reserve this little gem for "dressy" occasions, but will use it often.

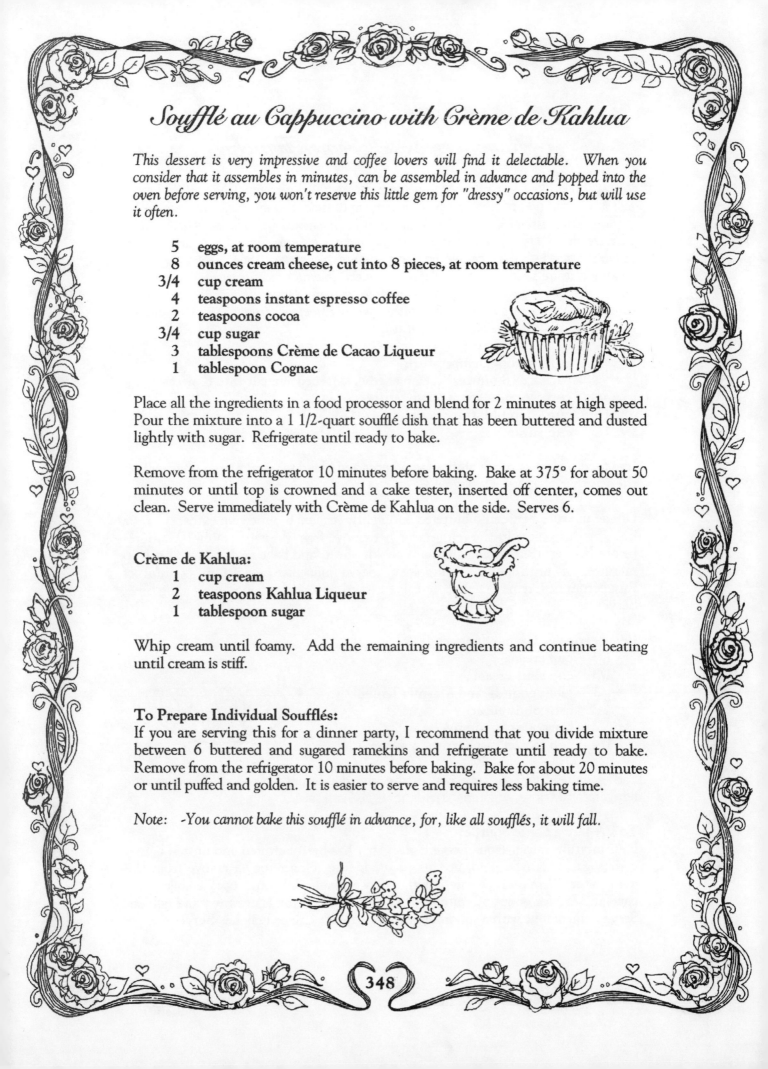

5	eggs, at room temperature
8	ounces cream cheese, cut into 8 pieces, at room temperature
3/4	cup cream
4	teaspoons instant espresso coffee
2	teaspoons cocoa
3/4	cup sugar
3	tablespoons Crème de Cacao Liqueur
1	tablespoon Cognac

Place all the ingredients in a food processor and blend for 2 minutes at high speed. Pour the mixture into a 1 1/2-quart soufflé dish that has been buttered and dusted lightly with sugar. Refrigerate until ready to bake.

Remove from the refrigerator 10 minutes before baking. Bake at 375° for about 50 minutes or until top is crowned and a cake tester, inserted off center, comes out clean. Serve immediately with Crème de Kahlua on the side. Serves 6.

Crème de Kahlua:

1	cup cream
2	teaspoons Kahlua Liqueur
1	tablespoon sugar

Whip cream until foamy. Add the remaining ingredients and continue beating until cream is stiff.

To Prepare Individual Soufflés:

If you are serving this for a dinner party, I recommend that you divide mixture between 6 buttered and sugared ramekins and refrigerate until ready to bake. Remove from the refrigerator 10 minutes before baking. Bake for about 20 minutes or until puffed and golden. It is easier to serve and requires less baking time.

Note: -You cannot bake this soufflé in advance, for, like all soufflés, it will fall.

Soufflé Cakes with Chocolate Ganache

This is a great dessert…easy to prepare and easy to serve. Little soufflé cakes, set on a creamy chocolate sauce and topped with a little vanilla ice cream is simply lovely. An extra bonus…eggs do not have to be separated and best of all the soufflés can be prepared in advance. We had a very similar dessert at a restaurant recently, but they wouldn't share the recipe. This is an exact duplicate and probably a lot easier to prepare.

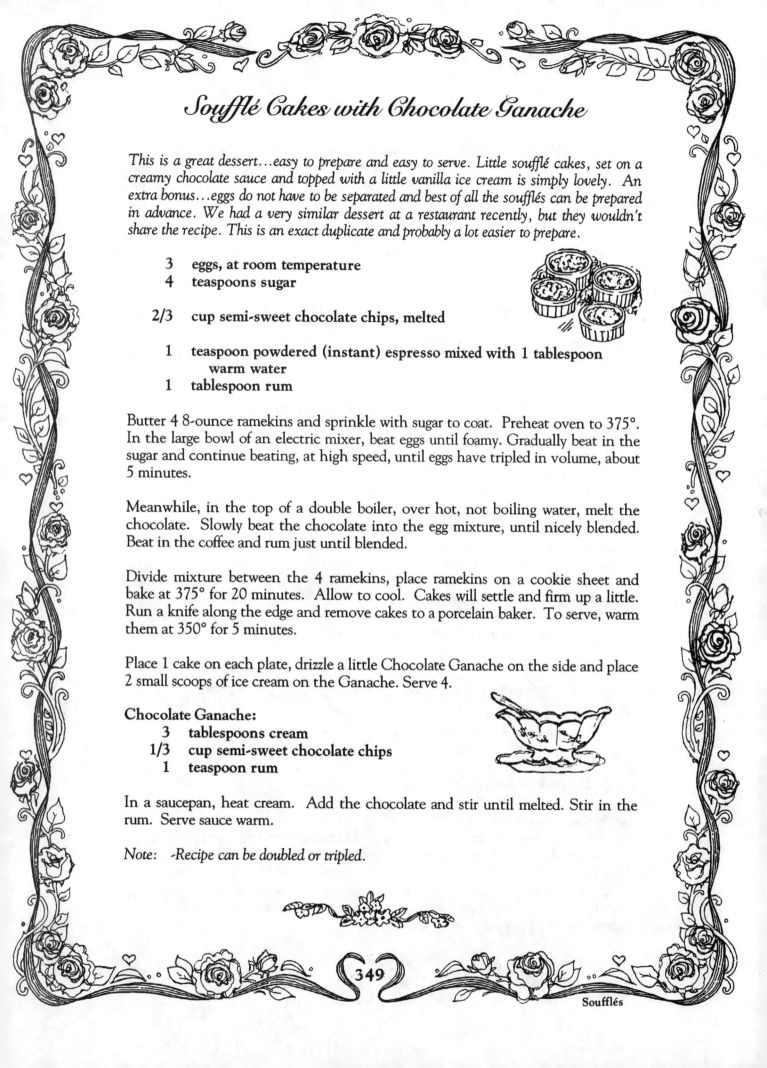

3	eggs, at room temperature
4	teaspoons sugar
2/3	cup semi-sweet chocolate chips, melted
1	teaspoon powdered (instant) espresso mixed with 1 tablespoon warm water
1	tablespoon rum

Butter 4 8-ounce ramekins and sprinkle with sugar to coat. Preheat oven to 375°. In the large bowl of an electric mixer, beat eggs until foamy. Gradually beat in the sugar and continue beating, at high speed, until eggs have tripled in volume, about 5 minutes.

Meanwhile, in the top of a double boiler, over hot, not boiling water, melt the chocolate. Slowly beat the chocolate into the egg mixture, until nicely blended. Beat in the coffee and rum just until blended.

Divide mixture between the 4 ramekins, place ramekins on a cookie sheet and bake at 375° for 20 minutes. Allow to cool. Cakes will settle and firm up a little. Run a knife along the edge and remove cakes to a porcelain baker. To serve, warm them at 350° for 5 minutes.

Place 1 cake on each plate, drizzle a little Chocolate Ganache on the side and place 2 small scoops of ice cream on the Ganache. Serve 4.

Chocolate Ganache:

3	tablespoons cream
1/3	cup semi-sweet chocolate chips
1	teaspoon rum

In a saucepan, heat cream. Add the chocolate and stir until melted. Stir in the rum. Serve sauce warm.

Note: -Recipe can be doubled or tripled.

Strudels & Danish

Strudels and Danish are also one of the most satisfying accompaniments to a cup of coffee or tea. These recipes are the stuff my memories are made of. The Sour Cream Quick Puff Pastry is one of my oldest recipes and still one of the very best. It handles easily and produces one of the finest tasting strudels. The Cream Cheese Quick Puff Pastry is a little sturdier and has a little more body, and is good for heavier fillings. But, they are both interchangeable, so use either one, as the spirit moves you. The fillings are all very delicious accompaniments and add a superb balance of flavors.

I grew up on Strudels and Danish, and my Mom always had them ready when a neighbor dropped in for coffee. The Viennese Crescents and the Danish Crescents were always in the freezer and I must confess, many were the times when they were eaten without first defrosting ... which I do not recommend ... except in emergencies.

Sour Cream Quick Puff Pastry

Sour Cream Pastry:
- 1 cup butter (2 sticks)
- 2 cups flour
- 1 cup sour cream

To Make the Dough:
Beat butter and flour in your electric mixer until the mixture resembles coarse meal. Add sour cream and beat for 30 seconds, until sour cream is lightly blended. Turn mixture out onto wax paper that is heavily dusted with flour. Sprinkle a little more flour over the dough for ease of handling. Shape into a 6-inch disc and wrap in the floured wax paper and then foil. Refrigerate overnight. Dough can be frozen, wrapped in plastic wrap and then foil.

Cream Cheese Quick Puff Pastry

Cream Cheese Pastry:
- 1 package (8 ounces) cream cheese
- 1 cup butter (2 sticks)
- 1 egg yolk
- 2 cups flour

To Make the Dough:
In the large bowl of an electric mixer, beat together the butter and cream cheese until the mixture is blended. Beat in the egg yolk. Add the flour and beat until blended. Do not overbeat. Turn dough out onto floured wax paper. With floured hands, form dough into a 6-inch disc, wrap it in the wax paper and then foil. Refrigerate it for several hours or overnight. Dough can be frozen, wrapped in plastic wrap and then foil.

Strudels & Danish Technique

To Shape the Strudels:
Take the dough from the refrigerator and divide it into 4 parts. Working one part at a time, roll it out on a floured pastry cloth until the dough measures about 10x10-inches. Spread 1/4 of the filling evenly over the dough. Fold the pastry in thirds ending with a strudel that measures approximately 3x10-inches and seam side down.

To Bake the Strudels:
Place strudel on a lightly greased 12x16-inch pan, so that you can bake the four strudels at one time. Repeat with the remaining 3 parts of dough. Bake in a preheated 350° oven for about 30 to 35 minutes or until top is lightly browned. Allow to cool in pan for 10 minutes, and then remove from the pan with two pancake turners and finish cooling on a brown paper bag. Sprinkle with sifted powdered sugar when cool.

To Freeze Strudels:
Do not sprinkle with sugar, or Vanilla Glaze. Wrap individual strudels in double thickness of plastic wrap and then foil. Place in a freezer bag. To defrost strudels, open the wrappers and allow to come to room temperature. Place on a baking pan, cut into 1-inch slices, and warm in a 350° oven for a few minutes to crisp. Now sprinkle with powdered sugar.

Strudel Fillings

Strawberry Coconut Filling:
- 1 cup strawberry jam
- 1 cup chopped walnuts
- 1 cup yellow raisins
- 1/2 cup flaked coconut

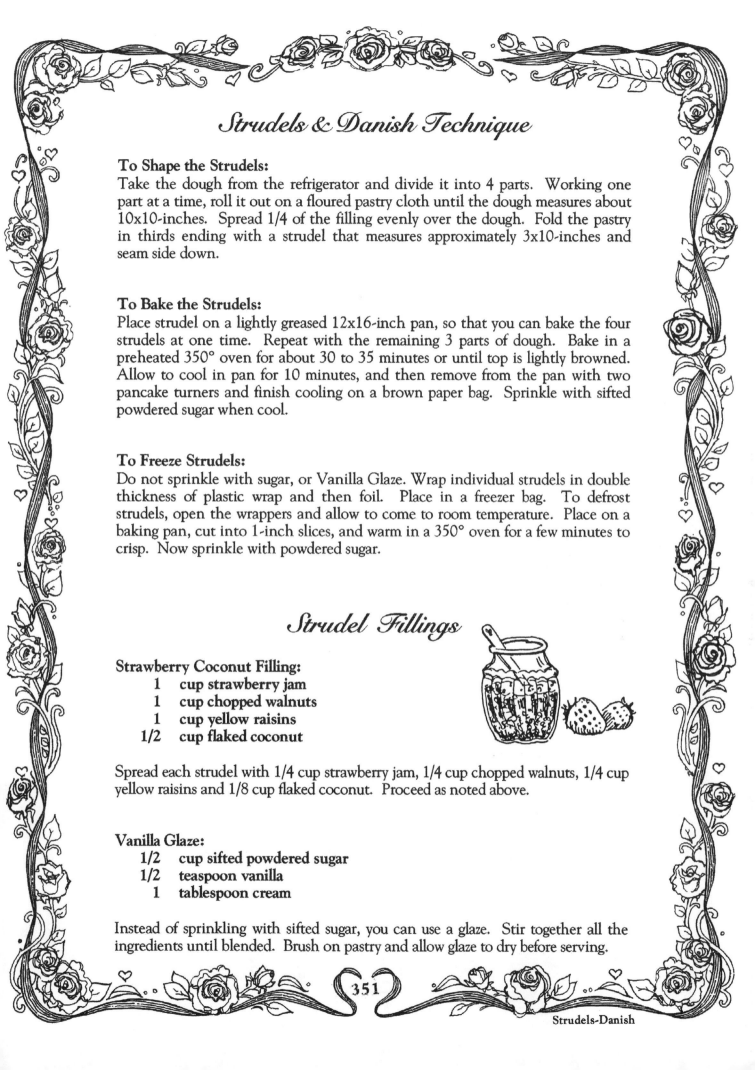

Spread each strudel with 1/4 cup strawberry jam, 1/4 cup chopped walnuts, 1/4 cup yellow raisins and 1/8 cup flaked coconut. Proceed as noted above.

Vanilla Glaze:
- 1/2 cup sifted powdered sugar
- 1/2 teaspoon vanilla
- 1 tablespoon cream

Instead of sprinkling with sifted sugar, you can use a glaze. Stir together all the ingredients until blended. Brush on pastry and allow glaze to dry before serving.

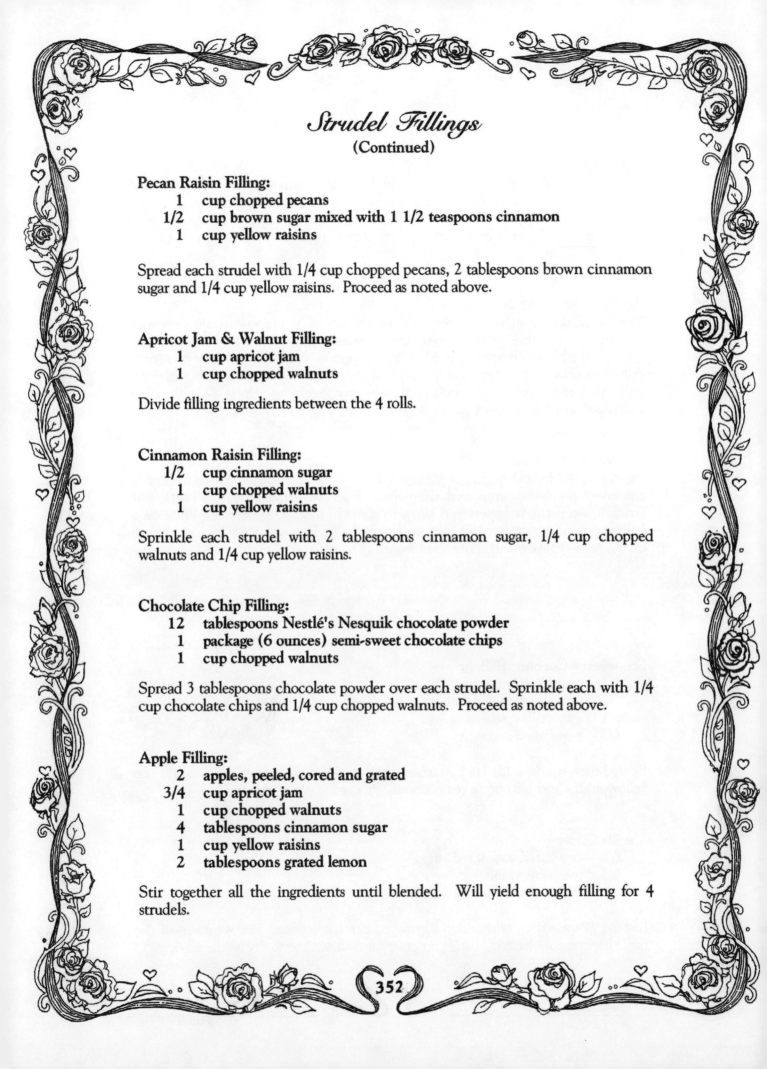

Strudel Fillings
(Continued)

Pecan Raisin Filling:

    1   cup chopped pecans
    1/2 cup brown sugar mixed with 1 1/2 teaspoons cinnamon
    1   cup yellow raisins

Spread each strudel with 1/4 cup chopped pecans, 2 tablespoons brown cinnamon sugar and 1/4 cup yellow raisins. Proceed as noted above.

Apricot Jam & Walnut Filling:

    1   cup apricot jam
    1   cup chopped walnuts

Divide filling ingredients between the 4 rolls.

Cinnamon Raisin Filling:

    1/2 cup cinnamon sugar
    1   cup chopped walnuts
    1   cup yellow raisins

Sprinkle each strudel with 2 tablespoons cinnamon sugar, 1/4 cup chopped walnuts and 1/4 cup yellow raisins.

Chocolate Chip Filling:

    12   tablespoons Nestlé's Nesquik chocolate powder
    1   package (6 ounces) semi-sweet chocolate chips
    1   cup chopped walnuts

Spread 3 tablespoons chocolate powder over each strudel. Sprinkle each with 1/4 cup chocolate chips and 1/4 cup chopped walnuts. Proceed as noted above.

Apple Filling:

    2   apples, peeled, cored and grated
    3/4 cup apricot jam
    1   cup chopped walnuts
    4   tablespoons cinnamon sugar
    1   cup yellow raisins
    2   tablespoons grated lemon

Stir together all the ingredients until blended. Will yield enough filling for 4 strudels.

Chocolate Chip Danish

This is the little children's favorite, without nuts. It is interesting to note that as they grow older, they love it with walnuts or pecans. So you have to be a little patient.

1	recipe Sour Cream Pastry
8	tablespoons Nestlé's Chocolate Nesquik
1	package (6 ounces) semi-sweet chocolate chips
1/2	cup chopped pecans, optional

Divide dough into 4 parts. Working one part at a time, roll it out on a floured pastry cloth until the dough measures about 10x10-inches. Spread 1/4 of the chocolate powder over the dough. Sprinkle with 1/4 of the chocolate chips. Roll dough into thirds, ending with a roll that is about 3x10-inches and is seam side down.

Place Danish roll on a lightly greased 12x16-inch pan so that you can bake the four pastries at one time. Repeat with the remaining 3 parts of dough and filling.

Bake in a preheated 350° oven for about 30 minutes or until top is golden. Cool in the pan for 10 minutes. Remove from pan and continue cooling on a rack or on brown paper. Sprinkle generously with powdered sugar. Cut into 1-inch slices when cool. Makes 28 to 32 slices.

Note: -Danish can be frozen after they are baked. Wrap them, uncut, in plastic wrap and then foil. Freeze them in freezer bags. This way, you can take out as many as you need, and have the rest ready for another time. Defrost them uncovered. Do not sprinkle powdered sugar on top, if you are planning to freeze them

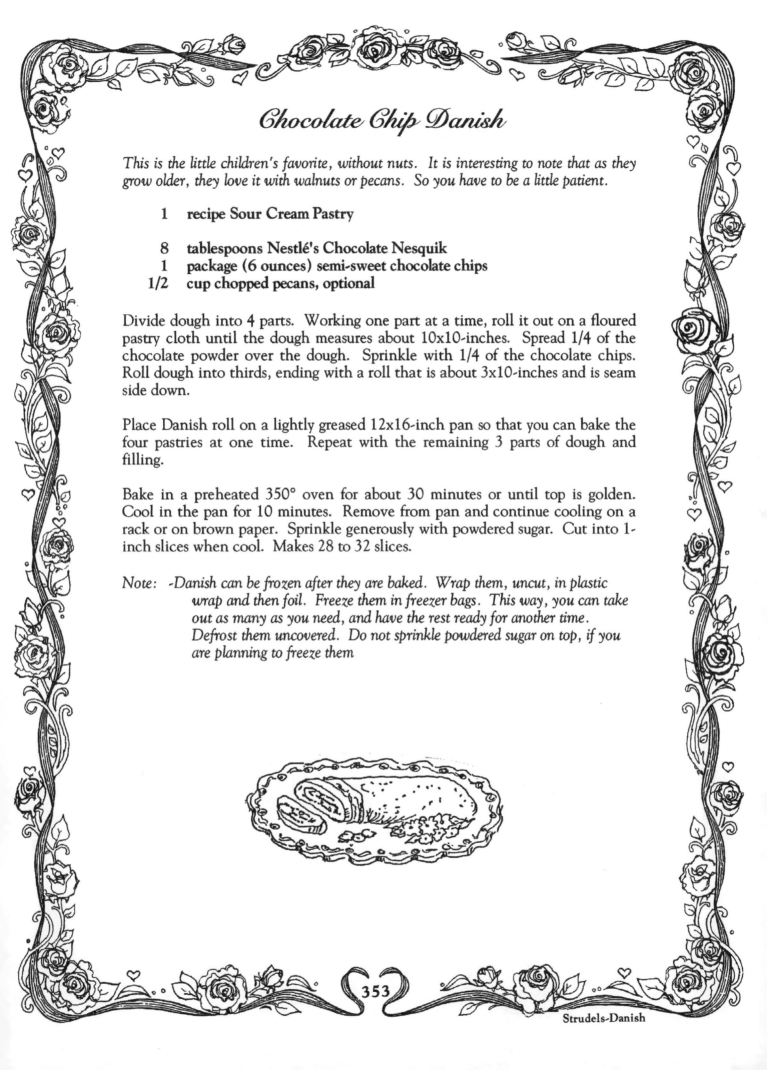

Strudels-Danish

Danish Apple Strudel with Cinnamon, Raisins & Walnuts

This is one of my husband's favorites. It can easily be prepared in 2 stages, making the dough early in the day (or even 1 or 2 days earlier), and rolling and baking on another day. The filling is delicious, filled with apples, raisins, walnuts, apricot jam and lemon. The pastry is flaky and tender.

1	cup butter (2 sticks)
2	cups flour
1	cup sour cream

In the bowl of an electric mixer, beat together butter and flour until mixture resembles coarse meal. Beat in the sour cream until blended (about 30 seconds). Turn dough out onto heavily floured wax paper and sprinkle a little more flour over the dough. Shape it into a 7-inch circle, wrap in the wax paper and refrigerate it for several hours or overnight.

Divide dough into 4 parts. Working one part at a time, roll it out on a floured pastry cloth to measure about 10x10-inches. Spread 1/4 of the Apple Filling down the center of the dough, fold in the sides of the dough over the apples (like a letter), and place, seam-side down, on a 12x16-inch baking pan. Repeat with remaining dough.

Bake at 350° for about 30 minutes, or until top is golden brown. Allow to cool in pan. Sprinkle generously with sifted powdered sugar and cut into slices to serve. Yields 24 to 30 slices.

Apple Filling:

2	apples, peeled, cored and grated
3/4	cup apricot jam
1	cup chopped walnuts
4	tablespoons cinnamon sugar
1	cup yellow raisins
2	tablespoons grated lemon

Stir together all the ingredients until blended. Will yield enough filling for 4 strudels.

Strudelettes with Walnuts, Coconut, & Strawberry Jam

This is another incredible pastry, that will grace a brunch or luncheon buffet. It can be sliced into small portions and enjoyed with a clear conscience.

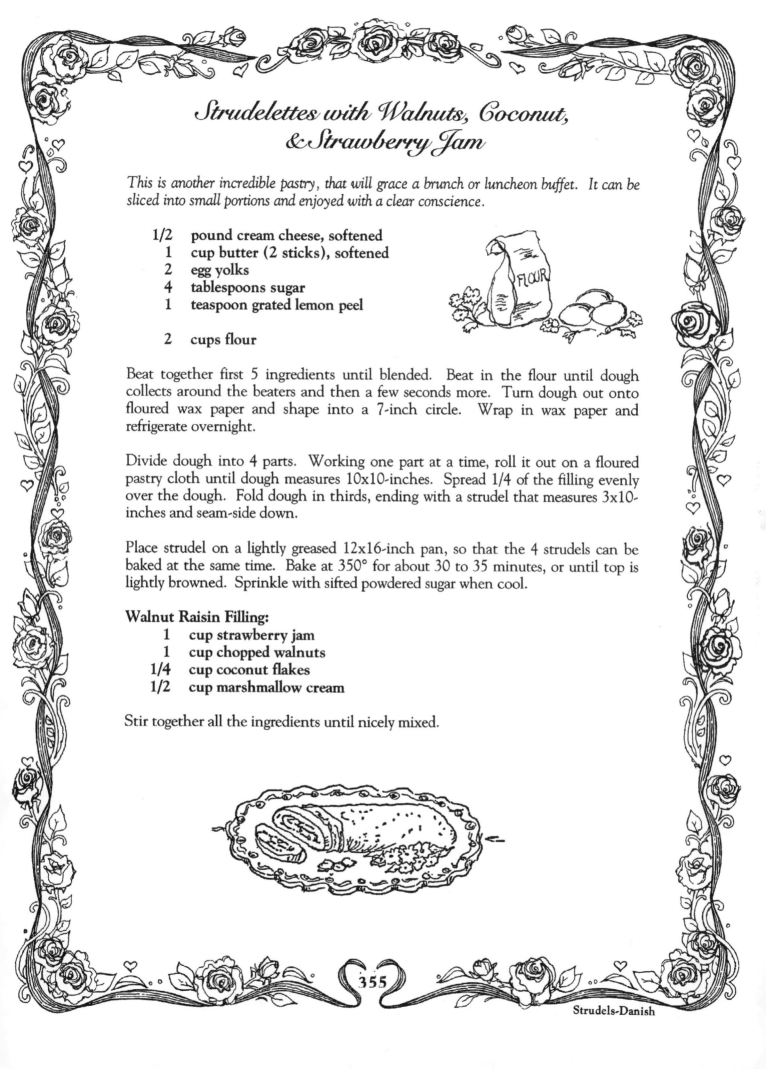

1/2	pound cream cheese, softened
1	cup butter (2 sticks), softened
2	egg yolks
4	tablespoons sugar
1	teaspoon grated lemon peel
2	cups flour

Beat together first 5 ingredients until blended. Beat in the flour until dough collects around the beaters and then a few seconds more. Turn dough out onto floured wax paper and shape into a 7-inch circle. Wrap in wax paper and refrigerate overnight.

Divide dough into 4 parts. Working one part at a time, roll it out on a floured pastry cloth until dough measures 10x10-inches. Spread 1/4 of the filling evenly over the dough. Fold dough in thirds, ending with a strudel that measures 3x10-inches and seam-side down.

Place strudel on a lightly greased 12x16-inch pan, so that the 4 strudels can be baked at the same time. Bake at 350° for about 30 to 35 minutes, or until top is lightly browned. Sprinkle with sifted powdered sugar when cool.

Walnut Raisin Filling:
1	cup strawberry jam
1	cup chopped walnuts
1/4	cup coconut flakes
1/2	cup marshmallow cream

Stir together all the ingredients until nicely mixed.

Strudels-Danish

Viennese Crescents with
Cinnamon & Walnuts & Vanilla Glaze

This is a divine pastry to serve with coffee. It is especially nice to serve at a ladies luncheon for the portions can be kept small and they are not sweet or cloying.

For the Dough:

1	cup butter (2 sticks)
1/2	cup sugar
2	cups flour
3/4	cup sour cream
1	egg yolk

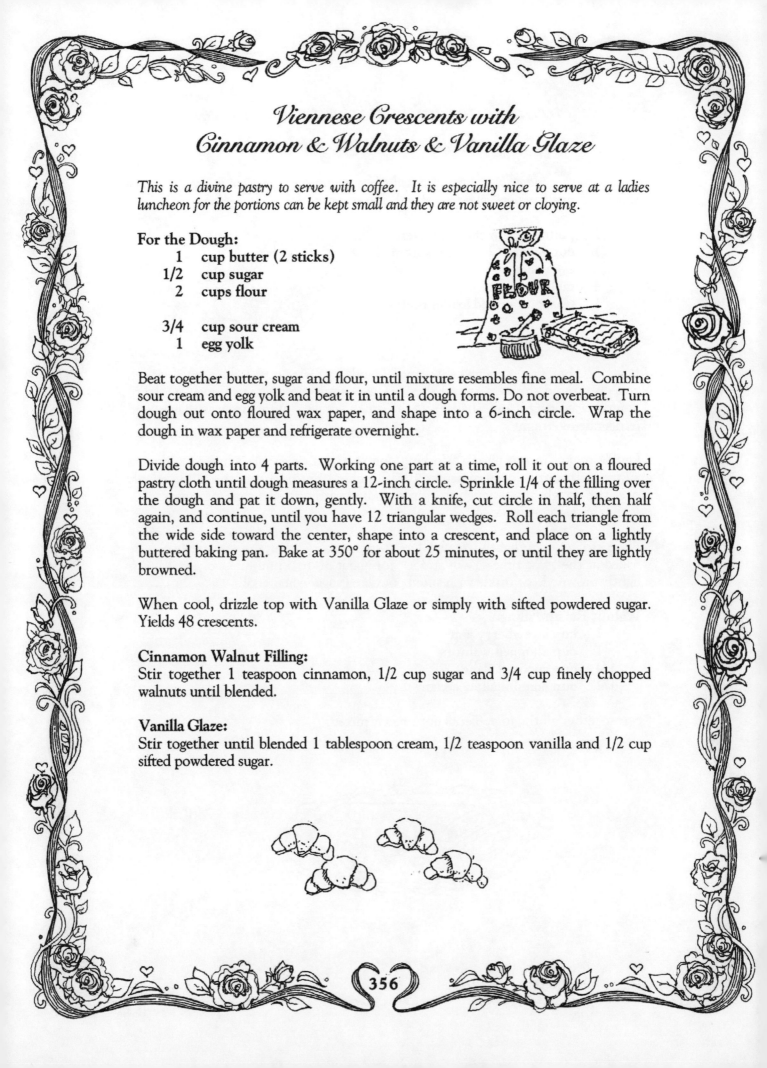

Beat together butter, sugar and flour, until mixture resembles fine meal. Combine sour cream and egg yolk and beat it in until a dough forms. Do not overbeat. Turn dough out onto floured wax paper, and shape into a 6-inch circle. Wrap the dough in wax paper and refrigerate overnight.

Divide dough into 4 parts. Working one part at a time, roll it out on a floured pastry cloth until dough measures a 12-inch circle. Sprinkle 1/4 of the filling over the dough and pat it down, gently. With a knife, cut circle in half, then half again, and continue, until you have 12 triangular wedges. Roll each triangle from the wide side toward the center, shape into a crescent, and place on a lightly buttered baking pan. Bake at 350° for about 25 minutes, or until they are lightly browned.

When cool, drizzle top with Vanilla Glaze or simply with sifted powdered sugar. Yields 48 crescents.

Cinnamon Walnut Filling:
Stir together 1 teaspoon cinnamon, 1/2 cup sugar and 3/4 cup finely chopped walnuts until blended.

Vanilla Glaze:
Stir together until blended 1 tablespoon cream, 1/2 teaspoon vanilla and 1/2 cup sifted powdered sugar.

Cinnamon Breakfast Croissants with Walnuts & Raisins

These lovely, delicate croissants are assembled in minutes. They look and taste as if they were made with yeast. They freeze beautifully and are nice to have on hand. But one word of caution...bake these on a day when no one is around, or they will never make it to the freezer.

For the Dough:

1	cup cottage cheese
3	ounces butter (3/4 stick), softened
1	cup flour
1/2	cup finely chopped walnuts
1/2	cup sugar
1/2	cup finely chopped raisins
1/2	teaspoon cinnamon (or more to taste)
	cinnamon sugar

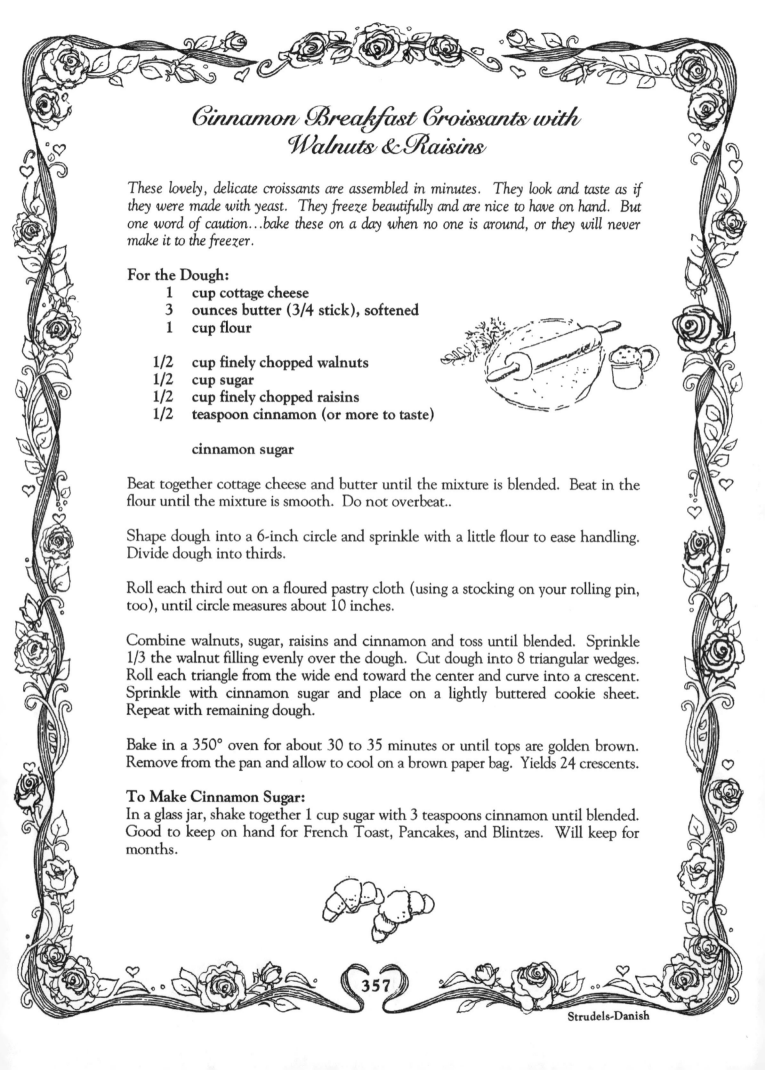

Beat together cottage cheese and butter until the mixture is blended. Beat in the flour until the mixture is smooth. Do not overbeat..

Shape dough into a 6-inch circle and sprinkle with a little flour to ease handling. Divide dough into thirds.

Roll each third out on a floured pastry cloth (using a stocking on your rolling pin, too), until circle measures about 10 inches.

Combine walnuts, sugar, raisins and cinnamon and toss until blended. Sprinkle 1/3 the walnut filling evenly over the dough. Cut dough into 8 triangular wedges. Roll each triangle from the wide end toward the center and curve into a crescent. Sprinkle with cinnamon sugar and place on a lightly buttered cookie sheet. Repeat with remaining dough.

Bake in a 350° oven for about 30 to 35 minutes or until tops are golden brown. Remove from the pan and allow to cool on a brown paper bag. Yields 24 crescents.

To Make Cinnamon Sugar:
In a glass jar, shake together 1 cup sugar with 3 teaspoons cinnamon until blended. Good to keep on hand for French Toast, Pancakes, and Blintzes. Will keep for months.

Strudels-Danish

Danish Crescents with
Strawberry Jam & Sour Cream Glaze

These little pastries can be stored in the freezer and are good to keep on hand in the event you are faced with unexpected company. They defrost in a matter of minutes. These are a bit more work, but very well worth the extra effort.

For the Dough:

2	1/2 cups flour
1	cup butter (2 sticks), cut into 8 pieces
2	egg yolks
1/2	cup sour cream

Beat together flour and butter until mixture resembles fine meal. Beat together yolks and sour cream until blended and add to the flour mixture. Beat until blended and a soft dough forms, about 15 seconds. Turn dough out onto heavily floured wax paper and shape into a 7-inch circle. Wrap in the wax paper and refrigerate for several hours or overnight.

Divide dough into 6 parts. Working one part at a time, roll it out on a floured pastry cloth until dough measures a 10-inch circle. Spread with 1/6 of the filling. With a knife, cut circle into 8 triangular wedges. (Cut in half, then half again and again.) Roll up each triangle from the wide side toward the center, shape into a crescent, and place on a lightly buttered baking pan. Bake at 350° for about 25 to 30 minutes, or until tops are lightly browned.

When cool, brush tops with Sour Cream Glaze. Yields 48 crescents.

Strawberry Pecan Filling:

2	cups finely grated pecans
2/3	cup strawberry jam
1/4	cup sugar
1/4	cup finely chopped raisins
1/3	cup finely chopped pecans

Stir together all the ingredients until blended.

Sour Cream Glaze:

Stir together until blended 2 tablespoons sour cream, 1 teaspoon vanilla and 1 cup sifted powdered sugar.

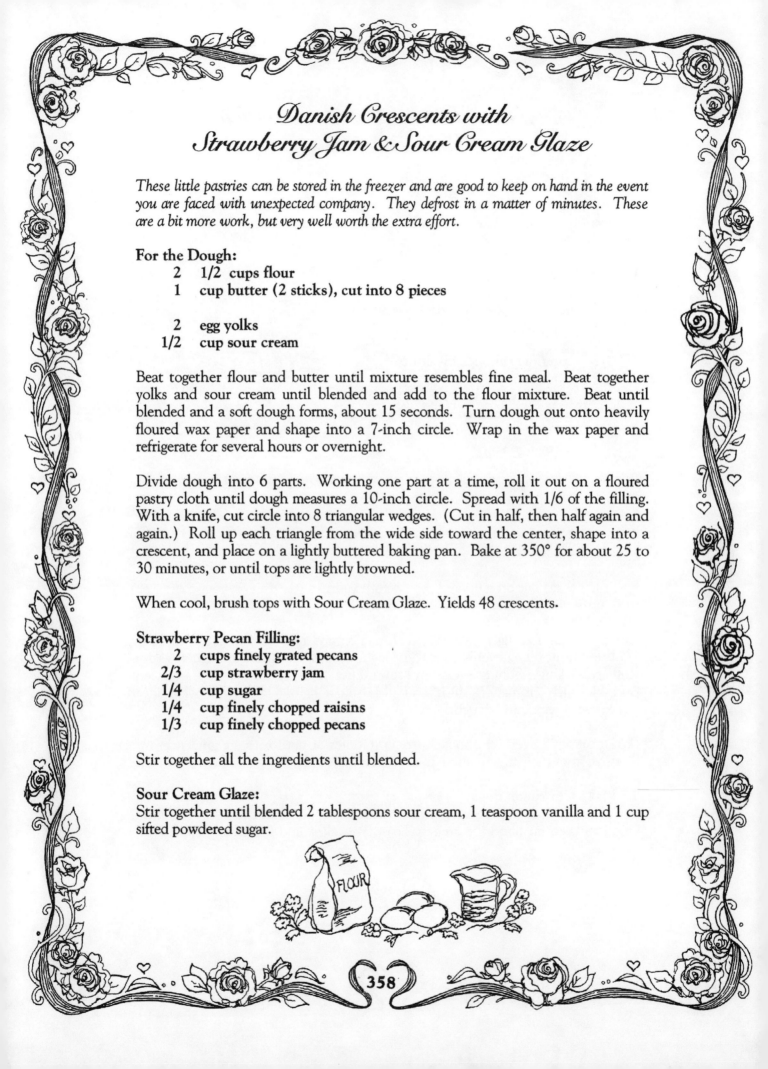

Old Fashioned Apple Strudel

Cream Cheese Pastry:
- 1   package (8 ounces) cream cheese
- 1   cup butter (2 sticks)
- 1   egg yolk
- 2   cups flour

Filling:
- 2   apples, peeled and grated
- 3/4 cup apricot jam
- 1   cup chopped walnuts
- 4   tablespoons cinnamon sugar

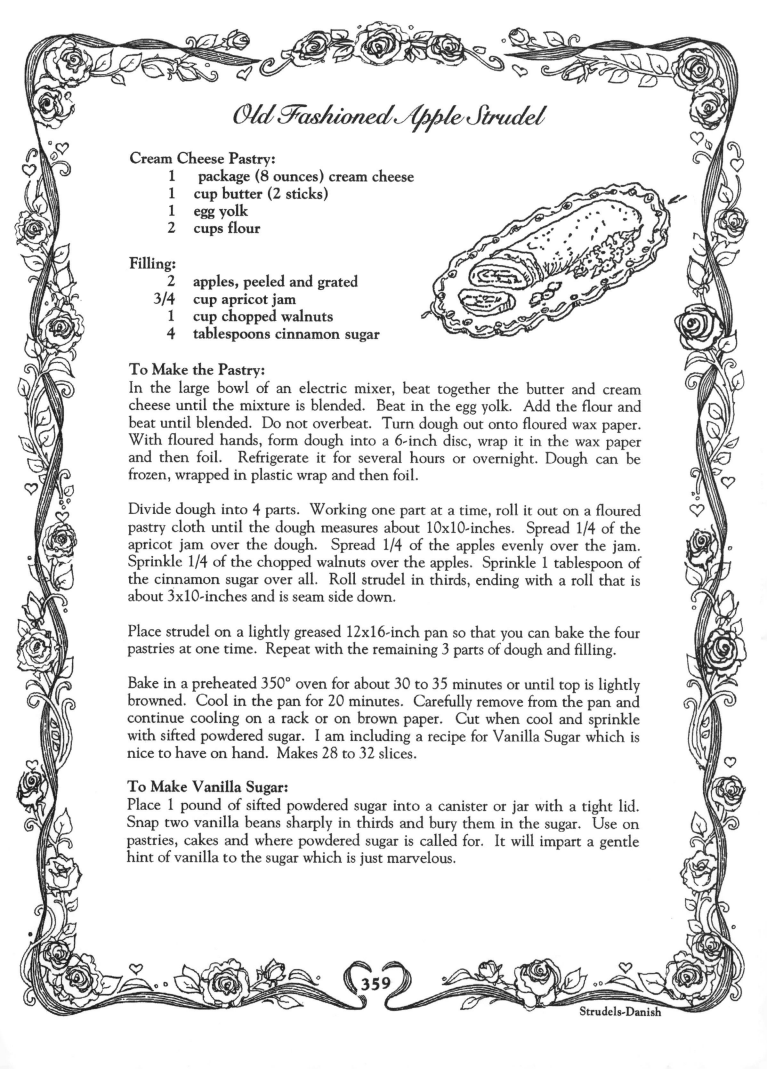

To Make the Pastry:

In the large bowl of an electric mixer, beat together the butter and cream cheese until the mixture is blended. Beat in the egg yolk. Add the flour and beat until blended. Do not overbeat. Turn dough out onto floured wax paper. With floured hands, form dough into a 6-inch disc, wrap it in the wax paper and then foil. Refrigerate it for several hours or overnight. Dough can be frozen, wrapped in plastic wrap and then foil.

Divide dough into 4 parts. Working one part at a time, roll it out on a floured pastry cloth until the dough measures about 10x10-inches. Spread 1/4 of the apricot jam over the dough. Spread 1/4 of the apples evenly over the jam. Sprinkle 1/4 of the chopped walnuts over the apples. Sprinkle 1 tablespoon of the cinnamon sugar over all. Roll strudel in thirds, ending with a roll that is about 3x10-inches and is seam side down.

Place strudel on a lightly greased 12x16-inch pan so that you can bake the four pastries at one time. Repeat with the remaining 3 parts of dough and filling.

Bake in a preheated 350° oven for about 30 to 35 minutes or until top is lightly browned. Cool in the pan for 20 minutes. Carefully remove from the pan and continue cooling on a rack or on brown paper. Cut when cool and sprinkle with sifted powdered sugar. I am including a recipe for Vanilla Sugar which is nice to have on hand. Makes 28 to 32 slices.

To Make Vanilla Sugar:

Place 1 pound of sifted powdered sugar into a canister or jar with a tight lid. Snap two vanilla beans sharply in thirds and bury them in the sugar. Use on pastries, cakes and where powdered sugar is called for. It will impart a gentle hint of vanilla to the sugar which is just marvelous.

Strudels-Danish

The Index

The Index

The Index

The Index

The Index

Additional Copies of the
RENNY DARLING COOKBOOKS
Can be purchased at your local book store or ordered directly from

ROYAL HOUSE PUBLISHING CO., INC
P.O. 5027 - Beverly Hills, CA 90210
1-800-277-5535
or
www.RennyDarling.com